Handbook of Pseudonyms and Personal Nicknames

compiled by
HAROLD S. SHARP

Volume I: A-J

The Scarecrow Press, Inc.
Metuchen, N.J. 1972

Library of Congress Cataloging in Publication Data

Sharp, Harold S
Handbook of pseudonyms and personal nicknames.

1. Anonyms and pseudonyms. 2. Nicknames.
I. Title.
Z1041.S43 929.4 71-189886
ISBN 0-8108-0460-3

Affectionately dedicated to the many persons who, for one reason or another, have earned nicknames which are unique, interesting and, unfortunately, unprintable.

FOREWORD

Nicknames and pseudonyms have been used for thousands of years. Lucius Junius Brutus, a Roman consul who flourished some 500 years before Christ, was called "Stupid." The ancient Egyptian pharaohs, many of the Roman emperors, medieval kings and modern rulers had nicknames bestowed upon them. This was by no means confined to royalty; it was the case with countless people, prominent and obscure, of both early and modern times. Homer, the Greek epic poet (c. 850 B.C., perhaps earlier, perhaps later), has been called "The Maeonian Swan" and "The Prince of Poets," although these and other appellations were given him after his death. Spenser, Shakespeare, Milton, Pope, Longfellow, and Frost, to mention only a few poets, had their sobriquets. The same is true of soldiers, politicians, judges, sports figures, musicians, and people of virtually all times and callings.

Many persons are better known by a nickname than by a birth name. Aristocles, the Greek philosopher (c. 427-347 B.C.) is far better known as "Plato," a name given him because of his broad shoulders. One of the all-time great professional baseball players was generally thought of as "Babe Ruth," "The Babe," and as "The Sultan of Swat" rather than as George Herman Ruth, his real name. Few people are aware that "Harry Houdini," called "The Handcuff King," "The King of Escapologists" and by other appellations, was christened Ehrich Weiss. Authors and actors frequently assume pen names and stage names and, as mentioned above, people from all walks of life acquire nicknames.

The essential difference between a pseudonym and a nickname is that the person using the pseudonym generally selects it himself, whereas the nickname is bestowed on one by others.

Why do such sobriquets abound? In the case of pseudonyms, including pen names used by authors and stage names of actors and actresses, there can be several reasons. A given name may be unwieldy. "Joseph Conrad" (pseudonym) is far more easily handled by English-speaking people than is Teodor Józef Konrad Korzeniowski, the Anglo-Polish author's real name. "W. C. Fields" fits better on a theater marquee than does the late American comedian's real name, William Claude Dukinfield.

An author may wish to conceal his identity. This was particularly true in the case of political pamphleteers. "Daniel Defoe" (actually Daniel Foe) held certain political beliefs which were not shared by the rulers then in power, and so published certain subversive tracts in which "Eye Witness" was indicated as the author.

In the 17th and 18th centuries, and even later, the world of the theater was regarded by some as tawdry. Various members of the nobility, however, felt the urge to write for the stage and, in so doing, preferred for social reasons to keep their identities unknown. This was the case of T. Southland, member of a noble English family who, in the year 1663, published a play called Love à la Mode, the manuscript of which indicates the author as "A Person of Honour," a pseudonym also used by Jonathan Swift. Another instance of anonymity was the use of initials, as with the play Orgula; or, The Fatal Error, a tragedy by "L. W.," published in 1658.

Frederick Schiller Faust, an extremely prolific modern writer, published his serious poetry and essays under his own name and his lighter efforts under such pseudonyms as "Max Brand," "George Owen Baxter," "David Manning," "Martin Dexter," "Hugh Owen," "Nicholas Silver," and others. He was also dubbed "The King of the Pulps," this attributable to the fact that much of his literary output appeared in this type of periodical. One issue of Western Story Magazine carried three stories by Faust, each under a different pseudonym.

Edward L. Stratemeyer, author of several series of books for juveniles, used over 20 pseudonyms, including "Harrison Adams," "Allen Chapman," "Jim Daly," "Spencer Davenport," and "Arthur M. Winfield," to mention only a few.

Dime novelists such as Colonel Prentiss Ingraham,

Frederick Van Rensselaer Dey, and John Russell Coryell used a remarkable number of pen names, not wishing to appear to flood the market with an oversupply of fiction by any one author. Again, dime novelists, under exclusive contract to one publisher, were known to write for other publishers under different names.

"Nick Carter," "Bertha M. Clay," and "W. B. Lawson," all being copyrighted pseudonyms belonging to specific publishers, were farmed out to various hack writers who composed stories to order. "Nick Carter" was used by at least seven writers and "Bertha M. Clay" and "W. B. Lawson" by no fewer than four each.

Nicknames may be contractions of real names, such as "Bill" for William, "Art" for Arthur, "Dick" for Richard and "Ted" for Theodore. Nicknames may stem from a physical characteristic of an individual, such as "Fats," "Slim," "Red," or "Shorty." They may be reflections of his character, as "The Cruel," "The Terrible," "The Good," "The Wise," or "The Magnificent." They may be the result of circumstances surrounding a person, as in the case of Abraham Lincoln, called, among other things, "The Martyr President," a term also applied to President Garfield. Again, Presidents Arthur, Cleveland, Fillmore, Andrew Johnson, and Tyler were all called "His Accidency."

Nicknames may be complimentary or otherwise. President Andrew Jackson, known as "Old Hickory," surely had no reason to feel that those who so designated him were not paying him a compliment. On the other hand, those who dubbed the weak Richard Cromwell "Queen Dick" were obviously not great admirers of the young Lord Protector of England.

Pen names, stage names, pseudonyms, appellations, sobriquets, nicknames--whatever they may be called: the purpose of this handbook is to identify real persons, both living and dead, behind the "other" names applied to them and/or used by them. Included are men and women from all walks of life: authors, actors, military figures, jazz and classical musicians, statesmen, rulers, popes, saints, criminals, bullfighters, sports personages and people of many other occupations. No time, geographical, or occupational limitations are imposed.

There are approximately 15,000 main entries, covering in most cases the real name of the individual cited, and some 25,000 nicknames and/or pseudonyms are indicated.

The book is so designed that one may (1) determine the nickname(s) or pseudonym(s) applied to a given person, and (2) learn the real name of the person(s) to whom a particular nickname or pseudonym applies. Real names are given in CAPITAL LETTERS and nicknames and pseudonyms are shown in lower case. The main entry consists of a person's real name--except in the case of joint pseudonyms as explained below--together with his birth date, death date where applicable, a short designation in square brackets of his nationality and occupation, and then his nickname(s) and/or pseudonym(s). All items are shown in one alphabetical listing and nicknames and pseudonyms are cross-indexed to the appropriate main entry or entries.

EXAMPLE

Main entry:	Cross references:
SPAETH, SIGMUND GOTTFRIED (1885-1965) [American musicologist, writer and lecturer] The Tune Detective	Tune Detective, The. See: SPAETH, SIGMUND GOTTFRIED
	Detective, The Tune. See: SPAETH, SIGMUND GOTTFRIED

Nicknames and pseudonyms, when consisting of two or more words, as in the example above, are indexed by all significant words. When two or more individuals have the same nickname, as in such cases as "Buster," "Red," "Spike," or "Fats," these are shown individually in the main entries and consolidated into a single entry in the cross reference.

EXAMPLE

<table>
<tr><td><u>Main entry:</u></td><td><u>Cross references (consolidated)</u></td></tr>
<tr><td>BAILEY, WILLIAM C. (1902-)
[American jazz musician (clarinet)]
Buster Bailey</td><td>Buster. See:
BAILEY, WILLIAM C.
COOPER, GEORGE
CRABBE, CLARENCE LINDEN
HARDING, LAVERE
KEATON, JOSEPH FRANCIS
SHAVER, FLOYD HERBERT</td></tr>
</table>

Where joint authors use a common pseudonym, such shared pseudonym is shown in lower case as the main entry, and "see" references are indicated from the individual real names of the writing team, shown in CAPITAL LETTERS.

When either or both of two joint authors also wrote separately, using individual pseudonyms, a main entry (IN CAPITAL LETTERS) appears for each such author, listing the pseudonyms used by each, in lower case, similar to the example shown for SIGMUND GOTTFRIED SPAETH. Cross references between the author main entries and the joint pseudonym main entry are also provided.

EXAMPLES

<table>
<tr><td><u>Main entry for joint authors using a common pseudonym:</u></td><td><u>Cross References:</u></td></tr>
<tr><td>Sisters of the West, joint pseud. of MRS. FRANCES FULLER BARRITT VICTOR (1826-1902) and her sister MRS. METTA VICTORIA FULLER MORSE VICTOR (1831-85) [American poets, editors and authors]</td><td>Sisters of the West. See also:
VICTOR, MRS. FRANCES FULLER BARRITT
VICTOR, MRS. METTA VICTORIA FULLER MORSE

West, Sisters of the. See:
Sisters of the West
VICTOR, MRS. FRANCES FULLER BARRITT VICTOR
MRS. METTA VICTORIA FULLER MORSE</td></tr>
</table>

Main entries for each individual author using individual pseudonym(s):

VICTOR, MRS. FRANCES FULLER BARRITT (1826-1902) [American author, poet and editor]
Florence Fane

VICTOR, MRS. METTA VICTORIA FULLER MORSE (1831-85) [American author, poet and editor]
Eleanor Lee Edwards
Walter T. Gray
Rose Kennedy
Mrs. Mark Peabody
Seeley Regester
The Singing Sybil

Cross References (cont.):

VICTOR, MRS. FRANCES FULLER BARRITT. See also: Sisters of the West

VICTOR, MRS. METTA VICTORIA FULLER MORSE. See also: Sisters of the West

Florence Fane. See: VICTOR, MRS. FRANCES FULLER BARRITT
Fane, Florence. See: VICTOR, MRS. FRANCES FULLER BARRITT
Eleanor Lee Edwards. See: VICTOR, MRS. METTA VICTORIA FULLER MORSE
Edwards, Eleanor Lee. See: VICTOR, MRS. METTA VICTORIA FULLER MORSE
Walter T. Gray. See: VICTOR, MRS. METTA VICTORIA FULLER MORSE
Gray, Walter T. See: VICTOR, MRS. METTA VICTORIA FULLER MORSE

"See also" references are included in instances of alternative spellings. "Alan," for example, is referred to "Allan," "Alain," "Allen," "Alleyn," and "Allyn," and each of these spellings is referred to the others. Similar names ("Smith-Smyth," the various forms of "Frederick" and "Catherine," "Crosbie-Crosby-Cosby" and the like are all cross-referenced. Hopefully this will make the various items easier to locate than might otherwise be the case.

In assembling material for this handbook the compiler was appalled to encounter a substantial number of discrepancies in the birth dates as reported by various standard reference sources. In some cases names were given contradictorily by these sources. While every effort was made to resolve such discrepancies, undoubtedly some have slipped through and appear as errata in this volume. It is hoped that readers who can furnish corrections in such instances will communicate them to the compiler.

In years to come this handbook could conceivably be revised and enlarged. Suggestions for additional names to be included in the revision, together with birth dates, death dates where applicable, an indication of the nationality and occupation of the person named and, of course, the nickname(s) and/or pseudonym(s) used, as well as the source of the information, would be most welcome.

During the period required to compile the material for this book many people gave willing assistance. Members of the faculty of the Department of Library Science, Indiana State University, including Mr. Ronald Haselhuhn, Dr. Choong Han Kim, Dr. Nancy Pillon and Miss Elizabeth Weller, were particularly helpful. Mr. O. Gene Norman, head of the Cunningham Memorial Library reference department of Indiana State University, as well as various members of his staff, gave valuable assistance, as did Mrs. David Anderson, assistant catalog librarian of the Cunningham Memorial Library. My wife Marjorie also deserves special thanks for her help in reading proof, in alphabetizing the 3" x 5" cards on which the information was assembled, and in other ways.

The compiler wishes to express his deep appreciation to these persons at this time.

Harold S. Sharp

Indiana State University
Terre Haute, Indiana
June 1971

HANDBOOK OF PSEUDONYMS AND PERSONAL NICKNAMES

A

A. See:
JOHNSON, ANNABELL JONES

A. A. Abbott. See:
SPEWACK, SAMUEL

A. A. Archer. See:
JOSCELYN, ARCHIE L.

A. A. Fair. See:
GARDNER, ERLE STANLEY

A. B. See:
GUTHRIE, ALFRED BERTRAM, JR.

A. B. Brooke. See:
JENNINGS, LESLIE NELSON

A. B. Carrick. See:
LINDSAY, HAROLD ARTHUR BILL

A Bludgeon Satirist. See:
HOPKINS, DR. LEMUEL

A Bostonian. See:
POE, EDGAR ALLAN

A Bystander. See:
SMITH, GOLDWIN

A Celebrated Actress. See:
AIKEN, ALBERT W.

A Celebrated Author. See:
DEY, FREDERICK VAN RENSSAELER

A Citizen of New York. See:
DUNLAP, WILLIAM

A Citizen of Philadelphia. See:
CAREY, MATHEW

A Civil War Captain. See:
ROLFE, MARO O.

A. D. B. See:
RAI, DEWAN BAHADUR DEWAN JAMIAT

A Dissenter. See:
SWIFT, JONATHAN

A. Don Adams. See:
CLEVELAND, PHILIP JEROME

A. E. See:
COPPARD, ALFRED EDGAR
HOUSMAN, ALFRED EDWARD
Johnson, A. E.

AE. See:
RUSSELL, GEORGE WILLIAM

A. E. F., The D'Artagnan of the. See: MacARTHUR, DOUGLAS

A. F. Grant, Major. See:
HARBAUGH, THOMAS CHALMERS

A. Fellow Feelin'. See:
FULLER, HENRY STARKEY

A Fighter Pilot. See:
JOHNSON, HUGH ANTHONY STEPHEN

A. G. See:
YATES, ALAN GEOFFREY

A Gentleman of Connecticut. See:
HOPKINS, DR. LEMUEL

A Gentleman of Maryland. See:
BRACKENRIDGE, HUGH HENRY

A Gentleman of Oxford. See:
SHELLEY, PERCY BYSSHE

A Gentleman of the Army. See:
STEELE, SIR RICHARD

A Gentleman with a Duster. See: BEGBIE, HAROLD

A Graduate of Oxford. See:
RUSKIN, JOHN

A Great Detective. See:
SCHINDLER, RAYMOND C.

A Greedy Woman. See:
PENNELL, ELIZABETH

A. H. Post. See:
BADGER, JOSEPH E., JR.

A. H. Z. See:
CARR, ALBERT ZOLOTKOFF

A Heaven-taught Plowman. See:
BURNS, ROBERT

A. J. See:
FOYT, ANTHONY JOSEPH, JR.

A.K. Laidlaw. See:
GRIEVE, CHRISTOPHER MURRAY
A.K. Roche. See:
KAPLAN, BOCHE
A.K. Sims, Lieut. See:
WHITSON, JOHN HARVEY
A.L.O.E. (A Lady of England). See: TUCKER, CHARLOTTE MARIA
A Lady. See:
AUSTEN, JANE
BOTSFORD, MARGARET
COOPER, SUSAN FENIMORE
FIELDING, SARAH
HOWE, JULIA WARD
SMITH, CLARA POGSON
WINCHILSEA, ANNE FINCH, COUNTESS OF
A Lady of England (A.L.O.E.). See: TUCKER, CHARLOTTE MARIA
A Lady of Maine. See:
BARRELL, SARAH SAYWARD
A Lady of Massachusetts. See:
BARRELL, SARAH SAYWARD
A Lady of Philadelphia. See:
BOTSFORD, MARGARET
A Lady of Quality. See:
BAGNOLD, ENID
A Lay Preacher to the Largest Congregation in the United States. See:
BOK, EDWARD WILLIAM
A. Lester-Rands. See:
JUDD, FREDERICK CHARLES
A Lover of Candour. See:
HOPKINSON, FRANCIS
A.M.D. See:
DENISON, MARY ANDREWS
A.M. Lightner. See:
HOPF, ALICE LIGHTNER
A.M.R. Gordon. See:
ROSE, A. McGREGOR
A.M. Renner. See:
GATTERMANN, EUGEN LUDWIG
A.N. Tyz. See:
TSEU, YIH-ZAN
A Native of America. See:
PARKE, JOHN
A.P. Yorick. See:
TINDALL, WILLIAM YORK
A Pennsylvania Farmer. See:
DICKINSON, JOHN
A Person of Honour. See:
SOUTHLAND, T.
SWIFT, JONATHAN
A Person of Quality. See:
SWIFT, JONATHAN
A Political Thor. See:
FARLEY, JAMES ALOYSIUS
A. Riposte. See:
MORDAUNT, MRS. EVELYN MAY CLOWES
A.S. See:
STARING, ADOLPH
A.S.M. See:
HUTCHINSON, ARTHUR STUART MENTETH
A. St. Laurence. See:
FELKIN, ALFRED LAURENCE
A Seafarer. See:
RUSSELL, WILLIAM CLARK
A Son of the Soil. See:
FLETCHER, JOSEPH SMITH
A Traveling Bachelor. See:
COOPER, JAMES FENIMORE
A U.S. Detective, E.S. St. Mox. See: ELLIS, EDWARD SYLVESTER
A.W. Rolker. See:
ROLFE, MARO O.
A Yankee. See:
WHITE, RICHARD GRANT
Aaron. See also:
ARON
Aaron the Upright. See:
HARUN AL-RASHID
AARTSEN, PETER (1507-73) [Flemish painter]
Long Peter
ABARBANELL, JACOB RALPH (1852-1922) [American attorney and author of dime novels]
Harrigan and Hart
Paul Revere
Ralph Royal

Abbé. See:
RAYNAL, GUILLAUME THOMAS FRANÇOIS
Abbé (Abt). See:
VOGLER, GEORG JOSEPH
ABBE, CLEVELAND (1838-1916) [American publisher of weather forecasts]
Old Prob
Old Probabilities
Abbé Edgeworth. See:
EDGEWORTH, HENRY ESSEX
Abbé Prévost, The. See:
PRÉVOST, ANTOINE FRANÇOIS
ABBITT, JIM (1916-) [American football player]
Jackrabbit
ABBOT, GEORGE (1603-49) [English scholar and writer]
The Puritan
Abbott, A. A. See:
SPEWACK, SAMUEL
Abbott, Anthony. See:
OURSLER, CHARLES FULTON
ABBOTT, AUSTIN. See:
Benauly
ABBOTT, BENJAMIN VAUGHAN. See:
Benauly
ABBOTT, GRACE (1878-1939) [American social worker]
The Second Mother of Everybody's Children
ABBOTT, LAWRENCE GILBERT (1901-) [American musician and teacher]
Larry Abbott
ABBOTT, LYMAN. See:
Benauly
Abbott, Manager Henry. See:
STRATEMEYER, EDWARD L.
ABBOTT, WILLIAM (1900-) [American comedian]
Bud Abbott
Abby, Dear. See:
PHILLIPS, PAULINE ESTHER FRIEDMAN
Abderite, The. See:
DEMOCRITUS
ABDUL HAMID II (1842-1918) [ruler of Ottoman empire]
Bloody Abdul
Abdul the Damned
Abdullah, Achmed. See:
SYYED SHAYKH ACHMED ABDULLAH NADIR KHAN EL-IDRISSVIEH EL-DURANI
Abe. See:
BURROWS, ABRAM S.
Abe, Honest. See:
LINCOLN, ABRAHAM
Abe Lyman. See:
SIMON, ABRAHAM
Abe Martin. See:
HUBBARD, FRANK McKINNEY
Abe, Old. See:
LINCOLN, ABRAHAM
Abe, Uncle. See:
LINCOLN, ABRAHAM
ABEL, ALAN IRWIN (1928-) [American lecturer, hoaxer, columnist and author]
Julius Bristol
Professor Bunker C. Hill
Dr. Bruce Spencer
ABEL, CHARLES WILLIAM (1863-1930) [English clergyman and missionary]
Apostle to the Papuans
ABEL, JEANNE (1937-) [American author and hoaxer]
Yetta Bronstein
Abel Shufflebottom. See:
SOUTHEY, ROBERT
Abelson, Ann. See:
CAVALLARO, ANN ABELSON
ABELSON, NATHAN (1906-) [American dress manufacturer]
Nat Abelson
Aber. See:
GRUNDY, WILFRED WALKER
ABERCROMBIE, LASCELLES (1881-1938) [English poet and critic]
The Georgian Laureate
ABERLE, KATHLEEN GOUGH (1925-) [British anthro-

pologist and author]
Kathleen Gough
ABERNETHY, JOHN (1764-1831) [English surgeon]
Doctor My-book
ABERSHAW, LOUIS JEREMIAH (c. 1773-95) [English highwayman]
Jerry Abershaw
Abigail Van Buren. See: PHILLIPS, PAULINE ESTHER FRIEDMAN
ABISCH, ROSLYN KROOP (1927-) [American copywriter, teacher and author]
Roz Abisch
Abolitionist Movement, Peter-the-Hermit of the. See: LUNDY, BENJAMIN
Abolitionist, The Martyr. See: LOVEJOY, ELIJAH PARRISH
About, Old Round. See: CLEVELAND, BENJAMIN
Above Grammar (Supra Grammaticam). See: SIGISMUND
ABRAHAM (c. 2866 B.C. -1700 B.C.) [traditional founder of the Hebrew people]
Father Abraham
Abraham-a-Santa Clara. See: MEGERLE, HANS ULRICH
Abraham, Father. See: FRANKLIN, BENJAMIN
LINCOLN, ABRAHAM
Abraham Lincoln of the Sea, The. See: FURUSETH, ANDREW
ABRAMOWITZ, SHALOM JACOB (1836-1917) [Hebrew writer]
Mendele Mocher Seforim
Abrams, Lee. See: ABRAMSON, LEON
Abrams, Ray. See: ABRAMSON, RAY
ABRAMSON, LEON (1925-) [American jazz musician (drums)]
Lee Abrams
ABRAMSON, RAYMOND (1920-) [American jazz musician (tenor saxophone)]
Ray Abrams
Abt (Abbé). See: VOGLER, GEORG JOSEPH
ABUL KALAM AZAD, MAULANA (1888-) [President of the Indian National Congress; scholar and author]
Azad (The Free)
ABUZA, SOPHIE (1884-1966) [Russian-American singer and entertainer]
The Last of the Red-Hot Mammas
The Queen of Jazz
Sophie Tucker
Abyssinian, The. See: BRUCE, JAMES
Academic Investor. See: REDDAWAY, WILLIAM BRIAN
Academic Pharisee, The. See: BONAPARTE, CHARLES JOSEPH
Academy, The Father of the United States Military. See: THAYER, SYLVANUS
Accidency, His. See: ARTHUR, CHESTER ALAN
CLEVELAND, STEPHEN GROVER
FILLMORE, MILLARD
JOHNSON, ANDREW
TYLER, JOHN
Accidental President, An. See: FILLMORE, MILLARD
Accidental President, The. See: ADAMS, JOHN QUINCY
TYLER, JOHN
Accomac, The Apostle of. See: MAKEMIE, FRANCIS
Accordion, The Liberace of the. See: WELK, LAWRENCE
Accordion, The Yankee Clipper of the. See: CONTINO, RICHARD
Accounts. See: WARREN, LINDSAY CARTER
Accursed Judas, A Thrice. See: BERIA, LAVRENTI PAVLOVICH
Ace. See: PANCOAST, ASA
SORRELL, VICTOR GARLAND
WILSON, JAMES

Ace Drummer Man, That. See:
KRUPA, EUGENE BERTRAM
Ace Investigator, Ohio's. See:
SLATER, ORA E.
Ace of Aces. See:
RICKENBACKER, EDWARD VERNON
Ace of Spades, Old. See:
LEE, ROBERT EDWARD
Ace, The Ukulele. See:
MARVIN, JOHN
Aces, Ace of. See:
RICKENBACKER, EDWARD VERNON
ACHA, DESIDERIO ALBERTO ARNAZ Y DE, 3D (1917-) [Cuban musician, actor and television producer]
Desi Arnaz
Achad Ha-am (One of the People). See: GINZBERG, ASCHER
Ache, Caran d'. See:
POIRÉ, EMMANUEL
Acher, Mathias. See:
BIRNBAUM, NATHAN
Achilles of England, The. See:
JOHN
Achilles of Germany, The. See:
ALBERT III
Achilles of the Gael, The. See:
SETANTA
Achilles, The English. See:
TALBOT, JOHN
WELLINGTON, ARTHUR WELLESLEY, 1ST DUKE OF
Achilles, The Roman. See:
SICINIUS DENATUS
ACHILLINI, ALESSANDRO (1463-1512) [Italian physician and philosopher]
The Second Aristotle
Achmed Abdullah. See:
SYYED SHAYKH ACHMED ABDULLAH NADIR KHAN EL-IDRISSVIEH EL-DURANI
Achyut. See:
BIRLA, LAKSHMINIWAS
ACKLON, RAUFF DE RYTHER DUAN (1902-) [Canadian motion picture and stage actor]
David Manners
Acre, Stephen. See:
GRUBER, FRANK
Act, The Father of the Homestead. See:
JOHNSON, ANDREW
Acting Governor of the English Nation. See:
CAXTON, WILLIAM
Action, The Pope of Catholic. See: SARTO, GIUSEPPE MELCHIORRE
Actius Syncerus. See:
SANNAZARO, JACOPO
Acton Bell. See:
BRONTË, ANNE
Actor, The. See:
SUTTON, WILLIAM
Actor, The Greatest English. See: GARRICK, DAVID
Actors, The Mercutio of. See:
LEWIS, WILLIAM THOMAS
Actress, A Celebrated. See:
AIKEN, ALBERT W.
Actress Without a Rival, The Poetic. See:
MURRAY, ALMA
Ada Clare. See:
McELHENEY, JANE
Ada Rehan. See:
CREHAN, ADA
Ada Rubin. See:
ROETER, ADA
Adah Bertha Menken. See:
FUERTES, DOLORES ADIOS
Adah Isaacs Menken. See:
FUERTES DOLORES ADIOS
Adair Aldon. See: MEIGS, CORNELIA LYNDE
ADAIR, THOMAS M. (1913-) [American writer of radio shows]
Tom Adair
Adam. See:
LEBENSOHN, ABRAHAM DOB
Adam, Allen. See:
Allen, Adam
EPSTEIN, BERYL WILLIAMS
Adam Bradford, M.D. See:
WASSERSUG, JOSEPH D.
Adam, Cornel. See:
LENGYEL, CORNEL ADAM

Adam Faith. See:
NELHAMS, TERENCE
Adam Fletcher. See:
FLEXNER, STUART BERG
Adam Greene. See:
SCOTT, PETER DALE
Adam Hall. See:
TREVOR, ELLESTON
Adam Hardwick. See:
CONNOR, JOHN ANTHONY
Adam Hornbook. See:
COOPER, THOMAS
Adam Knight. See:
LARIAR, LAWRENCE
Adam Smith. See:
GOODMAN, GEORGE J.W.
Adamantius (The Man of Steel).
See: ORIGEN
(ORIGENES)
Adamite, Pre. See:
HOAR, GEORGE FRISBIE
ADAMS [Adams]. See also:
Addums
Adams, A. Don. See:
CLEVELAND, PHILIP
JEROME
ADAMS, ALBERT J. (1844-1907)
[American gambler]
The Policy King
Adams, Annette. See:
ROWLAND, DONALD
SYDNEY
ADAMS, ARTHUR HENRY
(1872-1936) [New Zealand
novelist and poet]
James James
ADAMS, BERTRAM MARTIN
(1879-) [American
author]
Bill Adams
Adams, Betsy. See:
PITCHER, GLADYS
Adams, Captain Bruin. See:
ELLIS, EDWARD SYL-
VESTER
Adams, Captain J. F. C. See:
ELLIS, EDWARD
SYLVESTER
Adams, Charles. See:
SCHWANBECK, KARL
ADAM
Adams, Christopher. See:
HOPKINS, KENNETH
ADAMS, CLIFTON (1919-)
[American musician and
author]
Jonathan Gant
Matt Kinkaid
Clay Randall
Adams, Edie. See:
KOVACS, EDITH ENKE
ADAMS, FRANK RAMSAY
(1883-1963) [American
author]
Carl Dane
ADAMS, FRANKLIN PIERCE
(1881-1960) [American
author and newspaper
columnist]
F. P. A.
Adams, George. See:
LENGYEL, GEZA
ADAMS, HARRIET STRATEMEY-
ER (fl. late 19th, early
20th centuries) [American
author]
Carolyn Keene
Adams, Harrison. See:
RATHBONE, ST. GEORGE
HENRY
STRATEMEYER, EDWARD
L.
Adams, Henry, joint pseud. of
HENRY HITCH ADAMS
(1917-) and ALLEN B.
COOK (-) [American
authors]
ADAMS, HENRY BROOKS (1838-
1918 [American historian
and essayist]
Francis Snow Compton
ADAMS, HENRY JOSEPH (fl.
late 19th, early 20th cent.)
[English churchman and
author]
Ignotus
Adams, Henry T. See:
RANSOM, JAY ELLIS
Adams, James Fenimore Cooper.
See: ELLIS, EDWARD
SYLVESTER
ADAMS, JOHN (1735-1826)
[second President of the
United States]
Atlas of Independence
Colossus of American Inde-

pendence
Colossus of Debate
Colossus of Independence
Duke of Braintree
The Father of American Independence
The Father of the American Navy
His Rotundity
Novanglus
Old Sink or Swim
Partisan of Independence

Adams, John. See:
SMITH, ALEXANDER

ADAMS, JOHN QUINCY (1767-1848) [sixth President of the United States]
The Accidental President
Old Man Eloquent
Second John

Adams, Lowell. See:
JOSEPH, JAMES HERZ

Adams, Maude. See:
KISKADDEN, MAUDE

Adams, Moses. See:
BAGBY, GEORGE WILLIAM

Adams, Nick. See:
ADAMSHOCK, NICHOLAS

Adams of New Jersey, The Samuel. See:
FISHER, HENDRICK

Adams of North Carolina, The Samuel. See:
HARNETT, CORNELIUS

ADAMS, PARK (1930-) [American jazz musician (baritone saxophone)]
Pepper Adams

ADAMS, ROBERT MARTIN (1915-) [American educator and author]
R.M. Krapp

ADAMS, ROSE (1910-71) [American gypsy leader]
The Queen of the Gypsies

ADAMS, SAMUEL (1722-1803) [American Revolutionary statesman and patriot]
Amendment Monger
American Cato
The Brain of the Revolution
Chief Incendiary of the White House
Cromwell of New America
The Father of America
The Father of the American Revolution
The Last of the Puritans
Man of the Town Meeting
Psalm Singer
Sam the Maltster
Samuel the Publican
The Tribune of the People
Would-be Cromwell of America

ADAMS, SAMUEL HOPKINS (1871-1958) [American author]
Warner Fabian

ADAMS, WILLIAM TAYLOR (1822-97) [American writer of dime novels]
Warren T. Ashton
Irving Brown
Clingham Hunter, M.D.
Brooks McCormick
Old Stager
Oliver Optic
Oliver Optic, M.D.
Gale Winterton

ADAMSHOCK, NICHOLAS (1932-1968) [American motion picture actor]
Nick Adams

Adamson, Graham. See:
GROOM, ARTHUR WILLIAM

Adamus, Franz. See:
BRONNER, FERDINAND

ADCOCK, ARTHUR ST. JOHN (1864-) [British author]
Flecnoc
Arthur Rutland

ADDERLEY, JULIAN EDWIN (1928-) [American jazz musician (alto saxophone)]
Cannonball Adderley

ADDICKS, JOHN EDWARD O'SULLIVAN (1841-1919) [American industrialist and politician]
Gus Addicks
The Napoleon of Gas

ADDISON, JOSEPH (1672-1719) [English essayist, poet and statesman]
Clio

The English Atticus
Sir Roger de Coverley
Addison of the North, The.
See: MacKENZIE, HENRY
Addison Steele. See:
WHITSON, JOHN HARVEY
Addison, The American. See:
DENNIE, JOSEPH
Addison, The Northern. See:
MacKENZIE, HENRY
Addison, The Spanish. See:
MONTENEGRO, FREY
BENITO FEYJOO Y
ADDLEMAN, BONNIE JEAN
(1926-) [American jazz
musician (bass)]
Bonnie Wetzel
Addums. See also:
Adams
Addums, Mozis. See:
BAGBY, GEORGE WILLIAM
Addy, Ted. See:
WINTERBOTHAM, RUSSELL
ROBERT
Adelaide Davenport. See:
AIKEN, ALBERT W.
ADELBERT (c. 955-97) [Bohemian
prince and prelate]
St. Adelbert
The Apostle of the Prussians
Adele Astaire. See:
AUSTERLITZ, ADELE
Adele Mara. See:
DELGADO, ADELAIDA
Adeler. See also:
ADLER
Adler
Adeler, Max. See:
CLARKE, CHARLES HEBER
Adelphi Terriss, No. 1. See:
LEWIN, WILLIAM CHARLES
JAMES
ADELSTEIN, MILTON (1925-)
[American composer and
musician]
Milt Rogers
ADENAUER, KONRAD (1876-1967)
[German statesman]
Der Alte (The Old Man)
ADEODATUS (died 676) [Supreme
Pontiff of Roman Catholic
Church]
Pope Adeodatus II
St. Adeodatus
Adeodatus I, Pope. See:
DEUSDEDIT
ADER, PAUL FASSETT (1919-
) [American novelist]
James Allen
Adirondack. See:
MURRAY, WILLIAM HENRY
HARRISON
Adjutant, The Devil's. See:
WALLER, JOHN
Adkin, Knight. See:
KNIGHT-ADKIN, JAMES H.
ADKINSON, HARVEY E. (1934-
) [American composer]
Gene Adkinson
ADLAM, BASIL G. (191?-)
[English composer]
Buzz Adlam
ADLER [Adler]. See also:
Adeler
ADLER, E. MAURICE (1909-60)
[American motion picture
producer]
Buddy Adler
Adler, Irene. See:
STORR, CATHERINE COLE
ADLER, IRVING (1913-)
[American educator and
author]
Robert Irving
ADLER, LAWRENCE CECIL
(1914-) [American har-
monica virtuoso]
Larry Adler
ADLER, WILLIAM (1929-)
[American author]
Bill Adler
Administration, The Queen of
the Rosewater. See:
GREENHOW, ROSE O'NEAL
Admirable Crichton of our City
Politicians. See:
HALL, ABRAHAM OAKEY
Admirable Crichton, The. See:
CRICHTON, JAMES
Admirable Doctor, The. See:
BACON, ROGER
Admirable, The. See:
CRICHTON, JAMES
EZRA, ABRAHAM BEN
MEIR IBN
Admiral. See:
HOFFMAN, MICHAEL

Admiral of the Mosquitos. See:
COLUMBUS, CHRISTOPHER
Admiral of the Ocean Sea. See:
COLUMBUS, CHRISTOPHER
Admiral of the Trinity. See:
HATFIELD, BAZIL MUSE
Admiral, The Land. See:
REESIDE, JAMES
Admirari, Esq., Nil. See:
SHELTON, FREDERICK WILLIAM MAY
Admired Woman, The World's Most. See:
ROOSEVELT, ANNA ELEANOR
Adolescent of American Poetry, The Perpetual. See:
POUND, EZRA LOOMIS
Adolf Hitler's Evil Genius. See:
BORMANN, MARTIN
Adolf Schickelgrüber. See:
HITLER, ADOLF
Adolphus, Gustavus. See:
GUSTAVUS II
GUSTAVUS IV
Adonis of Forty (or Fifty), The Fat. See:
GEORGE IV
Adorée, Renée. See:
FONTE, JEANNE DE LA
Adria, The Blind Man of. See:
GROTO, LUIGI
ADRIAN. See also:
HADRIAN (ADRIAN)
ADRIAN (died 795) [Supreme Pontiff of Roman Catholic Church]
Pope Adrian I
ADRIAN (died 872) [Supreme Pontiff of Roman Catholic Church]
Pope Adrian II
ADRIAN (died 885) [Supreme Pontiff of Roman Catholic Church]
Pope Adrian III
St. Adrian
Adrian IV, Pope. See:
BREAKSPEAR, NICKOLAS
Adrian V, Pope. See:
FIESCHI, OTTOBONO
Adrian VI, Pope. See:
DEDEL, ADRIAN
Adrian, Iris. See:
HOSTETTER, IRIS A.
Adrian, Mary. See:
JORGENSEN, MARY VENN
Adrian Mason. See:
LEE, REV. ALBERT
Adrian Murray. See:
CURRAN, MONA ELISA
Adrian Ross. See:
ROPES, ARTHUR REED
ADRIANCE, JAN STERLING (1923) [American stage and motion picture actress]
Jan Sterling
ADULYADEJ, BHUMIBOL (1927-) [King of Thailand (Siam)]
Rama IX
Advance Agent of Emancipation, The. See:
MOTT, LUCRETIA
Advance Agent, Prosperity's. See: McKINLEY, WILLIAM
Adventurer, The Young. See:
STUART, CHARLES EDWARD LOUIS PHILIP CASIMIR
Adversity. See:
HUME, JOSEPH
Advertiser, The. See:
BARTON, BRUCE
Advertising King, The. See:
BARTON, BRUCE
Advertising, The Dean of Community. See:
HATFIELD, CHARLES FOLSOM
Adviser of Presidents, The. See: BARUCH, BERNARD MANNES
Advocate of Justice, Love and Humanity. The Sweet-Spirited. See:
MOTT, LUCRETIA
AEDILBERCT. See: ETHELBERT (AETHELBERT) (AEDILBERCT)
AEGIDIUS OF ASSISI (died 1262) [Italian friar and philosopher]
Blessed Giles
The Knight of Our Round Table
AELFGIFA, EMMA (died 1052)

[daughter of RICHARD II of Normandy]
The Gem of Normandy
AELFRED. See:
ALFRED (AELFRED)
AELFRIC (c.955-c.1020) [Anglo-Saxon religious writer]
Grammaticus
AELIANUS, CLAUDIUS (fl. c.220) [Latin writer]
The Sophist
Aeneas MacDonald. See:
THOMSON, GEORGE MALCOLM
Aeneas Silvius. See:
PICCOLOMINI, ENEA SILVIO DE
Aeon. See:
RUSSELL, GEORGE WILLIAM
Aëra, Per. See:
BOOTHBY, FREDERICK LEWIS MAITLAND
Aerial Photography, The Father of Modern. See:
GODDARD, GEORGE WILLIAM
AESCHYLUS (525-456 B.C.) [Greek tragic dramatist]
The Father of Greek Tragedy
Aesop of England, The. See:
GAY, JOHN
Aesop of France, The. See:
FONTAINE, JEAN DE LA
Aesop of Germany, The. See:
LESSING, GOTTHOLD EPHRAIM
AETHELBERT See:
ETHELBERT (AETHELBERT) (AEDILBERCT)
AETHELFLAED (died c.918) [daughter of ALFRED THE GREAT of England]
The Lady of the Mercians
AETHELRED. See:
ETHELRED (AETHELRED) II
AËTIUS (died c.367) [Anatolian churchman and theologian]
The Ungodly
Afer. See:
ARNOBIUS
Affable, The. See:
CHARLES VIII
Affidavit. See:
BOIES, HORACE
Affonso Henriques. See:
ALFONSO I
Affonso o Africano. See:
ALFONSO V
Africa, The Liberator of. See:
PHILIP, JOHN
African Astronomer, The. See:
BANNEKER, BENJAMIN
African Roscius, The. See:
ALDRIDGE, IRA
African, The. See:
ALFONSO V
Africano, Affonso o. See:
ALFONSO V
Africanus, Leo. See:
ALWAZZAN (ALWEZAZ), ALHASSAN IBN MOHAMMED
Afterwit, Anthony. See:
FRANKLIN, BENJAMIN
Aga Khan IV. See:
KARIM AL HUSSAINI SHAH
AGA SULTAN SIR MAHOMED SHAH (1877-1957) [Moslem religious leader]
Aga Khan III
Agamemnon, Old. See:
CARRINGTON, EDWARD
AGAPETUS (died 536) [Supreme Pontiff of Roman Catholic Church]
Pope Agapetus I
St. Agapetus
AGAPETUS (died 955) [Supreme Pontiff of Roman Catholic Church]
Pope Agapetus II
Agapida, Fray Antonio. See:
IRVING, WASHINGTON
Agar, Brian. See:
BALLARD, WILLIS TODHUNTER
Agard, H.E. See:
EVANS, HILARY
Agassiz, The Methodist. See:
MARCY, OLIVER
Agate. See:
REID, WHITELAW
Agatha Christie. See:
MILLER, AGATHA MARY CLARISSA

AGATHARCOS (c. 490-429 B.C.)
[Athenian artist]
The Founder of Scene Painting
AGATHO (died 681) [Supreme Pontiff of Roman Catholic Church]
Pope Agatho
St. Agatho
Age, The Apelles of His. See:
COOPER, SAMUEL
Age, The Censor of the. See:
CARLYLE, THOMAS
Age, The Homer of His. See:
ANGILBERT, ST.
Age, The Lord of the. See:
SULAIMAN I or II
Age, The Miracle of Our. See:
SIDNEY (SYDNEY), SIR PHILIP
Age, The Most Conspicuous Controversionalist of His. See:
CHILLINGWORTH, WILLIAM
Age, The Tibullus of His. See:
SEDLEY, SIR CHARLES
Age, The Translator-General in His. See:
HOLLAND, PHILEMON
Aged Eagle. See:
ELIOT, THOMAS STEARNS
Agent of Emancipation, The Advance. See:
MOTT, LUCRETIA
Agent, Prosperity's Advance.
See: McKINLEY, WILLIAM
Ages, The Walter Scott of the Middle. See:
FROISSART, JEAN
Aggressive Jack Benny, An. See:
KNIBERG, IRWIN ALAN
Agile Penne. See:
AIKEN, ALBERT W.
AGISILAUS (455-361 B.C.)
[King of Sparta]
The Great
Agitator, The Sand Lot. See:
KEARNEY, DENIS
Aglaius. See:
TIMROD, HENRY
AGNES, COUNTESS OF DUNBAR (c. 1312-69) [Scottish heroine]
Black Agnes
Agnes Goossen. See:
EPP, MARGARET
Agnes Rothery. See:
PRATT, AGNES EDWARDS ROTHERY
AGNEW, EDITH JOSEPHINE (1897-) [American Librarian, teacher and author]
Marcelino
AGNEW, ELIZA (1807-83) [American missionary to Ceylon]
The Mother of a Thousand Daughters
AGNEW, WALTER L. (c. 1880-1941) [American pugilist, vaudevillian and motion picture actor]
Stanley Fields
Agnostic, The Great. See:
INGERSOLL, ROBERT GREEN
Ago, Felix. See:
HALDEMAN, SAMUEL STEHMAN
AGOULT, COMTESSE D', MARIE CATHERINE SOPHIE DE FLAVIGNY (1805-76) [French author]
Daniel Stern
Agricola. See:
CRÈVECOEUR, MICHEL-GUILLAUME JEAN DE
AGRICOLA, GEORGIUS (1490-1555) [German scientist]
Georg Bauer
Agricola, Johannes. See:
SNEIDER (SCHNITTER), JOHANNES
Agricola, Martin. See:
SOHR (SORE), MARTIN
Agricola, Rodolphus. See:
HUYSMANN, ROELOF
Agricultural. See:
JONES, MARVIN
Agricultural Moses, The. See:
TILLMAN, BENJAMIN RYAN
Agriculture, The Father of Modern. See:
YOUNG, ARTHUR
Aguecheek. See:

FAIRBANKS, CHARLES BULLARD
Agujetas. See:
RIESGO, MANUEL MARTÍNEZ Y
Aherne, Owen. See:
CASSILL, RONALD VERLIN
Ahmad Jamal. See:
JONES, FRITZ
Ahmed Arabi. See:
AHMED PASHA
AHMED, MOHAMMED. See:
MOHAMMED AHMED
Aho Juhani. See:
BROFELDT, JUHANI
Ahrens, Thomas. See:
WILSON, ROGER C.
Aiglon, l' (The Eaglet). See:
BONAPARTE, NAPOLEON FRANÇOIS CHARLES JOSEPH
Aiguillette. See:
HARGREAVES, REGINALD CHARLES
AIKEN, ALBERT W. (1846-94) [American actor, playwright and author of dime novels]
A Celebrated Actress
Captain Frank P. Armstrong
Redmond Blake
Major Lewis W. Carson
Adelaide Davenport
Frances
Frances Helen Davenport
Agile Penne
Colonel Delle Sara
Lieut. Alfred B. Thorne
AIKEN, CONRAD POTTER (1889-) [American author]
Samuel Jeake, Jr.
AIKEN, GEORGE L. (1830-76) [American actor, playwright and author of dime novels]
Bernard Clyde
AIKEN, MARGARET (fl. late 16th cent.) [Scottish witch and informer]
The Great Witch of Balwery
AIKEN, LUCY (1781-1864) [British historian, biographer and writer of books for children]
Mary Godolphin
Aikman, Ann. See:
McQUADE, ANN AIKMAN
Aikman, Henry G. See:
ARMSTRONG, HAROLD HUNTER
Aileen Pringle. See:
BISBEE, AILEEN
AILLY, PIERRE D' (1350-1420) [French theologian and Nominalist writer]
The Eagle of the Doctors of France
The Hammer of the Heretics
Petrus de Alliaco
Aimard, Gustave. See:
GLOUX, OLIVIER
Aimé-Bien, Le (The Well-Beloved). See:
LOUIS XV
Aimee. See also:
AMY
Amy
Aimée, Anouk. See:
SORYA, FRANÇOISE
Aimee, Sister. See:
McPHERSON, AIMEE SEMPLE
Aimwell, Walter. See:
SIMONDS, WILLIAM
Ain Kalmus. See:
MAND, EWALD
Ainslie, Douglas. See:
DUFF, DOUGLAS AINSLIE GRANT
AINSWORTH, MARY DINSMORE SALTER (1913-) [American educator and author]
Mary D. Salter
AINSWORTH, NORMA (fl. 1932-64) [American columnist, feature writer and author]
Norma Paul Ruedi
Ainsworth, Ruth. See:
GILBERT, RUTH GALIARD AINSWORTH
Ain't Gonna Rain No Mo' Man,

The. See:
LEE, EDWARD D.
Air. See:
Sweethearts of the Air
Air, The Ambassador of the. See: LINDBERGH, CHARLES AUGUSTUS
Air, The Lonesome Singer of the. See:
MARVIN, JOHN
Air, The Prince of the. See:
WEISS, EHRICH (ERIK WEISZ)
Air Woman, America's Premier. See: PUTNAM, AMELIA EARHART
Aircraftsman Ross. See:
LAWRENCE, THOMAS EDWARD
Airlanes, The Idol of the. See:
GARBER, JAN
Airlie, Catherine. See:
MacLEOD, JEAN SUTHERLAND
Airplane Ears. See:
ANDERSON, JOHN Z.
AITKIN, ROBERT (1734-1802) [Scottish-American editor, publisher, printer and engraver]
Hudson Douglas
Ajax. See:
AVEN, ALGERNON JASPER
Akbar (The Great). See:
JELAL-ED-DIN-MOHAMMED
Akens, Floyd. See:
BAUM, LYMAN FRANK
AKENSIDE, MARK (1721-70) [English physician and poet]
The Bard of the Imagination
AKERS, ELIZABETH CHASE (1832-1911) [American poet and novelist]
Florence Percy
Akhmatova, Anna. See:
GORENKO, ANNA ANDREYEVNA
Akhnaton. See:
AMENHOTEP (AMENOPHIS)
Al. See:
ALCARO, ALFRED
CAPONE, ALPHONSE
DONAHUE, ALBERT FRANCIS
HIRT, ALOIS MAXWELL
LOPEZ, ALFONSO RAMÓN
MORRIS, ALVIN
ROSEN, ALBERT LEONARD
SCHACHT, ALEXANDER
SMITH, ALFRED EMANUEL
Al Avery. See:
MONTGOMERY, RUTHERFORD GEORGE
AL-BATTANI, ABDULLAH MUHAMMAD IBN-JABIR (fl. 850-929) [Arabian astronomer and mathematician]
Albategnius
Albatenius
Al, Big. See:
CAPONE, ALPHONSE
Al Bocca. See:
WINTER, BEVIS
Al Capp. See: CAPLIN, ALFRED GERALD
Al Cody. See:
JOSCELYN, ARCHIE L.
Al Edwards. See:
NOURSE, ALAN EDWARD
Al Foster. See:
FLEITMAN, ALEX O.
Al G. Barnes. See:
STONEHOUSE, ALPHEUS GEORGE BARNES
Al Jolson. See:
YOELSON, ASA
Al Mokanna (The Veiled). See:
DEN ATTA, HAKIM
Al Munger. See:
UNGER, MAURICE ALBERT
Al Shean. See:
SCHOENBERG, ALFRED
Al-Van-Gar. See:
RADWANSKI, PIERRE ARTHUR
Al Vega. See:
VAGRAMIAN, ARAM
Alabama Legislature, The Dean of the. See:
TUNSTALL, ALFRED MOORE
Alabama, The Father of the Public Schools of. See:
MEEK, ALEXANDER BEAUFORT

Aladdin. See:
PALLANTE, ALADDIN ABDULLAH
Alain. See:
Alan
ALLAN
Allan
ALLEN
Allen
Alleyn
Allyn
FOURNIER, HENRI ALAIN
ALAIN DE LILLE (ALANUS DE INSULIS) (1114?-1203?) [Flemish theologian and philosopher]
The Universal Doctor
Alamgir (Conqueror of the World) See: MOHAMMED
Alamo Boyd. See: BOSWORTH, ALLAN RUCKER
Alan. See:
ALAIN
Alain
ALLAN
Allan
ALLEN
Allen
Alleyn
Allyn
NAPIER-CLAVERING, ALAN
SCHNEIDER, ABRAM LEOPOLDOVICH
WATSON, WILLIAM ALEXANDER JARDINE
YOUNG, ANGUS
Alan Cowan. See:
GILCHRIST, ALAN W.
Alan Curtis. See:
NEBERROTH, HAROLD
Alan Dale. See:
COHEN, ALFRED J.
Alan Hale. See:
McKAHAN, RUFUS ALAN
Alan Hastings. See:
WILLIAMSON, GEOFFREY
Alan Kincaid. See:
RIKHOFF, JAMES C.
Alan King. See:
KNIBERG, IRWIN ALAN
Alan Monk. See:
KENDALL, WILLMOORE
Alan Muir. See:
MORRISON, THOMAS JAMES
Alan Random. See:
KAY, ERNEST
Alan Rayne. See:
TOBIN, JAMES EDWARD
Alan Shulberg. See:
WILKES-HUNTER, RICHARD
Alan Stone. See:
STRATEMEYER, EDWARD L.
ALANUS DE INSULIS. See:
ALAIN DE LILLE (ALANUS DE INSULIS)
Alaric-Cotin. See:
FREDERICK II
ALAS Y UREÑA, LEOPOLDO (1852-1901) [Spanish critic, novelist and short story writer]
Clarín
ALBACH-RETTY, ROSEMARIE (1938-) [Austrian motion picture actress]
Romy Schneider
Albaicín. See:
ESCUDERO, IGNACIO RAFAEL GARCÍA Y
ALBAN, ST. (died 303) [protomartyr of Britain]
The British St. Stephen
ALBANI (ALBANO), FRANCESCO (1578-1660) [Italian painter]
The Anacreon of Painters
ALBANI, GIAN FRANCESCO (1649-1721) [Supreme Pontiff of Roman Catholic Church]
Pope Clement II
ALBANI, MARIE LOUISE EMMA CÉCILE LAJEUNESSE (1852-1930) [Canadian singer]
Dame Emma
Albanian Alexander, The. See:
CASTRIOTA, GEORGE
ALBANO. See:
ALBANI (ALBANO), FRANCESCO
Albany, Count of . See:
STUART, CHARLES

EDWARD LOUIS PHILIP CASIMIR
STUART, JOHN SOBIESKI STOLBERG
Albany Regency, The Wizard of the. See:
VAN BUREN, MARTIN
ALBARRÁN, CARLOS RUFO (1819-1910) [torilero at Madrid bullring for over 60 years]
El Buñolero
Albategnius. See:
AL-BATTANI, ABDULLAH MUHAMMAD IBN-JABIR
Albatenius. See:
AL-BATTANI, ABDULLAH MUHAMMAD IBN-JABIR
Alben, Dear. See:
BARKLEY, ALBEN WILLIAM
ALBERSHART, HARRY (c. 1901-) [American cowboy motion picture actor]
Allan Lane
Rocky Lane
ALBERT (1100-70) [Count of Ballenstadt and Margrave of Brandenburg]
The Bear
ALBERT (1158-95) [Margrave of Meissen]
The Proud
ALBERT (1236-79) [Duke of Brunswick]
The Tall
ALBERT (died 1314) [Landgrave of Thuringia and Margrave of Meissen]
The Bad
ALBERT (1443-1500) [Duke of Saxony]
The Bold
ALBERT (1490-1545) [German Archbishop of Magdeburg and Elector of Mainz]
Albert of Brandenburg
ALBERT (1522-57) [Margrave of Brandenburg, Prince of Kulmbach-Bayreuth]
Alcibiades
ALBERT (1819-61) [naturalized English Prince Consort and husband of VICTORIA, Queen of England]
Consort of Her Most Gracious Majesty
The Good
Prince Albert
Royal Highness
Albert. See also:
ALBRECHT
Albrecht
GALLATIN, ABRAHAM ALPHONSE ALBERT
ALBERT III (1414-86) [German Elector of Brandenburg]
The Achilles of Germany
The Ulysses of Germany
ALBERT IV (1379-1414) [Duke of Austria]
The Pious
Albert Cecil Gaines. See:
GRISSOM, ARTHUR COLFAX
Albert, Charles. See:
CHARLES VIII
Albert Douglas. See:
ARMSTRONG, DOUGLAS ALBERT
Albert, Eddie. See:
HEIMBERGER, EDDIE ALBERT
Albert, George Frederick Ernest. See: GEORGE V
Albert Haddock. See:
HERBERT, SIR ALAN PATRICK
Albert, John. See:
JOHN I
Albert Lee Ford. See:
STRATEMEYER, EDWARD L.
Albert Michael. See:
LYONS, A. NEIL
Albert of Cologne. See:
ALBERTUS MAGNUS, SAINT, COUNT OF BOLLSTÄDT
Albert of Lauingen. See:
ALBERTUS MAGNUS, SAINT, COUNT OF BOLLSTÄDT
Albert Ross. See:
PORTER, LINN BOYD
Albert Russell. See:
BIXBY, JEROME LEWIS
Albert the Great. See:
ALBERTUS MAGNUS,

SAINT, COUNT OF BOLLSTÄDT
Albert the Great, St. See:
ALBERTUS MAGNUS, SAINT, COUNT OF BOLLSTÄDT
Alberto Moravia. See:
PINCHERLE, ALBERTO
ALBERTUS MAGNUS, SAINT, COUNT OF BOLLSTÄDT (c. 1193-1280) [Bavarian scholastic philosopher and theologian]
Albert of Cologne
Albert of Lauingen
Albert the Great
Doctor Universalis
St. Albert the Great
Albie. See:
SACHS, ALBERT LOUIS
Albinus. See:
ALCUIN
Albrand, Martha. See:
FREYBE, HEIDI HUBERTA
ALBRECHT (1559-1621) [Archduke of Austria]
The Pious
ALBRECHT [Albrecht]. See also:
ALBERT
Albert
Albrecht, Karl. See:
CHARLES VII
ALBRIDGE, IRA (c. 1810-67) [American Negro tragedian]
The African Roscius
ALBUQUERQUE, AFFONSO D' (1452/3-1515) [Portuguese navigator; viceroy of the Indies]
The Great
The Portuguese Mars
Alby, Little. See:
BARKLEY, ALBEN WILLIAM
Alcalow, Major G. W. See:
HARBAUGH, THOMAS CHALMERS
Alcalde, The Old. See:
ROBERTS, ORAN MILO
ALCARO, ALFRED (1906-) [American music teacher and conductor]
Al Alcaro
ALCAYAGA, LUCILLA GODOY DE (1889-1957) [Chilean poet]
Gabriela Mistral
Alchemy, The Prince of. See:
RUDOLF (RUDOLPH) II
Alcibiades. See:
ALBERT
TENNYSON, ALFRED, 1ST BARON TENNYSON
ALCINDOR, FERDINAND LEWIS, JR. (1947-) [American basketball player]
Lew Alcindor
ALCOFORADO, MARIANNA (1640-1723) [Portuguese nun and author]
The Portuguese Nun
Alcofribas Nasir. See:
RABELAIS, FRANÇOIS
Alcon, R. See:
BRONTË, EMILY JANE
ALCOTT, AMOS BRONSON (1799-1888) [American educator, mystic and author]
Potato Quixote
The Sage of Concord
ALCUIN (735-804) [adviser of CHARLEMAGNE, King of the Franks and Roman emperor]
Albinius
Ealhwine
Alda, Robert. See:
D'ABRUZZA, ALPHONSO
Aldanov, M. A. See:
LANDAU-ALDANOV, MARK
ALDEN, HENRY MILLS (1836-1919) [American editor, author and critic]
The Dean of American Magazine Editors
Metaphysics
ALDEN, ISABELLA MacDONALD (1841-1930) [American author of books for children]
Pansy
Alden, Jack. See:
BARROWS, MARJORIE
ALDERDICE, ALFRED (c. 1920-

) [American motion picture actor]
Tom Drake
ALDINGTON, HILDA DOOLITTLE (1886-1961) [American poet]
H. D.
ALDISS, BRIAN WILSON (1925-) [British film critic, book reviewer and author]
C.C. Shackleton
Aldo, G.R. See:
GRAZIATI, ALDO
Aldo Ray. See:
daRE, ALDO
ALDOBRANDINI, IPPOLITO (1536-1605) [Supreme Pontiff of Roman Catholic Church]
Pope Clement VIII
Aldon, Adair. See:
MEIGS, CORNELIA LYNDE
ALDOUS, DONALD WILLIAM (1914-) [English author]
Discobulus
ALDRICH [Aldrich]. See also:
ALDRIDGE
ALLDRIDGE
ALDRICH, BESS STREETER (1881-1954) [American novelist]
Margaret Dean Stevens
ALDRICH, CLARE CHAPLIN THOMAS (fl. 1917-50) [American novelist and playwright]
Darragh Aldrich
Aldrich, Louis. See:
LYON, LOUIS
ALDRIDGE. See also:
ALDRICH
Aldrich
ALLDRIDGE
ALDRIDGE, IRA (c.1810-66) [Negro tragic actor]
The African Roscius
Aleander. See also:
ALEANDRO
Alessandro
ALEXANDER
Alexander
ALEXANDRA
ALEXANDRIA
Alexandria
Aleander, Hieronymus. See:
ALEANDRO, GIROLAMO
ALEANDRO. See also:
Aleander
Alessandro
ALEXANDER
Alexander
ALEXANDRA
ALEXANDRIA
Alexandria
ALEANDRO, GIROLAMO (1480-1542) [Italian cardinal]
Hieronymus Aleander
Alec. See:
Aleck
Aleksis
Alex
ALEXEI (ALEXIS)
Alexis
CRAIG, ALEXANDER GEORGE
HARMAN, RICHARD ALEXANDER
McCOWEN, ALEXANDER DUNCAN
WAUGH, ALEXANDER RABAN
Alec Hudson. See:
HOLMES, WILFRED JAY
Aleck. See:
Alec
Aleksis
Alex
ALEXEI (ALEXIS)
Alexis
Aleck Forbes. See:
RATHBONE, ST. GEORGE HENRY
Aleck, Little. See:
STEPHENS, ALEXANDER HAMILTON
Aleichem, Shalom. See:
RABINOWITZ (RABINOVITZ), SOLOMON J.
Aleksis. See:
Alec
Aleck
Alex
ALEXEI (ALEXIS)
Alexis
Aleksis Kivi. See:
STENVALL, ALEKSIS
Alessandro. See also:

Aleander
ALEANDRO
ALEXANDER
Alexander
ALEXANDRA
ALEXANDRIA
Alexandria
Alessandro di Cagliostro, Count. See: BALSAMO, GIUSEPPE
Alex. See:
Alec
Aleck
Aleksis
ALEXEI (ALEXIS)
Alexis
STUART, VIVIAN FINLAY
Alex Cord. See: VIESPI, ALEXANDER
Alex Crane. See: WILKES-HUNTER, RICHARD
Alex D'Arcy. See: SARRUF, ALEXANDER
Alex Fraser. See: BRINTON, HENRY
Alex Frecke Turner. See: CRAWFURD, OSWALD
Alex Olmedo. See: RODRÍGUEZ, ALEJANDRO OLMEDO Y
Alex Robertson, M. D. See: RATHBONE, ST. GEORGE HENRY
Alex Rose. See: ROYZ, OLESH
ALEXANDER [Alexander]. See also: Aleander
ALEANDRO
Alessandro
ALEXANDRA
ALEXANDRIA
Alexandria
ALEXANDER (died c. 115) [Supreme Pontiff of Roman Catholic Church]
Pope Alexander I
St. Alexander
ALEXANDER I (c. 1078-1124) [King of Scotland]
The Fierce
Alexander I. See also: PTOLEMY IX
Alexander II. See: PTOLEMY X
ALEXANDER III (356-323 B.C.) [King of Macedon and conqueror of the eastern world]
Alexander the Great
The Conqueror of the World
The Madman of Macedonia
Alexander II, Pope. See: BAGGIO, ANSELMO DA
Alexander III, Pope. See: BANDINELLI, ROLAND
Alexander IV, Pope. See: CONTI, RINALDO
Alexander V, Pope. See: CANDIA, PIETRO DI
Alexander VI, Pope. See: BORGIA, RODRIGO
Alexander VII, Pope. See: CHIGI, FABIO
Alexander VIII, Pope. See: OTTOBONI, PIETRO
ALEXANDER, BEATRICE (1895-) [American doll designer and manufacturer
Madame Alexander
Alexander, Charles. See: HADFIELD, ELLIS CHARLES RAYMOND
ALEXANDER, CHARLES W. (fl. 1876) [American horse breaker]
Wild Horse Charlie
ALEXANDER, COLIN JAMES (1920-) [British physician and author]
Simon Jay
Alexander Cordell. See: GRABER, ALEXANDER
ALEXANDER, ELEANOR JANE (fl. early 20th cent.) [English author]
E. A.
Alexander Gode. See: GODE VON AESCH, ALEXANDER GOTTFRIED FRIEDRICH
ALEXANDER, GROVER CLEVELAND (1887-1950) [American professional baseball player]
Pete
Alexander Hazelton. See:

ARMSTRONG, WILLIAM ALEXANDER
ALEXANDER, JOCELYN ANNE ARUNDEL (1930-) [American author]
Jocelyn Arundel
Alexander Kent. See:
METHOLD, KENNETH WALTER
Alexander, Kyle. See:
MARLOWE, ALAN STEPHEN
ALEXANDER OF HALES (died 1245) [English theologian and philosopher]
Doctor Irrefragabilis
The Fountain of Life
The Irrefragable Doctor
The Monarch of Theologians
Alexander of the North. See:
CHARLES XII
Alexander Roth. See:
DUNNER, JOSEPH
Alexander, Sir George. See:
SAMSON, GEORGE ALEXANDER GIBB
Alexander, The Albanian. See:
CASTRIOTA, GEORGE
Alexander the Coppersmith. See:
HAMILTON, ALEXANDER
Alexander, The English. See:
HENRY V
Alexander the Great. See:
ALEXANDER III
DUMAS, ALEXANDRE
WILLIAMS, ALEX
ALEXANDER, WILLIAM (1726-83) [American general officer]
Lord Stirling
ALEXANDER, WILLIAM ANDERSON (1889-) [American football coach]
The Old Man
ALEXANDRA. See also:
Aleander
ALEANDRO
Alessandro
ALEXANDER
Alexander
ALEXANDRIA
Alexandria
ALEXANDRA, CAROLINE MARIE CHARLOTTE LOUISA JULIA (1844-1925) [Queen Consort of EDWARD VII of England]
The Sea King's Daughter
ALEXANDRIA [Alexandria]. See:
Aleander
ALEANDRO
Alessandro
ALEXANDER
Alexander
ALEXANDRA
DIDYMUS OF ALEXANDRIA
DIONYSIUS OF ALEXANDRIA, ST.
Alexandria, Lorez. See:
NELSON, DOLOREZ ALEXANDRIA
Alexandria, Philo of. See:
PHILO JUDAEUS
Alexandria, The Grand Old Man of. See:
DUNN, EMMETT CLARKE
Alexandria, The Little Giant of. See: NELSON, KNUTE
Alexandria Zenobia. See:
BRONTË, ANNE
ALEXEI. See also:
Alec
Aleck
Aleksis
Alex
Alexis
ALEXEI (ALEXIS) (1629-76) [second Russian czar of the house of Romanoff; father of PETER THE GREAT
Mikhailovich
ALEXEI (ALEXIS) (1690-1718) [Russian nobleman; eldest son of PETER THE GREAT]
Petrovich
ALEXEYEV, KONSTANTIN SERGEIVITCH (1865-1938) [Russian actor, producer and teacher]
Stanislavsky
Alexievna, Catherine. See:
SKAVRONSKAYA, MARFA
ALEXIS [Alexis]. See:
Alec
Aleck

Aleksis
Alex
ALEXEI (ALEXIS)
Alexis Brown. See:
BEECHING, AMY BROWN
Alexis, Willibald. See:
HÄRING, GEORG WILHELM HEINRICH
Alf. See:
LANDON, ALFRED MOSSMAN
Alf, Uncle. See:
TAYLOR, ALFRED ALEXANDER
TUNSTALL, ALFRED MOORE
Alfalfa. See:
SWITZER, CARL
Alfalfa Bill. See:
MURRAY, WILLIAM HENRY
Alfalfa Joe. See:
WING, JOSEPH ELWYN
ALFONSO I (693-757) [King of Asturias]
The Catholic
ALFONSO I (1030-1109) [King of Castile (as Alfonso I) and King of Léon and Castile (as Alfonso VI)]
Alfonso el Bravo (Alfonso the Brave
ALFONSO I (1104-34) [King of Aragon and Navarre]
El Batallador
The Fighter
ALFONSO I (1110-85) [King of Portugal]
Affonso Henriques
ALFONSO II (1185-1223) [King of Portugal]
Alfonso o Gordo (Alfonso the Fat)
ALFONSO III (848-912) [King of Léon, Asturias and Galacia]
The Great
ALFONSO IV (died c. 933) [King of Léon]
The Monk
ALFONSO IV (1290-1357) [King of Portugal]
Alfonso el Bravo (Alfonso the Brave)
The Fierce
ALFONSO V (1385-1458) [King of Aragon, Naples and Sicily]
Alfonso the Magnanimous
ALFONSO V (1432-81) [King of Portugal]
Affonso o Africano
The African
ALFONSO VI (1030-1109) [King of Léon]
The Valiant
ALFONSO VII (1106?-57) [King of Léon and Castile]
El Emperador (The Emperor)
ALFONSO IX (1155-1214) [King of Castile]
The Good
The Noble
ALFONSO IX (1299-1336) [King of Aragon]
The Good
The Noble
ALFONSO X (1226?-84) [King of Léon and Castile]
Alfonso the Learned
The Astronomer
El Sabio (The Wise)
ALFONSO (ALPHONSO) XI (died 1350) [King of Léon and Castile]
The Avenger
ALFRED. See: ALREDUS (ALURED) (ALUREDUS) (ALFRED)
Alfred. See:
Crowquill, Alfred.
ALFRED (AELFRED) (848-99) [King of the West Saxons]
Alfred the Great
Alfred Ayres. See:
OSMUN, THOMAS EMBLEY
Alfred B. Taylor, Captain. See:
INGRAHAM, COLONEL PRENTISS
Alfred B. Thorne, Lieut. See:
AIKEN, ALBERT W.
Alfred Burton. See:
MITFORD, JOHN
Alfred de Musset. See:
MUSSET, LOUIS CHARLES ALFRED DE

Alfred Drake. See:
CAPURRO, ALFRED
Alfred Drayton. See:
VARICK, ALFRED
Alfred Gwalia. See:
THOMAS, ALFRED
Alfred Herbert Theobald. See:
TUBBY, ALFRED HERBERT
Alfred, Lord Tennyson. See:
TENNYSON, ALFRED, 1ST BARON TENNYSON
Alfred of Beverley. See:
ALREDUS (ALURED) (ALUREDUS) (ALFRED)
Alfred Venison. See:
POUND, EZRA LOOMIS
Alfred Wynn. See:
BREWER, FRED ALDWYN
Algabeño. See:
GARCÍA, JOSÉ
ALGAROTTI, COUNT FRANCESCO (1712-64) [Italian art connoisseur and litérateur]
The Swan of Padua
Algebra, The Father of. See:
DIOPHANTUS
ALGER, HORATIO, JR. (1834-99) [American writer of inspirational books for boys]
Holy Horatio
ALI (1741-1822) [Turkish pasha]
Ali Pasha
The Lion of Janina
ALI, CALIPH (c. 600-61) [Son of ABU TALEB, uncle of MAHOMET]
The Lion of God
ALI, HASAAN IBN (1931-) [American jazz musician (piano, composer)]
Hasaan
Ali, Mohammed. See:
CLAY, CASSIUS MARCELLUS, JR.
ALI PASHA (1741-1822) [ruler of Albania]
Arslan
The Lion
Alice B. Emerson. See:
STRATEMEYER, EDWARD L.
Alice B. Haven. See:
HAVEN, EMILY BRADLEY NEAL
Alice Berend. See:
BREINLINGER, ALICE BEREND
Alice, Cousin. See:
BRADLEY, MARY EMILY
HAVEN, EMILY BRADLEY NEAL
Alice Dale Hardy. See:
STRATEMEYER, EDWARD L.
Alice Delysia. See:
LAPIZE, ALICE
Alice Duer Miller. See:
MILLER, MRS. HENRY WISE
Alice Eliot. See:
JEWETT, SARAH ORNE
Alice Faye. See:
LEPPERT, ALICE
Alice G. Lee. See:
HAVEN, EMILY BRADLEY NEAL
Alice Hamilton. See:
CROMIE, ALICE HAMILTON
Alice Hawthorne. See:
WINNER, SEPTIMUS
Alice, Princess. See:
LONGWORTH, ALICE LEE ROOSEVELT
Alice, Queen. See:
LONGWORTH, ALICE LEE ROOSEVELT
Alice Terry. See:
TAAFE, ALICE
Alice Tilton. See:
TAYLOR, PHOEBE ATWOOD
Alice Tisdale Hobart. See:
HOBART, ALICE NOURSE
Alice Tubbs, Poker. See:
TUBBS, ALICE
Alicia Markova. See:
MARKS, LILIAN ALICIA
Alida Valli. See:
ALTENBURGER, ALIDA MARIA
ALIGHIERI, DURANTE (1265-1321) [Italian poet]
Dante Alighieri
The Poet of the Damned
That Singular Splendor of the Italian Race
ALIGHIERI, DURANTE. See also:
Great Triumvirate of Italian

Literature, The
Immortal Four of Italy, The
Aliki. See:
BRANDENBERG, ALIKI LIACOURAS
Alison. See also:
Allison
ALLYSON
Alison Bray. See:
ROWLAND, DONALD SYDNEY
Alison Lascelles. See:
PARRIS, JOHN
Alive, The Luckiest Fool. See:
KELLY, ALVIN
All American, The Great. See:
FISH, HAMILTON, JR.
All Eyes. See:
WEBSTER, DANIEL
All Outdoors, The Bishop of. See: JACKSON, SHELDON
All the Doughboys, The Mother of. See:
SCHUMANN-HEINK, MME. ERNESTINE
All the Russians, The Little Mother of. See:
ANHALT-ZERBST, SOPHIA AUGUSTA FREDERICA OF
All Time, The Bard of. See:
SHAKESPEARE, WILLIAM
Allan. See:
ALAIN
Alain
Alan
ALLEN
Allen
Alleyn
Allyn
Martin, Allan Langdon
NEVINS, JOSEPH ALLAN
Allan Benarria. See:
GOLDENTHAL, ALLAN BENARRIA
Allan Cunningham, Honest. See:
CUNNINGHAM, ALLAN
ALLAN, DAVID (1744-96) [Scottish historical and portrait painter]
The Scottish Hogarth
Allan Dwight. See:
COLE, LOIS DWIGHT
Allan, Frank. See:
LUNGSTRUM, FRANK ALLAN
Allan, Honest. See:
CUNNINGHAM, ALLAN
Allan Lane. See:
ALBERSHART, HARRY
Allan, Luke. See:
AMY, WILLIAM LACEY
ALLAN, MABEL ESTHER (1915-) [British author]
Jean Estoril
Anne Pilgrim
Allan Sherman. See:
COPELON, ALLAN
Allan, Sidney. See:
HARTMANN, SADAKICHI
ALLDRIDGE. See also:
ALDRICH
Aldrich
ALDRIDGE
ALLDRIDGE, JOHN STRATTEN (1914-) [English author]
John Stratten
Alleghenies, The Apostle of the. See:
GALLITZIN, DEMETRIUS AUGUSTINE
Allegheny. See: JOHNSON, EDWARD
Allegheny, Old. See:
COLSTON, RALEIGH EDWARD
Allen. See:
ALAIN
Alain
Alan
ALLAN
Allan
Alleyn
Allyn
TATE, JOHN ORLEY ALLEN
Allen, Adam
Douglas Coe, joint pseuds. of SAMUEL EPSTEIN (1909-) and his wife BERYL WILLIAMS EPSTEIN (-) [American authors]
Allen, Adam. See also:
EPSTEIN, BERYL WILLIAMS
EPSTEIN, SAMUEL
Allen, Allyn. See:

EBERLE, IRMENGARDE
ALLEN, ARTHUR BRUCE (1903-) [British educator and author]
Borough Trice
ALLEN, BARBARA JO (c. 1904-) [American comedy actress]
Vera Vague
ALLEN, BENJAMIN (1789-1829) [American Episcopal clergyman and poet]
Juba
Osander
Allen, Betsy. See: CAVANNA, ELIZABETH ALLEN
Allen Chalmers. See: UPWARD, EDWARD FALASIE
Allen Chapman. See: STRATEMEYER, EDWARD L.
ALLEN, CHARLES GRANT BLAIRFINDIE (1848-99) [Canadian novelist, philosopher and scientific writer]
Grant Allen
Olive Pratt Raynor
Martin Leach Warborough
J. Arbuthnot Wilson
Allen, Ernie. See: BUNDGAARD, ERNEST
Allen, Esq., The Late Henry. See: HOPE, JAMES BARRON
ALLEN, ETHAN (1737-89) [American Revolutionary military leader]
The Robin Hood of the Forest
Allen, F. N. See: DOWNEY, EDMUND
Allen, Fred. See: SULLIVAN, JOHN FLORENCE
Allen, Gene. See: SUFANA, EUGENE
Allen, Graham. See: ARNOLD, GEORGE
Allen Grant. See: WILSON, JAMES GRANT
Allen, Hazel. See: HERSHBERGER, HAZEL KUHNS
ALLEN, HENRY, JR. (1908-) [American jazz musician (trumpet, singer, leader)]
Red Allen
ALLEN, HEYWOOD (1935-) [American comedian and writer]
Woody Allen
Allen, Hugh. See: MORRIS, CHARLES SMITH
ALLEN, IRA (1751-1814) [American pioneer and statesman in Vermont]
The Founder of Vermont
Allen, James. See: ADER, PAUL FASSETT
Allen Jenkins. See: McGONEGAL, AL
ALLEN, JOHN MILLS (1846-1917) [American statesman and Confederate soldier]
Private John
Allen, John W., Jr. See: LESLEY, PETER
ALLEN, LAURENCE (1908-) [American foreign correspondent]
Larry Allen
ALLEN, LT. THOMAS, R. N. See: STUART, JOHN SOBIESKI STOLBERG
ALLEN, MARION C. (1914-) [American Baptist clergyman, educator and author]
Sam Allen
ALLEN, MARY (1877-1955) [British stage and motion picture actress]
Mary Jerrold
ALLEN, PAUL (1775-1826) [American editor and poet]
Pasquin
St. Denis le Cadet
Allen Raine. See: PUDDICOMBE, ANNE ADALISA
ALLEN, RALPH (1694-1764) [English philanthropist]
The Man of Bath
ALLEN, REVEREND THOMAS (1743-1811) [American churchman and leader of Revolutionary volunteers]

The Fighting Parson
The Fighting Parson of Bennington Fields
Allen, Richard. See:
MARKOWITZ, RICHARD
Allen Richards. See:
ROSENTHAL, RICHARD A.
ALLEN, STEPHEN VALENTINE PATRICK WILLIAM (1921-) [American song-writer, pianist, author and comedian]
Steve Allen
Steverino
ALLEN, TERRY DE LA MESA (1888-) [American general officer]
The Firebrand
Terrible Terry
ALLEN, WILLIAM (1806-79) [American senator from Ohio]
Earthquake Allen
The Fog Horn
The Ohio Gong
Petticoat Allen
Rise Up William Allen
ALLEN, WILLIAM FRANKLIN (1883-1946) [American congressman from Delaware]
Lovebird Allen
ALLEN, WILLIAM HERVEY (1889-1949) [American author]
Hervey Allen
ALLEN, WILLIAM VINCENT (1847-1924) [American Populist senator from Nebraska]
The Intellectual Giant of Populism
ALLENBY, EDMUND HENRY HYNMAN, 1ST VISCOUNT (1861-1936) [British general officer]
The Bull
Allen's Wife, Josiah. See:
HOLLEY, MARIETTA
ALLERTON, ISAAC (c.1583-1659) [Anglo-American business pioneer]
The Father of New England Commerce
Allerton, Mary.
See:
GOVAN, CHRISTINE NOBLE
Alleyn. See also:
ALAIN
Alain
Alan
ALLAN
Allan
ALLEN
Allen
Allyn
Alleyn, Ellen. See:
ROSSETTI, CHRISTINA GEORGINA
ALLGOOD, MAIRE (1885-1952) [Irish stage and motion picture actress]
Maire O'Neill
ALLGOOD, MILES CLAYTON (1872-) [American congressman from Alabama]
Simon
Alliaco, Petrus de. See:
AILLY, PIERRE D'
Allie. See:
REYNOLDS, ALBERT PIERCE
ALLINE, HENRY (1748-84) [American preacher and religious leader]
The Whitfield of Nova Scotia
Allison. See:
Alison
ALLYSON
HAYES, MARY JANE
Allison, Clay. See:
KEEVIL, HENRY JOHN
Allison, Marian. See:
REID, FRANCES PUGH
Allison, Rand. See:
McCORMICK, WILFRED
Allison, Sam. See:
LOOMIS, NOEL MILLER
Allister, Claude. See:
PALMER, CLAUDE
ALLSTON, WASHINGTON (1779-1843) [American painter]
The American Titian
ALLUCINGOLI, UBALDO (c.1097-1185) [Supreme Pontiff of Roman Catholic Church]
Pope Lucius III
Ally of the Meddler,
The Schemer,

An. See:
TRUMBULL, JOHN
Ally Sloper. See:
ROSS, CHARLES HENRY
Allyn. See also:
ALAIN
Alain
Alan
ALLAN
Allan
ALLEN
Allen
Alleyn
Allyn Allen. See:
EBERLE, IRMENGARDE
Allyn, Paul. See:
SCHOSBERG, PAUL A.
ALLYSON. See also:
Alison
Allison
ALLYSON, JAN (1923-)
[American actress]
June Allyson
ALMAGRO, DIEGO DE (1520-42) [Spanish conquistador; Governor of Peru]
The Lad
The Youth
ALMAN, DAVID. See:
David, Emily
ALMAN, EMILY. See:
David, Emily
ALMEDINGEN, EDITH MARTHA (1898-) [Russian author]
Martha Edith von Almedingen
ALMEREYDA, JEAN (1905-34) [French motion picture director]
Jean Vigo
Almighty, Nephew of the. See:
BROTHERS, RICHARD
Alnaschar of Modern Literature, The. See:
COLERIDGE, SAMUEL TAYLOR
ALOMA, HAROLD DAVID (1908-) [American composer, author and musician]
Hal Aloma
ALONSO, LUIS ANTONIO DAMASO DE (1905-) [Mexican bullfighter; later motion picture actor]
Gilbert Roland
Aloysius. See: BERTRAND, LOUIS JACQUES NAPOLEON
Aloysius Harry Simmons. See:
SZYMANSKI, ALOYSIUS HARRY
Aloysius, St. See:
GONZAGA, LUIGI
ALPERT, HERMAN (1916-)
[American jazz musician (bass, arranger)]
Trigger Alpert
ALPERT, HOLLIS (1916-)
[American author]
Robert Carroll
ALPERT, MILTON I. (1904-65)
[American jazz musician (leader)]
Mickey Alpert
Alpha of the Plough. See:
GARDINER, ALFRED GEORGE
Alphabet, Old. See:
BEAUREGARD, PIERRE GUSTAVE TOUTANT
ALPHONSO. See:
ALFONSO (ALPHONSO) XI
Alphonsus, St. See:
LIGOURI, ALPHONSUS
Alps, Apostle of the . See:
BERNARD OF MENTHON, ST.
ALREDUS (ALURED) (ALUREDUS) (ALFRED) (1st half 12th cent.) [English chronicler]
Alfred of Beverley
ALSOP, RICHARD. See:
Hartford Wits, The
Alte, Der (The Old Man). See:
ADENAUER, KONRAD
Alte Dessauer, Der (The Old Dessauer). See:
LEOPOLD
ALTENBURGER, ALIDA MARIA (1921-) [Italian motion picture actress]
Alida Valli
ALTER, MOSHE JACOB (1862-1923) [Yiddish poet]
Morris Rosenfield
ALTER, ROBERT EDMOND (1925-65) [American author]
Robert Raymond
Robert Retla
ALTHORP. See:

LORD ALTHORP
ALTIERI, EMILIO (1590-1676) [Supreme Pontiff of Roman Catholic Church]
Pope Clement X
Alto Saxophone Player, The World's Greatest. See: DORSEY, JAMES
Alton, Josie. See: DEUBLER, MARY
Alton, Robert. See: HART, ROBERT ALTON
ALTWERGER, JOHN (1919-) [American jazz musician (saxophone, leader)]
Georgie Auld
Alumni Work at Fisk University, The Father of Organized. See: PROCTOR, HENRY HUGH
ALURED. See: ALREDUS (ALURED) (ALUREDUS) (ALFRED)
ALUREDUS. See: ALREDUS (ALURED) (ALUREDUS (ALFRED
ALVAREZ, ALFRED (1920-) [American jazz musician (trumpet)]
Chico Alvarez
ÁLVAREZ, JUAN DE YAPES Y (1542-91) [Cofounder of the Discalced Carmelites]
St. John of the Cross
ÁLVAREZ, MANUEL (1919-) [Spanish bullfighter]
Andaluz
Álvarez Quintero. See: Quintero, Álvarez
Alvin Karpis. See: KARPOVIECZ, FRANCIS ALBIN
Alvin Porter. See: ROWLAND, DONALD SYDNEY
Alvino Rey. See: McBURNEY, ALBERT
Always Prays, The Woman Who. See: DUCHESNE, ROSE PHILIPPINE
Always Speaks Her Mind, The Woman Who. See: COX-OLIVER, EDNA MAY
ALWAZZAN (ALWEZAZ), ALHASSAN IBN MOHAMMED (1494-1552) [Cordovan Moorish traveler and writer]
Leo Africanus
Eliberitanus
Johannes Leo
Giovanni Leone
Amabel Penfeather. See: COOPER, SUSAN FENIMORE
Amadeus. See: HOFFMAN, ERNST THEODOR WILHELM
AMADEUS V (1249-1323) [founder of Italian royal house of Savoy]
The Great
AMADEUS VI (1334-83) [ruler of Savoy, founder of the Order of the Annunziata]
The Green
The Green Count
AMADEUS VII (fl. late 14th cent.) [count of Savoy]
The Red
AMAMOO, JOSEPH GODSON (1931-) [African statesman and author]
Joseph Kambu
Amanda. See: WYNNE-TYSON, ESME
Amaryllis. See: DESHOULIÈRES, ANTOINETTE DU LIGIER DE LA GARDE
Amazing. See: MAYS, WILLIE HOWARD
Amazon of the Revolution, The. See: TERWAGNE, ANNE JOSEPH
Amazon, The British. See: TALBOT, MARY ANNE
Ambassador of Good Will, The. See: ROGERS, WILLIAM PENN ADAIR
Ambassador of the Air, The. See: LINDBERGH, CHARLES AUGUSTUS
Amber. See: HOLDEN, MARTHA EVERTS
AMBLER, ERIC. See: Reed, Eliot

AMBREE, MARY (fl. 1584)
[English heroine]
The English Joan of Arc
AMBROGINI, ANGELO (1454-94)
[Italian playwright, poet and essayist]
Politian
Poliziano
Ambrogio di Lorenzo. See:
LORENZETTI, AMBROGIO
Ambroise. See:
THOMAS, CHARLES LOUIS AMBROISE
AMBROS, MELISSA BROWN (1917-) [American author]
Melissa Mather
AMBROSE, ERIC (1908-)
[British architect and author]
Esor B. MacIre
Christopher Rennie
Edgar Vance
Ambrose Hoopington. See:
BINNEY, CECIL
AMBROSE, JAMES (182?-56)
[Irish-American prize fighter]
Yankee Sullivan
AMECHE, ALAN (1933-)
[American football player]
The Horse
Ameche, Don. See:
AMICI, DOMINIC
Amelia. See:
WELBY, AMELIA BALL COPPUCK
Amelia Earhart. See:
PUTNAM, AMELIA EARHART
Amélie Rives. See:
TROUBETZKOY, PRINCESS AMÉLIE RIVES
Amend-all, Jack. See:
CADE, JOHN
Amendment Monger. See:
ADAMS, SAMUEL
Amendment, The Father of the Eighteenth. See:
SHEPPARD, MORRIS
Amendment to the Constitution, The Father of the Twentieth. See: NORRIS, GEORGE WILLIAM
AMENHOTEP (AMENOPHIS) IV (14th cent. B.C.) [King of Egypt, 18th dynasty]
Akhnaton
AMENOPHIS. See: AMENHOTEP (AMENOPHIS)
America, A Native of. See:
PARKE, JOHN
America, Cromwell of New.
See: ADAMS, SAMUEL.
America, Gladstone of. See:
BLAINE, JAMES GILLESPIE
America, The Apostle of South.
See: FOWLER, CHARLES HENRY
America, The Atlas of. See:
WASHINGTON, GEORGE
America, The Baskerville of.
See: THOMAS, ISAIAH
America, The Black Spurgeon of. See:
WALKER, CHARLES THOMAS
America, The Brunel of. See:
ELLET, CHARLES
America, The Burns of. See:
RILEY, JAMES WHITCOMB
WHITTIER, JOHN GREENLEAF
America, The Cato of. See:
WHITE, HUGH LAWSON
America, The Cicero of. See:
LIVINGSTON, ROBERT R.
America, The Daisy Ashford of.
See: WAINWRIGHT, VIRGINIA
America, The Dean of Woman Authors of. See:
TARBELL, IDA MINERVA
America, The Deliverer of. See:
WASHINGTON, GEORGE
America, The Father of. See:
ADAMS, SAMUEL
WASHINGTON, GEORGE
America, The Father of Biblical Learning in. See:
STUART, MOSES
America, The Father of English Colonization in. See:
GORGES, FERDINANDO
America, The Father of Foreign Mission Work in Christian.
See: MILLS, SAMUEL JOHN

America, The Father of Historical Societies in. See:
PINTARD, JOHN
America, The Father of Homeopathy in. See:
HERING, CONSTANTINE
America, The Father of Iron Shipbuilding in. See:
ROACH, JOHN
America, The Father of More Brains Than Any Other Man in. See:
BEECHER, LYMAN
America, The Father of the Dry Plate Process in. See:
NEWTON, HENRY JOTHAM
America, The Father of the Dutch Reformed Church in. See:
LIVINGSTON, JOHN HENRY
America, The Father of Universalism in. See:
MURRAY, JOHN
America, The First Historian of. See: ANGHIERA, PIETRO MARTIRE
America, The Franconi of. See:
CHIARINI, SIGNOR G.
America, The Grace Darling of. See: WILSON, IDA LEWIS
America, The Hannah More of. See: MERCER, MARGARET
America, The Havelock of. See:
HOWARD, OLIVER OTIS
America, The Jean Ingelow of. See: CAREY, ALICE
America, The Leonidas of. See:
STARK, JOHN
America, The Millet of. See:
HIGGINS, EUGENE
America, The Missionary Bishop of. See:
DOANE, GEORGE WASHINGTON
America, The Mrs. Hemans of. See: SIGOURNEY, LYDIA HUNTLEY
America, The Moses of. See:
WISE, ISAAC MAYER
America, The Most Talented Young Composer in. See:
GOULD, MORTON
America, The Murat of. See:
WHEAT, CHATHAM ROBERDEAU
America, The Newman of. See:
HEWIT, AUGUSTINE FRANCIS
America, The Oliver Goldsmith of. See:
TAYLOR, BENJAMIN FRANKLIN
America, The Prince of. See:
TODD, JOHN PAYNE
America, The Sage of. See:
FRANKLIN, BENJAMIN
America, The Schoolmaster to. See: WEBSTER, NOAH
America, The Tiger of Central. See: GUARDIOLA, SANTOS
America, The Top Football Coach in. See:
PARKER, RAYMOND KLEIN
America, The Washington of South. See:
BOLÍVAR, SIMÓN
America, The Watt of. See:
EVANS, OLIVER
America, The Wire King of. See:
GATES, JOHN WARNE
America, Would-be Cromwell of. See: ADAMS, SAMUEL
Americaine, La Belle (The Beautiful American). See:
MONROE, ELIZABETH KORTRIGHT
American Addison, The. See:
DENNIE, JOSEPH
American, An. See:
CASS, LEWIS
CHURCH, BENJAMIN
COOPER, JAMES FENIMORE
DUNLAP, WILLIAM
EVERETT, EDWARD
American Anthracite Iron Industry, The Father of the. See:
THOMAS, DAVID
American Anthropology, The Father of. See:
MORGAN, LEWIS HENRY
American Apiculture, The Father of. See:
LANGSTROTH, LORENZO LORRAINE
American Artists, Founder of the Hudson River School of. See:

COLE, THOMAS
American Ballad Poetry, The Father of. See:
HEWITT, JOHN HENRY (HILL)
American Balzac, The. See:
FAULKNER, WILLIAM
American Baptists, The Father of. See:
CLARKE, JOHN
American Bar, The Erskine of the. See:
HOFFMAN, OGDEN
American Baseball, The Czar of. See:
LANDIS, KENESAW MOUNTAIN
American Bernhardt, The. See:
DUDLY, CAROLINE LOUISE
American Blackstone, The. See:
KENT, JAMES
TUCKER, SAINT GEORGE
American Botany, The Father of. See: BARTRAM, JOHN
American Botany, The Nestor of. See: DARLINGTON, WILLIAM
American Boxing, The Father of. See: MULDOON, WILLIAM
American Boy, The Idol of the See: RUTH, GEORGE HERMAN
American Bridge Building, The Father of. See:
WHIPPLE, SQUIRE
American Butler, The. See:
FESSENDEN, THOMAS GREEN
American Caesar, The. See:
GRANT, HIRAM ULYSSES
American Cato. See:
ADAMS, SAMUEL
American Church Music, The Father of. See:
MASON, LOWELL
American Cicero, The. See:
BERRIEN, JOHN Mac-PHERSON
LEE, RICHARD HENRY
American Clowns, The King of. See: RICE, DANIEL

American Commerce with India, The Father of. See:
DERBY, ELIAS HASKET
American Commoner, The Great. See:
STEVENS, THADDEUS
American Conchology, The Father of. See:
SAY, THOMAS
American Cotton Industry, The Father of the. See:
COXE, TENCH
American Criminologists, The Dean of the. See:
SUTHERLAND, DR. EDWIN H.
American Cruikshank, The. See:
JOHNSON, DAVID CLAY-POOLE
American Dance, The First Lady of the. See:
DENNIS, RUTH
American Democrat, The First Great. See:
WISE, JOHN
American Descriptive Entomology, The Father of. See:
SAY, THOMAS
American Devil, The. See:
McDOUGAL, DAVID STOCKTON
American Drama, The Father of. See: DUNLAP, WILLIAM
American Drama, The Wizard of. See:
BELASCO, DAVID
American Engineering, The Father of. See:
WRIGHT, BENJAMIN
American Entomology, The Father of. See:
SAY, THOMAS
American Ethnology, The Father of. See:
GALLATIN, ABRAHAM ALPHONSE ALBERT
American Experimental Physics, The Father of. See:
ROOD, OGDEN NICHOLAS
American Fabius, The. See:
WASHINGTON, GEORGE
American Football, The Dean of. See: CAMP, WALTER

American Football, The Father of. See: CAMP, WALTER
American Geography, The Father of. See: MORSE, JEDIDIAH
American Geology, The Father of. See: MACLURE, WILLIAM
American Geophysics, The Father of. See: GOLYER, EVERETTE LEE DE
American Goldsmith, The. See: IRVING, WASHINGTON
American Grape Culture, The Father of. See: LONGWORTH, NICHOLAS
American Hogarth, The. See: SHAHN, BENJAMIN
American Hemans, The. See: SIGOURNEY, LYDIA HUNTLEY
American History, The Father of. See: BRADFORD, WILLIAM
American History, The Sculptor of. See: KELLY, JAMES EDWARD
American Howard, The. See: EDDY, THOMAS
American Independence, Colossus of. See: ADAMS, JOHN
American Independence, The Father of. See: ADAMS, JOHN
American Journalists, The Nestor of the German. See: PREETORIUS, EMIL
American Jurist, The Greatest. See: MARSHALL, JOHN
American Kipling, The. See: LONDON, JOHN GRIFFITH
American Labor Movement, The Dean of the. See: FURUSETH, ANDREW
American Legion, The Mother of the. See: SCHUMANN-HEINK, MME. ERNESTINE
American Letters, The Dean of. See: HOWELLS, WILLIAM DEAN
American Letters, The Prince of. See: IRVING, WASHINGTON
American Literature, The Father of. See: IRVING, WASHINGTON
American Louis Philippe, The. See: FILLMORE, MILLARD
American Magazine Editors, The Dean of. See: ALDEN, HENRY MILLS
American Magicians, The Dean of. See: KELLAR, HARRY
American Manufacture, The Father of. See: SLATER, SAMUEL
American Map Making, The Father of. See: GANNETT, HENRY
American Maupassant, The. See: PORTER, WILLIAM SYDNEY
American Medical Association, The Father of the. See: DAVIS, NATHAN SMITH
American Meissonier, The. See: WATROUS, HARRY WILSON
American Milton, The. See: LORD, WILLIAM WILBER-FORCE
American Mineralogy, The Father of. See: CLEAVELAND, PARKER
American Minstrelsy, The Father of. See: RICE, THOMAS DARTMOUTH
American, Mr. See: TUGWELL, REXFORD GUY
American Montaigne, The. See: EMERSON, RALPH WALDO
American Music, The Dean of. See: DAMROSCH, WALTER JOHANNES
American Navy, The Father of the. See:
ADAMS, JOHN
BARRY, COMMODORE JOHN
HUMPHREYS, JOSHUA
American Navy, the Founder of the. See: PAUL, JOHN
American Negro Novelist, The

First. See:
CHESNUTT, CHARLES WADDELL
American Nehemiah, The. See: WINTHROP, JOHN
American Newspaper Woman, The First. See: CROLY, JANE CUNNINGHAM
American Newspapers, The Father of. See: HARRIS, BENJAMIN
American Orchards, The Patron Saint of. See: CHAPMAN, JOHN
American Orchestral Music, The Father of. See: GRAUPNER, JOHANN CHRISTIAN GOTTLIEB
American Pitt, The. See: STEVENS, THADDEUS
American Poet, The First. See: STEENDAM, JACOB
American Poetry, The Perpetual Adolescent of. See: POUND, EZRA LOOMIS
American Poets, The Father of. See: BRYANT, WILLIAM CULLEN
American Popular Music, The Dean of. See: WHITEMAN, PAUL
American Pre-Raphaelite, The. See: STILLMAN, WILLIAM JAMES
American Prodigy, The. See: SAUVOLLE, LE MOINE
American Professor, The. See: FELTON, CORNELIUS CONWAY
American Prose, The Father of. See: IRVING, WASHINGTON
American Psychiatry, The Father of. See: RUSH, BENJAMIN
American Revolution, The Father of the. See: ADAMS, SAMUEL
American Revolution, The Financier of the. See: MORRIS, ROBERT
American Revolution, The Navarre of the. See: BUTLER, THOMAS
American Revolution, The Penman of the American. See: DICKINSON, JOHN
American Revolution, The Poet of the. See: FRENAU, PHILIP MORIN
American Sappho, The. See: MORTON, SARAH WENTWORTH APTHORP
American Science, the Dean of. See: CATTELL, JAMES McKEEN
American Science, The Nestor of. See:
MITCHELL, SAMUEL LATHAM
SILLIMAN, BENJAMIN
American Scott, The. See: COOPER, JAMES FENIMORE
American Shipmaster. See: CODMAN, JOHN
American Showman, The Great. See: BARNUM, PHINEAS TAYLOR
American Socrates, The. See: FRANKLIN, BENJAMIN
American Sopranos, The Most Intelligent of. See: SMITH, PHYLLIS
American Stage, The Dean of the. See:
JEFFERSON, JOSEPH
SKINNER, OTIS
American Successor to Johann Strauss, The. See: ROMBERG, SIGMUND
American Surgery, The Father of. See: PHYSICK, PHILIP SYNG
American Talleyrand, The. See: VAN BUREN, MARTIN
American Tent-theater Showmen, The Dean of. See: ECCLES, GEORGE CLINTON, JR.
American, The Beautiful (La Belle Americaine). See: MONROE, ELIZABETH KORTRIGHT
American, The Great All. See: FISH, HAMILTON, JR.

American, The Syllable-accenting. See: WEISS, EHRICH (ERIK WEISZ)
American, The Typical. See: ROOSEVELT, THEODORE
American Theater, The Dean of the. See: SKINNER, OTIS
American Theater, The First Lady of the. See: BROWN, HELEN HAYES
American Titian, The. See: ALLSTON, WASHINGTON
American Traveler, The Great. See: PRATT, DANIEL
American Troubadour, The. See: SCOTT, THOMAS JEFFERSON
American Tupper, The. See: HOLLAND, JOSIAH GILBERT
American Universalism, The Father of. See: BALLOU, HOSEA
MURRAY, JOHN
American Watchmaking, The Father of. See: DENNISON, AARON LUFKIN
American Woodman, The. See: AUDUBON, JOHN JAMES FOUGÈRE
American Wordsworth, The. See: BRYANT, WILLIAM CULLEN
American Zoölogy, The Father of. See: SAY, THOMAS
Americans, The Cincinnatus of the. See: WASHINGTON, GEORGE
Americanus, Junius. See: ENDICOTT, CHARLES MOSES
LEE, ARTHUR
America's Answer to Brigitte Bardot. See: REMICK, LEE
America's Boyfriend. See: ROGERS, CHARLES
America's Favorite Television Comedian. See: JACOBS, AMOS
America's First Citizen. See: ELIOT, CHARLES WILLIAM
America's First Gentleman. See: ARTHUR, CHESTER ALAN
America's First Professional Playwright. See: DUNLAP, WILLIAM
America's Foremost Expatriate. See: STEARNS, HAROLD EDMUND
America's Foremost Master of Ceremonies. See: FAY, FRANCIS ANTHONY
America's Foremost Speculative Philosopher. See: WEISS, PAUL
America's Greatest Inventors, One of. See: BOYDEN, SETH
America's Most Honored Broadcaster. See: HARVEY, PAUL
America's No. 1 Boatbuilder. See: HIGGINS, ANDREW JACKSON
America's One-Eyed Jewish Negro. See: DAVIS, SAMMY, JR.
America's One-man Newspaper. See: WINCHEL, WALTER
America's Own Violinist. See: SPALDING, ALBERT
America's Premier Air Woman. See: PUTNAM, AMELIA EARHART
America's Show Music Composers, The Dean of. See: KERN, JEROME DAVID
America's Sweetheart. See: SMITH, GLADYS MARY
America's Sweetheart Emeritus. See: SMITH, GLADYS MARY
America's Tuning Fork. See: SEEGER, PETER
AMES, ELEANOR MARIA EASTERBROOK (1831-1908) [American author]
Eleanor Kirk
AMES, FISHER (1758-1808) [American Federalist orator

and essayist]
Camillus
AMES, FRANCIS H. (1900-). [American author]
Frank Watson
Ames, Jennifer. See: GREIG, MAYSIE COUCHER
AMES, JOSEPH (1689-1759) [English bibliographer and ironmonger]
The Historian of Printing
Ames, Leon. See: WYCOFF, LEON
AMES, NATHANIEL (1708-64) [American almanac maker, physician and innkeeper]
Student in Physick and Astronomy
Ames, Noel. See: BARROWS, MARJORIE
AMFRYE, GUILLAUME (1639-1720) [French churchman and poet]
The Anacreon of the Temple
Amgis. See: SARGENT, LUCIUS MANLIUS
Ami du Peuple, l' (The Friend of the People). See: MARAT, JEAN PAUL
AMICI, DOMINIC (c. 1908-) [American stage, radio and motion picture actor]
Don Ameche
Amicus Patriae. See: WISE, JOHN
Amiens, Peter of. See: PETER
Amis, Breton. See: RAYLEIGH BRETON AMIS
AMIS, KINGSLEY (1922-) [English author]
Robert Markham
Ammonia King, The. See: MALLINCKRODT, EDWARD
AMMONS, EUGENE (1925-) [American jazz musician (tenor saxophone)]
Gene Ammons
Jug Ammons
Amor, Amos. See: HARRELL, IRENE BURK
Amorian, The. See: MICHAEL II
AMORY, THOMAS (c. 1691-1788) [English author]
The English Rabelais
Amos Amor. See: HARRELL, IRENE BURK
Amos and Andy, joint stage name of CHARLES J. CORRELL (1890-) and FREEMAN S. GOSDEN (1899-) [American radio actors]
Amos and Andy. See also: CORRELL, CHARLES J. GOSDEN, FREEMAN F.
Amos Jones. See: GOSDEN, FREEMAN F.
Amos Winslow, Jr. See: COBB, SYLVANUS, JR.
Amos Wright. See: MAGOUN, FREDERICK ALEXANDER
Amphibian. See: ASHTON, SIR GEORGE GREY
Amphibious Warfare, The Father of Modern. See: SMITH, HOLLAND McTYEIRE
AMURATH. See: MURAD (AMURATH) I
AMY [Amy]. See also: Aimee
Amy Bell Marlowe. See: STRATEMEYER, EDWARD L.
Amy Leslie. See: WEST, LILLIE
Amy Lothrop. See: WARNER, ANNA BARTLETT
AMY, WILLIAM LACY (fl. 1921-40) [Canadian novelist]
Luke Allan
An Accidental President. See: FILLMORE, MILLARD
An Aggressive Jack Benny. See: KNIBERG, IRWIN ALAN
An American. See: CASS, LEWIS; CHURCH, BENJAMIN; COOPER, JAMES FENIMORE

DUNLAP, WILLIAM
EVERETT, EDWARD
An Elderly Spinster. See:
WILSON, MARGARET
An English Sappho. See:
PHILIPS, KATHERINE
An International Institution.
See: ANKA, PAUL ALBERT
An Irishman. See:
MOORE, THOMAS
An Old Bachelor. See:
CURTIS, GEORGE
WILLIAM
An Opera-goer. See:
MITCHELL, DONALD GRANT
Ana Dor. See:
CEDER, GEORGIANA
DORCAS
Anacharsis. See:
CLOOTZ, JEAN BAPTISTE
DU VAL DU GRÂCE
ANACLETUS (ANENCLETUS)
(CLETUS) (died c. 88)
[Supreme Pontiff of Roman
Catholic Church]
Pope Anacletus
St. Anacletus
Anacostia, The Sage of. See:
BAILEY, FREDERICK
AUGUST WASHINGTON
Anacreon. See: MOORE,
THOMAS
Anacreon of Painters, The.
See: ALBANI (ALBANO),
FRANCESCO
Anacreon of Persia, The. See:
SHAMS UD-DIN MOHAM-
MED
Anacreon of the Guillotine, The.
See: VIEUZAC, BERTRAND
BARÈRE DE
Anacreon of the Temple, The.
See: AMFRYE, GUILLAUME
Anacreon, The French. See:
THIARD, PONTUS DE
Anacreon, The Scottish. See:
SCOT, ALEXANDER
Anak of Publishers, The. See:
MURRAY, JOHN
Anak Sungel. See:
BROOKE, GILBERT
EDWARD
Ananias of Jazz, The. See:
MESIROW, MILTON
Ananias Twist. See:
NUNN, WILLIAM CURTIS
Anarchy, The Father of. See:
WARREN, JOSIAH
ANASTASIA, GRAND DUCHESS
ANASTASIA NIKOLAIEVNA.
See: ANDERSON, ANNA
ANASTASIUS (died 401) [Supreme
Pontiff of Roman Catholic
Church]
Pope Anastasius I
St. Anastasius
ANASTASIUS (died 498) [Supreme
Pontiff of Roman Catholic
Church]
Pope Anastasius II
St. Anastasius
ANASTASIUS (died 913) [Supreme
Pontiff of Roman Catholic
Church]
Pope Anastasius III
Anastasius IV, Pope. See:
SUBARRA, CORRADO
DELLA
Anastasius Grün. See:
AUERSPERG, ANTON
ALEXANDER GRAF VON
ANASTASIUS, ST. (died 628)
[Christian churchman]
The Apostle of the Hungarians
Anatole Bisque. See:
BOSQUET, ALAIN
Anatole France. See:
THIBAULT, JACQUES
ANATOLE FRANÇOIS
Anatomie Vivante, l' (The Liv-
ing Anatomy). See:
AROUET, FRANÇOIS
MARIE
Anatomist of Humanity, The.
See: POQUELIN, JEAN
BAPTISTE
Anatomy, The Living (l'Anatomie
Vivante). See:
AROUET, FRANÇOIS
MARIE
Ancha, Cara. See:
DEL CAMPO, JOSÉ
SANCHEZ
ANCHIETA (ANCHIETTA), JOSÉ
DE (1533-97) [Jesuit mis-
sionary]

The Apostle of Brazil
Ancient Comedy, The Prince of. See: ARISTOPHANES
Ancient, The. See: LINCOLN, ABRAHAM
Andalusia, The Apostle of. See: JUAN DE ÁVILA
Andaluz. See: ÁLVAREZ, MANUEL
ANDERS, EDITH MARY ENGLAND (1899-) [Australian journalist and author]
E.M. England
ANDERSEN, HANS CHRISTIAN (1805-75) [Danish writer of fairy tales]
The Children's Poet
ANDERSON, ALEXANDER (1845-1909) [Scottish poet]
Surfaceman
ANDERSON, ANNA, claimant to the name ANASTASIA, GRAND DUCHESS ANASTASIA NIKOLAIEVNA (1901-1918?) [daughter of CZAR NICHOLAS II of Russia]
Anderson, Clifford, joint pseud. of RICHARD GARDNER (1931-), ROBERT ANDERSON (-) and CLIFFORD IRVING (-) [American authors]
Anderson, Clifford. See also: GARDNER, RICHARD
ANDERSON, EDDIE (1905-) [American Negro comedian and actor]
Rochester
ANDERSON, G.M. (1882-) [American silent film actor]
Bronco Billy Anderson
Anderson, George. See: GROOM, ARTHUR WILLIAM
WEISSMAN, JACK
ANDERSON, GEORGE THOMAS (1824-1901) [American general officer]
Old Tige
ANDERSON, JAMES (fl. 1859) [American pioneer in North Dakota]
Robinson Crusoe Anderson
ANDERSON, JOHN HENRY (1814-74) [British illusionist and magician]
The Great Wizard of the North
ANDERSON, JOHN Z. (1904-) [American politician]
Airplane Ears
ANDERSON, MADELEINE PALTENGHI (1899-) [American concert singer and author]
Madeleine Paltenghi
ANDERSON, POUL WILLIAM (1926-) [American author]
Winston P. Sanders
ANDERSON, RICHARD HERON (1821-79) [Confederate general officer]
Fighting Dick
Anderson, Rosa. See: KAULITZ-NIEDECK, ROSA
ANDERSON, VIRGINIA R. CRONIN (1920-) [American poet]
Hyacinthe Hill
ANDERSON, VIVIAN (1895-1958) [American vaudevillian and motion picture actress]
Vivian Oakland
Anderson Wayne. See: DRESSER, DAVIS
ANDERSON, WILLIAM (1914-) [American singer and motion picture actor]
Leif Erickson
ANDERSON, WILLIAM ALONZO (1916-) [American jazz musician (trumpet, composer)]
Cat Anderson
ANDONOV-POLJANSKI, HRISTO (1927-) [Yugoslavian editor, educator and author]
Hristo Andonov Poljanski
ANDRADA, DJALMA DE (1928-) [Brazilian jazz musician (lute, guitar, composer)]
Bola Sete
André Baron. See: BOYRON, ANDRÉ

André Maurois. See:
HERZOG, ÉMILE SALAMON WILHELM
André Morell. See:
MESRITZ, ANDRÉ
André North. See:
NORTON, ALICE MARY
Andrea Blake. See:
WEALE, ANNE
Andrea de Pontedera. See:
PISANO, ANDREA
Andrea del Sarto. See:
VANNUCCHI, ANDREA DOMENICO D'AGNOLO DI FRANCESCO DI LUCA
Andrea del Verrocchio. See:
CIONE, ANDREA DI MICHELE DI FRANCESCO
Andrea King. See:
BARRY, GEORGETTA
Andrea Leeds. See:
LEES, ANTOINETTE
Andrea Thomas. See:
HILL, MARGARET OHLER
ANDREAS [Andreas]. See also:
ANDREWS
Andrews
ANDRIEUX
ANDRUS
ANDREAS, ANTONY (died 1320) [Spanish Minorite and theologian]
Doctor Dulcifuus
Andreas Osiander. See:
HOSEMANN, ANDREAS
ANDREW III (died 1301) [King of Hungary]
The Venetian
Andrew Barton. See:
FORREST, THOMAS
Andrew Bede. See:
BEHA, ERNEST
Andrew Blake. See:
JANIFER, LAURENCE MARK
Andrew Dearborn. See:
GARDNER, LEWIS J.
Andrew Dunstan. See:
CHANDLER, A. BERTRAM
Andrew Frazer. See:
MARLOWE, STEPHEN
Andrew Garve. See:
WINTERTON, PAUL
Andrew H. Brown. See:
CORRELL, CHARLES J.
Andrew Hedbrooke. See:
SILL, EDWARD ROWLAND
Andrew Hislop. See:
CLARKE, MARCUS
Andrew Hope. See:
HERN, GEORGE ANTHONY
Andrew James. See:
KIRKUP, JAMES
Andrew John Field. See:
WIEZELL, RICHARD JOHN
Andrew Lee. See:
AUCHINCLOSS, LOUIS STANTON
Andrew, Merry. See:
BORDE (BOORDE), ANDREW
Andrew Moreton, Merchant. See: FOE, DANIEL
Andrew North. See:
NORTON, ALICE MARY
Andrew Seth Pringle-Pattison. See: SETH, ANDREW
Andrew the First, King. See:
JACKSON, ANDREW
ANDREWS [Andrews]. See also:
ANDREAS
Andreas
ANDRIEUX
ANDRUS
ANDREWS, CHARLES ROBERT DOUGLAS HARDY (1908-) [American journalist, correspondent, producer and author]
Robert D. Andrews
Robert Douglas
Douglas Hardy
ANDREWS, CICILY ISABEL FAIRFIELD (1892-) [British novelist and critic]
Rebecca
ANDREWS, ELIZA FRANCES (born 1840) [American botanist and novelist]
Fanny
Elzey Hay
ANDREWS, GEORGE AUGUSTUS (1868-1946) [British stage and motion picture actor]
George Arliss
ANDREWS, IVY PAUL (1908-) [American professional base-

ball player
Poison Ivy
Andrews, John. See:
CAMPBELL, ANDREW
Andrews, Julie. See:
WALTON, JULIA ELIZABETH WELLS
Andrews, Lucilla. See:
CRICHTON, LUCILLA MATHEW
ANDREWS, WAYNE (1913-) [American editor and author]
Montagu O'Reilly
ANDREWS, WILLIAM FORREST (c.1925-) [American motion picture actor]
Steve Forrest
ANDREWS, WILLIAM LINTON (1886-) [British editor and author]
Edith Settle
ANDRIEUX. See also:
ANDREAS
Andreas
ANDREWS
Andrews
ANDRUS
ANDRIEUX, NICOLE (1930-) [French motion picture actress]
Nicole Courcel
ANDRONICUS (1st cent. B.C.) [Greek architect, born at Cyrrhus]
Cyrrhestes
ANDRONICUS OF RHODES (fl. 70-50 B.C.) [Greek peripatetic philosopher; editor of ARISTOTLE'S writings]
Rhodes
ANDROUET, JACQUES (1515?-84?) [French architect]
Du Cerceau (Hoop)
ANDRUS. See also:
ANDREAS
Andreas
ANDREWS
Andrews
ANDRIEUX
ANDRUS, CHARLES E. JR. (1928-) [American jazz musician (bass)]
Chuck Andrus
Andy. See:
Amos and Andy
BATHGATE, ANDREW JAMES
GIBSON, ALBERT ANDREW
GRANATELLI, ANDREW
GRIFFITH, ANDREW SAMUEL
KERR, ANDREW
WILLIAMS, ANDREW
Andy Burton, Major. See:
RATHBONE, ST. GEORGE HENRY
Andy, Faithful. See:
SOMMERVILLE, ANDREW
Andy, Handy. See:
SOMMERVILLE, ANDREW
Andy Iona. See:
LONG, ANDY IONA
Andy, King. See:
JOHNSON, ANDREW
Andy, Mischievous. See:
JACKSON, ANDREW
Andy, Old. See:
JOHNSON, ANDREW
Andy Razaf. See:
RAZAFKERIEFO, ANDREA PAUL
Andy the First, King. See:
JOHNSON, ANDREW
ANELLO. See:
MASANIELLO (TOMMASO ANIELLO) (ANELLO)
ANENCLETUS. See:
ANACLETUS (ANENCLETUS) (CLETUS)
Anet, Claude. See:
SCHOPFER, JEAN
Angel of Mercy and of Prison Reform, The Heaven-sent. See: DIX, DOROTHEA LYNDE
Angel of the Battlefield, The. See: BARTON, CLARISSA HARLOWE
Angel of the Prisons, The. See: TUTWILER, JULIA STRUDWICK
Angel of the Violin, The Dark. See: SOUTH, EDWARD OTHA
Angel, The Battlefield. See:
HANCOCK, CORNELIA

Angel, The Fire. See:
HUDLUN, ANNA ELIZABETH
Angeles, Victoria de Los. See:
CIMA, VICTORIA GAMEZ
Angelete. See:
FERNÁNDEZ, EUGENIO
Angeli, Pier. See:
PIERANGELI, ANNA MARIA
Angelic Doctor. See:
AQUINAS, ST. THOMAS
Angelico, Fra. See:
PIETRO, GUIDO DI
Angelicus, Doctor. See:
AQUINAS, ST. THOMAS
WICKLIFFE, JOHN
Angell, Norman. See:
LANE, RALPH NORMAN ANGELL
Angell, Sir Norman. See:
LANE, RALPH NORMAN ANGELL
Angelo, Michael. See:
BUONARROTTI, MICHELANGELO
Angelus, Muriel. See:
FINDLAY, MURIEL A.
Angelus Silesius. See:
SCHEFFLER, JOHANNES
ANGERMAYER, FRED ANTOINE (1889-) [German playwright]
LYNX
Angers, David d'. See:
DAVID, PIERRE JEAN
ANGHIERA, PIETRO MARTIRE (1455-1526) [Italian chaplain and historian]
The First Historian of America
Peter Martyr
ANGILBERT, ST. (c. 740-814) [Frankish poet]
The Homer of His Age
Angler, The Compleat. See:
WALTON, IZAAK
Anglican Church Music, The Father of. See:
PURCELL, HENRY
Anglicus, Joannes (John of England) See:
JOAN
Angling, The Father of. See:
WALTON, IZAAK
Anglo-Saxon Milton, The. See:
CAEDMON (CEDMON)
Anglo-Saxons, Apostle of the. See: AUGUSTINE (AUSTIN), ST.
ANGOFF, CHARLES (1902-) [Russian-American editor, educator and author]
Richard W. Hinton
Angoulême, Marguérite d'. See:
MARGARET OF NAVARRE
Angus Vicker. See:
FELSEN, HENRY GREGOR
ANHALT-ZERBST, SOPHIA AUGUSTA FREDERICA OF (1729-96) [Empress of Russia]
Catherine II
Catherine the Great
The Little Mother of all the Russians
The Modern Messalina
The Semiramis of the North
ANICETUS (died c. 166) [Supreme Pontiff of Roman Catholic Church]
Pope Anicetus
St. Anicetus
ANIELLO. See:
MASANIELLO (TOMMASO ANIELLO) (ANELLO)
Anita Louise. See:
FREMAULT, ANITA LOUISE
Anjou, Charles Robert of. See:
CHARLES I
Anjou, The Fair Maid of. See:
PLANTAGENET, LADY EDITH
ANKA, PAUL ALBERT (1941-) [Canadian composer and singer of popular songs]
An International Institution
ANKERSON, ARDIS (1915-) [American motion picture actress]
Brenda Marshall
ANLLÓ, JUAN (1898-1925) [Spanish bullfighter]
Nacional II
Anmar, Frank. See:
NOLAN, WILLIAM FRANCIS
ANN (1665-1714) [Queen of England]

Brandy Nan
Mrs. Bull
Mrs. Morley
Ann. See:
Anna
ANNE
Anne
SHERIDAN, CLARA LOU
Ann Abelson. See:
CAVALLARO, ANN ABELSON
Ann Aikman. See:
McQUADE, ANN AIKMAN
Ann Alexander Reid. See:
MARLOW, MRS. LOUIS
Ann Atom. See:
WALWORTH, JEANETTE RITCHIE HADERMAN
Ann Bridge. See:
O'MALLEY, MARY DOLLING SANDERS, LADY O'MALLEY
Ann Carmichael. See:
MACALPINE, MARGARET HESKETH MURRAY
Ann Compton. See:
PREBBLE, MARJORIE MARY CURTIS
Ann Dvorak. See:
McKIM, ANN
Ann Gillis. See:
O'CONNOR, ALMA
Ann Harding. See: GATLEY, DOROTHY
Ann Head. See:
MORSE, ANNE CHRISTENSEN
Ann Kilborn Cole. See:
CALLAHAN, CLAIRE WALLIS
Ann Landers. See:
FRIEDMAN, ESTHER PAULINE
Ann Lynton. See:
RAYNER, CLAIRE
Ann-Margret. See:
OLSON, ANN-MARGRET
Ann Marie Long. See:
JENSEN, PAULINE MARIE LONG
Ann Miller. See:
COLLIER, LUCY ANN
Ann, Mother. See:
LEE (LEES), ANN
Ann Mullins. See:
DALLY, ANN MULLINS
Ann of the Word. See:
LEE (LEES), ANN
Ann Patrice. See:
GALBRAITH, GEORGIE STARBUCK
Ann, Peggy. See:
MILLER, GEORGE AMOS
Ann Praize. See:
BLEWETT, DOROTHY EMILIE
Ann Sheldon. See:
STRATEMEYER, EDWARD L.
Ann Sothern. See:
LAKE, HARRIETTE
Ann Todd. See:
MAYFIELD, ANN TODD
Ann Weston. See:
PITCHER, GLADYS
Anna. See:
ANN
Ann
ANNE
Anne
RUSSELL-BROWN, CLAUDIA ANNA
Anna A. Robie, Mrs. See:
ROLFE, MARO O.
Anna Akhmatova. See:
GORENKO, ANNA ANDREYEVNA
Anna Blount. See:
GALLICHAN, WALTER M.
Anna Clark. See:
BENNINGHOFEN, MRS. ERNST
Anna Haynes. See:
MADLEE, DOROTHY HAYNES
Anna Kavan. See:
EDMONDS, HELEN WOODS
Anna Lee. See:
WINNIFRITH, JOANNA
Anna Maria Hirst. See:
HIRST, HENRY BECK
Anna Matilda. See:
COWLEY, MRS. HANNAH
Anna May Wong. See:
WONG LIU TSONG
Anna Neagle. See:

ROBERTSON, MARJORIE
Anna Sage. See:
CUMPANAS, ANA
Anna Seghers. See:
REILING, NETTY
Anna Sten. See:
SUJAKEVITCH, ANJUSCHLA STENSKI
Annabella. See:
CHARPENTIER, SUZANNE
Annan Dale. See:
JOHNSON, JAMES WESLEY
ANNE (died 1716) [Countess of Sutherland; second daughter of DUKE OF MARLBOROUGH]
The Little Whig
Anne. See:
ANN
Ann
Anna
Knish, Ann
OLDFIELD, NANCE
Anne Bancroft. See:
ITALIANO, ANNEMARIE (ANNA MARIA)
Anne Beaton. See:
WASHINGTON, MARGUERITE BEAU-CHAMP
Anne Bernays. See:
KAPLAN, ANNE BERNAYS
Anne Betteridge. See:
POTTER, MARGARET NEWMAN
Anne Blaisdell. See:
LININGTON, ELIZABETH
Anne Caldwell. See:
O'DEA, ANNE CALDWELL
Anne Carter. See:
BROOKS, ANNE TEDLOCK
Anne Caswell. See:
DENHAM, MARY ORR
ANNE, DUC DE MONTMORENCY (1492-1567) [Grand Constable of France]
The French Fabius
Anne Eliot. See:
COLE, LOIS DWIGHT
Anne Eyre Worboys. See:
WORBOYS, ANNETTE ISOBEL
Anne Fellowes. See
MANTLE, WINIFRED LANGFORD
Anne Frances Huether. See:
FREEMAN, ANNE FRANCIS
Anne Gwynne. See:
TRICE, MARGUERITE GWYNNE
Anne Heywood. See:
STROSS, MRS. RAYMOND
Anne Hill. See:
MUSKETT, NETTA
Anne Klainikite. See:
GEHMAN, BETSY HOLLAND
Anne Lorraine. See:
CHISHOLM, LILIAN MARY
Anne, Mad. See:
BAILEY, ANNE HENNIS TROTTER
Anne March. See:
WOOLSON, CONSTANCE FENIMORE
Anne Medley. See:
BORCHARD, RUTH BERENDSOHN
Anne Ophelia Todd. See:
DOWDEN, ANNE OPHELIA TODD
Anne Paterson. See:
EINSELEN, ANNE F.
Anne Penn. See:
PENDOWER, JACQUES
Anne Pilgrim. See:
ALLAN, MABEL ESTHER
Anne Powers. See:
SCHWARTZ, ANNE POWERS
Anne Royall, Godless. See:
ROYALL, ANNE NEWPORT
Anne S. Lee. See:
MURPHY, MABEL ANSLEY
Anne Savoy. See:
BROOKS, ANNE SOOY
Anne Shirley. See:
PARIS, DAWN
Anne Stafford. See:
PEDLER, ANNE I. STAFFORD
Anne Vernon. See: VIGNAUD, EDITH
Anne W. House. See:
McCAULEY, ELFRIEDA BABNICK
Anne Windsor. See:
DEWEY, ANNETTE BAR-RETT

Annett, Cora. See:
SCOTT, CORA ANNETT PEPITONE
Annette. See:
FUNICELLO, ANNETTE
Annette Adams. See:
ROWLAND, DONALD SYDNEY
Annette Eyre. See:
WORBOYS, ANNETTE ISOBEL
ANNICHIARICO, WALTER (1924-) [Italian comic actor]
Walter Chiari
Annie North Bedford. See:
WATSON, JANE WERNER
Annie Oakley. See:
MOZZEE, PHOEBE ANNE OAKLEY
Annie Ross. See:
SHORT, ANNABELLE
Annie Young. See:
DUPUY, ELIZA ANN
Annixter, Jane. See:
STURTZEL, JANE LEVINGTON
Annixetr, Paul. See:
STURTZEL, HOWARD ALLISON
Annunzio, Gabriele d'. See:
RAMPAGNETTO, GAETANO
Anny Ondra. See:
ONDRAKOVA, ANNY
Anouk. See:
SORYA, FRANÇOISE
Anouk Aimée. See:
SORYA, FRANÇOISE
Ans. See:
WEEKS, ANSON
ANSAGAR (ANSCHARIUS) (801-65) [Frankish missionary]
The Apostle of the North
ANSCHARIUS. See:
ANSAGAR (ANSCHARIUS)
ANSELM OF LAON (1030-1117) [French theologian]
The Scholastic Doctor
ANSON, ADRIAN CONSTANTINE (1852-1922) [American professional baseball player and manager]
Cap Anson
Anson Hunter. See:
ORRMONT, ARTHUR
Anson MacDonald. See:
HEINLEIN, ROBERT ANSON
Anspach, Caroline of. See:
FREDERICK, WILHELMINA CAROLINA
Anstey, F. See:
GUTHRIE, THOMAS ANSTEY
Answer to Brigitte Bardot, America's. See:
REMICK, LEE
Answers, The Man of Happy Unhappy. See:
TARLTON, RICHARD
ANTERUS (died 236) [Supreme Pontiff of Roman Catholic Church]
Pope Anterus
St. Anterus
Anthony. See:
Antonio
ANTONY (ANTHONY), ST.
Anthony A. Wood. See:
WOOD, ANTHONY
Anthony Abbott. See:
OURSLER, CHARLES FULTON
Anthony Afterwit. See:
FRANKLIN, BENJAMIN
Anthony Armstrong. See:
WILLIS, GEORGE ANTHONY ARMSTRONG
Anthony Berkeley. See:
COX, ANTHONY BERKELEY
Anthony Boucher. See:
WHITE, WILLIAM ANTHONY PARKER
Anthony, C.L. See:
SMITH, DODIE
Anthony Carson. See:
BROOKE, PETER
Anthony Dexter. See:
FLEISCHMANN, WALTER
ANTHONY, EDWARD (1895-) [American author]
Edar
Anthony, Evelyn. See:
WARD-THOMAS, EVELYN BRIDGET PATRICIA STEPHENS

Anthony Evergreen. See:
IRVING, WASHINGTON
Anthony Franciosa. See:
PAPALEO, ANTHONY
Anthony Grumbler. See:
HOFFMAN, DAVID
Anthony Hope. See:
HAWKINS, SIR ANTHONY HOPE
Anthony, John. See:
BECKETT, RONALD BRYMER
SABINI, JOHN ANTHONY
ANTHONY, JOHN ALSTON (1854-1927) [American educator]
Shelby's Man of Faith
ANTHONY, JOHN J. (1898-1970) [American radio program conductor]
Mr. Anthony
Anthony Lawless. See:
MACDONALD, PHILIP
ANTHONY, LEO (1925-) [American jazz musician (baritone saxophone, leader)]
Lee Roy Anthony
Anthony Morton. See:
CREASEY, JOHN
Anthony of Padua. See:
FERDINAND
Anthony Partridge. See:
OPPENHEIM, EDWARD PHILLIPS
Anthony Pasquin. See:
WILLIAMS, JOHN
Anthony, Piers. See:
JACOB, PIERS ANTHONY DILLINGHAM
Anthony Pryde. See:
WEEKES, AGNES RUSSELL
Anthony, Ray. See:
ANTONINI, RAYMOND
Anthony Roberts. See:
WATNEY, JOHN BASIL
Anthony Scott. See:
DRESSER, DAVIS
Anthony Sterling. See:
CAESAR, EUGENE LEE
Anthony Wayne, Mad. See:
WAYNE, ANTHONY
Anthony Webb. See:
WILSON, NORMAN SCARLYN
Anthony Wharton. See:
McALLISTER, ALISTER
Anthracite Iron Industry, The Father of the American. See: THOMAS, DAVID
Anthropology, The Father of American. See:
MORGAN, LEWIS HENRY
Anthropology, The Founder of the Science of. See:
BLUMENBACH, JOHANN FRIEDRICH
Anthropophagus Minor. See:
CONNIFF, JAMES CLIFFORD GREGORY
Anti-chain-store. See:
PATMAN, WRIGHT
Anti-McFarlane. See:
McFARLANE, WILLIAM DODDRIDGE
Anti-Masonry, The Arch-Priest of. See:
STEVENS, THADDEUS
Anti-war. See:
KNUTSON, HAROLD
Antigone, The Modern. See:
CHARLOTTE, MARIE THÉRÈSE
ANTIGONUS I (382-301 B.C.), [Macedonian king; general officer under ALEXANDER THE GREAT]
Cyclops
Monophthalmos (One-Eyed)
ANTIGONUS II (319?-239 B.C.) [Macedonian king]
Gonatas
Antilon. See:
DULANY, DANIEL
Antioch, John of.
See: CHRYSOSTOM, ST. JOHN
ANTIOCHUS I (323-261 B.C.) [King of Syria]
Soter (The Preserver)
ANTIOCHUS II (286-247 B.C.) [King of Syria]
Theos (God)
ANTIOCHUS III (242-187 B.C.) [King of Syria]
The Great

Megas
ANTIOCHUS IV (died 163 B.C.) [King of Syria]
Epiphanes
ANTIOCHUS VII (c.159-129 B.C.) [King of Syria]
Eurgetes (Benefactor)
Sidetes
ANTIOCHUS IX (died 95 B.C.) [King of Syria]
Cyzicenus
ANTIOCHUS XIII (died after 64 B.C.) [king of Syria]
Asiaticus
Antiquarian of Nassau Street, The. See:
GOWANS, WILLIAM
Antiquary, The. See:
LIVERMORE, GEORGE
Antiseptic Surgery, The Father of. See:
LISTER, JOSEPH
Antoine. See:
CIERPLIKOWSKI, ANTEK
Anton Burney. See:
HOPKINS, KENNETH
Anton Dolin. See:
HEALEY-KAY, PATRICK
ANTÓN, FRANCISCO (1939-) Spanish Bullfighter
Pacorro
Anton Hofman. See:
HOLLO, ANSELM
Anton Walbrook. See:
WOHLBRUCK, ADOLF
Antoñete. See:
CHENEL, ANTONIO
ANTONI, BOLESLAWOWICZ STANISLAW (1882-) [British-born orchestra conductor]
Leopold Stokowski
Antonia Molinera. See:
CARILLO, ROSITA FELIX
ANTONINI, RAYMOND (1922-) [American jazz musician (trumpet, leader)]
Ray Anthony
Antoninus. See:
VERUS, MARCUS ANNIUS
Antonio. See:
ANTHONY
Anthony
ANTONY
COLORADO CAPELIA, ANTONIO JULIO
SOLER, ANTONIO RUIZ
Antonio Agapida, Fray. See:
IRVING, WASHINGTON
Antonius, Brother. See:
EVERSON, WILLIAM OLIVER
ANTONY. See also:
ANTHONY
Anthony
Antonio
ANTONY (ANTHONY), ST. (c.250-c.350) [Christian churchman, monk and hermit]
Antony of Thebes
The Father of Christian Monachism
The Father of Monachism
The Father of Monks
The Founder of Christian Monasticism
The Great
St. Antony of Egypt
Antwerp, The Blacksmith of. See: MATSYS, QUENTIN
Anushirvan (Having an Immortal Soul). See:
KHOSRAU I
ANWYL, JOHN BODVAN (1875-) [British lexicographer]
Bodfan
ANZELEVITZ, BERNARD (1891-1943) [American jazz musician (violin, composer, leader, singer)]
Bernard Berni
Ben Bernie
The Old Maestro
Ap-i-juni. See:
SCHULTZ, JAMES WILLARD
APARICI, JULIO (1865-97) [Spanish bullfighter]
Fabrilo
Ape. See:
PELLEGRINI, CARLO
APELLES (fl. c.330 B.C.) [Greek painter]
The Prince of Painters
Apelles of His Age, The. See:
COOPER, SAMUEL

Apiculture, The Father of American. See: LANGSTROTH, LORENZO LORRAINE
Apollinaire, Guillaume. See: KOSTROWITZKY, APOLLINARIS
APOLLINARIS (fl. 4th cent. A.D.) [Prebister of Laodicea]
The Elder
APOLLINARIS (died 390) [Bishop of Laodicea]
The Younger
Apollo, The Portuguese. See: DE CAMOENS, LUIZ
APOLLODORUS (fl. 5th cent. B.C.) [Greek painter]
Skiagraphos (The Shadow Painter)
APOLLONIUS OF PERGA (fl. 3rd cent. B.C.) [Greek mathematician]
The Great Geometer
Apologist, The. See: TATIAN
Apostate, The. See: JULIANUS, FLAVIUS CLAUDIUS
Apostle of Accomac, The. See: MAKEMIE, FRANCIS
Apostle of Andalusia, The. See: JUAN DE ÁVILA
Apostle of Ardennes and of Brabant, The. See: HUBERT, ST.
Apostle of Armenia, The. See: GREGORY OF ARMENIA, ST.
Apostle of Brazil, The. See: ANCHIETA (ANCHIETTA), JOSÉ DE
Apostle of Caledonia, The. See: COLUMBA, ST.
Apostle of California, The. See: SALVATIERRA, JUAN MARÍADE
Apostle of Culture, The. See: ARNOLD, MATTHEW
Apostle of Disunion, The. See: JULIAN, GEORGE WASHINGTON
Apostle of Ethiopia, The. See: FRUMENTIUS, ST.
Apostle of Free Coinage for Silver, The. See: ST. JOHN, WILLIAM POPE
Apostle of Free Trade, The. See: BRIGHT, JOHN
COBDEN, RICHARD
Apostle of Germany, The. See: WINFRID (WYNFRITH)
Apostle of Greenland, The. See: EGEDE, HANS
Apostle of Infidelity, The. See: AROUET, FRANÇOIS MARIE
Apostle of Ireland, The. See: PATRICK, ST.
Apostle of Liberty, The. See: CLAY, HENRY
JEFFERSON, THOMAS
Apostle of Light and Power. See: LIEB, JOHN WILLIAM
Apostle of Methodism, The. See: LEE, JESSE
Apostle of Oregon, The. See: BLANCHET, FRANCIS HERBERT
Apostle of Organized Charity, The. See: VINCENT DE PAUL
Apostle of Peace, The. See: LADD, WILLIAM
Apostle of Persia, The. See: PERKINS, JUSTIN
Apostle of Peru, The. See: BARCENA (BARZENA), ALONSO DE
Apostle of Pomerania, The. See: OTTO OF BAMBERG
Apostle of Prohibition, The. See: HILL, WALTER BARNARD
Apostle of Quiet People, The. See: YOUNG, EMILY HILDA
Apostle of South America, The. See: FOWLER, CHARLES HENRY
Apostle of Sunshine, The. See: TAYLOR, ROBERT LOVE
Apostle of Temperance, The. See: MATTHEW, FATHER THEOBOLD
MURPHY, FRANCIS
Apostle of the Alleghenies, The. See: GALLITZIN, DEMETRIUS AUGUSTINE

Apostle of the Alps. See:
BERNARD OF MENTHON, ST.
Apostle of the Anglo-Saxons, The. See: AUGUSTINE (AUSTIN), ST.
Apostle of the English, The. See: AUGUSTINE (AUSTIN), ST.
Apostle of the French, The. See: DENIS (DENYS), ST.
Apostle of the Friesians, The. See: WILLIBRORD
Apostle of the Gauls, The. See: IRENAEUS, ST.
Apostle of the Gentiles, The. See: SAUL
Apostle of the Highlanders, The. See: COLUMBA, ST.
Apostle of the Hungarians, The. See: ANASTASIUS, ST.
Apostle of the Indians, The. See:
ELIOT, JOHN
LAS CASAS, BARTOLOMÉ DE
Apostle of the Indies, The. See: XAVIER, ST. FRANCIS
Apostle of the Netherlands, The. See: ARMAND, ST.
Apostle of the North, The. See:
ANSAGAR (ANSCHARIUS)
GILPIN, BERNARD
Apostle of the Peak, The. See: BAGSHAW, WILLIAM
Apostle of the Picts, The. See: NINIAN, ST.
Apostle of the Prussians, The. See: ADELBERT
BRUNO, ST.
Apostle of the Rocky Mountains, The. See:
DE SMET, PETER JOHN
Apostle of the Scots, The. See: KNOX, JOHN
Apostle of the Scottish Reformation, The. See:
KNOX, JOHN
Apostle of the Sword, The. See: MOHAMMED
Apostle of the Wilderness, The. See: BRECK, JAMES LLOYD
Apostle of Toleration, The. See:
WILLIAMS, ROGER
Apostle of Unitarianism, The. See: CHANNING, WILLIAM ELLERY
Apostle, The Thirteenth. See: CHRYSOSTOM, ST. JOHN
Apostle to the Germans, The. See: GULDIN, JOHN C.
Apostle to the Maoris. See: MARSDEN, SAMUEL
Apostle to the Papuans. See: ABEL, CHARLES WILLIAM
Apostle to the Sioux Indians, The. See:
HARE, WILLIAM HOBART
Apostle to the Slavs, The. See:
Apostles to the Slavs
CONSTANTINE
METHODIUS
SCHAUFFLER, HENRY ALBERT
Apostles to the Slavs, joint appellation of CONSTANTINE (St. Cyril) (827-69), and his brother METHODIUS (St. Methodius) (826-85), Thessalonian churchmen.
Appendixmonger. See: STRYPE, JOHN
APPERLEY, CHARLES JAMES (1777-1843) [English sporting writer and sportsman]
Nimrod
APPIANO, ANDREA (1754-1817) [Italian artist; court painter to NAPOLEON I]
The Painter of the Graces
Apple King. The. See: WELLHOUSE, FREDERICK
Appleseed, Johnny. See: CHAPMAN, JOHN
Appleton, Victor. See: STRATEMEYER, EDWARD L.
Appleton, Victor, II. See: STRATEMEYER, EDWARD L.
APPLEY, MORTIMER HERBERT (1921-) [American psychologist, educator and author]
M.H. Applezweig
Applezweig, N.H.
See:

APPLEY, MORTIMER HERBERT
APPOLONIUS (2d cent. A.D.) [Alexandrian grammarian]
Dyskolos (Ill Tempered)
Appomattox, Hero of. See: GRANT, HIRAM ULYSSES
Aquarian. See: OPPENHEIMER, JOEL LESTER
AQUINAS, ST. THOMAS (c.1227-74) [Italian scholastic theologian and philosopher]
Angelic Doctor
Doctor Angelicus
Doctor Universalis
Dumb Ox
Prince of Scholastics
Thomas of Aquino
Aquinian Sage, The. See: JUVENAL
AQUINO, FRANK J. (1906-) [American musician, conductor and composer]
Bernie Kane
Aquino, Thomas of. See: AQUINAS, ST. THOMAS
ARABI PASHA (c.1840-1911) [Egyptian rebel leader]
Ahmed Arabi
Arabia, Lawrence of. See: LAWRENCE, THOMAS EDWARD
Arabian Tailor, The. See: WILD, HENRY
Arabian, The. See: PHILIP I
Arabs, The Philosopher of the. See: KINDI, AL (ABU YUSUF YA IQUB IBN-ISHAQ AL-KINDI)
Aramis. See: SIMENON, GEORGES
ARANGO, DOROTEO (1877-1923) [Mexican revolutionary general officer]
Francisco Villa
Pancho Villa
ARBUCKLE, ROSCOE (1887-1932) [American silent film comedian]
Fatty Arbuckle
Will B. Good
ARC. See: JOAN OF ARC, ST. (JEANNE D'ARC)
Arc of the Modern Religious World, The Joan of. See: UTLEY, ULDINE
Arc, The English Joan of. See: AMBREE, MARY
Arch. See: WHITEHOUSE, ARTHUR GEORGE
Arch-Priest of Anti-Masonry, The. See: STEVENS, THADDEUS
ARCHAMBAULT, LOUIS-FRANÇOIS (1742-1812) [French actor and dramatist]
Dorvigny
Archbishop John I of Vancouver, The. See: WOLSEY, WILLIAM FRANKLYN
Archdruid, The. See: STUKELEY, WILLIAM
ARCHELAUS (40 B.C.-17 A.D.) [King of Cappadocia]
Sisines
Archer, A.A. See: JOSCELYN, ARCHIE L.
Archer, George. See: HARDWICK, ARCHER
Archer, Harry. See: AURACHER, HARRY
Archer, Heavenly (Alhuicamia). See: MONTEZUMA I
Archer, John. See: BOWMAN, RALPH
Archer, Lane. See: HAUCK, LOUISE PLATT
Archer, Ron. See: WHITE, THEODORE EDWIN
Archers," The Author of "The. See: DUNLAP, WILLIAM
Archibald Banks. See: CRAWFURD, OSEALD
Archibald, Mrs. George. See: PALMER, ANNA CAMPBELL
Archie. See: ARMSTRONG, ARCHIBALD
Archie Moore. See: WRIGHT, ARCHIBALD LEE
Archie the Manager. See: GARDNER, EDWARD FRANCIS

ARCHILOCHUS (fl. c. 700 B.C.)
[Greek lyric poet of Paros]
The Father of Iambic Verse
The Father of Satire
Architect Earl, The. See:
HERBERT, HENRY, 9TH EARL OF PEMBROKE
Architect of the Atomic Bomb, The. See:
FERMI, ENRICO
Architect, The World's No. 1 Industrial. See:
KAHN, ALBERT
Archy. See:
ARMSTRONG, ARCHIBALD
ARD, WILLIAM THOMAS (1922-) [American author]
Ben Kerr
Mike Moran
Jonas Ward
Thomas Wills
Arden, Barbie. See:
STOUTENBURG, ADRIEN PEARL
Arden, Elizabeth. See:
GRAHAM, FLORENCE NIGHTINGALE
Arden, Eve. See:
QUEDENS, EUNICE
Arden, J.E.M. See:
CONQUEST, GEORGE ROBERT ACWORTH
Ardennes and of Brabant, The Apostle of. See:
HUBERT, ST.
Areopagite, The. See:
DIONYSIUS
Areta, Mavis. See:
WINDER, MAVIS ARETA
Aretino. See:
BRUNI, LEONARDO
ARETINO, GUIDO. See:
GUIDO D'AREZZO (GUIDO ARETINO)
ARETINO, PIETRO (1492-1556)
[Italian writer and man of letters]
Censor of the Proud World
The Father of Journalism
The Scourge of Princes
Aretius Felinus. See:
KUHHORN, MARTIN
ARFONS, ARTHUR EUGENE (1926-) [American automobile racer and racing car designer]
Art Arfons
ARGENSOLA, BARTOLOMÉ LEONARDO DE. See:
Spanish Horaces, The
ARGENSOLA, LUPERCIO DE. See: Spanish Horaces, The
Argentinita. See:
LÓPEZ, ENCARNACIÓN
Argus. See:
PHILLIPS-BIRT, DOUGLAS
Ari. See:
LURIA, ISAAC BEN SOLOMON
ARIAS, BENITO (1527-98)
[Spanish theologian and linguist]
Montano
Arias, Dame Margot Fonteyn de. See: HOOKHAM, MARGARET
Ariel. See:
MORAES, FRANK ROBERT
ARIOSTO, LUDOVICO (1474-1533) [Italian poet]
The Homer of Ferrara
The Southern Scott
The Tuscan Poet
ARIOSTO, LUDOVICO. See also:
Immortal Four of Italy, The
Ariosto of the North, The.
See: SCOTT, SIR WALTER
ARISTARCHUS (fl. 2nd cent. B.C.) [Alexandrian grammarian]
The Coryphaeus of Grammarians
ARISTIDES (ARISTEIDES) (c. 530-468 B.C.) [Athenian statesman]
The Just
Aristides, Old. See:
BICKNELL, JOSHUA
Aristides, The British. See:
MARVELL, ANDREW
ARISTOCLES (427?-347 B.C.)
[Greek philosopher]
The Athenian Bee
The Attic Bee
The Homer of Philosophers
Plato

The Prince of Philosophers
ARISTOPHANES (c. 480-385 B.C.)
[Greek comic dramatist]
The Creator of the New Comedy
The Father of Comedy
The Prince of Ancient Comedy
Aristophanes, The English. See:
FOOTE, SAMUEL
Aristophanes, The French. See:
POQUELIN, JEAN BAPTISTE
Aristophanes, The Modern. See:
FOOTE, SAMUEL
ARISTOTLE (384-322 B.C.)
[Greek Philosopher]
The Stagirite
Aristotle, The Second. See:
ACHILLINI, ALESSANDRO
ARISZTID OLT. See:
BLASKO, BELA LUGOSI
Arizona Cy. See:
COWDRICK, JESSE C.
Arizona, The Father of. See:
POSTON, CHARLES
DEBRILL
Arjehir. See:
ARYABHATA (ARYA-
BHATTA)
Arkansas Humming Bird, The.
See: WARNECKE, LONNIE
Arkansas, Ol'. See:
WARNECKE, LONNIE
Arkie. See:
VAUGHAN, FLOYD E.
Arkwright, Peleg. See:
PROUDFIT, DAVID LAW
Arlen, Harold. See:
ARLUCK, HYMEN
Arlen, Michael. See:
KOUYOUMDJIAN, DIKRAN
Arlen, Richard. See:
VAN MATTIMORE,
RICHARD
Arlene Francis. See:
KAZANJIAN, ARLINE
FRANCIS
Arletty. See:
BATHIAT, LEONIE
Arlington B. Conway. See:
BURNS, EEDSON LOUIS
MILLARD
ARLINGTON, EARL OF (HENRY
BENNETT). See:
Cabal, The
Arlington, Josie. See:
DEUBLER, MARY
Arliss, George. See:
ANDREWS, GEORGE
AUGUSTUS
ARLUCK, HYMEN (1905-)
[American composer,
pianist and arranger]
Harold Arlen
Arm, Rubber. See:
CONNALLY, GEORGE
WALTER
Arm, The Man With the Golden.
See: KOUFAX, SANFORD
Armada, Captain General of
the. See:
COLUMBUS, CHRISTOPHER
ARMAND, LOUIS. See:
Three Wise Men
ARMAND, ST. (589-679)
[Christian churchman]
The Apostle of the Netherlands
Armansur. See:
CALIPH ABU-JAFAR
Armed Soldier of Democracy, The.
See: BONAPARTE,
NAPOLEON
Armée, Le Sage de la Grande.
See: DROUOT, ANTOINE,
COMTE
ARMENIA. See:
GREGORY OF ARMENIA,
ST.
Armenia, The Apostle of. See:
GREGORY OF ARMENIA,
ST.
Armenian, The. See:
LEO V
ARMERO, GIORGIO (1669-1707)
[Italian physician]
Baglivi
Armido. See:
TOYNE, CLARICE JOY
Armillita Chico. See:
ESPINOSA, FERMÍN
ARMIN, ROBERT (died 1615)
[English actor and play-
wright]
Robin Armin
Arminius, Jacobus. See:
HARMENSEN (HERMANSZ),
JACOB
ARMINUS (c. 17 B.C.-21 A.D.),

[German chief of the Cherusci; national hero]
Hermann
ARMSTEAD, GEORGE (1780-1818) [American Revolutionary officer]
The Hero of Fort McHenry
ARMITAGE, JOHN (188?-) [Australian author and journalist]
Hin me Geong
Armour, Gladys. See: OSBORNE, DOROTHY GLADYS YEO
Armstrong, Anthony. See: WILLIS, GEORGE ANTHONY ARMSTRONG
ARMSTRONG, ARCHIBALD (died 1672) [English jester]
Archie
Archy
Armstrong, Captain Frank P. See: AIKEN, ALBERT W.
ARMSTRONG, CHARLOTTE (1905-) [American author]
Jo Valentine
ARMSTRONG, DANIEL LOUIS (1900-71) [American jazz musician (trumpet, singer, leader and composer)]
Louie Armstrong
Pops
Satchmo
ARMSTRONG, DOUGLAS ALBERT (1920-) [British journalist and author]
Albert Douglas
Tribune
Rex Windsor
ARMSTRONG, HAROLD HUNTER (1884-) [American novelist]
Henry G. Aikman
Armstrong, Henry. See: JACKSON, HENRY
ARMSTRONG, HENRY W. (1879-) [American composer, pianist and talent agency executive]
Harry Armstrong
ARMSTRONG, JOHN BYRON (1917-) [American journalist, editor and author]
John Byron
Charles Willard
ARMSTRONG, PAUL (1869-1915) [American journalist and playwright]
Right Cross
ARMSTRONG, TERENCE IAN FYTTON (1912-) [British poet]
John Gawsworth
ARMSTRONG, WILLIAM (mid-16th cent.) [Dumfriesshire moss-trooper]
Kinmont Willy
ARMSTRONG, WILLIAM ALEXANDER (1912-) [Scottish educator and author]
Alexander Hazelton
Army, A Gentleman of the. See: STEELE, SIR RICHARD
Army, The Beau Brummel of the. See: MacARTHUR, DOUGLAS
Army, The Florence Nightingale of the Southern. See: TRADER, ELLA KING NEWSOM
Army, The Marion of the Mexican. See: LANE, JOSEPH
Army, The Murat of the Union. See: LOGAN, JOHN ALEXANDER
Army, The Poet Laureate of the. See: PATTEN, GEORGE WASHINGTON
Army's One-man Hit Parade, The. See: LOESSER, FRANK HENRY
ARNASON, JON (1819-88) [national librarian of Iceland]
The Grimm of Iceland
ARNAUD, ARSÈNE (1840-1913) [French novelist]
Jules Claretie
ARNAULD. See also: ARNOLD
Arnold
ARNAULD, ANTOINE (1612-94) [French theologian and philosopher]

The Great Arnauld
Arnaz, Desi. See:
ACHA, DESIDERIO ALBERTO ARNAZ Y DE, 3D
ARNDT, JOHN (1555-1621) [German theologian]
The Fénelon of the Reformation
ARNESS, PETER (1925-) [American television and motion picture actor]
Peter Graves
ARNHEIM, GUS (1897-1955) [American jazz musician (composer, leader)]
The Old Colonel
Arno, Curt. See:
PETERS, CURTIS ARNOUX
Arno, Peter. See:
PETERS, CURTIS ARNOUX
Arno, Sig. See:
ARON, SIEGFRIED
ARNOBIUS (died 327) [teacher of rhetoric at Sicca, Numidia]
The Elder
ARNOBIUS (fl. 300 A.D.) [early Christian apologist]
Arnobius Afer
The Younger
Arnold. See:
ARNAULD
BENNETT, ENOCH ARNOLD
ARNOLD, BENEDICT (1741-1801) [American general officer and traitor]
The Traitorous Hero
Arnold, Birch. See:
BARTLETT, ALICE ELINOR
Arnold, Edward. See:
SCHNEIDER, GUENTHER
ARNOLD, EDWIN LESTER (1856-) [English author]
Phra
Arnold Fredericks. See:
KUMMER, FREDERIC ARNOLD
ARNOLD, GEORGE (1834-65) [American journalist and poet]
Graham Allen
McArone
McArone
Pierrot
ARNOLD, HENRY HARLEY (1886-1950) [American general officer; Chief of Army Air Forces]
Hap Arnold
Arnold, Joseph H. See:
HAYES, JOSEPH
Arnold, L.J. See:
CAMERON, LOU
ARNOLD, MARGARET SHIPPEN (1760-1803) [American wife of BENEDICT ARNOLD]
Peggy
ARNOLD, MARY AUGUSTA (1851-1920) [English novelist]
Mrs. Humphrey Ward
ARNOLD, MATTHEW (1822-88) [English poet and critic]
The Apostle of Culture
The Sainte-Beuve of English Criticism
Arnold Meredith. See:
HOPKINS, KENNETH
ARNOLD, RICHARD (1912-) [Scottish author]
Coch-y-Bonddhu
ARNOLD, RICHARD EDWARD (1918-) [American Western singer]
Eddie Arnold
The Tennessee Plowboy
ARNOLD, THOMAS (1795-1842) [English educator and historian]
Arnold of Rugby
Arnoldy, Julie. See:
BISCHOFF, JULIA BRISTOL
Arnoul, Françoise. See:
GAUTSCH, FRANÇOISE
ARON. See also:
Aaron
ARON, SIEGFRIED (1895-) [German motion picture actor]
Sig Arno
Aroostook Potato, The. See:
BREWSTER, RALPH OWEN
AROUET, FRANÇOIS MARIE (1694-1778) [French wit, author and philosopher]
l'Anatomie Vivante (The Living

Anatomy)
The Apostle of Infidelity
The Dictator of Letters
The Great Pan
The Patriarch of Ferney
The Philosopher of Ferney
The Plato of the Eighteenth Century
Voltaire
Arp, Bill. See:
SMITH, CHARLES HENRY
ARP, JEAN (1887-1966) [Alsatian painter and sculptor]
Hans Arp
Arpino, Il Cavaliere d'. See:
CESARI, GIUSEPPE
ARQUETTE, CLIFFORD (1905-) [American entertainer]
Cliff Arquette
Charley Weaver
Arr, E.H. See:
ROLLINS, MRS. ELLEN CHAPMAN HOBBS
Arras, Le Bossu d'. See:
HALLE, ADAM DE LA
ARRINGTON, ALFRED W. (1810-67) [American lawyer, journalist, historian and poet]
Charles Summerfield
Arrow, The Pointed. See:
JACKSON, ANDREW
Arruza, Carlos. See:
RUIZ-CAMINO, CARLOS
ARSHAWSKY, ARTHUR (1910-) [American jazz musician (clarinet, composer, leader)]
Artie Shaw
Arslan. See:
ALI PASHA
Art. See:
ARFONS, ARTHUR EUGENE
BUCHWALD, ARTHUR
LINKLETTER, ARTHUR GORDON
MINEO, ATTILIO
TODD, ARTHUR W.
VAN DAMME, ARTHUR
WALL, ARTHUR JONATHAN, JR.
YOUNG, ARTHUR HENRY
ARTAXERXES I (fl. 465-425 B.C.) [Persian king]
Longimanus (Longhanded)
ARTAXERXES II (died 338 B.C.) [Persian king]
Ochus
Artemisia Gentileschi. See:
LOMI, ARTEMISIA
Artemus Ward. See:
BROWNE, CHARLES FARRAR
ARTHAUD, ROBERT (c.1922-) [American radio announcer and actor]
Robert Arthur
Arthur. See:
Artur
BRUHNS, GEORGE FREDERICK WILLIAM
GODFREY, ARTHUR MICHAEL
KING ARTHUR
RIMBAUD, JEAN NICHOLAS ARTHUR
Arthur, Burt. See:
SHAPPIRO, HERBERT ARTHUR
ARTHUR, CHESTER ALAN (1830-86) [twenty-first President of the United States]
America's First Gentleman
Arthur the Gentleman
The Dude President
Elegant Arthur
First Gentleman of the Land
His Accidency
Our Chet
Prince Arthur
Arthur Craik. See:
CRAIG, ALEXANDER GEORGE
Arthur Freed. See:
GROSSMAN, ARTHUR
Arthur, George K. See:
BREST, GEORGE K. ARTHUR
Arthur, Herbert. See:
SHAPPIRO, HERBERT ARTHUR
Arthur, Jean. See:
GREENE, GLADYS
Arthur King. See: CAIN,

ARTHUR HOMER
Arthur Lincoln. See:
HAYDON, ARTHUR LINCOLN
Arthur Loring Bruce. See:
CROWNINSHIELD, FRANK
Arthur M. Winfield. See:
STRATEMEYER, EDWARD L.
Arthur McCann. See:
CAMPBELL, JOHN WOOD
Arthur Merridew. See:
GASKOIN, CHARLES JACINTH BELLAIRS
Arthur Middleton. See:
O'BRIEN, EDWARD J.C. HARRINGTON
Arthur Murray. See:
TEICHMAN, ARTHUR MURRAY
Arthur Pendennis. See:
THACKERAY, WILLIAM MAKEPEACE
Arthur Penn. See:
MATTHEWS, JAMES BRANDER
Arthur. Robert. See:
ARTHAUD, ROBERT
FEDER, E.H.
Arthur Rutland. See:
ADCOCK, ARTHUR ST. JOHN
Arthur Sewell. See:
WHITSON, JOHN HARVEY
Arthur Singleton. See:
KNIGHT, HENRY COGSWELL
Arthur Sketchley. See:
ROSE, GEORGE
Arthur Stirling. See:
SINCLAIR, UPTON BEALL
Arthur Stone. See:
GLADSTONE, ARTHUR
Arthur Sylvester. See:
TUBBS, ARTHUR LEWIS
Arthur Tolby. See:
INFIELD, GLENN BERTON
Arthur Townley. See:
DUGANNE, AUGUSTINE JOSEPH HICKEY
Arthur Watkyn. See:
WATKINS, ARTHUR THOMAS LEVI
Arthur, William. See:
NEUBAUER, WILLIAM ARTHUR
Artie Shaw. See:
ARSHAWSKY, ARTHUR
Artifex. See:
GREEN, PETER
Artist of Damnation, The. See:
EDWARDS, JONATHAN
Artist of the Republic, People's. See: IPPOLITOV-IVANOV, MIKHAIL MIKHAILOVICH
Artists, Founder of the Hudson River School of American. See: COLE, THOMAS
Artists, The King of Escape. See: GARDNER, ROY
Artists, The Prince of. See:
DÜRER, ALBRECHT
Arts and Sciences, the Father of the Brooklyn Institute of. See: HEALY, AARON AUGUSTUS
Arts, The Savior of the. See:
SIROVICH, WILLIAM IRVING
Artur. See also:
ARTHUR
Arthur
Artur R. Kurz. See:
SCORTIA, THOMAS NICHOLAS
Arturo de Cordova. See:
GARCÍA, ARTURO
Arundel, Jocelyn. See:
ALEXANDER, JOCELYN ANNE ARUNDEL
ARYABHATA (ARYABHATTA) (b. 476) [Hindu astronomer and mathematician]
Arjehir
Asa Baker. See:
DRESSER, DAVIS
ASAOKA. See:
ASOKA (ASAOKA)
Asare. See:
KONADU, SAMUEL ASARE
ASCHAM, ROGER (1515-68) [English classical scholar and author]
The Father of English Prose
ASCHENBRENNER, PAUL (1891-) [German-American

theater orchestra conductor, pianist and song writer]
Paul Ash
Ascraean Sage, The. See:
HESIOD
Ash. See also:
Ashe
Ash Johnny, Soda. See:
HOBAN, JOHN MICHAEL
Ash, Paul. See:
ASCHENBRENNER, PAUL
Ash, Peter. See:
HAUCK, LOUISE PLATT
Ashby, Florine. See:
SHEAROUSE, FLORINE W.
ASHCROFT, EDITH MARGARET EMILY (1907-) [English actress]
Peggy Ashcroft
Ashdown, Clifford, joint pseud. of RICHARD AUSTIN FREEMAN (1862-1943) and UNKNOWN (-) [English detective story writers]
Ashdown, Clifford. See also:
FREEMAN, RICHARD AUSTIN
Ashe. See also:
Ash
Ashe, Gordon. See:
CREASEY, JOHN
Ashford, Jeffrey. See:
UNKNOWN
ASHFORD, MARGARET MARY (1910-) [English child author]
Daisy Ashford
Ashford of America, The Daisy See: WAINWRIGHT, VIRGINIA
Ashland, The Sage of. See:
CLAY, HENRY
LEE, HENRY
Ashley A. Royce. See:
HAWTHORNE, NATHANIEL
ASHLEY, ARTHUR ERNEST (1906-) [British author]
Francis Vivian
ASHLEY-COOPER, ANTHONY, 1st EARL OF SHAFTSBURY. See:
Cabal, The
Ashley, Graham. See:
ORGAN, JOHN
Ashley, Mary. See:
TOWNSEND, MARY ASHLEY VAN VOORHIS
Ashlin, John. See:
CUTFORTH, JOHN ASHLIN
Ashton Lamar. See:
SAYLER, HARRY LINCOLN
ASHTON, SIR GEORGE GREY (1861-) [British general officer and author]
Amphibian
George Southcote
Ashton, Warren T. See:
ADAMS, WILLIAM TAYLOR
ASHTON, WINIFRED (1888-1965) [English playwright and novelist]
Diana Cortis
Clemence Dane
ASHURBANIPAL (c. 822 B.C.) [King of Assyria]
Sardanapalus
ASHURST, HENRY FOUNTAIN (1874-) [American Democratic senator from Arizona]
The Cowboy Senator
The Fountain
Asia, The Bismarck of. See:
LI HUNG CHANG
Asiaticus. See:
ANTIOCHUS XIII
ASIMOV, ISAAC (1920-) [Russian author]
Paul French
Askari, Hussaini Muhammad. See: PEREIRA, HAROLD BERTRAM
Askham, Francis. See:
GREENWOOD, JULIA EILEEN COURTNEY
Aslan, Gregoire. See:
ASLANIAN, KRIDOR
ASLANIAN, KRIDOR (1908-) [Franco-Turkish character actor]
Gregoire Aslan
ASOKA (ASAOKA) (died 232 B.C.) [Indian king and patron of Buddhism]
Asaoka the Great
The Buddhist Constantine

Asquith, Nan. See:
PATTINSON, NANCY EVELYN
Assiac. See:
FRAENKEL, HEINRICH
ASSISI. See:
AEGIDIUS OF ASSISI
Assisi, St. Francis of. See:
BERNARDONE, GIOVANNI FRANCESCO
Association, The Father of the American Medical. See:
DAVIS, NATHAN SMITH
ASSUNTO, JACOB (1905-) [American jazz musician (trombone, banjo)]
Papa Jac
Astaire, Adele. See:
AUSTERLITZ, ADELE
Astaire, Fred. See:
AUSTERLITZ, FRED
Asterisk, John. See:
HILL, WILLIAM KIRK-PATRICK
Astor, Bob. See:
DADE, ROBERT E.
Astor, Mary. See:
LANGHANKE, LUCILE V.
Astraea. See:
BEHN, MRS. APHRA
Astrologer, The Last. See:
LILLY, WILLIAM
Astronomer, The. See:
ALFONSO X
Astronomer, The African. See:
BANNEKER, BENJAMIN
Astronomy, Student in Physick and. See:
AMES, NATHANIEL
Aswin. See:
NANDAKUMAR, PREMA
At the Sign of the Blue Moon. See: LEWIS, DOMINIC BEVAN WYNDHAM
ATAHUALPA (c.1495-1533) [Inca ruler of Peru]
The Last of the Incas
Atall, Peter. See:
WALN, ROBERT
Atall, Peter, Esq. See:
WALN, ROBERT
Atatürk, Kemal. See:
KEMAL, MUSTAFA (MUSTAPHA)
ATCHISON, SANDRA DALLAS (1939-) [American book reviewer and author]
Sandra Dallas
Athanasius of the West, The. See: HILARY OF POITIERS
ATHANASIUS, ST. (c.296-373) [early father of the Christian church]
The Father of Orthodoxy
Athanasius Y. Samuel. See:
SAMUEL, YESHUE
Atheling, William. See:
POUND, EZRA LOOMIS
ATHELSTAN (895-940) [King of the West Saxons and Mercia]
The Glorious
Athenaeum. See:
SHAW, WILLIAM SMITH
Athenian Bee, The. See:
ARISTOCLES
Athenian Stuart, The. See:
STUART, JAMES
Athens, The Grim Old Lion of. See: GROSVENOR, CHARLES HENRY
Athens, The Misanthrope of. See: TIMON
ATHERTON, CHARLES GORDON (1804-53) [American congressman from New Hampshire]
Gag Atherton
Athos. See:
WALKERLEY, RODNEY LEWIS
ATKINS, FREDERICK ANTHONY (1864-) [British editor and author]
Quousque
ATKINS, JAMES G. (1932-) [American newsman, photographer and author]
Jim Atkins
ATKINSON, JUSTIN BROOKS (1894-) [American drama critic and author
Brooks Atkinson
Atkinson, M.E. See:
FRANKAU, MARY EVELYN ATKINSON

Atlas of America, The. See:
WASHINGTON, GEORGE
Atlas of Independence. See:
ADAMS, JOHN
Atom, Ann. See:
WALWORTH, JEANETTE RITCHIE HADERMAN
Atomic Bomb, The Architect of the. See: FERMI, ENRICO
ATTALUS I (269-197 B.C.) [Hellenistic King of Pergamum]
Soter (The Preserver)
ATTALUS II (220-138 B.C.) [Hellenistic King of Pergamum]
Philadelphus
ATTALUS III (171-133 B.C.) [Hellenistic King of Pergamum]
Philometor
ATTENDOLO, MUZIO (1369-1424) [Italian soldier of fortune; founder of the house of Sforza]
Sforza (Stormer of Cities)
Atterdag. See:
WALDEMAR IV
Atterley, Joseph. See:
TUCKER, GEORGE
Attic Bee, The. See:
ARISTOCLES
SOPHOCLES
Attic Homer, The. See:
SOPHOCLES
Attic Muse, The. See:
XENOPHON
Atticus. See:
FLEMING, IAN LANCASTER
Atticus, The Christian. See:
HEBER, REGINALD
Atticus, The English. See:
ADDISON, JOSEPH
Atticus, The Irish. See:
FAULKNER, GEORGE
ATTILA (ETZEL) (ETHELE) (c. 406-453) [King of the Huns]
Attila the Hun
The Scourge of God
The Terror of the World
Attorney General for Runaway Slaves. See:
CHASE, SALMON PORTLAND
Attorney, The People's. See:
BRANDEIS, LOUIS DEMBITZ
ATWATER, RICHARD (1892-) [American author]
Riq
ATWELL, JEAN (1936-) [American jazz musician (singer)]
Jean Du Shon
AUBANEL, THEODORE (1829-86) [Provençal poet and playwright]
The French Petrarch
Auber Forestier. See:
WOODWARD, A. AUBERTINE
AUBERT, ETIENNE (died 1362) [Supreme Pontiff of Roman Catholic Church]
Pope Innocent VI
AUBREY-FLETCHER, HENRY LANCELOT (1887-) [English author]
Henry Wade
Aubry, Cécile. See:
BERNARD, ANNE-JOSE
Auburn, The Sage of. See:
SEWARD, WILLIAM HENRY
AUCHINCLOSS, LOUIS STANTON (1917-) [American author]
Andrew Lee
Auclair, Michel. See:
VUJOVIC, VLADIMIR
Auctioneer Mayor, The. See:
SHANK, SAMUEL LEWIS
AUDEN, WYSTAN HUGH (1907-) [English poet, playwright and essayist]
W. H. Auden
Audrey Hepburn. See:
VAN HEEMSTRA, EDDA HEPBURN
AUDUBON, JOHN JAMES FOUGÈRE (1785-1851) [American ornithologist and painter of birds]
The American Woodman
Auer, Mischa. See:
OUNSKOWSKY, MISCHA
AUERBACH, ARNOLD JACOB (1917-) [American professional basketball executive; former coach]

Red Auerbach
AUERSPERG, ANTON ALEXANDER, GRAF VON (1806-76) [Austrian poet]
Anastasius Grün
August. See:
STRINDBERG, JOHAN AUGUST
August, John. See:
DE VOTO, BERNARD AUGUSTINE
AUGUST, MARIO MORENO (1911-) [Mexican comedian]
Cantinflas
Augusta. See:
HELENA
Augusta, Clara. See:
TRASK, CLARA AUGUSTA JONES
Augusta Gregory, Lady. See:
PERSSE, ISABELLA AUGUSTA
Augusta Jane Evans. See:
WILSON, AUGUSTA JANE EVANS
Auguste Émile Carolus-Duran. See: DURAND, CHARLES AUGUSTE ÉMILE
Augustin. See:
DALY, JOHN AUGUSTIN
AUGUSTINE (AUSTIN), ST. (died 604) [English Benedictine monk and missionary]
The Apostle of the Anglo-Saxons
The Apostle of the English
Augustine, St. See:
AUGUSTINUS, AURELIUS
Augustine Smith. See:
GALLITZIN, DEMETRIUS AUGUSTINE
AUGUSTINUS, AURELIUS (354-430) [Numidian Christian churchman and philosopher]
The Bishop of Hippo
The Hammer of the Heretics
St. Augustine
AUGUSTUS II (1670-1733) [elector of Saxony and King of Poland]
The Strong
Augustus, Philip. See:
PHILIP II
AUKER, ELDEN LEROY (1910-) [American professional baseball player]
Big Six
Auld, Georgie. See:
ALTWERGER, J. JOHN
Auletes (The Piper). See:
PTOLEMY XI
AULLIER, PIERRE (1755-1834) [French military adventurer]
General Perron
Ault. See also:
OLT
Ault, Marie. See:
CRAGG, MARIE
AULUS PERSIUS FLACCUS (34-62 A.D.) [Roman satirist]
The Ligurian Sage
Aumont, Jean-Pierre. See:
SALOMONS, JEAN-PIERRE
Aun Foda. See:
FOXE, ARTHUR NORMAN
AUNO, MAUNG HTIN (1909-) [Burmese author]
The Fourth Brother
Aungerville. See:
DE BURY, RICHARD
Aunt Fanny. See:
BARROW, FRANCES ELIZABETH MEASE
GAGE, FRANCES DANA BARKER
Aunt Hattie. See:
BAKER, HARRIETTE NEWALL WOODS
Aunt Kitty. See:
McINTOSH, MARIA JANE
Aunt Maysie. See:
JEFFREY-SMITH, MAY THORNTON
Aunt Rachel. See:
JACKSON, RACHEL DONELSON
AURACHER, HARRY (1888-1960) [American composer and conductor]
Harry Archer
Aurangzeb (Ornament of the

Throne). See:
MOHAMMED
AURELIANUS, LUCIUS DOMITIUS (212?-75 A.D.) [Roman emperor]
Restitutor Orbis (Restorer of the Empire)
Aurelius, Marcus. See:
VERUS, MARCUS ANNIUS
Auren Paul. See:
URIS, AUREN
AUREOLUS, PETER (fl. 14th cent.) [Archbishop of Aix]
The Eloquent Doctor
Aurungzeb (Ornament of the Throne). See:
MOHAMMED
AUSTEN [Austen]. See also:
AUSTIN
Austin
AUSTEN, JANE (1775-1817) [English novelist]
A Lady
Austen Rhode. See:
FRANCIS, BASIL HOSKINS
AUSTERLITZ, ADELE (1897-) [American dancer]
Adele Astaire
AUSTERLITZ, FRED (1899-) [American dancer, actor and composer]
Fred Astaire
Austin. See:
AUGUSTINE (AUSTIN), ST.
AUSTEN
Austen
DOBSON, HENRY AUSTIN
AUSTIN, ALFRED (1835-1913) [English critic and poet laureate]
Lamia
Austin, Brett. See:
FLOREN, LEE
Austin C. Burdick. See:
COBB, SYLVANUS, JR.
AUSTIN, GENE (1900-72) [American singer and composer]
The Whispering Tenor
Austin Harding. See:
LENDON, ALFRED AUSTIN
Austin, Harry. See:
McINERNY, RALPH
AUSTIN, JAMES PHILIP (1879-) [American baseball coach]
Pepper Austin
Austin, Lovie. See:
CALHOUN, CORA
Austin Moore. See:
MUIR, CHARLES AUGUSTUS
AUSTIN, STEPHEN FULLER (1792-1836) [American pioneer in Texas]
The Father of Texas
Austin Trevor. See:
SCHILSKY, AUSTIN
Austral, Florence. See:
WILSON, FLORENCE
Australian Marie Lloyd, The. See: FLANAGAN, FLORENCE
Australia's Martin Luther King. See: PERKINS, CHARLES NELSON
Austria, Frederick of. See:
FREDERICK III
Austria, Juan de. See:
JOHN OF AUSTRIA
Austwick, John. See:
LEE, AUSTIN
Authentic Doctor, The. See:
GREGORY OF RIMINI
Author, A Celebrated. See:
DEY, FREDERICK VAN RENSSELAER
Author of "Elizabeth and Her German Garden," By the. See: BEAUCHAMP, MARY ANNETTE, COUNTESS RUSSELL (MRS. HENNING ARNIM)
Author of "Gentleman Joe," By the. See:
BADGER, JOSEPH E., JR.
Author of "M'Fingal," The Celebrated. See:
TRUMBULL, JOHN
Author of Palo Alto, The Hermit. See: HOOVER, HERBERT CLARK
Author of "Pamela," By the. See: RICHARDSON, SAMUEL
Author of "The Archers," The. See: DUNLAP, WILLIAM

Author of "The Father," The.
See: DUNLAP, WILLIAM
Author of the New Deal, The.
See: BURKE, EDWARD RAYMOND
Author of "Waverley," By The.
See: SCOTT, SIR WALTER
Author, The People's. See:
CLEMENS, SAMUEL LANGHORNE
Authors of America, The Dean of Women. See:
TARBELL, IDA MINERVA
Autocrat of the Quacks, The. See:
HEADLEY, JOEL TYLER
Autocrat, The. See:
HOLMES, OLIVER WENDELL
Autolycus. See:
BACON, LEONARD
Automatic. See:
MANDERS, JACK
Automatic Rifle, The Father of the. See:
BROWNING, JOHN MOSES
Automation, The Father of. See:
WIENER, NORBERT
Automobile Wizard, The. See:
FORD, HENRY
Autre, l (The Other One). See:
BONAPARTE, NAPOLEON
AUTRY, GENE ORVON (1908-) [American Western singer, actor and song writer]
Oklahoma's Yodeling Cowboy
AUTY, PHYLLIS (1910-) [British author]
Phyllis Richards
AVALLONE, FRANCIS (1939-) [American singer of popular songs]
Frankie Avalon
AVALLONE, MICHAEL ANGELO, JR. (1924-) [American author]
Mark Dane
Steve Michaels
Avalon, Frankie. See:
AVALLONE, FRANCIS
Avalon West. See:
CHAMBERS, BERTRAM MORDAUNT
AVEN, ALGERNON JASPER (1858-1935) [American professor of Latin]
Ajax
The Sage of Mississippi College
The Seer
Avenger, The. See:
ALFONSO (ALPHONSO) XI
Avery, Al. See:
MONTGOMERY, RUTHERFORD GEORGE
AVERY, CAPTAIN JOHN (1665-17??) [British pirate]
Every
Long Ben
AVERY, HENRY M. (1840-) [American frontiersman, Indian scout and author of dime novels]
Max Martine
Mohenesto
Avery Johns. See:
COUSINS, MARGARET
Avery, Lynn. See:
COLE, LOIS DWIGHT
Avery Mann. See:
BREETVELD, JIM PATRICK
Aviation, The Henry Ford of.
See: PIPER, WILLIAM THOMAS, SR.
Aviator, The Marine. See:
MAAS, MELVIN JOSEPH
Avicebron. See:
IBN GABIROL, SOLOMON BEN JUDAH
AVICENNA (980-1037) [Arabian physician and philosopher]
Ibn-Sina
The Prince of Physicians
ÁVILA. See:
JUAN DE ÁVILA
TERESA OF ÁVILA
Avis S. Spenser. See:
UNKNOWN
Avon Curry. See:
BOWDEN, JEAN
Avon, Sweet Swan of. See:
SHAKESPEARE, WILLIAM
Avon, The Bard of. See:
SHAKESPEARE, WILLIAM
Avram. See:
KAMPF, ABRAHAM
Axel Heyst. See:

GRABOWSKI, ZGIGNIEW
ANTHONY
Axis Sally. See:
SISK, MILDRED ELIZABETH
ZUCCA, RITA LOUISE
Ayala, The Chancellor. See:
LOPEZ DE AYALA, PEDRO
AYER, JOHN (1862-1936)
[American author and editor]
Guy Carlton Lee
AYER, LEWIS (1908-)
[American motion picture actor]
Lew Ayres
AYERS. See:
AYRES
Ayres
AYESHA (c. 611-c. 678) [favorite wife of MOHAMMED]
The Mother of Believers
Aylmer. See:
CADE, JOHN
Aylmer, Felix. See:
JONES, FELIX EDWARD
AYLMER
AYRES, AGNES (1890-1940)
[American motion picture actress]
The O. Henry Girl
Ayres, Alfred. See:
OSMUN, THOMAS EMBLEY
Ayres, Lew. See:
AYER, LEWIS
Ayrshire Poet, The. See:
BURNS, ROBERT
Ayrshire, The Bard of. See:
BURNS, ROBERT
AYRTON, MICHAEL (1921-)
[British painter, sculptor, and author]
Michael Gould
Ayscough, John. See:
BICKERSTAFFE-DREW,
FRANCIS BROWNING
DREW, COUNT
Azad (The Free). See:
ABUL KALAM AZAD,
MAULANA
Azarias, Brother. See:
MULLANY, PATRICK
FRANCIS

B

BB. See:
WATKINS-PITCHFORD,
DENYS JAMES
B. B. See:
KING, RILEY B.
B. Bolesławita. See:
KRASZEWSKI, JÓZEF
IGNACY
B. G. See:
DE SYLVA, GEORGE GARD
GOODMAN, BENJAMIN
DAVID
B. John. See:
JOHN, ELIZABETH BEAMAN
B. K. Ted Thorne. See:
THORNE, BLISS KIRBY
B. Kirby Thorne. See:
THORNE, BLISS KIRBY
B. L. See: JACOT DE
BOINOD, BERNARD LOUIS
B. L. T. See:
TAYLOR, BERT LESTON
B., Mr. See:
ECKSTINE, WILLIAM
CLARENCE
B. Suarez Lynch. See:
Domecq, Honorio Bustos
B. Traven. See:
TORSVAN, TRAVEN
B. V. See:
THOMSON, JAMES
B. W. See:
WELLER, BERNARD
WILLIAM
B. X. Sanborn. See:
BALLINGER, WILLIAM
SANBORN
Baal, The Grace of. See:
HANNIBAL
Baastad, Babbis Friis. See:
FRIIS-BAASTAD,
BABBIS ELINOR
Bab. See:
GILBERT, SIR WILLIAM
SCHWENCK
Bab-ed-din (Gate of Righteousness). See:
MOHAMMED, MIRZA ALI
Babbis. See:
FRIIS-BAASTAD, BABBIS

ELINOR
Babbis, Eleanor. See:
FRIIS-BAASTAD, BABBIS ELINOR
Babbis Friis. See:
FRIIS-BAASTAD, BABBIS ELINOR
Babbler. See:
LLOYD, JOHN IVESTER
Babbling Burglar, The. See:
MORRISON, RICHARD C.
BABCOCK, EDWARD CHESTER (1913-) [American composer and pianist]
James Van Heusen
BABCOCK, FREDERICK (1896-) [American editor and author]
Matthew Mark
BABCOCK, WINNIFRED EATON (1879-) [American writer of Japanese novels]
Onoto Watanna
Babe. See:
BROWN, JOHN H., JR.
HERMAN, FLOYD CAVES
RUSIN, IRVING
RUTH, GEORGE HERMAN
Babe Didrikson. See:
ZAHARIAS, MILDRED DIDRIKSON
Babe Ruth of the New Deal, The. See:
JOHNSON, HUGH SAMUEL
Baber (Babur) (Tiger). See:
MUHAMMAD, ZAHIR UD-DIN
Babette Deutsch. See:
YARMOLINSKY, MRS. AVRAHM
BABEUF, FRANÇOIS NOËL (1760-97) [French revolutionist; founder of revolutionary socialism]
Gracchus Babeuf
Babington White. See:
MAXWELL, MARY ELIZABETH BRADDON
Baboon, Lewis. See:
LOUIS XIV
Baboon, Philip. See:
PHILIP V
Baboon, The Illinois. See:
LINCOLN, ABRAHAM
BABSON, ROGER WARD (1875-1967) [American statistician and economist]
The Seer of Wellesley Hills
Babur (Baber) (Tiger). See:
MUHAMMAD, ZAHIR UD-DIN
Baby. See:
DODDS, WARREN
Baby Brother (El Tato). See:
SÁNCHEZ, ANTONIO
Baby-doll. See:
SORRELL, VICTOR GARLAND
Baby Face Nelson. See:
GILLIS, LESTER M.
Baby June, The Pocket Sized Pavlova, Dainty. See:
HOVICK, JUNE
Baby Le Roy. See:
WINNEBRENNER, LE ROY
Baby McKee's Grandfather. See:
HARRISON, BENJAMIN
Baby Snooks. See:
BORACH, FANNY
Baby Star. See:
WATERS, ETHEL
Baby, The Boston Tar. See:
LANGFORD, SAM
Baby, The Daddy of the. See:
JOHNSON, ANDREW
Baby, The Snow. See:
PEARY, MARIE AHNIGHITO
Baby Traps. See:
RICH, BERNARD
Baby Vamp, The. See:
WEST, MAE
Babylonian, The (Hababli). See:
HILLEL
Bacall, Betty. See:
BOGART, BETTY JOAN PEPSKE BACALL
Bacall, Lauren. See:
BOGART, BETTY JOAN PEPSKE BACALL
Baccio della Porta. See:
FATTORINO, BARTOLOMMEO DI PAGOLO DEL
BACH, JOHANN CHRISTIAN (1735-82) [German composer]
The London Bach
The Milan Bach

BACH, JOHANN CHRISTOPH FRIEDRICH (1732-95) [German composer]
The Bückeburg Bach
BACH, KARL PHILIPP EMANUEL (1714-88) [German composer]
The Berlin Bach
The Hamburg Bach
BACH, WILHELM FRIEDMANN (1710-84) [German composer]
The Halle Bach
BACHARACH, ISAAC (1870-) [American congressman from New Jersey]
Boardwalk Ike
Bachelor, A Traveling. See: COOPER, JAMES FENIMORE
Bachelor, An Old. See: CURTIS, GEORGE WILLIAM
Bachelor Governor, The. See: HILL, DAVID BENNETT
Bachelor President, The. See: BUCHANAN, JAMES
BACHO. See: BACONTHORPE (BACON) (BACHO), JOHN
BACKUS, JAMES (1913-) [American actor]
Jim Backus
BACKUS, JEAN (1914-) [American author]
David Montross
Backwoods Poet, The. See: BERRYHILL, S. NEWTON
BACON. See: BACONTHORPE (BACON) (BACHO), JOHN
BACON, LEONARD (1802-81) [American Congregational clergyman and writer]
The Congregational Pope of New England
The Nestor of Congregationalism
BACON, LEONARD (1887-1954) [American poet]
Autolycus
BACON, MARY SCHELL (1870-1934) [American author]
Dolores Marbourg
BACON, NATHANIEL (1647-76) [American colonial leader]
The Virginia Rebel
Bacon of Theology, The. See: BUTLER, BISHOP JOSEPH
BACON, ROGER (c. 1214-94) [English Franciscan philosopher and man of science]
The Admirable Doctor
The Father of Philosophy
The Wonderful Doctor (Doctor Mirabilis)
BACON, SIR FRANCIS (1561-1626) [British statesman, essayist and philosopher]
The British Socrates
BACONTHORPE (BACON) (BACHO), JOHN (died 1346) [English Carmelite monk and schoolman
The Resolute Doctor
Bactrian Sage, The. See: ZOROASTER
Bad Girl of the Mid-Victorians, The International. See: GILBERT, MARIE DOLORES ELIZA ROSANNA
Bad Girl, The Screen's. See: WEST, MAE
Bad Old Man, The. See: EARLY, JUBAL ANDERSON
Bad, The. See:
ALBERT
CHARLES II
LYTTELTON, THOMAS, 2ND LORD LYTTELTON
WILLIAM I
Baden Beatty. See: CASSON, FREDERICK RONALD CHRISTOPHER
BADEN-POWELL, ROBERT STEPHENSON SMYTHE, 1ST BARON BADEN-POWELL (1857-1941) [British general officer; founder of Boy Scouts and Girl Guides]
Bathing Towel
Badenoch, The Wolf of. See: STEWART, SIR ALEXANDER
BADGER, JOSEPH E., JR. (1848-1909) [American author of dime novels]

By the Author of "Gentleman Joe"
Harry Hazard
Harry Hazelton
A. H. Post
Badinguet. See:
BONAPARTE, CHARLES LOUIS NAPOLEON
BADONICUS. See:
SAPIENS (BADONICUS), GILDAS
BAEDA. See: BEDE (BEDA) (BAEDA), ST.
BAER, JACOB (191?-) [American professional heavyweight boxer and actor]
Buddy Baer
BAER, MAXIMILIAN ADELBERT (1909-59) [American professional boxer; world's heavyweight champion]
Max Baer
The Livermore Larruper
Madcap Maxie
BAER, MRS. (fl. 187?) [American author of dime novels]
K. F. Hill
Mrs. K. F. Hill
Kate F. Hill
BAEZ, JOAN (1941-) [American folk singer]
The Queen of the Folk Singers
BÁEZ, MANUEL (1905-26) [Spanish bullfighter]
Litri
BÁEZ, MIGUEL (1869-after 1911) [Spanish bullfighter]
Litri
BÁEZ, MIGUEL (c. 1912-) [Spanish bullfighter]
Litri
BÁEZ, MIGUEL (1930-) [Spanish bullfighter]
Litri
BAFFO (c. 1580-1600) [sultana and councillor of the sultan AMURATH III]
The Pure
Bagarag, Shibli. See:
LAWLOR, PATRICK ANTHONY
Bagby, George. See:
STEIN, AARON MARC
BAGBY, GEORGE WILLIAM (1828-83) [American editor, lecturer and author]
Moses Adams
Mozis Addums
BAGG, HELEN F. (fl. 1921-25) [American novelist and playwright]
Jarvis Hall
BAGGIO, ANSELMO DA (died 1073) [Supreme Pontiff of Roman Catholic Church]
Pope Alexander II
Baglivi. See:
AMERO, GIORGIO
Bagnacavallo. See:
RAMENGHI, BARTOLOMMEO
BAGNOLD, ENID (1889-) [British author and playwright]
A Lady of Quality
Bags. See:
JACKSON, MILTON
Bags, Old. See:
SCOTT, JOHN
BAGSHAW, WILLIAM (1628-1702) [British nonconformist divine]
The Apostle of the Peak
Bagster, Hubert. See:
TRUMPER, HUBERT BAGSTER
Baha Ullah (Splendor of God). See: MIRZA HUSEYN ALI
BAILEY [Bailey]. See also: BAYLY
BAILEY, ANNA WARNER (1758-1850) [American patriot]
The Heroine of Groton
Mother Bailey
BAILEY, ANNE HENNIS TROTTER (c. 1742-1825) [Anglo-American frontierswoman]
Mad Anne
BAILEY, DAVID ROY SHACKLETON (1917-) [British author]
D. R. Shackleton Bailey
BAILEY, DONALD ORLANDO (1934-) [American jazz musician (drums)]
Donald Duck
BAILEY, DULCIE (1919-)

[British stage and motion picture actress]
Dulcie Gray
BAILEY, ERNEST HAROLD (1925-) [American jazz musician (trumpet)]
Benny Bailey
BAILEY, FREDERICK AUGUST WASHINGTON (1817?-95) [American Negro abolitionist, orator and writer]
Frederick Douglass
The Sage of Anacostia
BAILEY, HOWARD HENRY (1913-) [American professional football player]
Screeno
BAILEY, IRENE TEMPLE (-1953) [American novelist]
Temple Bailey
Bailey, James. A. See: McGINNIS, JAMES ANTHONY
BAILEY, JAMES MONTGOMERY (1841-94) [American humorous journalist]
The Father of the "Colyumist"
The Danbury News Man
Bailey, Matilda. See: RADFORD, RUBY LORRAINE
BAILEY, PHILIP JAMES (1816-1903) [English poet]
The Nottingham Poet
BAILEY, WILLIAM C. (1902-) [American jazz musician (clarinet)]
Buster Bailey
BAILLIE, JOANNA (1762-1851) [Scotch dramatist and poet]
The Sister of Shakespeare
Bainbridge, Bryant. See: URNER, NATHAN DANE
Baïonette, General. See: CHASSÉ, DAVID HENDRIK, BARON
Baird Leonard. See: ZOGBAUM, BAIRD LEONARD
BAIRD, WILLIAM BRITTON (1904-) [American puppeteer]
Bil Baird
BAJAZET I (1347-1403) [Sultan of the Ottoman Empire]
Ilderim (Lightning)
The Thunderbolt
BAKER, ALPHEUS (1825-91) [American orator]
The Silver-tongued Orator of the South
BAKER, ANDERSON YANCEY (1876-1930) [American multimillionaire, sheriff and politician]
The Millionaire Sheriff
Baker, Asa. See: DRESSER, DAVIS
Baker, Betty. See: VENTURO, BETTY LOU BAKER
BAKER, BETTY DOREEN FLOOK (1916-) [British author]
Elizabeth Renier
BAKER, GEORGE (1877?-1965) [American Negro religious cult leader]
Joe Baker
Father Divine
Reverend Major J. Divine
Reverend Morgan J. Divine
Baker, George the. See: LEHMAN, GEORGE
BAKER, HAROLD J. (1914-) [American jazz musician (trumpet)]
Shorty Baker
BAKER, HARRIETTE NEWALL WOODS (1815-93) [American author]
Aunt Hattie
Mrs. Madeline Leslie
Baker, Henrietta. See: DAVIS, JEANNETTE
BAKER, HENRY (fl. 187-) [American author of dime novels]
H. Rebak
BAKER, JOHN FRANKLIN (1886-1963) [American professional baseball player]
Home Run Baker
BAKER, LAURA NELSON (1911-

[American author]
Nelson Minier
BAKER, MARY GLADYS (1892-) [Scottish journalist and author]
Sheila Stuart
BAKER, MRS. KARLE (1878-) [American author]
Charlotte Wilson
BAKER (MORTENSEN), NORMA JEAN (1926-62) [American actress and sex symbol]
Marilyn Monroe
BAKER, NORMAN (1918-) [American jazz musician (leader, piano, composer, arranger)]
Buddy Baker
BAKER, RAY STANNARD (1870-1946) [American journalist and author]
David Grayson
BAKER, RICHARD E. (1916-) [American jazz musician (piano, singer, actor)]
Two Ton Baker
Baker, The. See:
LOUIS XVI
BAKER, WILLIAM MUMFORD (1825-83) [American clergyman and miscellaneous writer]
George F. Harrington
Baker's Wife, The. See:
MARIE ANTOINETTE
Balanchine, George. See:
BALANCHIVADZE, GEORGEI MELITONOVITCH
BALANCHIVADZE, GEORGEI MELITONOVITCH (1904-) [Russian choreographer and author]
George Balanchine
BALASSONI, LOUIS (1924-) [American jazz musician (drums, arranger, composer)]
Louis Bellson
Balbus. See:
HUXLEY, JULIAN SORELL
BALCH, BENJAMIN (1743-1816) [American naval chaplain and naval hero]
The Fighting Parson
BALCHEN, BERNT (1899-) [Norwegian-American air force officer and pilot]
The Greatest Pilot in the World, Bar None
Bald Eagle of Edgefield, The. See:
GARY, MARTIN WITHERSPOON
Bald Eagle of Westchester, The. See: HUSTED, JAMES WILLIAM
Bald Eagle, The. See:
GARY MARTIN WITHERSPOON
Bald, Old. See:
PRESTON, JOHN THOMAS LEWIS
Bald, The. See:
CHARLES I
CHARLES II
Baldenne, F. See:
BALDENSPERGER, FERNAND
BALDENSPERGER, FERNAND (1871-1958) [French literary historian]
F. Baldenne
BALDWIN (died c. 879) [first Count of Flanders]
Bras de Fer
BALDWIN IV (fl. 12th cent.) [King of Jerusalem]
The Leper
Baldwin, Bates. See:
JENNINGS, JOHN E., JR.
BALDWIN, CHARLES CRITTENTON (1888-) [American author]
George Gordon
Baldwin, Edwin. See:
GODWIN, WILLIAM
BALDWIN, ELIAS JACKSON (1828-1909) [American frontiersman and fortune builder]
Lucky Baldwin
Baldwin, Faith. See:
CUTHRELL, MRS. FAITH BALDWIN
BALDWIN, GORDON C. (1908-) [American author]
Gordo Baldwin
Lew Gordon

BALDWIN, JAMES (1841-1925)
[American editor and author]
Robert Dudley
BALDWIN, MICHAEL (1930-)
[British educator and author]
Michael Jesse
Baldy. See:
SMITH, WILLIAM FARRAR
BALENCIAGA, CRISTOBAL
(1896?-) [Spanish fashion designer]
Balenciaga
Fashion's Picasso
Balfour Dangerfield. See:
McCLOSKEY, ROBERT
Balfour, Patrick. See:
KINROSS, PATRICK, LORD
BALFOUR, SIR JAMES (died 1583)
[Scottish judge and political intriguer]
Blasphemous Balfour
BALINE, ISRAEL (1888-) [Russian-American composer of popular music]
Irving Berlin
BALIOL. See:
JOHN DE BALIOL
Balkans, Crosser of the (Sabalkanski). See:
DIEBITSCH, HANS KARL FRIEDRICH, COUNT
BALL, DORIS BELL COLLIER
(1897-) [British author]
Josephine Bell
BALL, JOHN (died 1381) [English priest]
The Mad Priest
BALL, LUCILLE (1911-)
[American comedienne, actress and television producer]
The First Lady of Television
Lucy
Ball, Zachary. See:
MASTERS, KELLY R.
Ballad Poetry, The Father of American. See:
HEWITT, JOHN HENRY (HILL)
Ballard, Dean. See:
WILKES-HUNTER, RICHARD
BALLARD, FRANCIS DRAKE
(1899-1960) [American composer and author]
Pat Ballard
BALLARD, GEORGE (1918-)
[American jazz musician (drums)]
Butch Ballard
BALLARD, GUY WARREN (1878-1939) [English mining engineer, spiritualist and author]
Godfre Ray King
Ballard, J.D. See:
MORRIS, CHARLES SMITH
Ballard, K. G. See:
ROTH, HOLLY
Ballard, Kaye. See:
BALOTTA, CATHERINE GLORIA
BALLARD, WILLIS TODHUNTER
(1903-) [American author]
Brian Agar
P.D. Ballard
W. T. Ballard
Willis T. Ballard
Parker Bonner
Sam Bowie
Hunter D'Allard
Harrison Hunt
John Hunter
Neil MacNeil
John Shepherd
Ballengeigh, The Goodman of.
See: JAMES V
Ballerina, England's First Home-grown. See:
HOOKHAM, MARGARET
Ballet, The Father of Modern.
See: FOKINE, MICHEL
BALLINGER, WILLIAM SANBORN
(1912-) [American author]
Bill S. Ballinger
Frederic Freyer
B.X. Sanborn
Balloon. See:
TYTLER, JAMES
Balloon Buster, The. See:
LUKE, FRANK, JR.
Ballott Principle, The Father of the Short. See:
CHILDS, RICHARD SPENCER
BALLOU, HOSEA (1771-1852)
[American clergyman]

The Father of American Universalism
BALLOU, MATURIN MURRAY (1820-95) [American journalist, traveler and editor]
Lieut. Murray
BALOTTA, CATHERINE GLORIA (1926-) [American singer, comedienne and actress]
Kaye Ballard
BALSAMO, GIUSEPPE (1743-95) [Italian charlatan]
Count Alessandro di Cagliostro
BALSDON, JOHN PERCY VYVIAN DACRE (1901-) [British educator and author]
Dacre Balsdon
Balwery, The Great Witch of. See: AIKEN, MARGARET
BALZAC, JEAN LOUIS GUEZ DE (1594-1654) [French writer]
Le Grande Épistolier de France
The Solon of French Prose
Balzac, The American. See: FAULKNER, WILLIAM
BALZANO, JEANNE KOPPEL (1912-) [American journalist and author]
Gina Bell
Gina Bell-Zano
BAMBERG. See: OTTO OF BAMBERG
Bambino, The. See: RUTH, GEORGE HERMAN
Bambino, The Mighty. See: RUTH, GEORGE HERMAN
Bamboccio, Il (The Deformed). See: LAAR, PIETER VAN
Ban. See: JOHNSON, BYRON BANCROFT
Bancroft, Anne. See: ITALIANO, ANNEMARIE (ANNA MARIA)
Bandanna, Old. See: THURMAN, ALLAN GRANBERRY
BANDARRA, GONÇALO ANNES (15??-56) [Portuguese cobbler, rhymer and prophet]
The Portuguese Nostradamus
BANDINELLI, ROLAND (died 1181) [Supreme Pontiff of Roman Catholic Church]
Pope Alexander III
Bandit Queen, The. See: STARR, BELLE
BANÉR, JOHAN (1596-1641) [Swedish general officer]
The Lion of Sweden
Bangbang, Mr. Kisskiss. See: CONNERY, THOMAS
BANGS, JOHN KENDRICK (1862-1922) [American humorist, editor and author]
The Idiot
J.K.B.
Banished Preacher, The. See: WILLIAMS, ROGER
Banjo. See: PATERSON, ANDREW BARTON
Banjo Eyes. See: ISKOWITZ, EDWARD ISRAEL
Banjoist, Red Godfrey, The Warbling. See: GODFREY, ARTHUR MICHAEL
Bank, Emperor Nick of the Bribery. See: BIDDLE, NICHOLAS
Bank-Jensen. See: OTTESEN, THEA TAUBER
Bank, W. Dane. See: WILLIAMSON, WILLIAM HENRY
Banker-Poet, The. See: ROGERS, SAMUEL STEDMAN EDMUND CLARENCE
BANKHEAD, TALLULAH (1903-68) [American actress]
Tallu
BANKHEAD, WILLIAM BROCKMAN (1874-1940) [American statesman]
Tallulah's Papa
Banks, Archibald. See: CRAWFURD, OSWALD
BANKS, ERNEST (193?-) [American Negro baseball player]
Ernie Banks
Banks, Monty. See: BIANCHI, MARIO
BANKS, NATHANIEL PRENTISS (1816-94) [American congressman, governor and Union general officer]

The Bobbin Boy
BANKY, VILMA (1903-)
[Austrian actress]
The Hot Paprika from Hungary
BANNEKER, BENJAMIN (1731-1806) [American Negro mathematician]
The African Astronomer
BANNER, HERBERT STEWART (1891-1964) [British author]
Vexillum
Bannon, Peter. See:
DURST, PAUL
Banton, Coy. See:
NORWOOD, VICTOR GEORGE CHARLES
Banty. See:
HANCOCK, CLARENCE EUGENE
Baptistet. See:
DAUDET, ALPHONSE
Baptists, The Father of American. See: CLARKE, JOHN
Bapu. See:
KHARE, NARAYAN BHASKAR
BAR COCHEBA, SIMON (70-135 A.D.) [Jewish insurrectionist]
Son of the Star
Bar None, The Greatest Pilot in the World: See:
BALCHEN, BERNT
Bar of the State of New York, The Father of the. See:
VAN VECHEN, ABRAHAM
Bar, The Erskine of the American. See:
HOFFMAN, OGDEN
Bar, The Father of the Criminal. See: HOWE, WILLIAM FREDERICK
Bar, The Father of the Hampden County. See:
BATES, WILLIAM GELSTON
Bar, The Father of the New York: See: JONES, SAMUEL
Bar, The Father of the North Carolina. See:
MOORE, BARTHOLOMEW FIGURES
Bar, The Historian of the Hampden County. See:
BATES, WILLIAM GELSTON
Bar, The Napoleon of the California. See:
DELMAS, DELPHIN MICHAEL
Bar, The Nestor of the Hampden County. See:
BATES, WILLIAM GELSTON
Bar, The Scholar of the Georgia. See: HILL, WALTER BARNARD
Bara, Theda. See:
GOODMAN, THEODOSIA
BARBA, HARRY (1922-) [American author]
Baron Mikan
Ohon
Barbara. See:
COMYNS-CARR, BARBARA IRENE VERONICA
WRIGHT, MABEL OSGOOD
Barbara Allen. See:
STUART, VIVIAN FINLAY
Barbara Bel Geddes. See:
LEWIS, BARBARA GEDDES
Barbara Boyd. See:
BURR, AGNES RUSH
Barbara Britton. See:
CZUKOR, BARBARA BRANTINGHAM
Barbara Carroll. See:
COPPERSMITH, BARBARA
Barbara Christie. See:
CARLON, PATRICIA BERNARDETTE
Barbara Clayton. See:
PLUFF, BARBARA LITTLEFIELD
Barbara Fawcett. See:
UPSON, DOROTHY BARBARA
Barbara Herrnstein. See:
SMITH, BARBARA HERRNSTEIN
Barbara Howard. See:
CORYELL, JOHN RUSSELL
Barbara Kay. See:
KELLER, ETHEL MAY
Barbara Kaye.
MUIR, BARBARA KENRICK GOWING
Barbara Laage. See:
COLOMBAT, CLAIRE
Barbara La Marr. See:

WATSON REATHA
Barbara Michaels. See:
MERTZ, BARBARA GROSS
Barbara Redmayne. See:
HOWE, MURIEL
Barbara Rich. See:
JACKSON, LAURA RIDING
Barbara Stanwyck. See:
STEVENS, RUBY
Barbara Wentworth. See:
PITCHER, GLADYS
Barbara Yechton. See:
KRAUSE, LYDA FARRINGTON
BARBARELLI, GIORGIO (1478?-1511) [Venetian painter]
Il Georgione
Giorgione da Castelfranco
Barbarossa, Frederick. See:
FREDERICK I
BARBAROSSA, KHIZR (15??-46) [Barbary corsair]
Khaireddin
Barbary, James. See:
BEECHING, AMY BROWN
BEECHING, JACK
BARBAZAN, ARNAULD GUILHELM DE (died 1432) [French general officer]
The Knight Without Reproach
BARBE, JEHAN À LA. See:
Mandeville, Jehan de (Sir John)
Barbellion, W.N.P. See:
CUMMINGS, BRUCE FREDRICK
BARBER [Barber]. See also:
BARBOUR
BARBER, CARL JEROME (1916-) [American professional golfer]
Jerry Barber
BARBER, CHARLES ALFRED (1860-) [British author]
C.A.B.
BARBER, DONALD CHRISTOPHER (1930-) [American jazz musician (trombone, leader)]
Chris Barber
Barber, Jake the. See:
FACTOR, JOHN
BARBER, MARGARET FAIRLESS (1869-1901) [English nature writer and mystic]
Michael Fairless
BARBER, MARY (1690?-1757) [Irish poet]
Sapphira
Barber Poet, The. See:
BOÉ, JACQUES
BARBER, WALTER LANIER (1908-) [American sports commentator]
Red Barber
The Ol' Redhead
BARBERINI, MAFFEO (1568-) (1644) [Supreme Pontiff of Roman Catholic Church]
Pope Urban VIII
Barbette, Jay. See:
SPICER, BART
Barbie Arden. See:
STOUTENBURG, ADRIEN PEARL
BARBIERI, GIOVANNI FRANCESCO (1591-1666) [Italian painter of the Bolognese school]
Guercino [Squint-Eyed]
BARBIERI, LEANDRO (1933-) [Italian jazz musician (tenor saxophone)]
Gato
BARBIERI, NICCOLO (died c. 1640) [Italian actor and playwright]
Beltrame
BARBON, PRAISEGOD (1596?-1679) [English Puritan divine]
Praisegod Barebones
BARBOUR. See also:
BARBER
Barber
BARBOUR, DAVID MICHAEL (1912-) [American jazz musician (guitar, leader, composer, arranger)]
Dave Barbour
BARBOUR, JOHN (c. 1316-96) [Scottish poet and churchman]
The Father of Scottish Poetry and History
BARBOUR, RALPH HENRY (1870-1944) [American

author]
The Dean of Sports Writers for Boys
Richard Stillman Powell

BARBOUR, WILLIAM WARREN (1888-1943) [New Jersey politician and manufacturer]
Champ

BARCA. See: HAMILCAR BARCA

BARCENA (BARZENA), ALONSO DE (1526-98) [Spanish Jesuit]
The Apostle of Peru

BARCLAY-ALLARDICE, ROBERT (1779-1854) [Scottish soldier and sportsman]
Captain Barclay

Barclay Bennett. See: CROSSEN, KENDELL FOSTER

BARCLAY, DAVID (1912-) [American motion picture actor]
Dave O'Brien

Barclay, Isabel. See: DOBELL, ISABEL MARIAN BARCLAY

Barclays, One of the. See: OTIS, MRS. HARRISON GRAY (ELIZA HENDERSON BORDMAN)

Barcynska, Countess. See: EVANS, MARGUERITE FLORENCE HELENE

Bard. See: O'KELLY, PATRICK

Bard of All Time, The. See: SHAKESPEARE, WILLIAM

Bard of Avon, The. See: SHAKESPEARE, WILLIAM

Bard of Ayrshire, The. See: BURNS, ROBERT

Bard of Hope, The. See: CAMPBELL, THOMAS

Bard of Memory, The. See: ROGERS, SAMUEL

Bard of Olney, The. See: COWPER, WILLIAM

Bard of Prose, The. See: BOCCACCIO, GIOVANNI

Bard of Rydal Mount, The. See: WORDSWORTH, WILLIAM

Bard of Sheffield, The. See: MONTGOMERY, JAMES

Bard of the Chian Strand, The Blind. See: HOMER

Bard of the Imagination, The. See: AKENSIDE, MARK

Bard of Twickenham, The. See: POPE, ALEXANDER

Bard, Scio's Blind Old. See: HOMER

Bard, The Blind Old. See: HOMER

Bard, The Boston. See: COFFIN, ROBERT STEVENSON

Bard, The Immortal. See: SHAKESPEARE, WILLIAM

Bard, The Lynn. See: LEWIS, ALONZO

Bard, The Mantuan. See: MARO, PUBLIUS VERGILIUS

Bard, The Milford. See: LOFLAND, JOHN

Bard, The Peasant. See: BURNS, ROBERT; CANNING, JOSIAH DEAN

Bard, The Pilgrim. See: CUMMINGS, SCOTT

Bard, The Rustic. See: DINSMOOR, ROBERT

Bard, The Theban. See: PINDAR

BARDENS, DENNIS CONRAD (1911-) [British author]
Conrad Farel
Julian Roberts

BARDI, DONATO DI NICCOLÓ DI BETTO (1386?-1466) [Italian sculptor]
Donatello

Bardot, America's Answer to Brigitte. See: REMICK, LEE

Barebones, Praisegod. See: BARBON, PRAISEGOD

Barefoot, The. See: MAGNUS III

BARFIELD, OWEN (1898-) [British author]
G.A.L. Burgeon

Barge Canal, The Father of the. See: CLINTON, GEORGE

BARGONE, FRÉDERIC CHARLES PIERRE ÉDOUARD (1876-1957) [French novelist]
Claude Farrère
BARHAM, RICHARD HARRIS (1788-1845) [English humorist, novelist and clergyman]
Thomas Ingoldsby, Esq.
Bari. See also:
BARRIE
Barrie
BARRY
Barry
Bari, Joe. See:
BENEDETTO, ANTHONY DOMINICK
Bari, Lynn. See:
BITZER, MARJORIE
Bark, The King Of. See:
CHRISTOPHER III
BARKAN, STANLEY HOWARD (1936-) [American composer and author]
Sonny Hendrix
BARKER, ARTHUR (189?-1939) [American outlaw; member of the BARKER-KARPIS gang]
Dock Barker
BARKER, ARTHUR JAMES (1918-) [British soldier, gun expert and author]
Musketeer
BARKER, BENJAMIN (fl. 1845-47) [American novelist]
Egbert Augustus Cowslip, Esq.
BARKER, DUDLEY (1910-) [British author]
Lionel Black
BARKER, KATE CLARK (1879-1935) ["brains" of the BARKER-KARPIS gang of American outlaws]
Ma Barker
Mrs. Hunter
BARKER, S. OMAR (1894-) [American educator and author]
José Canusi
Dan Scott
Phil Squires
BARKER, WILL (1913-) [American author and editor]
Doug Demarest
BARKLEY, ALBEN WILLIAM (1877-1956) [American statesman; Vice President of the United States]
Dear Alben
Little Alby
The Veep
Barley King, The. See:
BUERGER, JOHN
BARLING, MURIEL VERE MANT (1904-) [British author]
Charles Barling
Pamela Barrington
P. V. Barrington
BARLING, PHILIP (1857-1936) [English actor-manager]
Phil Barling
Philip Ben
Sir Ben Greet
BARLOW, JOEL. See:
Hartford Wits, The
Barlow, Roger. See:
LECKIE, ROBERT HUGH
Barn Lock (Magnus Ladolas). See:
MAGNUS I
Barnaby Ross. See:
Queen, Ellery
Barnacle Bill. See:
SUTPHIN, WILLIAM HALSTEAD
Barnacle, Captain Robert. See:
NEWELL, CHARLES MARTIN
BARNARD. See also:
BERNARD
BARNARD, CHARLOTTE ALINGTON (1830-69) [English ballad composer]
Claribel
BARNATO, BARNETT ISAACS (1825-97) [Jewish speculator, capitalist and diamond mine operator in South Africa]
Barney Barnato
The Kaffir King
Barnes, Al G. See:
STONEHOUSE, ALPHEUS

GEORGE BARNES
BARNES, CLARA ERNST (1895-) [German-American artist and author]
Clara Ernst
BARNES, DJUNA (1892-) [British reporter, illustrator and author]
Lydia Steptoe
BARNES, PAUL D. (1901-) [American jazz musician (clarinet, saxophones)]
Polo Barnes
BARNES, WILLIAM (1801-86) [Scottish dialect poet]
The Dorsetshire Burns
BARNETT, CHARLES DALY (1913-) [American jazz musician, (tenor saxophone, leader)]
Charlie Barnett
Barnett, L. David. See:
LASCHEVER, BARNETT D.
Barney. See:
BARNATO, BARNETT ISAACS
BIGARD, LEON ALBANY
JOHNSON, WALTER PERRY
SHOTTON, BURTON EDWIN
Barney Ross. See:
ROSOFSKY, BARNEY
BARNHUM. See also:
BARNUM
Barnum
BARNHUM, H.B. (1936-) [American jazz musician (singer, arranger, leader, virtually all instruments)]
The Barnum Wonder Boy
BARNSLEY, ALAN GABRIEL (1916-) [British physician and author]
Gabriel Fielding
BARNUM [Barnum]. See also:
BARNHUM
Barnum of Broadway Producers, The. See:
MARGULOIS, DAVID
BARNUM, PHINEAS TAYLOR (1810-91) [American showman]
The Great American Showman
Prince of Humbugs
Prince of Showmen
Barnum, Richard. See:
STRATEMEYER, EDWARD L.
Barnum, The Greatest Showman Since. See:
NORTH, JOHN RINGLING
BARNUM, WILLIAM HENRY (1818-89) [American chairman of Democratic National Party]
Seven Mule Barnum
Barnum Wonder Boy, The. See:
BARNHUM, H.B.
BARNWELL, JOHN (1671-1724) [Irish-American pioneer; conqueror of Tuscarora Indians]
Tuscarora John
Baron. See:
Barron
MÜNCHAUSEN, EARL FRIEDRICH HIERONYMUS, BARON VON
Baron and Defender of the Holy Sepulcher. See:
GODFREY OF BOUILLON
Baron, André. See:
BOYRON, ANDRÉ
BARON (BOYRON), MICHEL (1653-1729) [French actor]
The French Roscius
Baron Cobham. See:
OLDCASTLE, SIR JOHN
Baron Corvo. See:
ROLFE, FREDERICK WILLIAM SERAFINO AUSTIN LEWIS MARY
Baron, David. See:
PINTER, HAROLD
Baron de Kalb. See:
KALB, JOHANN
Baron Ireland. See:
SALISBURY, NATE
Baron Mikan. See:
BARBA, HARRY
Baron Pomfret. See:
DAME, LAWRENCE
Baron, The Bloody Red. See:
VON RICHTHOFEN, BARON MANFRED
Baron, The Red. See:
VON RICHTHOFEN,

BARON MANFRED
Baron, Vic. See:
BARONI, VASCO
BARONDESS, SUE KAUFMAN (1926-) [American author]
Sue Kaufman
Baroness. See:
ORCZY, EMMUSKA
Baroness Julie Desplaines. See:
JENNINGS, LESLIE NELSON
BARONI, VASCO (1910-) [Italian-American accordionist and composer]
Vic Baron
Barons, The Last of the. See:
NEVIL (NEVILLE), RICHARD
BARR, BYRON (1913-) [American motion picture and television actor]
Gig Young
BARR, JOHN MARSHALL. See:
Hazard, Laurence
BARR, PATRICIA MIRIAM. See:
Hazard, Laurence
BARR, ROBERT (1850-1912) [Scottish novelist]
Luke Sharp
Barragán. See:
LLANO, ISIDRO SANTIAGO
Barrel-Mirabeau. See:
RIQUETI, ANDRÉ BONIFACE LOUIS
BARRELL, SARAH SAYWARD (1759-1855) [American novelist]
A Lady of Maine
A Lady of Massachusetts
BARREN, CHARLES (1913-) [British educator and author]
Thomas Rainham
BARRES, ADRIAN DES (died c. 1665) [French actor]
d'Orgemont
BARRETT, EMMA (1905-) [American jazz musician (piano, singer)]
Sweet Emma the Bell Gal
BARRETT, GEORGE HOOKER (HORTON) (1794-1860) [Anglo-American comedian]
Gentleman George
Barrett, Walter. See:
SCOVILLE, JOSEPH ALFRED
BARRETT, WILLIAM HENRY (1846-1904) [English actor, manager and dramatist]
Wilson Barrett
Barricades, The King of the. See: LOUIS PHILIPPE
BARRIE [Barrie]. See also:
Bari
BARRY
Barry
Barrie, Mona. See:
SMITH, MONA
BARRIE, SIR JAMES MATTHEW (1860-1937) [Scottish dramatist and novelist]
Gavin Ogilvy
Barrie, Wendy. See:
JENKINS, WENDY
Barrien, Edith Heal. See:
HEAL, EDITH
Barrington, E. See:
BECK, MRS. LILY MORESBY ADAMS
Barrington, P. V. See:
BARLING, MURIEL VERE MANT
Barrington, Pamela. See:
BARLING, MURIEL VERE MANT
BARRINGTON, WALDRON (1755-1804) [Irish writer]
George Barrington
BARRIOS, FRANCISCO (1936-) [Spanish bullfighter]
El Turia
Barron. See also:
BARON
Baron
Barron, Blue. See:
FRIEDLAND, HARRY
BARROS, JOÃO DE (1496-1570) [Portuguese historian]
The Livy of Portugal
The Portuguese Livy
BARROW, FRANCES ELIZABETH MEASE (1822-94) [American writer of children's books]
Aunt Fanny
BARROW, ISAAC (1630-77)

[English theologian, mathematician and classical scholar]
The Unfair Preacher
BARROW, JOSEPH LOUIS (1914-) [American professional Negro boxer; world's heavyweight champion
The Brown Bomber
The Dark Destroyer
Joe Louis
BARROWS, MARJORIE (fl. 1916-58) [American editor and author]
Jack Alden
Noel Ames
Ruth Barrows
Ruth Dixon
Hugh Graham
Barry. See:
Bari
BARRIE
Barrie
BENEFIELD, JOHN BARRY
Barry, Charles. See:
BRYSON, CHARLES
BARRY, COMMODORE JOHN (1745-1803) [American naval officer]
The father of the American Navy
Barry Cornwall. See:
PROCTOR, BRYAN WALLER
Barry, DeForest. See:
CLARK, CHARLES DUNNING
MANNING, WILLIAM HENRY
Barry, Don. See:
D'ACOSTA, DONALD BARRY
Barry Exall. See:
NUGENT, JOHN PEER
Barry Fitzgerald. See:
SHIELDS, WILLIAM JOSEPH
Barry, Gene. See:
KLASS, EUGENE
BARRY, GEORGETTA (1916-) [French-American stage and motion picture actress]
Andrea King
Barry Gray. See:
COFFIN, ROBERT BARRY
BARRY, SPRANGER (1719-77) [Irish actor]
The Irish Roscius
BARRY, WESLEY (1907-) [American motion picture actor]
Freckles Barry
Barrymore, Diana. See:
BLYTHE, DIANA
Barrymore, Ethel. See:
COLT, ETHEL BLYTHE
Barrymore, Jack. See:
BLYTHE, JOHN
Barrymore, John. See:
BLYTHE, JOHN
Barrymore, John, Jr. See:
BLYTHE, JOHN, JR.
Barrymore, Lionel. See:
BLYTHE, LIONEL
Barrymore, Maurice. See:
BLYTHE, HERBERT
Barrymore of the Brain Trust, The. See:
TUGWELL, REXFORD GUY
BARSTOW, NORAH LEE HAYMOND (1898-1941) [American composer]
Norah Lee
Bart. See:
BARTHOLOMEW, CHARLES L.
STARR, BRYAN BARTLETT
Bart, Black. See:
BOLTON, CHARLES E.
ROBERTS, CAPTAIN BARTHOLOMEW
Bart, Black, The Po8. See:
BOLTON, CHARLES E.
BART, JEAN (1650-1702) [French naval commander]
The French Devil
Bart Segundo. See:
ROWLAND, DONALD SYDNEY
BARTELL, RICHARD (1907-) [American professional baseball player]
Pepper Box
Barth, Lois. See:
FREIHOFER, LOIS DIANE
BARTHOLOMEW, CHARLES L. (1869-) [American cartoonist and teacher]
Bart
BARTIER, PIERRE (1945-) [Belgian author and motion

picture critic]
Peter Pan
Bartimeus. See:
COSTA RICCI, LEWIS DA
BARTLETT, ALICE ELINOR (1848-1920) [American author]
Birch Arnold
Bartlett, David. See:
MASON, MADELINE
BARTLETT, FREDERICK ORIN (1845-1912) [American poet and journalist]
Will Carleton
William Carleton
The Old Dog
BARTLETT, MARIE SWAN (1918-) [American author]
Billie Bartlett
Rowena Lee
Sara Linden
Valerie Rift
Marie Swan
Bartlett, Nancy. See:
STRONG, CHARLES STANLEY
Bartlett, Philip A. See:
STRATEMEYER, EDWARD L.
BARTLETT, VERNON (1894-) [English author]
Peter Oldfield
Bartley Campbell. See:
URNER, NATHAN DANE
Bartok, Eva. See:
SJÖKE, EVA
Bartolommeo, Fra. See:
FATTORINO, BARTOLOMMEO DI PAGOLO DEL
BARTOLOMMEO, MASO DI (1406-57) [Italian sculptor]
Masaccio
BARTOLOZZI, LUCIA ELIZABETH (1795-1856) [English actress and theater manager]
Madame Vestris
Barton, Andrew. See:
FORREST, THOMAS
BARTON, BERNARD (1784-1849) [English poet]
The Quaker Poet
BARTON, BRUCE (1886-1967) [American advertising executive, politician and author]
The Advertiser
The Advertising King
The Great Repealer
Barton, Caroline M. See:
BRAME, CHARLOTTE MARY
BARTON, CLARISSA HARLOWE (1821-1912) [American philanthropist and founder of American Red Cross]
The Angel of the Battlefield
Clara Barton
The Mother of the Red Cross
BARTON, DAVID (1783-1837) [American senator from Missouri]
Little Red
BARTON, ELIZABETH (c. 1506-34) [British domestic servant pretended prophetess]
The Maid of Kent
The Nun of Kent
Barton Gray. See:
SASS, GEORGE HERBERT
BARTON, JOHN (1880-1938) [American author of children's books]
Johnny Gruelle
Barton, May Hollis. See:
STRATEMEYER, EDWARD L.
Barton Shaw. See:
DRUMMOND, PATRICK HAMILTON
BARTRAM, JOHN (1699-1777) [American botanist]
Botanist to the King
The Father of American Botany
The Greatest Botanist in the World
BARUCH, BERNARD MANNES (1870-1965) [American financier and public servant]
The Adviser of Presidents
BARZENA. See:
BARCENA (BARZENA), ALONSO DE
BASCOMB, WILBUR ODELL (1916-) [American jazz musician (trumpet)]

Dud Bascomb
Baseball Eddy. See:
KELLY, EDWARD AUSTIN
Baseball Fandom, The Idol of. See: COBB, TYRUS RAYMOND
Baseball in the West, The Father of. See:
WALDO, HIRAM H.
Baseball, The Clown Prince of. See: SCHACHT, ALEXANDER
Baseball, The Cock o' the Walk of. See:
MAILS, WALTER
Baseball, The Czar of. See:
LANDIS, KENESAW MOUNTAIN
Baseball, The Czar of American-
See: LANDIS, KENESAW MOUNTAIN
Baseball, The Father of. See:
CHADWICK, HENRY
DOUBLEDAY, ABNER
Baseball, The Father of Modern. See: CARTWRIGHT, ALEXANDER JOY
Baseball, The Iron Man of. See: GEHRIG, HENRY LOUIS
Bashevis, Isaac. See:
SINGER, ISAAC
Bashkirtseff, The Butte. See:
MACLANE, MARY
BASIE, WILLIAM (1904-) [American jazz musician (leader, piano, organ, composer)]
Bill Basie
Count Basie
Basil. See:
KING, WILLIAM BASIL
BASIL I (812?-86) [Byzantine emperor]
Basil the Macedonian
The Macedonian
BASIL II (958?-1025) [Byzantine emperor]
Bulgaroktonos (Slayer of Bulgarians)
Basil Garstang. See:
BRERETON, JOHN LE GAY
BASIL, ST. (c. 329-379) [Greek churchman]
The Great
Basil, St. See:
SPENCE, SIR BASIL UNWIN
Basil Zaharoff, Sir. See:
ZACHARIAS, BASILEIOS
BASIT, ABDUL (1894-) [Indian author]
M. A. Basit
Baskerville of America, The. See: THOMAS, ISAIAH
Basket-Maker, The. See:
MILLER, THOMAS
Basketball, The Clown Prince of. See: LEMON, MEADOW GEORGE
Basketball, The Father of. See:
NAISMITH, DR. JAMES A.
BASON, FREDERICK THOMAS (1907-) [British bookseller, lecturer and author]
Fred Bason
The Gallerite
Bassano, Jacopo. See:
PONTE, GIACOMO DA
BASSELIN, OLIVER (fl. 15th cent.) [Norman poet and artisan]
The Joyous Father of the Vaudeville
Bassett, Jack. See:
ROWLAND, DONALD SYDNEY
Bassett, John Keith. See:
KEATING, LAWRENCE A.
BASSETT, WILLIAM B.K. (1908-) [American business executive and author]
Peter Darien
Bassetto, Corno di. See:
SHAW, GEORGE BERNARD
BASSIANUS, VARIUS AVITUS (204-22) [Emperor of Rome]
Heliogabalus (Elagabalus)
Bastard of Orleans, The. See:
DUNOIS, JEAN
Bastard, The. See:
JOHN I
WILLIAM I
Bastard, The Great. See:
BOURGOGNE, ANTOINE DE
Bastard, Thomas the. See:

FAUCONBERG, THOMAS
Bat. See:
MASTERSON, WILLIAM BARCLAY
Bat, Little. See:
GARNIER, BAPTISTE
Batallador, El. See:
ALFONSO I
BATES, ARLO (1850-1918) [American novelist, poet and teacher]
Eleanor Putnam
Bates, Baldwin. See:
JENNINGS, JOHN E., JR.
BATES, BARBARA SNEDEKER (1919-) [American editor and author]
Stephen Cuyler
Jim Roberts
Bates, Florence. See:
RABE, FLORENCE
BATES, HARRIET LEONORA VOSE (1856-86) [American author]
Eleanor Putnam
BATES, HERBERT ERNEST (1905-) [English novelist and short story writer]
H.E. Bates
Flying Officer X
BATES, WILLIAM (1625-99) [Puritan divine]
The Silver-tongued
BATES, WILLIAM GELSTON (1803-80) [American lawyer]
The Father of the Hampden County Bar
The Historian of the Hampden County Bar
The Nestor of the Hampden County Bar
Bath Murderer, The Brides in the. See:
SMITH, GEORGE JOSEPH
Bath, The King of. See:
NASH, RICHARD
Bath, The Maid of. See:
LINLEY, ELIZA ANN
Bath, The Man of. See:
ALLEN, RALPH
BATHGATE, ANDREW JAMES (1932-) [Canadian professional hockey player]
Andy Bathgate
BATHIAT, LEONIE (1898-) [French motion picture actress]
Arletty
Bathing Girl, The Original. See: STEADMAN, VERA
Bathing Towel. See:
BADEN-POWELL, ROBERT STEPHENSON SMYTHE, 1ST BARON BADEN-POWELL
Bathos, The Father of the, and indeed the Homer of it. See: BLACKMORE, SIR RICHARD
Batman. See:
ORTEGA, ANTHONY ROBERT
BATMAN, JOHN (1800-40) [Tasmanian colonist]
The Founder of Victoria
Batten, Joyce Mortimer. See:
MANKOWSKA, JOYCE KELLS BATTEN
Battery Dan. See:
FINN, DANIEL E.
BATTISCOMBE, ESTHER GEORGINA HARWOOD (1905-) [British author]
Gina Harwood
Battle-axe. See:
GLEASON, PATRICK JEROME
Battle Laureate, Our. See:
BROWNELL, HENRY HOWARD
Battle of Gettysburg, The Hero of. See:
BURNS, JOHN
Battlefield Angel, The. See:
HANCOCK, CORNELIA
Battlefield, The Angel of the. See: BARTON, CLARISSA HARLOWE
Battling Bob. See:
LA FOLLETTE, ROBERT MARION, SR.
BAUER, BRUNO (1809-82) [German theologian, historian and critic]
The Voltaire of Germany

BAUER, ERWIN A. (1919-) [American author and photographer]
Ken Bourbon
Tom Hardin
Charles W. North
Bauer, Georg. See:
AGRICOLA, GEORGIUS
BAUER, HENRY ALBERT (1922-) [American baseball manager]
Hank Bauer
BAUER, WILLIAM HENRY (1915-) [American jazz musician (guitar)]
Billy Bauer
BAUGH, EMMA (1912-) [American dance satirist, choreographer and costume designer]
Iva Kitchell
BAUGH, SAMUEL ADRIAN (1914-) [American athlete; baseball and football player]
Slinging Sammy
BAUGHAN, EDWARD ALGERNON (1865-) [English author]
E.A.B.
BAUM, LYMAN FRANK (1856-1919) [American playwright, novelist and writer of juvenile literature]
Floyd Akens
L. Frank Baum
Schuyler Staunton
Edith Van Dyne
BAUMGARNER, JAMES (1928-) [American motion picture and television actor]
James Garner
BAUMRIN, BERNARD HERBERT (1934-) [American educator and author]
Stefan Baumrin
Stefan Bernard
BAUTIER, JOSEPH (1848-1903) [French illusionist and magician]
Bautier de Kolta
Bavan, Yolande. See:
WOLFFE, YOLANDE MARI
BAVARIA. See:
COUNT POPPO OF BAVARIA
ISABELLA OF BAVARIA
Bavarian, The. See:
LOUIS IV
Bawden, Nina. See:
KARK, NINA MARY MABEY
Bawling. See:
JENKINS, JAMES
Bawn, Mary. See:
WRIGHT, MARY PAMELA GODWIN
Bax, Roger. See:
WINTERTON, PAUL
Baxter, George Owen. See:
FAUST, FREDERICK SCHILLER
Baxter, Hazel. See:
ROWLAND, DONALD SYDNEY
Baxter, Jane. See:
FORDE, FEODORA
Baxter, Larry. See:
SETARO, PETER D.
Baxter, Olive. See:
EASTWOOD, HELEN
Baxter, Shayne V. See:
NORWOOD, VICTOR GEORGE CHARLES
Baxter, Valerie. See:
MEYNELL, LAURENCE
Bay, The Hero of Mobile. See:
FARRAGUT, DAVID GLASGOW
Bayard. See:
BYARD
TAYLOR, JAMES BAYARD
BAYARD, JAMES ASHETON (1767-1815) [American senator from Delaware]
The Goliath of His Party
The High Priest of the Constitution
Bayard of India, The. See:
OUTRAM, SIR JAMES
Bayard of the Netherlands, The. See: NASSAU-DILLENBURG, COUNT LOUIS OF
Bayard of the Press, The. See:
PLEASANTS, JOHN HAMPDEN
Bayard of the Revolution, The.

See: LAURENS, GEORGE
Bayard of the Sea, The. See:
PAUL, JOHN
Bayard of the South, The. See:
MARION, FRANCIS
BAYARD, PIERRE DU TERRAIL, CHEVALIER DE (1476-1524) [French Knight]
Chevalier Bayard
The Knight Without Fear and Without Reproach
Bayard, The British. See:
SIDNEY (SYDNEY), SIR PHILIP
BAYLISS, JOHN CLIFFORD (1919-) [British editor and author]
John Clifford
BAYLY. See also:
BAILEY
Bailey
BAYLY, ADA ELLEN (1857-1903) [American author]
Edna Lyall
BAZZI, GIOVANNI ANTONIO DE' (1477?-1549) [Italian painter of the Sienese school]
Il Sodoma
Il Sodorna
Bea. See:
BEE
Bee
LILLIE, BEATRICE GLADYS
Beach, Charles Amory. See:
STRATEMEYER, EDWARD L.
BEACH, THOMAS (1840-94) [British spy]
Major Henri Le Caron
Beachcomber. See:
LEWIS, DOMINIC BEVAN WYNDHAM
MORTON, JOHN CAMERON ANDRIEU BINGHAM MICHAEL
BEADNELL, CHARLES MARSH (1872-) [English author]
Javali
BEAL, ABRAHAM (c. 1803-72) [Anglo-American philanthropist]
The Prisoner's Friend
Beal, John. See:
BLIEDUNG, ALEXANDER
BEAMISH, ANNIE O'MEARA DE VIC (1883-) [Irish novelist and language school director]
Noel de Vic Beamish
Bean. See:
HAWKINS, COLEMAN
BEAN, KEITH FENWICK (1911-) [Australian journalist and author]
Kay Fenwick
K. Harrington
Bean, Orson. See:
BURROWS, DALLAS FREDERICK
BEAN, ROY (c. 1825-1903) [American frontier justice of the peace]
Judge Bean
The Law West of the Pecos
Beanpole Jimmy. See:
JONES, JAMES C.
Bear, Honey. See:
SEDRIC, EUGENE PAUL
Bear, The. See:
ALBERT
BEARD, DANIEL CARTER (1850-1941) [American artist, author and naturalist]
Dan Beard
Uncle Dan
BEARD, FRANK (1939-) [American professional golfer]
A Nine-to-five Pro
BEARD, THOMAS FRANCIS (1842-1905) [American illustrator]
Frank Beard
Bearer, Christ. See:
CHRISTOPHER, ST.
Béarnais, Le. See:
HENRY IV
Beast Butler. See:
BUTLER, BENJAMIN FRANKLIN
Beast, The. See:
BUTLER, BENJAMIN FRANKLIN
Beatles, The, stage name of

Liverpudlian singing and instrumental group consisting of JOHN LENNON (1940-), GEORGE HARRISON (1943-), PAUL McCARTNEY (1942-) and RICHARD STARKEY (Ringo Starr), (1940-).

Beatles, The. See also:
Nurk Twins, The
STARKEY, RICHARD

Beaton, Anne. See:
WASHINGTON, MARGUERITE BEAUCHAMP

Beaton, George. See:
BRENAN, GERALD

Beatrice Fairfax. See:
GASCH, MARIE MANNING

Beatrice Plumb. See:
HUNZICKER, BEATRICE PLUMB

BEATTIE, JOHN McINTOSH (1905-) [Australian motion picture actor]
John Warwick

Beatty, Baden. See:
CASSON, FREDERICK RONALD CHRISTOPHER

Beatty, Elizabeth. See:
HOLLOWAY, TERESA BRAGUNIER

BEATTY, JAMES TULLY (1934-) [American middle distance runner]
Jim Beatty

BEATTY, JEROME, JR. (1918-) [American editor and author]
Aaron W. Stookey

BEATTY, LOUISE DILWORTH (1871-1947) [American operatic contralto]
Louise Homer

Beatty, Warren. See:
BEATY, WARREN

BEATY, SHIRLEY MACLEAN (1934-) [American dancer and actress]
Shirley MacLaine

BEATY, WARREN (1937-) [American motion actor and producer]
Warren Beatty

Beau. See:
BRUMMEL, GEORGE BRYAN
DAWSON, JOHN
FIELDING, ROBERT
NASH, RICHARD
NEILL, THOMAS HEWSON

Beau Brummel of Broadway, The. See:
FAY, LARRY

Beau Brummel of the Army, The, See: MacARTHUR, DOUGLAS

Beau Brummel of the Brooklyn Underworld, The. See:
UALE, FRANCESCO

Beau Brummel of the Senate, The. See:
LEWIS, JAMES HAMILTON

BEAU, HENRY J. (1911-) [American composer and arranger]
Heinie Beau

Beau James. See:
WALKER, JAMES JOHN

Beau Jonathan. See:
HAZARD, JONATHAN J.

Beau of Princes, The. See:
GEORGE IV

Beau Sabreur (Handsome Swordsman). See:
MURAT, JOACHIM

BEAUCHAMP, MARY ANNETTE, COUNTESS RUSSELL (MRS. HENNING ARNIM) (1866-1941) [English novelist]
By the Author of "Elizabeth and her German Garden"
Elizabeth

Beauchamp, Pat. See:
WASHINGTON, MARGUERITE BEAUCHAMP

BEAUCHAMP, WILLIAM MARTIN (1830-1925) [American Episcopal clergyman, archaeologist and author]
Wah-Kat-Yu-Ten (Beautiful Rainbow)

Beauclerc, Henry (Henry the Scholar). See:
HENRY I

BEAUDE, HENRI (1870-) [French author]
Henri D'Arles

BEAUFORT, DUC DE (1616-69)

[French nobleman]
The King of the Markets
BEAUFORT, PIERRE ROGER DE (1331-78) [Supreme Pontiff of Roman Catholic Church]
Pope Gregory XI
BEAUMONT, CHARLES (1929-) [American author]
Keith Grantland
C.B. Lovehill
S.M. Tenneshaw
BEAUMONT, FRANCIS (1584-1616) [British playwright]
The Twin of Heavenlier Birth
BEAUREGARD, PIERRE GUSTAVE TOUTANT (1818-93) [American Confederate general officer]
The Hero of Fort Sumter
The Little Napoleon
Old Alphabet
Old Bore
Old Bory
Prince John
BEAUREPAIRE. See: QUESNAY DE BEAUREPAIRE, JULES
Beauté. See also: Beauty
Beauté, La Dame de. See: SOREL, AGNES
Beautiful American, The (La Belle Américaine) See: MONROE, ELIZABETH KORTRIGHT
Beautiful Bob. See: BRUGH, SPANGLER ARLINGTON
Beautiful Corisande, The. See: D'ANDOUINS, DIANE
Beautiful Duchess of Gordon, The. See: GORDON, JANE MAXWELL
Beautiful Parricide, The. See: CENCI, BEATRICE
Beautiful Rainbow (Wah-Kat-Yu-Ten). See: BEAUCHAMP, WILLIAM MARTIN
Beautiful Rope Maker, The. (La Belle Cordière). See: LABÉ, LOUISE
Beauty. See: Beauté
STUART, JAMES EWELL BROWN
Beauty of Buttermere, The. See: ROBINSON, MARY
Beauty of Holiness. See: HURD, RICHARD
Beauty, The Ten Thousand Dollar. See: KELLY, MICHAEL J.
Beaver, The White. See: POWELL, DAVID FRANK
BEBAN, GARY JOSEPH (1946-) [American professional football player]
The Great One
Bebe. See: DANIELS, VIRGINIA
Bebop. See: CARROLL, JOE
BECCAFUMI, DOMENICO (1486-1551) [Italian painter, sculptor and engraver]
Il Meccherino
BECK, MRS. LILY MORESBY ADAMS (died 1931) [Canadian novelist and mystic]
E. Barrington
Louis Moresby
Beck, Phineas. See: CHAMBERLAIN, SAMUEL
BECK, WALTER WILLIAM (1906-) [American professional baseball player]
Elmer the Great
Becker, Florence. See: LENNON, FLORENCE BECKER TANNENBAUM
BECKER, STEPHEN DAVID (1927-) [American author, editor and translator]
Steve Dodge
BECKET, THOMAS À. (1118-70) [English prelate; Archbishop of Canterbury]
St. Thomas à Becket
Thomas Becket
St. Thomas of London
BECKETT, RONALD BRYMER

(1891-) [British civil servant and author]
John Anthony
Beckman, Ross. See:
DEY, FREDERICK VAN RENSSELAER
Beckwith, Lillian. See:
COMBER, LILLIAN
Becky Lynne. See:
ZAWADSKY, PATIENCE
BEDA. See:
BEDE (BEDA) (BAEDA), ST.
Bede, Andrew. See:
BEHA, ERNEST
BEDE, (BEDA) (BAEDA), ST. (c. 673-735) [English monk, historian and ecclesiastical writer]
The Father of Ecclesiastical History
The Venerable Bede
Bede, Cuthbert. See:
BRADLEY, EDWARD
Bede, The Venerable. See:
BEDE (BEDA) (BAEDA), ST.
EUSEBIUS OF CAESARIA
BEDEU, JULIEN (c. 1600-60) [French comedian]
Jodelet
Bedell, Lew. See:
BIDEU, LOU
Bedford, Annie North. See:
WATSON, JANE WERNER
Bedford, John. See:
HASTINGS, PHYLLIS DORA HODGE
BEDFORD-JONES, HENRY JAMES O'BRIEN (1887-1949) [Canadian author]
H. Bedford-Jones
John Wycliffe
Bedford, Sidney. See:
MEYNELL, LAURENCE
Bediako, K.A. See:
KONADU, SAMUEL ASARE
BEDNARIK, CHARLES (1925-) [American football player]
Chuck Bednarik
Bedott, The Widow. See:
WHITCHER, FRANCES MIRIAM BERRY
BEE [Bee]. See also:
Bea
Bee, Jay. See:
HUNTER, WILLIAM RANDOLPH
BEE, JOHN DAVID ASHFORD (1931-) [South African author]
David Bee
Bee, The Athenian. See:
ARISTOCLES
Bee, The Attic. See:
ARISTOCLES
SOPHOCLES
BEEBE, LUCIUS (1902-66) [American author, columnist and bon vivant]
The Social Historian of the Café Society
Beech, Webb. See:
BUTTERWORTH, WILLIAM EDMUND III
Beecher, Janet. See:
MEYSENBURG, JANET BEECHER
BEECHER, LYMAN (1775-1863) [American theologian]
The Father of More Brains Than Any Other Man in America
BEECHER, THOMAS KINNICUT (1824-1900) [American Congregational clergyman]
Father Tom
BEECHING, AMY BROWN (1922-) [American author]
James Barbary
Alexis Brown
BEECHING, JACK (192?-) [American author and poet]
James Barbary
Beeding, Francis
David Pilgrim, joint pseuds. of JOHN LESLIE PALMER (1885-1944) and HILARY AIDAN ST. GEORGE SAUNDERS (1898-) [English authors]
Beeding, Francis. See also:
PALMER, JOHN LESLIE
Beedle. See:
SMITH, WALTER BEDELL

BEEDLE, WILLIAM FRANKLIN (1918-) [American actor]
William Holden
BEEKS, CLARENCE (1922-) [American jazz musician (singer, composer)]
King Pleasure
Beer, Bottled. See:
NOWELL, ALEXANDER
BEER, ELOISE C.S. (1903-) [American artist and author]
Lisl Beer
Lisl Drake
BEER, JAKOB LIEBMANN (1791-1864) [German opera composer]
Giacomo Meyerbeer
Beer Poet, The Small. See:
FITZGERALD, WILLIAM THOMAS
BEERBOHM, SIR HENRY MAXIMILIAN (1872-1956) [English writer and caricaturist]
The Incomparable Max
Max Beerbohm
BEERS, ETHELINDA ELIOT (1827-79) [American poet and story writer]
E.B.
Ethel Lynn
Ethel Lynn Beers
Beeswax, Old. See:
SEMMES, RAPHAEL
Beetle. See:
SMITH, WALTER BEDELL
BEETS, NICHOLAAS (1814-1903) [Dutch poet and writer]
Hildebrand
Beets, Sugar. See:
CUMMINGS, FRED
BEFUMO, JOSEPH A. (1905-) [American jazz musician (tenor saxophone)]
Joe Holiday
Beg, Toran. See:
McKILLOP, NORMAN
BEGBIE, HAROLD (1871-1922) [British political writer]
A Gentleman With a Duster
Beggars, The King of the. See:
CAREW, BAMPFYLDE MOORE
Beggarstaff. See also:
Bickerstaff
BICKERSTAFFE
Beggarstaff, J. and W., pseud. of SIR WILLIAM NEWZAM PRIOR NICHOLSON (1872-1949) and his brother-in-law JAMES PRYDE (-) [English artists and poster designers]
BEGLEY, EDWARD (1901-) [American actor]
Ed Begley
BEHA, ERNEST (1908-) [British journalist and author]
Andrew Bede
Drake Elvin
BEHAM, BARTHEL. See:
Little Masters
BEHAM, HANS SEBALD. See:
Little Masters
Behemoth, Trumpeting. See:
HIRT, ALOIS MAXWELL
Behind the Throne Greater Than the Throne Itself, One. See: STUART, JOHN
BEHN, MRS. APHRA (c.1640-89) [English playwright and novelist]
Astraea
By Several Hands
BEIDERBECKE, LEON BISMARCK (1903-31) [American jazz musician (cornet, piano, composer, leader)]
Bix Beiderbecke
BEISSEL, JOHANN CONRAD (1690-1788) [German clergyman; founder of Seventh Day Dunkers]
Friedsam
BEITH, JOHN HAY (1876-1952) [Scottish general officer, novelist and dramatist]
Ian Hay
Junior Sub
Bejla, J. See:
RZEWUSKY, COUNT HENRYK
BEKESSY, JEAN (1911-)

[Hungarian-American author]
Hans Habe
Bel Geddes, Barbara. See: LEWIS, BARBARA GEDDES
Bela. See: MORKOVIN, BORIS VLADIMIR
Bela Lugosi. See: BLASKO, BELA LUGOSI
BELAFONTE, HAROLD GEORGE, JR. (1927-) [American singer, composer, author and producer]
Harry Belafonte
Belafré, Le (The Scarred). See: FRANÇOIS DE LORRAINE HENRI I
BELASCO, DAVID (1859-1931) [American playwright and theatrical producer]
The Wizard of American Drama
Belfast Chicken, The. See: CLARK, WILLIAM
Belfast Man, The. See: DAVIS, FRANCIS
BELFORD, JAMES BURNS (1837-1910) [American congressman from Colorado]
The Red-headed Rooster of the Rockies
Belgian Literature, The Father of. See: DE COSTER, CHARLES THEODORE HENRI
Belgium, The Carnegie of. See: SOLVAY, ERNEST
Belgium, The Walter Scott of. See: CONSCIENCE, HENDRICK
Believers, The Emperor of. See: OMAR I
Believers, The Mother of. See: AYESHA
Belinda Dell. See: BOWDEN, JEAN
Belita. See: JEPSON-TURNER, GLADYS
Belknap, Boynton, M.D. See: ELLIS, EDWARD SYLVESTER
Bell, Acton. See: BRONTË, ANNE
BELL, ALEXANDER GRAHAM (1847-1922) [Scottish teacher of the deaf and inventor of the telephone]
The Father of the Telephone
BELL, CHARLES JASPER (fl. late 1930's) [Missouri lawyer, politician and congressman]
The Investigator
Bell, Cobden. See: BELTON-COBB, GEOFFREY
Bell, Currer. See: BRONTË, CHARLOTTE
Bell, Ellis. See: BRONTË, EMILY JANE
Bell, Emily Mary. See: CASON, MABEL EARP
BELL, ERIC TEMPLE (1883-) [Scottish novelist]
E.T. Bell
John Taine
Bell Gal, Sweet Emma The. See: BARRETT, EMMA
Bell, Gina. See: BALZANO, JEANNE KOPPEL
BELL, JESSIE MARY ELEANOR (1901-) [Canadian author]
Eleanor Bell
Bell, John. See: JOHNSON, VICTOR HUGO
Bell, Josephine. See: BALL, DORIS BELL COLLIER
BELL, JOSHUA FRY (1811-70) [American orator]
The Silver-tongued Orator
BELL, LOUISE PRICE (fl. 1931-60) [American author]
Lita Bronson
Ruth Jeffrey
Bell, Neil. See: SOUTHWOLD, STEPHEN
Bell, Paul. See: CHORLEY, HENRY FOTHERGILL
Bell, Solomon. See: SNELLING, WILLIAM JOSEPH

Bell-the-Cat. See:
DOUGLAS, ARCHIBALD
Bell, The Dinner. See:
BURKE, EDMUND
Bell-Zano, Gina. See:
BALZANO, JEANNE KOPPEL
Bella Cohen. See:
SPEWACK, BELLA COHEN
Bella Darvi. See:
WEGIER, BELLA
Bellairs, George. See:
BLUNDELL, HAROLD
BELLAMY, ELIZABETH WHITFIELD CROOM (1837-1900) [American novelist and short story writer]
Kamba Thorpe
BELLAW, AMERICUS WELLINGTON (1842-) [American journalist and author of dime novels]
Frank Freelance
Joe Jot, Jr.
Jo King
Noah Nuff
Solomon Shingle
Washington Whitehorn
BELLAY, JOACHIM DU (c. 1524-60) [French poet and prose writer]
The French Ovid
The Prince of the Sonnet
Belle Américaine, La (The Beautiful American). See:
MONROE, ELIZABETH KORTRIGHT
Belle Cordière, La (The Beautiful Rope Maker). See:
LABÉ, LOUISE
Belle Gabrielle, La. See:
D'ESTRÉES, GABRIELLE
Belle Indienne, La. See:
MAINTENON, MADAME DE
Belle Laurette, La. See:
COONEY, HELEN LAURETTE MAGDALENE
Belle Liégeoise, La. See:
TERWAGNE, ANNE JOSEPH
Belle of the Union, The. See:
LE VERT, OCTAVIA WALTON
BELLEAU, REMI (1528-77) [French poet]
Le Gentil Belleau
The Painter of Nature
BELLEW, FRANK W. (1862-94) [American illustrator]
Chip
BELLEW, HAROLD KYRLE (1855-1911) [English actor]
Harold Kyrle
BELLOC, JOSEPH HILARY PIERRE (1870-1953) [English author]
Hilaire Belloc
Bellocq, Louise. See:
BOUDAT, MARIE-LOUISE
Bellona. See:
EATON, MARGARET O'NEILL
Belloy, Dormont de. See:
BUTRETTE, PIERRE LAURENT
Bellson, Louis. See:
BALASSONI, LOUIS
Bellwood, Bessie. See:
MAHONEY, BESSIE
Bellwood, Herbert. See:
PATTEN, WILLIAM GILBERT
BELMONTE. See:
CAMPOY, JUAN BELMONTE Y
Belmonte, Juan, Jr. See:
CAMPOY, JUAN BELMONTE Y
BELMONTE Y GARCÍA, JUAN (1892-) [Spanish bullfighter]
Juan Belmonte
Beloved Dean, The. See:
MOORE, WALTER HOMER
Beloved Jailer, The. See:
WHITTMAN, JOHN LORIN
Beloved Man of the Four Nations, The. See:
HAWKINS, BENJAMIN
Beloved Merchant, The. See:
POLE, MICHAEL DE LA
Beloved Physician, The. See:
LUKE, ST.

Beloved, The Well. See:
CHARLES VI
Beloved, The Well (Le Bien-Aimé). See:
LOUIS XV
Belshazzar, The Machiavellian. See: VAN BUREN, MARTIN
Belted Will. See:
HOWARD, LORD WILLIAM
BELTON-COBB, GEOFFREY (1892-) [English author]
Cobden Bell
Beltrame. See:
BARBIERI, NICCOLÒ
BEMBO, PIETRO (1470-1547) [Italian poet, scholar, critic and churchman]
The Miniature Petrarch
Ben. See:
BLACK, BENJAMIN
GAZZARA, BIAGO ANTHONY
GRAUER, BENJAMIN FRANKLIN
HOGAN, BENJAMIN WILLIAM
JONSON, BENJAMIN
LINDSEY, BENJAMIN BARR
SHAHN, BENJAMIN
TURPIN, C. MURRAY
WEBSTER, BENJAMIN FRANCIS
BEN ATTA, HAKIM (died 780) [Founder of Arabian religious sect]
Al Mokanna (The Veiled)
Ben Benny. See:
KUBELSKY, BENNY
Ben Bernie. See:
ANZELEVITZ, BERNARD
Ben Bite. See:
SCHNECK, STEPHEN
Ben Colder. See:
WOOLLEY, SHEB
Ben-Gorion, M.Y. See:
BERDICHEVSKY, MIKHAH YOSEF
Ben-Gurion, David. See:
GREEN, DAVID
Ben Halliday. See:
MANNING, WILLIAM HENRY
Ben Jonson. See:
JONSON, BENJAMIN
Ben Jonson, Rare. See:
JONSON, BENJAMIN
Ben Kerr. See:
ARD, WILLIAM THOMAS
Ben, Little. See:
HARRISON, BENJAMIN
Ben, Long. See:
AVERY, CAPTAIN JOHN
BEN MATTATHIAS, JOSEPH (c. 37-c. 101) [Jewish historian]
Flavius Josephus
Ben, Philip. See:
BARLING, PHILIP
Ben, Pitchfork. See:
TILLMAN, BENJAMIN RYAN
Ben Sarto. See:
FAWCETT, FRANK DUBREZ
Ben Smith, The Late. See:
MATHEWS, CORNELIUS
Ben Wade, Bluff. See:
WADE, BENJAMIN FRANKLIN
Ben Wade, Old. See:
WADE, BENJAMIN FRANKLIN
Benarria, Allan. See:
GOLDENTHAL, ALLAN BENARRIA
Benauly, joint pseud. of
AUSTIN ABBOTT (1831-96)
BENJAMIN VAUGHAN ABBOTT (1830-90), and
LYMAN ABBOTT (1835-1922), brothers
[American authors]
BENCHLEY, ROBERT (1889-1945) [American author, humorist and actor]
Bob Benchley
Bend, Palmer. See:
PUTNAM, GEORGE PALMER
BENDER, ARNOLD (1904-) [German author]
Mark Philippi
BENDER, CHARLES ALBERT (1883-1954) [American Indian professional baseball

player
Chief Bender
Bender, Jay. See:
DEINDORFER, ROBERT GREENE
BENDIT, GLADYS WILLIAMS (1885-) [Australian lecturer and author
John Presland
BENDIX, WILLIAM (1906-64) [American actor]
Bill Bendix
BENEDETTO, ANTHONY DOMINICK (1926-) [American popular singer]
Joe Bari
Tony Bennett
BENEDICT (died 579) [Supreme Pontiff of Roman Catholic Church]
Pope Benedict I
BENEDICT (died 685) [Supreme Pontiff of Roman Catholic Church]
Pope Benedict II
St. Benedict
BENEDICT (died 858) [Supreme Pontiff of Roman Catholic Church]
Pope Benedict III
BENEDICT (died 903) [Supreme Pontiff of Roman Catholic Church]
Pope Benedict IV
BENEDICT (died 966) [Supreme Pontiff of Roman Catholic Church]
Pope Benedict V
BENEDICT (died 974) [Supreme Pontiff of Roman Catholic Church]
Pope Benedict VI
BENEDICT (died 983) [Supreme Pontiff of Roman Catholic Church]
Pope Benedict VII
BENEDICT (died 1024) [Supreme Pontiff of Roman Catholic Church]
Pope Benedict VIII
BENEDICT (died 1055) [Supreme Pontiff of Roman Catholic Church; afterwards anti-pope]
Pope Benedict IX
Benedict X, Pope. See: JOHN, COUNT OF TUSCULUM
Benedict XI, Pope. See:
BOCCASINI, NICCOLÒ
Benedict XII, Pope. See:
FORNIER, JACQUES
Benedict XIII, Pope. See: ORSINI, PIETRO FRANCESCO
Benedict XIV, Pope. See:
LAMBERTINI, PROSPERO
Benedict XV, Pope. See:
CHIESA, GIACOMO DELLA
Benedict, Joseph. See:
DOLLEN, CHARLES JOSEPH
BENEDICT OF NURSIA, ST. (480?-543) [Italian prelate and monk]
The Founder of Peace
The Founder of Western Monasticism
BENEDUM, MICHAEL (1869-1961) [American petroleum executive]
The King of the Wildcatters
Benefactor (Euergetes). See:
ANTIOCHUS VII
DEMETRIUS III
PTOLEMY III
Benefactor (Euergetes II). See:
PTOLEMY VII (or VIII or IX)
BENEFIELD, JOHN BARRY (1877-) [American novelist]
Barry Benefield
BENEKE, GORDON (1914-) [American jazz musician (tenor saxophone, singer, leader)]
Tex Beneke
Benet, Edouard. See:
EDWARDS, WILLIAM BENNETT
BENEVENTO. See:
DESIDERIUS, PRINCE OF BENEVENTO
Bengal Tiger. See:
TWIGGS, DAVID EMANUEL
BENGE, RAY ADELPHIA (1905-) [American professional baseball player]
Silent Cal
Benicia Boy, The. See:

HEENAN, JOHN CAMEL
BENITEZ, MANUEL (1936-) [Spanish bullfighter]
El Córdobes (The Man from Cordoba)
Benjamin. See:
BRITTEN, EDWARD BENJAMIN
Benjamin Brace. See:
McCUTCHEON, BEN FREDERICK
Benjamin Brewster. See:
FOLSOM, FRANKLIN BREWSTER
Benjamin Broadaxe. See:
MUSICK, JOHN ROY
BENJAMIN, CLAUDE MAX EDWARD POHLMAN (1911-) [American physician and author]
Max Edwards
Marion E. George
Benjamin Constant. See:
DE REBECQUE, HENRI BENJAMIN CONSTANT
Benjamin F. Johnson of Boone. See: RILEY, JAMES WHITCOMB
BENJAMIN, JUDAH PHILIP (1811-84) [Attorney General of Southern Confederacy]
The Brains of the Confederacy
BENJAMIN, LEWIS SAUL (1874-1932) [English author, editor and actor]
Lewis Melville
Benjamin Miller. See:
LOOMIS, NOEL MILLER
Benjamin Swift. See:
PATERSON, WILLIAM ROMAINE
Bennett Barclay. See:
CROSSEN, KENDELL FOSTER
Bennett, Bruce. See:
BRIX, HERMAN
Bennett, Christine. See:
NEUBAUER, WILLIAM ARTHUR
Bennett Copplestone. See:
KITCHIN, FREDERICK HARCOURT
Bennett, Dorothea, See:
YOUNG, DOROTHEA BENNETT
Bennett, Dwight. See:
NEWTON, DWIGHT BENNETT
BENNETT, ENOCH ARNOLD (1867-1931)[English novelist]
Arnold Bennett
Jacob Tonson
Bennett Garland. See:
GARFIELD, BRIAN WYNNE
BENNETT, GEOFFREY MARTIN (1909-) [British naval officer and author]
Sea-Lion
Bennett, Hall. See:
HALL, BENNIE CAROLINE HUMBLE
BENNETT, HENRY, EARL OF ARLINGTON. See:
Cabal, The
BENNETT, JAMES O'DONNELL (1870-1940) [American correspondent and drama critic]
Eye Witness
BENNETT, JOHN JEROME NELSON (1939-) [British broadcaster and author]
Jeremy Bennett
Bennett, Lou. See:
BENOIT, LOUIS
Bennett, Rachel. See:
HILL, MARGARET OHLER
Bennett, Stanley. See:
HOUGH, STANLEY BENNETT
Bennett, Tony. See:
BENEDETTO, ANTHONY DOMINICK
BENNETT, WILLIAM (1824-87) [British poet and playwright]
Zavarr Wilmshurst
Bennie. See:
Benny
GAZZARA, BIAGO ANTHONY
BENNING, HENRY LEWIS (1814-75) [American

Civil War general officer]
Old Rock
BENNINGHOFEN, MRS. ERNEST (fl.late 19th-early 20th cents.) [American medium]
Anna Clark
The Mother Medium
Bennington Fields, The Fighting Parson of. See:
ALLEN, REVEREND THOMAS
Benny. See:
BAILEY, ERNEST HAROLD
Bennie
CARTER, BENNETT LESTER
GOODMAN, BENJAMIN DAVID
MORTON, HENRY STERLING
MOTEN, CLARENCE LEMONT
Benny, An Aggressive Jack. See:
KNIBERG, IRWIN ALAN
Benny, Ben. See:
KUBELSKY, BENNY
Benny, Jack. See:
KUBELSKY, BENNY
Benny Leonard. See:
LEINER, BENJAMIN
Benny, Little. See:
HARRIS, BENJAMIN
BENOIT, LOUIS (1926-) [American jazz musician (organ, composer)]
Lou Bennett
Benozzo Gozzoli. See:
SANDRO, BENOZZO DI LESE DI
BENSKIN, SAMUEL (1922-) [American composer, conductor and arranger]
Sammy Benskin
BENSMAN, JOSEPH (1922-) [American author]
Jay Bentham
Ian Lewis
Benson, Carl. See:
BRISTED, CHARLES ASTOR
BENSON, JOHN J. (1915-) [American composer, singer, dancer, and author]
Jack Benson
Benson, Richard. See:
COOPER, SAUL
Benson, Therese. See:
KNIPE, EMILIE BENSON
Bentham, Jay. See:
BENSMAN, JOSEPH
BENTHAM, JEREMY (1748-1832) [British philosopher and economist]
The Philosopher
Benthien, Fritz. See:
BONUS, ARTHUR
Bentley, William. See:
BLANCHARD, WILLIAM
Benton Price. See:
WILSON, ROGER C.
BENTON, THOMAS HART (1782-1858) [American statesman and senator from Missouri]
The Gold Bug
Gold Humbug
Old Bullion
Old Humbug
The Old Roman
Benton, Will. See:
PAINE, LAUREN
BENY, WILFRED ROY (1924-) [Canadian artist, photographer and author]
Roloff Beny
BEOLCO, ANGELO (1502-42) [Italian dramatist and actor]
Ruzzante
BÉRANGER, PIERRE-JEAN DE (1780-1857) [French song writer]
The French Burns
The French Horace
The Horace of France
Berch. See also:
Birch
Berch, William C. See:
COYNE, JOSEPH E.
BERCKMAN, EVELYN DOMINICA (1900-) [American author]
Joanna Wade
BERDICHEVSKY, MIKHAH YOSEF (1865-1921) [Hebrew scholar and writer]
M.Y. Ben Gorion
Berend, Alice. See:
BREINLINGER, ALICE BEREND
BERESFORD, MARCUS (1919-)

[Anglo-American novelist]
Marc Brandel
Beresford, Russell. See: ROBERTS, CECIL EDRIC MORINGTON
BERG, DAVID (1920-) [American cartoonist, artist, writer and editor]
Dave Berg
BERG, GENE (1920-) [American dancer and stage and motion picture actor]
Gene Nelson
Bergdahl, Enid. See: GILLETTE, LELAND J.
BERGE, CAROL (1928-) [American editor and poet]
Laura Keel
Berger, Colonel. See: MALRAUX, GEORGES-ANDRÉ
BERGER, JOSEF (1903-) [American writer of children's books]
Jeremiah Digges
BERGH, KARIN KROG (1937-) [Norwegian jazz singer]
Karin Krog
BERGHOFER, CHARLES CURTIS (1937-) [American jazz musician (bass)]
Chuck Berghofer
Beri Headin, From the Desk of. See: STORY, ISAAC
BERIA, LAVRENTI PAVLOVICH (1899-1953) [Soviet secret police chief]
The Himmler of Russia
A Thrice-Accursed Judas
BERIGAN, ROLAND BERNARD (1909-42) [American jazz musician (trumpet, leader)]
Bunny Berigan
BERINGER, JOSEPH AUGUST (1862-) [German author]
J. A. B.
BERKEBILE, FRED DONOVAN (1900-) [American educator, columnist and author]
William Donovan
William Ernest
Don Stauffer
Berkeley, Anthony. See: COX, ANTHONY BERKELEY
Berkeley, Busby. See: ENOS, WILLIAM BERKELEY
Berkeley, Helen. See: MOWATT, ANNA CORA OGDEN RITCHIE
Berkshire Lady, The. See: KENDRICK, FRANCES
BERKSON, WILLIAM C. (1939-) [American editor, journalist, poet and author]
Bill Berkson
Berle, Milton. See: BERLINGER, MILTON
Berlin Bach, The. See: BACH, KARL PHILIPP EMANUEL
BERLIN, ELAINE (1932?-) [American comedienne]
Elaine May
Berlin, Irving. See: BALINE, ISRAEL
BERLINGER, MILTON (1908-) [American actor and television personality]
Milton Berle
Mr. Television
Uncle Milty
BERMAN, SAUL (1924-47) [American jazz musician (trumpet)]
Sonny Berman
Bern. See also: BERNE
Berne
Bern, Paul. See: LEVY, PAUL
Bernadette, St. See: SOUBIROUS, MARIE BERNARDE
BERNADETTI, ERNEST MARCO (1884-) [American composer, pianist and organist]
Ernie Burnett
BERNADOTTE, JEAN BAPTISTE JULES (1763-1844)

[French marshal, later ruler of Sweden]
Charles XIV, King of Sweden
Charles John (Karl Johan)
Bernard. See:
BARNARD
SHAW, GEORGE BERNARD
BERNARD, ANNE-JOSE (1929-) [French actress]
Cécile Aubry
Bernard Berni. See:
ANZELEVITZ, BERNARD
Bernard Blackmantle. See:
WESTMACOTT, CHARLES MALLOY
Bernard Clyde. See:
AIKEN, GEORGE L.
BERNARD, HENRIETTE ROSINE (1844-1923) [French tragedienne]
Sarah Bernhardt
The Divine Sarah
BERNARD OF CLAIRVAUX (1091-1153) [French monk and teacher]
The Father of Western Mysticism
The Honeyed Teacher
The Last of the Fathers
The Mellifluous Doctor
The Oracle of the Church
St. Bernard
BERNARD OF MENTHON, ST. (923-1008) [French churchman; founder of hospices in Alps]
Apostle of the Alps
BERNARD, PAUL (1866-1947) [French novelist and dramatist]
Tristan
BERNARD, PIERRE A. (c.1875-1955) [American Yoga cult leader]
Peter Coon
Homer Stansbury Leeds
The Omnipotent
Oom
Bernard, Robert. See:
MARTIN, ROBERT BERNARD
BERNARD, ROGER (fl. 1223-41) [Comte de Foix]
The Great
Bernard, Stefan. See:
BAUMRIN, BERNARD HERBERT
BERNARDONE, GIOVANNI FRANCESCO (1182-1226) [Italian monk and preacher; founder of the Franciscans]
St. Francis of Assisi
The Seraphic Saint
Bernarn, Terrave. See:
BURNETT, DAVID
Bernays, Anne. See:
KAPLAN, ANNE BERNAYS
BERNE [Berne]. See also:
Bern
BERNE, ERIC LENNARD (1910-70) [Canadian-American author]
Lennard Gandalae
Ramsbottom Horsely
Peter Pinto
Cyprian St. Cyr
Berne, Leo. See:
DAVIES, LESLIE PURNELL
BERNERS, GERALD HUGH TYRWHITT-WILSON, 14TH BARON (1883-1950) [British composer]
Lord Berners
Gerald Tyrwhitt
Bernese Friendli, The. See:
MIND, GOTTFRIED
Bernhardt, Sarah. See:
BERNARD, HENRIETTE ROSINE
Bernhardt, The American. See: DUDLY, CAROLINE LOUISE
Berni. See also:
Bernie
BURNEY
Burney
Berni, Bernard. See:
ANZELEVITZ, BERNARD
Bernice May. See:
CROSS, ZORA BERNICE MAY
Bernie. See:
Berni
BIERMAN, BERNARD WILLIAM
BURNEY
Burney

Bernie, Ben. See:
ANZELEVITZ, BERNARD
Bernie Kane. See:
AQUINO, FRANK J.
BERNSTEIN, MORRIS (1916-) [American composer, author and publisher]
Morey Bernstein
BERQUIST, BERNARD H. (1903-62) [American composer and author]
Whitey Berquist
BERRA, LAWRENCE PETER (1925-) [American professional baseball player]
Yogi Berra
BERRIEN, JOHN Mac-PHERSON (1781-1856) [American statesman and senator from Georgia]
The American Cicero
Berrisford, Judith M., joint pseud. of CLIFFORD LEWIS (1912-) and his wife, MARY LEWIS (1921-) [English authors]
Berry Chetwynd. See:
RAYNER, CLAIRE
Berry, Erick. See:
BEST, MRS. ALLENA CHAMPLIN
Berry, Helen. See:
ROWLAND, DONALD SYDNEY
BERRY, JAMES (1932-) [American cartoonist and author]
Jim Berry
Berry, Jules. See:
PAUFICHET, JULES
BERRY, LEON (1910-41) [American jazz musician (tenor saxophone)]
Chu Berry
BERRY, MARTHA McCHESNEY (1866-1942) [American educator and philanthropist]
Distinguished Citizen of Georgia
BERRYHILL, S. NEWTON (1830-88) [American poet]
The Backwoods Poet
BERSHAD, SHELDON (1907-) [American stage and motion picture actor]
Sheldon Leonard
Bert. See:
BURT
Burt
Burte
DAHLANDER, NILS-BERTIL
LEIGHTON, JAMES ALBERT
STOUT, HERBERT E.
WILLIAMS, EGBERT AUSTIN
Bert Lahr. See:
LAHRHEIM, IRVING
Berta. See also:
Bertha
Birtha
Berta Ruck. See:
ONIONS, MRS. GEORGE OLIVER
BERTELSON, EMILY MARIE (1923-) [American stage, radio and motion picture actress]
Marie Windsor
Bertha. See also:
Berta
Birtha
Bertha M. Clay. See:
BRAME, CHARLOTTE MARY
CORYELL, JOHN RUSSELL
DEY, FREDERICK VAN RENSSELAER
HARBAUGH, THOMAS CHALMERS
Bertha T. Bishop. See:
RYMER, JAMES MALCOLM
Bertita Harding. See:
RADETZKY VON RADETZ, COUNTESS BERTHA LEONARZ DE HARDING
BERTOCCI, CHIARINA FRANCESCA (1924-) [American jazz musician (singer)]
Frances Wayne
BERTOCCI, NICHOLAS (1921-) [American jazz musician (clarinet, leader)]
Nick Jerret
Bertram. See:
EDWARDS, HERBERT

CHARLES
BERTRAM, CHARLES (1723-65) [English literary figure and forger]
Charles Julius
BERTRAND, LOUIS JACQUES NAPOLÉON (1807-41) [French writer of prose poems]
Aloysius
Berwick, Mary. See: PROCTOR, ADELAIDE ANNE
Berwick, Miss Mary. See: PROCTOR, ADELAIDE ANNE
Beryl Grey. See: SVENSON, MRS. SVEN GUSTAV
Beryl Moore. See: SMITH-WOODS, DOROTHY BERYL
Beryl Williams. See: EPSTEIN, BERYL WILLIAMS
Besieger of Cities (Poliorcetes). See: DEMETRIUS I
Bess. See: NORTON, OLIVE MARION
Bess, Edgeworth. See: LYON, BESS
Bess, Good Queen. See: ELIZABETH I
Bessie. See: BREUER, ELIZABETH
BESSIE, ALVAH. See: Hollywood Ten, The
Bessie Bellwood. See: MAHONEY, BESSIE
Bessie Love. See: HORTON, JUANITA
BEST, CAROL ANN (fl. mid-20th cent.) [English author]
Susan Ash
Best Foods Boys, The. See: Happiness Boys, The
BEST, MRS. ALLENA CHAMPLIN (1892-) [writer of children's stories]
Erick
Erick Berry
BEST, OSWALD HERBERT (1894-) [English actor]
Herbert Best
BEST, RAYLEIGH BRETON AMIS (1905-) [British journalist and author]
Breton Amis
Best Read Man of the Century, The. See: LOWELL, JAMES RUSSELL
Best Recruiting Sergeant, Our. See: NAST, THOMAS
BEST, WILLIE (1916-62) [American Negro motion picture actor]
Sleep'n Eat
Beston, Henry. See: SHEAHAN, HENRY BESTON
Beston, Henry B. See: SHEAHAN, HENRY BESTON
Bet-a-million. See: GATES, JOHN WARNE
Beth A. Retner. See: BROWN, BETH
Beth St. John. See: JOHN, ELIZABETH BEAMAN
Bethel. See: HILL, DANIEL HARVEY
BETHEL, DAWN (c. 1930-) [American dancer and motion picture actress]
Sheree North
Bethune, J. C. See: ELLIS, EDWARD SYLVESTER
BETHUNE, THOMAS GREEN (1849-1908) [American Negro musical prodigy]
Blind Tom
Betsy. See: WARREN, ELIZABETH AVERY
Betsy Adams. See: PITCHER, GLADYS
Betsy Allen. See: CAVANNA, ELIZABETH ALLEN
Betsy Blair. See: BOGER, BETSY
Betsy Hamilton. See: MOORE, IDORA McCLELLAN

Betta St. John. See:
STREIDLER, BETTY
Bette. See:
BETTI
Betty
DAVIS, RUTH ELIZABETH
Betteridge, Anne. See:
POTTER, MARGARET NEWMAN
BETTERTON, THOMAS (c.1635-1710) [English actor and dramatist]
The English Roscius
BETTI. See also:
Bette
Betty
BETTI, BERNARDINO DI (1454-1513) [Italian painter]
Pinturicchio
Bettina. See:
EHRLICH, BETTINA BAUER
VON HUTTON ZUM STOLZENBERG, BETSY RIDDLE, FREIFRAU
BETTS, WALTER M. (1898-) [American professional baseball player]
Huck
Betty. See:
Bette
BETTI
CAVANNA, ELIZABETH ALLEN
FURNESS, ELIZABETH MARY
JOHN, ELIZABETH BEAMAN
VAN DER SMISSEN, MARGARET ELISABETH
WASON, ELIZABETH
Betty Bacall. See:
BOGART, BETTY JOAN PEPSKE BACALL
Betty Baker. See:
VENTURO, BETTY LOU BAKER
Betty Blockinger. See:
BLOCKLINGER, PEGGY O'MORE
Betty Blythe. See:
SLAUGHTER, ELIZABETH BLYTHE
Betty Burke. See:
STUART, CHARLES EDWARD LOUIS PHILIP CASIMIR
Betty Carter. See:
JONES, LILLIE MAE
Betty Hutton. See:
THORNBURG, BETTY JANE
Betty MacDonald. See:
HESKETT, ANNE ELIZABETH CAMPBELL BARD
Betty Morgan Bowen. See:
WEST, BETTY
Betty Paoli. See:
GLUCK, BARBARA ELIZABETH
Betty Watson. See:
HALL, ELIZABETH WATSON
BETTY, WILLIAM HENRY WEST (1791-1874) [English actor and child prodigy]
Master Betty
The Infant Roscius
The Young Roscius
BETZ, EVA KELLY (fl. 1952-65) [American author]
Caroline Peters
Beverley. See:
TUCKER, NATHANIEL BEVERLEY
Beverley, Alfred of. See:
ALREDUS (ALURED) (ALUREDUS) (ALFRED)
Beverly Garland. See:
CAMPBELL, BEVERLY
Beverly Sills. See:
SILVERMAN, BELLE
BEVIN, ERNEST (1881-1951) [English labor statesman]
The Docker's K.C.
Bey, Kemal. See:
NAMIK, MEHMED
BEY, RAHMAN (c.1900-) [Egyptian illusionist]
The Egyptian Miracle Man
BEY, ROOSEVELT SYKES (1906-) [American jazz musician (singer, piano)]
Roosevelt Sykes

BEY, TURHAN SELAHATTIN SAHULTAVY (1920-) [Turkish motion picture actor]
Turhan Bey
BEYLE, MARIE HENRI (1783-1842) [French author]
Louis Alexandre César Bombet de Stendahl
Stendahl
BHARTRIHARI (BHARTRHARI) (fl. 1st half of 7th cent. A.D.) [Hindu poet, philosopher and legendary prince]
The Greatest Poet Who Wrote in Sanskrit
BHOSALE, YESHWANTRAO P. (1904-) [Indian author]
Pratap Roy Ramala
Ramala Pratap Roy
Bialk, Elisa. See: KRAUTTER, ELISA BIALK
BIANCHI, MARIO (1897-1950) [Italian silent motion picture comedian]
Monty Banks
BIAS. See: Seven Sages of Greece, The.
BIBERMAN, HERBERT J. See: Hollywood Ten, The
Bible-Class Man, The. See: STUART, JAMES EWELL BROWN
BIBLE, DANA XENOPHON (1891-) [American football coach]
D. X.
Biblical Learning in America, The Father of. See: STUART, MOSES
Bibliography, The Father of. See: TRITHEIM, JOHANNES
Bibliography, The Father of Universal. See: GESSNER, KONRAD VON
Bibliophile, P. L. Jacob. See: LACROIX, PAUL
BICKEL. See also: BICKLE
BICKEL, FREDERICK McINTYRE (1897-) [American stage and motion picture actor]
Frederick March
Bickerdyke, John. See: COOK, CHARLES HENRY
BICKERDYKE, MARY ANN BALL (1817-1901) [American nurse]
Brigadier Commanding Hospitals
Mother Bickerdyke
Bickerstaff. See also: Beggarstaff BICKERSTAFFE
Bickerstaff, Isaac. See: STEELE, SIR RICHARD SWIFT, JONATHAN WEST, BENJAMIN
BICKERSTAFFE. See also: Beggarstaff Bickerstaff
BICKERSTAFFE-DREW, FRANCIS BROWNING DREW, COUNT (1858-1928) [English priest, novelist and essayist]
John Ayscough
BICKHAM, JACK MILES (1930-) [American author]
Jeff Clinton
John Miles
BICKLE. See also: BICKEL
BICKLE, JUDITH BRUNDRETT (fl. 1930-62) [British author]
J. Tweedale
BICKLE, PHYLLIS (1915-) [British stage and motion picture actress]
Phyllis Calvert
BICKMORE, ALBERT SMITH (1839-1914) [American educator and naturalist]
The Father of the Museum
BICKNELL, JOSHUA (1759-1837) [American politician, active in Rhode Island politics]
Old Aristides
Biddenden Maids, The, nickname given MARY CHULKHURST (1100-34) and her sister,

ELIZABETH CHULKHURST (1100-34), twin English sisters born joined together
BIDDLE, CLEMENT (1740-1814) [American Revolutionary army officer; personal friend of GEORGE WASHINGTON]
The Quaker Soldier
BIDDLE, JOHN (1615-62) [English Unitarian clergyman]
The Father of English Unitarianism
BIDDLE, NICHOLAS (1786-1844) [American financier and bank president]
Emperor Nick of the Bribery Bank
Biddy. See:
REED, THOMAS BRACKETT
Bide. See:
DUDLEY, WALTER BRONSON
Bideford Postman, The. See:
CAPERN, EDWARD
BIDEN, EDMOND P. (1898-1959) [American playwright and motion picture director]
Preston Sturges
BIDEU, LOU (1919-) [American composer, comedian, author and publisher]
Lew Bedell
BIEDA, RANIERI DA (died 1118) [Supreme Pontiff of Roman Catholic Church]
Pope Paschal II
BIEL (BYLL), GABRIEL (died 1495) [German scholastic philosopher]
The Last of the Schoolmen
Bielyi, Sergei. See:
HOLLO, ANSELM
Bien-Aimé, Le (The Well-Beloved). See:
LOUIS XV
BIEN, ROBERT TAYLOR (1878-1965) [American motion picture actor]
Robert Warwick
Bienvenida. See:
MEJÍAS, ANTONIO
MEJÍAS, JOSÉ
MEJÍAS, JUAN
MEJÍAS, MANOLO
RAPELA, MANUEL MEJÍAS Y
BIERBOWER, ELSIE (1889-1956), [American variety performer, musical comedy librettist and composer]
Elsie Janis
BIERCE, AMBROSE GWINNETT (1842-1914?) [American author and journalist]
Bitter Bierce
Dod Grile
BIERMAN, BERNARD WILLIAM (1894-) [American football coach]
Bernie
The Silver Fox of the Northland
Big. See:
MILLER, CLARENCE H.
Big Al. See:
CAPONE, ALPHONSE
Big Bill. See:
BROONZY, WILLIAM LEE
DWYER, WILLIAM VINCENT
HAYWOOD, WILLIAM DUDLEY
PINKERTON, WILLIAM A.
THOMPSON, WILLIAM HALE
TILDEN, WILLIAM TATEM, JR.
Big Black. See:
RAY, DANNY
Big Boy. See:
WILLIAMS, GUINN
Big Boy, The. See:
CAPONE, ALPHONSE
Big Buckeye, The. See:
SPROAT, EBENEZER
Big Captain, The. See:
CRAWFORD, WILLIAM
Big Chief. See:
CURTIS, CHARLES
MOORE, RUSSELL
Big Eye. See:
NELSON, LOUIS DELISLE
Big Feller, The. See:
SULLIVAN, TIMOTHY DANIEL

Big Four, The, collective nickname of COLLIS POTTER HUNTINGTON (1821-1900), CHARLES CROCKER (1822--88), AMASA LELAND STANFORD (1824-93) and MARK HOPKINS (1813-78) [American railroad builders]
Big Game Hunter, The. See: TINKHAM, GEORGE HOLDEN
Big Guy, The. See: DIMAGGIO, JOSEPH PAUL, JR.
WILLIAMS, THEODORE SAMUEL
Big Hal. See: SHARP, HAROLD SPENCER
Big Jake. See: KRAMER, JOHN ALBERT
Big Jim. See: COLOSIMO, JAMES
FARLEY, JAMES ALOYSIUS
Big Joe. See: TURNER, JOSEPH
Big John. See: PATTON, JOHN
Big Judge. See: CONNOLLY, RICHARD
POWELL, JOHN STEPHEN
Big Lip, The. See: MAILS, WALTER
Big Man from Little Egypt, The. See: KELLER, KENT ELLSWORTH
Big Medicine. See: KELLY, CLINTON WAYNE
Big Moose. See: EARNSHAW, GEORGE LIVINGSTON
WALSH, EDWARD AUGUSTIN
Big-Navy Claude. See: SWANSON, CLAUDE AUGUSTUS
Big O, The. See: ROBERTSON, OSCAR PALMER
Big Poison. See: WANER, PAUL GLEE
Big Red, See: LITTLE, MALCOLM
Big Sid. See: CATLETT, SIDNEY
Big Six. See: AUKER, ELDEN LEROY
MATHEWSON, CHRISTOPHER
Big Steve. See: OWEN, STEPHEN JOSEPH
Big T. See: TEAGARDEN, WELDON JOHN
Big Three, The, collective nickname of THOMAS WOODROW WILSON (1856-1924), DAVID LLOYD GEORGE (1863-1945) and GEORGES CLEMENCEAU (1841-1929) [American, English and French representatives of their countries at the 1919 Peace Conference in Paris, France]
Big Three, The, collective nickname of SIR WINSTON LEONARD SPENCER CHURCHILL (1871-1965), YOSIF VISSARIONOVICH DJUGASHVILI (Joseph Stalin) (1879-1953) and FRANKLIN DELANO ROOSEVELT (1882-1945), [English, Russian and American representatives of their countries during World War II]
Big Three, The. See also: CHURCHILL, SIR WINSTON LEONARD SPENCER
CLEMENCEAU, GEORGES
DJUGASHVILI, YOSIF VISSARIONOVICH
GEORGE, DAVID LLOYD
ROOSEVELT, FRANKLIN DELANO
WILSON, THOMAS WOODROW
Big Thunder. See: WAYNE, ANTHONY
Big Tim. See: SULLIVAN, TIMOTHY DANIEL
Big Tiny. See: LITTLE, DUDLEY
Big Train, The. See:

JOHNSON, WALTER PERRY
SISK, JOHN

BIGARD, LEON ALBANY (1906-) [American jazz musician (clarinet)]
Barney Bigard

BIGELOW. See also:
Biglow

BIGELOW, WILLIAM FREDERICK (1879-) [American editor]
Charles Chatterbox

Bigfoot. See:
WALLACE, WILLIAM ALEXANDER ANDERSON

Biggest Hotel Man in the World, The. See:
HILTON, CONRAD NICHOLSON

BIGGS, BENJAMIN THOMAS (1821-93) [American statesman; governor of Delaware]
The Delaware Plowboy

Biglow. See also:
BIGELOW

Biglow, Hosea. See:
LOWELL, JAMES RUSSELL

Bigly, Cantrell A. See:
PECK, GEORGE WASHINGTON

BIGORDI, RIDOLFO (1483-1561) [Florentine painter, goldsmith and silversmith]
Ghirlandajo
Grillandajo

BIGORDI, TOMMASO (1449-98) [Florentine painter, goldsmith and silversmith]
Ghirlandajo
Grillandajo

Bil. See:
BAIRD, WILLIAM BRITTON
BIEL
Bill

Bilbao, Cocherito de. See:
IBARRA, CASTOR JAUREGUIBEITIA

BILBO, THEODORE GILMORE (1877-1947) [American senator from Mississippi]
The Two-edged Knife

Bill. See:
ADAMS, BERTRAM MARTIN
ADLER, WILLIAM
BALLINGER, WILLIAM SANBORN
BASIE, WILLIAM
BENDIX, WILLIAM
BERKSON, WILLIAM C.
BIEL
Bil
BLASS, WILLIAM
BOYD, WILLIAM LAWRENCE
BROWN, WILLIAM LOUIS
BUDINGTON, WILLIAM STONE
COSBY, WILLIAM HENRY, JR.
CULLEN, WILLIAM LAWRENCE
CUNNINGHAM, ELIJAH WILLIAM
DANA, WILLIAM
DICKEY, WILLIAM MALCOLM
FINEGAN, WILLIAM I.
GUNN, WILLIAM HARRISON
HART, WILLIAM S.
KNOTT, WILLIAM CECIL, JR.
KNOX, WILLIAM
KNUDSEN, WILLIAM S.
LEONARD, WILLIAM AUGUSTUS
MAULDIN, WILLIAM
MOYERS, BILLY DON
NYE, EDGAR WILSON
PORTER, WILLIAM SYDNEY
RIVIERE, WILLIAM ALEXANDER
ROBINSON, WILLIAM
ROBINSON, WILLIAM WHEELER
RUDOLPH, WILLIAM
SEVERN, WILLIAM IRVING
SNYDER, WILLIAM

SPIVERY, WILLIAM
SURFACE, WILLIAM E.
TERRY, WILLIAM HAROLD
TILDEN, WILLIAM TATEM, JR.
TURNER, WILLIAM PRICE
VAUGHAN, WILLIAM EDWARD
VEECK, WILLIAM LOUIS, JR.
WALLACE, WILLIAM N.
WANNAN, WILLIAM FIELDING

Bill, Alfalfa. See:
MURRAY, WILLIAM HENRY

Bill Arp. See:
SMITH, CHARLES HENRY

Bill, Barnacle. See:
SUTPHIN, WILLIAM HALSTEAD

Bill, Big. See:
BROONZY, WILLIAM LEE
DWYER, WILLIAM VINCENT
HAYWOOD, WILLIAM DUDLEY
PINKERTON, WILLIAM A.
THOMPSON, WILLIAM HALE
TILDEN, WILLIAM TATEM, JR.

Bill Bonney. See:
KEEVIL, HENRY JOHN

Bill, Breezy. See:
LEWIN, WILLIAM CHARLES JAMES

Bill, Bristol. See:
UNKNOWN

Bill, Buffalo. See:
CODY, WILLIAM FREDERICK
MATTHEWSON, WILLIAM

Bill, Cherokee. See:
HASTINGS, WILLIAM WIRT

Bill, Cockle-bur. See:
MURRAY, WILLIAM HENRY

Bill Cody the Scout. See:
CODY, WILLIAM FREDERICK

Bill Cody the Wagonmaster. See: CODY, WILLIAM FREDERICK

Bill, Duch. See:
HICKOCK, JAMES BUTLER

Bill, Duck. See:
HICKOCK, JAMES BUTLER

Bill, Dutch. See:
HICKOCK, JAMES BUTLER

Bill Fields. See:
DUKINFIELD, WILLIAM CLAUDE

Bill Gray, Captain. See:
GRAY, WILLIAM BITTLE

Bill Haywood, Big. See:
HAYWOOD, WILLIAM DUDLEY

Bill, Horizontal. See:
MORRISON, WILLIAM RALLS

Bill J. Carol. See:
KNOTT, WILLIAM CECIL, JR.

Bill, Kaiser. See:
WILLIAM II

Bill, Little. See:
JOHNSTON, WILLIAM M.

Bill, Memphis. See:
TERRY, WILLIAM HAROLD

Bill, Moratorium. See:
LENKE, WILLIAM

Bill Owen. See:
ROWBOTHAM, BILL

Bill Parker. See:
PARSONS, WILLIAM

Bill, Pawnee. See:
LILLIE, MAJOR GORDON W.

Bill Pembury, See:
GROOM, ARTHUR WILLIAM

Bill Poole, Butcher. See:
POOLE, WILLIAM

Bill, Shanghai. See:
HICKOCK, JAMES BUTLER

Bill the Builder. See:
McADOO, WILLIAM GIBBS

Bill the Butcher. See:
POOLE, WILLIAM

Bill, The Father of the New York State Boxing. See:
WALKER, JAMES JOHN
Bill the Pony Express Rider, Wild. See:
CODY, WILLIAM FREDERICK
Bill, Uncle. See:
WOLSEY, WILLIAM FRANKLYN
Bill, Wild. See:
DAVIS, WILLIAM STRETHEN
DAVISON, WILLIAM
ELLIOTT, GORDON
HICKOCK, JAMES BUTLER
Bill Williams. See:
KATT, WILLIAM
Bill, Wyoming. See:
PATTEN, WILLIAM GILBERT
BILLECARD, DENISE (1925-) [French motion picture actress]
Denise Darcel
Billex Muller. See:
ELLIS, EDWARD SYLVESTER
Billie. See:
BARTLETT, MARIE SWAN
Billy
BURKE, MARY WILLIAM ETHELBERT APPLETON
Billie Dove. See:
BOHNY, LILIAN
Billie Holiday. See:
McKAY, ELEANOR GOUGH
Billie the Kid. See:
Billy the Kid.
RUSSELL, WILLIAM EUSTIS
Billings, Josh. See:
SHAW, HENRY WHEELER
Billy. See:
BAUER, WILLIAM HENRY
Billie
CASPER, WILLIAM EARL, JR.
ECKSTINE, WILLIAM CLARENCE
GRAHAM, WILLIAM FRANKLIN
HILL, WILLIAM JOSEPH
MAY, WILLIAM
MILLS, WILLIAM R.
MITCHELL, WILLIAM
SOUTHWORTH, WILLIAM H.
STRAYHORN, WILLIAM
SUNDAY, WILLIAM ASHLEY
TALBERT, WILLIAM FRANKLIN, III
TAYLOR, WILLIAM
VER PLANCK, JOHN
WARREN, WILLIAM STEPHEN
Billy, Bronco. See:
ANDERSON, G. M.
Billy, Captain. See:
FAWCETT, WILLIAM HAMILTON
McCUE, WILLIAM
Billy Cody the Messenger, Little. See:
CODY, WILLIAM FREDERICK
Billy de Wolfe. See:
JONES, WILLIAM ANDREW
Billy Duke. See:
TESONE, WILLIAM N.
Billy, Dutch. See:
WILLIAM III
Billy, Extra. See:
SMITH, WILLIAM
Billy Graham. See:
GRAHAM, WILLIAM FRANKLIN
Billy Graham, Dr. See:
GRAHAM, WILLIAM FRANKLIN
Billy Jones. See:
Happiness Boys, The
Billy, Little. See:
SMITH, WILLIAM RUSSELL
Billy Merson. See:
THOMPSON, WILLIAM HENRY
Billy, Old. See:
SHERMAN, WILLIAM TECUMSEH
Billy Rose. See:
ROSENBERG, WILLIAM SAMUEL
Billy, Silly. See:

WILLIAM IV
WILLIAM FREDERICK
Billy Snel. See:
SNELL, WILLIAM
Billy Sunday. See:
SUNDAY, WILLIAM ASHLEY
Billy Sunday of Japan, The. See: KIMURA, HENRY SEIMATSU
Billy Sunday, The Black. See:
WILLBANKS, ALEXANDER
Billy the Kid. See:
Billie the Kid
BONNEY, WILLIAM H.
SOUTHWORTH, WILLIAM H.
Billy, Uncle. See:
SHERMAN, WILLIAM TECUMSEH
SMITH, WILLIAM
WORKMAN, WILLIAM HENRY
Billy Young. See:
D'ARCY, COLIN
BINDER, OTTO OSCAR (1911-) [American author]
Eando Binder
John Coleridge
Gordon A. Giles
Dean D. O'Brien
Bing. See:
CROSBY, HARRY LILLIS
Bingham, Carson. See:
CASSIDAY, BRUCE BINGHAM
BINGHAM, HENRY HARRISON (1841-1912) [American statesman; representative from Pennsylvania]
The Father of the House
BINGHAM, MADELEINE (1912-) [British author and playwright]
Julia Mannering
Bingham, Sallie. See:
ELLSWORTH, SALLIE BINGHAM
Bingle, Der. See:
CROSBY, HARRY LILLIS
Bink. See:
NOLL, LOU BARKER
BINNEY, CECIL (1897-) [British barrister and author]
Ambrose Hoopington
Binnie Hale. See:
MUNRO, BERNICE HALE
Biographer, The First Professional English. See:
WALTON, IZAAK
Bion. See:
SOUTHEY, ROBERT
BIONDOLILLO, GASPARE (1903-) [American motion picture actor]
Jack La Rue
Bip. See:
MARCEAU, MARCEL
Birch. See also:
Berch
Birch Arnold. See:
BARTLETT, ALICE ELINOR
Bird. See:
BYRD
Byrd
PARKER, CHARLES
Bird, Brandon
Harris Evans, joint pseuds. of GEORGE BIRD EVANS (1906-) and his wife KAY HARRIS EVANS (1906-) [American authors]
BIRD, CYRIL KENNETH (1887-) [British artist and editor]
Fougasse
BIRD, FRANCIS WILLIAM (1809-94) [American scholar]
The Sage of Walpole
BIRD, FREDERIC MAYER (1838-1908) [American Episcopal clergyman, novelist, hymnologist and editor]
Robert Timsol
Bird, Isabella. See:
BISHOP, ISABELLA BIRD
Bird, Lady. See:
JOHNSON, CLAUDIA ALTA TAYLOR
Bird, Little. See:
HEATH, JAMES EDWARD
Bird, Swift. See:

HARE, WILLIAM
HOBART
Bird, The Arkansas Humming. See:
WARNECKE, LONNIE
BIRD, WILLIAM RICHARD
(1891-) [American
author and government
official]
Will R. Bird
Bird Woman, The. See:
SACAJAWEA (SACAGAWEA)
Bird, Yellow (Chees-quat-a-
law-ny). See:
RIDGE, JOHN ROLLIN
Bird, Zenobia. See:
LEFEVRE, LAURA
ZENOBIA
BIRDE. See:
BYRD (BIRDE), WILLIAM
Birds, John o'. See:
BURROUGHS, JOHN
BIRLA, LAKSHMINIWAS (1909-)
[Indian business executive
and author]
Achyut
Birmingham, G.A. See:
HANNAY, JAMES OWEN
Birmingham, George A. See:
HANNAY, JAMES OWEN
Birmingham Poet, The. See:
FREETH, JOHN
Birmingham, The Duke of. See:
POWELL, JAMES ROBERT
BIRNBAUM, NATHAN (1864-)
[German author]
Mathias Acher
BIRNBAUM, NATHAN (1896-)
[American comedian and
actor]
George Burns
BIRREN, FABER (1900-)
[American color con-
sultant and author]
Gregor Lang
Martin Lang
Birth, The Twin of Heavenlier.
See: BEAUMONT,
FRANCIS
Birtha. See:
Berta
Bertha
Ella
BISBEE, AILEEN (c.1885-)
[American silent motion
picture actress]
Aileen Pringle
BISCH, EDITH (1907-)
[Austrian author]
Edith de Born
BISCHOFF, JULIA BRISTOL
(1909-) [American
teacher, editor and writer]
Julie Arnoldy
Bish. See:
BISHOP, WILLIAM AVERY
Bishop. See:
BUNYAN, JOHN
SHEEN, FULTON JOHN
HATTO II
Bishop, Bertha T. See:
RYMER, JAMES MALCOLM
BISHOP, CURTIS KENT
(1912-) [American author]
Curt Brandon
Curt Carroll
Bishop, E. Morchard. See:
STONOR, OLIVER
Bishop, Evelyn Morchard. See:
STONOR, OLIVER
Bishop from Virginia, The Dry.
See: CANNON, BISHOP
JAMES, JR.
BISHOP, ISABELLA BIRD
(1831-1904) [British
travel author]
Isabella Bird
Bishop, Jack. See:
DORMAN, MICHAEL
BISHOP, JAMES ALONZO
(1907-) [American
journalist and author]
Jim Bishop
Bishop, Joey. See:
GOTTLIEB, JOSEPH
ABRAHAM
Bishop, Morchard. See:
STONOR, OLIVER
BISHOP, MORRIS (1893-)
[American author]
W. Bolingbroke Johnson
Bishop of All Outdoors, The.
See: JACKSON, SHELDON
Bishop of America, The Mis-
sionary. See:
DOANE, GEORGE WASHING-
TON

Bishop of Congregational
Churches. See:
WEEDEN, CHARLES
FOSTER
Bishop of Hippo, The. See:
AUGUSTINIUS,
AURELIUS
Bishop, The Boy. See:
NICOLAUS, ST.
Bishop, The Fighting. See:
POLK, LEONIDAS
Bishop, The Good. See:
OTEY, JAMES
HARVEY
Bishop, The Mormon. See:
KING, WILLIAM HENRY
Bishop, The Singing. See:
McCABE, CHARLES
CARDWELL
BISHOP, WILLIAM AVERY
(1894-1956) [Canadian
military aviator; World
War I ace]
Billy Bishop
Bish
BISMARCK. See:
VON BISMARCK, PRINCE
OTTO EDUARD
LEOPOLD
Bismarck of Asia, The. See:
LI HUNG CHANG
Bisque, Anatole. See:
BOSQUET, ALAIN
Bitch of Buchenwald, The. See:
KOCH, ILSE
Bite, Ben. See:
SCHNECK, STEPHEN
Bitter. See:
BIERCE, AMBROSE
GWINNETT
BITZER, MARJORIE (1916-)
[American motion picture
actress]
Lynn Bari
BITZIUS, ALBERT (1797-1854)
[Swiss novelist and pastor]
Jeremias Gotthelf
Bix. See:
BEIDERBECKE, LEON
BISMARCK
BIXBY, HORACE EZRA (1829-
1912) [Mississippi River
pilot]
The Lightning Pilot
BIXBY, JEROME LEWIS
(1923-) [American
author]
Jay B. Drexel
Emerson Jans
D. B. Lewis
Harry Neal
Albert Russell
J. Russell
M. St. Vivant
Bixby, Ray Z. See:
TRALINS, S. ROBERT
Black. See:
AGNES, COUNTESS OF
DUNBAR
Black Bart. See:
BOLTON, CHARLES E.
ROBERTS, CAPTAIN
BARTHOLOMEW
Black Bart the Po8. See:
BOLTON, CHARLES E.
BLACK, BENJAMIN (1889-1950)
[Anglo-American theater
orchestra conductor]
Ben Black
Black, Big. See:
RAY, DANNY
Black Billy Sunday, The. See:
WILLBANKS, ALEXANDER
Black Captain, The. See:
DAVIDOV, DENIS
VASSILIEVITCH
Black Charlie. See:
NAPIER, SIR CHARLES
Black Crows. See:
Two Black Crows
Black Dan. See:
McFARLAND, DANIEL
WEBSTER, DANIEL
Black Dan, Little. See:
WEBSTER, DANIEL
Black David. See:
FORMAN, DAVID
Black Diamond, The. See:
CRIBB, TOM
Black Dick. See:
HOWE, RICHARD, 1ST
EARL
Black Douglas, The. See:
DOUGLAS, ARCHIBALD
DOUGLAS, JAMES
DOUGLAS, SIR JAMES

DOUGLAS, WILLIAM
Black Eagle of Illinois. See:
LOGAN, JOHN ALEXANDER
Black, Gavin. See:
WYND, OSWALD MORRIS
Black George (Karadjordje). See: CZERNY, GEORGE
Black Giant, The. See:
WEBSTER, DANIEL
Black Hobart. See:
SANDERS, ED
Black Horowitz, The. See:
WALLER, THOMAS WRIGHT
Black Hussar of Literature, The. See: SCOTT, SIR WALTER
Black, Ivory. See:
JANVIER, THOMAS ALLIBONE
Black Jack. See:
KEMBLE, JOHN PHILIP
LOGAN, JOHN ALEXANDER
PERSHING, JOHN JOSEPH
BLACK, JAMES (1728-99) [Scottish chemist]
The Nestor of the Chemical Revolution
Black Knight of the Border, The. See:
MALONE, PERCY LAY
Black Knight of the South, The. See: McCLUNG, ALEXANDER
Black, Lionel. See:
BARKER, DUDLEY
Black, Mansell. See:
TREVOR, ELLESTON
Black Patti. See:
JONES, SISSIERRETTA JOYNER
Black Prince of Cricketers, The. See:
RANJITSINHJI, PRINCE
Black Prince, The. See:
EDWARD, PRINCE OF WALES
Black Republican Blair. See:
BLAIR, FRANCIS PRESTON, JR.
Black Republican, The. See:
BLAIR, FRANCIS PRESTON, JR.
Black Roger. See:
TOUHY, ROGER
Black Snake, The. See:
WAYNE, ANTHONY
Black Spurgeon of America, The. See:
WALKER, CHARLES THOMAS
Black Swan, The. See:
GREENFIELD, ELIZABETH TAYLOR
Black, The. See:
FULC (FULK) (FOULQUES) III
HENRY III
Black, The Woman In. See:
GILBERT, MARIE DOLORES ELIZA ROSANNA
Black Tom. See:
CORWIN, THOMAS
Black, Vince. See:
CERNEY, JAMES VINCENT
Blackbeard. See:
TEACH (THATCH), EDWARD
Blackbeard the Buccaneer. See:
TEACH (THATCH), EDWARD
BLACKBURN, VICTORIA GRACE (18??-1928) [Canadian author and journalist]
Fan Fan
BLACKBURNE, RUSSELL (1886-) [American professional baseball coach]
Lena
BLACKETT, VERONICA HEATH STUART (1927-) [English author]
Veronica Heath
Blackguard Charlie. See:
PINCKNEY, CHARLES
Blackie. See:
Blacky
MANCUSO, AUGUST RODNEY
Blackie, Boston. See:
MORRIS, CHESTER
Blackmantle, Bernard. See:
WESTMACOTT, CHARLES MALLOY
BLACKMORE, RICHARD DODDRIDGE (1825-1900)

[English author]
The Market Gardener
BLACKMORE, SIR RICHARD (1654-1729) [English physician and writer]
The Father of the Bathos and Indeed the Homer of it
Blacksmith of Antwerp, The. See: MATSYS, QUENTIN
Blacksmith, The Flemish. See: MATSYS, QUENTIN
Blacksmith, The Learned. See: BURRITT, ELIHU
Blackstone, The American. See: KENT, JAMES
TUCKER, SAINT GEORGE
BLACKWELL, MRS. HENRY BROWN (1818-93) [American feminist]
Lucy Stone
BLACKWOOD, WILLIAM (1777-1834) [English magazine publisher]
Ebony
Blacky. See:
Blackie
MANGUM, LEO ALLAN
BLAICH, HANS ERICH (1873-1945) [German writer and translator]
Dr. Owlglass
Ratatöskr
BLAIK, EARL HENRY (1897-) [American football coach]
Colonel
Red
BLAIKLOCK, EDWARD MUSGRAVE (1903-) [British educator and author]
Grammaticus
BLAINE [Blaine]. See also: Blane
BLAINE, JAMES GILLESPIE (1830-93) [American statesman; Secretary of State]
Gladstone of America
Guano Statesman
Henry of Navarre
Magnetic Man
Magnetic Statesman
Man from Maine
Plumed Knight
Premier Blaine
Tattooed Knight
Tattooed Man
Uncrowned King
Blaine, John. See: GOODWIN, HAROLD LELAND
Blaine, Sara. See: MORGAN, DIANA
Blaine, Vivian. See: STAPLETON, VIVIENNE
Blaine's Irishman. See: EGAN, PATRICK
Blair, Betsy. See: BOGER, BETSY
Blair, David. See: BUTTERFIELD, DAVID
BLAIR, DOROTHY. See: Scarlett, Roger
BLAIR, ERIC (1903-50) [English essayist and novelist]
George Orwell
BLAIR-FISH, WALLACE WILFRID (1889-) [English author]
Blair
BLAIR, FRANCIS PRESTON, JR. (1821-75) [American statesman; congressman from Missouri]
The Black Republican
Black Republican Blair
Blair, Lucile. See: YEAKLEY, MARJORY HALL
Blairman, Jacqueline. See: PINTO, JACQUELINE HARRIS
Blaisdell, Anne. See: LININGTON, ELIZABETH
Blake, Andrea. See: WEALE, ANNE
Blake, Andrew. See: JANIFER, LAURENCE MARK
BLAKE, JAMES HUBERT (1883-) [American jazz musician (piano, composer)]
Eubie Blake
BLAKE, JOHN FRED (1889-)

[American professional baseball player]
Sheriff Blake
BLAKE, JOSEPH (died 1723) [English burglar]
Blueskin
Blake, Katherine. See: WALTER, DOROTHY BLAKE
Blake, Kay. See: WALTER, DOROTHY BLAKE
BLAKE, LILLIE DEVEREUX (1835-1913) [American novelist and reformer]
Tiger Lily
Blake, Lowell. See: SCHOENFELD, WILLIAM C.
Blake, Monica. See: MUIR, MARIE
Blake, Nicholas. See: DAY-LEWIS, CECIL
Blake, Redmond. See: AIKEN, ALBERT W. MORRIS, CHARLES SMITH
Blake, Robert. See: DAVIES, LESLIE PURNELL
Blake Savage. See: GOODWIN, HAROLD LELAND
Blake, Walker E. See: BUTTERWORTH, WILLIAM EDMUND III
BLAMAUER, KAROLINE (fl. 1920-35) [German singer and actress]
Lotta Lenya
BLAMIRE, SUSANNA (1747-94) [English poet]
The Muse of Cumberland
BLANC, DAMITA JO DE (1933?-) [American jazz musician (singer)]
Damita Jo
Blanc, The Monarch of Mont. See: SMITH, ALBERT RICHARD
Blanchan, Neltze. See: DOUBLEDAY, NELTZE DE GRAFF
BLANCHARD, FELIX ANTHONY (1924-) [former U.S. army cadet and football star]
Doc Blanchard
Mr. Inside
BLANCHARD, JACQUES (1600-38) [French painter]
The French Titian
BLANCHARD, JEAN PIERRE (1753-1809) [French aeronaut]
François Blanchard
BLANCHARD, WILLIAM (1769-1825) [English actor]
William Bentley
Blanche. See: FEARING, LILIAN BLANCHE
BLANCHET, FRANCIS HERBERT (1795-1883) [first Roman Catholic Archbishop of Oregon)]
The Apostle of Oregon
Blanco, Giuseppe. See: WHITE, JOSEPH BLANCO
BLAND, GEORGE (died 1806) [English actor]
George Wilson
Bland, Lizzie. See: BROWN, ELIZABETH ANN
BLAND, MRS. HUBERT (from 1917 MRS. THOMAS TUCKER) (1858-1924) [English writer]
Edith Nesbit
BLAND, RICHARD (1710-76) [American patriot]
The Cato of the Revolution
BLAND, RICHARD PARKS (1835-99) [American representative from Missouri; leader of the Free Silver movement]
The Father of Free Silver
Silver Dick
BLAND, SCHUYLER OTIS (1872-) [American congressman from Virginia]
Bridge Builder Bland
Blane. See also: BLAINE Blaine
Blane, Daphne du. See: GROOM, ARTHUR WILLIAM
BLANKENBURG, RUDOLPH (1843-1918) [German-American humanitarian; Mayor of Philadelphia]

Old Dutch Cleanser
The Old War Horse of Reform
BLANTON, THOMAS LINDSAY (1872-) [American congressman from Texas]
The Czar of the District
Hold That Line
The Scourge of the District Police
Talkative Tom
The Watchdog of the Treasury
BLASKO, BELA LUGOSI, or ARISZTID OLT (1882-1956) [Hungarian stage and motion picture actor]
Bela Lugosi
Blasphemous. See: BALFOUR, SIR JAMES
BLASS, WILLIAM (1922-) [American fashion designer]
Bill Blass
BLATCHFORD, ROBERT (1851-1943) [English socialist journalist]
Nunquam
BLATTY, WILLIAM PETER (1928-) [American editor and author]
Terence Clyne
BLAU, VICENTE (1935-) [Spanish bullfighter]
El Tino
BLAZE, ANGE HENRI (1813-88) [French poet and translator]
Henri Blaze
Blaze de Bury
F. de Lagenevais
Hans Warner
Bledlow, John. See: VALE, HENRY EDMUND THEODORIC
Bleeker, Sonia. See: ZIM, SONIA BLEEKER
BLESH, RUDOLPH PICKETT (1899-) [American artist and writer on jazz]
Rudi Blesh
Blessed Giles. See: AEGIDIUS OF ASSISI
Blessed, The. See: CADWALADER (CADWALLADER) GERARD
Blessed Virgin Mary, The. See: MARY, ST.
BLEWETT, DOROTHY EMILIE (1898-) [Australian author]
Ann Praize
BLIEDUNG, ALEXANDER (1909-) [American actor]
John Beal
Bligh, Norman. See: NEUBAUER, WILLIAM ARTHUR
BLIGH, WILLIAM (c. 1753-1817) [British sailor, captain of the "Bounty"]
Bread-fruit Bligh
Blind. See: HARRY, BLIND
Blind Bard of the Chian Strand, The. See: HOMER
Blind Boss. See: BUCKLEY, CHRISTOPHER A.
Blind Emperor, The. See: LOUIS III
Blind Jack of Knaresborough. See: METCALF, JACK
Blind Man Eloquent. See: WEST, WILLIAM HENRY
Blind Man of Adria, The. See: GROTO, LUIGI
Blind, Mathilde. See: COHEN, MATHILDE
Blind Mechanician, The. See: STRONG, JOHN
Blind Minister, The. See: WOODBRIDGE, TIMOTHY
Blind Naturalist, The. See: HUBER, FRANÇOIS
Blind Old Bard, Scio's. See: HOMER
Blind Old Bard, The. See: HOMER
Blind Old Man of Scio's Rocky Isle, The. See: HOMER
Blind Poet, The. See: GROTO, LUIGI
MILTON, JOHN

Blind Preacher, The. See:
MILBURN, WILLIAM HENRY
WADDELL, JAMES
Blind Savant, The. See:
GORE, THOMAS PRYOR
Blind, The. See:
DIDYMUS OF ALEXANDRIA
LOUIS III
MAGNUS IV
Blind Tom. See:
BETHUNE, THOMAS GREEN
Blind Traveler, The. See:
HOLMAN, JAMES
Blind White Devil, The. See:
BUCKLEY, CHRISTOPHER A.
Blind Willie Dunn. See:
MASSARO, SALVATORE
Bliss, James L. See:
PORTER, WILLIAM SYDNEY
Bliss Lomax. See:
DRAGO, HENRY SINCLAIR
Bliss, Reginald. See:
WELLS, HERBERT GEORGE
BLIXEN-FINECKE, BARONESS KAREN (1885-) [Danish author]
Isak Dinesen
Blizzards, Old. See:
LORING, WILLIAM WING
BLOCH, RAYMOND A. (1902-) American orchestra conductor]
Ray Bloch
BLOCH, RUDOLPH EDGAR (1870-1940) [American newspaper columnist and editor]
Bruno Lessing
Block, The Old. See:
DELANO, ALONZO
Blockinger, Betty. See:
BLOCKLINGER, PEGGY O'MORE
BLOCKLINGER, PEGGY O'MORE (1895-) [American reporter, editor, librarian and author]
Betty Blockinger
Jeanne Bowman
Peggy O'More
BLOEDE, GERTRUDE (1845-1905) [German-American poet]
Stuart Sterne
BLOFELD, JOHN EATON CALTHORPE (1913-) [English educator and author]
Chu Fêng
Blondin, Charles. See:
GRAVELET, JEAN FRANÇOIS
Blood and Guts, Old. See:
PATTON, GEORGE SMITH, JR.
Blood and Iron, The Man of. See: VON BISMARCK, PRINCE OTTO EDUARD LEOPOLD
Blood, Matthew. See:
DRESSER, DAVIS
Blood, The Man of. See:
CHARLES I
SIMMONS, THOMAS
BLOOD, THOMAS (1618?-80) [Irish adventurer]
Colonel Blood
Bloody. See:
ABDUL HAMID II
MACKENZIE, SIR GEORGE
Bloody Bridles. See:
WAITE, DAVID HANSON
Bloody Butcher, The. See:
CUMBERLAND, WILLIAM AUGUSTUS, DUKE OF
Bloody Claverse. See:
GRAHAM, JOHN
Bloody Duke of Cumberland, The. See: CUMBERLAND, WILLIAM AUGUSTUS, DUKE OF
Bloody Mary. See:
MARY I
Bloody Red Baron, The. See:
VON RICHTHOFEN, BARON MANFRED
Bloody Shirt. See:
FORAKER, JOSEPH B.
BLOOM, MILTON (1906-) [American composer, trumpeter, and pianist]

Mickey Bloom
BLOOM, MURRAY (1889-) [American composer, author, and publisher]
Donald Murray
BLOOM, SEYMOUR I. (1911-) [American author and television writer]
Si Bloom
BLOOM, SOL (1870-1949) [American journalist, publisher and politician]
George Washington Bloom
The Savior of the Constitution
Bloomfield H. Moore, Mrs. See: MOORE, CLARA SOPHIA JESSUP
Bloomfield-Moore, Mrs. See: MOORE, CLARA SOPHIA JESSUP
BLOOMGARDEN, SOLOMON (1870-1927) [Lithuanian poet, essayist and translator]
Yehoash
Blossom. See: MILES, MAXINE FRANCES MARY FORBES-ROBERTSON
BLOUET, PAUL (1848-1903) [French author, journalist, lecturer and critic]
Max O'Rell
Blount, Anna. See: GALLICHAN, WALTER M.
BLOW, SUSAN ELIZABETH (1843-1916) [American educator]
The Mother of the Kindergarten
BLÜCHER, GEBHARD LEBERECHT VON, PRINCE OF WAHLSTADT (1742-1819) [Prussian field marshal]
Marshal Forwards
Bludgeon Satirist, A. See: HOPKINS, DR. LEMUEL
Blue. See: MITCHELL, RICHARD ALLEN
Blue Barron. See: FRIEDLAND, HARRY
Blue Jeans. See: WILLIAMS, JAMES DOUGLAS
Blue Light Elder, The. See: JACKSON, THOMAS JONATHAN
Blue Moon, At the Sign of the. See: LEWIS, DOMINIC BEVAN WYNDHAM
Blue-tooth. See: HAROLD
Blue, Wallace. See: KRAENZEL, MARGARET POWELL
Bluebeard. See: CONOMOR (COMORRE) RAIS (RETZ), GILLES DE
BLUEGE, OTTO ADAM (1910-) [American professional baseball player]
Squeaky
Blues Boy King. See: KING, RILEY B.
Blues, The Empress of the. See: SMITH, BESSIE
Blues, The Father of the. See: HANDY, WILLIAM CHRISTOPHER
Blueskin. See: BLAKE, JOSEPH
Bluestockings, Laureate of the. See: MORE, HANNAH
Bluestring, Robin. See: WALPOLE, SIR ROBERT
Bluff Ben Wade. See: WADE, BENJAMIN FRANKLIN
Bluff, Harry. See: MAURY, MATTHEW FONTAINE
Bluff King Hal. See: HENRY VIII
BLUMENBACH, JOHANN FRIEDRICH (1752-1840) [German naturalist, physiologist and anthropologist]
The Founder of the Science of Anthropology
BLUNCK, HANS FRIEDRICH (1888-) [German author]
Johann Friedrich Blunck
BLUNDELL, HAROLD (1902-) [English author]
George Bellairs

BLUNDELL, MRS. FRANCIS SWEETMAN (1930-) [English author, dramatist and novelist]
Mary E. Francis
Blunt, Don. See:
BOOTH, EDWIN
Bluphocks, Lucien. See:
SELDES, GILBERT VIVIAN
Blusa, Chico de la. See:
PASTOR, VICENTE
Blutig, Eduard. See:
GOREY, EDWARD St JOHN
Bly, Nellie. See:
SEAMAN, ELIZABETH COCHRAN
Blythe, Betty. See:
SLAUGHTER, ELIZABETH BLYTHE
BLYTHE, DIANA (1921-60) [American actress]
Diana Barrymore
BLYTHE, HERBERT (1847-1905) [Anglo-American actor]
Maurice Barrymore
BLYTHE, JOHN (1882-1942) [American stage and motion picture actor]
Jack Barrymore
John Barrymore
The Great Profile
BLYTHE, JOHN, JR. (1932-) [American actor]
John Barrymore, Jr.
BLYTHE, LIONEL (1878-1954) [American stage and motion picture actor]
Lionel Barrymore
Hollywood's Grand Old Man
BLYTHE, VERNON (1887-1918) [American ballroom dancer]
Vernon Castle
Boanerges. See:
Scottish Boanerges, The.
Boar, The. See:
RICHARD III
Board, Chairman of the. See:
SINATRA, FRANCIS ALBERT
Boardwalk Ike. See:
BACHARACH, ISAAC
BOAS, GUY HERMAN SIDNEY (1896-) [British educator and author]
G.B.
Boas, Marie. See:
HALL, MARIE BOAS
Boatbuilder, America's No. 1 See: HIGGINS, ANDREW JACKSON
Boatmen, The Last of the. See: FINK, MIKE
Bob. See:
BENCHLEY, ROBERT
BROWN, ROBERT JOSEPH
CHESTER, ROBERT ST.
CONSIDINE, ROBERT BERNARD
CROSBY, GEORGE ROBERT
DRUM, ROBERT F.
FELLER, ROBERT WILLIAM ANDREW
FITZSIMMONS, ROBERT PROMETHEUS
FORD, ROBERT
GIBSON, ROBERT
HAYES, ROBERT LEE
HOLLAND, ROBERT EMORY
HOPE, EMORY TOWNES
HOPE, LESLIE TOWNES
KEESHAN, ROBERT JAMES
KRAUSS, ROBERT G.
NEWHART, GEORGE ROBERT
RIZZO, ANTHONY
RUSSELL, SIDNEY KEITH
SCOBEY, ROBERT
SWINFORD, BETTY JUNE WELLS
TRALINS, S. ROBERT
WATERFIELD, ROBERT
YOUNG, ROBERT WILLIAM
ZURKE, ROBERT
Bob and Ray, joint pseud. of ROBERT B. ELLIOTT (1923-) and RAYMOND W. GOULDING (1922-) [American radio comedians and satirists]
Bob Astor. See:
DADE, ROBERT E.
Bob, Battling. See:
LA FOLLETTE, ROBERT MARION, SR.
Bob, Beautiful. See:

BRUGH, SPANGLER
ARLINGTON
Bob Carter. See:
KAHAKALAU, ROBERT
Bob Dylan. See:
ZIMMERMAN, ROBERT
Bob, Farmer. See:
DOUGHTON, ROBERT L.
SCOTT, ROBERT WALTER
Bob, Fiddling. See:
TAYLOR, ROBERT LOVE
Bob, Fighting. See:
EVANS, ROBLEY
DUNGLISON
Bob Keene. See:
KUHN, ROBERT
Bob Levinson. See:
WELLS, ROBERT
Bob, Marine. See:
MOUTON, ROBERT L.
Bob Miketta. See:
MORRIS, ROBERT
Bob, Our. See:
REYNOLDS, ROBERT RICE
TAYLOR, ROBERT LOVE
Bob, Pony. See:
HASLAM, ROBERT
Bob, Quicksilver. See:
FULTON, ROBERT
Bob Rodney. See:
RODRIGO, ROBERT
Bob Scott, Farmer. See:
SCOTT, ROBERT WALTER
Bob Short. See:
POPE, ALEXANDER
Bob Steele. See:
BRADBURY, ROBERT
Bob Tremaine. See:
STEINDLER, ROBERT A.
Bob White. See:
HOLLAND, RAY P.
Bob, Woolly. See:
RICH, ROBERT FLEMING
Bobbie. See:
Bobby
BURNS, ROBERT
KENNEDY, ROBERT
Bobbin Boy, The. See:
BANKS, NATHANIEL
PRENTISS
Bobbin, Tim. See:
COLLIER, JOHN
Bobbing Joan. See:
MAR, JOHN ERSKINE,
6TH or 11TH EARL OF
Bobby. See:
Bobbie
CLARK, ROBERT EDWIN
FISCHER, ROBERT JAMES
HARRON, ROBERT
HULL, ROBERT MARVIN,
JR.
JONES, ROBERT TYRE,
JR.
ORR, ROBERT
RICHARDSON, ROBERT
CLINTON, JR.
SCOTT, ROBERT W.
TROUP, ROBERT WILLIAM
VINTON, STANLEY ROBERT
Bobby Collazo. See:
PENA, ROBERTO CO-
LLAZO
Bobby Darin. See:
CASOTTO, ROBERT
WALDEN
Bobby the Cofferer. See:
MORRIS, ROBERT
Bobby the Treasurer. See:
MORRIS, ROBERT
Bobette. See:
SIMENON, GEORGES
Bobo, Willie. See:
CORREA, WILLIAM
Bocanegra. See:
FUENTES, MANUEL
Bocca, Al. See:
WINTER, BEVIS
BOCCACCIO, GIOVANNI (1313-
75) [Italian novelist and
poet]
The Bard of Prose
The Father of Italian Prose
The Prince of Story-tellers
BOCCACCIO, GIOVANNI.
See also: Great Tri-
umvirate of Italian Litera-
ture, The
BOCCASINI, NICCOLÒ (1240-
1304) [Supreme Pontiff of
Roman Catholic Church]
Pope Benedict XI
BOCCHERINI, LUIGI (1740-1805)
[Italian composer]
Haydn's Wife
BOCHENSKI, JOSEPH M.

(1902-) [Polish Dominican educator and author]
Innocentius M. Bochenski
Josef Miche
BOCHER, MAIN (1891?-) [American fashion designer]
Mainbocher
Bodell, Mary. See:
PECSOC, MARY BODELL
Boden, Hilda. See:
BODENHEIM, HILDA MORRIS
BODENHEIM, HILDA MORRIS (1901-) [British author]
Hilda Boden
Pauline Welch
BODENSTEIN, ANDREAS RUDOLF (prior to 1483-1541) [Bavarian reformer]
Carlstadt
Bodfan. See:
ANWYL, JOHN BODVAN
Body, The. See:
FRYE, MARIE
BOÉ, JACQUES (1798-1864) [Gascon wigmaker and poet]
The Barber Poet
The Burns of France
Jacques Jasmin
The Last of the Troubadours
BOETTICHER, OSCAR (1916-) [American motion picture director]
Budd Boetticher
BOËX, JOSEPH HENRI HONORÉ (1856-1940) [French novelist]
J.H. Rosny the Elder
BOËX, JOSEPH HENRI HONORÉ See also: Rosny, Joseph Henri
BOËX, SERAPHIN JUSTIN FRANÇOIS (1859-1948) [French novelist]
J.H. Rosny the Younger
BOËX, SERAPHIN JUSTIN FRANÇOIS. See also: Rosny, Joseph Henri
Bogaduck. See:
LINDSAY, HAROLD ARTHUR BILL
BOGAERDE, DEREK JULES GASPARD ULRIC NIVEN VAN DEN (1921-) [British actor]
Dirk Bogarde
Bogarde, Dirk. See:
BOGAERDE, DEREK JULES GASPARD ULRIC NIVEN VAN DEN
BOGART, BETTY JOAN PEPSKE BACALL (1924-) [American actress]
Betty Bacall
Lauren Bacall
BOGART, HUMPHREY (1899-1957) [American stage and motion picture actor]
Bogey
BOGART, WILLIAM HENRY (1810-88) [American author]
Sentinel
Bogen, Miss Ellen. See:
ELLENBOGEN, HENRY
BOGER, BETSY (1923-) [American motion picture actress]
Betsy Blair
Bogey. See:
BOGART, HUMPHREY
Bogle, George. See:
DUKINFIELD, WILLIAM CLAUDE
Bohemia, The Queen of. See:
McELHENEY, JANE
Bohemian. See:
CHANNING-RENTON, LIEUT. ERNEST MATTHEWS
Bohemians, The King of the. See: CLAPP, HENRY, JR.
COLLINS, MORTIMER
BOHLMAN, EDNA McCAULL (1897-) [American educator and author]
M.E. McCaull
BOHME, DAVID M. (1916-) [Polish-American composer, violinist and author]
David Romaine
BOHNY, LILIAN (1903-) [American silent motion picture actress]
Billie Dove

BOIES, HORACE (1827-1923)
[American statesman; Governor of Iowa]
Affidavit Boies
BOILEAU-DESPRÉAUX, NICHOLAS (1636-1711)
[French critic and poet]
The Lawgiver of Parnassus
The Poet of Reason
The Solon of Parnassus
Boiling Water. See:
LEE, CHARLES
Bojangles. See:
ROBINSON, WILLIAM
BOK, EDWARD WILLIAM (1863-1930) [Dutch-American journalist]
A Lay Preacher to the Largest Congregation in the United States
Bola Sete. See:
ANDRADA, DJALMA DE
BOLAND, FRANÇOIS (1929-)
[Belgian jazz musician (composer, leader, piano)]
Francy Boland
Bold, The. See:
ALBERT
BOLESLAV II
CHARLES
PHILIP
PHILIP III
BOLDEN, CHARLES (1868-1931)
[American jazz musician (cornet, leader)]
Buddy Bolden
King Bolden
Boldrewood, Rolf. See:
BROWNE, THOMAS ALEXANDER
BOLESLAV I (died 1025)
[King of Poland]
The Mighty
BOLESLAV II (1039?-83)
[King of Poland]
The Bold
BOLESLAV III (1086-1138)
[King of Poland]
Wry-Mouthed
BOLESLAV V (1221-79)
[King of Poland]
The Chaste
Boleslaw Prus. See:
GLOWACKI, ALEXANDER
Bolesławita, B. See:
KRASEWSKI, JÓZEF IGNACY
BOLGER, RAYMOND WALLACE (1904-) [American dancer and actor]
Ray Bolger
BOLIN, NICOLAI P. (1908-) [Russian-American composer, choirmaster, and author]
Nick Bolin
Bolina, Jack La. See:
VECCHI, AUGUSTUS VICTOR
Bolingbroke. See:
HENRY IV
Bolingbroke, Viscount. See:
ST. JOHN, HENRY
Bolitho, William. See:
RYALL, WILLIAM BOLITHO
BOLÍVAR, SIMÓN (1783-1830)
[Venezuelan general officer and statesman]
The Liberator (El Libertador)
The Washington of Colombia
The Washington of South America
BOLLSTÄDT. See:
ALBERTUS MAGNUS, SAINT, COUNT OF BOLLSTÄDT
Bolo, Solomon, joint pseud. of WILLIAM ISAAC GOLDSTEIN (1932-) and JAMES NELSON WHITON (1932-) [American writers]
Bolo, Solomon. See also:
GOLDSTEIN, WILLIAM ISAAC
WHITON, JAMES NELSON
BOLTON, CHARLES E. (fl. 1876-83) [California highwayman and road agent]
Black Bart
Black Bart the Po8
Bolton, Isabel. See:
MILLER, MARY BRITTON
BOLTON, MAISIE SHARMAN

(1915-) [Scottish author]
Stratford Davis
Maisie Sharman
Bomba. See:
FERDINAND II
Bomba, King. See:
FERDINAND II
Bomber. See:
HARRIS, SIR ARTHUR TRAVERS
Bomber, The Brown. See:
BARROW, JOSEPH LOUIS
Bombet, Louis Alexandre César. See:
BEYLE, MARIE-HENRI
Bombita. See:
TORRES, EMILIO
TORRES, RICARDO
Bombshell, The Brazilian. See:
CUNHA, MARÍA DE CARMO MIRANDA DE
Bon Gaultier. See:
MARTIN, SIR THEODORE
Bon, Le (The Good). See:
JOHN II
Bon Roi René, Le. See:
RENÉ I
Bona Fide, Old. See:
LOUIS XIV
BONAL, FRANCISCO (1871-1956) [Spanish bullfighter]
Bonarillo
BONANO, JOSEPH (1904-) [American jazz musician (trumpet, singer)]
Sharkey Bonano
BONAPARTE, CHARLES JOSEPH (1851-1921) [American lawyer, scholar and humanitarian]
The Academic Pharisee
The Imperial Peacock of Park Avenue
Souphouse Charlie
BONAPARTE, CHARLES LOUIS NAPOLÉON (1808-73) [Emperor of the French]
Badinguet
Boustrapa
The Man of December (L'Homme de Décembre)
The Man of Sedan
The Man of Silence
Napoleon III
Louis Napoleon
The Prisoner of Ham
The Savior of Society
BONAPARTE, JOSEPH (1768-1844) [King of Naples and King of Spain]
Comte de Survilliers
BONAPARTE, JOSEPH CHARLES PAUL (1822-91) [French General officer]
Plon-Plon
Prince Napoleon
BONAPARTE, NAPOLÉON (1769-1821) [Corsican general officer and Emperor of France]
The Armed Soldier of Democracy
l'Autre (The Other One)
Boney
The Colossus of the Nineteenth Century
The Corsican
The Corsican Fiend
The Corsican General
The Corsican Ogre
The Corsican Seostris
Le Général Entrepreneur (The Contractor General)
The Great
The Heir of the Republic
The Little Corporal (Le Petit Caporal)
The Man of Destiny
The Modern Seostris
Napoléon I
The Nightmare of Europe
Old Boney
Redingote Grise
Jupiter Scapin
BONAPARTE, NAPOLÉON FRANÇOIS CHARLES JOSEPH (1811-32) [titular Emperor of France]
Duke of Reichstadt
The Eaglet (l'Aiglon)
King of Rome
Napoléon II
The Son of the Man
Bonar Colleano. See:
SULLIVAN, BONAR
Bonarillo. See:

BONAL, FRANCISCO
Bonaventura, Father. See:
STUART, CHARLES EDWARD LOUIS PHILIP CASIMIR
Bonaventura, Giovanni. See:
FIDANZA, GIOVANNI DI
Bonaventura, St. See:
FIDANZA, GIOVANNI DI
BOND, GLADYS PARKER (1912-) [American journalist and author]
Jo Mendel
Bond, Ian. See:
WILLETT, BROTHER FRANCISCUS
Bond, J. Harvey. See:
WINTERBOTHAM, RUSSELL ROBERT
BOND, MARY FANNING WICKHAM (1898-) [American poet and author]
Mrs. James Bond
Mary F.W. Lewis
Mary F. Wickham
Mary F. Wickham Porcher
Mary Fanning Wickham
BOND, WALTER (1896-) [British stage and motion picture actor]
Walter Fitzgerald
Bonddhu, Coch-y. See:
ARNOLD, RICHARD
BONDONE, GIOTTO DI (1276?-1337?) [Florentine painter, sculptor and architect]
Giotto
Bonehead. See:
MERKLE, FREDERICK C.
Bonehill, Captain Ralph. See:
STRATEMEYER, EDWARD L.
Bonerge (Son of Thunder). See:
JAMES THE GREATER, ST.
JOHN THE EVANGELIST, ST.
BONESTEELE, LAURA JUSTINE (1872-1932) [American actress and theater manager]
Jessie Bonstelle
The Maker of Stars
Bonett, Emery. See:
COULSON, FELICITY CARTER
Bonett, John. See:
COULSON, JOHN HUBERT ARTHUR
Boney. See:
BONAPARTE, NAPOLÉON
Boney, Old. See:
BONAPARTE, NAPOLÉON
Bonhomme, Jacques. See:
CAILLET, GUILLAUME
BONIFACE (died 422) [Supreme Pontiff of Roman Catholic Church]
Pope Boniface I
St. Boniface
BONIFACE (died 532) [Supreme Pontiff of Roman Catholic Church]
Pope Boniface II
BONIFACE (died 607) [Supreme Pontiff of Roman Catholic Church]
Pope Boniface III
BONIFACE (died 615) [Supreme Pontiff of Roman Catholic Church]
Pope Boniface IV
St. Boniface
BONIFACE (died 625) [Supreme Pontiff of Roman Catholic Church]
Pope Boniface V
BONIFACE (died 896) [Supreme Pontiff of Roman Catholic Church]
Pope Boniface VI
BONIFACE (died 985) [Supreme Pontiff of Catholic Church]
Pope Boniface VII
Boniface VIII, Pope. See:
CAETANI, BENEDETTO
Boniface IX, Pope. See:
TOMACELLI, PIETRO
Boniface, St. See:
WINFRID (WYNFRITH)
Bonifazio Veneziano. See:
PITATI, BONIFAZIO DI
Bonifazio Veronese. See:
PITATI, BONIFAZIO DI
BONN, MORITZ JULIUS (1873-) [German

economist, political
scientist and author]
Moritz Julius
Bonne Reine, La. See:
FRANCE, CLAUDE DE
BONNER, CAREY (1859-)
[British clergyman, composer and author]
Vincent Percival
Bonner, Michael. See:
GLASSCOCK, ANNE
BONNER
Bonner, Parker. See:
BALLARD, WILLIS TODHUNTER
Bonner, Sherwood. See:
MACDOWELL, KATHERINE
SHERWOOD BONNER
Bonnette, Victor. See:
ROY, EWELL PAUL
Bonney, Bill. See:
KEEVIL, HENRY JOHN
BONNEY, WILLIAM H. (1859-81)
[American cowboy and
outlaw]
Billy the Kid
Bonnie Wetzel. See:
ADDLEMAN, BONNIE
JEAN
BONNIVARD, FRANÇOIS DE
(1496-c. 1570) [Genevan
prelate and politician]
The Prisoner of Chillon
Bonny Brown Wife, The. See:
JACKSON, RACHEL
DONELSON
Bonny Dundee. See:
GRAHAM, JOHN
Bonny Prince Charlie. See:
STUART, CHARLES
EDWARD LOUIS PHILIP
CASIMIR
Bonstelle, Jessie. See:
BONESTEELE, LAURA
JUSTINE
Bontemps, Roger. See:
COLLERYE, ROGER DE
BONUS, ARTHUR (1864-)
[German author]
Fritz Benthien
Franz Brand
George Stolterfoth
Bonus, The Father of the. See:
PATMAN, WRIGHT
VAN ZANT, JAMES E.
BONVICINO, ALESSANDRO
(1498-1554) [Italian painter]
Il Moretto
Moretto Da Brescia
Boob. See:
McNUTT, PAUL VORIES
Boomie. See:
RICHMAN, ABRAHAM
SAMUEL
Boone, Benjamin F. Johnson of.
See: RILEY, JAMES
WHITCOMB
BOONE, CHARLES EUGENE
(1934-) [American
popular singer, author and
actor]
Pat Boone
Boone, Denver. See:
RENNIE, JAMES ALAN
Boone, Henry L. See:
ST. JOHN, PERCY
BOLLINGBROKE
Boone of Southern Kentucky, The
Daniel. See:
LYNN, BENJAMIN
Boone of the Rockies, The
Daniel. See:
BRIDGER, JAMES
BOORDE. See:
BORDE (BOORDE),
ANDREW
Booth. See:
TARKINGTON, NEWTON
BOOTH
BOOTH, EDWIN (fl. 1933-63)
[American accountant and
author]
Don Blunt
Jack Hazard
Booth, Edwina. See:
WOODRUFF, EDWINA
Booth, Mrs. Letitia. See:
RUSSELL, WILLIAM
CLARK
Booth, Shirley. See:
FORD, THELMA BOOTH
BOOTH, WILLIAM (1829-1912)
[English preacher; founder
of the Salvation Army]
General Booth
BOOTHBY, FREDERICK LEWIS

MAITLAND (fl. early 20th cent.) [British naval officer and author]
Per Aëra
Per Mare
Bootleggers, The King of the. See: DWYER, WILLIAM VINCENT
Boots. See:
GRANTHAM, GEORGE FARLEY
MUSSULLI, HENRY W.
Boots-and-Saddle Star, The World's Top. See:
SLYE, LEONARD
BORACH, FANNY (1891-1951) [American actress and comedienne]
Fanny Brice
Baby Snooks
BORAH, WILLIAM EDGAR (1865-1940) [American senator from Idaho]
The Idaho Lion
The Lion of the Senate
The Lone Lion
Borax. See:
SMITH, FRANCIS MARION
Borax King, The. See:
SMITH, FRANCIS MARION
BORBÓN. See also:
BOURBON
Bourbon
BORBÓN, CARLOS LUIS FERNANDO DE, CONDE DE MONTEMOLÍN (1818-61) [Spanish prince]
Don Carlos
BORBÓN, CARLOS MARÍA DE, INFANTE DE ESPAÑA (1870-1949) [Spanish prince]
Don Carlos
BORBÓN, CARLOS MARÍA DE LOS DOLORES DE, DUQUE DE MADRID (1848-1909) [Spanish prince]
Don Carlos
BORBÓN, CARLOS MARÍA ISIDRO DE, CONDE DE MOLINA (1788-1855) [Spanish prince]
Don Carlos
Borch, Ted. See:
LUND, A. MORTEN
BORCHARD, RUTH BERENDSOHN (1910-) [German author]
Iqua
Anne Medley
BORDE (BOORDE), ANDREW (1490?-1549) [English author and physician]
Merry Andrew
Borden, Lee. See:
DEAL, BORDEN
Borden, M. See:
SAXON, GLADYS RELYEA
BORDEN, MARY (1886-) [American author]
Bridget MacLagan
Border Minstrel, The. See:
SCOTT, SIR WALTER
Border, The Black Knight of the. See:
MALONE, PERCY LAY
Border, The King of the. See:
SCOTT, ADAM, OF TUSHIELAW
Border, The Minstrel of the. See: SCOTT, SIR WALTER
BORDMAN, ELIZA HENDERSON. See: OTIS, MRS. HARRISON GRAY (ELIZA HENDERSON BORDMAN)
Bore, Old. See:
BEAUREGARD, PIERRE GUSTAVE TOUTANT
Borel. See:
HUGUES (HUGH) II
Borge, Victor. See:
ROSENBAUM, BORGE
BORGES, JORGE LUIS. See:
Domecq, Honorio Bustos
BORGHESE, CAMILLO (1552-1621) [Supreme Pontiff of Roman Catholic Church]
Pope Paul V
BORGIA, ALONSO (1378-1458) [Supreme Pontiff of Roman Catholic Church]
Pope Callistus III
BORGIA, RODRIGO (1431-1503) [Supreme Pontiff of

Roman Catholic Church]
Pope Alexander VI
BORGMANN, DMITRI ALFRED (1927-) [German-American actuary, word-play expert and writer]
El Uqsor
BORGNINE, ERMES EFFRON (1917-) [American actor]
Ernest Borgnine
Boris Karloff. See:
PRATT, WILLIAM HENRY
Boris Morros. See:
MIKHAILOVITCH, BORIS
Boris Pilnyak. See:
VOGAU, BORIS ANDREYEVICH
Boris Sherashevski. See:
BROWN, JOHN J.
BORLAND, HAROLD GLEN (1900-) [American author]
Hal Borland
Ward West
BORMANN, MARTIN (1900-45?) [German Nazi party leader]
Adolf Hitler's Evil Genius
The Brown Eminence
Born, Edith de. See:
BISCH, EDITH
Berne, Dorothy. See:
RICE, DOROTHY MARY
BORNEMAN, ERNEST (1915-) [German author, playwright, radio and television producer]
Cameron McCabe
Borneman, H. See:
GOTTSHALL, FRANKLIN HENRY
BORNET, FRANÇOIS (1915-) [American composer, author, director and singer]
Fred Bornet
Boroimhe, Brian. See:
BRIAN
BOROSON, WARREN (1935-) [American reporter, editor and author]
Warner Brown
Borough Trice. See:
ALLEN, ARTHUR BRUCE
BORRAS, JORGE AUGUSTÍN NICOLÁS RUIZ DE SANTAYANA Y (1863-1952) [Spanish-American poet and philosopher]
George Santayana
BORRERO, ANTONIO (1936-) [Spanish bullfighter]
Chamaco
BORROW, GEORGE HENRY (1803-81) [English author and linguist]
Lavengro (Word Master)
Taylor of Norwich
Boru, Brian (Brian of the Tribute). See:
BRIAN
Bory, Old. See:
BEAUREGARD, PIERRE GUSTAVE TOUTANT
Bos. See:
Boz
UNKNOWN
Bos (Bosch), Hieronymus. See:
VAN AEKEN, HIERONYMUS
BOSCAWEN, EDWARD (1711-61) [English admiral]
Old Dreadnaught
Boscawen, Linda. See:
SMITHELLS, ANABEL DOREEN
Bosch (Bos), Hieronymus. See :
VAN AEKEN, HIERONYMUS
BOSE, NIRMAL KUMAR (1901-) [Indian anthropologist, educator and author]
Nirmala-Kumara Vasu
BOSEN, JENS CRUZ (1884-1942) [Danish-American motion picture director]
James Cruze
BOSQUET, ALAIN (1919-) [Russian-American editor, publisher and poet]
Anatole Bisque
Boss. See:
CROKER, RICHARD
CRUMP, EDWARD HULL
HAGUE, FRANK

KELLY, JOHN
KETTERING, CHARLES FRANKLIN
TWEED, WILLIAM MARCY
Boss Buckley, Blind. See:
BUCKLEY, CHRISTOPHER A.
Boss Platt, Easy. See:
PLATT, THOMAS COLLIER
Boss, The. See:
LAFITTE, JEAN
ROOSEVELT, FRANKLIN DELANO
Bossu d'Arras, Le. See:
HALLE, ADAM DE LA
BOSSUET, JACQUES BÉNIGNE (1627-1704) [French prelate, pulpit orator and theological writer]
The Eagle of Meaux
BOSTICK, CALVIN T. (1928-) [American composer, author and pianist]
Cal Bostic
Boston Bard, The. See:
COFFIN, ROBERT STEVENSON
Boston Blackie. See:
MORRIS, CHESTER
Boston, Charles K. See:
GRUBER, FRANK
Bostón, El Rubio de. See:
TUCK, PORTER
Boston Medium, Margery the. See: CRANDON, MINA
Boston Strangler, The. See:
DE SALVO, ALBERT H.
Boston Strong Boy, The. See:
SULLIVAN, JOHN LAWRENCE
Boston Tar Baby, The. See:
LANGFORD, SAM
Boston, The Father and Glory of. See: COTTON, JOHN
Boston, The Grandmother of. See: PEABODY, ELIZABETH PALMER
Boston, The Strong Boy of. See: SULLIVAN, JOHN LAWRENCE
Boston Tim. See:
SULLIVAN, TIMOTHY P.
Bostonian, A. See:
POE, EDGAR ALLAN
Bostonian, By a. See:
POE, EDGAR ALLAN
Bostwick, Colonel T. B. See:
HARBAUGH, THOMAS CHALMERS
Boswell Butt, Esq. See:
ROSS, CHARLES HENRY
BOSWELL, JAMES (1740-95) English friend and biographer of DR. SAMUEL JOHNSON
Bozzy
Boswell, John. See:
KING, JOHN BOSWELL
BOSWORTH, ALLAN RUCKER (1901-) [American author]
Alamo Boyd
Botanicus Regius Primarius. See:
PARKINSON, JOHN
Botanist in the World, The Greatest. See:
BARTRAM, JOHN
Botanist to the King. See:
BARTRAM, JOHN
Botany, The Father of American. See: BARTRAM, JOHN
Botany, The Father of English. See: RAY, JOHN
Botany, The Nestor of American. See: DARLINGTON, WILLIAM
BOTETOURT, LORD NORBORNE BERKELEY (1718-70) [colonial governor of Virginia]
The Good Governor of Virginia
BOTSFORD, MARGARET (fl. 1816-30) [American novelist and poet]
A Lady
A Lady of Philadelphia
Bott, Elizabeth. See:
SPILLUS, ELIZABETH JANE
Botticelli, Sandro. See:
FILIPEPI, ALESSANDRO DI MARIANO DEI
Bottled Beer. See:
NOWELL, ALEXANDER

Bottomless Pit, The. See:
PITT, WILLIAM
BOTZARIS. See:
BOZZARIS (BOTZARIS), MARKOS
Boucher, Anthony, See:
WHITE, WILLIAM ANTHONY PARKER
Boucher, Le Royaliste. See:
LASSERAN-MASSENCOME, SEIGNEUR DE MONT-LUC
BOUCICAULT, DIONYSIUS LARDNER (1822-90) [Irish playwright and actor]
Dion Boucicault
Lee Moreton
BOUCK, WILLIAM C. (1786-1859) [Governor of New York]
The Farmer Governor
BOUDAT, MARIE-LOUISE (1909-) [French author]
Louise Bellocq
Boudinot, Elias. See:
GALAGINA
BOUILLON. See:
GODFREY OF BOUILLON
BOUILLON, HENRI DE LA TOUR D'AUVERGNE, DUKE DE (1555-1623) [French marshal]
The Father of Turenne
BOUILLY, JEAN NICOLAS (1762-1842) [French dramatist]
The Poète Lacrymal
BOULANGER, GEORGES ERNEST JEAN MARIE (1837-91) [French general officer and politician]
The Man on Horseback
Boulevard(s), The Corneille of the. See:
PIXÉRÉCOURT, GUILBERT DE
Boulevard(s), The Shakespeare of the. See:
PIXERECOURT, GUILBERT DE
BOULTING, SYDNEY (1912-) [British actor, producer and author]
Peter Cotes
Peter Northcote
BOURBON [Bourbon]. See also:
BORBÓN
BOURBON, DUC CHARLES DE (1490-1527) [French general officer]
Connétable de Bourbon
Bourbon, Ken. See:
BAUER, ERWIN A.
BOURDALONE, LOUIS (1632-1704) [French preacher]
The Founder of Christian Eloquence
The King of Preachers
BOURGEOIS, JEANNE MARIE (1874-1956) [French dancer and actress]
Mistinguett
BOURGOGNE, ANTOINE DE (1421-1504) [Duke of Burgundy; natural son of PHILIP THE GOOD]
The Great Bastard
BOURGOGNE, JEHAN DE. See:
Mandeville, Jehan de (Sir John)
BOURGUIGNON, LOUIS-DOMINIQUE (1693-1721) [notorious French robber]
Cartouche
The Dick Turpin of France
BOURILLON, PIERRE (1876-) [French author]
Pierre Hamp
Bourne, Lesley. See:
MARSHALL, EVELYN
Boustrapa. See:
BONAPARTE, CHARLES LOUIS NAPOLÉON
BOUTELLEAU, JACQUES (1884-) [French writer]
Jacques Chardonne
BOW, CLARA (1905-65) [American motion picture actress]
The It Girl
The Red Head
BOWDEN, JEAN (1920-) [Scottish author]
Avon Curry
Belinda Dell
BOWDITCH, FREDERICK W.

(1906-) [American motion picture actor]
Kane Richmond
Bowen, Betty Morgan. See:
WEST, BETTY
BOWEN, GEORGE (1816-88) [American missionary to India]
The Nestor of the Methodist Conference in India
Bowen, Marjorie. See:
LONG, MRS. GABRIELLE MARGARET VERE CAMPBELL
BOWEN-ROWLANDS, ERNEST BOWEN BROWN (fl. early 20th cent.) [British barrister and author]
Member for Treorky
BOWER, MAURICE (1922-) [American composer, conductor and trumpeter]
Bugs Bower
BOWER, SIR GRAHAM JOHN (1848-) [British naval officer and author]
Centurion
BOWERING, GEORGE (1935-) [Canadian educator, editor, poet and author]
The Panavision Kid
BOWERS, SANTHA RAMA RAU (1923-) [Indian author and lecturer]
Santha Rama Rau
BOWES, EDWARD (1874-1946) [American radio program director, soldier, corporation executive and real estate operator]
Major Bowes
BOWIE, JAMES (1799-1836) [American soldier; reputed inventor of the bowie knife]
Jim Bowie
Bowie, Jim. See:
BOWIE, JAMES
NORWOOD, VICTOR GEORGE CHARLES
STRATEMEYER, EDWARD L.
Bowie, Sam. See:
BALLARD, WILLIS TODHUNTER
Bowman, Jeanne. See:
BLOCKLINGER, PEGGY O'MORE
BOWMAN, RALPH (1915-) [American motion picture actor]
John Archer
Bowood, Richard. See:
DANIELL, ALBERT SCOTT
BOWRAN, JOHN GEORGE (1869-) [British clergyman and author]
Ramsay Guthrie
BOWYER, WILLIAM (1699-1777) [English printer, scholar and editor]
The Learned Printer
Box, Edgar. See:
VIDAL, GORE
Box Office Girl, The. See:
MICHAELSKA, MARIANNE
Box, Pepper. See:
BARTELL, RICHARD
Box, Peter Pepper. See:
FESSENDEN, THOMAS GREEN
Boxing Bill, The Father of the New York State. See:
WALKER, JAMES JOHN
Boxing, The Czar of. See:
MULDOON, WILLIAM
Boxing, The Father of American. See: MULDOON, WILLIAM
Boy, Big. See:
WILLIAMS, GUINN
Boy Bishop, The. See:
NICOLAUS, ST.
Boy General, The. See:
CUSTER, GEORGE ARMSTRONG
Boy Geologist of Michigan, The. See: HOUGHTON, DOUGLASS
Boy, Golden. See:
HORNUNG, PAUL VERNON
Boy Governor, The. See:
MASON, STEVENS THOMSON
Boy Guard, The. See:
WHITMAN, JOHN LORIN
Boy-hero of the Confederacy, The. See:

DAVIS, SAM
Boy, Hollywood's No. 1 Glamour. See: MATURE, VICTOR JOHN
Boy, Honey. See: EVANS, CHARLES E.
Boy in Specs, The Old. See: DAVIS, MATHEW LIVINGSTON
Boy King, Blues. See: KING, RILEY B.
Boy Major, The. See: PELHAM, JOHN
Boy Mayor, The. See: RUSSELL, WILLIAM EUSTIS
Boy Monologist, The. See: JESSEL, GEORGE
Boy of Boston, The Strong. See: SULLIVAN, JOHN LAWRENCE
Boy of the Rappahannock, The Drummer. See: HENDERSHOT, ROBERT HENRY
Boy of the Slashes, The Mill. See: CLAY, HENRY
Boy Orator of the Platte, The. See: BRYAN, WILLIAM JENNINGS
Boy Orator, The. See: LEE, JOSHUA BRYAN
Boy Poet of Nottingham, The. See: WHITE, HENRY KIRKE
Boy Pope, The. See: OTTAVIANO
Boy Preacher of Los Angeles, The. See: IRONSIDE, HENRY ALLAN
Boy Preacher, The. See: FURMAN, RICHARD
KENNEDY, CRAMMOND
LIPSCOMB, ANDREW ADGATE
Boy Producer, The. See: THALBERG, IRVING GRANT
Boy Robot, The. See: FISCHER, ROBERT JAMES
Boy Socialist, The. See: LONDON, JOHN GRIFFITH
Boy, The Barnum Wonder. See: BARNHUM, H. B.
Boy, The Benicia. See: HEENAN, JOHN CAMEL
Boy, The Big. See: CAPONE, ALPHONSE
Boy, The Bobbin. See: BANKS, NATHANIEL PRENTISS
Boy, The Boston Strong. See: SULLIVAN, JOHN LAWRENCE
Boy, The Bristol. See: CHATTERTON, THOMAS
Boy, The Butcher. See: WANDERER, CARL
Boy, The Canal. See: GARFIELD, JAMES ABRAM
Boy, The Elephant. See: DASTAGIR, SABU
Boy, The Ferry. See: CHASE, SALMON PORTLAND
Boy, The Gipsy. See: SMITH, RODNEY
Boy, The Idol of the American. See: RUTH, GEORGE HERMAN
Boy, The Lord's Chore. See: MAY, SAMUEL JOSEPH
Boy, The Marvellous. See: CHATTERTON, THOMAS
Boy, The Norfolk. See: PORSON, RICHARD
Boy, The Wagon. See: CORWIN, THOMAS
Boy, The Wild. See: HAUSER, KASPAR
PETER THE WILD BOY
Boy, Wonder. See: KRAMER, STANLEY E.
Boy Wonder, The. See: HARRIS, STANLEY RAYMOND
HOPPE, WILLIAM FREDERICK
LEE, JOSHUA BRYAN
Boyd, Alamo. See: BOSWORTH, ALLAN RUCKER
Boyd, Barbara. See: BURR, AGNES RUSH
Boyd Boylan. See: WHITON, JAMES NELSON
Boyd Cable. See: EWART, ERNEST ANDREW

Boyd, Frank. See:
KANE, FRANK
Boyd, Nancy. See:
MILLAY, EDNA ST. VINCENT
Boyd, Stephen. See:
MILLAR (MILLER), WILLIAM
BOYD, WILLIAM LAWRENCE (1898-) [American actor]
Bill Boyd
BOYDEN, SETH (1788-1890) [American inventor]
One of America's Greatest Inventors
BOYER, KENTON LLOYD (1931-) [American professional baseball player]
Ken Boyer
Boyfriend, America's. See:
ROGERS, CHARLES
Boylan, Boyd. See:
WHITON, JAMES NELSON
BOYLE, HAROLD VINCENT (1911-) [American journalist and columnist]
Hal Boyle
BOYLE, RICHARD, 1ST EARL OF CORK (1566-1643) [Irish administrator]
The Great Earl
BOYLE, RICHARD (1695-1753) [English architect]
The High Priest of English Palladianism
BOYLE, SIR ROBERT (1627-91) [British chemist and physicist]
The Father of Modern Chemistry
BOYLE, WILLIAM ANTHONY (1907-) [American labor union official]
Tony Boyle
BOYLES, CLARENCE SCOTT, JR. (1905-) [American editor and author]
Will C. Brown
Boylston, Peter. See:
CURTIS, GEORGE TICKNOR
Boynton Belknap, M.D. See:
ELLIS, EDWARD SYLVESTER
BOYRON. See:
BARON (BOYRON), MICHEL
BYRON
Byron
BOYRON, ANDRÉ (c. 1602-55) [French actor]
André Baron
Boys. See:
Happiness Boys, The
Boys, The Best Foods. See:
Happiness Boys, The
Boys, The Dean of Sports Writers for. See:
BARBOUR, RALPH HENRY
Boz. See:
Bos
DICKENS, CHARLES JOHN HUFFAM
BOZZARIS (BOTZARIS), MARKOS (c. 1788-1823) [Greek soldier and patriot]
The Leonidas of Modern Greece
Bozzy. See:
BOSWELL, JAMES
Brabant, The Apostle of Ardennes and of. See:
HUBERT, ST.
Brace, Benjamin. See:
McCUTCHEON, BEN FREDERICK
Brace, Timothy. See:
PRATT, THEODORE
Bracefield, Richard. See:
WOOLEY, EDWARD MOTT
Bracefield, Robert. See:
WOOLEY, EDWARD MOTT
BRACEGIRDLE, MRS. ANNE (c. 1663-1748) [English actress]
The Diana of the Stage
BRACKENRIDGE, HUGH HENRY (1748-1816) [Scottish-American author and judge]
A Gentleman of Maryland
Brad. See:
GOWANS, ARTHUR BRADFORD
Brad Regan. See:
NORWOOD, VICTOR GEORGE CHARLES

BRADBURY, RAY DOUGLAS (1920-) [American author]
Ray Bradbury
Leonard Spaulding
BRADBURY, ROBERT (1907-) [American Western motion picture actor]
Bob Steele
BRADDOCK, JAMES J. (1905-) [American professional boxer; world's heavyweight champion]
The Cinderella Man
The Forgotten Man
BRADDON, MARY ELIZABETH (1837-1915) [English author and poet]
Lady Caroline Lascelles
BRADFIELD, ROGER (1924-) [American illustrator and author of books for children]
Jolly Roger Bradfield
Bradford, Adam, M.D. See: WASSERSUG, JOSEPH D.
BRADFORD, JOHN (1749-1830) [American pioneer newspaper publisher]
The Franklin of the West
Bradford, Joseph. See: HUNTER, WILLIAM RANDOLPH
BRADFORD, SARAH ELIZABETH HOPKINS (1818-) [American author]
Cousin Cicely
BRADFORD, WILLIAM (1590-1657) [Anglo-American Settler at Plymouth Colony, Massachusetts]
The Father of American History
BRADFORD, WILLIAM (1721/22-91) [American printer and publisher]
The Patriot Printer of 1776
BRADLAUGH, CHARLES (1833-91)[English reformer]
Iconoclast
BRADLEY-BIRT, FRANCIS BRADLEY (1874-) [British novelist]
Shelland Bradley
BRADLEY, EDWARD (1827-89) [English author and clergyman]
Cuthbert Bede
BRADLEY, KATHARINE HARRIS. See: Field, Michael
BRADLEY, MARY EMILY (1835-98) [American novelist and poet]
Cousin Alice
BRADLEY, OMAR NELSON (1893-) [American general officer]
The Doughboy's General
BRADLEY, WARREN IVES (1847-68) [American author]
Glance Gaylord
Bradley, Will. See: SCHWICHTENBERG, WILBUR
Bradly, Mr. See: BURROUGHS, WILLIAM SEWARD
Bradshaw, Wesley. See: UNKNOWN
BRADSTREET, ANNE DUDLEY (c. 1612-72) [Anglo-American poet]
The Tenth Muse
BRADWARDINE, THOMAS (1290-1349) [English prelate, theologian and mathematician]
The Profound Doctor (Doctor Profundus)
The Solid Doctor
BRADY, JAMES BUCHANAN (1856-1917) [American business executive, philanthropist and man-about-town]
Diamond Jim Brady
Brady, Scott. See: TIERNEY, GERALD
BRAFF, REUBEN (1927-) [American jazz musician]
Ruby Braff
Brag, Sir Jack. See: BURGOYNE, JOHN
BRAGDON, ELSPETH MacDUFFIE (1897-) [American teacher, advertising executive and author]
Elspeth
BRAHE, TYCHO (1546-1601) [Danish astronomer]
Golden Nose
BRAHM, HANS (1893-)

[German motion picture director]
John Brahm
Brain of the Revolution, The. See: ADAMS, SAMUEL
Brain, The. See: RICKEY, WESLEY BRANCH
Brain Trust, The Barrymore of the. See: TUGWELL, REXFORD GUY
Brainerd, Norman. See: FULLER, SAMUEL RICHARD, JR.
Brains. See: SWEENEY, PETER BARR
Brains of the Confederacy, The. See: BENJAMIN, JUDAH PHILIP
Brains, Old. See: HALLECK, HENRY WAGER
Brains Than Any Other Man in America, The Father of More. See: BEECHER, LYMAN
Braintree, Duke of. See: ADAMS, JOHN
Braith, George. See: BRAITHWAITE, GEORGE
BRAITHWAIT (BRAITHWAITE), RICHARD (1588?-1673) [British poet]
Corymbaeus
BRAITHWAITE, GEORGE (1939-) [American jazz musician (saxophone)]
George Braith
BRALY, MALCOLM (1925-) [American author]
Ray Lorning
Bram. See: STOKER, ABRAHAM
Bramah, Ernest. See: SMITH, ERNEST BRAMAH
Bramante. See: D'AGNOLO, DONATO
Bramante Lazzari. See: D'AGNOLO, DONATO
BRAME, CHARLOTTE MARY (1836-84) [English author of love stories]
Caroline M. Barton
C. M. B.
Bertha M. Clay
Mrs. Florice Norton
Dora Thorne
BRAMER, JENNIE PERKINS (1900-) [American reporter, columnist and author]
Faith Perkins
BRAMWELL, JAMES GUY (1911-) [British editor, educator and author]
James Byrom
Bran Meal and Pumpkins, The Poet of. See: GRAHAM, SYLVESTER
Branch. See: RICKEY, WESLEY BRANCH
Branch, The Fair. See: HYDE, DOUGLAS
BRAND [Brand]. See also: Brandt Brant
BRAND, ADOLF JOHANNES (1934-) [South African jazz musician (piano, composer)]
Dollar
Brand, Clay. See: NORWOOD, VICTOR GEORGE CHARLES
Brand, Franz. See: BONUS, ARTHUR
Brand, Max. See: FAUST, FREDERICK SCHILLER
Brand, Peter. See: LARSEN, ERLING
Brandane, John. See: MACINTYRE, DR. JOHN
BRANDEIS, LOUIS DEMBITZ (1856-1941) [American jurist; Associate Justice of U.S. Supreme Court]
The People's Attorney
The People's Lawyer
Brandel, Marc. See: BERESFORD, MARCUS
BRANDENBERG, ALIKI LIACOURAS (1929-) [American author]
Aliki
Brandenburg, Albert of. See: ALBERT
Brander. See: MATTHEWS,

JAMES BRANDER
Brandon, Curt. See:
BISHOP, CURTIS KENT
Brandon, Joe. See:
DAVIS, ROBERT P.
Brandon, Sheila. See:
RAYNER, CLAIRE
Brandt. See also:
BRAND
Brand
Brant
Brandt, Harvey. See:
EDWARDS, WILLIAM BENNETT
Brandt, Tom. See:
DEWEY, THOMAS BLANCHARD
Brandt, Willy. See:
FRAHM, HERBERT ERNST KARL
BRANDWEIN, CHAIM NAFTALI (1920-) [Israeli educator and author]
Ch. Naftali
Brandy Nan. See:
ANN
BRANN, WILLIAM COWPER (1855-98) [American editor, reformer and iconoclast]
Brann the Iconoclast
BRANNON. See also:
BRENAN
BRENNAN
Brennan
Brennand
BRANNON, WILLIAM T. (1906-) [American journalist, columnist and author]
Lawrence Gardner
Jack Hamilton
Peter Hermanns
Dwight McGlinn
Peter Oberholtzer
S. T. Peters
William Tibbetts
Bransby Williams. See:
PHAREZ, BRANSBY WILLIAM
Brant. See also:
BRAND
Brand
Brandt
Brant, Cyr de. See:
HIGGINSON, JOSEPH VINCENT
Brant, Joseph. See:
THAYENDANEGEA
Brant, Lewis. See:
ROWLAND, DONALD SYDNEY
Bras de Fer. See:
BALDWIN
NOUE, FRANÇOIS DE
BRASCHI, GIOVANNI ANGELO (1717-99) [Supreme Pontiff of Roman Catholic Church]
Pope Pius VI
Brashest, Cassius the. See:
CLAY, CASSIUS MARCELLUS, JR.
Brat Fink. See:
DAVIS, GWEN
BRATSBURG, HARRY (1915-) [American stage, motion picture and television actor]
Harry Morgan
Brave. See:
BROKE, SIR PHILIP BOWES VERE
Brave, Alfonso the (Alfonso el Bravo). See:
ALFONSO I
ALFONSO IV
Brave, Bravest of the. See:
NEY, MICHEL
Brave Men, The King of. See:
HENRY IV
Bravest of the Brave. See:
NEY, MICHEL
Bravo, Alfonso el (Alfonso the Brave). See:
ALFONSO I
ALFONSO IV
BRAWNER, HELEN. See:
Coffin, Geoffrey
Bray, Alison. See:
ROWLAND, DONALD SYDNEY
Brayce, William. See:
ROWLAND, DONALD SYDNEY
BRAYMAN, JAMES O. (1815-87) [American journalist, editor and author]

Harley Thorne
Braza, Jacque. See:
McKEAG, ERNEST LIONEL
Brazil, The Apostle of. See:
ANCHIETA (ANCHIETTA), JOSÉ DE
Brazilian Bombshell, The. See:
CUNHA, MARÍA DE CARMO MIRANDA DE
Bread-father, The. (Der Brodvater). See:
SOWER, CHRISTOPHER
Bread-fruit. See:
BLIGH, WILLIAM
Breaker, Champion Jail. See:
WEISS, EHRICH (ERIK WEISZ)
Breaker, The Father of the. See:
MARKLE, GEORGE BUSHER
BREAKSPEAR, NICKOLAS (c. 1100-59) [Supreme Pontiff of Roman Catholic Church]
Pope Adrian IV
BREAU, LOUIS (1893-1928) [American composer, conductor and publisher]
Lew Breau
BRECK [Breck]. See also:
Brick
BRECK, JAMES LLOYD (1818-76) [American Episcopal clergyman and missionary]
The Apostle of the Wilderness
Breck, Vivian. See:
BRECKENFELD, VIVIAN GURNEY
BRECKENFELD, VIVIAN GURNEY (1895-) [American educator and author]
Vivian Breck
Brécourt. See:
MARCOUREAU, GUILLAUME
Breda, Tjalmar. See:
DeJONG, DAVID CORNEL
Bredow, Miriam. See:
WOLF, MIRIAM BREDOW
Breeches, Little. See:
HAY, JOHN MILTON
BREEN, MAY SINGHI (190?-) [American composer, ukulele player and radio entertainer]
The Ukulele Lady
BREEN, MAY SINGHI. See also:
Sweethearts of the Air
BREETVELD, JIM PATRICK (1925-) [American author]
Avery Mann
Breezy Bill. See:
LEWIN, WILLIAM CHARLES JAMES
BREINLINGER, ALICE BEREND (1878-) [German author]
Alice Berend
Breitmann, Hans. See:
LELAND, CHARLES GODFREY
Bremer, Carl. See:
GUSTAFSON, AXEL
BRENAN. See also:
BRANNON
BRENNAN
Brennan
Brennand
BRENAN, GERALD (1894-) [British soldier and author]
George Beaton
Brenda Gray. See:
MACKINLAY, LEILA ANTOINETTE STERLING
Brenda Joyce. See:
LEABO, BETTY
Brenda Marshall. See:
ANKERSON, ARDIS
BRENNAN [Brennan]. See also:
BRANNON
BRENAN
Brennand
BRENNAN, JOHN NEEDHAM HUGGARD (1914-) [Irish author]
John Welcome
BRENNAN, JOSEPH LOMAS (1903-) [American author]
Steve Lomas
Brennan, Tim. See:
CONROY, JOHN WESLEY
Brennand. See also:
BRANNON
BRENAN
BRENNAN
Brennan
Brennand, Frank. See:
LAMBERT, ERIC

Brent, Carl. See:
WILLETT, EDWARD
Brent, George. See:
NOLAN, GEORGE
Brent, Loring. See:
WORTS, GEORGE FRANK
Brent, Romney. See:
LARRALDE, ROMULO
Brentford, Burke. See:
URNER, NATHAN DANE
Breon, Edmund. See:
MacLAVERTY, EDMUND
BRERETON, JOHN LE GAY (1871-) [Australian educator, essayist and poet]
Basil Garstang
Brescia, Moretto Da. See:
BONVICINO, ALESSANDRO
BRESHKOVSKY, CATHERINE (1844-1934) [Russian revolutionary leader]
The Little Grandmother of the Russian Revolution
BRESNAHAN, ROGER PATRICK (1880-1944) [Irish-American professional baseball player]
The Duke of Tralee
BREST, GEORGE K. ARTHUR (1899-) [British motion picture actor]
George K. Arthur
BRESTOWSKI, CARL AUGUST (1861-) [Austrian chemist and author]
Gustav Troll
Bret. See:
BRETT
Brett
Britt
HARTE, FRANCIS BRETT
Breton Amis. See:
BEST, RAYLEIGH BRETON AMIS
BRETON, EMILY CHARLOTTE LE (1852-1929) [English actress]
The Jersey Lily
Lily Langtry
BRETON, PHILLIPPE (1916-) [Canadian pianist, composer, music publisher and singer]
Phil Breton
Bretonne, Restif de la. See:
RESTIF, NICOLAS EDME
BRETT [Brett]. See also:
Bret
Britt
Brett Austin. See:
FLOREN, LEE
Brett, David. See:
CAMPBELL, WILL DAVIS
Brett Halliday. See:
DRESSER, DAVIS
BRETT, MARY ELIZABETH (fl. 1936-62) [British commercial artist and author]
Molly Brett
Brett, Michael. See:
TRIPP, MILES
Brett Rand. See:
NORWOOD, VICTOR GEORGE CHARLES
Bretwalda (Ruler of the British). See:
ETHELBERT (AETHELBERT) (AEDILBERCT)
BREUER, ELIZABETH (1893-) [American novelist]
Bessie Breuer
BREUGHEL. See:
BRUEGHEL (BREUGHEL), JAN
BRUEGHEL (BREUGHEL), PIETER
BREVAL, JOHN DURANT (c. 1680-1738) [English writer]
Joseph Gay
Brew. See: MOORE, WILLIAM A.
BREWER, FRED ALDWYN (1921-) [American journalist, educator and author]
Alfred Wynn
Brewer of Ghent, The. See:
VAN ARTEVELDE, JACOB
Brewster, Benjamin. See:
FOLSOM, FRANKLIN BREWSTER
Brewster, Eliot. See:

GIFFORD, JAMES NOBLE
BREWSTER, RALPH OWEN (1888-) [Maine politician]
The Aroostook Potato
BRIAN (926-1014) [King of Ireland]
Brian Boroimhe
Brian Boru (Brian of the Tribute)
Brian. See also:
Brien
HOOKER, WILLIAM BRIAN
KEITH, ROBERT, JR.
SULLIVAN, HARRY JOSEPH
Brian Agar. See:
BALLARD, WILLIS TODHUNTER
Brian Harwin. See:
HENDERSON, LeGRAND
Brian, James. See:
THOMAS, GORDON
TIERNEY, JOHN LAWRENCE
Brian Lynch. See:
LIDDY, JAMES DANIEL REEVES
Brian, Mary. See:
DANTZLER, LOUISE
Brian Nolan. See:
O'NUALLAIN, BRIAN
Brian O'Nolan. See:
O'NUALLAIN, BRIAN
Brian Wynne. See:
GARFIELD, BRIAN WYNNE
Bribery Bank, Emperor Nick of the. See:
BIDDLE, NICHOLAS
Brice, Fanny. See:
BORACH, FANNY
Brick. See:
BRECK
Breck
FLEAGLE, JACOB ROGER
MULLER, HAROLD
OWENS, CLARENCE B.
POMEROY, MARCUS MILLS
BRICKER, JOHN WILLIAM (1893-) [American statesman; Governor of Ohio]
Honest John
Brides in the Bath Murderer, The. See: SMITH, GEORGE JOSEPH
Bridge, Ann. See:
O'MALLEY, MARY DOLLING SANDERS, LADY O'MALLEY
Bridge Builder Bland. See:
BLAND, SCHUYLER OTIS
Bridge Building, The Father of American. See:
WHIPPLE, SQUIRE
Bridge, The Father of the Triborough. See:
FRANKLIN, BENJAMIN
BRIDGER, JAMES (1804-81) [American pioneer, scout, and settler]
The Daniel Boone of the Rockies
Jim Bridger
BRIDGES [Bridges]. See also:
BRYDGES
Bridges, Madeline. See:
DE VERE, MARY AINGE
BRIDGES, ROBERT SEYMOUR (1844-1930) [English poet laureate]
Droch
Bridget Elia. See:
LAMB, MARY ANN
Bridget Maclagan. See:
BORDEN, MARY
BRIDGET, ST. (died 523) [Patron saint of Ireland]
The Pearl of Ireland
Bridgman, Richard. See:
DAVIES, LESLIE PURNELL
Bridie, James. See:
MAVOR, DR. OSBORNE HENRY
Bridles Waite, Bloody. See:
WAITE, DAVID HANSON
Brien. See also:
BRIAN
Brian
Brien, Raley. See:
McCULLEY, JOHNSTON
Brigade, The General of the Mackerel. See:
McCLELLAN, GEORGE BRINTON
Brigadier. See:
ENGLISH, THOMAS DUNN

Brigadier Commanding Hospitals. See: BICKERDYKE, MARY ANN BALL
BRIGGS, CHARLES FREDERICK (1804-77) [American editor and author]
Harry Franco
BRIGHAM, GERTRUDE RICHARDSON (fl. 1917-26) [American editor, writer, lecturer and traveler]
Viktor Flambeau
Bright Eyes (Inshtatheanba). See: LA FLESCHE, SUZETTE
BRIGHT, JOHN (1811-89) [English Liberal statesman and orator]
The Apostle of Free Trade
The Tribune of the People
BRIGHT, MRS. MARY CHAVELITA DUNNE (1860-1945) [English novelist, dramatist and translator]
George Egerton
Bright Path (Wa-Tho-Huck). See: THORPE, JAMES FRANCIS
BRIGHT, TIMOTHY (1551-1615) [English physician and cleric; inventor of modern shorthand]
The Father of Shorthand
Brigitte Bardot, America's Answer to. See: REMICK, LEE
Brigitte Helm. See: SCHITTENHELM, GISELE EVE
BRILL, ETHEL CLAIRE (1877-)[American author]
Edwin C. Burritt
BRILLAT-SAVARIN, ANTHELME (1755-1826) [French lawyer and authority on gastronomy]
The Prince of Gourmets
Brilliant Madman, The. See: CHARLES XII
BRIMMER, ERNEST (1894-1949) [American motion picture actor]
Richard Dix
BRIND, SMYLLA (1928-) [American motion picture actress]
Vanessa Brown
BRINITZER, CARL (1907-) [Russian lawyer, broadcaster and author]
Usikota
BRINSMEAD, HESBA FAY (1922-) [Australian speech therapist, educator and author]
Pixie Hungerford
BRINTON, HENRY (1901-) [British author]
Alex Fraser
BRION, SIMON DE (c.1210-85) [Supreme Pontiff of Roman Catholic Church]
Pope Martin IV
BRISBANE, ARTHUR (1864-1936) [American editorialist, columnist and newspaper editor]
Old Double Dome
Brisbane, Major Walter. See: HARBAUGH, THOMAS CHALMERS
Brisson, Carl. See: PEDERSEN, CARL
BRISSOT, JACQUES PIERRE (1754-93) [French journalist and revolutionist]
De Warville
BRISTED, CHARLES ASTOR (1820-74) [American scholar, sports writer and author]
Carl Benson
BRISTER, RICHARD (1915-) [American author]
Will O. Grove
C.L. Lewin
George Richmond
Bristol Bill. See: UNKNOWN
Bristol Boy, The. See: CHATTERTON, THOMAS
Bristol, Julius. See: ABEL, ALAN IRWIN
Bristoliensis, Dunelmus. See: CHATTERTON, THOMAS
Britain. See:

BRITTEN
BRITTON
Britton
BRITTANY
Brittany
British Amazon, The. See: TALBOT, MARY ANNE
British Aristides, The. See: MARVELL, ANDREW
British Bayard, The. See: SIDNEY (SYDNEY), SIR PHILIP
British Cicero, The. See: PITT, WILLIAM
British Columbia, The Father of. See: DOUGLAS, SIR JAMES
British Homer, The. See: MILTON, JOHN
British Inland Navigation, The Father of. See: EGERTON, FRANCIS
British Jeremiah, The. See: GILDAS (GILDUS)
British Martial, The. See: OWEN, JOHN
British Novelists, The Salvator Rosa of. See: RADCLIFFE, ANN WARD
British Pausanias, The. See: CAMDEN, WILLIAM
British Pindar, The. See: GRAY, THOMAS
British Plastics, The Father of. See: SWINBURNE, SIR JAMES, 9TH BARONET
British, Ruler of the (Bretwalda). See: ETHELBERT (AETHELBERT) (AEDILBERCT)
British St. Stephen, The. See: ALBAN, ST.
British Samson, The. See: TOPHAM, THOMAS
British Senate, The Cicero of the. See: CANNING, GEORGE
British Skeptic of the Eighteenth Century, The Most Thoroughgoing. See: HUME, DAVID
British Socrates, The. See: BACON, SIR FRANCIS
British Solomon, The. See: JAMES I
British Strabo, The. See: CAMDEN, WILLIAM
British Varro, The. See: TUSSER, THOMAS
Brito, Phil. See: COLOMBRITO, PHILIP
Britt. See also:
Bret
BRETT
Brett
Britt, May. See: WILKENS, MAYBRITT
BRITTANY. See: ELEANOR OF BRITTANY
Brittany, The Damsel of. See: ELEANOR OF BRITTANY
Brittany, The Eagle of. See: GUESCLIN (DUGUESCLIN), BERTRAND DU
BRITTEN, EDWARD BENJAMIN (1913-) [English composer, pianist and conductor]
Benjamin Britten
Britton, Barbara. See: CZUKOR, BARBARA BRANTINGHAM
BRITTON, MATTIE LULA COOPER (1914-) [American educator and author]
Jane Patterson
BRITTON, THOMAS (1654?-1714) [founder of musical club in London]
The Musical Small-coal Man
BRIX, HERMAN (1909-) [American motion picture actor]
Bruce Bennett
Broad Shouldered (Herdebred). See: HAAKON II
Broadaxe, Benjamin. See: MUSICK, JOHN ROY
BROADBENT, DORA (1923-) [British stage and motion picture comedienne]
Dora Bryan
Broadbottom, Geffery. See: STANHOPE, PHILIP DORMER
Broadbrim, Old. See: RATHBONE, ST. GEORGE HENRY

Broadcaster, America's Most
Honored. See:
HARVEY, PAUL
Broadcasting, The Father of Radio.
See: DAVIS, HARRY PHILLIP
Broadway Joe. See:
NAMATH, JOSEPH
WILLIAM
Broadway, Mr. See:
COHAN, GEORGE MICHAEL
Broadway Producers, The Barnum of. See:
MARGULOIS, DAVID
Broadway, The Beau Brummel of.
See: FAY, LARRY
Broadway, The Mad Poet of.
See: CLARKE, McDONALD
Brock, Gavin. See:
LINDSAY, JOHN MAURICE
Brock, Lynn. See:
McALLISTER, ALISTER
Brock, Stuart. See:
TRIMBLE, LOUIS P.
BROCK, WILLIAM EMERSON
(1872-) [American candy
manufacturer and senator
from Tennessee]
The Candy Kid
BROCKWAY, JENNIE M. (1886-)
[American composer and
author]
Mary Jane Owen
Brod-vater, Der (The Bread-father). See:
SOWER, CHRISTOPHER
BRODELL, JOAN (1925-)
[American vaudeville and
motion picture actress]
Joan Leslie
Brodie, Steve. See:
STEVENS, JOHN
BRODRIBB, JOHN HENRY
(1838-1905) [British
actor and theater manager]
Sir Henry Irving
Brody, Marc. See:
WILKES-HUNTER, RICHARD
BROFELDT, JUHANI (1861-1921)
[Finnish writer]
Aho Juhani
BROKE, SIR PHILIP BOWES
VERE (1776-1841) [English
rear admiral]
Brave Broke

Broken Hand. See:
FITZPATRICK, THOMAS
Brom. See:
BROMLEY, ISAAC HILL
BROMFIELD, FARRON (1922-)
[American motion picture
actor]
John Bromfield
BROMLEY, ISAAC HILL (1833-98)
[American journalist]
Brom
Bronco Billy. See:
ANDERSON, G. M.
Bronco Carlos. See:
MILLER, CHARLES
Bronco Charlie. See:
MILLER, CHARLES
BRONNER, FERDINAND (1867-)
[Austrian educator and
dramatic author]
Franz Adamus
Bronson, Charles. See:
BUCHINSKY, CHARLES
Bronson, Howitzer. See:
HARDMAN, RICHARDS
LYNDEN
Bronson, Lita. See:
BELL, LOUISE PRICE
Bronson, Lynn. See:
LAMPMAN, EVELYN SIBLEY
Bronson, Oliver. See:
ROWLAND, DONALD SYDNEY
BRONSTEIN, LEV DAVIDOVICH
(1879-1940) [Russian
Jewish revolutionary]
Leon Trotsky
Bronstein, Yetta. See:
ABEL, JEANNE
BRONTË, ANNE (1820-49)
[English author]
Acton Bell
Lady Geralda
Olivia Vernon
Alexandria Zenobia
BRONTË, BRANWELL (1817-48)
[English author]
John Bud
Captain John Flower, M. P.
BRONTË, CHARLOTTE (1816-55)
[English author]
Currer Bell
Genius C. B.

Lord Charles Wellesley
The Marquis of Douro
BRONTË, EMILY JANE (1818-48) [English author]
R. Alcon
Ellis Bell
Bronzino, Il. See: COSIMO, AGNOLO (ANGIOLO) DI
BROOK, CLIFFORD (1891-) [British stage and motion picture actor]
Clive Brook
BROOK-SHEPHERD, GORDON (1918-) [English author]
Gordon Shepherd
Brooke, A. B. See: JENNINGS, LESLIE NELSON
Brooke, Carole. See: RAMSKILL, VALERIE PATRICIA ROSKAMS
BROOKE, GILBERT EDWARD (1873-) [British physician and author]
Anak Sungel
BROOKE, PETER (1907-) [English author]
Anthony Carson
BROOKER, BERTRAM (1888-) [English author]
Huxley Hearne
Richard Surrey
Brooker, Clark. See: FOWLER, KENNETH ABRAMS
Brooklyn Institute of Arts and Sciences, The Father of the. See: HEALY, AARON AUGUSTUS
Brooklyn, The First Citizen of. See: STRANAHAN, JAMES SAMUEL THOMAS
Brooklyn, Underworld, The Beau Brummel of the. See: UALE, FRANCESCO
Brooks, See: ATKINSON, JUSTIN BROOKS
BROOKS, ANNE SOOY (1911-) [American composer, author and singer]
Anne Savoy
BROOKS, ANNE TEDLOCK (1905-) [American author]
Anne Carter
Cynthia Millburn
Brooks, Geraldine. See: STROOCK, GERALDINE
Brooks Henderley. See: STRATEMEYER, EDWARD L.
BROOKS, JAMES GORDON (1801-41) [American editor and poet]
Florio
BROOKS, JEREMY (1926-) [British journalist, critic and author]
Clive Meikle
Brooks, Jonathan. See: MELLETT, JOHN CALVIN
Brooks McCormick. See: ADAMS, WILLIAM TAYLOR
BROOKS, MARIA GOWEN (c. 1794-1845) [American poet and novelist]
Maria del Occidente
BROOKS, NOAH (1830-1903) [American journalist, government official and author]
Uncle Noah
BROOKS, PRESTON SMITH (1819-57) [American statesman; senator from South Carolina]
Bully Brooks
BROONZY, WILLIAM LEE (1893-) [American jazz musician (singer, guitar)]
Big Bill Broonzy
BROSCHI, CARLO (1705-82) [Italian castrato singer]
Farinelli
BROSNAN, JAMES PATRICK (1929-) [American author]
Jim Brosnan
Brother Antonius. See: EVERSON, WILLIAM OLIVER
Brother Azarias. See: MULLANY, PATRICK FRANCIS
Brother, Baby (El Tato) See: SÁNCHEZ, ANTONIO
Brother Choleric. See: VAN ZELLER, HUBERT

Brother Devil (Fra Diavolo). See:
PEZZA, MICHELE
Brother Flavius. See:
ELLISON JAMES E.
Brother George. See:
LIBERACE, GEORGE J.
Brother Jack McDuff. See:
McDUFFY, EUGENE
Brother Jeremy Premont. See:
WILLETT, BROTHER
FRANCISCUS
Brother John Sellers. See:
SELLERS, JOHN B.
Brother Jonathan. See:
LAMBERT, JONATHAN
TRUMBULL, JONATHAN
Brother Lawrence. See:
HERMAN, NICHOLAS
Brother of the Lord, The. See:
JAMES THE LESS
Brother Orrin Primm. See:
WILLETT, BROTHER
FRANCISCUS
Brother Paul (Fra Paolo). See:
SARPI, PIETRO (PAOLO)
Brother, The Fourth. See:
AUNG, MAUNG HTIN
Brotherly, The (Philadelphus).
See: PTOLEMY II
Brothers. See:
Four Marx Brothers, The
Brothers Grimm, The, joint
pseud. of JACOB LUDWIG
KARL GRIMM (1785-1863) and
WILHELM KARL GRIMM
(1786-1859) [German
philologists and mythologists;
authors of Grimm's Fairy
Tales]
BROTHERS, JOYCE DIANE
BAUER (1927-) [American
psychologist, author and
broadcaster]
Dr. Joyce Brothers
Brothers Quintero, The. See:
Quintero, Álvarez
BROTHERS, RICHARD (1757-
1824) [English religious
fanatic]
Nephew of the Almighty
BROUGHAM, HENRY PETER
(1778-1868) [Baron
Brougham and Vaux;
English statesman, orator,
jurist and scientist]
Harry Twitcher
Brougham, J. T. See:
ST. JOHN, PERCY
BOLLINGBROKE
Broward, Donn. See:
HALLERAN, EUGENE
EDWARD
BROWIN, FRANCES WILLIAMS
(1898-) [American
editor, art director and
author]
Francis B. Williams
BROWN [Brown]. See also:
BROWNE
Browne
Brown, Alexis. See:
BEECHING, AMY BROWN
BROWN, ALICE (1857-1948)
[American novelist]
Martin Redfield
Brown, Andrew H. See:
CORRELL, CHARLES J.
BROWN, BETH (Fl. 1927-68)
[American author]
Beth A. Retner
Brown Bomber, The. See:
BARROW, JOSEPH LOUIS
Brown, Caroline. See:
KROUT, CAROLINE
VIRGINIA
Brown, Carter. See:
YATES, ALAN GEOFFREY
BROWN, CLAUDE (1937-)
[American Negro author]
Sonny
BROWN, DAVID (18??-73)
[American recluse and
book collector]
The Hermit of Newfane
BROWN, EDMUND GERALD
(1905-) [American
politician; governor of
California]
Pat Brown
Patrick Henry Brown
BROWN, ELIZABETH ANN
(1848-80) [English
actress]
Lizzie Bland
Lilian Adelaide Neilson
The Queen of the English Stage

Brown, Emily. See:
STERNE, EMMA GELDERS
Brown Eminence, The. See:
BORMANN, MARTIN
Brown, F. See:
MACKINNON, CHARLES ROY
BROWN, GEORGE (1847-) [British editor and author]
Campbell Brown
BROWN, GEORGE DOUGLAS (1869-1902) [Scottish author]
George Douglas
BROWN, H. CLARK (1898-) [American author and poet]
Donald Thistle
BROWN, HELEN HAYES (1900-) [American actress]
The First Lady of the American Theater
Helen Hayes
Brown, Irving. See:
ADAMS, WILLIAM TAYLOR
BROWN, JAMES NATHANIEL (1936-) [American Negro professional football player]
Jimmy Brown
BROWN, JAMES OSTEND (1906-63) [American jazz musician (saxophone)]
Pete Brown
BROWN, JOHN (c.1627-85) [Scotch Covenanter martyr]
The Christian Carrier
BROWN, JOHN (1800-59) [American abolitionist]
The Martyr Hero
Shubel Morgan
Old Brown of Ossawatomie
Old Ossawatomie
Ossawatomie Brown
BROWN, JOHN H., JR. (1891-) [American football player]
Babe Brown
BROWN, JOHN J. (1916-) [Canadian editor, management consultant and author]
Boris Sherashevski
BROWN, JOHN JACKSON (1820-91) [American educator]
The Cyclopedia of Knowledge
BROWN, LANCELOT (1715-83) [English landscape gardener]
Capability Brown
Brown, Mahlon A. See:
PECK, WILLIAM HENRY
BROWN, MARGARET WISE (1910-) [American writer of juvenile fiction]
Golden MacDonald
BROWN, MARGARET WISE. See also:
Sage, Juniper
BROWN, MAUREEN FITZSIMONS (1921-) [Irish motion picture actress]
Maureen O'Hara
The Queen of Technicolor
Brown, Mr. See:
THACKERAY, WILLIAM MAKEPEACE
BROWN, MORDECAI PETER CENTENNIAL (1876-1948) [American professional baseball player]
Three-Finger Brown
BROWN, MORNA DORIS (1907-) [British author]
Elizabeth Ferrars
E.X. Ferrars
Brown, Myra. See:
COOK, MYRA B.
BROWN, ROBERT JOSEPH (1907-) [American newspaper panel author]
Bob Brown
BROWN, ROSALIE GERTRUDE MOORE (1910-) [American poet and author]
Rosalie Brown
Rosalie Moore
Brown the Younger, Thomas. See: MOORE, THOMAS
BROWN, THEOPHILIS (1811-79?) [American tailor and man of letters]
The Literary Tailor
BROWN, THERON (1832-1914) [American Baptist clergy-

man, editor and author]
Park Ludlow
BROWN, THOMAS (1663-1704) [English satirical poet and prose writer]
Tom Brown
Brown, Three-Finger. See:
BROWN, MORDECAI PETER CENTENNIAL
LUCHESE, GAETANO
Brown, Tom. See:
BROWN, THOMAS
HUGHES, THOMAS
Brown, Tommy. See:
LUCHESE, GAETANO
Brown, Vanessa. See:
BRIND, SMYLLA
BROWN, VIRGINIA SHARPE (1916-) [American author]
Ginny Brown
Brown, Warner. See:
BOROSON, WARREN
Brown Wife, The Bonny. See:
JACKSON, RACHEL DONELSON
Brown, Will C. See:
BOYLES, CLARENCE SCOTT, JR;
BROWN, WILLIAM JAMES CLARK (1910-) [Australian author]
Jamieson Brown
BROWN, WILLIAM JOHN (1805-57) [American statesman; representative from Indiana]
Done Brown
BROWN, WILLIAM LOUIS (1910-64) [American author]
Bill Brown
BROWN, WILLIAM PERRY (1847-1923) [American journalist and author]
Captain William B. Perry
BROWN, ZENITH JONES (1898-) [American writer of mystery stories]
Leslie Ford
David Frome
BROWNE [Browne]. See also:
BROWN
Brown
BROWNE, CHARLES FARRAR (1834-67) [American humorist]
The Genial Showman
Artemus Ward
BROWNE, DOROTHY MARGARET STUART (fl. 1925-30) [British author]
Dorothy Margaret Stuart
Browne, Dunn. See:
FISKE, SAMUEL WHEELOCK
BROWNE, ERNEST D. (1900-) [American composer]
Irving Rose
BROWNE, GEORGE WALDO (1851-1930) [American lecturer and author of boys' books]
G. Waldo Browne
Victor St. Clair
BROWNE, HABLOT KNIGHT (1815-82) [English caricaturist]
Nemo
Phiz
Browne, Matthew. See:
RANDS, WILLIAM BRIGHTY
BROWNE, RILMA MARION (fl. early 20th cent.) [American educator and author]
Stanley Castle
Browne, Sam. See:
SMITH, RONALD GREGOR
BROWNE, THOMAS ALEXANDER (1826-1915) [Australian novelist]
Rolf Boldrewood
BROWNELL, HENRY HOWARD (1820-79) [American poet]
Our Battle Laureate
Brownie. See:
McGHEE, WALTER
BROWNING, EDWARD (1874-1934) [American real estate dealer and financier; figure in notorious lawsuit]
The Cinderella Man
Daddy Browning
BROWNING, ELIZABETH BARRETT (1806-61) [English poet]
E. B. B.
My Little Portuguese

Browning, Henry C. See:
MOWATT, ANNA CORA OGDEN RITCHIE
BROWNING, JOHN MOSES (1855-1926) [American firearms inventor]
The Father of the Automatic Rifle
BROWNLOW, WILLIAM CANNAWAY (1805-77) [American political and theological writer]
Parson Brownlow
The Fighting Parson
BROZ, JOSIP (1892-) [Yugoslav leader]
Marshal Tito
BROZA, ELLIOT LAWRENCE (1925-) [American jazz musician (leader, piano, singer)]
Elliot Lawrence
Bruce, Arthur Loring. See:
CROWNINSHIELD, FRANK
Bruce Bennett. See:
BRIX, HERMAN
Bruce Cabot. See:
BUJAC, JACQUES DE
Bruce Campbell. See:
EPSTEIN, SAMUEL
Bruce Carter. See:
HOUGH, RICHARD
Bruce, David. See:
McBROOM, MARDEN
Bruce, Guy. See:
PUNNETT, IVOR McCAULEY
BRUCE, JAMES (1730-94) [Scottish explorer]
The Abyssinian
Bruce Lester. See:
LISTER, BRUCE
Bruce Morgan. See:
HUESTON, BILLY
BRUCE, ROBERT (1915-) [American composer, author and violinist]
Robert B. Wright
Bruce Spencer, Dr. See:
ABEL, ALAN IRWIN
Bruce, The. See:
ROBERT I
BRUCE, WALLACE (1844-1914) [American poet]
Thursty McQuill
Bruder Klaus. See:
LOWENBRUGGER, NIKOLAS
BRUEGHEL (BREUGHEL), JAN (1568-1625) [Flemish painter]
Jan the Elder
Flower Brueghel
Velvet Brueghel
BRUEGHEL (BREUGHEL), JAN (1601-78) [Flemish painter]
Jan the Younger
BRUEGHEL (BREUGHEL), PIETER (1520?-69) [Flemish painter]
The Droll
Peasant Brueghel
Pieter the Elder
BRUEGHEL (BREUGHEL), PIETER (1564?-1638) [Flemish painter]
Hell Brueghel
Pieter the Younger
Bruff, Nancy. See:
GARDNER, NANCY BRUFF
BRUGH, SPANGLER ARLINGTON (1911-69) [American motion picture actor]
Beautiful Bob
Robert Taylor
BRUHNS, GEORGE FREDERICK WILLIAM (1874-1963) [German-American pianist, organist, composer and conductor]
Arthur Bruhns
Bruin Adams, Captain. See:
ELLIS, EDWARD SYLVESTER
Brulls, Christian. See:
SIMENON, GEORGES
BRUMBAUGH, CARL (1907-) [American footabll player and coach]
Little Napoleon
BRUMM, GEORGE FRANKLIN (1878-) [American statesman; representative from Pennsylvania]
Three-minute Brumm

BRUMMEL, GEORGE BRYAN
(1778-1840) [English dandy
and arbiter of dress]
Beau Brummel
Brummel of Broadway, The Beau.
See: FAY, LARRY
Brummel of the Army, The
Beau. See:
MacARTHUR, DOUGLAS
Brummel of the Brooklyn Underworld, The Beau. See:
UALE, FRANCESCO
Brummel of the Senate, The
Beau. See:
LEWIS, JAMES HAMILTON
BRUN. See:
BRUNO (BRUN), ST.
Brunel of America, The. See:
ELLET, CHARLES
BRUNET, MARGUERITE (1730-1820) [French actress and
theater manager]
Marguérite Montansier
BRUNI, LEONARDO (1369-1444)
[Italian humanist]
Aretino
Brunne, Robert de. See:
MANNYNG, ROBERT
BRUNNER, JOHN KILIAN HOUSTON (1934-) [British author]
Keith Woodcott
BRUNO (BRUN), ST. (925-65)
[Archbishop of Cologne and
Duke of Lorraine; scholar
and churchman]
Bruno the Great
BRUNO, COUNT OF EGISHEIM-DAGSBURG (died 1054)
[Supreme Pontiff of Roman
Catholic Church]
Pope Leo IX
St. Leo
Bruno, Frank. See:
ST. BRUNO, ALBERT
FRANCIS
BRUNO, JAMES (1917-)
[American composer,
singer and guitarist]
Jimmy Bruno
Bruno Lessing. See:
BLOCK, RUDOLPH EDGAR
BRUNO, ST. (c. 970-1009)
[Christian churchman and
martyr]
The Apostle of the Prussians
Bruno Walter. See:
SCHLESINGER, BRUNO
Brunswick, Otto of.
See: OTTO IV
Brutus. See:
SIMPSON, STEPHEN
BRUTUS, LUCIUS JUNIUS
(fl. 500 B.C.) [Roman
consul]
Stupid
Brutus, The Spanish. See:
GUZMÁN, ALONSO
PÉREZ DE
BRUYÈRE, JEAN DE LA (1645-96) [French moralist]
The Theophrastus of
France
Bryan, Dora. See:
BROADBENT, DORA
Bryan Green. See:
DAVIS, HORACE BANCROFT
Bryan, Jane. See:
O'BRIEN, JANE
Bryan, The Second William
Jennings. See:
LEE, JOSHUA BRYAN
BRYAN, WILLIAM JENNINGS
(1860-1925) [American
statesman, editor and
lecturer]
The Boy Orator of the Platte
The Great Commoner
The Silver-tongued Orator
BRYANS, ROBERT HARBINSON
(1928-) [Irish author]
Robin Bryans
Robert Harbinson
Bryant Bainbridge. See:
URNER, NATHAN DANE
BRYANT, RAPHAEL (1931-)
[American jazz musician
(piano, composer)]
Ray Bryant
BRYANT, WILLIAM CULLEN
(1794-1878) [American editor
and poet]
The American Wordsworth
C. B.
The Father of American Poets
Francis Herbert
Bryce, Ronald. See:

BRYDGES. See also:
BRIDGES
Bridges
ROCKEY, HOWARD
BRYDGES, GREY (died 1621)
[Lord Chandos]
The King of Cotswold
BRYER, WILLIAM FREDERICK
(1846-1908)[English comedian]
Willie Edouin
Brynner, Yul. See:
KHAN, TAIDJE
BRYSON, CHARLES (1877-)
[English writer of detective stories]
Charles Barry
BSCHLIESSMAYER, OSKAR
JOSEPH (1922-) [Austrian actor and director]
Oskar Werner
Bubber. See:
MILEY, JAMES
Bubbles. See:
SILVERMAN, BELLE
Buccaneer, Blackbeard the. See:
TEACH (THATCH), EDWARD
Buccer (Butzer), Martin.
See: KUHHORN, MARTIN
BUCCI, VINCENT (1921-)
[American jazz musician (leader, bass)]
Vinnie Burke
BUCHAN, ANNA (-1948)
[Scottish author]
Olive Douglas
Buchan, John. See:
TWEEDSMUIR, BARON
JOHN BUCHAN
Buchanan, Chuck. See:
ROWLAND, DONALD
SYDNEY
BUCHANAN, DUGALD (1716-68)
[Scottish schoolmaster, preacher and religious poet]
The Cowper of the Highlands
BUCHANAN, JAMES (1791-1858)
[Fifteenth President of the United States]
The Bachelor President
Old Buck
Old Public Functionary
The Sage of Wheatland
Ten-cent Jimmy
Buchanan, William. See:
BUCK, WILLIAM RAY
Buchenwald, The Bitch of.
See: KOCH, ILSE
BUCHHOLZ, ROBERT WERNER
(1933-) [German actor]
Hotte
The Teutonic James Dean
BUCHINSKY, CHARLES (c.1920-)
[American motion picture actor]
Charles Bronson
BUCHWALD, ARTHUR (1925-)
[American columnist]
Art Buchwald
Buck. See:
CLAYTON, WILBUR
EWING, WILLIAM
JONES, CHARLES
WASHINGTON, FORD LEE
WHITTEMORE, ARTHUR
BUCK, EDWARD EUGENE
(1885-1957) [American author, artist, director and producer]
Gene Buck
Buck, Old. See:
BUCHANAN, JAMES
BUCK, PEARL SYDENSTRICKER
(1892-) [American author]
John Sedges
Buck Private's Gary Cooper, The.
See: MacARTHUR,
DOUGLAS
BUCK, WILLIAM RAY (1930-)
[American author]
William Buchanan
Buckduck. See:
MAYS, WILLIE HOWARD
Bückeburg Bach, The. See:
BACH, JOHANN CHRISTOPH
FRIEDRICH
Bucketfoot. See:
SZYMANSKI, ALOYSIUS
HARRY
Buckeye, The Big. See:
SPROAT, EBENEZER
BUCKINGHAM, GEORGE
VILLIERS, 1ST DUKE OF
(1592-1628) [English statesman]
Steenie
BUCKINGHAM, GEORGE
VILLIERS, 2ND DUKE OF
(1628-87) [English

nobleman and playwright]
Zimri
BUCKINGHAM, GEORGE VILLIERS, 2ND DUKE OF
See also:
Cabal, The
BUCKINGHAM, WILLIAM ALFRED (1804-75) [Governor of Connecticut; staunch Union sympathizer]
Staunch Buckingham
BUCKLEY, CHRISTOPHER A. (1845-1922) [Democratic boss of San Francisco]
Blind Boss Buckley
The Blind White Devil
BUCKLEY, FERGUS REID (1930-) [American business executive and author]
Peter Crumpet
Buckrose, J. E. See
JAMESON, ANNIE EDITH
Buckshot. See:
WRIGHT, FORREST GLENN
Buckskin Sam. See:
HALL, MAJOR SAMUEL STONE
Buckwheat. See:
FRAZIER, JAMEL
Bucky. See:
HARRIS, STANLEY RAYMOND
JORDON, BAXTER BYERLY
Bud. See:
ABBOTT, WILLIAM
BUDD
Budd
BUDDE
FISHER, HARRY CONWAY
FLANAGAN, EDWARD
FREEMAN, LAWRENCE
JOHNSON, HOWARD BRENNAN
KELLAND, CLARENCE BUDINGTON
POWELL, EARL
SCOTT, ARTHUR BUDD
SHANK, CLIFFORD EVERETT, JR.
WILKINSON, CHARLES BURNHAM
YORKIN, ALAN
Bud Flanagan. See:
FLANAGAN, EDWARD WINTHROP, ROBERT
Bud, John. See:
BRONTË, BRANWELL
BUDAEUS. See:
BUDÉ (BUDAEUS), GUILLAUME
Budd. See:
BOETTICHER, OSCAR
Bud
BUDDE
JOHNSON, ALBERT J.
BUDD, JOHN (1913-) [English author]
Julian Prescot
BUDDE. See also:
Bud
BUDD
Budd
Buddy
BUDDE, GERHARD AUGUST (1865-) [German educator]
Dr. Edzard Friese
Buddha. See:
GAUTAMA SIDDHARTHA
BUDDHA LOES-LA, P'RA (1768-1824) [King of Thailand (Siam)]
Rama II
BUDDHA YOD FA, P'RA (1737-1809) [King of Thailand (Siam)]
Rama I
Buddhist Constantine, The. See:
ASOKA (ASAOKA)
BUDDICOM, JACINTHA LAURA MAY (fl. 1929) [British author]
Cini Willoughby Dering
Buddy. See:
ADLER, E. MAURICE
BAER, JACOB
BAKER, NORMAN
BOLDEN, CHARLES
BUDDE
CATLETT, GEORGE JAMES
CHILDERS, MARION
COLE, EDWIN LE MAR
COLLETTE, WILLIAM

MARCELL
DE FRANCO, BONIFACE FERDINAND LEONARDO
DE SYLVA, GEORGE GARD
EBSEN, CHRISTIAN RUDOLF
FIELDS, ARTHUR B.
GRECO, ARMANDO
JOHNSON, WOODROW WILSON
JONES, BURGHER WILLIAM
MONTGOMERY, CHARLES F.
PARKER, RAYMOND KLEIN
RAY, ROBERT J.
RICH, BERNARD
ROGERS, CHARLES
TATE, GEORGE HOLMES
WEED, HAROLD
WISE, ROBERT RAYMOND

Buddy Hackett. See: HACKER, LEONARD

Buddy Morrow. See: ZUDEKOFF, MOE

BUDÉ (BUDAEUS), GUILLAUME (1467-1540) [French savant]
The Prodigy of France

Budget, Genius on a Low. See: KRAMER, STANLEY E.

BUDINGTON, WILLIAM STONE (1919-) [American librarian]
Bill Budington

Buena Vista, Old. See: TAYLOR, ZACHARY

BUERGER, JOHN (1845-1927) [German-American grain merchant and speculator]
The Barley King

Buffalo. See: JONES, CHARLES JESSE

Buffalo Bill. See:
CODY, WILLIAM FREDERICK
MATTHEWSON, WILLIAM

Buffalo Chips. See: WHITE, JAMES

Buffalo Hangman, The. See: CLEVELAND, STEPHEN GROVER

Buffalo Hunter of the Plains, The Champion. See: CODY, WILLIAM FREDERICK

Buffalo Killer, The. See: MATTHEWSON, WILLIAM

Buffalo Sheriff, The. See: CLEVELAND, STEPHEN GROVER

Buffalo, The Father of. See: ELLICOT, JOSEPH

Buffalo, The Hangman of. See: CLEVELAND, STEPHEN GROVER

Buffoon, The. See: LINCOLN, ABRAHAM

Buffoon, The Pulpit. See: PETERS, HUGH

Buffy. See: SAINTE-MARIE, BEVERLY

Bug, The Gold. See: BENTON, THOMAS HART

BUGBEE, RUTH CARSON (1903-) [American author]
Ruth Carson

BUGENHAGEN, JOHANN (1485-1558) [German religious reformer]
Dr. Pommer
Pomeranus

Bugs. See:
BOWER, MAURICE
MORAN, GEORGE C.

Builder, Bill the. See: McADOO, WILLIAM GIBBS

Builder Bland, Bridge. See: BLAND, SCHUYLER OTIS

Builder of the Chattanooga, The. See: OCHS, ADOLPH SIMON

Builder of the City of Houston, The. See: WILSON, WILLIAM ABNER

Builder, The Empire. See: HILL, JAMES JEROME

Building in America, The Father of Iron Ship. See: ROACH, JOHN

Building, The Father of American Bridge. See:

WHIPPLE, SQUIRE
Building, The Father of Ship. See: DICKIE, GEORGE WILLIAM
BUJAC, JACQUES DE (1904-) [American motion picture actor]
Bruce Cabot
Bulgarians, Slayer of (Bulgaroktonos). See:
BASIL II
Bulgaroktonos (Slayer of Bulgarians). See:
BASIL II
Bull. See:
DURHAM, EDWARD FANT
HALSEY, WILLIAM FREDERICK
NELSON, WILLIAM
RUTHER, WYATT
Bull-dog. See also:
Bulldog
Bull-dog, The Federal. See:
MARTIN, LUTHER
Bull, Mrs. See:
ANN
Bull Moose, The. See:
ROOSEVELT, THEODORE
Bull of the Pampas, The Wild. See: FIRPO, LUIS ANGEL
Bull of the Woods, The. See:
SUMNER, CHARLES
Bull, Sitting. See:
LAWSON, JOHN DANIEL
NORTON, OLIVER HAZARD PERRY THROCK
SUMMERALL, CHARLES PELOT
TATANKA YOTANKA
Bull, The. See:
ALLENBY, EDMUND HENRY HYNMAN, 1ST VISCOUNT
Bull, The Eretrian. See:
MENEDEMUS OF ERETRIA
Bull, The Geneva. See:
MARSHALL, STEPHEN
Bulldog. See:
Bull-dog
CHEATHAM, BENJAMIN FRANKLIN
SMITH, WALTER BEDELL
Bulldog, The. See:
LONGSTREET, JAMES
BULLEID, H.A.V. (1912-) [British engineer and author]
D. Collins
Bullfighting, The Pontiff of. See:
GÓMEZ, JOSÉ
Bullingham, Rodney. See:
SLADEN, NORMAN ST. BARBE
Bullion, Old. See:
BENTON, THOMAS HART
BULLITT, JOHN CHRISTIAN (1824-1902) [American lawyer; instrumental in developing the city of Philadelphia]
The Father of Greater Philadelphia
BULLOCK, MICHAEL (1918-) [British translator and author]
Michael Hale
Bully. See:
BROOKS, PRESTON SMITH
BULMER, HENRY KENNETH (1921-) [British author]
Ernest Corley
Philip Kent
Karl Maras
BULMER, HENRY KENNETH. See also:
Johns, Kenneth
Bump. See:
HADLEY, IRVING D.
BUMP, MERCY LAVINIA WARREN (1841-1919) [American midget exhibited by PHINEAS TAYLOR BARNUM]
Lavinia Warren
BUNCE, CORAJANE DIANE (1919-) [American composer, singer and actress]
Diane Ward
BUNDGAARD, ERNEST (1920-) [American radio announcer and disc jockey]
Ernie Allen
BUNGAY, THOMAS (fl. c.1290) [English Franciscan monk

and teacher]
Friar Bungay
Bunk. See:
JOHNSON, WILLIAM GEARY
Bunker C. Hill, Professor. See: ABEL, ALAN IRWIN
BUNKER, CHANG. See:
Siamese Twins, The
BUNKER, ENG. See:
Siamese Twins, The
Bunky. See:
GREEN, VERNICE, JR.
BUNN, ALFRED (c.1796-1860) [English theater manager; writer and translator of libretti]
The Poet Bunn
BUNN, ALFRED (fl. 1819-26) [English lessee of Drury Lane Theater, London]
The Napoleon of the Drama
Bunny. See:
BERIGAN, ROLAND BERNARD
SCHULTZE, CARL EMIL
Buñolero, El. See:
ALBARRÁN, CARLOS RUFO
Buntline, Ned. See:
JUDSON, EDWARD ZANE CARROLL
BUNYAN, JOHN (1628-88) [English religious author and preacher]
Bishop Bunyan
The Immortal Dreamer
The Immortal Tinker
Bunyan, The Modern. See:
MILLER, JAMES RUSSELL
Bunyan, The Shipyard. See:
HIGGINS, ANDREW JACKSON
BUONACCORSO, LORENZO DI CIONE DI SER (1378-1455) [Florentine sculptor, goldsmith and painter]
Lorenzo Ghiberti
BUONARROTI, MICHELANGELO (1475-1564) [Italian Renaissance sculptor, painter, architect and poet]
The Divine Madman
Michael Angelo
Michelangelo
BUONCOMPAGNI, UGO (1502-85) [Supreme Pontiff of Roman Catholic Church]
Pope Gregory XIII
BURACK, SYLVIA (1916-) [American editor]
Sylvia E. Kamerman
BURBAGE, RICHARD (c.1567-1619) [English actor and theater owner]
Roscius
BURBANK, LUTHER (1849-1926) [American horticulturist]
The Plant Wizard
BURCE, SUZANNE (c.1928-) [American singer and motion picture actress]
Jane Powell
BURCHARD, SAMUEL DICKINSON (1812-91) [American Presbyterian clergyman]
The Student Nurse of Danville
BURDETTE, ROBERT JONES (1844-1913) [American journalist and humorist]
The Burlington Hawkeye Man
Burdick, Austin C. See:
COBB, SYLVANUS, JR.
BURDICK, USHER L. (1879-) [American lawyer and politician; representative from North Dakota]
Chief Burdick
Burford, Eleanor. See:
HIBBERT, ELEANOR BURFORD
Burgeon, G. A. L. See:
BARFIELD, OWEN
Burger, John. See:
MARQUARD, LEOPOLD
Burgess. See:
TREVOR, ELLESTON
BURGESS, ANTHONY (1917-) [British author]
Joseph Kell
John Burgess Wilson
Burgess, Lord. See:
BURGIE, IRVING
BURGIE, IRVING (1924-) [American composer, singer and guitarist]

Lord Burgess
Burglar, The Babbling. See:
MORRISON, RICHARD C.
Burgoyne, Elizabeth. See:
PICKLES, MABEL
ELIZABETH
BURGOYNE, JOHN (1722-92)
[British general officer
and dramatist]
Gentlemanly Johnny
Sir Jack Brag
Burguillos, Tome. See:
CARPIO, LOPE FÉLIX
DE VEGA
BURGUNDY. See:
GERHARD OF BURGUNDY
GUY OF BURGUNDY
Burke, Betty. See:
STUART, CHARLES EDWARD LOUIS PHILIP
CASIMIR
Burke Brentford. See:
URNER, NATHAN DANE
BURKE (CANARY), MARTHA
JANE (1852-1903) [American
frontier character]
Calamity Jane
BURKE, EDMUND (1729-97)
[British statesman, orator
and writer]
The Dinner-Bell
The First Man in the Commons
BURKE, EDMUND. See also:
Wondrous Three, The.
BURKE, EDWARD RAYMOND
(1880-) [American
lawyer and politician;
senator from Nebraska]
The Author of the New Deal
Burke, Fielding. See:
DARGAN, OLIVE TILFORD
BURKE, J. FRANCIS
(1914-) [American conductor, arranger and recording executive]
Sonny Burke
BURKE, JOHN FREDERICK
(1922-) [British editor
and author]
Jonathan Burke
Sara Morris
Burke, Leda. See:
GARNETT, DAVID

BURKE, MARY WILLIAM
ETHELBERT APPLETON
(1885-1970) [American
stage and motion picture
actress]
Billie Burke
Burke, Vinnie. See:
BUCCI, VINCENT
BURKE, WILLIAM (c.1870-)
[American ex-convict;
later member of the Philadelphia City Council]
The Prince of Flatworkers
Philadelphia's Jean
Valjean
Burl Ives. See:
IVANHOE, BURL ICLE
BURLEIGH (BURLEY),
WALTER (1274/5-c.1345)
[English scholar]
The Plain and Perspicuous
Doctor
Burlesque Poetry, The Father of.
See: HIPPONAX
BURLEY. See:
BURLEIGH (BURLEY),
WALTER
Burley, Mary Lou. See:
SCRUGGS, MARY
ELFRIEDA
BURLINGAME, VIRGINIA
STRUBLE (1900-)
[American librarian,
teacher and author]
Virginia Struble
Burlington Hawkeye Man, The.
See: BURDETTE,
ROBERT JONES
BURMAN (BURMANN), PIETER
(1668-1741) [Dutch
classical scholar]
Pieter the Elder
BURMAN (BURMANN), PIETER
(1714-78) [Dutch
classical scholar]
Pieter the Younger
BURNETT, CAROL (1934?-)
[American comedienne,
singer and television personality]
Hot Lips
BURNETT, DAVID (1931-)
[American editor and author]

Terrave Bernarn
Peter Pace
Burnett, Ernie. See:
BERNADETTI, ERNEST MARCO
BURNETT, WILLIAM RILEY (1899-) [American author]
W.R. Burnett
James Updyke
BURNEY [Burney]. See also:
Berni
Bernie
Burney, Anton. See:
HOPKINS, KENNETH
BURNEY, FRANCES (1752-1840) [British novelist and diarist]
Madame D'Arblay
Fanny Burney
BURNFORD, SHEILA PHILIP COCHRANE AVERY (1918-) [Scottish author]
S. D. Burnford
BURNHAM, GEORGE P. See:
Old 'un
Burns. See:
BYRNES
MANTLE, ROBERT BURNS
BURNS, EEDSON LOUIS MILLARD (1897-) [Canadian general officer and author]
Arlington B. Conway
Burns, George. See:
BIRNBAUM, NATHAN
BURNS, JOHN (1793-1872) [American soldier, distinguished for bravery in battle]
The Hero of the Battle of Gettysburg
BURNS, JOHN IRVING (1907-) [American professional baseball player]
Slugger Burns
Burns of America, The. See:
RILEY, JAMES WHITCOMB
WHITTIER, JOHN GREENLEAF
Burns of France, The. See:
BOÉ, JACQUES
Burns of New England. See:
EASTMAN, CHARLES GAMAGE
Burns of the Green Mountain See: EASTMAN, CHARLES GAMAGE
BURNS, ROBERT (1759-96) [Scottish poet]
The Ayrshire Poet
The Bard of Ayrshire
Bobbie Burns
A Heaven-taught Plowman
The Peasant Bard
Sylvander
Burns, Tex. See:
L'AMOUR, LOUIS DEARBORN
Burns, The Dorsetshire. See:
BARNES, WILLIAM
Burns, The French. See:
BÉRANGER, PIERRE-JEAN DE
Burns, The Lancashire. See:
WAUGH, EDWIN
BURNS, WILLIAM (1904-54) [American Western motion picture actor]
Tom Tyler
BURNS, WILLIAM JOHN (1861-1932) [American detective]
Never Fail Burns
BURNSON, GEORGE (1921-) [American opera singer]
George London
BURR, AGNES RUSH (fl. 1905-29) [American journalist and author]
Barbara Boyd
Burr, Dangerfield. See:
INGRAHAM, COLONEL PRENTISS
Burr, Jane. See:
WINSLOW, ROSE GUGGENHEIM
Burritt, Edwin C. See:
BRILL, ETHEL CLAIRE
BURRITT, ELIHU (1811-79) [American blacksmith, Biblical student and reformer]
The Learned Blacksmith
Burroughs, Ellen. See:
JEWETT, SOPHIE
BURROUGHS, JOHN (1837-1921)

[American ornithologist and naturalist]
The Grey-crested Flycatcher
The Hermit of Slabsides
John o' Birds
The Laird of Woodchuck Lodge

BURROUGHS, MARGARET TAYLOR (1917-) [American teacher and author]
Margaret Taylor

BURROUGHS, WILLIAM SEWARD (1914-) [American author]
Mr. Bradly
William Lee
Mr. Martin

BURROWS, ABRAM S. (1910-) [American producer, writer and comedian]
Abe Burroughs

BURROWS, DALLAS FREDERICK (1928-) [American actor and comedian]
Orson Bean

Burt. See:
Bert
Burte
LANCASTER, BURTON STEPHEN
SHOTTON, BURTON EDWIN

Burt Arthur. See:
SHAPPIRO, HERBERT ARTHUR

Burt Farnham. See:
CLIFFORD, HAROLD B.

BURT, KATHERINE NEWLIN (1882-) [American novelist]
Rebecca Scarlett

Burt Kroll. See:
ROWLAND, DONALD SYDNEY

Burt L. Standish. See:
PATTEN, WILLIAM GILBERT
WHITSON, JOHN HARVEY

Burte. See:
Bert
BURT
Burt

Burte, Hermann. See:
STRUBE, HERMANN

Burton, Alfred. See:
MITFORD, JOHN

BURTON, EDWARD J. (1917-) [American correspondent and author]
Michael Carey

BURTON, JENNIE DAVIS (fl. 1871-90) [American author]
Gipsy Glenn

BURTON, JOAN EILEEN VERONICA (1921-) [English author]
Cecil Vincent
Suzy Yorke

Burton Lane. See:
LEVY, BURTON

Burton, Major Andy. See:
RATHBONE, ST. GEORGE HENRY

Burton, Miles. See:
STREET, CECIL JOHN CHARLES

Burton, Richard. See:
JENKINS, RICHARD

BURTON, ROBERT (1577-1640) [English author and student]
Democritus Junior

Burton Saxe. See:
SIKES, WILLIAM WIRT

Burton, Thomas. See:
LONGSTREET, STEPHEN

BURWELL, CLIFFORD R. (1898-) [American composer, pianist and arranger]
Cliff Burwell

Busby Berkeley. See:
ENOS, WILLIAM BERKELEY

Busby of New England, The. See: LOVELL, JOHN

BUSCH, LOUIS F. (1910-) [American jazz musician (piano)]
Joe Fingers Carr

BUSHKIN, JOSEPH (1916-) [American composer, pianist, trumpeter and conductor]
Joe Bushkin

BUSHNELL, MRS. WILLIAM R. (fl. mid 19th cent.) [American author]
Helen Luqueer

BUSHNELL, WILLIAM H. (1823-9?) [American

attorney, journalist, poet and author]
Frank Webber
Busiest and Most Versatile Woman, Hollywood's. See: HOPPER, ELDA FURRY
Business Scene We Have, The Most Helpful Philosopher About the. See: DRUCKER, PETER FERDINAND
Business, The King of the Marine Insurance. See: TOWNSEND, HAWORTH NOTTINGHAM
Buster. See:
BAILEY, WILLIAM C.
COOPER, GEORGE
CRABBE, CLARENCE LINDEN
HARDING, LAVERE
KEATON, JOSEPH FRANCIS
SHAVER, FLOYD HERBERT
Buster, The Balloon. See: LUKE, FRANK, JR.
Buster, The Trust. See: ROOSEVELT, THEODORE
Busting President, The Trust. See: ROOSEVELT, THEODORE
Busybody, The. See: FRANKLIN, BENJAMIN
Butch. See:
BALLARD, GEORGE
JENKINS, JACKIE
LA GUARDIA, FIORELLO HENRY
WARREN, EDWARD
Butcher. See:
CUMBERLAND, WILLIAM AUGUSTUS, DUKE OF
GRANT, HIRAM ULYSSES
HOOD, JOHN BELL
WEYLER Y NICOLAU, VALERIANO
Butcher Bill Poole. See: POOLE, WILLIAM
Butcher, Bill the. See: POOLE, WILLIAM
Butcher Boy, The. See: WANDERER, CARL
Butcher from Galena. See: GRANT, HIRAM ULYSSES
Butcher of England, The. See: TIPTOFT, JOHN
Butcher, The Bloody. See: CUMBERLAND, WILLIAM AUGUSTUS, DUKE OF
Butcher, The (Makeles). See: LEO I
BUTLER, BENJAMIN FRANKLIN (1818-93) [American general officer, in charge of New Orleans during Civil War]
The Beast
Beast Butler
Old Cockeye
Silver Spoon Butler
Spoon Butler
Spoon Stealer
BUTLER, BISHOP JOSEPH (1692-1752) [British churchman]
The Bacon of Theology
BUTLER, LADY ELEANOR (1745-1829) [Irish recluse]
Lady of the Vale
Maid of Llangollen
BUTLER, MARION (1863-1938) [American senator from North Carolina; active in establishing rural free delivery of mail]
The Father of Rural Free Delivery
BUTLER, REGINALD COTTERELL (1913-) [British sculptor]
Reg Butler
BUTLER, SAMUEL (1835-1902) [British painter, philosophical, miscellaneous writer]
Eubulus
John Pickard Owen
BUTLER, SMEDLEY DARLINGTON (1881-1940) [American general officer]
Duckboard
Hell's Devil Butler
Old Gimlet Eye
Butler, The American. See: FESSENDEN, THOMAS GREEN
BUTLER, THOMAS (1748-18??) [Irish-American military officer, distinguished for

bravery]
The Navarre of the American Revolution
Butt, Boswell, Esq. See:
ROSS, CHARLES HENRY
Butte Bashkirtseff, The. See:
MACLANE, MARY
Butter. See:
JACKSON, QUENTIN LEONARD
BUTTERFIELD, DAVID (1932-) [British ballet dancer]
David Blair
Butterfly Farmer, The. See:
NEWMAN, LEONARD HUGH
Buttermere, The Beauty of. See:
ROBINSON, MARY
BUTTERS, DOROTHY GILMAN (1923-) [American author]
Dorothy Gilman
BUTTERWORTH, WILLIAM EDMUND III (1929-) [American author]
Webb Beech
Walker E. Blake
Edmund O. Scholefield
Buttle, Myra. See:
PURCELL, VICTOR
BUTTON, RICHARD TOTTEN (1929-) [American figure skater]
Dick Button
Buttons, Red. See:
SCHWATT, AARON
BUTTS, JAMES WALLACE, JR. (1907-) [American football coach]
The Little Round Man
Wally Butts
Butzer (Buccer), Martin. See:
KUHHORN, MARTIN
BUXBAUM, MARTIN (1913-) [American editor, photographer and writer]
Martin Noll
BUXTON, JEDEDIAH (1705-72) [English mathematical prodigy]
The Calculator
BUYRETTE, PIERRE LAURENT (1727-75) [French dramatist]
Dormant de Belloy
Buzz. See:
ADLAM, BASIL G.
BUZZELL, EDWARD (1900-) [American author, director and producer]
Eddie Buzzell
Buzzy. See:
DROOTIN, BENJAMIN
WARES, CLYDE
By. See:
DUNHAM, WILLIAM D.
By a Bostonian. See:
POE, EDGAR ALLAN
By a Gentleman of Virginia. See:
DAWSON, WILLIAM
By Ganny Cross. See:
CROSS, OLIVER HARLAN
By Miss Ella Vator. See:
SMITH, HARRY ALLEN
By Professor Wilden-Hart. See:
WILSON-HART, BERNARD JOHN
By Several Hands. See:
BEHN, MRS. APHRA
By the Author of "Elizabeth and her German Garden." See:
BEAUCHAMP, MARY ANNETTE, COUNTESS RUSSELL (MRS. HENNING ARNIM)
By the Author of "Gentlemen Joe." See: BADGER, JOSEPH E., JR.
By the Author of "Pamela." See:
RICHARDSON, SAMUEL
By the Author of "Waverley." See: SCOTT, SIR WALTER
BYARD. See:
BAYARD
Bayard
BYARD, JOHN A., JR. (1922-) [American jazz musician (piano, other instruments, composer)]
Jaki Byard
BYLES, MATHER (1706/7-88) [American Congregationalist minister, poet and writer]
Punning Byles
BYLL. See:
Bil
Bill
BIEL (BYLL), GABRIEL

BYNNER, WITTER. See:
Knish, Anne
BYRD [Byrd]. See:
BIRD
Bird
BYRD (BIRDE), WILLIAM (1543-1623) [English organist and composer]
The Father of Musick
BYRD, GENE (1933-) [American jazz musician (bass, guitar, flute)]
Joe Byrd
BYRD, HARRY FLOOD (1887-1966) [American farmer, publisher and U.S. senator from Virginia]
Mr. Economy
The Watchdog of the Treasury
Byrd Hooper. See:
ST. CLAIR, BYRD HOOPER
BYRD, SAMUEL ARMANIE (1908-) [American actor, author and theatrical producer]
Sam Byrd
Byrne, Donn. See:
DONN-BYRNE, BRIAN OSWALD
BYRNES. See also:
BURNS
Burns
BYRNES, EDD (1933-) [American teenage television actor]
Kookie
BYRNES, JAMES FRANCIS (1879-) [American politician; Governor of South Carolina, U.S. Supreme Court Justice]
Jimmy Byrnes
Byrom, James. See:
BRAMWELL, JAMES GUY
BYRON [Byron]. See also:
BOYRON
BYRON, CAPTAIN JOHN (-1791) [father of GEORGE GORDON NOEL BYRON
Mad Jack
BYRON, GEORGE GORDON NOEL (1788-1824) [English poet]
Lord Byron
BYRON, JAMES (1931-55) [American motion picture actor]
James Dean
Byron Janis. See:
YANKS, BYRON
BYRON, JOHN (1723-86) [English admiral]
Foul Weather Jack
Byron, John. See:
ARMSTRONG, JOHN BYRON
Byron, The French. See:
MUSSET, LOUIS CHARLES ALFRED DE
Byron, The Oregon. See:
MILLER, CINCINNATUS HEINE (HEINER)
Byron, The Russian. See:
PUSHKIN, ALEXANDER
Bysshe Vanolis. See:
THOMSON, JAMES
Bystander, A. See:
SMITH, GOLDWIN

C

C.A.B. See:
BARBER, CHARLES ALFRED
C.B. See:
BRYANT, WILLIAM CULLEN
DE MILLE, CECIL BLOUNT
C.B., Genius. See:
BRONTË, CHARLOTTE
C. Busby Smith. See:
SMITH, JOHN
C.C. Shackleton. See:
ALDISS, BRIAN WILSON
C.E. Raimond. See:
ROBINS, ELIZABETH
C.E. Tripp. See:
MORRIS, CHARLES SMITH
C.F. Griffin. See:
FISKO, EUNICE CLELAND
C.H. Frick. See:
IRWIN, CONSTANCE FRICK

C.H. Thames. See:
MARLOWE, STEPHEN
C. Humfrey. See:
OSBORNE, CHARLES HUMFREY CAULFIELD
C.J. Pennethorne Hughes. See:
HUGHES, CHARLES JAMES PENNETHORNE
C.K. Munro. See:
MACMULLEN, CHARLES KIRKPATRICK
C.L. See:
MAIZEL, CLARICE MATTHEWS
C.L. Anthony. See:
SMITH, DODIE
C.L. Lewin. See:
BRISTER, RICHARD
C. Lenanton. See:
OMAN, CAROLA MARY ANIMA
C.M.B. See:
BRAME, CHARLOTTE MARY
C.M. Cornwall. See:
ROE, MARY ABIGAIL
C.M. O'Neill. See:
WILKES-HUNTER, RICHARD
C. O'Malley. See:
LEVER, CHARLES JAMES
C.R. Mill. See:
CNRJANSKI, MILOS
C. Raymond Dyer. See:
DYER, CHARLES
C.S. See:
FORESTER, CECIL SCOTT
LEWIS, CLIVE STAPLES
C.S. Jennison. See:
STARBIRD, KAYE
C. Sharpe. See:
HOUGH, CLARA SHARPE
C. Sydney. See:
TRALINS, S. ROBERT
C. 3. 3. See:
WILDE, OSCAR FINGAL O'FLAHERTIE WILLS
C.V. Terry. See:
SLAUGHTER, FRANK GILL
C.W. Ceram. See:
MAREK, KURT WILLI
Cab. See:
CALLOWAY, CABELL, 3RD
Cabal, The, joint nickname of THOMAS CLIFFORD, 1ST BARON CLIFFORD OF CHUDLEIGH (1630-73); ANTHONY ASHLEY-COOPER, 1ST EARL OF SHAFTSBURY (1621-83); GEORGE VILLIERS, 2ND DUKE OF BUCKINGHAM (1628-87); HENRY BENNETT, EARL OF ARLINGTON (1618-85) and JOHN MAITLAND, DUKE OF LAUDERDALE (1616-82), [members of the ministry of CHARLES II, King of England]
Cabal, The. See also:
BUCKINGHAM, GEORGE VILLIERS, 2ND DUKE OF
Caballero, Fernán. See:
FABER, CECILIA BÖHL DE
Cabin Candidate, The Log. See:
HARRISON, WILLIAM HENRY
Cabin Harrison, Log. See:
HARRISON, WILLIAM HENRY
Cable, Boyd. See:
EWART, ERNEST ANDREW
CABLE, GEORGE WASHINGTON (1844-1925) [American novelist]
Drop Shot
Cabot, Bruce. See:
BUJAC, JACQUES DE
CABRINI, MARY FRANCES (1850-1917) [Italian Roman Catholic nun]
Frances Xavier Cabrini
Mother Cabrini
CACCIANEMICI, GHERARDO (died 1145) [Supreme Pontiff of Roman Catholic Church]
Pope Lucius II
CACCINI, GIULIO (1550?-1618) [Italian composer]
Giulio Romano
Cactus Jack. See:
GARNER, JOHN NANCE
CADE, JOHN (died 1450)

[Irish leader of insurgents in England]
Aylmer
The Captain of Kent
Jack Amend-all
Jack Cade
Mortimer
Cadet, St. Denis le. See:
ALLEN, PAUL
Cadmus. See:
ZACHOS, JOHN CELIVERGOS
Cadore, Da. See:
VECELLI (VECELLIO), TIZIANO
CADWALADER (CADWALLADER) (died c. 664) [British king]
The Blessed
CAEDMON (CEDMON), ST. (fl. c. 670) [Anglo-Saxon (Northumbrian) poet]
The Anglo-Saxon Milton
Caedmon, Father. See:
WAHL, CAEDMON THOMAS
Caesar. See:
CESARI
CESARIO
HAMILTON, ALEXANDER
LINCOLN, ABRAHAM
CAESAR, EUGENE LEE (1927-) [American author]
Johnny Laredo
Anthony Sterling
Caesar of Football, The. See:
LITTLE, LOUIS LAWRENCE
Caesar, Philopator Philometer. See: PTOLEMY XIV
CAESAR, R.D. See:
James, Dynely
Caesar, Sawdust. See:
GOEHRING, HERMANN WILHELM
CAESAR, SIDNEY (1922-) [American comedian]
Sid Caesar
Caesar Smith. See:
TREVOR, ELLESTON
Caesar, The American. See:
GRANT, HIRAM ULYSSES
CAESAREA. See:
EUSEBIUS OF CAESAREA
CAETANI, BENEDETTO (c. 1235-1303) [Supreme Pontiff of Roman Catholic Church]
Pope Boniface VIII
Café Society, The Social Historian of the. See:
BEEBE, LUCIUS
Cagancho. See:
RODRÍGUEZ, JOAQUIN
CAGLIARI (CALIARI) PAOLO (1528-88) [Italian Venetian painter]
The Painter of Pageants
Paolo Veronese
Cagliostro, Count Alessandro di. See:
BALSAMO, GIUSEPPE
CAGNEY, JAMES (1904-) [American actor]
Jimmy Cagney
Cagney, Peter. See:
WINTER, BEVIS
CAHN, ZVI (1896-) [Polish educator, editor and author]
Harry C. Laurie
CAIANI, JOSEPH (1929-) [American conductor, arranger and publisher]
Joe Cain
CAILLET, GUILLAUME (fl. 1358) [French peasant leader of the Jacquerie]
Jacques Bonhomme
CAIN [Cain]. See:
CAINE
Caine
KANE
Kane
Kayne
CAIN, ARTHUR HOMER (1913-) [American author]
Arthur King
Cain, Christopher. See:
FLEMING, THOMAS JAMES
CAÏN, HENRI-LOUIS (1729-78) [French actor]
Henri-Louis Lekain
CAIN, JACQUELINE RUTH (1928-) [American jazz musician (singer)]

Jackie Cain
Cain, Joe. See:
CAIANI, JOSEPH
CAIN, MERRITT PATRICK (1908-) [American professional baseball player]
Sugar
Sugar Cain
Cain, Tubal. See:
SPOTSWOOD, ALEXANDER
CAINE [Caine]. See also:
CAIN
Cain
KANE
Kane
Kayne
Caine, Mark, joint pseud. of TOM MASCHLER (-) and FREDERIC MICHAEL RAPHAEL (1931-) [British authors]
Caine, Michael. See:
MICKELWHITE, MAURICE JOSEPH
CAINE, THOMAS HENRY HALL (1853-1931) [English novelist and dramatist]
Hall Caine
Sir Hall Caine
Cainneach, O'Maonaigh. See:
MOONEY, CANICE ALBERT JAMES
CAIRD, ALICE MONA (1858-1932) [English feminist and novelist]
G. Noel Hatton
Caissa. See:
FRAENKEL, HEINRICH
CAIUS (died 296) [Supreme Pontiff of Roman Catholic Church]
Pope Caius
St. Caius
CAIUS MARIUS (c. 115-86 B.C.) [Roman general officer]
The Third Founder of Rome
Cal. See:
TINNEY, CALVIN LAWRENCE
Cal Bostic. See:
BOSTICK, CALVIN T.
Cal, Silent. See:
BENGE, RAY ADELPHIA
COOLIDGE, JOHN CALVIN
CALABRO, JOHN A. (1909-) [American composer and author]
Johnny Cale
Calamity Jane. See:
BURKE (CANARY), MARTHA JANE
CALAMY, EDMUND (1600-66) [English churchman and pamphleteer]
The Elder
CALAMY, EDMUND. See also:
Smectymnuus
Calcraft, John William. See:
COLE, JOHN WILLIAM
Calculator, The. See:
BUXTON, JEDEDIAH
CALDARA, POLIDORO (1495?-1543) [Italian painter]
Polidoro da Caravaggio
CALDWELL. See also:
Caudwell
Cauldwell
CALDWELL, ALBERT (1903-) [American jazz musician (tenor saxophone)]
Happy Caldwell
Caldwell, Anne. See:
O'DEA, ANNE CALDWELL
CALDWELL, JAMES (1734-81) [American Presbyterian clergyman; chaplain in Continental Army during Revolutionary War]
The Fighting Chaplain
The Soldier Parson
CALDWELL, TAYLOR (1900-) [Anglo-American author]
Max Reiner
Cale, Johnny. See:
CALABRO, JOHN A.
Caleb Clootz. See:
SMITH, FRANCIS SHUABEL
Caleb Saunders. See:
HEINLEIN, ROBERT ANSON
Caledonia, The Apostle of. See:
COLUMBA, ST.
Calesero, El. See:
RAMÍREZ, ALFONSO
CALETTI-BRUNI, FRANCESCO (c. 1600-76) [Italian composer]

Francesco Cavalli
Calhern, Louis. See:
VOGT, CARL
CALHOUN, CORA (1895-)
[American jazz musician (singer, arranger)]
Lovie Austin
CALHOUN, JOHN CALDWELL (1782-1850) [American statesman and orator]
The Eagle Orator of South Carolina
The Father of States' Rights
The Great Nullifier
The Napoleon of Slavery
Warhawk
CALHOUN, JOHN CALDWELL. See also:
Great Triumvirate, The
Calhoun, Rory. See:
DURGIN, FRANCIS TIMOTHY
CALIARI. See:
CAGLIARI (CALIARI), PAOLO
Caliban. See:
REID, JOHN COWIE
Caliban of Science, The. See:
RAMSEY, ALEXANDER
Calico Jack. See:
RACKHAM, JOHN
California Bar, The Napoleon of the. See:
DELMAS, DELPHIN MICHAEL
California Joe. See:
MILNER, MOSES EMBREE
California, The Apostle of. See:
SALVATIERRA, JUAN MARÍA DE
California, The Father of the Union Party of. See:
VAN DYKE, WALTER
California, The Mad Poet of. See:
KENDALL, W.S.
California, The Poet Laureate of. See:
COOLBRITH, IDA DONNA
McGROARTY, JOHN STEVEN
Caligula. See:
GAIUS JULIUS CAESAR GERMANICUS
CALIPH ABU-JAFAR (died 775) [Founder of Bagdad]
Armansur
The Victorious
CALISCH, EDITH (1898-)
[American composer]
Edith Lindeman
Calker, The. See:
MICHAEL V
Calkins, Franklin. See:
STRATEMEYER, EDWARD L.
CALLAHAN, CLAIRE WALLIS (1890-) [American author]
Ann Kilborn Cole
Nancy Hartwell
Callao, El. See:
REYES, FERNANDO DE LOS
CALLARD, MAURICE FREDERICK THOMAS (1912-) [English author]
Sutherland Rose
Callas, Theo. See:
McCARTHY, SHAUN
CALLENDER, GEORGE (1918-)
[American jazz musician (bass)]
Red Callender
Callender, Julian. See:
LEE, AUSTIN
Calli Goran. See:
GERRITY, DAVID JAMES
Calligrapher, The. See:
THEODOSIUS II
Callinicus. See:
SELEUCUS II
Calliope, The French. See:
DESHOULIÈRES, ANTOINETTE DU LIGIER DE LA GARDE
CALLISTUS (died 222) [Supreme pontiff of Roman Catholic Church]
Pope Callistus I
St. Callistus
Callistus II, Pope. See:
GUY OF BURGUNDY
Callistus III, Pope. See:
BORGIA, ALONSO
Callman Rawley. See:
RAKOSI, CARL
CALLOWAY. See also:

GALLOWAY
Galloway
CALLOWAY, CABELL, 3RD (1907-) [American actor and jazz musician (singer, leader)]
Cab Calloway
The Hi De Ho Man
The King of Hi De Ho
Calumet. See:
HOPKINSON, FRANCIS
Calvé, Emma. See:
ROQUER, EMMA DE
Calvert, Phyllis. See:
BICKLE, PHYLLIS
Calves. See:
Golden Calves of the People, The
Calvet, Corinne. See:
DIBOS, CORINNE
Calvin. See:
COOLIDGE, JOHN CALVIN
GALVIN
Calvin, Henry. See:
HANLEY, CLIFFORD
CALVIN, JOHN (1509-64) [Protestant reformer]
The Democritus of the Sixteenth Century
Calvin M. Knox. See:
SILVERBERG, ROBERT
Camará. See:
FLORES, JOSÉ
Cambridge, Elizabeth. See:
HODGES, BARBARA K.
Cambridge, John Smith of. See: SMITH, JOHN
Cambridge Platonist, The. See:
MORE, HENRY
CAMBYSES II (died 522 B.C.] [second king of the Medes and Persians]
Kambujiya
CAMDEN, WILLIAM (1551-1623) [English historian and antiquary]
The British Pausanias
The British Strabo
Camel-driver of Mecca, The. See: MOHAMMED
Camel, The. See:
HUMPHREYS, MURRAY
Camerarius, Joachim. See:
LIEBHARD, JOACHIM
CAMERO, CANDIDO (1921-) [Cuban jazz musician (banjo, drums)]
Candido
CAMERON, DONALD ALLEN (1937-) [Canadian educator and author]
D.A. Cameron
CAMERON, DONALD, OF LOCHIEL (c.1695-1748) [Scotch Highland chieftain]
Gentle Lochiel
Cameron, Elizabeth. See:
ROBINSON, ELIZABETH CAMERON
CAMERON, ELIZABETH JANE (1910-) [American author]
Jane Duncan
Cameron, Ian. See:
PAYNE, DONALD GORDON
CAMERON, JOHN (c.1579-1625) [Scotch educator and theologian]
The Walking Library
Cameron, John. See:
MACDONELL, ARCHIBALD GORDON
CAMERON, KENNETH NEILL (1908-) [American educator and author]
Warren Madden
CAMERON, LOU (1924-) [American author]
L.J. Arnold
Steve Cartier
W.R. Marvin
Cameron McCabe. See:
BORNEMAN, ERNEST
Cameron, Rod. See:
COX, ROD
CAMERON, SIMON (1799-1889) [American statesman; senator from Pennsylvania]
The Czar of Pennsylvania Politics
CAMERON, SIR EVAN (1629-1719) [Lord of Lochiel; Scottish nobleman]
The Ulysses of the Highlands
Cameron Vandal. See:
THORNE, BLISS KIRBY

Camille Davied. See:
ROSE, CAMILLE DAVIED
Camille Querno, Poet Laureate to the Congress. See: ODELL, JONATHAN
Camillus. See:
AMES, FISHER
Camilo, Don. See:
CELA, CAMILO JOSÉ
CAMINO. See:
RUIZ-CAMINO, CARLOS
CAMINO, FRANCISCO (1943-) [Spanish bullfighter]
Paco Camino
Camisero. See:
CARMONA, ANGEL
CAMOENS, LUIZ DE (c. 1524-80) [Portuguese poet]
The Homer of Portugal
CAMP, WALTER (1859-1925) [pioneer in establishing the game of football as a major American sport]
The Dean of American Football
The Father of American Football
CAMPANELLA, ROY (1921-) [American professional baseball player]
Campy
Campbell. See:
BROWN, GEORGE
MACGREGOR, ROBERT
CAMPBELL, ANDREW (1910-) [English author]
John Andrews
Campbell, Bartley. See:
URNER, NATHAN DANE
CAMPBELL, BARTLEY T. (1843-88) [American journalist, poet, novelist, dramatist and theatrical manager]
Edwin South
CAMPBELL, BEATRICE STELLA TANNER (1865-1940) [British actress]
Mrs. Patrick Campbell
CAMPBELL, BEVERLY (1926-) [American motion picture and television actress]
Beverly Garland
CAMPBELL, BLANCHE (1902-) [American author
Julian Fish
Campbell, Bruce. See:
EPSTEIN, SAMUEL
CAMPBELL, BRUCE DOUGLAS (1909-) [American professional baseball player]
Hump
Campbell, Clive. See:
MACRAE, DONALD G.
Campbell, Donald. See:
GILFORD, CHARLES BERNARD
Campbell, Francis Stuart. See:
KUEHNELT-LEDDIHN, ERIK RITTER VON
CAMPBELL, HANNAH (fl. 1964) [American editor and author]
Elizabeth Franklin
Campbell, Jane. See:
EDWARDS, JANE CAMPBELL
CAMPBELL, JOHN WOOD (1910-) [American author]
Arthur McCann
Don A. Stuart
Karl Van Kampen
Campbell, Judith. See:
PARES, MARION STAPYLTON
Campbell, Judy. See:
GAMBLE, JUDY
CAMPBELL, LITTA BELLE (1886-) [American attorney and author]
Mrs. Kemper Campbell
CAMPBELL, MARY (fl. last part of 18th cent.) [sweetheart of ROBERT BURNS]
Highland Mary
Campbell Praed, Mrs. See:
PRAED, ROSA CAROLINE
CAMPBELL, ROSEMAE WELLS (1909-) [American librarian and author]
R. W. Campbell
Campbell, Scott. See:
DAVIS, FREDERICK WILLIAM

Campbell Tatham. See:
ELTING, MARY
CAMPBELL, THOMAS (1777-1844) [British poet and miscellaneous writer]
The Bard of Hope
CAMPBELL, THOMAS F. (1924-) [Irish educator and author]
Crosscountry
CAMPBELL, WALTER STANLEY (1887-1957) [American educator and author]
Stanley Vestal
CAMPBELL, WILL DAVIS (1924-) [American churchman and author]
David Brett
CAMPBELL, WILLIAM EDWARD MARCH (1893-1954) [American novelist]
William March
Campeador, El Cid. See:
VIVAR, RODRIGO DÍAZ DE
Camper, Shirley. See:
SOMAN, SHIRLEY
CAMPIN, ROBERT (c.1375-1444) [Dutch artist]
Master of Flémalle
CAMPION, EDMUND (1540-81) [English Jesuit martyr]
The Seditious Jesuit
CAMPION, SIDNEY RONALD (1891-) [British barrister, journalist, educator and author]
Geoffrey Swayne
CAMPISTRON, JEAN GALABERT DE (1656-1723) [French dramatic poet]
Le Singe de Racine
The Monkey
CAMPO. See:
DEL CAMPO, JOSÉ SANCHEZ
CAMPOY, JUAN BELMONTE Y (1918-) [Spanish bullfighter]
Juan Belmonte, Jr.
Juanito
Camps, The Evil Genius of the German Horror. See:
HIMMLER, HEINRICH
Campy. See:
CAMPANELLA, ROY
Canada Lee. See:
CANEGATA, LEONARD LIONEL CORNELIUS
Canada, The Ugliest Man in. See: CHAPELSKI, ALEX SAMUEL
CANADAY, JOHN EDWIN (1907-) [American educator and author]
Matthew Head
Canadian Laureate, The. See:
FRÉCHETTE, LOUIS HONORÉ
Canal Boy, The. See:
GARFIELD, JAMES ABRAM
Canal, The Father of the Barge. See: CLINTON, GEORGE
CANARY. See:
BURKE (CANARY), MARTHA JANE
CANDELON, CATHERINE (c.1852-1903) [English comedy actress]
Kate Vaughan
CANDIA, DON GIOVANNI DE (1810-83) [Italian tenor]
Giuseppe Mario
CANDIA, PIETRO DI (1340?-1410) [Supreme Pontiff of Roman Catholic Church]
Pope Alexander V
Candid Spoilsman, That. See:
FARLEY, JAMES ALOYSIUS
Candidate, The Log Cabin. See:
HARRISON, WILLIAM HENRY
Candidate, The Perpetual. See:
CLEVELAND, STEPHEN GROVER
Candido. See:
CAMERO, CANDIDO
Candie. See:
CANDY
Candy
CARAWAN, CAROLANNE M.
CANDOLI, SECONDO (1927-) [American jazz musician

(trumpet)]
Conte Candoli
CANDOLI, WALTER JOSEPH (1923-) [American jazz musician (trumpet, composer)]
Pete Candoli
Candour, A Lover of. See: HOPKINSON, FRANCIS
CANDY [Candy]. See also: Candie
Candy, Edward. See: NEVILLE, BARBARA ALISON BOODSON
CANDY, HUGH CHARLES HERBERT (fl. late 18th-early 19th cents.) [British chemist, lecturer and author]
H.C.H.C.
Candy Jones. See: WILCOX, JESSICA
Candy Kid, The. See: BROCK, WILLIAM EMERSON
Candy King, The Pittsburgh. See: CLARK, DAVID LYTLE
CANEGATA, LEONARD LIONEL CORNELIUS (1907-) [American Negro actor]
Canada Lee
Canfield, Dorothy. See: FISHER, DOROTHY CANFIELD
CANFIELD, RICHARD A. (1855-1914) [American gambling house proprietor]
The Greatest Gambler
Cañitas. See: VERA, CARLOS
Canmore (Great Head). See: MALCOLM III
CANNING, CHARLES JOHN, 1ST EARL (1812-62) [English statesman]
Clemency Canning
CANNING, GEORGE (1770-1827) [British statesman and orator]
The Cicero of the British Senate
Clemency Canning
The Zany of Debate
CANNING, JOSIAH DEAN (1816-92) [American poet]
The Peasant Bard
CANNING, SIR STRATFORD (1786-1880) [English diplomat; 1st Viscount Stratford de Redcliffe]
The Great Elchi
CANNON, ANTHONY (1857-91) [American actor]
Tony Hart
CANNON, BISHOP JAMES, JR. (1864-1944) [American Methodist-Episcopal clergyman and prohibitionist]
The Dry Bishop from Virginia
CANNON, CHARLES A. (1893-1971) [American textile executive]
Mr. Charlie
CANNON, CHARLES JAMES (1800-60) [American poet, storyteller and playwright]
Grandfather Greenway
CANNON, CLARENCE (1879-) [American educator, parliamentarian and politician]
Parliamentary Procedure
CANNON, JOSEPH GURNEY (1836-1926) [American statesman; Speaker of the House of Representatives]
Uncle Joe Cannon
The Watchdog of the Treasury
Cannonball. See: ADDERLEY, JULIAN EDWIN
CANO, ALONSO (1601-67) [Spanish painter, sculptor and architect]
The Spanish Michelangelo
CANO, EDWARD, JR. (1927-) [American composer, pianist and conductor]
Eddie Cano
Cano, El. See: JIMÉNEZ, MANUEL
CANO, ENRIQUE (1893-1927) [Spanish bullfighter]
Gavira
CANO, FRANCISCO SEGURA

(1921-) [Ecuadorean tennis player]
Francisco Segura
Pancho Segura
Canon Wace. See:
UNKNOWN
CANSINO, MARGARITA CARMEN (1918-) [American actress]
Rita Hayworth
Cantacuzene. See:
JOHN VI (or V)
CANTARINI, SIMONE (1612-48) [Italian painter]
Il Pesarese
Cantinflas. See:
AUGUST, MARIO MORENO
Cantor, Eddie. See:
ISKOWITZ, EDWARD ISRAEL
Cantrell A. Bigly. See:
PECK, GEORGE WASHINGTON
Canusi, José. See:
BARKER, S. OMAR
CANUTE (CNUT) (KNUT) II (944?-1035) [King of England, Denmark and Norway]
Canute the Great
King Canute
Cap. See:
ANSON, ADRIAN CONSTANTINE
Cap Collier, Old. See:
IRON, NATHANIEL COLCHESTER
SAWYER, EUGENE TAYLOR
Cap, Red. See:
POWELL, RANSOM T.
Capability. See:
BROWN, LANCELOT
Capel, Roger. See:
SHEPPARD, LANCELOT CAPEL
CAPERN, EDWARD (1819-94) [English letter carrier and versifier]
The Bideford Postman
The Postman Poet
CAPETILLO, MANUEL. See:
Three Musketeers, The
Capitán. See also:
Captain
Capitán, El Gran (The Great Captain). See:
GONZALO DE CÓRDOBA (GONSALVO DI CORDOVA)
CAPLI, ERDOGAN (1926-) [Turkish-American composer, musician and teacher]
Pasha
CAPLIN, ALFRED GERALD (1909-) [American cartoonist]
Al Capp
Capnio. See:
REUCHLIN, JOHANN
Capon, Peter. See:
OAKLEY, ERIC GILBERT
CAPONE, ALPHONSE (1898-1947) [American gangster and racketeer]
Al Capone
Big Al
The Big Boy
Scarface
Caporal, Le Petit (The Little Corporal). See:
BONAPARTE, NAPOLEON
Capote, Truman. See:
PERSONS, TRUMAN STRECKFUS
Capp, Al. See:
CAPLIN, ALFRED GERALD
CAPPELLARI, BARTOLOMMEO ALBERTO (1765-1846) [Supreme Pontiff of Roman Catholic Church]
Pope Gregory XVI
CAPPER, ARTHUR (1865-) [American publisher and statesman; Governor of Kansas]
Farmer's Friend
CAPRA, FRANK (1897-) [Italian-American motion picture director and producer]
Picture-maker's Picture-maker
Capsadell, Lou. See:
HAMMOND, HENRIETTA HARDY
Captain. See:

BARCLAY-ALLARDICE, ROBERT
Capitán
CLARK, CHARLES DUNNING
COOK, JAMES
HARPER, JAMES CUNNINGHAM
KIDD, WILLIAM
MARRYAT, FREDERICK
SMITH, ALEXANDER
STANDISH, MILES (MYLES)
STEELE, SIR RICHARD
SUTTER, JOHN AUGUSTUS

Captain, A Civil War. See: ROLFE, MARO O.

Captain Alfred B. Taylor. See: INGRAHAM, COLONEL PRENTISS

Captain Bill Gray. See: GRAY, WILLIAM BITTLE

Captain Billy. See: FAWCETT, WILLIAM HAMILTON; McCUE, WILLIAM

Captain Bruin Adams. See: ELLIS, EDWARD SYLVESTER

Captain Clutterbuck. See: SCOTT, SIR WALTER

Captain Dick Steadman. See: HARBAUGH, THOMAS CHALMERS

Captain Dominique. See: YOU, DOMINIQUE

Captain Ezekiel, Old. See: GREELEY, EZEKIEL

Captain Frank P. Armstrong. See: AIKEN, ALBERT W.

Captain General of the Armada. See: COLUMBUS, CHRISTOPHER

Captain H.R. Millbank. See: ELLIS, EDWARD SYLVESTER

Captain Hamilton Holmes. See: HARBAUGH, THOMAS CHALMERS

Captain Hazelton. See: WHITSON, JOHN HARVEY

Captain Hercules Vinegar. See: FIELDING, HENRY

Captain Howard Holmes. See: HARBAUGH, THOMAS CHALMERS

Captain Howard, Police. See: SENARENS, LUIS PHILIP

Captain J.F.C. Adams. See: ELLIS, EDWARD SYLVESTER

Captain J.L. Kennedy. See: HARBAUGH, THOMAS CHALMERS

Captain Jack. See: CRAWFORD, JOHN WALLACE

Captain Jafah Clarke. See: NESMITH, ROBERT I.

Captain James Carson. See: STRATEMEYER, EDWARD L.

Captain John Flower, M.P. See: BRONTË, BRANWELL

Captain John Smith. See: SMITH, JOHN

Captain Latham C. Carleton. See: ELLIS, EDWARD SYLVESTER

Captain McKeen. See: ST. JOHN, PERCY BOLLINGBROKE

Captain Mark Wilton. See: MANNING, WILLIAM HENRY

Captain Merry, U.S.N. See: RYMER, JAMES MALCOLM

Captain Miles Standish. See: STANDISH, MILES (MYLES)

Captain Molly. See: McCAULEY, MARY LUDWIG HAYS

Captain of Kent, The. See: CADE, JOHN

Captain R.M. Hawthorne. See: ELLIS, EDWARD SYLVESTER

Captain Ralph Bonehill. See: STRATEMEYER, EDWARD L.

Captain Ringbolt. See: CODMAN, JOHN

Captain Robert Barnacle. See: NEWELL, CHARLES MARTIN

Captain Roberts. See:
HOBART-HAMPDEN, AUGUST CHARLES
Captain, The Big. See:
CRAWFORD, WILLIAM
Captain, The Black. See:
DAVIDOV, DENIS VASSILIEVITCH
Captain, The Great (El Gran Capitán). See:
GONZALO DE CÓRDOBA (GONSALVO DI CORDOVA)
Captain Walt Winton. See:
HARBAUGH, THOMAS CHALMERS
Captain Wheeler. See:
ELLIS, EDWARD SYLVESTER
Captain Wilbur Jones. See:
EDWARDS, WILLIAM BENNETT
Captain William B. Perry. See: BROWN, WILLIAM PERRY
Captive, The Redeemed. See:
WILLIAMS, JOHN
Capucine. See:
LEFEBVRE, GERMAINE
CAPURRO, ALFRED (1914-) [American singer and actor]
Alfred Drake
Cara-Ancha. See:
DEL CAMPO, JOSÉ SANCHEZ
Caracalla. See:
MARCUS AURELIUS ANTONINUS
Caracci of France, The. See:
JOUVENET, JEAN
Caradoc. See:
EVANS, DAVID
CARADOG (died c. 1247) [Welsh historian]
Caradog of Llancarvan
Caradon, Lord. See:
FOOT, HUGH MACKINTOSH
CARAFFA, GIAMPIETRO (1476-1559) [Supreme Pontiff of Roman Catholic Church]
Pope Paul IV
Caraman, Georges. See:
SIMENON, GEORGES
Caran d'Ache. See:
POIRÉ, EMMANUEL
Caravaggio, Michelangelo da. See: MERISI (MERISIO), MICHELANGELO
Caravaggio, Polidoro da. See:
CALDARA, POLIDORO
CARAWAN, CAROLANNE M. (1939-) [American compiler of song collections]
Candie Carawan
CARAWAY, HATTIE WYATT (1878-1950) [American stateswoman; senator from Arkansas]
Knitting Hattie
Carco, Francis. See:
CARCO-PINO-TUSOLI, FRANCIS
CARCOPINO-TUSOLI, FRANCIS (1886-1958) [French author]
Francis Carco
CÁRDENAS, SIMÓN (1882-) [Mexican "monosabio" (bull ring attendant)]
Simón
Carder, Leigh. See:
CUNNINGHAM, EUGENE
CARDI, LUDOVICO (1559-1613) [Italian painter and architect]
Cigoli
Cardinal. See:
RICHELIEU, DUC DE, ARMAND JEAN DU PLESSIS
SPELLMAN, FRANCIS JOSEPH
WOLSEY, THOMAS
YORK, HENRY BENEDICT MARIA CLEMENT STUART
Cardinal of England. See:
POLE, REGINALD
CARDINAL, PIERRE (died c. 1305) [French troubadour]
The Juvenal of the Provençals
Cardinal Ximínes. See:
CISNEROS, FRANCISCO XIMÍNES DE
CARDOZO, LOIS STEINMETZ (1934-) [American author]

Lois Duncan
Lois Kerry
CARDUCCI, GIOSUE (1835-1907) [Italian poet, critic and teacher]
Enotrio Romano
CARETTE, LOUIS-ALBERT (1913-) [Belgian author]
Felicien Marceau
CAREW, BAMPFYLDE MOORE (1693-c. 1770) [English vagabond]
The King of the Beggars
CAREW, JOHN MOHUN (1921-) [British soldier, journalist and author]
Tim Carew
CAREY [Carey]. See also:
CARY
Cary
CAREY, ALICE (1820-71) [American poet, author and hymn writer]
The Jean Ingelow of America
Patty Lee
CAREY, ALICE. See also:
Sweet Singers of the West, The
Carey, Edmund. See:
KEAN, EDMUND
CAREY, HENRY DE WITT (1878-1947) [American motion picture actor]
Harry Carey.
Carey, Joyce. See:
LAWRENCE, JOYCE
CAREY, MATHEW (1760-1839) [American publisher, bookseller and economist]
A Citizen of Philadelphia
CAREY, MAX GEORGE (1890-) [American professional baseball executive]
Carnarius
Carey, Michael. See:
BURTON, EDWARD J.
CAREY, PHOEBE. See:
Sweet Singers of the West, The.
CAREY, REGINALD (1908-) [British stage and motion picture actor]
Rex Harrison
CAREY, RICHARD DURANT (1916-) [American conductor, arranger and composer]
Dick Carey
CAREY, THOMAS (1891-1948) [American jazz musician (trumpet)]
Papa Mutt Carey
CAREY, WILLIAM (1761-1834) [English missionary to India]
The Father of Modern Missions
Carfagne, Cyril. See:
JENNINGS, LESLIE NELSON
CARHART, ARTHUR HAWTHORNE (1892-) [American author]
Hart Thorne
V.A. Van Sickle
CARILLO, JOAQUIN (1832-53) [Mexican outlaw in California]
Robin Hood of the Sierras
Joaquin Murieta
CARILLO, ROSITA FELIX (1834?-) [wife of JOAQUIN CARILLO (Joaquin Murieta) Mexican outlaw in California]
Antonia Molinera
Carl. See:
Carle
Karl
McKINLEY, CARLYLE
Carl Benson. See:
BRISTED, CHARLES ASTOR
Carl Bremer. See:
GUSTAFSON, AXEL
Carl Brent. See:
WILLETT, EDWARD
Carl Brisson. See:
PEDERSEN, CARL
Carl Courteney. See:
URNER, NATHAN DANE
Carl, Cowboy. See:
HATCH, CARL ATWOOD
Carl Dane. See:
ADAMS, FRANK RAMSAY
Carl Esmond. See:
EICHBERGER, WILLY
Carl H. Thomas. See:
DOERFFLER, ALFRED
Carl, Karl. See:
VON BERNBRUNN, KARL ANDREAS

Carl Sturdy. See:
STRONG, CHARLES STANLEY
Carle. See:
Carl
Karl
VERNET, ANTOINE CHARLES HORACE
Carle, Frankie. See:
CARLONE, FRANCIS N.
Carle, Richard. See:
CARLETON, CHARLES NICHOLS
Carleton. See:
Carlton
COFFIN, CHARLES CARLETON
Carleton, Captain Latham C. See: ELLIS, EDWARD SYLVESTER
CARLETON, CHARLES NICHOLS (1871-) [American actor and playwright]
Richard Carle
Carleton, Cousin May. See:
FLEMING, MAY AGNES
Carleton, JAMES O. (1906-) [American professional baseball player]
Tex Carleton
Carleton Kendrake. See:
GARDNER, ERLE STANLEY
Carleton, Will. See:
BARTLETT, FREDERICK ORIN
Carleton, William. See:
BARTLETT, FREDERICK ORIN
CARLEY, PATRICK J. (1866-1936) [American statesman; congressman from New York]
The Fire Chief
Carli. See:
Laklan, Carli
CARLILE. See also:
CARLYLE
CARLILE, JOHN CHARLES (fl. late 19th-early 20th cent.) [British editor and author]
John Iron
Carlin, Francis. See:
MACDONNELL, JAMES FRANCIS CARLIN
Carlo Collodi. See:
LORENZINI, CARLO
Carlo, Johnny. See:
SELVAGGIO, JOHN R.
Carlo Khan. See:
FOX, CHARLES JAMES
Carlo, Yvonne de. See:
MIDDLETON, PEGGY YVONNE
CARLON, PATRICIA BERNARDETTE (fl. mid 20th cent.) [Australian author]
Patricia Charters
Barbara Christie
Patricia Curtis
CARLONE, FRANCIS N. (1903-) [American jazz musician (leader, piano)]
Frankie Carle
Carlos, Bronco. See:
MILLER, CHARLES
Carlos, Don. See:
BORBÓN, CARLOS LUIS FERNANDO DE, CONDE DE MONTEMOLÍN
BORBÓN, CARLOS MARÍA DE, INFANTE DE ESPAÑA
BORBÓN, CARLOS MARÍA DE LOS DOLORES DE, DUQUE DE MADRID
BORBÓN, CARLOS MARÍA ISIDRO DE, CONDE DE MOLINA
CHARLES IV
Carlson, John Roy. See:
DEROUNIAN, ARTHUR
CARLSON, JULES (1904-) [American professional football player and coach]
Old Reliable
CARLSON, VADA F. (1897-) [American editor and author]
Florella Rose
Carlstadt. See:
BODENSTEIN, ANDREA RUDOLF
Carlton. See also:

CARLETON
Carleton
Carlton Keith. See:
ROBERTSON, KEITH
Carlton, Robert. See:
HALL, BAYNARD RUSH
CARLYLE. See also:
CARLILE
CARLYLE, ALEXANDER (1722-1805) [Scottish divine]
Jupiter Carlyle
CARLYLE, THOMAS (1795-1881) [Scottish essayist and historian]
The Censor of the Age
The Chelsea Philosopher
The Sage of Chelsea
Teufelsdröch
Carman, Dulce. See:
DRUMMOND, MARIE DULCE CARMAN
Carmen, Felix. See:
SHERMAN, FRANK DEMPSTER
Carmen Miranda. See:
CUNHA, MARÍA DE CARMO MIRANDA DE
Carmen on Record, The Prettiest. See:
SWARTHOUT, GLADYS
Carmen Sylva. See:
ELISABETH
Carmi, T. See:
CHARNEY, CARMI
Carmichael, Ann. See:
MACALPINE, MARGARET HESKETH MURRAY
Carmichael, Harry. See:
OGNALL, LEOPOLD HORACE
CARMICHAEL, HOAGLAND HOWARD (1899-) [American jazz musician (songwriter, singer, piano)]
Hoagy Carmichael
Carmichael, Marie. See:
STOPES, MRS. MARIE CHARLOTTE CARMICHAEL
Carmichael Smith. See:
LINEBARGER, PAUL MYRON ANTHONY
CARMONA, ANGEL (1874-1960) [Spanish bullfighter]
Camisero
CARMONA, ANTONIO (1838-1920) [Spanish bullfighter]
Gordito
CARNAHAN, SUZANNE (1921-52) [American motion picture actress]
Susan Peters
Carnarius. See:
CAREY, MAX GEORGE
Carnarvon, Edward of. See:
EDWARD II
CARNEGIE, ANDREW (1835-1919) [Scottish-American industrialist and philanthropist]
The Laird of Skibo
The Laird of Skibo Castle
Carnegie of Belgium, The. See:
SOLVAY, ERNEST
CARNEGIE, RAYMOND ALEXANDER (1920-) [Scottish soldier and author]
Sacha Carnegie
CARNEY, THOMAS PATRICK (1914-) [Irish educator and poet]
Seumas O. Ceithearnaigh
Carnicerito de México. See:
GONZÁLEZ, JOSÉ
CARNOT, LAZARE-NICHOLAS MARGUÉRITE (1753-1823) [French statesman and scientist]
The Organizer of Victory
CARO. See also:
CAROE
CARO, ELME MARIE (1826-87) [French educator]
Le Philosophe des Dames
CARO, FRANCISCO MARTÍN (1915-) [Spanish bullfighter]
Curro Caro
Carobert, Charles Robert of. See: CHARLES I
CAROE. See also:
CARO
CAROE, WILLIAM DOUGLAS (1857-) [British writer on architectural subjects]
Wedecee

Carol. See also:
Carole
Carrel
CARROLL
Carroll
Karol
Carol I. See:
FRIEDRICH, KARL EITEL
Carol, Bill J. See:
KNOTT, WILLIAM CECIL, JR.
Carol Lawrence. See:
LARAIA, CAROL MARIA
Carol Lee. See:
FLETCHER, HELEN JILL
Carol Marsh. See:
SIMPSON, NORMA
Carol, Martine. See:
MOURER, MARYSE
Carol Morse. See:
YEAKLEY, MARJORY HALL
Carol Norton. See:
NORTH, GRACE MAY
Carol Raye. See:
CORKREY, KATHLEEN
Carola Oman. See:
OMAN, CAROLA MARY ANIMA
Carole. See also:
Carol
Carrel
CARROLL
Carroll
Karol
Carole Brooke. See:
RAMSKILL, VALERIE PATRICIA ROSKAMS
Carole Landis. See:
RIDSTE, FRANCES
Carole Lombard. See:
PETERS, JANE
Carolina. See also:
Caroline
Carolyn
Carolina Lee. See:
DERN, PEGGY GADDIS
Caroline. See also:
Carolina
Carolyn
Caroline Brown. See:
KROUT, CAROLINE VIRGINIA
Caroline Chesebro'. See:
CHESEBROUGH, CAROLINE
Caroline, John Taylor of. See:
TAYLOR, JOHN
Caroline Lascelles, Lady. See:
BRADDON, MARY ELIZABETH
Caroline M. Barton. See:
BRAME, CHARLOTTE MARY
Caroline More. See:
CONE, MOLLY LAMKEN
STRACHAN, MARGARET PITCAIRN
Caroline of Anspach. See:
FREDERICK, WILHELMINA CAROLINA
Caroline Peters. See:
BETZ, EVA KELLY
Caroline Silver June. See:
SMITH, LAURA ROUNTREE
Caroline Thomas. See:
DORR, JULIA CAROLINE RIPLEY
Caroline Tucker. See:
NOLAN, JEANNETTE COVERT
Carolinian Gamecock, The. See:
SUMTER, THOMAS
Carolus Duran. See:
DURAND, CHARLES AUGUSTE ÉMILE
Carolus-Duren, Augusta Émile. See: DURAND, CHARLES AUGUSTE ÉMILE
Carolus Linnaeus. See:
VON LINNÉ, CARL
Carolus Magnus. See:
CHARLEMAGNE
Carolyn. See also:
Carolina
Caroline
Carolyn Keene. See:
ADAMS, HARRIET STRATEMEYER
KARIG, WALTER
STRATEMEYER, EDWARD L.
Caron, Major Henri Le. See:
BEACH, THOMAS
CARPENTER. See also:
CARPENTIER
CHARPENTIER
CARPENTER, HARLEAN (1911-37) [American motion picture

actress]
Jean Harlow
CARPENTER, TERRY Mc-GOVERN (1900-) [American statesman; representative from Nebraska]
Cut Rate Carpenter
CARPENTIER. See also:
CARPENTER
CHARPENTIER
CARPENTIER, GEORGES (1894-) [French professional boxer; world's light heavyweight champion]
The Orchid Man
CARPIO, LOPE FÉLIX DE VEGA (1562-1635) [Spanish dramatic poet]
The Father of the Spanish Drama
Lope de Vega
Tome Burguillos
CARR, ALBERT ZOLOTKOFF (1902-) [American author]
A. H. Z. Carr
Carr, Catherine. See:
WADE, ROSALIND HERSCHEL
CARR, DOROTHY STEVENSON LAIRD (1912-) [British author]
Dorothy Laird
Carr, Glyn. See:
STYLES, FRANK SHOWELL
Carr, Joe Fingers. See:
BUSCH, LOUIS F.
CARR, JOHN DICKSON (1905-) [Anglo-American writer of detective stories]
Carr Dickson
Carter Dickson
Carr, Roberta. See:
ROBERTS, IRENE
CARR, T. See:
Edwards, Norman
Carra, Emma. See:
UNKNOWN
CARRADINE, RICHMOND REED (1906-) [American stage and motion picture actor]
John Carradine
CARRARIO, ANGELO (1327-1415) [Supreme Pontiff of Roman Catholic Church]
Pope Gregory XII
CARRÉ [Carré]. See also:
CURRIE
Currie
Curry
Carré, John le. See:
CORNWELL, DAVID JOHN MOORE
CARRÉ, LILLIAN (1905-) [French actress and motion picture star]
Lili Damita
Carrel. See also:
Carol
Carole
CARROLL
Carroll
Karol
Carrel, Mark. See:
PAINE, LAUREN
Carrick, A. B. See:
LINDSAY, HAROLD ARTHUR BILL
Carrick, Edward. See:
CRAIG, EDWARD ANTHONY
Carrick, John. See:
CROSBIE, HUGH PROVAN
Carrier, The Christian. See:
BROWN, JOHN
CARRIÈRE, EUGÈNE (1849-1906) [French artist]
The Modern Madonna Painter
Carrier's Friend, The Letter. See: COX, SAMUEL SULLIVAN
CARRIGAN, WILLIAM F. (1883-) [American professional baseball player and manager]
Rough Carrigan
Carriles. See:
MARTÍN, MARIANO

CARRINGTON, CHARLES EDMUND (1897-) [British author]
Charles Edmonds
CARRINGTON, EDWARD (fl. late 18th cent.) [Quartermaster General of the Continental Army]
Old Agamemnon
CARROLL [Carroll]. See also:
Carol
Carole
Carrel
Karol
Carroll, Barbara. See: COPPERSMITH, BARBARA
CARROLL, CHARLES (1737-1832) [American patriot; signer of the Declaration of Independence]
Charles Carroll of Carrollton
Carroll, Curt. See: BISHOP, CURTIS KENT
Carroll, Diahann. See: JOHNSON, CAROL DIAHANN
Carroll, Irv. See: GELLERS, IRVING
CARROLL, JOE (1919-) [American jazz musician (singer)]
Bepop
Carroll, John. See: FAYE, JULIAN LA
Carroll, Lewis. See: DODGSON, CHARLES LUTWIDGE
Carroll, Robert. See: ALPERT, HOLLIS
Carroll, Sydney W. See: WHITEMAN, GEORGE FREDERICK CARL
CARROLL, THOMAS THEODORE, JR. (1925-) [American journalist, editor and author]
Ted Carroll
Carrollton, Charles Carroll of. See: CARROLL, CHARLES
Carrots. See: GUICHE, LILLIAN DE
CARRUCCI, JACOPO (1494-1557) [Italian painter of the Florentine School]
Jacopo da Pontormo
CARRUTH, WILLIAM HERBERT (1859-1924) [American educator, author and poet]
The Evolution Poet
CARRUTHERS, MRS. JAMES (1872-) [British social worker and author]
Violet Rosa Markham
CARRY, GEORGE DORMAN (1915-) [American jazz musician (alto saxophone, clarinet)]
Scoops Carry
Carson. See: McCULLERS, LULA CARSON
Carson, Anthony. See: BROOKE, PETER
Carson, Bingham. See: CASSIDAY, BRUCE BINGHAM
Carson, Captain James. See: STRATEMEYER, EDWARD L.
CARSON, CHRISTOPHER (1809-68) [American pioneer scout and Indian agent]
Father Kit
Kit Carson
The Monarch of the Prairies
The Nestor of the Rocky Mountains
Carson, Jeannie. See: SHUFFLEBOTTOM, JEAN
CARSON, JOHN (1925-) [American television personality and master of ceremonies]
Johnny Carson
CARSON, JOHN MILLER (1838-1912) [American newspaper man; organizer, charter member and president of the Gridiron Club]
The Father and Nursing

Mother of the Gridiron Club
Carson, Major Lewis W. See:
AIKEN, ALBERT W.
Carson, Ruth. See:
BUGBEE, RUTH CARSON
CARSON, WALTER LLOYD (1913-) [American professional baseball player]
Kit Carson
CARTER [Carter]. See also:
Cartier
Carter, Anne. See:
BROOKS, ANNE TEDLOCK
CARTER, BENNETT LESTER (1907-) [American jazz musician (composer, leader, saxophones, arranger)]
Benny Carter
Carter, Betty. See:
JONES, LILLIE MAE
Carter, Bob. See:
KAHAKALAU, ROBERT
Carter Brown. See:
YATES, ALAN GEOFFREY
Carter, Bruce. See:
HOUGH, RICHARD
CARTER, CHARLES J. (fl. early 20th cent.) [American illusionist and magician]
Carter The Great
The Eminent Prestidigitateur
Carter Dickson. See:
CARR, JOHN DICKSON
CARTER, DONALD JAMES (1926-) [American professional bowler]
Don Carter
Carter, Helena. See:
RICKERTS, HELEN
CARTER, HENRY (1821-80) [Anglo-American wood engraver, publisher and editor]
Frank Leslie
Carter, Herbert. See:
RATHBONE, ST. GEORGE HENRY
Carter, Janis. See:
DREMANN, JANIS
CARTER, JOHN FRANKLIN (1897-) [American journalist and writer of detective stories]
Diplomat
Jay Franklin
Carter, Mrs. Leslie. See:
DUDLY, CAROLINE LOUISE
Carter, Nicholas. See:
CORYELL, JOHN RUSSELL
DAVIS, FREDERICK WILLIAM
DEY, FREDERIC VAN RENSSELAER
JENKS, GEORGE CHARLES
SAWYER, EUGENE TAYLOR
Carter, Nick. See:
CARTER, VINCENT
CORYELL, JOHN RUSSELL
DAVIS, FREDERICK WILLIAM
DEY, FREDERICK VAN RENSSELAER
HARBAUGH, THOMAS CHALMERS
JENKS, GEORGE CHARLES
SAWYER, EUGENE TAYLOR
Carter, Phyllis Ann. See:
EBERLE, IRMENGARDE
Carter, Ralph. See:
NEUBAUER, WILLIAM ARTHUR
Carter, Ray. See:
KRUMBEIN, MAURICE
CARTER, ROBERT (1663-1732) [American landowner and politician; governor of the Virginia Colony]
King Carter
CARTER, VINCENT (1891-) [American statesman; representative from Wyoming]

Nick Carter
Cartesius. See:
DESCARTES, RENÉ
Carthaginian Lion, The.
See: HANNIBAL
Cartier. See also:
CARTER
Carter
Cartier, Steve. See:
CAMERON, LOU
Carton, R.C. See:
CRITCHETT, RICHARD
CLAUDE
Cartoonists, The Mark Twain
of. See:
WEBSTER, HAROLD
TUCKER
Cartouche. See:
BOURGUIGNON, LOUIS-
DOMINIQUE
Cartwheel. See:
CARTWRIGHT, WILBURN
CARTWRIGHT, ALEXANDER
JOY (c.1800-92) [organizer
of the Knickerbocker
Club of New York, the
world's first baseball
club]
The Father of Modern
Baseball
Cartwright, James McGregor.
See: JENNINGS,
LESLIE NELSON
CARTWRIGHT, JOHN
(1740-1824)
[English politician and
abolitionist]
The Father of Reform
CARTWRIGHT, WILBURN
(1891-)
[American lawyer and
politician; congressman
from Oklahoma]
Cartwheel
Good Roads Cartwright
CARVER, DR. GEORGE
WASHINGTON (c.1864-
1943) [American
Negro botanist]
The Peanut Man
The Plant Doctor
The Sweet-potato Man
Carver, John. See:
GARDNER, RICHARD
CARVER, RICHARD
MICHAEL POWER
(1915-) [English
author]
Michael Carver
CARY [Cary]. See also:
CAREY
Carey
CARY, ARTHUR JOYCE
LUNEL (1888-)
[English novelist]
Joyce Cary
Cary Grant. See:
LEACH, ALEXANDER
ARCHIBALD
CARYL, WARREN
(1920-) [American
educator and author]
Moss Tadrack
Casalandra, Estelle. See:
ESTELLE, SISTER
MARY
CASARES, ADOLFO BIOY.
See: Domecq, Honorio
Bustos
Casca. See:
PIKE, ALBERT
CASCALES, JOHN (1911-)
[American jazz musician
(arranger, composer)]
Johnny Richards
Case, Justin. See:
GLEADOW, RUPERT
SEELEY
Case, L. L. See:
LEWIN, LEONARD CASE
Case, Michael. See:
HOWARD, ROBERT
WEST
CASE, RUSSELL D.
(1912-64) [American
composer, arranger,
conductor, and
trumpeter]
Russ Case
CASELEYR, CAMILLE
AUGUSTE MARIE (1909-)
[Belgian author)
Jack Danvers
CASEWIT, CURTIS
(1922-) [German-
American author]

D. Green
D. Vernor
K. Werner

Casey. See:
JONES, JOHN LUTHER
STENGEL, CHARLES DILLON

CASEY, JOHN (1880-1964) [Irish playwright]
Sean O'Casey

CASEY, MICHAEL T. (1922-) [American educator and author]
Mart Casey

CASEY, WESLEY EUGENE (1933-) [American composer, conductor and arranger]
Gene Casey

CASH, GRACE (1915-) [American author]
Grady Cash

CASH, JOHN R. (1932-) [American guitarist, composer and country music singer]
Johnny Cash

Cash, Sebastian. See:
SMITHELLS, ROGER WILLIAM

Casimir. See:
JOHN II

CASIMIR II (1138-94) [King of Poland]
The Just

CASIMIR III (1309-70) [King of Poland]
The Great

Casimir V. See:
JOHN II

Casimir Sarbievius. See:
SARBIEWSKI, MACIEJ KAZIMIERZ

Caskoden, Edwin. See:
MAJOR, CHARLES

CASON, MABEL EARP (1892-) [American teacher, illustrator and author]
Emily Mary Bell

CASSOTTO, ROBERT WALDEN (1936-) [American popular singer and motion picture actor]
Bobby Darin

CASPER, WILLIAM EARL, JR. (1931-) [American professional golfer]
Billy Casper

Caspipina, T. See:
DUCHÉ, JACOB

Casque, Sammy. See:
DAVIS, SYDNEY CHARLES HOUGHTON

Cass Daley. See:
DAILEY, CATHERINE

CASS, LEWIS (1782-1866) [Superintendent of Indian Affairs in the Michigan Territory]
An American
The Father of the Old Northwest
The Great Father of Detroit

CASS, MARY MARGARET (1926-) [American actress]
Peggy Cass

Cass Mayo. See:
STEVENS, CASANDRA MAYO

Cassandra of the Columnists, The. See:
LEWIS, MRS. SINCLAIR

Cassandra, The Contemporary. See: LEWIS, MRS. SINCLAIR

Cassells, John. See:
DUNCAN, WILLIAM MURDOCH

CASSIANUS, JOHANNES (360?-435?) [Christian monk and theologian]
Johannes Eremita
Johannes Massiliensis

CASSIDAY, BRUCE BINGHAM (1920-) [American author]
Carson Bingham
Max Day

CASSILL, RONALD VERLIN (1919-) [American teacher and author]
Owen Aherne
Jesse Webster

CASSIN. See also:
CASSON

CASSIN, BILLIE. See:

LE SUEUR, LUCILLE
CASSINI, OLEG LOIEWSKI (1913-) [Italian-American fashion designer]
The Fashion World's Most Irrepressible Master of Ceremonies
The Rebel of Seventh Avenue
Cassius, Gaseous. See: CLAY, CASSIUS MARCELLUS, JR.
Cassius the Brashest. See: CLAY, CASSIUS MARCELLUS, JR.
CASSON. See also: CASSIN
CASSON, FREDERICK RONALD CHRISTOPHER (1910-) [English author]
Baden Beatty
CASTAGNA, GIAMBATTISTA (1521-90) [Supreme Pontiff of Roman Catholic Church]
Pope Urban VII
Castelar, Isabella. See: WINTER, ELIZABETH CAMPBELL
Castelfranco, Giorgione da. See: BARBARELLI, GIORGIO
Castello, De. See: VERGIL, POLYDORE
CASTELLO, GUIDO DI (died 1144) [Supreme Pontiff of Roman Catholic Church]
Pope Celestine II
CASTIGLIONE, FRANCESCO XAVERIO (1761-1830) [Supreme Pontiff of Roman Catholic Church]
Pope Pius VIII
CASTIGLIONE, GOFFREDO (died 1241) [Supreme Pontiff of Roman Catholic Church]
Pope Celestine IV
CASTILLA, MARÍA MARGUERITA GUADELUPE BOLDAO Y (1918-) [Spanish dancer and motion picture actress]
Margo
CASTLE, MRS. GEOFFREY L. (1905-) [English author and playwright]
Margery Sharp
CASTLE, NICHOLAS (1910-) [American composer, author and choreographer]
Nick Castle
Castle, Stanley. See: BROWNE, RILMA MARION
Castle, The Laird of Skibo. See: CARNEGIE, ANDREW
Castle, Vernon. See: BLYTHE, VERNON
Castlemon, Harry. See: FOSDICK, CHARLES AUSTIN
Castleton, Charles. See: COBB, SYLVANUS, JR.
Castor and Pollux of Georgia, The, joint nickname of ALEXANDER HAMILTON STEPHENS (1812-83) [Vice President of the Confederacy] and ROBERT TOOMBS (1810-85) [American politician active in Georgia politics]
Castor and Pollux of Georgia, The. See also: STEPHENS, ALEXANDER HAMILTON
TOOMBS, ROBERT
CASTRIOTA, GEORGE (1403-68) [Albanian commander]
The Albanian Alexander
Scanderbeg
Skanderbeg
The White Devil of Wallachia
CASTRO, LUIS (1912-) [Mexican bullfighter]
El Soldado
Castro, Thomas. See: ORTON, ARTHUR
CASWALL, E. (1814-78) [English author, imitator of CHARLES JOHN HUFFAM DICKENS]
Quiz
Caswell, Anne. See: DENHAM, MARY ORR
Cat. See:

ANDERSON, WILLIAM
ALONZO
KATT
Cat, Bell-the. See:
DOUGLAS, ARCHIBALD
Cat, The Hillbilly. See:
PRESLEY, ELVIS ARON
CATALANI, ANGELICA (1779-1849) [Italian singer]
The Italian Nightingale
The Queen of Song
Cataline, Crispin. See:
D'ÉPRÉMESNIL, JEAN JACQUES DUVAL
Catalog, The Father of the Mail Order. See:
FRANKLIN, BENJAMIN
Cathal O'Dubh. See:
DUFF, CHARLES ST. LAWRENCE
CATHCART, CHARLES MURRAY, 2ND EARL (1783-1895) [British general officer]
Lord Greenock
Cathedral Music, The Father of English. See:
TALLIS, THOMAS
Catherine I. See:
SKAVRONSKAYA, MARFA
CATHERINE[Catherine]. See also:
Cathrine
Katharine
Katherine
Kathryn
Katrin
Katrina
Catherine II. See:
ANHALT-ZERBST, SOPHIA AUGUSTA FREDERICA OF
Catherine Airlie. See:
MACLEOD, JEAN SUTHERLAND
Catherine Alexievna. See:
SKAVRONSKAYA, MARFA
Catherine Carr. See:
WADE, ROSALIND HERSCHEL
Catherine Marchant. See:
COOKSON, CATHERINE McMULLEN
Catherine the Great. See:
ANHALT-ZERBST, SOPHIA AUGUSTA FREDERICA OF
Cathie. See:
Cathy
Kathey
TAYLOR, CATHERINE
Catholic Action, The Pope of. See: SARTO, GIUSEPPE MELCHIORRE
Catholic Schleiermacher, The. See: MOHLER, JOHANN ADAM
Catholic, The. See:
ALFONSO I
FERDINAND II
FERDINAND V
ISABELLA I
Cathrine. See:
CATHERINE
Catherine
CLEVEN, KATHRYN SEWARD
Katharine
Katherine
Kathryn
Katrin
Katrina
WILDE, CLEO
Cathy. See also:
Cathie
Kathey
Cathy O'Donnell. See:
STEELY, ANN
CATINAT, NICOLAS (1637-1712) [French marshal]
The Father of Thought
CATLETT, GEORGE JAMES (1933-) [American jazz musician (bass, saxophone, clarinet)]
Buddy Catlett
CATLETT, SIDNEY (1910-51) [American jazz musician (drums)]
Big Sid Catlett
Catlow, Joanna. See:
LOWRY, JOAN CATLOW
Cato, joint pseud. of PETER DUNSMORE HOWARD (1908-65), FRANK OWEN (-) and MICHAEL FOOTE (-) [British authors]

Cato. See also:
CLINTON, GEORGE
Cato, American. See:
ADAMS, SAMUEL
CATO, MARCUS PORCIUS (234-149 B.C.) [Roman soldier and statesman]
Censor
The Elder
CATO, MARCUS PORCIUS (95-46 B.C.) [Roman soldier and statesman]
Uticensis
The Younger
Cato of America, The. See:
WHITE, HUGH LAWSON
Cato of the Revolution. See:
BLAND, RICHARD
Cato of the Senate, The. See:
WHITE, HUGH LAWSON
WRIGHT, SILAS
CATS [Cats]. See also:
Catz
KATZ
CATS, JACOB (1577-1660) [Dutch poet and statesman]
Father Cats
Cats, The Raphael of. See:
MIND, GOTTFRIED
CATSOS, NICHOLAS A. (1912-) [American composer and producer]
Gary Romero
CATTELL, JAMES McKEEN (1860-1944 [American psychologist, educator and author]
The Dean of American Science
Cattle King, The. See:
KLEBERG, RICHARD MIFFIN
Catullus, The Oriental. See:
MUSLIH-UD-DIN
Catz. See also:
CATS
Cats
KATZ
Catz, Max. See:
GLASER, MILTON
Caucus, King. See:
STILWELL, SILAS MOORE
Caudwell. See also:
CALDWELL
Cauldwell
Caudwell, Christopher. See:
SPRIGG, CHRISTOPHER ST. JOHN
Cauldwell. See also:
CALDWELL
Caudwell
Cauldwell, Frank. See:
KING, FRANCIS HENRY
CAULEY, TROY JESSE (1902-) [American economist and author]
Terry Cauley
Cauliflower, Sebastian. See:
SELDES, GILBERT VIVIAN
Causes, The Invincible Warrior in Righteous. See:
MOTT, LUCRETIA
Caustic, Christopher. See:
FESSENDEN, THOMAS GREEN
Caustic, Dr. See:
FESSENDEN, THOMAS GREEN
Caution, Takkie. See:
HATFIELD, CLARENCE E.
Cautious. See:
HOPKINSON, FRANCIS
Cavalier, The. See:
HUNTER, THOMAS LOMAX
Cavalier, The Last Literary. See: HAYNE, PAUL HAMILTON
Cavalier, The Mad. See:
PRINCE RUPERT
Cavaliere d'Arpino, Il. See:
CESARI, GIUSEPPE
Cavalli, Francesco. See:
CALETTI-BRUNI, FRANCESCO
CAVALLARO, ANN ABELSON (1918-) [American social worker and author]
Ann Abelson
CAVANNA, ELIZABETH ALLEN (1909-) [American journalist and author]
Betsy Allen
Betty Cavanna
Elizabeth Headley

Cave. See:
WILSON, JOHN
CAVE, EDWARD (1691-1754) [printer and publisher of the "Gentleman's Magazine"]
Sylvanus Urban
CAVE, RODERICK GEORGE JAMES MUNRO (1935-) [British librarian and author]
James Munro
Cavendish. See:
JONES, HENRY
Cavendish, Harry. See:
ST. JOHN, PERCY BOLLINGBROKE
CAVENDISH, RICHARD (1930-) [British insurance company executive and author]
Martin Cornwall
CAWEIN, MADISON JULIUS (1865-1914) [American poet]
The Keats of Kentucky
CAWSTON, FREDERICK GORDON (1885-) [British medical practitioner and author]
Juvenis
CAXTON, WILLIAM (c. 1422-91) [First printer in the English language]
Acting Governor of the English Nation
The Father of English Printing
Cayley, Rod. See:
ROWLAND, DONALD SYDNEY
Cecil Home. See:
WEBSTER, JULIA AUGUSTA
Cecil Mack. See:
McPHERSON, RICHARD C.
Cecil Parker. See:
SCHWABE, CECIL
Cecil Vincent. See:
BURTON, JOAN EILEEN VERONICA
Cecile. See:
LEE, MARY EMILY FRANCES
Cecile Aubry. See:
BERNARD, ANNE-JOSE
CEDER, GEORGIANA DORCAS (19??-) [American author]
Ana Dor
CEDMON. See:
(CAEDMON (CEDMON)
Ceiriog. See:
HUGHES, JOHN CIERIOG
Ceithearnaigh, Seumas O. See:
CARNEY, THOMAS PATRICK
CELA, CAMILO JOSÉ (1916-) [Spanish author]
Don Camilo
Matilde Verdu
Celebrated Actress, A. See:
AIKEN, ALBERT W.
Celebrated Author, A. See:
DEY, FREDERICK VAN RENSSELAER
Celebrated Author of "M'Fingal," The. See:
TRUMBULL, JOHN
CELESTIN, OSCAR (1884-1954) [American jazz musician (cornet, leader)]
Papa Celestin
CELESTINE (died 432) [Supreme Pontiff of Roman Catholic Church]
Pope Celestine I
St. Celestine
Celestine II, Pope. See:
CASTELLO, GUIDO DI
Celestine III, Pope. See:
ORSINI, GIACINTO BOBONI
Celestine IV, Pope. See:
CASTIGLIONE, GOFFREDO
Celestine V, Pope. See:
MURRONE, PIETRO ANGELARI DA
Celia Fremlin. See:
GOLLER, CELIA FREMLIN
Céline, Louis-Ferdinand. See:
DESTOUCHES, LOUIS FUCH
CELLINI, BENVENUTO (1500-71) [Italian goldsmith, sculptor and engraver]
The Firebrand of Florence
CELSUS, AULUS CORNELIUS (1st cent. A.D.) [Latin physician and writer]
The Roman Hippocrates

CENCI, BEATRICE (1577-99) [Italian noblewoman]
The Beautiful Parricide
Censor. See:
CATO, MARCUS PORCIUS
Censor of the Age, The. See:
CARLYLE, THOMAS
Censor of the Proud World. See: ARETINO, PIETRO
Centennial President, The. See:
HARRISON, BENJAMIN
CENTLIVRE, SUSANNAH (1667?-1723) [English actress and dramatist]
Mrs. Centlivre
Central America, The Tiger of. See: GUARDIOLA, SANTOS
Central Park, The Watchdog of. See:
OCHS, ADOLPH SIMON
Centurion. See:
BOWER, SIR GRAHAM JOHN
Century. See:
WHITE, JOHN
Century Moses, Twentieth. See:
CHAPLIN, CHARLES SPENCER
Century, The Best Read Man of the. See:
LOWELL, JAMES RUSSELL
Century, The Colossus of the Nineteenth. See:
BONAPARTE, NAPOLEON
Century, The Democritus of the Sixteenth. See:
CALVIN, JOHN
Century, The Greatest Theoretical Physicist of the Nineteenth. See:
MAXWELL, JAMES CLERK
Century, The Most Thoroughgoing British Skeptic of the. See:
HUME, DAVID
Century, The Plato of the Eighteenth. See:
AROUET, FRANÇOIS MARIE
CEPHISODOTUS (fl. early 4th cent. B.C.) [Greek sculptor, elder brother or possibly father of PRAXITELES]
Cephisodotus the Elder
CEPHISODOTUS (fl. late 4th cent. B.C.) [Greek sculptor, son of PRAXITELES]
Cephisodotus the Younger
CERAGIOLI, PETER A. (1932-) [American jazz musician (piano, accordion)]
Pete Jolly
Ceram, C.W. See:
MAREK, KURT WILLI
Cerberus of the Treasury, The. See: ELLSWORTH, OLIVER
Cerceau, Du (Hoop). See:
ANDROUET, JACQUES
Ceremonies, America's Foremost Master of. See:
FAY, FRANCIS ANTHONY
Ceremonies, The Fashion World's Most Irrepressible Master of. See:
CASSINI, OLEG LOIEWSKI
Ceremonious, The. See:
PEDRO IV
CERNEY, JAMES VINCENT (1914-) [American podiatrist and author]
Vince Black
Cerro Gordo. See:
KELLY, JONATHAN FALCONBRIDGE
Cervantes, The Modern. See:
PEREDA, JOSÉ MARÍA DE
CESARI. See also:
CAESAR
Caesar
CESARIÒ
CESARI, GIUSEPPE (c. 1568-1640) [Italian painter]
Il Cavaliere d'Arpino
CESARIÒ. See also:
CAESAR
Caesar
CESARI
CESARIÒ, SIMONETTA COLONNA DI (1922-) [Italian dress designer]
Simonetta
Cesarion. See:
PTOLEMY XIV

CÉZANNE, PAUL (1839-1906)
[French painter]
The Father of Modernism
Ch. Naftali. See:
BRANDWEIN, CHAIM
NAFTALI
Chaber, M. E. See:
CROSSEN, KENDELL
FOSTER
Chad. See:
KIMSEY, CLYDE
CHADWICK, HENRY (1824-1908)
[Anglo-American
organizer of professional
baseball]
The Father of Baseball
Chadwick, Lester. See:
STRATEMEYER,
EDWARD L.
CHAFFEE, ADNA ROMANZA
(1884-1941) [American
general officer]
The Father of the Mechanized
Forces
Chairman of the Board. See:
SINATRA, FRANCIS
ALBERT
CHALIANS, MARY (1905-)
[English author]
Mary Renault
Challis, George. See:
FAUST, FREDERICK
SCHILLER
Chalmers, Allen. See:
UPWARD, EDWARD
FALASIE
CHALMERS, JAMES
(1841-1901) [Scottish
missionary to South Sea
Islands]
Tamate
CHALUPEK, APPOLONIA
(1897-) [Polish-born
stage and silent motion
picture actress]
Pola Negri
Cham (Ham). See:
NOÉ, AMÉDÉE DE
Cham of Literature, The
Great. See:
JOHNSON, DR. SAMUEL
Chamaco. See:
BORRERO, ANTONIO
Chamber. See:
CHANG, MITCHELL
CHAMBERLAIN, JOSEPH
(1836-1914) [British
statesman]
Pushful Joe
CHAMBERLAIN, JOSHUA
LAWRENCE (1828-1914)
[American general officer;
fought gallantly in the bat-
tle of Gettysburg]
The Hero of Little Round Top
CHAMBERLAIN, SAMUEL
(1895-) [American edu-
cator, author and
illustrator]
Phineas Beck
Chamberlain, Theodore, joint
pseud. of RONALD
JOHNSON (1935-) and
JONATHAN CHAMBERLAIN
WILLIAMS (1929-)
[American authors]
CHAMBERLAIN, WILTON
NORMAN (1936-)
[American professional
basketball player]
Wilt Chamberlain
Wilt the Stilt
CHAMBERS, BERTRAM
MORDAUNT (1866-)
[British naval officer and
author]
Avalon West
CHAMBERS, JESSIE RALPH
(1864-1944) [American
motion picture actress]
Jessie Ralph
CHAMBERS, MARGARET ADA
EASTWOOD (1911-)
[British author]
Peggy Chambers
Chambers, Peter. See:
PHILLIPS, DENNIS JOHN
ANDREW
CHAMBORD, HENRI CHARLES
DIEUPONNÉ, COMTE DE
(1820-83) [claimant of
the French throne]
The Citizen King
Henry V
l'Enfant du Miracle
CHAMFORT, NICOLAS

SÉBASTIAN ROCH
(1741-94) [French
writer]
La Rouchefoucauld-Chamfort
Champ. See:
BARBOUR, WILLIAM
WARREN
Champ, The. See:
DEMPSEY, WILLIAM
HARRISON
Champagne, Robert of. See:
ROBERT DE MOLESME
CHAMPEAUX, GUILLAUME DE
(c. 1070-1121) [French
scholastic philosopher]
Doctor Venerabilis
(Venerable Doctor)
The Pillar of the Doctors
Champfleury. See:
FLEURY-HUSSON, JULES
Champion Buffalo Hunter of
the Plains, The. See:
CODY, WILLIAM
FREDERICK
Champion Jail Breaker. See:
WEISS, EHRICH
(ERIK WEISZ)
CHAMPION, MARJORIE CELESTE
BELCHER (1923-)
[American dancer]
Marge Champion
Champion of Champions. See:
FITZSIMMONS, ROBERT
PROMETHEUS
Champion of Orthodoxy. See:
PUSEY, EDWARD
BOUVERIE
Champion of the English Theater,
The Present. See:
OLIVIER, SIR LAURENCE
Champion of the Virgin, The.
See: CYRIL OF ALEXAN-
DRIA, ST.
Champions, Champion of. See:
FITZSIMMONS, ROBERT
PROMETHEUS
CHAMPLAIN, SAMUEL DE
(1567?-1635) [French ex-
plorer in North America]
The Father of New France
CHAMPLIN, EDWIN ROSS
(1854-1828) [American
editor and poet]
Clarence Fairchild
CHAMPNEY, ELIZABETH
WILLIAMS (1850-1922)
[American novelist and
traveler]
Lizzie W. Champney
CHAMSON, ANDRÉ JULES
LOUIS (1900-) [French
museum curator and
author]
Lauter
Chan. See:
GURNEY, JOHN CHANDLER
Chanakya. See:
PANIKKAR, KAVALAM
MADHAVA
CHANCE, FRANK LeROY
(1877-1924) [American
professional baseball
player]
Husk
The Peerless Leader
CHANCE, JULIE GRINNELL
(fl. 1890-1905) [American
novelist]
Julien Gordon
Chancellor. See also:
CHANSLOR
Chancellor Ayala, The. See:
LÓPEZ DE AYALA,
PEDRO
Chancellor of the Rising State
of New Jersey, Extra-
ordinary. See:
LIVINGSTON, WILLIAM
Chancellor, The. See:
SMITH, FRANCIS
SHUBAEL
Chancellor, The Dancing. See:
HATTON, CHRISTOPHER
Chancellor, The Iron. See:
VON BISMARCK, PRINCE
OTTO EDUARD LEO-
POLD
CHANDLER, A. BERTRAM
(1912-) [British sailor and
author]
Andrew Dunstan
George Whitley
CHANDLER, ALBERT BEN-
JAMIN (1898-) [Amer-
ican statesman; Governor
of Kentucky, U.S. senator
and High Commissioner of
Baseball]

Happy Chandler
CHANDLER, CHARLES (1905-) [American motion picture actor]
Chuck Chandler
Chandler, Jeff. See: GROSSEL, IRA
CHANDLER, RAYMOND (1888-1959) [American author of detective stories]
The Poet of Violence
CHANDLER, WILLIAM EATON (1835-1917) [American statesman; U.S. senator from New Hampshire and Secretary of the Navy]
The Father of Our Modern Navy
Stormy Petrel
Chandos, Fay. See: TEMPEST, JAN
CHANDRA GUPTA (CHANDRA GUPTA MAURYA) (d. 286 B.C.) [First king of the Maurya dynasty of the ancient kingdom of Magadha]
Sandrocottus
CHANEL. See also: Chenal CHENEL
CHANEL, GABRIELLE (1884-1971) [French parfumier and high fashion dictator]
Coco
CHANEY, CREIGHTON (1907?-1912?-) [American motion picture actor]
Lon Chaney, Jr.
CHANEY, LON (1883-1930) [American motion picture actor; adept in the use of bizarre makeup]
The Man of a Thousand Faces
CHANG. See: LI HUNG CHANG
CHANG BUNKER. See: Siamese Twins, The
CHANG HSUEH-LIANG (1898-) [Chinese soldier]
The Young Marshal
CHANG, MITCHELL (1880-) [Chinese editor and author]
Chamber
CHANNING-RENTON, LIEUT. ERNEST MATTHEWS (1895-) [British army officer and author]
Bohemian
E. Channing Matthews
CHANNING, WILLIAM ELLERY (1780-1842) [American Unitarian clergyman]
The Apostle of Unitarianism
The Elder
Little King Pepin
The Peacemaker
CHANNING, WILLIAM ELLERY (1818-1901) [American poet and essayist]
The Younger
Chano Pozo. See: GONZALES, LUCIANO
CHANSLOR. See also: Chancellor
CHANSLOR, MARJORIE TORREY HOOD (1899-) [writer of literature for juveniles]
Marjorie Torrey
Chao, Y.R. See: JAW-YUARENN
CHAPELSKI, ALEX SAMUEL (1932-70) [Canadian convict]
Lumpy Willie
The Ugliest Man in Canada
Chaplain, The Fighting. See: CALDWELL, JAMES
Chaplain, The Singing. See: McCABE, CHARLES CARDWELL
CHAPLIN, CHARLES SPENCER (1889-) [British-born motion picture comedian, producer and screen writer]
Charlie Chaplin
The Little Tramp
Twentieth Century Moses
Chapman, Allen. See: STRATEMEYER, EDWARD L.

CHAPMAN, GEORGE WARREN VERNON (1925-) [English author]
Vernon Warren
CHAPMAN, J. DUDLEY (1928-) [American physician and author]
Jay Dudley
CHAPMAN, JOHN (1768? 1775?-1847) [American planter of apple seeds in the wilderness]
Johnny Appleseed
The Patron Saint of American Orchards
Chapman, Maristan, joint pseud. of JOHN STANTON HIGHAM CHAPMAN (1891-) and his wife, MARY HAMILTON ILLSLEY CHAPMAN (1895-) [Anglo-American novelists]
CHAPMAN-MORTIMER, WILLIAM CHARLES (1907-) [Scottish author]
Chapman Mortimer
CHAPMAN, RAYMOND (1924-) [British educator and author]
Simon Nash
Chapman, Walker. See: SILVERBERG, ROBERT
Chappaqua, The Sage of. See: GREELEY, HORACE
CHAPPELL, GEORGE SHEPARD (1878-1946) [American author and architect]
Walter Traprock
Walter E. Traprock
Chapultepec, Old. See: SCOTT, WINFIELD
Chardonne, Jacques. See: BOUTELLEAU, JACQUES
Charisse, Cyd. See: FINKLEA, TULA ELLICE
Charity, The Apostle of Organized. See: VINCENT DE PAUL
CHARLAP, MORRIS (1928-) [American composer]
Moose Charlap
CHARLEMAGNE (742-814) [King of France and Emperor of the West]
Carolus Magnus
Charles the Great
Charlemagne, The Second. See: CHARLES V
CHARLES (1433-77) [Last Duke of Burgundy]
Charles the Bold
Charles. See:
BARLING, MURIEL VERE MANT
Collins, Charles
DE COSTER, CHARLES THEODORE HENRI
GRAY, HAROLD M.
Merriman, Charles Eustace
WHITE, JAMES
CHARLES I (823-77) [King of France]
The Bald
CHARLES I (1246-1309) [King of Naples]
The Lame
CHARLES I (1288-1342) [King of Hungary]
Charles Robert of Anjou
Charles Robert of Carobert
CHARLES I (1600-49) [King of England]
The Last Man
The Man of Blood
The Martyr
The Royal Martyr
The White King
CHARLES II (823-77) [Holy Roman Emperor]
Charles the Bald
CHARLES II (839-88) [King of France (and Holy Roman Emperor as CHARLES III)]
Charles the Fat
CHARLES II (1332-87) [King of Navarre]
Charles the Bad
CHARLES II (1604-75) [Duke of Lorraine]
The Great
CHARLES II (1630-85) [King of England]
The Merry Monarch
Old Rowley

The Satyr
The Son of the Last Man
CHARLES II (1661-1700) [King of Spain]
Lord Strutt
CHARLES III (879-929) [King of France]
Charles the Simple
CHARLES III (1345-86) [King of Naples]
Charles of Durazzo
CHARLES III (1361-1425) [King of Navarre]
Charles the Noble
CHARLES IV (1294-1328) [King of France]
Charles the Fair
CHARLES IV (1316-78) [Emperor of the Holy Roman Empire and King of Germany]
Parson's Emperor
CHARLES IV (1421-61) [King of Navarre]
Don Carlos
Prince of Viana
CHARLES V (1337-80) [King of France]
Charles the Wise
The Solomon of France
CHARLES V (1500-58) [Holy Roman Emperor]
The Second Charlemagne
CHARLES VI (1368-1422) [King of France]
Charles the Silly
Charles the Well-Beloved
The Foolish
CHARLES VII (1403-61) [King of France]
The Victorious
CHARLES VII (1697-1745) [Holy Roman Emperor]
Karl Albrecht
CHARLES VIII (1408?-70) [King of Sweden]
Karl Knutsson
CHARLES VIII (1470-98) [King of France]
Charles the Affable
CHARLES VIII (1697-1745) [Holy Roman Emperor]
Charles Albert
CHARLES XII (1682-1718) [King of Sweden]
Alexander of the North
The Brilliant Madman
The Madman of the North
The Quixote of the North
CHARLES XIV [King of Sweden] See: BERNADOTTE, JEAN BAPTISTE JULES
Charles A. Sandburg. See: SANDBURG, CARL AUGUST
Charles Adams. See: SCHWANBECK, KARL ADAM
Charles Alexander. See: HADFIELD, ELLIS CHARLES RAYMOND
Charles Amory Beach. See: STRATEMEYER, EDWARD L.
Charles Augustus Conybeare. See: ELIOT, THOMAS STEARNS
Charles Barry. See: BRYSON, CHARLES
Charles Blondin. See: GRAVELET, JEAN FRANÇOIS
Charles Bronson. See: BUCHINSKY, CHARLES
Charles Carroll of Carrollton. See: CARROLL, CHARLES
Charles Castleton. See: COBB, SYLVANUS, JR.
Charles Chatterbox. See: BIGELOW, WILLIAM FREDERICK
Charles Coborn. See: McCALLUM, COLIN WHITTON
Charles de France, Louis. See: LOUIS XVII
Charles Drake. See: RUPPERT, CHARLES
Charles E. LaSalle. See: ELLIS, EDWARD SYLVESTER
Charles Edmonds. See: CARRINGTON, CHARLES EDMUND
Charles-Edward Jeanneret. See:

JEANNERET-GRIS,
CHARLES EDOUARD

Charles Edward Stuart. See:
STUART, CHARLES
EDWARD LOUIS PHILIP
CASIMIR

Charles Egbert Craddock. See:
MURFREE, MARY
NOAILLES

CHARLES EMMANUEL I
(1562-1630) [Duke of
Savoy]
The Great

Charles Erskine White, D. D.
See: OSBORN, LAUGHTON

CHARLES, EZZARD (1921-)
[American professional
boxer; world's heavyweight
champion]
The Hawk

Charles Field. See:
ROWLAND, DONALD
SYDNEY

Charles Franklin. See:
USHER, FRANK

Charles Geoffrey. See:
MULLER, CHARLES
GEORGE

Charles Gorney. See:
RUDOLPH, WILLIAM

Charles Grant. See:
LENGEL, WILLIAM
CHARLES

Charles H. Cranston. See:
JUDSON, EDWARD ZANE
CARROLL

Charles Harmon. See:
FLAGENHEIMER, ARTHUR

Charles Harvard. See:
GIBBS-SMITH, CHARLES
HARVARD

Charles Hawtrey. See:
HARTREE, CHARLES

Charles Henry Percy. See:
SMITH, DODIE

Charles Hooton. See:
ROWE, VIVIAN CLAUDE

Charles Howard. See:
HARBAUGH, THOMAS
CHALMERS

Charles J. Kenny. See:
GARDNER, ERLE
STANLEY

Charles James Grimble,
Reverend. See:
ELIOT, THOMAS STEARNS

Charles John (Karl Johan). See:
BERNADOTTE, JEAN
BAPTISTE JULES

Charles Julius. See:
BERTRAM, CHARLES

Charles K. Boston. See:
GRUBER, FRANK

Charles, Louis. See:
STRATEMEYER,
EDWARD L.

Charles Luciano. See:
LUCIANA, SALVATORE

Charles M. Clay. See:
CLARK, CHARLOTTE
MOON

Charles M. Green. See:
GARDNER, ERLE STAN-
LEY

Charles Marie Franzero. See:
FRANZERO, CARLO
MARIA

Charles Marlowe. See:
JAY, HARRIET

CHARLES MARTEL (689-741)
[Frankish leader; grand-
father of CHARLEMAGNE]
Charles the Hammer
The Hammer

Charles Morey. See:
FLETCHER, HELEN JILL

Charles Norden. See:
DURRELL, LAWRENCE
GEORGE

Charles Proteus Steinmetz. See:
STEINMETZ, KARL
AUGUST RUDOLF

Charles, Ray. See:
ROBINSON, RAY CHARLES

Charles Richards. See:
MARVIN, JOHN T.

Charles, Riff. See:
EMBREE, CHARLES, JR.

Charles Roscoe. See:
ROWLAND, DONALD
SYDNEY

Charles S. Johnson. See:
EDWARDS, WILLIAM
BENNETT

Charles Sealsfield See:
POSTL, KARL ANTON

Charles Sidons. See:
POSTL, KARL ANTON
Charles, Sir. See:
THOMPSON, CHARLES PHILIP
Charles Stretton. See:
DYER, CHARLES
Charles Strong. See:
EPSTEIN, SAMUEL
Charles Stuart. See:
MACKINNON, CHARLES ROY
Charles Summerfield. See:
ARRINGTON, ALFRED W.
Charles Sumner. See:
HALL, HOWARD
Charles, Teddy. See:
COHEN, THEODORE CHARLES
Charles Tennyson Turner. See:
TENNYSON, CHARLES
Charles the Great. See:
CHARLEMAGNE
Charles, Theresa, joint pseud. of CHARLES SWATRIDGE (fl. 1940-65) and his wife, IRENE SWATRIDGE (fl. 1940-65) [British authors]
Charles W. North. See:
BAUER, ERWIN A.
Charles Wellesley, Lord. See:
BRONTË, CHARLOTTE
Charles Willard. See:
ARMSTRONG, JOHN BYRON
Charles Winterfield. See:
WEBBER, CHARLES WILKINS
Charles Wynn. See:
WEINBERG, CHARLES
Charles Yellowplush, Esq. See:
THACKERAY, WILLIAM MAKEPEACE
Charleston, The Hero of. See:
LEE, CHARLES
Charleston, The Poet of. See:
HAYNE, PAUL HAMILTON
Charley. See:
Charlie
CHORLEY
STRAIGHT, CHARLES
Charley, Lonesome. See:
REYNOLDS, CHARLES ALEXANDER
Charley, Poker. See:
FARWELL, CHARLES BENJAMIN
Charley, Prince. See:
GALLOWAY, CHARLES BETTS
Charley, Silent. See:
MURPHY, CHARLES FRANCIS
Charley, Slingshot. See:
TAYLOR, CHARLEY
Charley Weaver. See:
ARQUETTE, CLIFFORD
Charley, Wise. See:
McNARY, CHARLES LINZA
Charlie. See:
BARNETT, CHARLES DALY
CHAPLIN, CHARLES SPENCER
Charley
CHORLEY
CHRISTIAN, CHARLES
CONERLY, CHARLES
MANNA, CHARLES J.
PARKER, CHARLES
TEAGARDEN, CHARLES
Charlie, Black. See:
NAPIER, SIR CHARLES
Charlie, Blackguard. See:
PINCKNEY, CHARLES
Charlie, Bonny Prince. See:
STUART, CHARLES EDWARD LOUIS PHILIP CASIMIR
Charlie, Bronco. See:
MILLER, CHARLES
Charlie, Doctor. See:
MAYO, CHARLES HORACE
Charlie, Dutch. See:
DUANE, CHARLES P.
Charlie May Simon. See:
FLETCHER, CHARLIE MAY HOGUE
Charlie, Mr. See:
CANNON, CHARLES A.
Charlie, Souphouse. See:
BONAPARTE, CHARLES JOSEPH
Charlie Ventura. See:
VENTURO, CHARLES

Charlie, Wild Horse. See:
ALEXANDER, CHARLES W.
CHARLIEU. See:
LABÉ (CHARLIEU), LOUISE
Charlotte Corday. See:
D'ARMONT, MARIE ANNE CHARLOTTE CORDAY
Charlotte Dunning. See:
WOOD, CHARLOTTE DUNNING
CHARLOTTE, MARIE THÉRÈSE (1778-1851) [Daughter of LOUIS XVI of France]
The Daughter of Sorrow
The Modern Antigone
The Orphan of the Temple
Charlotte Morrow. See:
KIRWAN, MOLLY MORROW
Charlotte Olmsted. See:
KURSH, CHARLOTTE OLMSTED
Charlotte Steer. See:
HUNTER, MAUD LILY
Charlotte Wilson. See:
BAKER, MRS. KARLE
Charlson, David. See:
HOLMES, DAVID CHARLES
Charlton, John. See:
WOODHOUSE, MARTIN
Charming, Prince. See:
FAROUK I
CHARNEY, CARMI (1925-) [American-Israeli editor and author]
T. Carmi
CHARPENTIER. See also:
CARPENTER
CARPENTIER
CHARPENTIER, SUZANNE (1910-) [French motion picture actress]
Annabella
Charteris, Leslie. See:
LIN, LESLIE CHARLES BOWYER
Charters, Patricia. See:
CARLON, PATRICIA BERNADETTE
Chartist Clergyman, The. See:
KINGSLEY, REV. CHARLES
Chartist Preacher, The. See:
KINGSLEY, REV. CHARLES
Chase, James Hadley. See:
RAYMOND, RENÉ
CHASE, SALMON PORTLAND (1803-73) [American lawyer and statesman]
Attorney General for Runaway Slaves
The Father of Greenbacks
The Ferry Boy
CHASSAGNE, MICHELINE (1922-) [French stage and motion picture actress]
Micheline Presle
CHASSÉ, DAVID HENDRIK, BARON (1765-1849) [Dutch soldier; served under NAPOLEON]
General Baïonette
Chaste, The. See:
BOLESLAV V
CHATMAN, PETER (1915-) [American jazz musician (piano, singer, songwriter)]
Memphis Slim
Chatrian. See:
Erckmann-Chatrian
CHATRIAN, ALEXANDRE. See:
Erckmann-Chatrian
Chatta Johnson. See:
GIOVANNONE, ANTHONY J.
Chattanooga, The Builder of. See: OCHS, ADOLPH SIMON
Chatterbox, Charles. See:
BIGELOW, WILLIAM FREDERICK
CHATTERTON, THOMAS (1752-70) [English poet, author and juvenile prodigy]
The Bristol Boy
Dunelmus Bristoliensis
Decimus
The Marvellous Boy
Thomas Rowley
Chatty Cheerful, Old. See:
MARTIN, WILLIAM
CHAUCER, GEOFFREY (c.1340-

1400) [English poet]
The Father of English Poetry
The Flower of Poets
The Morning Star of Song
Tityrus
Chaucer of France, The. See:
MAROT, CLÉMENT
Chaucerians, The Last of the Scottish. See:
LINDSAY (LYNDSAY), SIR DAVID
CHAUCHOIN, CLAUDETTE (1905-) [French-American motion picture actress]
Claudette Colbert
Lily
Chautauqua County, The Father of. See:
FOOTE, ELIAL TODD
CHAVARRI, EMPERATRIZ (1927-) [Peruvian singer]
Yma Sumac
Che. See:
GUEVARA, DR. SERNA ERNESTO
CHEATHAM, ADOLPHUS (1905-) [American jazz musician (trumpet)]
Doc Cheatham
CHEATHAM, BENJAMIN FRANKLIN (1820-86) [American general officer]
Bulldog Cheatham
Ney of the Confederacy
Old Frank
CHEATHAM, KATHERINE SMILEY (fl. 2nd decade of 20th cent.) [American singer, lecturer and interpreter of children's stories]
Kitty Cheatham
Cheche. See:
MARRERO, JOSÉ
Checker, Chubby. See:
EVANS, ERNEST
Cheerful, Old Chatty. See:
MARTIN, WILLIAM
Chees-quat-a-law-ny (Yellow Bird). See:
RIDGE, JOHN ROLLIN
Chefs, The King of. See:
ESCOFFIER, AUGUSTE
Chelsea Philosopher, The. See:
CARLYLE, THOMAS
Chelsea, The Sage of. See:
CARLYLE, THOMAS
Chelton, John. See:
DURST, PAUL
Chemical Revolution, The Nestor of the. See:
BLACK, JAMES
Chemistry, The Father of. See:
VILLENEUVA, ARNAUD DE
Chemistry, The Father of Modern. See:
BOYLE, SIR ROBERT
Chen Hwei. See:
STEVENSON, WILLIAM
Chenal. See also:
CHANEL
CHENEL
Chenal, Pierre. See:
COHEN, PIERRE
Chenault, Nell. See:
SMITH, LINELL NASH
CHENEL. See also:
CHANEL
Chenal
CHENEL, ANTONIO (1932-) [Spanish bullfighter]
Antoñete
CHENEY, SOPHIE H. (fl. mid-19th cent.) [American philanthropist]
Santa Claus of the Manchester Poor
CHENG, CHU-YUAN (1927-) [Chinese educator, scientist and author]
Cheng Tek-cheung
Cheng, Prince. See:
SHIN HUANG TI
CHEOPS (died 2877 B.C.) [Pharaoh of Egypt; builder of Great Pyramid at Gizeh]
Khufu
Cher, Marie. See:
SCHERR, MARIE
CHERKOSE, EDWARD (1912-) [American musician]
Eddie Maxwell
CHEROCK, CLARENCE FRANCIS

(1915-) [American jazz musician (trumpet)]
Shorty Sherock
Cherokee. See:
JOHNSON, ROBERT LEE
Cherokee Bill. See:
HASTINGS, WILLIAM WIRT
Cherokee Kid, The. See:
ROGERS, WILLIAM PENN ADAIR
Cheronean Sage, The. See:
PLUTARCH
Cherry-trees Nemesis, The. See:
JENCKES, VIRGINIA ELLIS
Cherubic Master of Suspense, The. See:
HITCHCOCK, ALFRED JOSEPH
CHESDA (1788-1851) [King of Thailand (Siam)]
Rama III
Chesebro', Caroline. See:
CHESEBROUGH, CAROLINE
CHESEBROUGH, CAROLINE (1825-73) [American novelist]
Caroline Chesebro'
CHESNUTT, CHARLES WADDELL (1858-1932) [American Negro author]
The First American Negro Novelist
Chester F. O'Leary. See:
KEUHNELT-LEDDIHN, ERIK RITTER VON
Chester, John. See:
MITCHELL, DR. SILAS WEIR
Chester K. Steele. See:
STRATEMEYER, EDWARD L.
Chester, Peter. See:
PHILLIPS, DENNIS JOHN ANDREW
CHESTER, ROBERT T. (1908-) [American jazz musician (composer, leader)]
Bob Chester
Chesterfield of the Navy, The. See: LE ROY, WILLIAM EDGAR
CHESTERTON, GILBERT KEITH (1874-1936) [English author]
G.K.C.
Master of Paradox
Chet. See:
FORREST, GEORGE
HOLIFIELD, CHESTER EARL
HUNTLEY, CHESTER ROBERT
Chet, Our. See:
ARTHUR, CHESTER ALAN
CHETHAM-STRODE, WARREN (1896-) [British businessman, playwright and author]
Michael Hamilton
Chetwynd, Berry. See:
RAYNER, CLAIRE
Chevalier. See:
BAYARD, PIERRE DU TERRAIL, CHEVALIER DE
Chevalier d'Éon, The. See:
ÉON DE BEAUMONT, TIMOTHÉE D'
Chevalier de Parcieux. See:
RIVAROL (RIVAROLI), ANTOINE
Chevalier de Ramsay. See:
RAMSAY, ANDREW MICHAEL
Chevalier de St. George, The. See: STUART, JAMES FRANCIS EDWARD
Chevalier, H.W. See:
SEARS, EDWARD I.
CHEVALIER, MAURICE AUGUSTE (1888-1972) [French singer, actor and entertainer]
The Man in the Straw Hat
CHEVALIER, SULPICE GUILLAUME (1804-66) [French caricaturist and illustrator]
Gavarni
Paul Gavarni
Chevalier, The Young. See:
STUART, CHARLES EDWARD LOUIS PHILIP CASIMIR

Cheviot of the Field. See:
PARKER, ERIC
Cheyney, Peter. See:
SOUTHOUSE-CHEYNEY, REGINALD EVELYN PETER
Chi Chi. See:
RODRIGUEZ, JUAN A.
CHIABRERA, GABRIELLO (1552-1637) [Italian lyric poet]
The Italian Pindar
Chian Strand, The Blind Bard of the. See:
HOMER
CHIANG CHUNG-CHENG (1886-) [Chinese soldier and statesman]
Chiang Chieh-Shih
Chiang Kai-Shek
CHIARAMONTI, LUIGI BARNABA (1740-1823) [Supreme Pontiff of Roman Catholic Church]
Pope Pius VII
Chiari, Walter. See:
ANNICHIARICO, WALTER
CHIARINI, SIGNOR G. (1823-97) [Italian-American circus impresario]
The Franconi of America
Chic. See:
Chick
SALE, CHARLES PARTLOW
Chic Conwell. See:
UNKNOWN
Chicago's Grand Old Lady. See:
HUDLUN, ANNA ELIZABETH
Chichester, Jane. See:
LONGRIGG, JANE CHICHESTER
Chick. See:
Chic
COOMBS, CHARLES IRA
WEBB, WILLIAM
Chick, The Day-old. See:
WENE, ELMER H.
Chickamauga, Old. See:
STEEDMAN, JAMES BARRETT
Chickamauga, The Rock of. See: THOMAS, GEORGE HENRY
Chicken, The Belfast. See:
CLARK, WILLIAM
Chiclanero, El. See:
REDONDO, JOSÉ
Chico. See:
ÁLVAREZ, ALFRED
HAMILTON, FORESTORN
O'FARRILL, ARTURO
Chico, Armillita. See:
ESPINOSA, FERMÍN
Chico de la Blusa. See:
PASTOR, VICENTE
Chico Marx. See:
Four Marx Brothers, The
Chicuelo. See:
JIMÉNEZ, RAFAEL
MORENO, MANUEL JIMÉNEZ
Chicuelo II. See:
JIMÉNEZ, MANUEL
Chief. See:
BENDER, CHARLES ALBERT
BURDICK, USHER L.
HALE, ARNELL ODELL
HARDER, MELVIN LEROY
HOGSETT, ELON CHESTER
Chief, Big. See:
CURTIS, CHARLES
MOORE, RUSSELL
Chief Executioner, The. See:
ROPER, DANIEL CALHOUN
Chief, Great White. See:
ROOSEVELT, THEODORE
Chief Incendiary of the White House. See:
ADAMS, SAMUEL
Chief, Little. See:
THATCHER, MOSES
Chief of the Pawnees, The White. See: LILLIE, MAJOR GORDON W.
Chief, Old. See:
CLAY, HENRY
Chief Old Woman, The. See:
STEVENS, THADDEUS
Chief, The. See:
HOOVER, HERBERT CLARK
Chief, The Fire. See:
CARLEY, PATRICK J.
LEOPOLD, ISAIAH EDWIN
Chief Who Never Sleeps, The. See: WAYNE, ANTHONY
Chiefs of Staff, The Disraeli of the. See:

MacARTHUR, DOUGLAS
Chieftain, The Grim. See:
LANE, JAMES HENRY
Chieh-Shih, Chiang. See:
CHIANG CHUNG-CHENG
CHIESA, GIACOMO DELLA (1854-1922) [Supreme Pontiff of Roman Catholic Church]
Pope Benedict XV
CHIGI, FABIO (1599-1667) [Supreme Pontiff of Roman Catholic Church]
Pope Alexander VII
Chignon, Niles. See:
LINGEMAN, RICHARD ROBERTS
Child, Alan
Isabelle Loudon, joint psueds. of LAWRENCE LANGNER (1890-) and his wife ARMINA MARSHALL LANGNER [Anglo-American playwrights]
Child, Julia. See:
McWILLIAMS, JULIA
Child, The. See:
LOUIS III
Child, Victory's Darling. See: MASSÉNA, ANDRÉ
Child Wonder Magician, The. See: DUNNINGER, JOSEPH
CHILDERS, MARION (1926-) [American jazz musician trumpet)]
Buddy Childers
Childhood, The Poet of. See:
FIELD, EUGENE
Children, The Friend of Helpless. See: HOOVER, HERBERT CLARK
Children, The Second Mother of Everybody's. See:
ABBOTT, GRACE
Children's Poet, The. See:
ANDERSEN, HANS CHRISTIAN
LONGFELLOW, HENRY WADSWORTH
RILEY, JAMES WHITCOMB
CHILDS, ELEANOR STUART (1876-) [American author]
Eleanor Stuart
CHILDS, RICHARD SPENCER (1882-) [American business executive and organization official]
The Father of the City Manager Plan of Municipal Government
The Father of the Short Ballot Principle
CHILLINGWORTH, WILLIAM (1602-44) [British theologian]
The Most Conspicuous Controversialist of His Age
Chillon, The Prisoner of. See:
BONNIVARD, FRANÇOIS DE
CHILO (CHILON). See:
Seven Sages of Greece, The.
China, The Christian General of. See:
FENG, YU-HSIANG
China, The Philosopher of. See:
CONFUCIUS
Chinese. See:
GORDON, CHARLES GEORGE
HARRISON, BENJAMIN
MORRISON, GEORGE ERNEST
Chinese Republic, The Father of the. See:
SUN YAT-SEN
Ching, Prince. See:
SHIH HUANG TI
Ching, Wen. See:
LIM, BOON KENG
Chinghiz Khan (Precious Warrior). See: TEMUJIN
Chinnubbie Harjo. See:
POSEY, ALEXANDER LAWRENCE
Chino. See: POZO, FRANCISCO
Chinook, Old. See:
WISE, HENRY ALEXANDER
Chios, The Man of. See:
HOMER
Chip. See:
BALLEW, FRANK W.
ROBERT, LAWRENCE WOOD
CHIPPERFIELD, JOSEPH EUGENE (1912-) [British editor, film writer and author]
John Eland Craig

Chipperfield, Robert Orr. See:
OSTRANDER, ISABEL
Chippewa, The Hero of. See:
SCOTT, WINFIELD
Chippie. See:
HILL, BERTHA
Chips, Buffalo. See:
WHITE, JAMES
Chips Rafferty. See:
GOFFAGE, JOHN
CHISHOLM, LILIAN MARY
(1906-) [English author]
Anne Lorraine
Chivalry, The Flower of. See:
DOUGLAS, SIR WILLIAM
SIDNEY (SYDNEY), SIR
PHILIP
CHOATE, GWEN PETERSON
(1922-) [American
author]
R. G. Choate
Chochlik. See:
RADWANSKI, PIERRE
ARTHUR
Choirmaster of the House, The.
See: WOODRUM,
CLIFTON ALEXANDER
CHOISEUL-AMBOISE, ÉTIENNE
FRANÇOIS, DUC DE (1719-
85) [French minister to
King LOUIS XV]
Le Cocher de L'Europe (The
Coachman of Europe)
Comte de Stainville
Choleric, Brother. See:
VAN VELLER, HUBERT
Cholly Knickerbocker. See:
PAUL, MAURY HENRY
BIDDLE
CHOLMONDELEY, MARY (-
1925) [English novelist]
Pax
CHOMETTE, RENÉ (1898-)
[French film producer,
director and writer]
René Clair
Choni, El. See:
MARCO, JAIME
Chore Boy, The Lord's. See:
MAY, SAMUEL JOSEPH
CHORLEY. See also:
Charley
Charlie
CHORLEY, HENRY FOTHER-
GILL (1808-72) [British
critic, poet and novelist]
Paul Bell
CHOSROES. See:
KRUSRAU (CHOSROES) I
Chris. See:
BARBER, DONALD CHRIS-
TOPHER
Cris
Kris
Christ-Bearer. See:
CHRISTOPHER, ST.
Christendom, The Most
Learned Fool in. See:
JAMES I
Christendom, The Wisest Fool
in. See:
JAMES I
CHRISTIAN [Christian]. See also:
Kristian
CHRISTIAN II (1481-1569) (King
of Denmark and Norway]
The Cruel
The Nero of the North
CHRISTIAN III (1502-59) [King
of Denmark]
The Father of the People
Christian America, The Father
of Foreign Mission Work
in. See:
MILLS, SAMUEL JOHN
Christian Atticus, The. See:
HEBER, REGINALD
Christian Brulls. See:
SIMENON, GEORGES
Christian Carrier, The. See:
BROWN, JOHN
CHRISTIAN, CHARLES (1916-42)
[American jazz musician
(guitar, bass)]
Charlie Christian
Christian Eloquence, The
Founder of. See:
BOURDALONE, LOUIS
Christian, Frederick. See:
GEHMAN, RICHARD
BOYD
Christian General of China, The.
See: FENG YU-HSIANG
Christian Hero, The. See:
GEORGE, ST.
Christian-Jacque. See:

MAUDET, CHRISTIAN
Christian, Jill. See:
DILCOCK, NOREEN
Christian, Linda. See:
WELTER, BLANCA ROSA
Christian Monachism, The Father of. See:
ANTONY (ANTHONY) ST.
Christian Monasticism, The Founder of. See:
ANTONY (ANTHONY), ST.
Christian Reid. See:
TIERNAN, FRANCES CHRISTINE FISHER
Christian Seneca, The. See:
HALL, JOSEPH
Christian Statesman, The. See:
FRELINGHUYSEN, THEODORE
Christian Virgil, The. See:
SANNAZARO, JACOPO
VIDA, MARCO GIROLAMO
Christianissimus, Doctor. See:
GERSON, JEAN CHARLIER DE
CHRISTIANS, MARGUERITA MARIA (1900-) [Viennese actress]
Madi Christians
Mady Christians
CHRISTIE [Christie]. See also:
CHRISTY
Christy
Christie, Agatha. See:
MILLER, AGATHA MARY CLARISSA
Christie, Barbara. See:
CARLON, PATRICIA BERNARDETTE
Christie, Keith. See:
HAYNES, ALFRED HENRY
CHRISTINA (1626-89) [Queen of Sweden]
The Miracle of Nature
CHRISTINA, MARIA. See:
MARIA CHRISTINA
Christina of Spain. See:
MARIA CHRISTINA
Christine. See:
HUNTER, MAUD LILY
Christine Bennett. See:
NEUBAUER, WILLIAM ARTHUR
Christine Keir. See:
POPESCU, CHRISTINE PULLEIN-THOMPSON
Christine Lambert. See:
FREYBE, HEIDI HUBERTA
Christine Pullein-Thompson. See: POPESCU, CHRISTINE PULLEIN-THOMPSON
CHRISTOPHER III (died 1448) [King of Sweden and Denmark]
The King of Bark
Christopher Adams. See:
HOPKINS, KENNETH
Christopher Cain. See:
FLEMING, THOMAS JAMES
Christopher Caudwell. See:
SPRIGG, CHRISTOPHER ST. JOHN
Christopher Caustic. See:
FESSENDEN, THOMAS GREEN
Christopher Columbus. See:
COLUMBUS, CHRISTOPHER
MORRIS, JOSEPH CHRISTOPHER COLUMBUS
Christopher Crowfield. See:
STOWE, HARRIET BEECHER
Christopher Druce. See:
PULLING, CHRISTOPHER ROBERT DRUCE
Christopher Fry. See:
HARRIS, CHRISTOPHER
Christopher Haddon. See:
PALMER, JOHN LESLIE
Christopher Irving. See:
JOHNSTON, SIR REGINALD FLEMING
Christopher, Louise. See:
HALE, ARLENE
CHRISTOPHER, MATTHEW F. (1917-) [American author]
Frederic Martin
Christopher Monig. See:
CROSSEN, KENDELL FOSTER

Christopher North. See:
WILSON, JOHN
Christopher Penn. See:
LAWLOR, PATRICK ANTHONY
Christopher Rennie. See:
AMBROSE, ERIC
CHRISTOPHER, ST. (3rd cent. A.D.) [Syrian saint and martyr]
Christ-Bearer
Christopher Storm. See:
OLSEN, THEODORE VICTOR
Christ's, The Lady of. See:
MILTON, JOHN
Christy. See:
CHRISTIE
Christie
MATHEWSON, CHRISTOPHER
Christy, June. See:
LUSTER, SHIRLEY
Christy Munro. See:
TAVES, ISABELLA
CHRISTY, WILLIAM (1791-1865) [American soldier; outstanding for bravery]
The Hero of Fort Meigs
Chrysorrhoas (Stream of Gold) See: JOHN OF DAMASCUS (JOHANNES DAMASCENUS)
Chrysostom of the Middle Ages, The. See:
VON REGENSBURG, BERTHOLD
CHRYSOSTOM, ST. JOHN (c.347-407) [Early Christian churchman]
The Glorious Preacher
Golden Mouthed
The Homer of Orators
John of Antioch
The Thirteenth Apostle
Chu. See:
BERRY, LEON
Chu Fêng. See:
BLOFELD, JOHN EATON CALTHORPE
CHU TEH (1886-) [Chinese Communist leader]
The Supreme Military Commander of the State
Chubbuck, Emily. See:
JUDSON, EMILY CHUBBUCK
Chubby. See:
JACKSON, GREIG STEWART
Chubby Checker. See:
EVANS, ERNEST
Chuck. See:
ANDRUS, CHARLES E., JR.
BEDNARIK, CHARLES
BERGHOFER, CHARLES CURTIS
CHANDLER, CHARLES
CONERLY, CHARLES
DRESSEN, CHARLES WALTER
ISRAELS, CHARLES H.
KEENEY, CHARLES JAMES
McKINLEY, CHARLES ROBERT
MANGIONE, CHARLES FRANK
REISNER, CHARLES
Chuck Buchanan. See:
ROWLAND, DONALD SYDNEY
Chuck Connors. See:
CONNOR, KEVIN JOSEPH
Chuck Mason. See:
ROWLAND, DONALD SYDNEY
Chuck Wayne. See:
JAGELKA, CHARLES
CHUDLEIGH, THOMAS CLIFFORD, 1ST BARON CLIFFORD OF. See:
Cabal, The
CHUDNICK, ROBERT (1927-) [American jazz musician (trumpet)]
Red Rodney
CHULALONGKORN (1853-1910) [King of Thailand (Siam)]
The Great
Rama V
CHULKHURST, ELIZABETH. See:
Biddenden Maids, The
CHULKHURST, MARY. See:
Biddenden Maids, The

Chummy. See:
MACGREGOR, JOHN CHALMERS
Chung Ling Soo. See:
ROBINSON, WILLIAM ELLSWORTH
CHURCH, BENJAMIN (1734-c. 78) [American physician and traitor]
An American
Church History, The Father of. See: EUSEBIUS OF CAESAREA
Church in America, The Father of the Dutch Reformed. See:
LIVINGSTON, JOHN HENRY
Church, Jeffrey. See:
KIRK, RICHARD EDMUND
Church Music, The Father of American. See:
MASON, LOWELL
Church Music, The Father of Anglican. See:
PURCELL, HENRY
Church Music, The Savior of. See: PALESTRINA, GIOVANNI PIERLUIGI DA
Church, The Oracle of the. See: BERNARD OF CLAIRVAUX
Churches, Bishop of Congregational. See:
WEEDEN, CHARLES FOSTER
Churches, The Light of the Western. See:
HOOKER, THOMAS
CHURCHILL, JOHN (1650-1722) [Duke of Marlborough]
Corporal John
The Handsome Englishman
Humphrey Hocus
The Silly Duke
CHURCHILL, RANDOLPH HENRY SPENCER (1849-95) [English statesman]
Lord Randolph Churchill
CHURCHILL, SIR WINSTON LEONARD SPENCER (1874-1965) [British statesman and author]
Winnie
CHURCHILL, SIR WINSTON LEONARD SPENCER. See also: Big Three, The
Churton, Henry. See:
TOURGEE, ALBION WINEGAR
Chute, Rupert. See:
CLEVELAND, PHILIP JEROME
Cialente, Fausta. See:
TERNI, FAUSTA CIALENTE
CIBBER, COLLEY (1671-1757) [English actor, playwright and theater manager]
The King of Dullness
The King of Dunces
CIBO, GIOVANNI BATTISTA (1432-92) [Supreme Pontiff of Roman Catholic Church]
Pope Innocent VIII
Cicely, Cousin. See:
BRADFORD, SARAH ELIZABETH HOPKINS
CICERO, MARCUS TULLIUS (106-43 B.C.) [Roman orator, man of letters and statesman]
Pater Patriae (The Father of His Country)
The Father of Roman Philosophy
The Father of the Country
The God of All Philosophers
Tully
Cicero of America, The. See:
LIVINGSTON, ROBERT R.
Cicero of France, The. See:
MASSILLON, JEAN BAPTISTE
Cicero of Germany, The. See:
JOHANN
Cicero of the British Senate, The. See:
CANNING, GEORGE
Cicero, The American. See:
BERRIEN, JOHN MacPHERSON
LEE, RICHARD HENRY
Cicero, The British. See:
PITT, WILLIAM
Cicero, The New England. See:
WEBSTER, DANIEL
Cicero's Mouth. See:
POT, PHILIPPE

Cid Campeador, El. See:
VIVAR, RODRIGO DÍAZ DE
Cid, El. See:
VIVAR, RODRIGO DÍAZ DE
Cid, The. See:
VIVAR, RODRIGO DÍAZ DE
Cid, The Portuguese. See:
PEREIRA, D. NUNO ÁLVARES
CIERPLIKOWSKI, ANTEK (1884-) [Polish hairdresser]
Antoine
Cigoli. See:
CARDI, LUDOVICO
CIMA, GIOVANNI BATTISTA (1459?-1517) [Italian painter]
Cima de Conegliano
CIMA, VICTORIA GAMEZ (1923-) [Spanish opera singer]
Victoria de Los Angeles
CIMABUE, GIOVANNI (1240-c. 1302) [Italian painter]
The Father of Modern Painting
Cincinnatus of the Americans, The. See:
WASHINGTON, GEORGE
Cincinnatus of the West, The. See: WASHINGTON, GEORGE
Cinderella Man, The. See:
BRADDOCK, JAMES J.
BROWNING, EDWARD
Cini Willoughby Dering. See:
BUDDICOM, JACINTHA LAURA MAY
Cinna. See:
FRAENKEL, HEINRICH
Cino da Pistoia. See:
SIGHIBULDI, GUITTONCINO DEI
Cinthio (Cintio). See:
GIRALDI, GIOVANNI BATTISTA
CINTRON, JOSÉ VINCENTE FERRER OTERO Y (1912-) [Puerto Rican-American stage and motion picture actor]
José Ferrer
CIO. See:
HOFFMAN, CLARE E.
CIONE, ANDREA DI (1308?-68?) [Italian painter, sculptor, mosaicist and architect]
Orcagna
CIONE, ANDREA DI MICHELE DI FRANCESCO (1435-88) [Italian sculptor, painter and goldsmith]
Andrea del Verrocchio
Circe of the Revolution, The. See: ROLAND DE LA PLATIÈRE, JEANNE MANON PHILIPON
Circus, Jim. See:
ROSEVEAR, JOHN
Circus King, The. See:
RINGLING, JOHN
Cire. See:
HAYDEN, ERIC WILLIAM
CISNEROS, FRANCISCO XIMÍNES DE (1436-1517) [Spanish churchman and statesman]
Cardinal Ximînes
Cissie. See:
LOFTUS, MARIE CECILIA
PATTERSON, ELEANOR MEDILL
Citeaux, Robert of. See:
ROBERT DE MOLESME
CITERIORE, VASTO ABRUZZO (1783-1854) [Italian poet]
Gabriele Rossetti
Cities, Besieger of (Poliorcetes). See: DEMETRIUS I
Cities, Stormer of (Sforza). See:
ATTENDOLO, MUZIO
Citizen, America's First. See:
ELIOT, CHARLES WILLIAM
Citizen in the United States, The Greatest. See:
ELIOT, CHARLES WILLIAM
Citizen King, The. See:
CHAMBORD, HENRI CHARLES DIEUPONNÉ, COMTE DE
LOUIS PHILIPPE
Citizen No. 1, World. See:
DAVIS, GARRY
Citizen of Brooklyn, The First.

See: STRANAHAN, JAMES SAMUEL THOMAS
Citizen of Geneva. See: ROUSSEAU, JEAN-JACQUES
Citizen of Georgia, Distinguished. See: BERRY, MARTHA McCHESNEY
Citizen of New York, A. See: DUNLAP, WILLIAM
Citizen of New York, The First. See: McINTYRE, OSCAR ODD
Citizen of Philadelphia, A. See: CAREY, MATHEW
Citizen of St. Anthony, The First. See:
STEELE, FRANKLIN
City-items Scribe, The. See:
COWDRICK, JESSE C.
City Manager Plan of Municipal Government, The Father of the. See:
CHILDS, RICHARD SPENCER
City of Houston, The Builder of the. See:
WILSON, WILLIAM ABNER
City Politicians, The Admirable Crichton of Our. See:
HALL, ABRAHAM OAKEY
Civil Service Reform, The Father of. See:
JENCKES, THOMAS ALLEN
PENDLETON, GEORGE HUNT
Civil Service, The Guardian of. See:
RAMSPECK, ROBERT
Civil War Captain, A. See:
ROLFE, MARO O.
CLAASEN, HAROLD (1905-) [American journalist and writer on football]
Hub Pomeroy
Clabe Hankins. See:
McDONALD, ERWIN LAWRENCE
Claibe. See:
RICHARDSON, CLAIBORNE F.
CLAIBORNE. See also:
CLEBURNE
CLAIBORNE, WILLIAM (c.1589-c.1676) [claimant to Kent Island which also claimed by both Virginia and Maryland]
The Evil Genius of Maryland
Claimant, The. See:
CLEVELAND, STEPHEN GROVER
Clair. See also:
Claire
CLARE
Clare
Clair, René. See:
CHOMETTE, RENÉ
Claire. See:
Clair
CLAIRMONT, CLARA MARY JANE
CLARE
Clare
Claire France. See:
DORE, CLAIRE MORIN
Claire, Ina. See:
FAGAN, INA
Claire Morin. See:
DORE, CLAIRE MORIN
Claire Trevor. See:
WEMLINGER, CLAIRE
CLAIRMONT, CLARA MARY JANE (1798-1879) [step-daughter of WILLIAM GODWIN; mother of LORD BYRON'S daughter ALLEGRA]
Claire Clairmont
Clairon. See:
TUDE, CLAIRE JOSEPHE HIPPOLYTE LEYRIS DE LA
CLAIRVAUX. See:
BERNARD OF CLAIRVAUX
Clâna, Henrich von der. See:
WEISS, ALBERT MARIA
Clancool, Clarence. See:
URNER, NATHAN DANE
Clancy. See:
HAYES, CLARENCE
CLAPP, CHARLES (1899-1962) [American jazz musician (trombone, composer, leader)]

Sunny Clapp
CLAPP, GEORGE ALFRED (1856-1924) [American blackface minstrel]
Lew Dockstader
CLAPP, HENRY, JR. (1814-75) [American humorist and journalist]
Figaro
The King of the Bohemians
CLAPPE, LOUISE AMELIA KNAPP (1819-1906) [American author]
Dame Shirley
Clara. See:
BARTON, CLARISSA HARLOWE
Clara Augusta. See:
TRASK, CLARA AUGUSTA JONES
Clara Cushman. See:
HAVEN, EMILY BRADLEY NEAL
Clara Ernst. See:
BARNES, CLARA ERNST
Clara Erskine Clement. See:
WATERS, CLARA ERSKINE CLEMENT
Clara Gazul. See:
MÉRIMÉE, PROSPER
Clara Moreton. See:
MOORE, CLARA SOPHIA JESSUP
Clara Morris. See:
MORRISON, CLARA
Clara Vance. See:
DENISON, MARY ANDREWS
Clare. See:
Clair
Claire
Jaynes, Clare
Clare, Ada. See:
McELHENEY, JANE
CLARE, GLADYS (1902-54) [American stage and motion picture actress]
Gladys George
CLARE, JOHN (1793-1864) [British poet]
Northamptonshire Peasant Poet
Clare, Margaret. See:
MAISON, MARGARET MARY BOWLES
Clarence Clancool. See:
URNER, NATHAN DANE
Clarence Fairchild. See:
CHAMPLIN, EDWIN ROSS
Clarence Young. See:
STRATEMEYER, EDWARD L.
Claretie, Jules. See:
ARNAUD, ARSÈNE
Claribel. See:
BARNARD, CHARLOTTE ALINGTON
Clarín. See:
ALAS Y UREÑA, LEOPOLDO
Clarinda. See:
MACLEHOSE, AGNES CRAIG
Clarissa Packard, Mrs. See:
GILMAN, CAROLINE HOWARD
Clark. See:
GABLE, WILLIAM CLARK
McMeekin, Clark
CLARK, ABRAHAM (1726-94) [American lawyer; signer of Declaration of Independence]
The Poor Man's Counsellor
Clark, Anna. See:
BENNINGHOFEN, MRS. ERNEST
Clark Broker. See:
FOWLER, KENNETH ABRAMS
CLARK, CHARLES DUNNING (1843-92) [American teacher, journalist and writer of historical and dime novels]
Captain Clark
Barry DeForest
W. J. Hamilton
CLARK, CHARLES HEBER (1847-1915) [American novelist, journalist and humorist]
Max Adeler
CLARK, CHARLOTTE MOON (fl. 1878-82) [American author]
Charles M. Clay
CLARK, CONRAD YEATIS

(1931-) [American jazz musician (piano)]
Sonny Clark
Clark, Dane. See:
ZANVILLE, BERNARD
CLARK, DAVID LYTLE (1864-1939) [Irish-American confectionery manufacturer]
The Pittsburgh Candy King
CLARK, DOROTHY PARK. See:
McMeekin, Clark
CLARK, EARL (1906-) [American professional football coach]
Dutch Clark
Clark Fitch. See:
SINCLAIR, UPTON BEALL
Clark Fitch, U.S.N., Ensign, See: SINCLAIR, UPTON BEALL
Clark, Francis Edward. See:
SYMNES, FRANCIS EDWARD
CLARK, FREDERICK STEPHEN (1908-) [British correspondent and author]
Clive Dalton
CLARK, GEORGE (1896-) [American professional football coach]
Potsy
CLARK, GEORGE ROGERS (1752-1818) [American general officer]
The Hero of Vincennes
The Washington of the West
Clark, Howard. See:
HASKIN, DOROTHY CLARK
PORTER, WILLIAM SYDNEY
CLARK, M. JEROME (fl. 1861-65) [American soldier; member of Quantrill's guerrillas]
Sue Mundy
CLARK, RICHARD (1845-1930) [South Dakota pioneer and stagecoach driver]
Deadwood Dick
CLARK, RICHARD WAGSTAFF (1929-) [American television personality]
Dick Clark
CLARK, ROBERT EDWIN (1888-1960) [American actor and comedian]
Bobby Clark
The Funniest Clown in the World
Clark South. See:
SWAIN, DWIGHT VREELAND
Clark, T. See:
GALT, JOHN
CLARK, WILLIAM (1828-) [Irish prize fighter and swimming instructor]
The Belfast Chicken
Clarke, Captain Jafah. See:
NESMITH, ROBERT I.
Clarke, Covington. See:
VENABLE, CLARKE
CLARKE, DAVID WALDO (1907-) [British educator and author]
Dave Waldo
CLARKE, GEORGE R. (1827-92) [American missionary and businessman]
Colonel Clarke
CLARKE, JOHN (1609-76) [Anglo-American Baptist clergyman; one of the founders of Rhode Island]
The Father of American Baptists
The Father of Rhode Island
Clarke, John. See:
LAUGHLIN, VIRGINIA CARLI
SONTUP, DANIEL
CLARKE, JOHN CAMPBELL (1913-) [British journalist and author]
Hugh Cleland
Robert Kingsley
CLARKE, KENNETH SPEARMAN (1914-) [American jazz musician (drums, leader, composer)]
Kenny Clarke
Klook Clarke
Liaqat Ali Salaam
CLARKE, McDONALD (1798-1842) [American poet]
The Mad Poet
The Mad Poet of Broadway

The Mad Poet of New York
CLARKE, MARCUS (1846-81) [British novelist and dramatist]
Andrew Hislop
CLARKE, REBECCA SOPHIA (1840-1929) [Author of juvenile books]
Sophie May
CLARKE, SARAH DUNN (1835-1917) [American missionary]
Mother Clarke
CLARKE, SARAH J. (1840-) [American author of juvenile books]
Penn Shirley
CLARKSON, JAMES SULLIVAN (1842-1918) [American first Assistant Postmaster General]
Headsman Clarkson
CLATTEN, LILIAN (1882-) [American actress and playwright]
Margaret Mayo
Claud. See:
VAN ZELLER, HUBERT
Claude Allister. See:
PALMER, CLAUDE
Claude Anet. See:
SCHOPFER, JEAN
Claude, Big-Navy. See:
SWANSON, CLAUDE AUGUSTUS
Claude Dampier. See:
COWAN, CLAUDE
Claude Dauphin. See:
FRANC-NOHAIN, CLAUDE
CLAUDE DE FRANCE. See:
FRANCE, CLAUDE DE
Claude Farrère. See:
BARGONE, FRÉDÉRIC CHARLES PIERRE EDOUARD
Claude Houghton. See:
OLDFIELD, CLAUDE HOUGHTON
Claude Lorraine. See:
GELÉE, CLAUDE
Claudette Colbert. See:
CHAUCHOIN, CLAUDETTE
Claudia Hall. See:
FLOREN, LEE
CLAUDIUS. See:
MARCELLUS (MARCUS CLAUDIUS)
Claudius Clear. See:
NICOLL, SIR WILLIAM ROBERTSON
CLAUDIUS (MARCUS AURELIUS CLAUDIUS) (214-70 A.D.) [Roman emperor]
Gothicus
Claus, Santa. See:
COLEMAN, LEIGHTON
NICOLAUS, ST.
CLAUSSEN, RAELENE SUE (1940-) [American jazz musician (singer, song-writer)]
Sue Raney
Clavell, Stauffer. See:
NAGELE, ANTON
Claverhouse, Graham of. See:
GRAHAM, JOHN
Clavers, Mrs. Mary. See:
KIRKLAND, CAROLINE MATILDA STANDBURY
Claverse, Bloody. See:
GRAHAM, JOHN
Clay. See:
PERRY, CLAIR WILLARD
Clay Allison. See:
KEEVIL, HENRY JOHN
Clay Brand. See:
NORWOOD, VICTOR GEORGE CHARLES
Clay, Bertha M. See:
BRAME, CHARLOTTE MARY
CORYELL, JOHN RUSSELL
DEY, FREDERICK VAN RENSSELAER
HARBAUGH, THOMAS CHALMERS
CLAY, CASSIUS MARCELLUS, SR. (1810-1903) [American journalist and politician]
The Kentucky Duel Fighter
CLAY, CASSIUS MARCELLUS, JR. (1942-) [American Negro professional boxer; world's heavyweight champion]
Cassius the Brashest

Gaseous Cassius
The Louisville Lip
Mohammed Ali
Clay, Charles M. See:
CLARK, CHARLOTTE MOON
Clay, Duncan. See:
DIEHL, WILLIAM WELLS
CLAY, HENRY (1777-1852) [American statesman and lawyer]
The Apostle of Liberty
The Father of the National Road
The Father of the Protective Policy
The Great Commoner
The Great Compromiser
The Great Pacificator
Harry of the West
The Mill Boy of the Slashes
Old Chief
The President Maker
The Sage of Ashland
The Same Old Coon
The Second Washington
Warhawk
CLAY, HENRY. See also:
Great Triumvirate, The
CLAY, JAMES (1924-) [American press secretary and author]
Jim Clay
Clay Randall. See:
ADAMS, CLIFTON
Clay Richards. See:
CROSSEN, KENDELL FOSTER
Clay Stuart. See:
WHITTINGTON, HARRY
Clayton, Barbara. See:
PLUFF, BARBARA LITTLEFIELD
CLAYTON, RICHARD HENRY MICHAEL (1907-) [British civil servant and author]
William Haggard
CLAYTON, WILBUR (1911-) [American jazz musician (trumpet, composer)]
Buck Clayton
Clean, The Mean Mr. See:
LEONARD, JACK E.
Cleanser, Old Dutch. See:
BLANKENBURG, RUDOLPH
Clear, Claudius. See:
NICOLL, SIR WILLIAM ROBERTSON
CLEAVELAND. See also:
CLEVELAND
Cleveland
CLEAVELAND, PARKER (1780-1858) [American pioneer in mineralogy]
The Father of American Mineralogy
Cleaver, Nancy. See:
MATHEWS, EVELYN CRAW
CLEBURNE. See also:
CLAIBORNE
CLEBURNE, PATRICK RONAYNE (1828-64) [Irish-American Confederate Army general officer]
The Stonewall of the West
Cleisbotham, Jedediah. See:
SCOTT, SIR WALTER
Cleland, Hugh. See:
CLARKE, JOHN CAMPBELL
Cleland, Mabel. See:
WIDDEMER, MABEL CLELAND
Cleland, Morton. See:
RENNIE, JAMES ALAN
Clem Colt. See:
NYE, NELSON CORAL
Clemence Dane. See:
ASHTON, WINIFRED
CLEMENCEAU, GEORGES (1841-1929) [French statesman]
The Tiger
CLEMENCEAU, GEORGES. See also: Big Three, The
Clemency. See:
CANNING, CHARLES JOHN, 1ST EARL
CANNING, GEORGE
CLEMENS. See also:
Clemons
CLEMENS, SAMUEL LANGHORNE (1835-1910)

[American humorist, author and lecturer]
Mark Twain
The Master Pilot of the Mississippi
The Moralist of the Main
The People's Author
The Prince of Humorists
The Wild Humorist of the Pacific Slope
CLEMENT (died c. 97) [Supreme Pontiff of Roman Catholic Church]
Pope Clement I
St. Clement
Clement II, Pope. See: SUITGER, COUNT OF MORSLEBEN
Clement III, Pope. See: SCOLARI, PAOLO
Clement IV, Pope. See: FOULQUES, GUY LE GROS
Clement V, Pope. See: GOT, BERTRAND DE
Clement VI, Pope. See: ROGER, PIERRE
Clement VII, Pope. See: MEDICI, GIULIO DE'
Clement VIII, Pope. See: ALDOBRANDINI, IPPOLITO
Clement IX, Pope. See: ROSPIGLIOSI, GIULIO
Clement X, Pope. See: ALTIERI, EMILIO
Clement XI, Pope. See: ALBANI, GIAN FRANCESCO
Clement XII, Pope. See: CORSINI, LORENZO
Clement XIII, Pope. See: REZZONICO, CARLO DELLA TORRE
Clement XIV, Pope. See: GANGANELLI, GIOVANNI
Clement, Clara Erskine. See: WATERS, CLARA ERSKINE CLEMENT
Clement, Hal. See: STUBBS, HARRY CLEMENT
Clement Hardin. See: NEWTON, DWIGHT BENNETT
Clementine. See: HOWARTH, ELLEN C.
Clements, E.H. See: HUNTER, EILEEN HELEN
CLEMO, REGINALD JOHN (1916-) [British author and poet]
Jack Clemo
Clemons. See also: CLEMENS
Clemons, Elizabeth. See: ROBINSON, ELIZABETH CAMERON
CLEOBULUS. See: Seven Sages of Greece, The
CLEOPATRA (69-30 B.C.) [Last queen of Egypt]
The Queen of Queens
Clergy, The Patriarch of the New England. See: NOTT, SAMUEL
Clergyman, The Chartist. See: KINGSLEY, REV. CHARLES
CLETUS. See: ANACLETUS (ANENCLETUS) (CLETUS)
CLEVELAND [Cleveland]. See also: CLEAVELAND
CLEVELAND, BENJAMIN (1738-1806) [American Revolutionary War Colonel]
The Hero of King's Mountain
Old Round About
Cleveland, John. See: McELFRESH, ELIZABETH ADELINE
CLEVELAND, PHILIP JEROME (1903-) [American Congregational minister and author]
A. Don Adams
Rupert Chute
CLEVELAND, STEPHEN GROVER (1837-1908) [22nd and 24th President of the United States]
The Buffalo Hangman
The Buffalo Sheriff
The Claimant
Grover Cleveland

The Dumb Prophet
Grover the Good
The Hangman of Buffalo
His Accidency
The Man of Destiny
Old Grover
Old Veto
Our Grover
The People's President
The Perpetual Candidate
The Pretender
The Reform Governor
The Sage of Princeton
The Stuffed Prophet
Uncle Jumbo
The Veto Governor
The Veto Mayor
The Veto President

CLEVEN, KATHRYN SEWARD (19??-) [American author]
Cathrine Cleven

Clew Garnet. See:
JUDSON, EDWARD ZANE CARROLL

Cliff. See:
ARQUETTE, CLIFFORD
BURWELL, CLIFFORD R.
ROBERTSON, CLIFFORD PARKER, 3RD

Cliff Richards. See:
WEBB, HAROLD

Clifford. See:
Anderson, Clifford
Ashdown, Clifford

CLIFFORD, HAROLD B. (1893-) [American educator and author]
Burt Farnham

CLIFFORD, HENRY DE (c. 1455-1523) [English nobleman; 14th Baron Clifford]
The Shepherd Lord

Clifford, John. See:
BAYLISS, JOHN CLIFFORD

CLIFFORD, ROSAMOND (fl. 12th cent.) [mistress of HENRY II of England]
Fair Rosamond

CLIFFORD, THOMAS, 1ST BARON CLIFFORD OF CHUDLEIGH. See:
Cabal, The

Clifford's Inn, Gent., Thomas Morton of. See:
MORTON, THOMAS

Clifton Fourth. See:
MORSE, H. CLIFTON

CLIFTON, HERMAN E. (1910-) [American professional baseball player]
Flea

Clifton, Oliver Lee. See:
RATHBONE, ST. GEORGE HENRY

Clifton Webb. See:
HOLLENBECK, WEBB PARMELEE

CLINCH, JOSEPH (fl. late 18th cent.) [American Revolutionary War lieutenant]
The Terror of the Tories

Clingham Hunter, M.D. See:
ADAMS, WILLIAM TAYLOR

Clint Dangerfield. See:
NORWOOD, VICTOR GEORGE CHARLES

CLINTON, GEORGE (1739-1812) [American Revolutionary War general officer and statesman]
Cato

CLINTON, GEORGE (1846-1934) [American lawyer, instrumental in securing construction of New York State Barge Canal
The Father of the Barge Canal

CLINTON, IRIS A. CORBIN (1901-) [British editor and author]
Iris Corbin

Clinton, Jeff. See:
BICKHAM, JACK MILES

CLINTON, LARRY (1900-) [American jazz musician (leader, composer, trumpet, trombone, vibraphone, arranger)]
The Dipsy Doodler

Clinton Spurr. See:
ROWLAND, DONALD SYDNEY
Clinton W. Locke. See:
STRATEMEYER, EDWARD L.
Clio. See:
ADDISON, JOSEPH H.
Clipper of the Accordion, The Yankee. See:
CONTINO, RICHARD
Clipper, The Yankee. See:
DIMAGGIO, JOSEPH PAUL, JR.
CLITHEROW, MARGARET MIDDLETON (1556-86) [English Catholic martyr]
The Pearl of York
Clive. See:
BROOK, CLIFFORD
Clive Campbell. See:
MACRAE, DONALD G.
Clive Dalton. See:
CLARK, FREDERICK STEPHEN
Clive Hamilton. See:
LEWIS, CLIVE STAPLES
Clive Holland. See:
HANKINSON, CHARLES JAMES
Clive, Kitty. See:
RAFTOR, CATHERINE
Clive Meikle. See:
BROOKS, JEREMY
CLIVE, ROBERT, BARON CLIVE OF PLASSEY (1725-74) [English general officer and statesman]
Clive of India
Clodion. See:
MICHEL, CLAUDE
CLOETE, EDWARD FAIRLIE STUART GRAHAM (1897-) [English author]
Stuart Cloete
Clootz, Caleb. See:
SMITH, FRANCIS SHUBAEL
CLOOTZ, JEAN BAPTISTE DU VAL DE GRÂCE (1755-94) [French fanatical social reformer]
Anacharsis Clootz
The Orator of the Human Race
CLOPINEL, JEAN (c. 1250-c. 1305) [French poet]
Jean de Meung
The French Ennius
CLOSE, JOHN (1816-91) [British versifier]
Poet Close
Close, Upton. See:
HALL, JOSEF WASHINGTON
CLOTILDA (c. 475-c. 545) [Queen of the Franks; wife of CLOVIS, afterwards churchwoman]
St. Clotilda
Clout, Colin. See:
SPENSER, EDMUND
CLOVIO, GIULIO (1498-1578) [Croatian miniaturist]
Jurni Glovichisch
CLOVIS II (died 656) [King of Neustria]
The Do-nothing King
Clown in the World, The Funniest. See:
CLARK, ROBERT EDWIN
Clown Prince of Baseball, The. See:
SCHACHT, ALEXANDER
Clown Prince of Basketball, The. See:
LEMON, MEADOW GEORGE
Clown, The Shakespeare. See:
RICE, DANIEL
Clowns, The King of American. See:
RICE, DANIEL
Club, Old. See:
COLSTON, RALEIGH EDWARD
Club, The Father and Nursing Mother of the Gridiron. See: CARSON, JOHN MILLER
Clubby, Old. See:
COLSTON, RALEIGH EDWARD

Clubs, The First Lady of Supper. See: SELL, HILDEGARDE LORETTA
Clubs, The Jack of. See: SHERIDAN, PHILIP HENRY
CLUETT, ERNEST HAROLD (1874-1954) [American manufacturer and politician]
Collars and Cuffs
CLUNE, FRANCIS PATRICK (1893-) [Australian soldier and author]
Frank Clune
Clusius. See: LÉCLUSE, CHARLES DE
CLUTHA, JANET PATERSON FRAME (1924-) [New Zealand author]
Janet Frame
Clutterbuck, Captain. See: SCOTT, SIR WALTER
CLUTTERBUCK, RICHARD (1917-) [British general officer and author]
Richard Jocelyn
Clyde. See: FITCH, WILLIAM CLYDE
Clyde, Bernard. See: AIKEN, GEORGE L.
Clyde, Kit. See: SENARENS, LUIS PHILIP
Clynder, Monica. See: MUIR, MARIE
Clyne, Terence. See: BLATTY, WILLIAM PETER
Clysle Stevens. See: WADE, JOHN STEVENS
CNUT. See: CANUTE (CNUT) (KNUT) II
Coach, Football's Greatest. See: NEYLAND, GENERAL ROBERT REESE, JR.
Coach in America, The Top Football. See: PARKER, RAYMOND KLEIN
Coachman of Europe, The (Le Cocher de l'Europe). See: CHOISEUL-AMBOISE, ÉTIENNE FRANÇOIS, DUC DE
Coal Man, The Musical Small. See: BRITTON, THOMAS
Coalfleet, Pierre. See: DAVISON, FRANK CYRIL
Coast, The Host to the. See: GRIER, JAMES W.
Coast, The Silver-tongued Spellbinder of the Pacific. See: DELMAS, DELPHIN MICHAEL
COBB, ARNETT CLEOPHUS (1918-) [American jazz musician (tenor saxophone)]
The World's Wildest Tenor Man
COBB, GERALDYN M. (1931-) [American aeroplane pilot]
Jerrie Cobb
Cobb, Lee J. See: JACOBY, LEE
COBB, SYLVANUS, JR. (1823-87) [American author of dime novels]
Austin C. Burdick
Charles Castleton
Colonel Walter B. Dunlap
Enoch Fitzwhistler, C.C.B.
Symus, the Pilgrim
Amos Winslow, Jr.
COBB, TYRUS RAYMOND (1886-1961) [American professional baseball player]
The Georgia Peach
The Idol of Baseball Fandom
Ty Cobb
COBB, WELDON J. (fl. 1866-95) [American author, journalist, editor and real estate dealer]
Genevieve Ulmar
Cobbett. See: LUDOVICI, ANTHONY MARIO
COBBETT, WILLIAM (1763-1835) [English journalist, publisher, political radical and agriculturist]

Peter Porcupine
Cobbler, The. See:
WILSON, HENRY
Cobbler, The Natick. See:
WILSON, HENRY
Cobden Bell. See:
BELTON-COBB, GEOFFREY
COBDEN, RICHARD (1804-65)
[English political economist and statesman]
The Apostle of Free Trade
Cobham, Baron. See:
OLDCASTLE, SIR JOHN
Cobham, The Good Lord.
See: OLDCASTLE, SIR JOHN
Cobleigh, Tom. See:
RAYMOND, WALTER
Coborn, Charles. See:
McCALLUM, COLIN WHITTON
Cobwallis. See:
CORNWALLIS, CHARLES CORNWALLIS, 1ST MARQUIS
Coccaius, Merlinus. See:
FOLENGO, TEOFILO
Cocceianus. See:
DIO (DION) CASSIUS
Coch-y-Bonddhu. See:
ARNOLD, RICHARD
Cocher de l'Europe, Le (The Coachman of Europe).
See: CHOISEUL-AMBOISE ÉTIENNE FRANÇOIS, DUC DE
Cocherito de Bilbao. See:
IBARRA, CASTOR JAUREGUIBEITIA
COCHLAEUS (DOBNECK), JOHANN (1479-1552)
[German humanist and controversialist]
Wendelstein
Cochran, Jeff. See:
DURST, PAUL
COCHRANE, CLARK BETTON (1817-67) [American politician]
The Great Pacificator
Cochrane, Corinna. See:
PETERSON, CORINNA
COCHRANE DE ALENCAR, GERTRUDE E. L. (1906-)
[Austrian author]
Gertrude von Schwarzenfeld
COCHRANE, GORDON STANLEY (1903-62) [American professional baseball player]
Mickey Cochrane
Cock o' the Walk of Baseball.
See: MAILS, WALTER
Cock of the North, The.
See: GEORGE, DUKE OF GORDON
COCKBURN, CATHERINE TROTTER (1679-1749)
[Scottish dramatist and controversial writer]
The Scotch Sappho
Cocked Hat, The Last. See:
MONROE, JAMES
Cocked Hats, The Last of the.
See: MEASE, JOHN
Cockeye, Old. See:
BUTLER, BENJAMIN FRANKLIN
Cockle-bur Bill. See:
MURRAY, WILLIAM HENRY
Cocles of the Tyrol, Horatius.
See: DUMAS, ALEXANDRE DAVY DE LA PAILLETERIE
Coco. See:
CHANEL, GABRIELLE
COCOZZA, ALFRED (1921-59)
[American opera singer and motion picture actor]
Mario Lanza
Code, The Father of the. See:
FIELD, DAVID DUDLEY
Codes, Robbie of the. See:
ROBINSON, FRANCES M.
CODIAN, MICHAEL (1915-)
[American jazz musician (composer, leader, trumpet)]
Mickey Codian
CODMAN, JOHN (1814-1900)
[American sea captain and author]
American Shipmaster
Captain Ringbolt
Codomannus. See:
DARIUS III
Cody, Al. See:

JOSCELYN, ARCHIE L.
Cody, Lew. See:
COTÉ, LOUIS JOSEPH
Cody, Walt. See:
NORWOOD, VICTOR GEORGE CHARLES
CODY, WILLIAM FREDERICK (1846-1917) [American Indian scout, author and showman]
Bill Cody the Scout
Bill Cody the Wagonmaster
Buffalo Bill
The Champion Buffalo Hunter of the Plains
Colonel William F. Cody
The Last of the Great Scouts
Little Billy Cody the Messenger
Pahaska
Pa-he-haska
Wild Bill the Pony Express Rider
Coe, Douglas. See:
Allen, Adam
EPSTEIN, BERYL WILLIAMS
COE, FREDERICK (1914-) [American television producer]
Fred Coe
COELLO, ALONSO SANCHEZ (c. 1520-90) [Spanish portrait painter]
The Portuguese Titian
Coeur de Lion (The Lion Hearted). See:
LOUIS VIII
RICHARD I
Cofferer, Bobby the. See:
MORRIS, ROBERT
COFFEY, EDWARD HOPE (1896-1958) [American author]
Edward Hope
COFFIN, CHARLES CARLETON (1823-96) [American war correspondent and historical novelist]
Carleton
Coffin, Geoffrey, joint pseud. of HELEN BRAWNER (-) and FRANCIS VAN WYCK MASON (1901-) [American novelists]
Coffin, Geoffrey. See also:
MASON, FRANCIS VAN WYCK
Coffin, Joshua. See:
LONGFELLOW, HENRY WADSWORTH
COFFIN, ROBERT BARRY (1826-86) [American journalist and author]
Barry Gray
COFFIN, ROBERT STEVENSON (1797-1827) [American poet]
The Boston Bard
COFFMAN, RAMON PEYTON (1896-) [American reporter, editor, columnist and writer]
Uncle Ray
COGSWELL, CORALIE NORRIS (1930-) [American librarian and author]
Coralie Howard
COGSWELL, FREDERICK WILLIAM (1917-) [Canadian author]
Fred Cogswell
COHAN, GEORGE MICHAEL (1878-1942) [American actor, song-writer, comedian, playwright and producer]
Mr. Broadway
COHEN, ALFRED J. (1861-1928) [Anglo-American drama critic and novelist]
Alan Dale
Cohen, Bella. See:
SPEWACK, BELLA COHEN
COHEN, MATHILDE (1841-96) [German poet]
Mathilde Blind
COHEN, MORTON NORTON (1921-) [Canadian author]
John Moreton
COHEN, PIERRE (1903-) [French motion picture director]
Pierre Chenal

Cohen, Rosalyn. See:
HIGGINS, ROSALYN COHEN

COHEN, THEODORE CHARLES (1928-) [American jazz musician (vibraphone, composer)]
Teddy Charles

COHN, EMIL (1881-1948) [German man of letters)
Emil Ludwig

COHN, GEORGE THOMAS (1925-) [American jazz musician (trumpet)]
Sonny Cohn

COIFFIER, ANTOINE (1581-1632) [Marquis d'Effiat; marshal of France]
Ruzé

Coin. See:
HARVEY, WILLIAM HOPE

Coinage for Silver, The Apostle of Free. See:
ST. JOHN, WILLIAM POPE

Coiner of Weasel Words. See:
WILSON, THOMAS WOODROW

COKER, CHARLES MITCHELL (1927-) [American jazz musician (piano, alto saxophone)]
Dolo

COLBATH, JEREMIAH JONES (1812-73) [American statesman; Vice President of the United States]
Henry Wilson

Colbert, Claudette. See:
CHAUCHOIN, CLAUDETTE

Colder, Ben. See:
WOOLEY, SHEB

Cole. See:
COLL
Kole
YOUNGER, THOMAS COLEMAN

COLE, AMBROSE N. (fl. mid 19th cent.) [American politician; active in establishing the Republican Party]
Father Cole
The Father of the Republican Party

Cole, Ann Kilborn. See:
CALLAHAN, CLAIRE WALLIS

Cole, Davis. See:
ELTING, MARY

COLE, EDWIN LE MAR (1916-64) [American jazz musician (piano, organ)]
Buddy Cole

COLE, JANET (1922-) [American stage and motion picture actress]
Kim Hunter

COLE, JOHN WILLIAM (fl. last half of the 19th cent.) [English miscellaneous writer]
John William Calcraft

COLE, LESTER. See:
Hollywood Ten, The.

COLE, LOIS DWIGHT (19??-) [American editor and author]
Lynn Avery
Nancy Dudley
Allan Dwight
Anne Eliot

COLE, MARGARET ALICE (fl. 1957-63) [British educator and author]
Rosemary Manning
Julia Renton
Ione Saunders

Cole, Nat King. See:
COLES, NATHANIEL ADAMS

COLE, SIR HENRY (1808-82) [English writer and art critic]
Felix Summerley

Cole, Stephen. See:
WEBBE, GALE DUDLEY

COLE, THOMAS (1801-48) [Anglo-American artist]
Founder of the Hudson River School of the American Artists

COLE, WILLIAM R. (1909-) (American jazz musician (drums)]
Cozy Cole

Coleen Gray. See:
JENSEN, DORIS
COLEMAN. See also:
COLMAN
COLEMAN, LEIGHTON (1837-1907) [American Episcopal bishop]
Santa Claus
COLEMAN, ROBERT WILLIAM ALFRED (1916-) [British clergyman and author]
James Insight
COLERIDGE, DAVID HARTLEY (1796-1849) [English poet]
Little Hartley
Coleridge, John. See:
BINDER, OTTO OSCAR
COLERIDGE, SAMUEL TAYLOR (1772-1834) [English poet, philosopher and literary critic]
The Alnaschar of Modern Literature
Old Man Eloquent
Coles, Manning
Francis Gaite, joint pseuds. of CYRIL HENRY COLES (1899-) and ADELAIDE FRANCIS OKE MANNING (-) [British authors]
COLES, NATHANIEL ADAMS (1917-65) [American jazz musician (singer, piano, leader)]
Nat King Cole
COLETTE, SIDONIE GABRIELLE (1873-1954) [French novelist]
Colette
Willy
COLETTE, SIDONIE GABRIELLE. See also:
Willy
Colin. See also:
COLLINS
Collins
Colin Clout. See:
SPENSER, EDMUND
Colin Lochlons. See:
JACKSON, CAARY PAUL
Colin Murry. See:
MIDDLETON-MURRY, JOHN
Colin Ross. See:
ROSKOLENKO, HARRY
COLL. See also:
COLE
Cole
Kole
COLL, VINCENT (1909-32) [American gangster]
The Mad Dog of Gangland
Collars and Cuffs. See:
CLUETT, ERNEST HAROLD
Collazo, Bobby. See:
PENA, ROBERTO COLLAZO
Colleano, Bonar. See:
SULLIVAN, BONAR
Colleen Moore. See:
MORRISON, KATHLEEN
College Puritan. See:
SHERMAN, JOHN
College, The Sage of Mississippi. See:
AVEN, ALGERNON JASPER
Collen, Neil. See:
LEE, LINCOLN
COLLERYE, ROGER DE (1470?-1540) [French poet]
Roger Bontemps
COLLETTE, WILLIAM MARCELL (1921-) [American jazz musician (saxophone, flute, clarinet, arranger)]
Buddy Collette
COLLIER [Collier]. See also:
COLLYER
Collier, Constance. See:
HARDIE, LAURA CONSTANCE
Collier, Douglas. See:
FELLOWES-GORDON, IAN DOUGLAS
Collier, Jane. See:
SHUMSKY, ZENA FELDMAN
COLLIER, JOHN (1708-86) [Lancashire poet]
Tim Bobbin
COLLIER, LUCY ANN (1919-)

[American dancer and motion picture actress]
Ann Miller
Collier, Old Cap. See:
IRON, NATHANIEL COLCHESTER
SAWYER, EUGENE TAYLOR
Collier Santee. See:
FLEXNER, STUART BERG
Collier, Zena. See:
SHUMSKY, ZENA FELDMAN
Colline. See:
DE ANGELIS, ALBERTO
COLLINS [Collins]. See also:
Colin
Collins, Charles, possible joint pseud. of WILLIAM WILKIE COLLINS (1824-89) and CHARLES JOHN HUFFAM DICKENS (1812-70) [English novelists]
Collins, Charles. See also:
COLLINS, WILLIAM WILKIE
DICKENS, CHARLES JOHN HUFFAM
Collins, D. See:
BULLEID, H.A.V.
COLLINS, EDWARD TROWBRIDGE (1887-1951) [American professional baseball player]
Eddie Collins
COLLINS, FREDERICA JOAN HALE (1904-) [British author]
Freda Collins
COLLINS, HERMAN LEROY (1865-1940) [American journalist and columnist]
Girard
Collins, Hunt. See:
HUNTER, EVAN
COLLINS, JAMES ANTHONY (1905-) [American professional baseball player]
Ripper Collins
Collins, Jeffrey. See:
WILCOX, COLLIN
COLLINS, JOHN (1624-83) [English mathematician and physicist]
The English Mercenne
Collins, Joyce. See:
SEARLE, JOYCE COLLINS
COLLINS, LESTER RALLINGSTON (1910-) [American jazz musician (trumpet)]
Shad Collins
COLLINS, MORTIMER (1827-76) [English poet and novelist]
The King of the Bohemians
COLLINS, PHIL EUGENE (1903-) [American professional baseball player]
Fidgety
Collins, Sam. See:
VAGG, SAMUEL
Collins, Tom. See:
MURPHY, JOSEPH
COLLINS, WILLIAM WILKIE (1824-89) [British novelist]
Wilkie Collins
COLLINS, WILLIAM WILKIE
See also:
Collins, Charles
Collinson, Peter. See:
HAMMETT, SAMUEL DASHIELL
Collodi, Carlo. See:
LORENZINI, CARLO
COLLYER. See also:
COLLIER
Collier
Collyer, Doric. See:
HUNT, DOROTHY ALICE
COLMAN. See also:
COLEMAN
COLMAN, GEORGE (1732-94) [English playwright and theater manager]
The Elder
COLMAN, GEORGE (1762-1836) [English playwright and theater manager]
The Younger
Cologne, Albert of. See:
ALBERTUS MAGNUS, SAINT, COUNT OF BOLLSTÄDT
COLOMBAT, CLAIRE (1925-)

[French motion picture actress]
Barbara Laage
Colombia. See also:
COLUMBA
Columbia
Colombia, Joselillo de. See:
ZUÑIGA, JOSÉ
Colombia, The Washington of. See: BOLÍVAR, SIMÓN
Colombo, Cristoforo. See:
COLUMBUS, CHRISTOPHER
Colombo, Dale. See:
MONROE, KEITH
COLOMBRITO, PHILIP (1915-)
[American composer, author and singer]
Phil Brito
Colon. See:
DENNIE, JOSEPH
Colón, Cristóbal. See:
COLUMBUS, CHRISTOPHER
Colonel. See:
BLAIK, EARL HENRY
BLOOD, THOMAS
CLARKE, GEORGE R.
CUSHING, JOSEPH
FICKINGER, JAMES ALBERT
FISK, JAMES, JR.
HOUSE, EDWARD MANDELL
MEEK, JOSEPH L.
Colonel Berger. See:
MALRAUX, GEORGES-ANDRÉ
Colonel Cris Forrest. See:
STODDARD, WILLIAM OSBORN
Colonel Delle Sara. See:
AIKEN, ALBERT W.
Colonel H.R. Gordon. See:
ELLIS, EDWARD SYLVESTER
Colonel Hazelton. See:
WHITSON, JOHN HARVEY
Colonel Jack. See:
KROHN, JOHN ALBERT
Colonel Lawrence Leslie. See:
RATHBONE, ST. GEORGE HENRY
Colonel Leon Lafitte. See:
INGRAHAM, COLONEL PRENTISS
Colonel Oram Eflor. See:
ROLFE, MARO O.
Colonel Oram R. McHenry. See: ROLFE, MARO O.
Colonel Red Reeder. See:
REEDER, RUSSELL P., JR.
Colonel Stoopnagle. See:
TAYLOR, FREDERICK CHASE
Colonel Surry. See:
COOKE, JOHN ESTEN
Colonel T.B. Bostwick. See:
HARBAUGH, THOMAS CHALMERS
Colonel, The. See:
RUPPERT, JACOB, SR.
Colonel, The Fighting. See:
GALBRAITH, FREDERICK WILLIAM
Colonel, The Little. See:
SHARP, HAROLD SPENCER
Colonel, The Old. See:
ARNHEIM, GUS
Colonel Walter P. Dunlap. See: COBB, SYLVANUS, JR.
Colonel William F. Cody. See:
CODY, WILLIAM FREDERICK
Colonial. See:
WALLIS, FRANK EDWIN
Colonization in America, The Father of English. See:
GORGES, FERDINANDO
COLONNA. See:
ROMANUS, AGAEDIUS, OF COLONNA
COLONNA, GERARD (1905-)
[American comedian, singer and musician]
Jerry Colonna
The Professor
COLONNA, ODDONE (1368-1431) [Supreme Pontiff of Roman Catholic Church]
Pope Martin V
COLORADO CAPELLA, ANTONIO JULIO (1903-)

[Puerto Rican educator and author]
Antonio J. Colorado
Colorists of the World, One of the Supreme. See: TURNER, JOSEPH MALLORD WILLIAM
COLOSIMO, JAMES (-1920) [American pander and gangster]
Big Jim Colosimo
Colossus of American Independence. See: ADAMS, JOHN
Colossus of Debate. See: ADAMS, JOHN
Colossus of Independence. See: ADAMS, JOHN
Colossus of the Nineteenth Century, The. See: BONAPARTE, NAPOLEON
Colossus of the Roads, The. See: HARRIMAN, EDWARD H.
Colossus, The Literary. See: JOHNSON, DR. SAMUEL
COLSTON, RALEIGH EDWARD (1825-96) [French-born general officer in American Confederate Army and teacher of French]
Old Allegheny
Old Club
Old Clubby
Old Polly
Old Parlez
Colt, Clem. See: NYE, NELSON CORAL
COLT, ETHEL BLYTHE (1879-1959) [American actress]
Ethel Barrymore
Colt, Martin. See: EPSTEIN, SAMUEL
Colter, Shayne. See: NORWOOD, VICTOR GEORGE CHARLES
COLTMAN-ALLEN, ERNEST (1908-) [British contract writer and broadcaster]
Ernest Vivian Coltman
Ernest Dudley
COLTON, CALVIN (1789-1857) [American Episcopal clergyman, journalist, educator and biographer]
Junius
Colum. See: COLUMBA, ST.
COLUMBA. See also: Colombia Columbia
COLUMBA, ST. (521-97) [Irish monk and missionary]
The Apostle of Caledonia
The Apostle of the Highlanders
Colum
Columcille
COLUMBAN (COLUMBANUS), ST. (543-615) [Celtic churchman]
The Younger Columbia
Columbia. See also: COLOMBA Colombia
Columbia, The Father of British. See: DOUGLAS, SIR JAMES
Columbia, The Patriarch of. See: TAYLOR, THOMAS
Columbia, The Younger. See: COLUMBAN (COLUMBANUS), ST.
COLUMBO, RUGGIERO DE RUDOLPHO (1908-34) [American singer, musician, orchestra leader and motion picture actor]
Russ Columbo
COLUMBUS, CHRISTOPHER (1446?-1506) [Italian discoverer of America]
Admiral of the Mosquitos
Admiral of the Ocean Sea
Captain General of the Armada
Cristoforo Colombo
Cristóbal Colón
Columbus, Christopher. See: MORRIS, JOSEPH CHRISTOPHER COLUMBUS

Columbus of Modern Thought, The.
See: EMERSON,
RALPH WALDO
Columcille. See:
COLUMBA, ST.
Columella of the New England
States. See:
LOWELL, JOHN, JR.
Columnist. See:
"Colyumnist"
Columnists, The Cassandra of
the. See:
LEWIS, MRS. SINCLAIR
"Colyumnist," The Father of
the. See:
BAILEY, JAMES MONT-
GOMERY
Comancho, El. See:
PHILLIPS, WALTER
SHELLEY
COMBER, LILLIAN (1916-)
[British teacher, farmer
and author]
Lillian Beckwith
Combs, Robert. See:
MURRAY, JOHN
Comedian, America's
Favorite Television. See:
JACOBS, AMOS
Comedy, The Creator of the
New. See:
ARISTOPHANES
MENANDER
Comedy, The Father of. See:
ARISTOPHANES
Comedy, The King of. See:
SENNETT, MACK
Comedy, The Prince of Ancient.
See:
ARISTOPHANES
Comedy, The Teniers of. See:
DANCOURT, FLORENT
CARTON
Comfort, Jane Levington. See:
STURTZEL, JANE
LEVINGTON
COMINI, RAILBERTO (1907-)
[Italian composer, author
and photographer]
Tino Comini
COMISKEY, CHARLES ALBERT
(1859-1931) [American
professional baseball
player]
Commy
The Old Roman
Commander. See:
WHITEHEAD, WALTER
EDWARD
Commander of the Faithful.
See: OMAR I
Commander of the State, The
Supreme Military. See:
CHU TEH
Commanding Hospitals,
Brigadier. See:
BICKERDYKE, MARY
ANN BALL
Commentator, The Greek. See:
GUZMAN, FERNANDO
NUÑEZ DE
Commentators, The Puck of.
See: STEEVENS,
GEORGE
Commerce, The Father of New
England. See:
ALLERTON, ISAAC
Commerce with India, The
Father of American.
See: DERBY, ELIAS
HASKET
Commissary, The Fighting.
See: GINTER, LEWIS
Commodore. See:
VAN SANTVOORD,
ALFRED
VANDERBILT,
CORNELIUS
Commodore Nutt. See:
McNUTT, GEORGE
WASHINGTON MOR-
RISON
COMMODUS, LUCIUS AELIUS
AURELIUS (161-92 A.D.)
[Roman emperor]
Hercules Romanus
Common People, The Poet of
the. See:
RILEY, JAMES
WHITCOMB
Common-School Education,
The Father of the
System of. See:
TREADWELL, JOHN
Commoner, The Great. See:
BRYAN, WILLIAM
JENNINGS

CLAY, HENRY
FOWLER, CHARLES HENRY
GLADSTONE, WILLIAM EWART
HOGG, JAMES STEPHEN
PITT, WILLIAM
STEVENS, THADDEUS

Commoner, The Great American. See:
STEVENS, THADDEUS

Commoner, The Nevada. See:
JONES, JOHN PERCIVAL

Commoner, The Old. See:
STEVENS, THADDEUS

Commonplace, The Poet of the See: LONGFELLOW, HENRY WADSWORTH

Commons, The Father of the House of. See:
O'CONNOR, THOMAS POWER
VILLIERS, CHARLES PELHAM

Commons, The First Man in the. See: BURKE, EDMUND

Commons, The King of the. See: JAMES V

Community Advertising, The Dean of. See:
HATFIELD, CHARLES FOLSOM

Commy. See:
COMISKEY, CHARLES ALBERT

Comnenus. See:
JOHN II
MANUEL I

COMO, PIERINO (1913-) [American popular singer and television personality]
Perry Como
The King of the Jukes

COMORRE. See:
CONOMOR (COMORRE)

Company, The One-man Trust. See: WILSON, CHARLES MOSEMAN

Compere, Mickie. See:
DAVIDSON, MICKIE COMPERE

Compleat Angler, The. See:
WALTON, IZAAK

Composer in America, The Most Talented Young. See: GOULD, MORTON

Composers, The Dean of America's Show Music. See: KERN, JEROME DAVID

Composers, The King of the Ragtime. See:
JOPLIN, SCOTT

Composition, The Father of the Czech Nationalist School of. See:
SMETANA, BEDŘICH

Compromiser, The Great. See: CLAY, HENRY

COMPSON, BETTY (1897-) [American motion picture actress]
The Minx of the Movies

Compton, Ann. See:
PREBBLE, MARJORIE MARY CURTIS

Compton, Francis Snow. See:
ADAM, HENRY BROOKS

Compton, Henry. See:
MACKENZIE, CHARLES

COMSTOCK, ANTHONY (1844-1915) [American reformer and author]
The Roundsman of the Lord

COMSTOCK, AUGUSTUS (1837-19??) [American author of dime novels]
Roger Starbuck

COMSTOCK, HENRY TOMKINS PAIGE (1820-70) [Canadian prospector in Nevada]
Old Pancake

COMSTOCK, PETER (c. 1840-) [American businessman]
The Napoleon of the North

Comte de Lautréamont, Le. See: DUCASSE, ISIDORE LUCIEN

Comte de Mirabeau. See:
RIQUETI, HONORÉ GABRIEL

Comte de Rivarol. See:
RIVAROL (RIVAROLI), ANTOINE

Comte de Stainville. See:
CHOISEUL-AMBOISE, ÉTIENNE FRANÇOIS, DUC DE
Comte de Survilliers. See:
BONAPARTE, JOSEPH
Comte de Voilemont. See:
ESTERHAZY, MARIE CHARLES FERDINAND WALSIN
COMYNS-CARR, BARBARA IRENE VERONICA (1912-) [British author]
Barbara Comyns
Con Conrad. See:
DOBER, CONRAD K.
Concepción, The Hero of. See:
FANNIN, JAMES W.
Conchology, The Father of American. See:
SAY, THOMAS
Concord, The Sage of. See:
ALCOTT, AMOS BRONSON
EMERSON, RALPH WALDO
Concrete Roads in New York, The Father of. See:
GREENE, FREDERICK STUART
CONDÉ, LOUIS II, PRINCE DE (1621-86) [French military leader, son of Henry II]
The Great Condé
CONDON. See also:
CONGDON
CONDON, ALBERT EDWARD (1905-) [American jazz musician (banjo, guitar, leader)]
Eddie Condon
CONDON, DR. JOHN FRANCIS (1860-1945) [American go-between in kidnapping of the son of CHARLES AUGUSTUS LINDBERGH]
Jafsie
Condor, Gladys. See:
DAVISON, GLADYS PATTON
Conductor, France's Greatest. See: MÜNCH, CHARLES
CONDULMER, GABRIELE (1383-1447) [Supreme Pontiff of Roman Catholic Church]
Pope Eugene IV
CONE, MOLLY LAMKEN (1918-) [American author]
Caroline More
Conegliano, Cima de. See:
CIMA, GIOVANNI BATTISTA
CONEGLIANO, EMANUELE (1749-1838) [Italian poet and librettist]
Lorenzo Da Ponte
CONERLY, CHARLES (1921-) [American football player]
Charlie Conerly
Chuck Conerly
Confederacy, Ney of the. See:
CHEATHAM, BENJAMIN FRANKLIN
Confederacy, The Boy Hero of the. See:
DAVIS, SAM
Confederacy, The Brains of the. See:
BENJAMIN, JUDAH PHILIP
Confederacy, The Daughter of the. See:
DAVIS, VARINA ANNE JEFFERSON
Confederacy, The Mother of the. See:
LAW, SALLIE CHAPMAN GORDON
Confederacy, The Plumed Knight of the. See:
STUART, JAMES EWELL BROWN
Confederacy, The Poet Laureate of the. See:
TIMROD, HENRY
Confederacy, The Poet of the. See: RYAN, ABRAM JOSEPH
Confederacy, The Prince Rupert of the. See:
STUART, JAMES EWELL BROWN
Confederacy, The Sword of the. See:
JACKSON, THOMAS JONATHAN
Confederacy, The War Horse

of the. See:
LONGSTREET, JAMES
Confederacy, Winnie Davis, The Daughter of the. See: DAVIS, VARINA ANNE JEFFERSON
Conference in India, The Nestor of the Methodist. See: BOWEN, GEORGE
Confessor, The. See: EDWARD (EADWARD) MAXIMUS, ST.
CONFREY, EDWARD E. (1895-) [American pianist and composer]
Zez Confrey
CONFUCIUS (c. 550-478 B.C.) [Chinese philosopher]
The Philosopher of China
Confucius, The European. See: QUESNAY, FRANÇOIS
CONGDON. See also: CONDON
CONGDON, CHARLES TABER (1821-91) [American editor and poet]
Paul Potter
Conger, Lesley. See: SUTTLES, SHIRLEY SMITH
Congregation in the United States, A Lay Preacher to the Largest. See: BOK, EDWARD WILLIAM
Congregational Churches, Bishop of. See: WEEDEN, CHARLES FOSTER
Congregational Pope of New England, The. See: BACON, LEONARD
Congregationalism, The Nestor of. See: BACON, LEONARD
Congress, Camillo Querno, Poet Laureate to the. See: ODELL, JONATHAN
Congress, The Father of the Continental. See: FRANKLIN, BENJAMIN
Congress, The Hand and Pen of the. See: THOMPSON, CHARLIE
Congressional Playboy, The. See: ZIONCHECK, MARION A.
Congresswoman, The Farm Woman's. See: KNUTSON, CORNELIA GJESDAL
CONIUOLO, GIOVANNI (died 1119) [Supreme Pontiff of Roman Catholic Church]
Pope Gelasius II
CONKLING, ROSCOE (1816-91) [American statesman; senator from New York]
The Peacock Senator
CONLIN, BERNARD (1831-91) [American actor]
William James Florence
CONNALLY. See also: CONNELLY CONNOLLY
CONNALLY, GEORGE WALTER (1898-) [American professional baseball player]
Rip
Rubber Arm
Sarge
Snorter
CONNALLY, THOMAS TERRY (1877-) [American politician; congressman from Texas]
Texas Tom
Tom Connally
Connecticut, A Gentleman of. See: HOPKINS, DR. LEMUEL
Connecticut Jurisprudence, The Father of. See: LUDLOW, ROGER
Connection, The Countess of Huntingdon's. See: HUNTINGDON, SELINA, COUNTESS OF
Connell, Norreys. See: O'RIORDAN, CONAL O'CONNELL
CONNELLY, LELIA LOGAN (1837-1904) [American journalist, novelist and playwright]
L. Fairfax

CONNELLY, MARCUS COOK (1890-) [American playwright]
Marc Connelly
CONNELLY. See also:
CONNALLY
CONNOLLY
CONNERY, THOMAS (1930-) [British actor]
Sean Connery
Mr. Kisskiss Bangbang
Connétable de Bourbon. See:
BOURBON, DUC CHARLES DE
CONNETT, EUGENE VIRGINIUS III (1891-) [American businessman, politician, editor and author]
Virginius
Connie Fennell. See:
VAYSSE, CHARLES
Connie Francis. See:
FRANCONERO, CONCETTA
Connie Mack. See:
McGILLICUDDY, CORNELIUS
Connie Stevens. See:
INGOLIA, CONCETTA
CONNIFF, JAMES CLIFFORD GREGORY (1920-) [American public relations executive and author]
John Coolwater
Anthropophagus Minor
Connington, J.J. See:
STEWART, ALFRED WALTER
Connington, John Jervis. See:
STEWARD, ALFRED WALTER
CONNOLLY. See also:
CONNALLY
CONNELLY
CONNOLLY, CYRIL VERNON (1903-) [British author]
Palinurus
Vercors
CONNOLLY, RICHARD (fl. late 19th cent.) [American politician; member of Tweed Ring]
Big Judge
Slippery Dick
CONNOR, JOHN ANTHONY (1930-) [British poet, designer and educator]
Tony Connor
Adam Hardwick
CONNOR, KEVIN JOSEPH (1921-) [American motion picture and television actor]
Chuck Connors
CONNOR, PATRICK REARDON (1907-) [Irish author]
Reardon Connor
Peter Malin
Connor, Ralph. See:
GORDON, CHARLES WILLIAM
CONNOR, REV. JOSEPH P. (1895-) [American priest and composer]
Pierre Norman Connor
Connors, Chuck. See:
CONNOR, KEVIN JOSEPH
Conny Keyber, Mr. See:
FIELDING, HENRY
CONOMOR (COMORRE) (fl. 6th cent.) [Breton chief; put several wives to death]
Bluebeard
The Cursed
CONON (died 687) [Supreme Pontiff of Roman Catholic Church]
Pope Conon
Conqueror of the World (Alamgir). See:
MOHAMMED
Conqueror of the World, The. See:
ALEXANDER III
JAHINGIR
Conqueror, The. See:
MOHAMMED II
NADIR, SHAH
WILLIAM I
Conqueror, The (El Conquistador). See:
JAMES I
PIZARRO, FRANCISCO
CONQUEST, GEORGE ROBERT ACWORTH (1917-)

[British civil servant, editor and author]
J.E.M. Arden
Conquistador, El (The Conqueror). See: JAMES I
PIZARRO, FRANCISCO
CONRAD (died 955) [Duke of Lorraine]
Conrad the Red
CONRAD II (990?-1039) [Holy Roman Emperor and King of Germany]
The Salian
Conrad, Con. See: DOBER, CONRAD K.
Conrad Farel. See: BARDENS, DENNIS CONRAD
Conrad, Hugh. See: SCHOENFELD, WILLIAM C.
Conrad, Joseph. See: KORZENIOWSKI, TEODOR JOZEF KONRAD
Conrad, Kenneth. See: LOTTICH, KENNETH VERNE
Conrad Pendleton. See: KIDD, WALTER E.
Conrad, Robert Arnold. See: HART, MOSS
Conrad, Tod. See: WILKES-HUNTER, RICHARD
Conroy, J.D. See: RYMER, JAMES MALCOLM
CONROY, JOHN WESLEY (1899-) [American editor and author]
Tim Brennan
Jack Conroy
John Norcross
CONROY, PATRICK DOMINIC (1900-) [Canadian government official]
Pat Conroy
CONSCIENCE, HENDRICK (1812-83) [Flemish novelist]
The Walter Scott of Belgium
CONSIDINE, ROBERT BERNARD (1906-) [American journalist]
Bob Considine
Consort of Her Most Gracious Majesty. See: ALBERT
Conspicuous Controversialist of His Age, The Most. See: CHILLINGWORTH, WILLIAM
Constance Collier. See: HARDIE, LAURA CONSTANCE
Constance Cummings. See: HALVERSTADT, CONSTANCE
Constance Frick. See: IRWIN, CONSTANCE FRICK
Constance Howard. See: WHITE, CONSTANCE M.
Constance Tomkinson. See: WEEKS, CONSTANCE TOMPKINSON
Constant, Benjamin. See: DE REBECQUE, HENRI BENJAMIN CONSTANT
Constant Reader. See: PARKER, DOROTHY ROTHSCHILD
Constant, The. See: JOHN (JOHANN)
CONSTANTELOS, DEMETRIOS J. (1927-) [Greek-American clergyman and author]
Dimitris Stachys
Constantia. See: MURRAY, JUDITH SARGENT STEVENS
CONSTANTINE. See also: Apostle to the Slavs
CONSTANTINE (died 715) [Supreme Pontiff of Roman Catholic Church]
Pope Constantine I
CONSTANTINE (827-69) [Thessalonian churchman]
The Apostle to the Slavs
St. Cyril
The Philosopher
Constantine I. See: CONSTANTINIUS, FLAVIUS VALERIUS AURELIUS
CONSTANTINE V (719-75)

[Emperor of the Byzantine Empire]
Copronymus
Constantine, The Buddhist. See: ASOKA (ASAOKA)
Constantine the Great. See: CONSTANTINIUS, FLAVIUS VALERIUS AURELIUS
CONSTANTINI, CONSTANTINO (fl. 1668-96) [Italian actor]
Gradelino
CONSTANTINIUS, FLAVIUS VALERIUS AURELIUS (c. 280-337) [Roman emperor]
Constantine I
Constantine the Great
CONSTANTOPOULOS, KATINA (1900-) [Greek actress]
Katina Paxinou
Constitution, The Defender of the. See: WEBSTER, DANIEL
Constitution, The Expounder of the. See: WEBSTER, DANIEL
Constitution, The Father of the. See: MADISON, JAMES
Constitution, The Father of the Twentieth Amendment to the. See: NORRIS, GEORGE WILLIAM
Constitution, The High Priest of the. See: BAYARD, JAMES ASHETON
Constitution, The Legal Interpreter of the. See: MARSHALL, JOHN
Constitution, The Pillar of the. See: WEBSTER, DANIEL
Constitution, The Savior of the. See: BLOOM, SOL
Constitution, The Upholder of the. See: WEBSTER, DANIEL
CONTANDIN, FERNAND JOSEPH DÉSIRÉ (1903-71) [French actor and comedian]
Fernandel
Conte. See: CANDOLI, SECONDO
Contemporary Cassandra, The. See: LEWIS, MRS. SINCLAIR
Contemporary English Novelists, The Dean of. See: FORSTER, EDWARD MORGAN
Contentment, The Pied Piper of. See: COUÉ, ÉMILE
CONTI, MICHELANGELO (1655-1724) [Supreme Pontiff of Roman Catholic Church]
Pope Innocent XIII
CONTI, RINALDO (died 1261) [Supreme Pontiff of Roman Catholic Church]
Pope Alexander IV
Continental Congress, The Father of the. See: FRANKLIN, BENJAMIN
CONTINO, RICHARD (1930-) [American accordionist]
Dick Contino
The Yankee Clipper of the Accordion
Contractor General, The (Le Général Entrepreneur). See: BONAPARTE, NAPOLEON
Contractors, The Prince of Mail. See: REESIDE, JAMES
Contributor, The Fat. See: GRISWALD, A. MINER
THACKERAY, WILLIAM MAKEPEACE
Controversialist of His Age, The Most Conspicuous. See: CHILLINGWORTH, WILLIAM
CONTUCCI, ANDREA (1460-1529) [Italian sculptor]
Sansovino
Conventions, The Flea of the. See: FOLSOM, ABIGAIL
Conway, Arlington B. See: BURNS, EEDSON LOUIS MILLARD
Conway, Denise. See:

PREBBLE, MARJORIE
MARY CURTIS
Conway, Faulkner. See:
PRICE, FRANK J.
Conway, Handsome. See:
RUGG, WILLIAM
AUGUSTUS
Conway, Hugh. See:
FARGUS, FREDERICK
JOHN
Conway Tearle. See:
LEVY, FREDERICK
Conway, Tom. See:
SANDERS, THOMAS
Conway, William Augustus.
See: RUGG, WILLIAM
AUGUSTUS
Conwell, Chic. See:
UNKNOWN
Conybeare, Charles Augustus.
See: ELIOT, THOMAS
STEARNS
Coody, King. See:
TANEY, ROGER BROOKE
COOK, ALLEN B. See:
Adams, Henry
COOK, CHARLES HENRY
(1858-1933) [British
barrister and author]
John Bickerdyke
COOK, FLAVIUS JOSEPHUS
(1838-1901) [American
author and lecturer]
Joseph Cook
COOK, HERMAN (1934-)
[American jazz musician
(tenor saxophone)]
Junior Cook
COOK, JAMES (1728-79)
[English explorer and
navigator]
Captain Cook
COOK, JOHN (1923-)
[American jazz musician
(trumpet)]
Willie Cook
COOK, MYRA B. (1933-)
[American teacher and
author]
Myra Brown
COOK, PHILIP (1817-94)
[American Civil War
soldier; distinguished for
bravery]
The Old War Horse
COOK, PROCTOR FYFFE
(1891-) [American
humorist, editor and
columnist]
Ted Cook
COOK, RAMONA GRAHAM (fl.
1936-66) [American
educator, poet and author]
Ramona Graham
COOK, WILLIAM EVERETT
(1921-) [American
author]
Wade Everett
James Keene
COOK, WILLIAM WALLACE
(1867-1933) [American
writer of dime novels]
John Milton Edwards
W. B. Lawson
COOKE, ALLEN LINDSEY
(1907-) [American pro-
fessional baseball player]
Dusty Cooke
COOKE, JOHN ESTEN (1830-86)
[American author and
biographer]
Colonel Surry
COOKE, THOMAS (1703-56)
[English writer and trans-
lator]
Hesiod Cooke
COOKSON, CATHERINE Mc-
MULLEN (1906-)
[British lecturer and
author]
Catherine Marchant
COOLBRITH, IDA DONNA
(1842-1928) [American
poet and librarian]
The Poet Laureate of
California
COOLBRITH, IDA DONNA. See:
also: Golden Gate Trinity,
The
Coole, W.W. See:
KULSKI, WLADYSLAW
WSZEBOR
COOLIDGE, CHARLES WILLIAM
(1912-62) [American jazz
musician (trombone, drums)]
Skip Morr

COOLIDGE, JOHN CALVIN (1872-1933) [thirtieth President of the United States]
Calvin Coolidge
Red
Silent Cal
Coolidge McCann. See: FAWCETT, FRANK DUBREZ
Coolidge of the West, The. See: LANDON, ALFRED MOSSMAN
Coolidge, Susan. See: WOOLSEY, SARAH CHAUNCEY
Coolidge, The Kansas. See: LANDON, ALFRED MOSSMAN
Coolwater, John. See: CONNIFF, JAMES CLIFFORD GREGORY
COOMBS, CHARLES IRA (1914-) [American author]
Chick Coombs
COOMES, OLIVER (1845-1921) [American author of dime novels]
Oil Coomes
Will Dexter
Coon, Peter. See: BERNARD, PIERRE A.
Coon, The Same Old. See: CLAY, HENRY
COONEY, HELEN LAURETTE MAGDALENE (1884-) [American actress]
La Belle Laurette
Laurette Taylor
COOPER, ALFRED BENJAMIN (1863-) [British author]
Paul Preston
COOPER, ALFRED MORTON (1890-) [American educator and author]
Morley Cooper
COOPER, EDITH EMMA. See: Field, Michael
Cooper, Esther. See: KELLNER, ESTHER
Cooper, Frank. See: SIMMS, WILLIAM GILMORE
COOPER, FRANK J. (1901-61) [American motion picture actor]
Gary Cooper
COOPER, GEORGE (1929-) [American jazz musician (trombone)]
Buster Cooper
COOPER, JAMES FENIMORE (1789-1851) [American author]
An American
The American Scott
Cornelius Littlepage
A Traveling Bachelor
Cooper, James R. See: STRATEMEYER, EDWARD L.
Cooper, Jefferson. See: FOX, GARDNER FRANCIS
Cooper, John R. See: STRATEMEYER, EDWARD L.
Cooper of the South, The. See: SIMMS, WILLIAM GILMORE
COOPER, PETER (1791-1883) [American manufacturer and philanthropist]
The Father of Railroads
COOPER, RICHARD (1740-c.1814) [English painter and engraver]
The English Poussin
The Younger
COOPER, SAMUEL (1609-72) [English miniaturist]
The Apelles of His Age
Van Dyck in Little
COOPER, SAUL (1934-) [American author]
Richard Benson
Michael Milner
COOPER, SUSAN FENIMORE (1813-94) [American author]
A Lady
Amabel Penfeather
COOPER, SYLVIA (1903-) [American author]
Sylvia Paul Jerman
Cooper, The Buck Private's Gary.

See: MacARTHUR, DOUGLAS
Cooper, The French Fenimore.
See: GLOUX, OLIVIER
Cooper, The Southern. See:
SIMMS, WILLIAM GILMORE
COOPER, THOMAS (1759-1839)
[Anglo-American educator, scientist and political economist]
Adam Hornbook
Cooper, William. See:
HOFF, HARRY SUMMERFIELD
Cootie. See:
WILLIAMS, CHARLES MELVIN
COOWESCOOWE (KOOWESKOOWE) (1790-1866)
[Chief of Cherokee Indian Nation]
John Ross
COPE, ROBERT KNOX (1913-)
[South African journalist and author]
Jack Cope
COPE, VINCENT ZACHARY
(1881-) [British surgeon and author]
Zeta
COPELON, ALLAN (1924-)
[American comedian, television writer and producer]
Allan Sherman
Copernicus of the Mind, The.
See: FREUD, SIGMUND
COPPARD, ALFRED EDGAR
(1878-1957) [English poet and short story writer]
A. E. Coppard
Coppersmith, Alexander the.
See: HAMILTON, ALEXANDER
COPPERSMITH, BARBARA
(1925-) [American composer and pianist]
Barbara Carroll
Copplestone, Bennett. See:
KITCHIN, FREDERICK HARCOURT
Copronymus. See:
CONSTANTINE V
COPWAY, GEORGE (1818-c.1863)
[Canadian Ojibway Indian chief, missionary and author]
Kah-Ge-Ga-Gah-Bowh
Coquina. See:
SHIELDS, GEORGE OLIVER
Cora Annett. See:
SCOTT, CORA ANNETT PEPITONE
Cora Sandel. See:
FABRICIUS, SARA
CORAK, MIA (1917-)
[Yugoslavian ballet dancer and choreographer]
Mia Slavenska
Coralie Howard. See:
COGSWELL, CORALIE NORRIS
Coralie Stanton. See:
HOSKEN, ALICE CECIL SEYMOUR
CORBETT, JAMES JOHN
(1866-1933) [American professional boxer; world's heavyweight champion]
Gentleman Jim
Corbin, Iris. See:
CLINTON, IRIS A. CORBIN
Corbusier, Le. See:
JEANNERET-GRIS, CHARLES ÉDOUARD
Corchaito. See:
MUÑOZ, FERMÍN
CORCORAN, GENE PATRICK
(1924-) [American jazz musician (tenor saxophone)]
Corky Corcoran
CORCORAN, THOMAS GARDINER
(1900-) [American politician; unofficial adviser to President FRANKLIN DELANO ROOSEVELT]
Tommy the Cork
White House Tommy
Cord. See:
HULL, CORDELL
Cord, Alex. See:
VIESPI, ALEXANDER
Cord Wainer. See:

DEWEY, THOMAS BLANCHARD
Corday, Charlotte. See: D'ARMONT, MARIE ANNE CHARLOTTE CORDAY
CORDAY, PAULA (1924-) [Anglo-Swiss motion picture actress]
Rita Corday
Paule Croset
Cordell, Alexander. See: GRABER, ALEXANDER
CORDIAUX, RAYMOND (1898-1956) [French motion picture actor]
Raymond Cordy
Cordière, La Belle (The Beautiful Rope Maker). See: LABÉ, LOUISE
CORDOBA. See:
CORDOVA
Cordova
GONZALO DE CÓRDOBA (GONSALVO DI CORDOVA)
CORDOBA, JESÚS. See: Three Musketeers, The
Córdoba, The Man from (El Córdobes). See: BENITEZ, MANUEL
Cordobes, El (The Man from Córdoba). See: BENÍTEZ, MANUEL
CORDOVA. See:
CÓRDOBA
Córdoba
GONZALO DE CORDOBA (GONSALVO DI CORDOVA)
Córdova, Arturo de. See: GARCÍA, ARTURO
Corduroy Killer, The. See: FISCHER, ROBERT JAMES
Cordy, Raymond. See: CORDIAUX, RAYMOND
Corelli, Marie. See: MACKAY, MARY
COREY, FRANCIS ADELBERT (1843-1934) [American author of dime novels]
Frank Corey
Rett Winwood
Corinna Cochrane. See: PETERSON, CORINNA
Corinne Calvet. See: DIBOS, CORINNE
Corinne Holt Rickert. See: SAWYER, CORINNE HOLT
Corinne L'Estrange. See: HARTSHORNE, HENRY
Corisande, The Beautiful. See: D'ANDOUINS, DIANE
Cork, Tommy the. See: CORCORAN, THOMAS GARDINER
CORKREY, KATHLEEN (1923-) [British motion picture actress]
Carol Raye
Corky. See: CORCORAN, GENE PATRICK
Corley, Ernest. See: BULMER, HENRY KENNETH
Corn-law Rhymer, The. See: ELLIOTT, EBENEZER
Corn, The King of Musical. See: WELK, LAWRENCE
Corneille of the Boulevard(s), The. See: PIXÉRÉCOURT, GUILBERT DE
CORNEILLE, PIERRE (1606-84) [French dramatist]
The Father of French Tragedy
The French Shakespeare
Le Grand Corneille
The Homer of the French Drama
Cornel. See also:
CORNELL
Cornell
Cornel Adam. See: LENGYEL, CORNEL ADAM
Cornelia Jessey. See: SUSSMAN, CORNELIA SILVER
Cornelia Spencer. See: YAUKEY, GRACE SYDENSTRICKER
CORNELIUS (died 253) [Supreme Pontiff of Roman Catholic Church]
Pope Cornelius
St. Cornelius
Cornelius Littlepage. See: COOPER, JAMES FENIMORE
Cornelius O'Dowd. See: LEVER, CHARLES JAMES
CORNELL [Cornell]. See also:

Cornel
CORNELL, KATHERINE (1898-) [American actress]
Kit Cornell
Cornell Woolrich. See: HOPLEY-WOOLRICH CORNELL GEORGE
CORNING, ERASTUS (1794-1872) [American developer of railroads in New York State]
The Railway King
Cornish Metaphysician, The. See: DREW, SAMUEL
Cornish Wonder, The. See: OPIE, JOHN
Corno di Bassetto. See: SHAW, GEORGE BERNARD
Cornwall. See also: CORNWELL
Cornwall, Barry. See: PROCTOR, BRYAN WALLER
Cornwall, C. M. See: ROE, MARY ABIGAIL
Cornwall, Jim. See: RIKHOFF, JAMES C.
Cornwall, Martin. See: CAVENDISH, RICHARD
CORNWALLIS, CHARLES CORNWALLIS, 1ST MARQUIS (1738-1805) [English general officer and statesman]
Cobwallis
Viceroy of India
CORNWELL. See also: Cornwall
CORNWELL, DAVID JOHN MOORE (1931-) [English author]
John le Carré
Coroner. See: FERNÁNDEZ, JOACHIM OCTAVE
Corporal John. See: CHURCHILL, JOHN
Corporal of Unsought Fields, Little. See: McCLELLAN, GEORGE BRINTON
Corporal, The Little. See: NELSON, KNUTE
Corporal, The Little (Le Petit Caporal). See: BONAPARTE, NAPOLEON
CORRALL, ALICE ENID (1916-) [British columnist and author]
Justine Glass
CORREA, WILLIAM (1934-) [American jazz musician (bongos, conga drums, timbals)]
Willie Bobo
Corrector, The. See: CRUDEN, ALEXANDER
Correggio of Sculpture, The. See: GOUJON, JEAN
CORRELL, CHARLES J. (1890-) [American radio actor]
Andrew H. Brown
Henry van Porter
CORRELL, CHARLES J. See: also: Amos and Andy
CORRIGAN, DOUGLAS GEORGE (1907-) [American aviator]
Wrong-way Corrigan
Corrupter, The Grand. See: WALPOLE, SIR ROBERT
CORSI, FRANCO ZEFFIRELLI (1923-) [Italian theatrical and operatic director and designer]
Franco Zeffirelli
Corsica, Theodore, King of. See: VAN NEUHOFF, BARON
Corsican Fiend, The. See: BONAPARTE, NAPOLEON
Corsican General, The. See: BONAPARTE, NAPOLEON
Corsican Ogre, The. See: BONAPARTE, NAPOLEON
Corsican Seostris, The. See: BONAPARTE, NAPOLEON
Corsican, The. See: BONAPARTE, NAPOLEON
CORSINI, LORENZO (1652-1740) [Supreme Pontiff of Roman Catholic Church]
Pope Clement XII
The Protestant Pope
Corson, Geoffrey. See:

IRVING, WASHINGTON
SHOLL, ANNA McCLURE
Corteen, Wes. See:
NORWOOD, VICTOR GEORGE CHARLES
CORTÉS, HERNÁN (1485-1547) [Spanish conquistador; conqueror of Mexico] thought by MONTEZUMA II to be
The Fair God (Quetzalcoátl)
Cortez, Ricardo. See:
KRANZ, JACOB
Cortez, Stanley. See:
KRANZ, STANISLAUS
Cortis, Diana. See:
ASHTON, WINIFRED
Corvin, Eugen Alban. See:
GATTERMANN, EUGEN LUDWIG
Corvinus, Jakob. See:
RAABE, WILHELM
Corvo, Baron. See:
ROLFE, FREDERICK WILLIAM SERAFINO AUSTIN LEWIS MARY
CORWIN, THOMAS (1794-1865) [American lawyer and politician; senator from and Governor of Ohio]
Black Tom
The Wagon Boy
Cory, Desmond. See:
McCARTHY, SHAUN
Cory, Howard L., joint pseud. of CORRIE HOWARD (-) and JACK JARDINE (1931-) [American authors]
CORY, WINIFRED MURIEL (fl. early 20th cent.) [British author]
Winifred Graham
CORYELL, JOHN RUSSELL (c. 1852-1924) [American writer of dime novels]
Nick Carter
Nicholas Carter
Bertha M. Clay
Tyman Currio
Lillian R. Drayton
Julia Edwards
Geraldine Fleming
Margaret Grant
Barbara Howard
Harry Dubois Milman
Milton Quarterly
Lucy May Russell
Corymbaeus. See:
BRAITHWAIT (BRAITHWAITE), RICHARD
Coryphaeus of Grammarians, The. See:
ARISTARCHUS
COSBY. See also:
CROSBIE
CROSBY
Crosby
COSBY, WILLIAM HENRY, JR. (1938-) [American Negro actor and comedian]
Bill Cosby
COSIMO, AGNOLO (ANGIOLO) DI (1502-72) [Florentine painter]
Il Bronzino
COSIMO, PIERO DI (1462-1521) [Italian Renaissance painter]
Piero di Lorenzo
Cosimo The Elder. See:
MEDICI, COSIMO DE'
Cosimo the Great. See:
MEDICI, COSIMO DE'
Cosmo Hamilton. See:
GIBBS, COSMO HAMILTON
Cossack, Vian of the. See:
VIAN, SIR PHILIP LOUIS
Cossacks of the Don, Hetman of the. See:
PLATOV, MATVEI IVANOVICH COUNT
COSTA RICCI, LEWIS DA (1886-) [British naval officer and author]
Bartimeus
Costello, Lou. See:
CRISTELLO, LOUIS
Costello, Michael. See:
DETZER, KARL
Costello, Pierre. See:
HOSKEN, ERNEST CHARLES HEATH
Coster. See:
JANSZOON, LAURENS

Costillares. See:
RODRÍGUEZ, JOAQUIN
COTÉ, LOUIS JOSEPH (1884-1934) [American silent motion picture actor]
Lew Cody
Cotes, Peter. See:
BOULTING, SYDNEY
Cotin, Alaric. See:
FREDERICK II
Cotswold, The King of. See:
BRYDGES, GREY
COTTLE, JOSEPHINE (1922-) [American motion picture actress]
Gale Storm
Cotton Ed. See:
SMITH, ELLISON DuRANT
Cotton Gin, The Father of the. See:
WHITNEY, ELI
Cotton Industry, The Father of the American. See:
COXE, TENCH
COTTON, JOHN (1584-1652) [Anglo-American Puritan divine]
The Father and Glory of Boston
The Patriarch of New England
Cotton Row, The Dean of. See:
DOUGHTY, JAMES P.
COUCH, HELEN FOX (1907-) [American writer of worship materials]
V. Helen Fox
COUÉ, ÉMILE (1857-1926) [French healer by auto-suggestion]
The Pied Piper of Contentment
COUGHLAN, FRANK (1916-) [American motion picture actor]
Junior Coughlan
COUGHRAN, LARRY C. (1925-) [American writer on judo and self-defense]
Larry Craig
COULSON, FELICITY CARTER (1907-) [British author]
Emery Bonett
COULSON, JOHN HUBERT ARTHUR (1906-) [British banker, business executive and author]
John Bonett
Coulson Kernahan, Mrs. See:
KERNAHAN, JEAN GWYNNE
COULSON, ROBERT S. See:
Stratton, Thomas
Council, Stern in (Hardrata). See: HAROLD III
Counsellor, The Poor Man's. See: CLARK, ABRAHAM
Count. See:
BASIE, WILLIAM
Count Alessandro di Cagliostro, See: BALSAMO, GIUSEPPE
Count of Albany. See:
STUART, CHARLES EDWARD LOUIS PHILIP CASIMIR
STUART, JOHN SOBIESKI STOLBERG
COUNT OF BOLLSTÄDT. See:
ALBERTUS MAGNUS, SAINT, COUNT OF BOLLSTÄDT
Count of Dunois and Longueville. See: DUNOIS, JEAN
COUNT OF HIRSCHBERG. See:
GEBHARD, COUNT OF HIRSCHBERG
COUNT OF MORSLEBEN. See:
SUITGER, COUNT OF MORSLEBEN
COUNT OF SEGNI. See:
UGOLINO, COUNT OF SEGNI
COUNT OF TUSCULUM. See:
JOHN, COUNT OF TUSCULUM
COUNT POPPO OF BAVARIA (died 1048) [Supreme Pontiff of Roman Catholic Church]
Pope Damasus II
Count, The Green. See:
AMADEUS VI
Countess Barcynska. See:

EVANS, MARGUERITE FLORENCE HELENE
Countess of Huntingdon's Connection, The. See: HUNTINGDON, SELINA, COUNTESS OF
Countess of Landsfield, The. See: GILBERT, MARIE DOLORES ELIZA ROSANNA
Country. See also: WARNECKE, LONNIE
WASHBURNE, JOSEPH
Country, Liberator and Father of His. See: DORIA, ANDREA
Country Music, The Dandy of. See: DEAN, JIMMY RAY
Country, The Father of His. See: WASHINGTON, GEORGE
Country, The Father of His (Pater Patriae). See: ADRIAN (HARDIAN)
CICERO, MARCUS TULLIUS
MEDICI, COSIMO DE'
Country, The Father of the. See: CICERO, MARCUS TULLIUS
Country, The Savior of His. See: OATES, TITUS
WASHINGTON, GEORGE
Country, The Stepfather of His. See: WASHINGTON, GEORGE
County Bar, The Father of the Hampden. See: BATES, WILLIAM GELSTON
County Bar, The Historian of the Hampden. See: BATES, WILLIAM GELSTON
County Bar, The Nestor of the Hampden. See: BATES, WILLIAM GELSTON
County, The Father of Chautaqua. See: FOOTE, ELIAL TODD
County, The Marrying Justice of Worcester. See: DAVIS, WALTER ALONZO
County, The War Horse of Sumner. See: TROUSDALE, WILLIAM
Coupling, J. J. See: PIERCE, JOHN ROBINSON
Courcel, Nicole. See: ANDRIEUX, NICOLE
COURNOS, HELEN SYBIL NORTON (1893-) [American author]
Sybil Norton
COURNOS, JOHN (1881-) [Russian-American editor, intelligence officer and author]
John Courtney
Mark Gault
Court Nez, Marquis au (Marquis Short-nose). See: GUILLAUME D'ORANGE
Court, The Father of the Juvenile. See: LINDSEY, BENJAMIN BARR
Courtenay, Sir William. See: THOM, JOHN NICHOLS
COURTENAY, THOMAS DANIEL (1937-) [British actor]
Tom Courtenay
Courteney, Carl. See: URNER, NATHAN DANE
Courtland, Roberta. See: DERN, PEGGY GADDIS
Courtney. See: DAINTON, WILLIAM COURTNEY
Courtney, John. See: COURNOS, JOHN
JUDD, FREDERICK CHARLES
Courtney Melmoth. See: PRATT, SAMUEL JACKSON
COUSIN [Cousin]. See also: Couzin
Cousin Alice. See: BRADLEY, MARY EMILY
HAVEN, EMILY BRADLEY NEAL
Cousin Cicely. See: BRADFORD, SARAH ELIZABETH HOPKINS
Cousin Ern. See: FORD, ERNEST JENNINGS
COUSIN, JEAN (c-1500-90) [French painter, engraver and sculptor]
The French Michelangelo

Cousin May Carleton. See:
FLEMING, MAY AGNES
Cousin Virginia. See:
JOHNSON, VIRGINIA WALES
COUSINS. See also:
COUZENS
COZZENS
COUSINS, MARGARET (1905-)
[American author]
Avery Johns
William Masters
Mary Parrish
COUZENS. See also:
COUSINS
COZZENS
COUZENS, JAMES (1872-1936)
[American businessman and senator from Michigan]
The Croesus of the Senate
The Poor Man's Friend
Couzin. See also:
COUSIN
Cousin
Couzin Dud. See:
LEBLANC, DUDLEY J.
Coventry, John. See:
PALMER, JOHN WILLIAMSON
Coverley, Sir Roger de. See:
ADDISON, JOSEPH
SEWALL, JONATHAN
Covington Clarke. See:
VENABLE, CLARK
COVODE, JOHN (1808-71)
[American politician; congressman from Pennsylvania]
Honest John Covode
Cow Cow. See:
DAVENPORT, CHARLES
COWAN [Cowan]. See also:
Cowen
Cowan, Alan. See:
GILCHRIST, ALAN W.
COWAN, CLAUDE (1885-1955)
[British motion picture comedian]
Claude Dampier
COWARD, NOEL PEIRCE
(1899-) [British playwright composer and actor]
Hernia Whittlebot
Coward, The Dirty Little
See: FORD, ROBERT
Cowboy Carl. See:
HATCH, CARL ATWOOD
Cowboy, Oklahoma's Yodeling.
See: AUTREY, GENE ORVON

Cowboy Philosopher, The. See:
ROGERS, WILLIAM PENN ADAIR
Cowboy Senator, The. See:
ASHURST, HENRY FOUNTAIN
COWDRICK, JESSE C. (1859-99)
[American author of dime novels]
Arizona Cy
The City-items Scribe
Cowen. See also:
COWAN
Cowan
Cowen, Frances. See:
MUNTHE, FRANCES
Cowgirls, The Queen of the.
See: SMITH, FRANCES OCTAVIA
COWL, JANE. See:
Martin, Allan Langdon
COWLEY, MRS. HANNAH (1743-1809) [American dramatist and poet]
Anna Matilda
Cowlin, Dorothy. See:
WHALLEY, DOROTHY
COWLISHAW, RANSON
(1894-) [British author]
R.A. Woodrook
COWPER, FRANK (1849-)
[British author]
Diogenes Junior
Jack-all-alone
Cowper of Our Modern Poetesses, The. See:
SOUTHEY, CAROLINE ANNE BOWLES
Cowper of the Highlands, The.
See: BUCHANAN, DUGALD
COWPER, WILLIAM (1731-1800)
[English poet]
The Bard of Olney
The Domestic Poet
Cowslip, Egbert Augustus, Esq.
See: BARKER, BENJAMIN
COX. See also:
COXE
COX, ANTHONY BERKELEY

detective stories]
Anthony Berkeley
Francis Iles
COX, DOROTHY ISOBEL (1906-64) [British stage and motion picture actress]
Diana Wynyard
COX, JAMES R. (fl. 1932-38) [American Catholic clergyman]
The Pastor of the Poor
COX, JOHN (1913-) [American motion picture actor]
John Howard
COX-OLIVER, EDNA MAY (1883-1942) [American stage and motion picture actress]
Edna May Oliver
The Woman Who Always Speaks Her Mind
COX, ROD (1910-) [Canadian motion picture actor]
Rod Cameron
COX, SAMUEL SULLIVAN (1824-89) [American newspaperman and politician; congressman from Ohio]
The Letter Carrier's Friend
Sunset Cox
COX, WALLACE MAYNARD (1924-) [American actor, radio and television personality]
Wally Cox
Mr. Peepers
COX, WILLIAM R. (fl. 1956-65) [American author]
Joel Reeve
Coxcombs, The Prince of. See: JOSEPH, CHARLES
COXE. See also: COX
COXE, TENCH (1755-1824) [American pioneer in the textile industry]
The Father of the American Cotton Industry
COXEY, JACOB SECHLER (1854-1951) [American politician; leader of "Coxey's Army"]
General Coxey
Coy Banton. See: NORWOOD, VICTOR GEORGE CHARLES
Coya. See: KNUTSON, CORNELIA GJESDAL
COYNE, JOSEPH E. (1918-) [American reporter, editor and author]
William O. Berch
COYSEVOX, ANTOINE (1640-1720) [French sculptor of Spanish origin]
The Van Dyck of Sculpture
Cozy. See: COLE, WILLIAM R.
COZZENS. See also: COUSINS
COUZENS
COZZENS, FREDERICK SWARTWOUT (1818-69) [American humorist, essayist and poet]
Richard Haywarde
Crab. See: EVERS, JOHN JOSEPH
CRABBE, CLARENCE LINDEN (1909-) [American swimming star and motion picture actor]
Buster Crabbe
Crabshaw, Timothy. See: LONGSTREET, AUGUSTUS BALDWIN
CRABTREE CHARLOTTE (1847-1924) [American actress]
Lotta Crabtree
Crack-Down. See: JOHNSON, HUGH SAMUEL
Crack-Down Czar of the N.R.A., The. See: JOHNSON, HUGH SAMUEL
Crack Downs, King of the Never-Made-Good. See: JOHNSON, HUGH SAMUEL
Cracker. See: SCHALK, RAYMOND WILLIAM
Crackers. See: EARLY, JUBAL ANDERSON
Craddock, Charles Egbert. See: MURFREE, MARY NOAILLES

Craft, The Laureate of the
Gentle. See:
SACHS, HANS
CRAGG, MARIE (1870-1951)
[British stage and screen character actress]
Marie Ault
CRAIG, ALEXANDER GEORGE (1897-) [British poet and author]
Alec Craig
Arthur Craik
Craig, David. See:
TUCKER, JAMES
Craig, Denys. See:
STOLL, DENNIS GRAY
CRAIG, EDWARD ANTHONY (1905-) [British art director]
Edward Carrick
Craig, Georgia. See:
DERN, PEGGY GADDIS
CRAIG, ISA (1831-1903)
[Scottish author and poet]
Isa
Craig, James. See:
MEADOR, JAMES
Craig, John Eland. See:
CHIPPERFIELD, JOSEPH EUGENE
Craig, Larry. See:
COUGHRAN, LARRY C.
Craig, Lee. See:
SANDS, LEO GEORGE
CRAIG, MARY FRANCIS (1923-)
[American author]
Mary Francis Shura
Craig, Michael. See:
GREGSON, MICHAEL
Craig, Peggy. See:
KREIG, MARGARET B.
Craig Stevens. See:
SHEKLES, GAIL
CRAIGHILL, WILLIAM PRICE (1833-1909) [American general officer and construction engineer]
The Father of Our Modern Fortifications
CRAIGIE, PEARL MARY TERESA RICHARDS (1867-1906)
[American novelist and playwright]
John Oliver Hobbes
Craik, Arthur. See:
CRAIG, ALEXANDER GEORGE
CRAIK, DINAH MARIA MULOCK (1826-87) [English novelist]
Miss Mulock
Craille, Wesley. See:
ROWLAND, DONALD SYDNEY
CRAMER. See also:
KRAMER
KREMER
CRAMER, ROGER M. (1906-)
[American professional baseball player]
Doc Cramer
CRANACH, LUCAS (1515-86)
[German painter and etcher]
The Younger
Cranberry. See:
GIFFORD, CHARLES L.
Cranbrook, James L. See:
EDWARDS, WILLIAM BENNETT
CRANDALL, MILTON (fl. 1928)
[American marathon dance promoter]
Doc Crandall
The Professor
CRANDON, MINA (1897-)
[Canadian-American fraudulent medium; exposed by ERICH WEISS (Harry Houdini)]
Margery the Boston Medium
Crane, Alex. See:
WILKES-HUNTER, RICHARD
Crane, Edna Temple. See:
EICHER, ETHEL ELIZABETH
CRANE, HAROLD HARTE (1899-1932) [American poet]
Hart Crane
Crane, Ichabod, Jr. See:
SMITH, FRANCIS SHUBAEL
CRANE, JAMES GORDON (1927-)

[American educator, artist and author]
Jim Crane
CRANE, RANDOLPH (1903-) [American stage and motion picture actor]
Randolph Scott
Crane, Robert. See: ROBERTSON, FRANK CHESTER
CRANE, STEPHEN (1871-1900) [American novelist]
Johnston Smith
Cranston, Charles H. See: JUDSON, EDWARD ZANE CARROLL
CRASSUS, MARCUS LICINIUS (115?-53 A.D.) [Roman politician and speculator]
Dives (The Rich)
Crater, The Hero of the. See: MAHONE, WILLIAM
Craven, Hawes, See: GREEN, HENRY HAWES CRAVEN
CRAWFORD, ABEL (c.1793-c.1850) [American pioneer in American White Mountains]
The Patriarch of the Hills
The Patriarch of the Mountains
CRAWFORD, BENNY ROSS, JR. (1934-) [American jazz musician (saxophones, piano, composer)]
Hank Crawford
CRAWFORD, CLIFFORD RANKIN (1902-) [American professional baseball player]
Pat
CRAWFORD, DANIEL (1870-1926) [Scottish missionary to Central Africa]
Dan Crawford
CRAWFORD, ETHAN ALLEN (1792-1848) [American strong man; resident of White Mountains in New Hampshire]
The Giant of the Hills
The White Mountain Giant
CRAWFORD, JESSE (1895-1962) [American organist, pianist and composer]
The Poet of the Organ
Crawford, Joan. See: LE SUEUR, LUCILLE
CRAWFORD, JOHN WALLACE (1847-1917) [American frontier scout and writer]
Captain Jack
CRAWFORD, SAMUEL EARL (1880-) [American professional baseball player]
Wahoo Sam
CRAWFORD, WILLIAM (1732-82) [American army officer and Indian fighter]
The Big Captain
CRAWFURD, OSWALD (1834-1909) [English author and poet]
Archibald Banks
John Dangerfield
John Latouche
Humphrey St. Kayne
George Windle Sandys
Joseph Strange
Alex Frecke Turner
Crayon, Geoffrey. See: IRVING, WASHINGTON
Crayon, Geoffrey, Gent. See: IRVING, WASHINGTON
Crayon, Porte. See: STROTHER, DAVID HUNTER
Crazy. See: DOW, LORENZO; MARSH, SYLVESTER
Crazy Jane. See: LA LOCA, JOANNA
CREAM, ARNOLA RAYMOND (1914-) [American professional boxer; world's heavyweight champion]
Jersey Joe Walcott
CREASEY, JOHN (1908-) [British author of detective stories]
Gordon Ashe
Norman Deane
Michael Halliday
Kyle Hunt
Peter Manton

J. J. Marric
Richard Martin
Anthony Morton
Ken Ranger
William K. Reilly
Tex Riley
Jeremy York
Creator of French Landscape Gardening, The. See: LENÔTRE, ANDRÉ
Creator of the New Comedy, The. See: ARISTOPHANES
MENANDER
Crébillon. See: JOLYOT, PROSPER, SIEUR DE CRAIS-BILLON
Credit in North Carolina, The Father of Rural. See: HILL, JOHN SPRUNT
CREECH, WILLIAM (1745-1815) [Scottish essayist, letter writer and publisher]
Theophrastus
Creepy, Old. See: KARPOVIECZ, FRANCIS ALBIN
CREESE, IRENE (1912-) [British stage and motion picture actress]
René Ray
CREHAN, ADA (1860-1916) [American actress]
Ada Rehan
Creighton. See also: Creyton
Creighton Hale. See: FITZGERALD, PATRICK
Creston. See: LANE-JACKSON, NICHOLAS
CRÈVECOEUR, MICHEL-GUILLAUME JEAN DE (1735-1813) [French-American agriculturist and travel writer]
Agricola
J. Hector St. John
St. John De Crèvecoeur
Creyton. See also: Creighton
Creyton, Paul. See: TROWBRIDGE, JOHN TOWNSEND
Crib, Tom. See: MOORE, THOMAS
CRIBB, TOM (1781-1848) [English pugilist]
The Black Diamond
Criblecoblis, Otis. See: DUKINFIELD, WILLIAM CLAUDE
CRICHTON, JAMES (1560-82) [Scottish athlete, scholar, poet and linguist]
The Admirable
The Admirable Crichton
CRICHTON, KYLE SAMUEL (1896-1960) [American editor and author]
Robert Forsythe
Crichton of Our City Politicians, The Admirable. See: HALL, ABRAHAM OAKEY
Cricketers, The Black Prince of. See: RANJITSINHJI, PRINCE
Crier, The Town. See: WOOLLCOTT, ALEXANDER HUMPHREYS
Crime Detection, The Edison of. See: HEINRICH, EDWARD OSCAR
Crime, The Napoleon of. See: WORTH, ADAM
Criminal Bar, The Father of the. See: HOWE, WILLIAM FREDERICK
Criminologists, The Dean of the American. See: SUTHERLAND, DR. EDWIN H.
Crinkle, Nym. See: WHEELER, ANDREW CARPENTER
CRIPPEN, DR. HAWLEY HARVEY (1860?-1910) [American murderer of his wife CORA]
John Philo Robinson
Dr. Crippen
Cris. See also: Chris
Kris
Cris Williams. See: DE CRISTOFORO, R.J.

CRISLER, HERBERT ORIN (1899-) [American football coach]
Fritz Crisler
The Lord
Crispin-Cataline. See: D'EPREMESNIL, JEAN JACQUES DUVAL
Crispin, Edmund. See: MONTGOMERY, ROBERT BRUCE
CRISS, WILLIAM (1927-) [American jazz musician (alto saxophone)]
Sonny Criss
CRISTILLO, LOUIS (1906-59) [American comedian]
Lou Costello
Cristóbal Colón. See: COLUMBUS, CHRISTOPHER
Cristoforo Colombo. See: COLUMBUS, CHRISTOPHER
Cristy, R.J. See: DE CRISTOFORO, R.J.
CRITCHETT, RICHARD CLAUDE (1853-1928) [American author]
R.C. Carton
Critic. See: MARTIN, BASIL KINGSLEY
Critical Philosophy, The Founder of the. See: KANT, IMMANUEL
Criticism, The Father of English. See: DRYDEN, JOHN
Criticism, The Father of German. See: LESSING, GOTTHOLD EPHRAIM
Criticism, The Sainte-Beuve of English. See: ARNOLD, MATTHEW
Critics, The Dean of the Dramatic. See: MANTLE, ROBERT BURNS
Criticus. See: HARCOURT, MELVILLE
ROE, FREDERIC GORDON
CRITTENTON, CHARLES NELSON (1833-1909) [American businessman, evangelist and humanitarian]
The Merchant Evangelist
CRIVELLI, UBERTO (died 1187) [Supreme Pontiff of Roman Catholic Church]
Pope Urban III
CRNJANSKI, MILOS (1893-) Hungarian-British educator and author]
C.R. Mill
Croakers & Co., joint pseud. of JOSEPH RODMAN DRAKE (1795-1820) and FITZ-GREEN HALLECK (1790-1867) [American poets]
CROALL, JOHN (1898-) [British motion picture actor]
John Stuart
CROCETTI, DINO (1917-) [American singer, actor and entertainer]
Dean Martin
CROCKER, CHARLES. See: Big Four, The
CROCKETT, DAVID (1786-1836) [American pioneer, hunter and politician]
Davy Crockett
The Münchausen of the West
Crockett Johnson. See: LEISK, DAVID JOHNSON
Croesus of the Senate, The. See: COUZENS, JAMES
Croesus, The World War. See: McADOO, WILLIAM GIBBS
Crofts, James. See: SCOTT, JAMES
Croise, Jacques. See: SCHAKOVSKOY, PRINCESS ZINAIDA
CROKER, RICHARD (1841-1922) [Irish-American politician]
Boss Croker
Dick Croker
CROLY, JANE CUNNINGHAM (1829-1901) [American journalist]
The First American Newspaper woman
Jenny June
CROME, JOHN (1768-1821) [English landscape painter]
The English Hobbema
Old Crome

CROME, JOHN BERNAY (1794-1842) [English landscape painter]
Young Crome
CROMIE, ALICE HAMILTON (1914-) [American author]
Alice Hamilton
Vivian Mort
Crompton, John. See: LAMBURN, JOHN BATTERSBY CROMPTON
CROMPTON, MARGARET NORAH MAIR (1901-) [British author]
Margaret Mair
Crompton, Richmal. See: LAMBURN, RICHMAL CROMPTON
Cromwell, Grandison. See: MOTIER, MARIE JEAN PAUL ROCH YVES GILBERT
Cromwell Murray. See: MORGAN, MURRAY
Cromwell of America, Would-be. See: ADAMS, SAMUEL
Cromwell of New America. See: ADAMS, SAMUEL
CROMWELL, OLIVER (1599-1658) [English revolutionist, general officer and statesman]
Ironsides
Lord Protector of England
The Man of Sin
Noll
Nosey
Old Noll
The Sagest of the Usurpers
CROMWELL, RICHARD (1626-1712) [English statesman]
Lord Protector of England
Queen Dick
Cromwell, Richard. See: RADEBAUGH, ROY
CROMWELL, THOMAS (c.1485-1540) [English statesman; Earl of Essex]
The Hammer of the Monks
The Maul of the Monks
CRONIN, JOSEPH EDWARD (1906-) [American sports executive; former professional baseball player]
Joe Cronin
Cronus, Diodorus. See: TAYLOR, RICHARD
CROOK, GEORGE (1828-90) [American general officer]
The Gray Fox
Crookback. See: RICHARD III
Crooner, The. See: VALLEE, HUBERT PRIOR
Crooning Troubadour, The. See: LUCANESE, NICK
CROSBIE. See also: COSBY
CROSBY
Crosby
CROSBIE, HUGH PROVAN (1912-) [Scottish banker and author]
John Carrick
CROSBY [Crosby]. See also: COSBY
CROSBIE
Crosby, Fanny. See: VAN ALSTYNE, MRS. FRANCES JANE CROSBY
CROSBY, GEORGE ROBERT (1913-) [American jazz musician (leader, singer)]
Bob Crosby
CROSBY, HARRY LILLIS (1904-) [American singer and actor]
Bing Crosby
Der Bingle
The Groaner
Croset, Paule. See: CORDAY, PAULA
CROSS, CLAIRE (1932-) [English educator, archivist and author]
M. Claire Cross
CROSS, COLIN JOHN (1928-) [British journalist and author]
John Weir
Cross, James. See: PARRY, HUGH JONES
Cross Knight, The Red. See: GEORGE, ST.
CROSS, MARY ANN (MARIAN) EVANS (1819-80) [English novelist]

George Eliot
CROSS, OLIVER HARLAN (1870-) [American politician, representative from Texas]
By Ganny Cross
Cross, Right. See: ARMSTRONG, PAUL
Cross, St. John of the. See: ÁLVAREZ, JUAN DE YAPES
Cross, Stewart. See: DRAGO, HENRY SINCLAIR
Cross, The Mother of the Red. See: BARTON, CLARISSA HARLOWE
CROSS, WILBUR LUCIUS (1862-1948) [American politician; Governor of Connecticut]
Uncle Toby
CROSS, ZORA BERNICE MAY (1890-) [Australian author]
Bernice May
Crosscountry. See: CAMPBELL, THOMAS F.
CROSSEN, KENDELL FOSTER (1910-) [American author]
Bennett Barclay
M.E. Chaber
Ken Crossen
Richard Foster
Christopher Monig
Clay Richards
Crosser of the Balkans (Sabalkanski). See: DIEBITSCH, HANS KARL FRIEDRICH, COUNT
CROSSER, ROBERT (1874-) [Scottish-born American lawyer and politician]
The Father of Ohio Labor
CROTHERS, SHERMAN (1910-) [American jazz musician (guitar, singer, comedian)]
Scat Man
CROUCH, JACK ALBERT (1905-) [American professional baseball player]
Roxey
Crouchback. See: EDMUND
RICHARD III
CROW, FRANCIS LUTHER (1905-) [American jazz musician (singer and composer)]
Frank Luther
Crowd. See: Jim-Jim Crowd, The
CROWE, BETTINA LUM (1911-) [American author
Peter Lum
CROWELL, MRS. MARY REED (1847-1934) [American author]
Emerce
Crowfield, Christopher. See: STOWE, HARRIET BEECHER
Crown Prince of the New Deal, The. See: ROOSEVELT, JAMES
Crown Prince, The. See: McADOO, WILLIAM GIBBS
CROWNE, JOHN (1640-1712) [Anglo-American playwright]
The First Harvard Playwright
CROWNINSHIELD, FRANK (1872-1947) [American editor and author]
Arthur Loring Bruce
Crowquill, Alfred, joint pseud. of ALFRED HENRY FORRESTER (1804-72) and his brother CHARLES ROBERT FORRESTER (1803-50) [British authors and illustrators]
Crowquill, Alfred. See also: FORRESTER, CHARLES ROBERT
Crows. See: Two Black Crows
CROWTHER, WILMA BERYL (1918-) [English author]
Wilma George
CRUDEN, ALEXANDER (1701-70) [London bookseller and author]
The Corrector
Cruel, Pedro el. See: PEDRO (PETER)
Cruel, Peter the. See: PEDRO (PETER)
Cruel, The. See: CHRISTIAN II

Cruikshank, The American.
See: JOHNSON, DAVID CLAYPOOLE
CRUMP, EDWARD HULL (1875-1954) [American politician]
Boss Crump
CRUMP, JAMES IRVING (1887-) [American editor and author]
Irving Crump
Crumpet, Peter. See:
BUCKLEY, FERGUS REID
Crusader. See:
SALEEBY, CALEB WILLIAMS
Crusca, Della. See:
MERRY, ROBERT
CRUSE, HELOISE (1919-) [American newspaper columnist]
Heloise
Crusoe, Robinson. See:
ANDERSON, JAMES
CRUZ, JUANA INÉS DE LA (1651-95) [Mexican poet, scholar and nun]
The Tenth Muse
Cruze, James. See:
BOSEN, JENS CRUZ
Cu Cullin. See:
SETANTA
Cub. See:
TEAGARDEN, CLOIS LEE
Cub, The Young. See:
FOX, CHARLES JAMES
Cubism, The Father of. See:
PICASSO, PABLO RUIZ Y
Cúchares. See:
HERRERA, FRANCISCO ARJONA
Cuchulain. See:
SETANTA
Cuevas, Ramón de las. See:
HARRINGTON, MARK RAYMOND
Cuffs, Collars and. See:
CLUETT, ERNEST HAROLD
CUGAT, XAVIER (1900-) [Spanish-American caricaturist and jazz musician (violin, leader, composer)]
Cugie
Cugie. See:
CUGAT, XAVIER
CULLEN, HUGH TROY (1881-) [American oilman, business executive and philanthropist]
The King of the Texas Wildcatters
CULLEN, WILLIAM LAWRENCE (1920-) [American radio and television entertainer]
Bill Cullen
Cullin, Cu. See:
SETANTA
Culture, The Apostle of. See:
ARNOLD, MATTHEW
Culture, The Father of American Grape. See:
LONGWORTH, NICHOLAS
Cultured Perelman. See:
SHULMAN, MAX
Culver, Kathryn. See:
DRESSER, DAVIS
CULVER, ROLLAND PIERCE (1908-) [American jazz musician (drums)]
Rollie Culver
CUMBERLAND, MARTEN (1892-) [British editor and author]
R. Laugier
Kevin O'Hara
Cumberland, Muse of. See:
BLAMIRE, SUSANNA
Cumberland Poet, The. See:
WORDSWORTH, WILLIAM
CUMBERLAND, RICHARD (1631-1718) [English philosopher]
Founder of the Utilitarian School of Philosophy
CUMBERLAND, RICHARD (1732-1811) [English playwright]
The English Terence
The Man Without a Skin
The Terence of England
Cumberland, The Spy of the.
See: CUSHMAN, PAULINE
CUMBERLAND, WILLIAM AUGUSTUS, DUKE OF (1721-65) [British general officer; 3rd son of

GEORGE II of England
The Bloody Butcher
The Bloody Duke of Cumberland
Butcher Cumberland
CUMMING, ROUALEYN GEORGE GORDON (1820-66) [Scottish traveler and sportsman in South Africa]
The Lion Hunter
CUMMINGS, BRUCE FREDERICK (1889-1919) [English diarist and essayist]
W. N. P. Barbellion
Cummings, Constance. See: HALVERSTADT, CONSTANCE
CUMMINGS, EDWARD ESTLIN (1894-) [American author]
E. E. Cummings
Lower Case Cummings
CUMMINGS, FRED (18??-1945) [Colorado farmer and politician]
Sugar Beets
Cummings, Richard. See: GARDNER, RICHARD
CUMMINGS, SCOTT (1846-) [American poet]
The Pilgrim Bard
CUMPANAS, ANA (1891-1947) [Rumanian-American procuress; friend of JOHN HERBERT DILLINGER]
Anna Sage
Katie from the Kostur Hotel
CUNATI, EDWIGE (1907-) [French actress]
Edwige Feuillère
Cunctator (The Delayer). See: VERROCOSUS, QUINTUS FABIUS MAXIMUS
CUNHA, MARÍA DE CARMO MIRANDA DE (1904-55) [Brazilian singer, dancer and motion picture actress]
The Brazilian Bombshell
Carmen Miranda
Cunning President, The. See: MESSER, DOCTOR ASA
Cunning Teacher, The (Doctor Subtilis). See: DUNS SCOTUS, JOHN
CUNNINGHAM, ALBERT BENJAMIN (1888-) [American author]
Garth Hale
CUNNINGHAM, ALLAN (1784-1842) [Scottish poet and man of letters]
Honest Allan
Honest Allan Cunningham
Cunningham, E. V. See: FAST, HOWARD MELVIN
CUNNINGHAM, ELIJAH WILLIAM (1896-1960) [American writer]
Bill Cunningham
CUNNINGHAM, EUGENE (1896-1957) [American author]
Leigh Carder
CUNNINGHAM, JAMES (1823-64) [Irish-American comedian]
James Seymour
CUPPY, WILLIAM JACOB (1884-1949) [American humorist]
Will Cuppy
Curator of the Secrets of 82 Nations, The. See: HAMMARSKJÖLD, DAG HJALMAR CARL AGNE
Curé de Meúdon, The (The Parish Priest of Meudon). See: RABELAIS, FRANÇOIS
Curé, The Perfect. See: STEAD, JAMES HENRY
CURIE, MARIE SKLODOWSKA (1867-1934) [French physicist]
Madame Curie
Curley. See: MAHR, HERMAN CARL
CURLEY, DOROTHY NYREN (1927-) [American author]
Dorothy Nyren
Curly. See: RUSSELL, DILLON
Curly Howard. See:

Stooges, The Three
Curmudgeon, The. See:
ICKES, HAROLD LeCLAIR
CURRAN, MONA ELISA (fl. 1951-63) [British journalist and author]
Giles Merton
Adrian Murray
Mervyn Thomas
Currer Bell. See:
BRONTË, CHARLOTTE
CURRIE [Currie]. See also:
CARRÉ
Carré
Curry
CURRIE, LADY MARY MONTGOMERY LAMB (1843-1905) [British poet, novelist, story writer and essayist]
Violet Fane
Currie, Thomas Stewart. See:
RICHARDSON, ANTHONY
Currio, Tyman. See:
CORYELL, JOHN RUSSELL
Curro. See:
CARO, FRANCISCO MARTÍN
GIRÓN, FRANCISCO
Curro Guillén. See:
RODRÍGUEZ, FRANCISCO HERRERA
Curry. See also:
CARRÉ
Carré
CURRIE
Currie
Curry, Avon. See:
BOWDEN, JEAN
Cursed, The. See:
CONOMOR (COMORRE)
Curt. See:
GOWDY, CURTIS
MASSEY, D. CURTIS
Curt Arno. See:
PETERS, CURTIS ARNOUX
Curt Brandon. See:
BISHOP, CURTIS KENT
Curt Carroll. See:
BISHOP, CURTIS KENT
Curt-hose. See:
ROBERT II
CURTIN, ANDREW GREGG (fl. mid 19th cent.) [American politician; Governor of Pennsylvania during Civil War period]
The Great War Governor
The Soldier's Friend
Curtin, Phyllis. See:
SMITH, PHYLLIS
Curtis, Alan. See:
NEBERROTH, HAROLD
Curtis Bill Pepper. See:
PEPPER, CURTIS G.
CURTIS, CHARLES (1860-1936) [American statesman; Vice President of the United States]
Big Chief
CURTIS-GAGLIARDI, ANTONIO FURST DE (1901-) [Italian comedian]
Toto
CURTIS, GEORGE TICKNOR (1812-94) [American constitutional author and lawyer]
Peter Boylston
CURTIS, GEORGE WILLIAM (1824-92) [American editor, orator and author]
An Old Bachelor
Howadji
Curtis, John. See:
PREBBLE, JOHN EDWARD CURTIS
Curtis, Mann. See:
KURTZ, MANNY
Curtis, Marjorie. See:
PREBBLE, MARJORIE MARY CURTIS
Curtis, Patricia. See:
CARLON, PATRICIA BERNARDETTE
Curtis, Peter. See:
LOFTS, NORAH ROBINSON
Curtis, Tom. See:
PENDOWER, JACQUES
Curtis, Tony. See:
SCHWARTZ, BERNARD
Curtis, Will. See:
NUNN, WILLIAM CURTIS
Curtiz, Michael. See:
KERTESZ, MIHALY
Curtmantle. See:
HENRY II
ROBERT II

Curzon, Sam. See:
KRASNEY, SAMUEL A.
CURZON-SUGGERS, WILLIAM (1860-) [British clergyman and author]
Esegar
Curzon, Virginia. See:
HAWTON, HECTOR
CUSHING, CHARLES CYPRIAN STRONG (1874-1941) [American playwright]
Tom Cushing
CUSHING, JOSEPH (1818-84) [American circus impresario]
Colonel Cushing
Cushman, Clara. See:
HAVEN, EMILY BRADLEY NEAL
CUSHMAN, PAULINE (1835-93) [American actress and Civil War spy]
The Spy of the Cumberland
CUSTER, GEORGE ARMSTRONG (1839-76) [American general officer]
The Boy General
CUSTIS, GEORGE WASHINGTON PARKE (1781-1857) [American playwright]
Old Man Eloquent
Cut Rate. See:
CARPENTER, TERRY McGOVERN
CUTFORTH, JOHN ASHLIN (1911-) [British educator and author]
John Ashlin
Cuthbert Bede. See:
BRADLEY, EDWARD
CUTHRELL, MRS. FAITH BALDWIN (1893-) [American author]
Faith Baldwin
CUTLER, AUGUSTUS WILLIAM (1829-97) [American educator]
The Father of the Free School System in New Jersey
CUTLER, IVOR (1923-) [British singer, humorist and author]
Knifesmith
CUTLER, MANASSEH (1742-1823) [American educator; active in the establishment of Ohio University]
The Father of Ohio University
The Father of State Universities
Cutler, Samuel. See:
FOLSOM, FRANKLIN BREWSTER
CUTNER, SOLOMON (1902-) [English pianist]
Solomon
Cutpurse, Moll. See:
FRITH, MARY
CUTSHALL, ROBERT DEWEES (1911-) [American jazz musician (trombone)]
Cutty Cutshall
CUTTING, BRONSON (1910-35) [American politician; senator from New Mexico]
Harvard's Gift to the West
Cutty. See:
CUTSHALL, ROBERT DEWEES
Cuy. See:
CUYLER, HAZEN S.
Cuyler, Duke. See:
MESERVE, COLONEL ARTHUR LIVERMORE
CUYLER, HAZEN S. (1899-) [American professional baseball player]
Cuy.
Kiki
Cuyler Pine. See:
PECK, ELLEN
Cuyler, Stephen. See:
BATES, BARBARA SNEDEKER
CUYP, JACOB GERRITS (c.1575-1649) [Dutch portrait painter]
Old Cuyp
Cy. See:
PFIRMAN, CHARLES H.
YOUNG, DENTON TRUE
Cy, Arizona. See:
COWDRICK, JESSE C.
Cyclone, The Pacific. See:
SMITH, HOLLAND McTYEIRE

Cyclopedia of Knowledge, The.
See: BROWN, JOHN JACKSON
Cyclops. See:
ANTIGONUS I
Cyd. See also:
Sid
Cyd Charisse. See:
FINKLEA, TULA ELLICE
Cymon. See:
SIMON
Simon
Simeon
SOMERBY, FREDERICK THOMAS
Cynam. See:
EVANS-JONES, ALBERT
Cynthia Millburn. See:
BROOKS, ANNE TEDLOCK
Cynthia Pilkington. See:
HORNE, CYNTHIA MIRIAM
Cyprian. See:
CYPRIANUS, THASCIUS CAECILIUS
Cyprian St. Cyr. See:
BERNE, ERIC LENNARD
CYPRIANUS, THASCIUS CAECILIUS (c. 200-258) [Christian church father and martyr]
Cyprian
Cyr de Brant. See:
HIGGINSON, JOSEPH VINCENT
Cyril. See:
Judd, Cyril
Cyril Carfage. See:
JENNINGS, LESLIE NELSON
CYRIL OF ALEXANDRIA, ST. (376-444) [Christian ecclesiastic and theologian]
The Champion of the Virgin
The Doctor of the Incarnation
Cyril, St. See:
Apostles to the Slavs
CONSTANTINE
Cyrrhestes. See:
ANDRONICUS
CYRUS (c. 600-529 B.C.) [King of Persia]
The Elder
The Great
Kurshu
CYRUS (424-401 B.C.) [Persian prince and satrap]
The Younger
CYRUS [Cyrus]. See also:
SYRUS
Cyrus Fisher. See:
TEILHET, DARWIN
Cyzicenus. See:
ANTIOCHUS IX
Czar. See:
REED, THOMAS BRACKETT
Czar of American Baseball, The. See:
LANDIS, KENESAW MOUNTAIN
Czar of Baseball, The. See:
LANDIS, KENESAW MOUNTAIN
Czar of Boxing, The. See:
MULDOON, WILLIAM
Czar of Pennsylvania Politics, The. See:
CAMERON, SIMON
Czar of the District, The. See:
BLANTON, GEORGE LINDSAY
Czar of the Liquor Industry, The. See:
MORGAN, WILLIAM FORBES
Czar of the N.R.A., The Crack-Down. See:
JOHNSON, HUGH SAMUEL
Czar of the National Pastime, The. See:
LANDIS, KENESAW MOUNTAIN
Czar, The Iron. See:
NICHOLAS I
Czar, The Liquor. See:
MORGAN, WILLIAM FORBES
Czar, The N.R.A. See:
JOHNSON, HUGH SAMUEL
Czech Nationalist School of Composition, The Father of the. See:
SMETANA, BEDŘICH
CZERNY, GEORGE (1766-1817)

[Serbian prince and governor]
Karadjordje (Black George)
CZUKOR. See also:
ZUKOR
CZUKOR, BARBARA BRANTINGHAM (1920-) [American motion picture actress]
Barbara Britton

D

D. A. See:
CAMERON, DONALD ALLEN
D. A. Esrom. See:
MORSE, THEODORA
D. B. Lewis. See:
BIXBY, JEROME LEWIS
D. Collins. See:
BULLEID, H. A. V.
D. Green. See:
CASEWIT, CURTIS
D. H. See:
LAWRENCE, DAVID HERBERT
D. J. Mann. See:
FREEMAN, JAMES DILLET
D. L. See:
PAPE, DONNA LUGG
D. R. Shackleton Bailey. See:
BAILEY, DAVID ROY SHACKLETON
D. Vernor. See:
CASEWIT, CURTIS
D. X. See:
BIBLE, DANA XENOPHON
DABOLL, NATHAN (1750-1818) [American educator and almanac maker]
Edmund Freebetter
D'ABRUZZA, ALPHONSO (1914-) [American radio, stage and motion picture actor]
Robert Alda
Da Cadore. See:
VECELLI (VECELLIO) TIZIANO
D'ACOSTA, DONALD BARRY (c. 1916-) [American motion picture actor]
Don Barry
DA COSTA, JACOB MENDEZ (1833-1900) [American physician]
The Physician's Physician
Dacre. See:
BALSDON, JOHN PERCY VYVIAN DACRE
Dad. See:
NELSON, WILLIAM
PRICE, STERLING C.
ROBERTS, THEODORE
Daddy. See:
BROWNING, EDWARD
EDWARDS, EDWIN BRANFORD
Daddy Longlegs. See:
McADOO, WILLIAM GIBBS
Daddy of the Baby, The. See:
JOHNSON, ANDREW
DADE, ROBERT E. (1915-) [American jazz musician (leader, trumpet, drums)]
Bob Astor
Daffy. See:
DEAN, PAUL DEE
Daft, Tennyson J. See:
MORGAN, THOMAS P.
D'AGNOLO, DONATO (1444-1514) [Italian architect]
Bramante
Bramante Lazzari
Dago, The. See:
SINATRA, FRANCIS ALBERT
Dagonet. See:
SIMS, GEORGE ROBERT
Dagover, Lil. See:
LILETTS, MARTA MARIA
DAHLANDER, NILS-BERTIL (1928-) [Swedish jazz musician (drums)]
Bert Dahlander
DAILEY. See also:
Daley
DALLY
DALY
Daly
DAILEY, CATHERINE (1915-) [American comedienne, singer and actress]
Cass Daley

DAINTON. See also:
DANTON
DAINTON, WILLIAM COURTNEY (1920-) [English author]
Courtney Dainton
Dainty Baby June the Pocket-Sized Pavlova. See:
HOVICK, JUNE
Daisey. See: SMITH, FRANCIS SHUBAEL
Daisy. See:
ASHFORD, MARGARET MARY
Daisy Ashford of America, The. See: WAINRIGHT, VIRGINIA
Dale. See:
MESSICK, DALIA
Dale, Alan. See:
COHEN, ALFRED J.
Dale, Annan. See:
JOHNSON, JAMES WESLEY
Dale Colombo. See:
MONROE, KEITH
Dale, Darley. See:
STEELE, FRANCESCA MARIA
Dale, Dash. See:
RATHBONE, ST. GEORGE HENRY
Dale Evans. See:
SMITH, FRANCES OCTAVIA
Dale, J.S. of. See:
STIMSON, FREDERIC JESUP
Dale, Jean. See:
DIESTELHORST, H. JEAN
DALE, MARGARET JESSY (1911-) [English author]
Margaret J. Miller
Dale Michaels. See:
RIFKIN, SHEPARD
Dale O'Hara. See:
GILLESE, JOHN PATRICK
DALE, RICHARD (1756-1826) [American commodore and naval hero]
Fighting Dick Dale
Dale White. See:
PLACE, MARIAN TEMPLETON
Dale Wilmer. See:
Miller, Wade
Daley. See also:
DAILEY
DALLY
DALY
Daly
Daley, Cass. See:
DAILEY, CATHERINE
Dall, John. See:
THOMPSON, JOHN JENNER
D'Allard, Hunter. See:
BALLARD, WILLIS TODHUNTER
Dallas, Sandra. See:
ATCHINSON, SANDRA DALLAS
DALLWITZ-WEGNER, RICHARD VON (1873-) [German author]
Richard Weda
Richard Wegner
DALLY. See also:
DAILEY
Daley
DALY
Daly
DALLY, ANN MULLINS (1926-) [British physician and author]
Ann Mullins
Dalton, Clive. See:
CLARK, FREDERICK STEPHEN
Dalton, Dorothy. See:
KUEHN, DOROTHY DALTON
DALTON, WILLIAM (1883-1941) [American actor and female impersonator]
Julian Eltinge
DALY [Daly]. See:
DAILEY
Daley
DALLY
Daly, Jim. See:
STRATEMEYER, EDWARD L.
DALY, JOHN AUGUSTIN (1838-99) [American playwright and theatrical producer]
Augustin Daly
Daly, Maureen. See:

McGIVERN, MAUREEN DALY

DALYELL (DALZELL), THOMAS (1599-1685) [British soldier; afterwards in the service of the Russians]
The Muscovy General

DALZEL, JOB PATRICK (1913-) [British sailor and author]
Peter Dalzel

DALZELL. See:
DALYELL (DALZELL)

DALZELL, JOHN (1845-1927) [American politician; congressman from Pennsylvania]
The Father of the House

DAMASCENUS. See:
JOHN OF DAMASCUS (JOHANNES DAMASCENUS)

DAMASCUS. See:
JOHN OF DAMASCUS (JOHANNES DAMASCENUS)

DAMASUS (died 384) [Supreme Pontiff of Roman Catholic Church]
Pope Damasus I
St. Damasus

Damasus II, Pope. See:
COUNT POPPO OF BAVARIA

Dame de Beauté, La. See:
SOREL, AGNES

Dame Emma. See:
ALBANI, MARIE LOUISE EMMA CÉCILE LA JEUNESSE

DAME, LAWRENCE (1898-) [American journalist, lecturer, correspondent and author]
Baron Pomfret

Dame Margot Fonteyn de Arias. See: HOOKHAM, MARGARET

Dame Shirley. See:
CLAPPE, LOUISE AMELIA KNAPP

DAMERON, TADLEY EWING (1917-65) [American jazz musician (piano, composer)]
Tadd Dameron

Dames, Le Philosophe des. See:
CARO, ELME MARIE

D'AMICO, HENRY JOHN (1915-) [American jazz musician (clarinet)]
Hank d'Amico

Damien, Father. See:
VEUSTER, JOSEPH DAMIEN DE

Damita Jo. See:
BLANC, DAMITA JO DE

Damita, Lili. See:
CARRÉ, LILLIAN

Damnation, The Artist of. See:
EDWARDS, JONATHAN

Damned, Abdul the. See:
ABDUL HAMID II

Damned, The Poet of the. See: ALIGHIERI, DURANTE

Damon. See:
RUNYON, ALFRED DAMON

Damone, Vic. See:
FARINOLA, VITO

Dampier, Claude. See:
COWAN, CLAUDE

DAMROSCH, WALTER JOHANNES (1862-1950) [German-American composer, conductor and music commentator]
The Dean of American Music

Damsel of Brittany, The. See:
ELEANOR OF BRITTANY

Dan. See:
BEARD, DANIEL CARTER
CRAWFORD, DANIEL
DILLINGER, JOHN HERBERT
GALLERY, DANIEL V.
McCARTY, DANIEL THOMAS, JR.
MARBLE, DANFORTH
THORNTON, DANIEL I. J.

Dan, Battery. See:
FINN, DANIEL E.

Dan, Black. See:
McFARLAND, DANIEL
WEBSTER, DANIEL

Dan De Quille. See:

WRIGHT, WILLIAM
Dan, Desperate. See: DILLINGER, JOHN HERBERT
Dan, Indian. See:
WEBSTER, DANIEL
Dan J. Stevens. See:
OVERHOLSER, WAYNE D.
Dan Leno. See:
GALVIN, GEORGE
Dan, Little Black. See:
WEBSTER, DANIEL
Dan Quin. See:
LEWIS, ALFRED HENRY
Dan Rice. See:
McLAREN, DANIEL
Dan Scott. See:
BARKER, S. OMAR
STRATEMEYER, EDWARD L.
Dan Temple. See: NEWTON, DWIGHT BENNETT
Dan Terry. See:
KOSTRABA, DANIEL
Dan, Uncle. See:
BEARD, DANIEL CARTER
Dana. See:
WYNTER, DAGMAR
Dana Scott. See:
ROBERTSON, CONSTANCE NOYES
DANA, WILLIAM (1924-) [American composer, actor and comedian]
Bill Dana
José Jiménez
Danari, Pochi (The Penniless) See: MAXIMILIAN I
Danbury News Man, The. See:
BAILEY, JAMES MONTGOMERY
Danby, Frank. See:
FRANKAU, JULIA
Dance, The Duse of the. See:
KOREFF, NORA
Dance, The First Lady of the American. See:
DENNIS, RUTH
DANCER, DANIEL (1716-94) [British miser]
The Pinner Miser
Dancing Chancellor, The. See:
HATTON, CHRISTOPHER
Dancing Fool, The. See:
McADOO, WILLIAM GIBBS
Dancing Hamlet. See:
DRAPER, PAUL
Dancing, The God of. See:
VESTRIS, GAETANO APOLLINO
DANCOURT, FLORENT CARTON (1661-1725) [French playwright and comedian]
The Teniers of Comedy
Dandies, The Last of the. See:
D'ORSAY, ALFRED GUILLAUME GABRIEL, COUNT
D'ANDOUINS, DIANE (died 1620) [Countess of Guiche and Grammont]
The Beautiful Corisande
Dandy. See:
WAYNE, ANTHONY
Dandy King, The. See:
MURAT, JOACHIM
Dandy of Country Music, The. See: DEAN, JIMMY RAY
Dandy, The Sublime. See:
LEWIS, MERIWETHER
Dane, Carl. See:
ADAMS, FRANK RAMSAY
Dane Clark. See:
ZANVILLE, BERNARD
Dane, Clemence. See:
ASHTON, WINIFRED
Dane, Hal. See:
MACFALL, CHAMBERS HALDANE COOKE
Dane, Mark. See:
AVALLONE, MICHAEL ANGELO, JR.
Dane, The Unmelancholy. See:
ROSENBAUM, BORGE
Dangerfield, Balfour. See:
McCLOSKEY, ROBERT
Dangerfield Burr. See:
INGRAHAM, COLONEL PRENTISS
Dangerfield, Clint. See:
NORWOOD, VICTOR GEORGE CHARLES
Dangerfield, Harry. See:
PATTEN, WILLIAM GILBERT
Dangerfield, John. See:
CRAWFURD, OSWALD
d'Angers, David. See:

DAVID, PIERRE JEAN
Dangle. See:
THOMPSON, ALEXANDER MATTOCK
DANICAN, FRANÇOIS ANDRÉ (1726-95) [French composer and chess player]
Philidor
DANIEL [Daniel]. See also:
Daniele
DANIELL
DANIELS
Daniels
Dan'l.
DANIEL, ARNAUD (ARNAUT) (fl. 12th cent.) [Provençal troubadour]
The Great Master of Love
Daniel Boone of Southern Kentucky, The. See:
LYNN, BENJAMIN
Daniel Boone of the Rockies, The. See:
BRIDGER, JAMES
Daniel De Foe. See:
FOE, DANIEL
Daniel Defoe. See:
FOE, DANIEL
Daniel Henry, Jun. See:
HOLMES, HENRY DANIEL
Daniel Lesueur. See:
LAPAUZE, JEANNE LOISEAU
Daniel Nash. See:
LOADER, WILLIAM REGINALD
Daniel Paul. See:
KESSEL, LIPMANN
Daniel-Rops. See:
PETIOT DANIEL-ROPS, HENRY
DANIEL, SAMUEL (1562-1616) [English poet]
The Well-languaged Daniel
Daniel Stern. See:
AGOULT, COMTESSE D', MARIE CATHERINE SOPHIE DE FLAVIGNY
Daniel, The God-like. See:
WEBSTER, DANIEL
Daniele. See also:
DANIEL
Daniel
DANIELL
DANIELS
Daniels
Dan'l
Daniele Delorme. See:
GIRARD, GABRIELLE
DANIELL. See also:
DANIEL
Daniel
Daniele
DANIELS
Daniels
Dan'l
DANIELL, ALBERT SCOTT (1906-) [British author]
David Scott Daniell
Richard Bowood
DANIELS [Daniels]. See also:
DANIEL
Daniel
Daniele
DANIELL
Dan'l
DANIELS, CHARLES N. (1878-1943) [American composer and publisher]
Neil Moret
Daniels, John S. See:
OVERHOLSER, WAYNE D.
DANIELS, VIRGINIA (1901-71) [American silent film actress]
Bebe Daniels
Danish Literature, The Founder of. See:
HOLBERG, LUDVIG
Danish Luther, The. See:
TAUSEN, HANS
Dan'l. See also:
DANIEL
Daniel
Daniele
DANIELL
DANIELS
Daniels
Dan'l, Uncle. See:
DREW, DANIEL
Dannay, Frederic. See:
Queen, Ellery
d'Annunzio, Gaetano. See:
RAMPAGNETTO, GAETANO
Danny Kaye. See:
KAMINSKY, DAVID DANIEL

Danny Thomas. See:
JACOBS, AMOS
Dano, Tony. See:
SOLDANO, ANTHONY
Dante Alighieri. See:
ALIGHIERI, DURANTE
Great Triumvirate of Italian Literature, The
Immortal Four of Italy, The.
Dante Gabriel Rossetti. See:
ROSSETTI, GABRIEL CHARLES DANTE
D'Antibes, Germain. See:
SIMENON, GEORGES
DANTON. See also:
DAINTON
DANTON, GEORGES JACQUES (1759-94) [French Revolutionist]
The Mirabeau of the Mob
D'ANTONGUOLLA, RODOLPHO ALFONSO RAFAELO PIERRE FILIBERT GUGLIELMO DI VALENTIN (1895-1926) [Italian-American motion picture actor]
Rudolph Guglielmi
The Screen's Greatest Lover
Rudolph Valentino
DANTZLER, LOUISE (1908-) [American motion picture actress]
Mary Brian
Danube, The Peasant of the. See: LEGENDRE, LOUIS
Danvers, Jack. See:
CASELEYR, CAMILLE AUGUSTE MARIE
Danville, The Student Nurse of. See:
BURCHARD, SAMUEL DICKINSON
Daphne du Blane. See:
GROOM, ARTHUR WILLIAM
Daphne Machin Goodall. See:
MACHIN GOODALL, DAPHNE
D'AQUINO, IVA IKUKO TOGURI (1916-) [American-born Japanese radio propagandist]
Tokyo Rose
D'Arblay, Madame. See:
BURNEY, FRANCES
Darby, J.N. See:
GOVAN, CHRISTINE NOBLE
Darby, John. See:
GARRETSON, JAMES EDMUND
DARBY, KENNETH LORIN (1909-) [American composer, conductor, arranger and singer]
Ken Darby
Darcel, Denise. See:
BILLECARD, DENISE
D'Arcy, Alex. See:
SARRUF, ALEXANDER
D'ARCY, COLIN (1912-) [American composer, conductor, arranger and pianist]
Billy Young
daRE, ALDO (1926-) [American motion picture actor]
Aldo Ray
Dare, Roland. See:
MORRIS, CHARLES SMITH
DARGAN, OLIVE TILFORD (fl. 1904-58) [American playwright and poet]
Fielding Burke
Darien, Peter. See:
BASSETT, WILLIAM B.K.
Darin. See also:
Darren
Darin, Bobby. See:
CASOTTO, ROBERT WALDEN
Daring, Hope. See:
JOHNSON, ANNA
Darío Rubén. See:
SARMIENTO, FELIX RUBÉN GARCÍA
DARIUS I (c. 550 B.C.-486 B.C.) [King of Persia]
The Great
The Huckster
Hystaspis
DARIUS II (died 404 B.C.) [King of Persia]
Ochus
DARIUS III (died 330 B.C.) [King of Persia]
Codomannus

Dark Angel of the Violin, The. See: SOUTH, EDWARD OTHA
Dark Destroyer, The. See: BARROW, JOSEPH LOUIS
Dark Horse President, The. See: HAYES, RUTHERFORD BIRCHARD
Dark Horse, The First. See: POLK, JAMES KNOX
Dark, Johnny. See: NORWOOD, VICTOR GEORGE CHARLES
Dark Philosopher, The. See: HERACLITUS
D'Arles, Henri. See: BEAUDE, HENRI
Darley Dale. See: STEELE, FRANCESCA MARIA
DARLEY, GEORGE (1795-1846) [English poet, novelist and critic]
John Lacy
DARLING [Darling]. See also: DORLING
Darling Child, Victory's. See: MASSÉNA, ANDRÉ
DARLING, JAY NORWOOD (1876-1962) [American cartoonist, author and leader in wild life conservation]
J.N. Ding
Ding Darling
Darling of America, The Grace. See: WILSON, IDA LEWIS
Darling of Spanish Romanticism, The Spoiled. See: MORAL, JOSÉ ZORRILLAY
DARLING, WILLIAM YOUNG (1885-) [Scottish author]
Sacheverell Smith
d'Arlington, Lobrano. See: DEUBLER, MARY
DARLINGTON, WILLIAM (1782-1863) [American botanist]
The Nestor of American Botany
D'ARMONT, MARIE ANNE CHARLOTTE CORDAY (1768-93) [French assassin of JEAN PAUL MARAT
Charlotte Corday
DARNELL, MANETTA ELOISA (1923-65) [American stage, television and motion picture actress]
Linda Darnell
Darragh. See: ALDRICH, CLARE CHAPLIN THOMAS
Darren. See also: Darin
Darren, James. See: ERCOLANI, JAMES
Darro, Frankie. See: JOHNSON, FRANK
Darry Dover. See: KHAURY, HERBERT BUCKINGHAM
D'Artagnan of the A.E.F., The. See: MacARTHUR, DOUGLAS
Darvi, Bella. See: WEGIER, BELLA
Darwell, Jane. See: WOODWARD, PATTI
DAS, PRAFULLA CHANDRA (1927-) [Indian author]
Subhadra-Nandan
Dash. See:
HAMMETT, SAMUEL DASHIELL
WEISS, THEO
Dash Dale. See: RATHBONE, ST. GEORGE HENRY
Dashiell. See: HAMMETT, SAMUEL DASHIELL
Dashing Phil. See: KEARNY, PHILIP
Dashmore, Frank. See: DOWNING, FRANCES MURDAUGH
DASHWOOD, MRS. EDMÉE ELIZABETH MONICA (1890-1943) [English novelist and short story writer]
E.M. Delafield
DASHWOOD, ROBERT JULIAN (1899-) [British politician and author]
Julian Hillas
DASS, PETER (1647-1708) [Norwegian poet]

The Father of Modern Norwegian Poetry
DASTAGIR SABU (1924-63) [Indian motion picture actor]
The Elephant Boy
Sabu
DAUDET, ALPHONSE (1840-97) [French novelist and humorist]
Baptistet
The French Dickens
Jean Froissart
Marie Gaston
Tartarin
Daugé, Henri. See: HAMMOND, HENRIETTA HARDY
Daughter of Sorrow, The. See: CHARLOTTE, MARIE THÉRÈSE
Daughter of the Confederacy, The. See: DAVIS, VARINA ANNE JEFFERSON
Daughter of the Confederacy. Winnie Davis, The. See: DAVIS, VARINA ANNE JEFFERSON
Daughter, The Sea King's. See: ALEXANDRA, CAROLINE MARIE CHARLOTTE LOUISA JULIA
Daughters, The Mother of a Thousand. See: AGNEW, ELIZA
Dauphin, Claude. See: FRANC-NOHAIN, CLAUDE
Dauphin, The Lost. See: WILLIAMS, ELEAZAR
Dauphin, The Second. See: LOUIS
DAVAUX, J.B. (died 1822) [French composer]
Father Rondo
Dave. See:
BARBOUR, DAVID MICHAEL
BERG, DAVID
GARROWAY, DAVID CUNNINGHAM
HILL, DAVID CHARLES
MORRAH, DAVID WARDLAW, JR.
RUBINOFF, DAVID
Dave Gardner. See: WEINGARTEN, DAVID
Dave Nichols. See: FROST, HELEN
Dave O'Brien. See: BARCLAY, DAVID
Dave, Red River. See: McENERY, DAVID
Dave Waldo. See: CLARKE, DAVID WALDO
Dave Warren. See: WIERSBE, WARREN WENDELL
Dave Wilson. See: FLOREN, LEE
Davenport, Adelaide. See: AIKEN, ALBERT W.
DAVENPORT, CHARLES (1895-1955) [American jazz musician (piano, singer)]
Cow Cow Davenport
Davenport, Frances Helen. See: AIKEN, ALBERT W.
Davenport, Francine. See: TATE, VELMA
Davenport, Spencer. See: STRATEMEYER, EDWARD L.
DAVEY [Davey]. See also:
DAVIE
Davy
Davey, Little. See: LEWIS, DAVID JOHN
DAVEY, MARIE AUGUSTA (1865-1932) [American actress]
Little Minnie Maddern
Minnie Maddern Fiske
David. See:
BEE, JOHN DAVID ASHFORD
WYSS, JOHANN RUDOLF
David Baron. See: PINTER, HAROLD
David Bartlett. See: MASON, MADELINE
David Ben-Gurion. See: GREEN, DAVID
David, Black. See: FORMAN, DAVID
David Blair. See:

BUTTERFIELD, DAVID
David Brett. See:
CAMPBELL, WILL DAVIS
David Bruce. See:
McBROOM, MARDEN
David Charlson. See:
HOLMES, DAVID CHARLES
David, Devil. See:
FORMAN, DAVID
David, Emily, joint pseud. of DAVID ALMAN (1919-) and his wife EMILY ALMAN (-) [American authors and film producers]
David Farrell. See:
SMITH, FREDERICK ESCREET
David Fox. See:
OSTRANDER, ISABEL
David Frome. See:
BROWN, ZENITH JONES
David Grayson. See:
BAKER, RAY STANNARD
David Grinnell. See:
WOLLHEIM, DONALD ALLEN
David Hextall. See:
PHILLIPS-BIRT, DOUGLAS
David Irland. See:
GREEN, JULIEN HARTRIDGE
David Janssen. See:
MEYER, DAVID HAROLD
David, Julian. See:
MacKaye, Loring
David Knight. See:
PRATHER, RICHARD SCOTT
David Lindsay. See:
WALLS, IAN GASCOIGNE
David, Little. See:
RANDOLPH, JOHN
David Manners. See:
ACKLON, RAUFF DE RYTHER DUAN
David Manning. See:
FAUST, FREDERICK SCHILLER
David Margerson. See:
DAVIES, DAVID MARGERISON
David Merrick. See:
MARGULOIS, DAVID
David Montross. See:
BACKUS, JEAN
David, Nicholas. See:
MORGAN, THOMAS BRUCE
David Ormsbee. See:
LONGSTREET, STEPHEN
David Osborne. See:
SILVERBERG, ROBERT
DAVID, PIERRE JEAN (1789-1856) [French sculptor]
David d'Angers
David Pilgrim. See:
Beeding, Francis
David Romaine. See:
BOHME, DAVID M.
David Saunders. See:
SONTUP, DANIEL
David Scott Daniell. See:
DANIELL, ALBERT SCOTT
David Severn. See:
UNWIN, DAVID STORR
David Sommers. See:
SMITH, HOWARD VAN
David Stewart. See:
POLITELLA, DARIO
David Valentine. See:
LUDOVICI, ANTHONY MARIO
David Wayne. See:
McMEEKAN, DAVID
David William Meredith. See:
MIERS, EARL SCHENCK
DAVIDOV, DENIS VASSILIEVITCH (1784-1839) [Russian army officer and poet]
The Black Captain
David's Harp of the North. See:
WALLIN, JOHAN OLOF
DAVIDSON. See also:
DAVISON
DAVIDSON, HILDA RODERICK ELLIS (1914-) [British educator and author]
Hilda Roderick Ellis
DAVIDSON, JO (1883-1952) [American sculptor]
The Dean of United States Sculptors
The Plastic Historian

DAVIDSON, MICKIE COMPERE (1936-) [American teacher and author]
Mickie Compere
DAVIDSON, THOMAS (1837-70) [Scottish poet]
The Scottish Probationer
DAVIE. See also:
DAVEY
Davey
Davy
DAVIE, WILLIAM RICHARDSON (1756-1820) [Anglo-American soldier, politician and educator]
The Father of the University of North Carolina
Davied, Camille. See:
ROSE, CAMILLE DAVIED
DAVIES [Davies]. See also:
DAVIS
Davis
DAVIES, ANDREW JACKSON (1826-1910) [American spiritualist and mesmerist]
The Poughkeepsie Seer
DAVIES, CHARLES (1798-1876) [American professor of mathematics at West Point]
Old Tush
DAVIES, CHARLES STEWART (1788-1865) [American lawyer]
Grecian Davies
DAVIES, CHRISTIAN (1667-1739) [Irish female soldier; served under MARLBOROUGH]
Mother Ross
DAVIES, DAVID MARGERISON (1923-) [British physician and author]
David Margerson
DAVIES, EILEEN WINIFRED (1910-) [British journalist and author
Eileen Elias
DAVIES, IVOR NOVELLO (1893-1951) [Welsh actor, composer and dramatist]
Ivor Novello
DAVIES, LESLIE PURNELL (1914-) [British artist and author]
Leo Berne
Robert Blake
Richard Bridgman
Morgan Evans
Ian Jefferson
Lawrence Peters
Thomas Philips
G.K. Thomas
Leslie Vardre
Rowland Welch
Davies, Marion. See:
DOURAS, MARION
DAVIES, MARY CAROLYN (fl. 1918-27) [American poet and author]
Pautuxie
DAVIES, ROBERTSON (1913-) [Canadian author]
Samuel Marchbanks
DA VINCI. See:
VINCI, LEONARDO DA
Daviot, Gordon. See:
MACINTOSH, ELIZABETH
DAVIS [Davis]. See also:
DAVIES
Davies
DAVIS, CHARLES AUGUSTUS (1795-1867) [American merchant and author]
J. Downing
Davis Cole. See:
ELTING, MARY
Davis, Don. See:
DRESSER, DAVIS
DAVIS, EDDIE (1921-) [American jazz musician (tenor saxophone)]
Lockjaw
DAVIS, FRANCIS (1810-85) [Irish poet]
The Belfast Man
DAVIS, FREDERICK WILLIAM (1858-1933) [American writer of dime novels]
Scott Campbell
Nicholas Carter
Nick Carter
DAVIS, GARRY (1921-) [American World War II bomber pilot; renounced U.S. citizenship, later applied for reinstatement]

World Citizen No. 1
DAVIS, GEORGE WILLIS (1904-) [American professional baseball player]
Kiddo
DAVIS, GLENN (1924-) [Former U.S. army cadet and football star]
Junior
Mr. Outside
Davis, Gordon. See: DIETRICH, ROBERT SALISBURY
DAVIS, GWEN (1936-) [American author]
Brat Fink
DAVIS, HAROLD LENOIR (1896-) [American author]
H. L. Davis
DAVIS, HARRY ALBERT (1910-) [American professional baseball player]
Stinky
DAVIS, HARRY PHILLIPS (1868-1931) [American pioneer in radio broadcasting]
The Father of Radio Broadcasting
DAVIS, HORACE BANCROFT (1898-) [American educator and author]
Bryan Green
Jan Reling
Lowell E. Willis
DAVIS, JACKSON (1920-) [American composer, pianist and organist]
Jackie Davis
DAVIS, JAMES (1848-1907) [American writer of musical comedies]
Owen Hall
DAVIS, JAMES JOHN (1873-1947) [Anglo-American politician; senator from Pennsylvania]
Puddler Jim
The Welsh Parson
DAVIS, JEANNETTE (1837-1909) [American actress]
Henrietta Baker
DAVIS, JOAN (1912-) [American actress and comedienne]
The World's Funniest Woman
DAVIS, JULIA (1904-) [American author]
F. Draco
Davis, Kay. See: WIMP, KATHRYN ELIZABETH
Davis, Maralee G. See: THIBAULT, MARALEE G.
DAVIS, MARY EVELYN MOORE (1852-1900) [American novelist and poet]
Mollie E. Moore Davis
DAVIS, MATHEW LIVINGSTON (1773-1850) [American politician and journalist]
The Old Boy in Specs
DAVIS, NATHAN SMITH (1817-1904) [American physician, editor and lecturer]
The Father of the American Medical Association
Davis, Norman. See: LUCAS, CHRISTOPHER NORMAN
DAVIS, ROBERT P. (1929-) [American advertising writer and author]
Joe Brandon
Davis, Rosemary L., joint pseud. of ROSEMARY DAVIS (fl. 1944-64) and her mother LILY MAY DAVIS (fl. 1944-64) British authors
DAVIS, RUTH ELIZABETH (1908-) [American actress]
Bette Davis
DAVIS, SAM (1842-63) [American Civil War Confederate spy]
The Boy-hero of the Confederacy
The Nathan Hale of the South
DAVIS, SAMMY, JR. (1925-) [American Negro entertainer, television

personality and actor]
America's One-eyed Jewish Negro
Davis, Stratford. See:
BOLTON, MAISIE SHARMAN
DAVIS, SYDNEY CHARLES HOUGHTON (1887-) [British artist and author of automobile books]
Sammy Casque
DAVIS, VARINA ANNE JEFFERSON (1864-98) [American author; daughter of JEFFERSON DAVIS]
The Daughter of the Confederacy
Winnie Davis, The Daughter of the Confederacy
DAVIS, VIRGIL LAWRENCE (1904-) [American professional baseball player]
Spud
DAVIS, WALTER ALONZO (1846-1921) [City clerk in Fitchburg, Worcester County, Massachusetts]
The Marrying Justice of Worcester County
DAVIS, WILLIAM (1727-90) [British highwayman]
The Golden Farmer
DAVIS, WILLIAM MORRIS (1850-1934) [American geologist and geographer]
The Father of the Science of Physiography
DAVIS, WILLIAM STRETHEN (1918-) [American jazz musician (organ, piano, composer)]
Wild Bill Davis
DAVISON. See also:
DAVIDSON
DAVISON, FRANK CYRIL (1893-) [American author]
Pierre Coalfleet
DAVISON, GLADYS PATTON (1905-) [American author]
Gladys Condor
DAVISON, WILLIAM (1906-) [American jazz musician (cornet, leader)]
Wild Bill Davison
Davy. See:
CROCKETT, DAVID
DAVEY
Davey
DAVIE
Davy, Old. See:
TWIGGS, DAVID EMANUEL
DAWE, ROBERT SHAEN (c. 1910-) [American motion picture actor]
Robert Shayne
DAWES, CHARLES GATES (1865-1951) [American financier, general officer, and Vice President of the U.S.]
Hell and Maria Dawes
DAWES, HENRY LAURENS (1816-1903) [American politician; congressman and senator from Massachusetts]
The Sage of Pittsfield
Dawn, Dolly. See:
STABILE, THERESA
Dawn O'Day. See:
PARIS, DAWN
Dawson, Elmer A. See:
STRATEMEYER, EDWARD L.
DAWSON, FLORENCE (1905-) [British dancer, impersonator and motion picture actress]
Florence Desmond
DAWSON, JOHN (1762-1814) [American statesman; congressman from Virginia]
Beau
Dawson, Lawrence H. See:
LAWRENCE, DAVID HERBERT
Dawson, Peter. See:
FAUST, FREDERICK SCHILLER
DAWSON, WILLIAM (1704-52) [Anglo-American poet]
By a Gentleman of Virginia

Day. See also:
Dey
DAY, BETH FEAGLES (1924-) [American educator and writer]
Elizabeth Feagles
Day, Doris. See:
VON KAPPELHOFF, DORIS
DAY, GEORGE HAROLD (1900-) [British physician and author]
Peter Quince
Day, Irene. See:
ORME, EVE
Day, Lady. See:
McKAY, ELEANOR GOUGH
Day, Laraine. See:
JOHNSON, LARAINE
DAY-LEWIS, CECIL (1904-) [British poet, critic and detective story writer]
Nicholas Blake
DAY, MARGARET (1916-) [British motion picture actress]
Margaret Lockwood
Day, Max. See:
CASSIDAY, BRUCE BINGHAM
Day, Michael. See:
DEMPEWOLFF, RICHARD FREDERIC
Day-old Chick, The. See:
WENE, ELMER H.
Day-star of the Revolution, The. See: HAMILTON, ANDREW
DAYMORE, REGINALD LEIGH (1891-) [British stage and motion picture actor]
Reginald Denny
Days' King, The Seven. See:
MASANIELLO (TOMMASO ANIELLO) (ANELLO)
Dazzy. See:
Dizzy
VANCE, CLARENCE ARTHUR
DE [De]. Those not listed below may be found under their respective surnames
Deacon, Paul the. See:
PAULUS DIACONUS
Dead End Kids, The
The East Side Kids, stage names of LEO GORCEY (1917-), HENRY HALL (Huntz Hall) (1920-) and BILLY HALOP (1920-) [American actors]
Dead End Kids, The. See also:
HALL, HENRY
Dead Man Who Won a Fight, The. See: DOUGLAS, JAMES
Deadwood Dick. See:
CLARK, RICHARD
Deaf and Dumb Poet, The. See:
NACK, JAMES M.
Deafman Eloquent, The. See:
POTTS, JAMES HENRY
DEAL, BORDEN (1922-) [American author]
Lee Borden
Deal, Crown Prince of the New. See:
ROOSEVELT, JAMES
Deal, The Author of the New. See: BURKE, EDWARD RAYMOND
Deal, The Babe Ruth of the New. See: JOHNSON, HUGH SAMUEL
DEALE, KENNETH EDWIN LEE (1907-) [Irish writer, speaker and broadcaster]
Paul Martin
Dealers, The King of the New. See: MINTON, SHERMAN
DEALEY, EDWARD MUSGROVE (1892-) [American journalist, publisher and author]
Ted Dealey
Dean Ballard. See:
WILKES-HUNTER, RICHARD
Dean D. O'Brien. See:
BINDER, OTTO OSCAR
Dean, Eddie. See:
GLOSSUP, EDGAR D.
Dean, Isabel. See:

HODGKINSON, ISABEL
Dean, James. See:
BYRON, JAMES
DEAN, JEROME HANNA (1911-) [American professional baseball player and sports announcer]
Dizzy Dean
DEAN, JIMMY RAY (1928-) [American country and Western singer]
The Dandy of Country Music
Dean Martin. See:
CROCETTI, DINO
DEAN, NELL MARR (1910-) [American journalist, librarian and author]
Virginia Roberts
Dean of American Criminologists, The. See:
SUTHERLAND, DR. EDWIN H.
Dean of American Football, The. See: CAMP, WALTER
Dean of American Letters, The. See: HOWELLS, WILLIAM DEAN
Dean of American Magazine Editors, The. See:
ALDEN, HENRY MILLS
Dean of American Magicians, The. See:
KELLAR, HARRY
Dean of American Music, The. See: DAMROSCH, WALTER JOHANNES
Dean of American Popular Music, The. See:
WHITEMAN, PAUL
Dean of American Science, The. See: CATTELL, JAMES McKEEN
Dean of American Tent-theater Showmen, The. See:
ECCLES, GEORGE CLINTON, JR.
Dean of America's Show Music Composers, The. See:
KERN, JEROME DAVID
Dean of Community Advertising, The. See:
HATFIELD, CHARLES FOLSOM
Dean of Contemporary English Novelists, The. See:
FORSTER, EDWARD MORGAN
Dean of Cotton Row, The. See:
DOUGHTY, JAMES P.
Dean of St. Patrick's, The. See:
SWIFT, JONATHAN
Dean of Sports Writers for Boys, The. See:
BARBOUR, RALPH HENRY
Dean of the Alabama Legislature, The. See:
TUNSTALL, ALFRED MOORE
Dean of the American Labor Movement, The. See:
FURUSETH, ANDREW
Dean of the American Stage, The. See:
JEFFERSON, JOSEPH
SKINNER, OTIS
Dean of the American Theater, The. See:
SKINNER, OTIS
Dean of the Dramatic Critics, The. See:
MANTLE, ROBERT BURNS
Dean of the House, The. See:
SABATH, ADOLPH JOACHIM
Dean of the Liberals, The. See:
NORRIS, GEORGE WILLIAM
Dean of the United States Sculptors, The. See:
DAVIDSON, JO
Dean of Woman Authors of America, The. See:
TARBELL, IDA MINERVA
DEAN, PAUL DEE (1913-) [American professional baseball player]
Daffy Dean
Dean, The Beloved. See:
MOORE, WALTER HOMER
Dean, The Gloomy. See:
INGE, WILLIAM RALPH
SWIFT, JONATHAN
Dean, The Red. See:
JOHNSON, HEWLETT
Dean, The Teutonic James. See:
BUCHOLZ, HORST WERNER

Deane, Lorna. See:
WILKINSON, LORNA HILDA KATHLEEN
Deane Monahan. See:
STEELE, JAMES
Deane, Norman. See:
CREASEY, JOHN
Deane Sears. See:
RYWELL, MARTIN
Deane, Sonia. See:
SOUTAR, GWENDOLNIE AMY
DE ANGELIS, ALBERTO (1885-) [Italian author]
Colline
Deanna. See:
DURBIN, EDNA MAE
Dear Abby. See:
PHILLIPS, PAULINE ESTHER FRIEDMAN
Dear Alben. See:
BARKLEY, ALBEN WILLIAM
Dearborn, Andrew. See:
GARDNER, LEWIS J.
Death on a Pale Horse. See:
WIRZ, CAPTAIN HENRY
Debate, Colossus of. See:
ADAMS, JOHN
Debate, The Hotspur of. See:
LORD STANLEY
Debate, The Rupert of. See:
LORD STANLEY
Debate, The Zany of. See:
CANNING, GEORGE
Debbie. See:
MEYER, DEBORAH ELIZABETH
REYNOLDS, MARIE FRANCES
DE BERNARDINIS, WILLIAM (1926-65) [American jazz musician (trombone)]
Willie Dennis
DE BOIS. See also:
DuBOSE
DUBUS
DE BOIS, WILHELMINA, J.E. (1923-) [Dutch author]
Helma de Bois
Debonaire, The. (Le Débonnaire). See:
LOUIS I
Débonnaire, Le (The Debonaire). See: LOUIS I
Deborah. See:
KERR-TRIMMER, DEBORAH JANE
de Born, Edith. See:
BISCH, EDITH
Debra Paget. See:
GRIFFIN, DEBRALEE
de Brant, Cyr. See:
HIGGINSON, JOSEPH VINCENT
Debrett, Hal, joint pseud. of DAVIS DRESSER (1904-) and KATHLEEN ROLLINS (-) [American authors of mystery stories]
Debrett, Hal. See also:
DRESSER, DAVIS
de Bury, Blaze. See:
BLAZE, ANGE HENRI
DE BURY, RICHARD (1287-1345) [English churchman]
Aungerville
DE CAMOENS, LUIZ (c.1524-80) [Portuguese poet]
The Portuguese Apollo
DE CAMP, LYON SPRAGUE (1907-) [American author]
Lyman R. Lyon
J. Washington Wells
de Carlo, Yvonne. See:
MIDDLETON, PEGGY YVONNE
De Castello. See:
VERGIL, POLYDORE
December, The Man of (l'Homme de Décembre). See: BONAPARTE, CHARLES LOUIS NAPOLEON
Décember, l'Homme de (The Man of December). See:
BONAPARTE, CHARLES LOUIS NAPOLEON
DECHEZ, LOUIS A. (1808-30) [French author]
Jenneval
Decimus. See:
CHATTERTON, THOMAS
DECKER. See also:
DEKKER
DECKER, DUANE (1910-)

[American author]
Richard Wayne
Declaration of Independence, The Father of the. See: JEFFERSON, THOMAS
DE CLARK, RICHARD (died 1176) [Earl of Pembroke and Strigul]
Strongbow
DE COLLIBUS, NICHOLAS (1913-) [American composer, violinist, teacher]
Don Nicholas
DE COSTER, CHARLES THEODORE HENRI (1827-79) [Belgian author]
Charles de Coster
The Father of Belgian Literature
de Coverley, Sir Roger. See: ADDISON, JOSEPH
SEWALL, JONATHAN
DE CRISTOFORO, R. J. (1917-) [American educator and author]
R. J. Cristy
Cris Williams
Dede. See: PIERCE, JOSEPH DE LACROIS
DEDEL, ADRIAN (1459-1523) [Supreme Pontiff of Roman Catholic Church]
Pope Adrian VI
Dee, Frances. See: DEE, JEAN
Dee Francis. See: HAAS, DOROTHY F.
Dee, Henry. See: TORBETT, HARVEY DOUGLAS LOUIS
Dee Hill. See: ZUCKER, DOLORES MAE BOLTON
DEE, JEAN (1908-) [American motion picture actress]
Frances Dee
Dee, Sandra. See: DOUVAIN, SANDRA
Dee, Sylvia. See: PROFFITT, JOSEPHINE MOORE
Deed-doer, The. See: EDMUND (EADMUND) I
Deems. See: TAYLOR, JOSEPH DEEMS
DEEPING, GEORGE WARWICK (1877-1950) [English novelist]
Warwick Deeping
George Warwick
de facto President, The. See: HAYES, RUTHERFORD BIRCHARD
de Falla, Manuel. See: FALLA Y MATHEU, MANUEL MARÍA DE
Defaulter, The Unintentional. See: WEBSTER, DANIEL
Defender of the Constitution, The. See: WEBSTER, DANIEL
Defender of the Faith, The. See: ROBERTS, BRIGHAM HENRY
Defender of the Holy Sepulcher. See: GODFREY OF BOUILLON
Defender of the Holy Sepulcher, Baron and. See: GODFREY OF BOUILLON
Defender of the Kingdom, Protector and. See: JOHN OF LANCASTER
Defender of the Union, The. See: WEBSTER, DANIEL
Defender, The Illustrious. See: WEBSTER, DANIEL
de Fer, Bras. See: BALDWIN
NOUE, FRANÇOIS DE
DE FILIPPI, AMEDEO (1900-) [Italian-American composer, conductor and violinist]
Philip Weston
De Firmont. See: EDGEWORTH, HENRY ESSEX
De Foe, Daniel. See: FOE, DANIEL
Defoe, Daniel. See: FOE, DANIEL
Defoe, The French. See: RESTIF, NICOLAS EDME
De Forbes. See: FORBES, DELORIS STANTON

DeForest, Barry. See:
CLARK, CHARLES DUNNING
MANNING, WILLIAM HENRY
DEFORGE, EVARISTE DÉSIRÉ (1753-1814) [Chevalier de Parny; French elegian and erotic poet]
The French Tibullus
Deformed, The (Il Bamboccio) See: LAAR, PIETER VAN
DE FRANCO, BONIFACE FERDINAND LEONARDO (1923-) [American jazz musician (clarinet, bass clarinet, leader)]
Buddy De Franco
de Frece, Lady. See:
POWLES, MATILDA ALICE
DEGHY, GUY. See:
Froy, Herald
DEGNI, LOU (1933-) [American athlete, gymnast and motion picture actor]
Mark Forest
DE GONCOURT, EDMOND LOUIS ANTOINE HUOT. See: Goncourts, The
DE GONCOURT, JULES ALFRED HUOT. See: Goncourts, The
Dehan, Richard. See:
GRAVES, CLOTILDE INEZ AUGUSTA MARY
DE HARTOG, JAN (1914-) [Dutch author]
F. R. Eckmar
Deh-he-wö-mis. See:
JEMISON, MARY
DEINDORFER, ROBERT GREENE (1922-) [American author]
Jay Bender
Jay Dender
Robert Greene
Dejaz Kassai. See:
JOHN IV
DeJONG, DAVID CORNEL (1905-) [Dutch-American teacher and author]
Tjalmar Breda
Deke. See:
MOFFITT, DE LOYCE
DEKKER. See also:
DECKER
DEKKER, EDUARD DOUWES (1820-87) [Dutch novelist, essayist and satirist]
Multatuli
De Kolta. See:
BAUTIER, JOSEPH
DE KOVEN, HENRY LOUIS REGINALD (1859-1920) [American composer and music critic]
Reginald de Koven
DEL [Del]. Those not listed below may be found under their respective surnames.
Del. See:
RENTZEL, DELOS WILSON
de Lagenevais, F. See:
BLAZE, ANGE HENRI
DE LA MARE, WALTER JOHN (1873-1956) [English poet and novelist]
Walter Ramel
DE LANCEY, JAMES (1732-1800) [American politician and turfman]
The Father of the New York Turf
DE LANGE, EDGAR (1904-49) [American composer and conductor]
Eddie DeLange
de la Pluche, Jeames. See:
THACKERAY, WILLIAM MAKEPEACE
de la Torre-Bueno, Lillian. See: McCUE, LILLIAN BUENO
de la Torre, Lillian. See:
McCUR, LILLIAN BUENO
DEL CAMPO, DOMINGO (1873-1900) [Spanish bull-fighter]
Dominguín
DEL CAMPO, JOSÉ SANCHEZ (1848-1925) [Spanish bull-fighter]
Cara-Ancha
Delafield, E. M. See:

DASHWOOD, MRS. EDMÉE
ELIZABETH MONICA
Delaney, Denis. See:
GREEN, PETER MORRIS
Delaney, Francey. See:
O'HARA, JOHN HENRY
DELANO, ALONZO (1806-74)
[California pioneer and
correspondent]
The Old Block
Delaporte, Theophile. See:
GREEN, JULIEN
HARTRIDGE
DELAROCHE, HIPPOLYTE
(1797-1856) [French
painter]
Paul
Delaware Plowboy, The. See:
BIGGS, BENJAMIN
THOMAS
Delayer, The (Cunctator). See:
VERRUCOSUS, QUINTUS
FABIUS MAXIMUS
DE LEATH, VAUGHN (1896-
1943) [American popular
singer]
The Original Radio Girl
DE LEEUW, CATEAU WIL-
HELMINA (1903-)
[American author]
Kay Hamilton
Jessica Lyon
de Lenclos, Ninon. See:
LENCLOS, ANNE
DE LEO, LIONARDO ORONZO
SALVATORE (1694-1744)
[Italian composer]
Leo Leonardo
Delft, Jan Van Der Meer Van.
See: VERMEER, JAN
Delgadillo, Monico. See:
YAÑEZ, AGUSTÍN
DELGADO, ADELAÏDA (1923-)
[Spanish-American dancer
and motion picture actress]
Adele Mara
DELGADO, JOSÉ (1754-1801)
[Spanish bullfighter]
Pepe-Hillo
Deliberate Pedant. See:
ELIOT, THOMAS
STEARNS
Delight of Mankind. See:
MAXIMILIAN II
VESPASIANUS, TITUS
FLAVIUS SALINUS
Deliverer of America, The.
See: WASHINGTON,
GEORGE
Delivery, The Father of Rural
Free. See:
BUTLER, MARION
Dell, Belinda. See:
BOWDEN, JEAN
Dell Shannon. See:
LININGTON, ELIZABETH
Della Crusca. See:
MERRY, ROBERT
Della Francesca, Piero. See:
FRANCHESI, PIERO DEI
della Porta, Baccio. See:
FATTORINO, BARTOLOM-
MEO DI PAGOLO DEL
Delle Sara, Colonel. See:
AIKEN, ALBERT W.
DELMAS, DELPHIN MICHAEL
(1844-1928) [Franco-
American lawyer]
The Napoleon of the California
Bar
The Silver-tongued Spell-
binder of the Pacific Coast
DE LONGPRÉ, PAUL (1855-
1911/12) [Franco-American
painter]
The King of the Flower
Painters
Delorme, Daniele. See:
GIRARD, GABRIELLE
de Loyola, Ignatius. See:
RECALDE, IÑIGO LÓPEZ DE
Delphi. See:
HODSON, ARNOLD WEIN-
HOLT
Delta. See:
DENNETT, HERBERT
VICTOR
MOIR, DAVID MACBETH
Delysia, Alice. See:
LAPIZE, ALICE
Demaine, Don. See:
DRINKALL, GORDON DON
de Mar, Paul. See:
FOLEY, PEARL
Demarest, Doug. See:
BARKER, WILL
Demaris, Ovid.
See:

DESMARAIS, OVIDE E.
DE MAUPASSANT, HENRI RENÉ ALBERT GUY (1850-93) [French author]
Guy de Maupassant
Dembry, R. Emmett. See: MURFREE, MARY NOAILLES
DE MENDELSSOHN, HILDE MARIA (1911-) [Viennese educator and author]
Hilde Spiel
DEMETRIUS I (337?-283 B.C.) [King of Macedonia]
Poliorcetes (Besieger of Cities)
DEMETRIUS I (died c. 150 B.C.) [Ruler of Syria]
Soter (The Preserver)
DEMETRIUS II (died c.125 B.C.) [Ruler of Syria]
Nicator
DEMETRIUS III (died c.88 B.C.) [King of Egypt]
Euergetes (Benefactor)
Eukairos
Philometor
de Meung, Jean. See: CLOPINEL, JEAN
Demijohn, Thom, joint pseud. of THOMAS M. DISCH (1940-) and JOHN SLADEK (-) [American authors]
DE MILLE, CECIL BLOUNT (1881-1959) [American actor, playwright and motion picture director and producer]
C.B.
Deming, Kirk. See: DRAGO, HENRY SINCLAIR
DEMING, RICHARD (1915-) [American social worker and author]
Max Franklin
Democracy, Old Wheel-horse of. See: MEDARY, SAMUEL
Democracy, The Armed Soldier of. See: BONAPARTE, NAPOLEON
Democracy, The Philosopher of. See: JEFFERSON, THOMAS
Democrat, The First. See: HOOKER, THOMAS
Democrat, The First Great American. See: WISE, JOHN
Democratiad, The. See: HOPKINS, DR. LEMUEL
Democratic War Horse of Tennessee, The. See: McMILLIN, BENTON
Democratic War Horse, The. See: McMILLIN, BENTON
Democratic Warwick, The Great. See: SWEENEY, PETER BARR
DEMOCRITUS (c.450-370 B.C.) [Greek philosopher]
The Abderite
The Laughing Philosopher
Democritus Junior. See: BURTON, ROBERT
Democritus of the Sixteenth Century, The. See: CALVIN, JOHN
Demon, The. See: SPOFFORTH, FREDERICK ROBERT
de Montfort, Guy. See: JOHNSON, DONALD McINTOSH
de Morny, Peter. See: WYNNE-TYSON, ESME
DEMOSTHENES (c.384-322 B.C.) [Greek orator]
The Prince of Orators
Demosthenes of Texas, The. See: HUBBARD, RICHARD BENNETT
Demosthenes of the Mountains, The. See: MILLER, HOMER VIRGIL MILTON
Demosthenes, The Forest-born. See: HENRY, PATRICK
Demosthenes, The High-born. See: WILLIAM I
Demosthenes, The New Hampshire. See: WEBSTER, DANIEL
DEMPEWOLFF, RICHARD FREDERIC (1914-).

[American author]
Michael Day
Dick Frederick
Frederick Wolf
Dempsey, Jack. See:
DEMPSEY, WILLIAM HARRISON
KELLY, JOHN
DEMPSEY, JAMES E. (1876-1918) [American author, composer and singer]
Powell I. Ford
Paul Grayson
DEMPSEY, MILES CHRISTOPHER (1896-) [British general officer]
Lucky Dempsey
DEMPSEY, WILLIAM HARRISON (1895-) [American professional boxer; world's heavyweight champion]
The Champ
Jack Dempsey
Jack the Giant-killer
The Manassa Mauler
DEMSKY, ISSUR DANIELOVITCH (1916-) [American stage and motion picture actor]
Kirk Douglas
DeNAUT, GEORGE MATTHEWS (1915-) [American jazz musician (composer, arranger, bass)]
Jud DeNaut
Dender, Jay. See:
DEINDORFER, ROBERT GREENE
DENHAM, MARY ORR (19??-) [American author]
Anne Caswell
Mary Orr
DENHOLM, THERESE MARY ZITA WHITE (1933-) [Australian teacher, editor and author]
Zita White
DENIS [Denis]. See also:
Denise
DENNIS
Dennis
DENYS
Denys
DINIZ (DENIS)
Denis Delaney. See:
GREEN, PETER MORRIS
DENIS (DENYS), ST. (died c. 272) [patron saint of France]
The Apostle of the French
Denis le Cadet, St. See:
ALLEN, PAUL
Denis Thévenin. See:
DUHAMEL, GEORGES
Denise. See also:
DENIS
Denis
DENNIS
Dennis
DENYS
Denys
DINIZ (DENIS)
Denise Conway. See:
PREBBLE, MARJORIE MARY CURTIS
Denise Darcel. See:
BILLECARD, DENISE
Denise Egerton. See:
DUGGAN, DENISE VALERIE
Denise Trez. See:
TREDEZ, DENISE
DENISON. See also:
DENNISON
DENISON, CHARLES WHEELER (1809-81) [American editor, clergyman, poet and consul]
Major Penniman
DENISON, MARY ANDREWS (1826-1911) [American author]
A. M. D.
M. A. D.
N. I. Edson
Clara Vance
Denmark, Harrison. See:
ZELAZNY, ROGER
Denmark, Old. See:
FEBIGER, CHRISTIAN
Denmark, The Oracle of. See:
VON BERNSTORFF, COUNT JOHANN HARTWIG ERNST
DENNETT, HERBERT VICTOR

(1893-) [British advertising manager and author]
Delta
John Syntax
Ned Tent
DENNIE, JOSEPH (1768-1812) [American editor and essayist]
The American Addison
Colon
Lay Preacher
Oliver Oldschool, Esq.
Denning, Patricia. See:
WILLIS, CORINNE DENNENY
Denning, Richard. See:
DENNINGER, LOUIS A.
DENNINGER. See also:
DUNNINGER
DENNINGER, LOUIS A. (1916-) [American motion picture actor]
Richard Denning
DENNIS [Dennis]. See also:
DENIS
Denis
Denise
DENYS
Denys
DINIZ (DENIS)
Dennis, Derrick. See:
TERRY, DENNIS
Dennis Hoey. See:
HYAMS, SAMUEL DAVID
Dennis King. See:
PRATT, DENNIS
Dennis Montclair. See:
SLADEN, NORMAN ST. BARBE
Dennis Morgan. See:
MORNER, STANLEY
Dennis O'Keefe. See:
FLANAGAN, EDWARD
Dennis Price. See:
ROSEPRICE, DENNISTOUN FRANKLYN JOHN
DENNIS, RUTH (1878?-1968) [American dancer and choreographer]
The First Lady of the American Dance
The Mother of the Strip Tease
Miss Ruth
Ruth St. Denis
DENNIS, SANDRA DALE (1937-) [American actress]
Sandy Dennis
Dennis, Willie. See:
DE BERARDINIS, WILLIAM
DENNISON. See also:
DENISON
DENNISON, AARON LUFKIN (1812-95) [American pioneer watch manufacturer]
The Father of American Watchmaking
Denny. See:
McLAIN, DENNIS DALE
Denny, Reginald. See:
DAYMORE, REGINALD LEIGH
DENTATUS. See:
SICINIUS DENTATUS
Denton, James. See:
HUGHES, ROBERT J.
Denver, Boone. See:
RENNIE, JAMES ALAN
Denver, Drake C. See:
NYE, NELSON CORAL
Denys. See also:
DENIS
Denis
DENIS (DENYS), ST.
Denise
DENNIS
Dennis
DINIZ (DENIS)
Denys Craig. See:
STOLL, DENNIS GRAY
Denys Rutledge, Dom. See:
RUTLEDGE, EDWARD WILLIAM
DEPEW, CHAUNCEY MITCHELL (1834-1928) [American railroad executive and politician; Senator from New York]
The Peach
D'Épinay, Louise Florence Pétronille de la Live. See:
D'ESCLAVELLES, LOUISE TARDIEU

de Pontedera, Andrea. See:
PISANO, ANDREA
D'EPREMESNIL, JEAN JACQUES DUVAL (1746-94) [French revolutionist]
Crispin-Cataline
De Quille, Dan. See:
WRIGHT, WILLIAM
DE QUINCEY, THOMAS (1785-1859) [English essayist and miscellaneous writer]
The English Opium-Eater
Der Alte (The Old Man). See:
ADENAUER, KONRAD
Der Alte Dessauer (The Old Dessauer). See:
LEOPOLD
de Ramsay, Chevalier. See:
RAMSAY, ANDREW MICHAEL
Der Bingle. See:
CROSBY, HARRY LILLIS
Der Führer. See:
HITLER, ADOLF
Der Max. See:
KLEIN-LUCKOW, MAX
Der Meister (The Master). See: VON GOETHE, JOHANN WOLFGANG
WIELAND, CHRISTOPHER MARTIN
DERBY, ELIAS HASKET (1739-99) [American shipping magnate]
The Father of American Commerce with India
DERBY, GEORGE HORATIO (1823-61) [American humorist]
John Phoenix
John P. Squibob
Squibob
Derby, Wright of. See:
WRIGHT, JOSEPH
DE REBECQUE, HENRI BENJAMIN CONSTANT (1767-1830) [French author and political leader]
Benjamin Constant
Derel Pilgrim. See:
KANTO, PETER
Derème, Tristan. See:
HUC, PHILIPPE
DeRENEVILLE, MARY MARGARET MOTLEY SHERIDAN (1912-) [British author]
Mary Motley
Dering, Cini Willoughby. See:
BUDDICOM, JACINTHA LAURA MAY
DERLETH, AUGUST WILLIAM (1909-) [American author]
Stephen Grendon
Tally Mason
DERMOT, JESSIE (1868-1940) [American actress]
Maxine Elliott
DERN, PEGGY GADDIS (1895-1966) [American author]
Roberta Courtland
Georgia Craig
Peggy Gaddis
Gail Jordan
Carolina Lee
Perry Lindsay
Joan Sherman
DE ROSE, PETER. See:
Sweethearts of the Air
DEROUNIAN, ARTHUR (1909-) [Armenian-American author]
John Roy Carlson
George Pagnanelli
Derrick, Dennis. See:
TERRY, DENNIS
DERRINGER, PAUL (1907-) [American professional baseball player]
Duke Derringer
Dersonne, Jacques. See:
SIMENON, GEORGES
DE RUYSBROECK, JEAN (1294-1381) [celebrated mystic]
The Divine Doctor
The Ecstatic Doctor
DE SALVO, ALBERT H. (1932-) [American murderer of thirteen women]
The Boston Strangler

The Green Man
The Measuring Man
DESCARTES, RENÉ (1586-1650) [French philosopher and mathematician]
Cartesius
The Father of Modern Philosophy
DESCHAMPS, EUSTACHE (c.1346-c.1406) [French poet]
Morel
D'ESCLAVELLES, LOUISE TARDIEU (1726-83) [French author]
Louise Florence Pétronille de la Live D'Épinay
Descriptive Entomology, The Father of American. See: SAY, THOMAS
Desert Fox, The. See: ROMMEL, ERWIN JOHANNES EUGEN
DESGILBERTS, GUILLAUME (1594-1651) [French actor]
Montdory
Deshabilleuse, La. See: SIMENON, GEORGES
DESHOULIÈRES, ANTOINETTE DU LIGIER DE LA GARDE (c.1635-94) [French poet]
Amaryllis
The French Calliope
The Tenth Muse
Desi Arnaz. See: ACHA, DESIDERIO ALBERTO ARNAZ Y DE, 3D
Desiderius Erasmus. See: GERHARDS, GERHARD (GEERT GEERTS)
DESIDERIUS, PRINCE OF BENEVENTO (c.1027-87) [Supreme Pontiff of Roman Catholic Church]
Pope Victor III
Désiré, Louis de. See: LOUIS XVIII
Desk of Beri Headin, From The. See: STORY, ISAAC
DESLYS, GABRIELLE (1884-1920) [French singer and music-hall artist]
Gaby Deslys
DESMARAIS, OVIDE E. (1919-) [American author]
Ovid Demaris
DE SMET, PETER JOHN (1801-72) [Belgian Jesuit priest; missionary to American Indians in Rocky Mountain area]
The Apostle of the Rocky Mountains
Desmond Cory. See: McCARTHY, SHAUN
Desmond Dunne. See: LEE-RICHARDSON, JAMES
Desmond Farrell. See: ORGAN, JOHN
Desmond, Florence. See: DAWSON, FLORENCE
Desmond Meiring. See: RICE, DESMOND CHARLES
Desoeillets, Mademoiselle. See: FAVIOT, ALIX
de Souza, Madame. See: FILLEUL, ADÉLAÏDE MARIE ÉMILE
Despair, The Poet of. See: THOMSON, JAMES
Desperate Dan. See: DILLINGER, JOHN HERBERT
Desperdicios. See: DOMÍNGUEZ, MANUEL
Desplaines, Baroness Julie. See: JENNINGS, LESLIE NELSON
Despot-in-Chief in and over the Rising State of New Jersey. See: LIVINGSTON, WILLIAM
Dessauer, Der Alte (The Old Dessauer). See: LEOPOLD
Dessauer, The Old (Der Alte Dessauer). See: LEOPOLD

de Staël, Madame. See:
STAËL-HOLSTEIN, ANNE LOUISE GERMAINE, BARONNE DE
de Stendahl. See:
BEYLE, MARIE HENRI
Destiny, The Green-eyed Man of. See:
WALKER, WILLIAM
Destiny, The Grey-eyed Man of. See:
WALKER, WILLIAM
Destiny, The Man of. See:
BONAPARTE, NAPOLEON
CLEVELAND, STEPHEN GROVER
DESTOUCHES, LOUIS FUCH (1894-1961) [French author]
Louis-Ferdinand Céline
D'ESTRÉES, GABRIELLE (1571-99) [mistress of HENRY IV, King of France]
La Belle Gabrielle
Destroyer, The Dark. See:
BARROW, JOSEPH LOUIS
Destruction, The Prince of. See: TIMUR LENK
Destry, Vince. See:
NORWOOD, VICTOR GEORGE CHARLES
DE SYLVA, GEORGE GARD (1896-1950) [American song writer and theatrical producer]
B.G. De Sylva
Buddy De Sylva
Detection, The Edison of Crime. See: HEINRICH, EDWARD OSCAR
Detective, A Great. See:
SCHINDLER, RAYMOND C.
Detective, A U.S.--E. S. St. Mox. See:
ELLIS, EDWARD SYLVESTER
Detective, Hawkshaw the. See:
IRON, NATHANIEL COLCHESTER
Detective Novelist, M.O. Rolfe, The. See:
ROLFE, MARO O.
Detective Stories, The Godmother of. See:
GREEN, ANNA KATHARINE
Detective Stories, The Mother of. See: GREEN, ANNA KATHARINE
Detective, The. See:
VIDOCQ, EUGÉNE FRANÇOIS
Detective, The Old. See:
ROLFE, MARO O.
Detective, The Tune. See:
SPAETH, SIGMUND GOTTFRIED
Detective, The Young. See:
ROLFE, MARO O.
Detroit, The Great Father of. See: CASS, LEWIS
Detroit's Greatest Traveler. See: STEARNS, FREDERICK KIMBALL
DETZER, KARL (1891-) [American journalist and author]
Michael Costello
DEUBLER, MARY (c.1864-1914) [American prostitute and New Orleans brothel keeper]
Josie Alton
Josie Arlington
Lobrano d'Arlington
DEUSDEDIT (died 618) [Supreme Pontiff of Roman Catholic Church]
Pope Adeodatus I
Pope Deusdedit I
St. Deusdedit
D'EUSE, JACQUES (1249-1334) [Supreme Pontiff of Roman Catholic Church]
Pope John XXII
Deutsch, Babette. See:
YARMOLINSKY, MRS. AVRAHM
DEUTSCHER, ISAAC (1907-) [Polish journalist, editor and author]
Peregrine
de Vega, Lope. See:
CARPIO, LOPE FÉLIX DE VEGA

Devera Myles. See:
ZUCKER, DOLORES MAE BOLTON
DE VERE, MARY AINGE (fl. 1870-1915) [American poet]
Madaline Bridges
Devil, Brother (Fra Diavolo) See: PEZZA, MICHELE
Devil Butler, Hell's. See:
BUTLER, SMEDLEY DARLINGTON
Devil David. See:
FORMAN, DAVID
Devil Dick. See:
PORSON, RICHARD
Devil of Wallachia, The White. See: CASTRIOTA, GEORGE
Devil, Old Kill. See:
FREEMAN, AUSTIN
Devil on Two Sticks, The. See:
MORTON, OLIVER HAZARD PERRY THROCK
Devil Pete. See:
MUHLENBERG, JOHN PETER GABRIEL
Devil, Robert the. See:
ROBERT I
Devil, The American. See:
McDOUGAL, DAVID STOCKTON
Devil, The Blind White. See:
BUCKLEY, CHRISTOPHER A.
Devil, The French. See:
BART, JEAN
Devil, The Great White. See:
VAN CORTLANDT, PHILIP
Devil, The Holy. See:
RASPUTIN, GREGORY
Devil, The One-armed. See:
KEARNY, PHILIP
Devil, The Sea. See:
VON LUCKNER, COUNT FELIX
Devil's Adjutant, The. See:
WALLER, JOHN
DEVIN, THOMAS CASIMIR (1822-78) [American Union Army soldier and Indian fighter]
The Old War Horse
DEVLAN, EUGENE (1890-1960) [American biographer and novelist]
Gene Fowler
The Pride of the Rockies
de Voilemont, Comte. See:
ESTERHAZY, MARIE CHARLES FERDINAND WALSIN
Devon, W.A. See:
SMITH, FRANCIS SHUBAEL
DE VOTO, BERNARD AUGUSTINE (1897-) [American novelist]
John August
DE VRIENDT, FRANS FLORIS (1520-70) [Flemish historical painter]
The Flemish Raphael
De Warville. See:
BRISSOT, JACQUES PIERRE
DeWEESE, GENE. See:
Stratton, Thomas
Dewes, Simon. See:
MURIEL, JOHN
DEWEY, ANNETTE BARRETT (1884-) [American poet]
Anne Windsor
DEWEY, GEORGE (1837-1917) [American admiral]
The Hero of Manila
Dewey, James. See:
McNEILLY, MILDRED MASTERSON
DEWEY, JEDEDIAH (1714-78) [American clergyman]
The Fighting Parson
DEWEY, MELVILLE LOUIS KOSSUTH (1851-1931) [American pioneer librarian]
Melvil Dewey
Dewey, Missouri's Tom. See:
MILLIGAN, MAURICE MORTON
Dewey of Manzanillo, The. See:
TODD, CHAPMAN C.
Dewey, The New Deal's Tom.

See: MURPHY, FRANK
DEWEY, THOMAS BLANCHARD (1915-) [American author]
Tom Brandt
Cord Wainer
DEWEY, THOMAS EDMUND (1902-71) [American lawyer and statesman]
Tom Dewey
DeWitt, James. See:
LEWIS, MILDRED D.
De Wolf. See:
HOPPER, WILLIAM DE WOLF
d'Exiles, Prévost. See:
PRÉJOST, ANTOINE FRANÇOIS
Dexter, Anthony. See:
FLEISCHMANN, WALTER
Dexter, John. See:
KANTO, PETER
Dexter, Martin. See:
FAUST, FREDERICK SCHILLER
DEXTER, TIMOTHY (1747-1806) [American merchant, eccentric and author]
Lord Timothy Dexter
Peter Quince
Dexter, Will. See:
COOMES, OLIVER
DEY [Dey]. See also:
Day
DEY, FREDERICK VAN RENSSELAER (1861-1922) [American writer of dime novels]
A Celebrated Author
Ross Beckman
Nicholas Carter
Nick Carter
Bertha M. Clay
Frederick M. Dey
Marmaduke Dey
Marian Gilmore
Frederic Ormund
Dirck Van Doren
Varick Venardy
Dey, Larry. See:
DEYBROOK, L. M.
DEYBROOK, L. M. (1910-) [American author and composer]
Larry Dey
Diahann Carroll. See:
JOHNSON, CAROL DIAHANN
Diamond Jim. See:
BRADY, JAMES BUCHANAN
Diamond Lil. See:
WEST, MAE
Diamond, The Black. See:
CRIBB, TOM
Diana Barrymore. See:
BLYTHE, DIANA
Diana Cortis. See:
ASHTON, WINIFRED
Diana Dors. See:
FLUCK, DIANA
Diana Lynn. See:
LOEHR, DELORES
Diana Maugham. See:
MARR-JOHNSON, DIANA MAUGHAM
Diana Napier. See:
ELLIS, MOLLY
Diana of the Stage, The. See:
BRACEGIRDLE, MRS. ANNE
Diana Pullein-Thompson. See:
FARR, DIANA PULLEIN-THOMPSON
Diana Wynyard. See:
COX, DOROTHY ISOBEL
Diane Wakoski-Sherbell. See:
WAKOSKI, DIANE
Diane Ward. See:
BUNCE, CORAJANE DIANE
Dianne Foster. See:
LURASKA, DIANNE
Diavolo, Fra (Brother Devil). See: PEZZA, MICHELE
DIAZ, DON JUAN MARTÍN (1775-1823) [Spanish general officer]
Empecinado
di Bassetto, Corno. See:
SHAW, GEORGE BERNARD
DIBOS, CORINNE (1925-) [French motion picture actress]
Corinne Calvet
Dic. See:
Dick
DIKE

Dirk
GARDNER, RICHARD
Dick. See:
BUTTON, RICHARD TOTTEN
CAREY, RICHARD DURANT
CLARK, RICHARD WAGSTAFF
CONTINO, RICHARD
CROKER, RICHARD
Dic
DIKE
Dirk
FRIENDLICH, RICHARD J.
GROAT, RICHARD MORROW
HIGGINS, RICHARD C.
HILLIS, CHARLES RICHARD
JURGENS, RICHARD HENRY
LIEB, ZISKIND
LUPOFF, RICHARD ALLEN
MOORE, JOHN RICHARD, JR.
PEARCE, RICHARD ELMO
POWELL, RICHARD EWING
RIDDLE, R. RICHARD
SHEPPARD, HUGH RICHARD LAWRIE
SMITH, RICHARD EMERSON
SMOTHERS, RICHARD
TURPIN, RICHARD
WEBER, RICHARD ANTHONY
WHITTINGTON, RICHARD
Dick, Black. See:
HOWE, RICHARD, 1ST EARL
Dick Dale, Fighting. See:
DALE, RICHARD
Dick, Deadwood. See:
CLARK, RICHARD
Dick, Devil. See:
PORSON, RICHARD
Dick Donovan. See:
MUDDOCK, JOYCE EMERSON PRESTON
Dick, Farmers'. See:
OGLESBY, RICHARD JAMES
Dick, Fighting. See:
ANDERSON, RICHARD HERON
DALE, RICHARD
RICHARDSON, ISRAEL BUSH
Dick Frederick. See:
DEMPEWOLFF, RICHARD FREDERIC
Dick, Galloping. See:
FERGUSON, RICHARD
Dick, Queen. See:
CROMWELL, RICHARD
Dick St. John. See:
GOSTING, RICHARD
Dick Shawn. See:
SCHULEFAND, RICHARD
Dick, Silver. See:
BLAND, RICHARD PARKS
Dick, Slippery. See:
CONNOLLY, RICHARD
Dick Steadman, Captain. See:
HARBAUGH, THOMAS CHALMERS
Dick Sutton. See:
SCHWARTZ, RICHARD
Dick Talbot, Lying. See:
TALBOT, RICHARD
Dick Tinto. See:
GOODRICH, FRANK BOOTT
Dick, Tricky. See:
NIXON, RICHARD MILHOUS
Dick Turpin of France, The. See: BOURGUIGNON, LOUIS-DOMINIQUE
Dick, Uncle. See:
OGLESBY, RICHARD JAMES
DICKENS, CHARLES JOHN HUFFAM (1812-70) [English novelist and playwright]
Boz
Pickwick
Timothy Sparks
Tibbs
DICKENS, CHARLES JOHN HUFFAM. See also:
Collins, Charles
Dickens, The French. See:
DAUDET, ALPHONSE
DICKENSON, ALBERT VICTOR (1906-) [American jazz

musician (trombone, leader)]
Vic Dickenson
DICKEY. See also:
DICKIE
Dickie
Dicky
DICKEY, WILLIAM MALCOLM (1907-) [American professional baseball player]
Bill Dickey
Dickie. See:
DICKEY
Dicky
MOOR, JOHN RICHARD, JR.
DICKIE, GEORGE WILLIAM (1844-1918) [Scottish-American naval architect and shipbuilder]
The Father of Shipbuilding
DICKINSON, HAROLD H., JR. (1913-) [American composer, singer, and producer]
Hal Dickinson
DICKINSON, JOHN (1732-1808) [American political pamphleteer; Governor of Pennsylvania]
Fabius
The Penman of the American Revolution
The Pennsylvania Farmer
Dickson. See:
DIXON
Dixon
REYNOLDS, HELEN MARY GREENWOOD
Dickson, Carr. See:
CARR, JOHN DICKSON
Dickson, Carter. See:
CARR, JOHN DICKSON
Dickson, Helen. See:
REYNOLDS, HELEN MARY GREENWOOD
Dicky. See:
DICKEY
DICKIE
Dickie
SUETT, RICHARD
WELLS, WILLIAM
Dictator. See:
GOEBEL, WILLIAM
Dictator of Jersey City, The. See: HAGUE, FRANK
Dictator of Letters, The. See: AROUET, FRANÇOIS MARIE
Dictator of Louisiana, The. See: LONG, HUEY PIERCE
Didrikson, Babe. See:
ZAHARIAS, MILDRED DIDRIKSON
DIDYMUS OF ALEXANDRIA (c. 313-98) [Alexandrian churchman]
The Blind
DIEBITSCH, HANS KARL FRIEDRICH, COUNT (1785-1831) [Russian field marshal]
Sabalkanski (Crosser of the Balkans)
Diedrich. See also:
DIETRICH
Dietrich
Diedrich Knickerbocker. See:
IRVING, WASHINGTON
Diego Rivera. See:
RODRÍGUEZ, DIEGO MARÍA CONCEPCIÓN JUAN NEPOMUCENTO ESTANISLAO DE LA RIVERA Y BARRIENTOS ACOSTA Y
DIEHL, WILLIAM WELLS (1916-) [American journalist, photographer, editor and author]
Duncan Clay
DIESTELHORST, H. JEAN (1904-) [American composer, singer and publisher]
Jean Dale
DIETERLE, WILHELM (1893-) [German-American motion picture director and producer]
William Dieterle
The Hollywood Plutarch
DIETRICH [Dietrich]. See also:
Diedrich
Dietrich, Marlene. See:

VON LOSCH, MARIA MAGDALENE
DIETRICH, ROBERT SALISBURY (1928-) [American author]
Gordon Davis
Dietrich von Bern. See: THEODORIC
Digger, The Well. See: MATTHEWS, JOSEPH W.
Digges, Jeremiah. See: BERGER, JOSEF
Dighton Morel. See: WARNER, KENNETH LEWIS
Digna, Osman. See: NISBET, GEORGE
DIKE. See also:
Dic
Dick
Dirk
DIKE, PHILIP LATIMER (1906-) [American artist]
Phil Dike
Dil, Zakhmi. See: HILTON, RICHARD
DILCOCK, NOREEN (1907-) [English author]
Jill Christian
Norrey Dilcock
Norrey Ford
DILLES, JAMES (1923-) [American author]
Jim Dilles
DILLINGER, JOHN HERBERT (1903-34) [American bank robber and outlaw]
Desperate Dan
Dan Dillinger
Kill Crazy Dillinger
John Donovan
Johnnie
Jimmie Lawrence
Public Enemy No. 1
Frank Sullivan
Dillingham, Robert Barclay. See: FOULKE, WILLIAM DUDLEY
DILLON, JOHN BROWN (1808-79) [American librarian and historian]
The Father of Indiana History
DILLON, WILLIAM A. (1877-1966) [American composer and actor]
Will Dillon
Dilly Tante. See: KUNITZ, STANLEY JASSPON
DIMAGGIO, JOSEPH PAUL, JR. (1914-) [American professional baseball player]
The Big Guy
Joe DiMaggio
The Yankee Clipper
Di Martino. See: MARTINI, SIMONE
Dimitris Stachys. See: CONSTANTELOS, DEMETRIOS J.
DIMITRY, CHARLES PATTON (1837-1910) [American journalist and novelist]
Tobias Guarnerius, Jr.
Dinah. See:
FÉLIX, MELANIE EMILIE
SHORE, FRANCES ROSE
Dinah Washington. See: JONES, RUTH
DI NAPOLI, MARIO (1914-) [American pianist and conductor]
Mike Di Napoli
DINEMANDY (DORAT), JEAN (c. 1510-88) [French poet]
The French Pindar
Dinesen, Isak. See: BLIXEN-FINECKE, BARONESS KAREN
Ding. See: DARLING, JAY NORWOOD
Ding, J. N. See: DARLING, JAY NORWOOD
DINGELL, JOHN DAVID (1894-) [American journalist, politician and congressman from Michigan]
Owski
Witz

DINIZ (DENIS) (1261-1325)
[King of Portugal]
Rei Lavrador (Farmer King)
DINIZ (DENIS). See also:
DENIS
Denis
Denise
DENNIS
Dennis
DENYS
Denys
Dinner-bell, The. See:
BURKE, EDMUND
DINSMOOR, ROBERT (1757-1836) [American poet]
The Rustic Bard
DIO (DION) CASSIUS (155?-235? A.D.) [Roman historian and politician]
Cocceianus
Diodorus Cronus. See:
TAYLOR, RICHARD
Diogenes. See:
POWELL, THOMAS
Diogenes Junior. See:
COWPER, FRANK
Dion. See:
BOUCICAULT, DIONYSIUS LARDNER
DION. See:
DIO (DION) CASSIUS
DION, SISTER RAYMOND DE JESUS (1918-) [American Roman Catholic nun and author]
Mother Raymond de Jesus
Dionne Warwick. See:
WARRICK, MARIE DIONNE
DIONYSIUS (fl. 1st cent. A.D.) [Greek convert to Christianity]
The Areopagite
DIONYSIUS (died 268) [Supreme Pontiff of Roman Catholic Church]
Pope Dionysius
St. Dionysius
DIONYSIUS OF ALEXANDRIA, ST. (c. 190/200-c. 264) [Bishop of Alexandria]
The Great
Dionysos. See:
PTOLEMY XII
Dionysos, Philopator Neos. See: PTOLEMY XI
DIOPHANTUS (fl. 3rd cent. A.D. or later) [Greek mathematician]
The Father of Algebra
Diotima. See:
WYNNE-TYSON, ESME
Diplomat. See:
CARTER, JOHN FRANKLIN
Diplomatists, The Prince of. See: TALLEYRAND-PÉRIGORD, CHARLES MAURICE DE
Dipsy Doodler, The. See:
CLINTON, LARRY
Dircaean Swan, The. See:
PINDAR
Dirceu. See:
GONZAGA, TOMAZ ANTÔNIO
Dirck Van Doren. See:
DEY, FREDERICK VAN RENSSELAER
Dirk. See:
Dic
Dick
DIKE
Dirck
DIRKSEN, EVERETT McKINLEY
GRINGHUIS, RICHARD H.
Dirk Bogarde. See:
BOGAERDE, DEREK JULES GASPARD ULRIC NIVEN VAN DEN
DIRKSEN, EVERETT McKINLEY (1896-1969) [American politician; Congressman from Illinois]
Dirk
The Distillery King
Dirt, The Orator of Free. See:
JULIAN, GEORGE WASHINGTON
Dirty Little Coward, The. See:
FORD, ROBERT
DISCH, THOMAS M. (1940-) [American author]
Dobbin Thorpe

DISCH, THOMAS M. See also:
Demijohn, Thom
Discobulus. See:
ALDOUS, DONALD WILLIAM
D'Isly, Georges. See:
SIMENON, GEORGES
DISNEY, WALTER ELIAS (1901-66) [American cartoonist and motion picture producer]
Walt Disney
DISNEY, WESLEY ERNEST (1883-) [American politician, Congressman from Oklahoma]
Pipe-line Disney
DISRAELI, BENJAMIN, 1ST EARL OF BEACONSFIELD (1804-81) [British novelist, statesman and prime minister]
Dizzy
Laelius
Runnymede
Disraeli of the Chiefs of Staff, The. See:
MacARTHUR, DOUGLAS
Dissenter, A. See:
SWIFT, JONATHAN
Distillery King, The. See:
DIRKSEN, EVERETT McKINLEY
Distinguished Citizen of Georgia. See: BERRY, MARTHA McCHESNEY
Distressed Statesman, The. See: PITT, WILLIAM
District, King of the. See:
KING, WILLIAM HENRY
District Police, The Scourge of the. See: BLANTON, THOMAS LINDSAY
District, The Czar of the. See:
BLANTON, THOMAS LINDSAY
Disunion, The Apostle of. See:
JULIAN, GEORGE WASHINGTON
DITMAS, FRANCIS IVAN LESLIE (fl. early 20th cent.) [British engineer and author]
Ivan Rosedale
DITZEN, RUDOLPH (1893-1947) [German novelist]
Hans Fallada
Dives (The Rich). See:
CRASSUS, MARCUS LICINIUS
Divine Doctor, The. See:
DE RUYSBROECK, JEAN
Divine Empress, The. See:
WU, LADY
Divine, Father. See:
BAKER, GEORGE
Divine Madman, The. See:
BUONARROTI, MICHELANGELO
Divine, Reverend Major J. See:
BAKER, GEORGE
Divine, Reverend Morgan J. See: BAKER, GEORGE
Divine, St. John the. See:
JOHN THE EVANGELIST, ST.
Divine Sarah, The. See:
BERNARD, HENRIETTE ROSINE
Divines, The Shakespeare of. See: TAYLOR, JEREMY
Divino, Il. See:
VECELLI (VECELLIO) TIZIANO
DIX, DOROTHEA LYNDE (1802-87) [American humanitarian]
The Heaven-sent Angel of Mercy and of Prison Reform
Dix, Dorothy. See:
GILMER, ELIZABETH MERIWETHER
Dix, Richard. See:
BRIMMER, ERNEST
Dixie. See:
WALKER, FRED
WARNECKE, LONNIE
DIXON [Dixon]. See also:
Dickson
Dixon, Franklin W. See:
STRATEMEYER, EDWARD L.
Dixon, Granby. See:
KINGSLEY, HENRY
DIXON, HENRY HALL

(1822-70) [British sporting and agricultural writer]
The Druid
DIXON, MARJORIE MACK (1887-) [British author]
Marjorie Mack
Dixon, Ruth. See:
BARROWS, MARJORIE
Dizzy. See:
Dazzy
DEAN, JEROME HANNA
DISRAELI, BENJAMIN, 1ST EARL OF BEACONSFIELD
GILLESPIE, JOHN BIRKS
REECE, ALPHONSO SON
DJANG, YUAN SHAN (1892-) [Chinese author]
Wise
Django. See:
REINHARDT, JEAN BAPTISTE
Djanira. See:
PAIVA, DJANIRA
DJUGASHVILI, YOSIF VISSARIONOVICH (1879-1953) [Russian revolutionist and Soviet dictator]
Joseph Stalin
DJUGASHVILI, YOSIF VISSARIONOVICH. See also:
Big Three, The
D'Lynn. See:
WALDRON-SHAH, DIANE LYNN
DMYTRYK, EDWARD. See:
Hollywood Ten, The
Do-nothing King, The. See:
CLOVIS II
DOANE, GEORGE WASHINGTON (1799-1859) [American churchman; Bishop of New Jersey]
The Missionary Bishop of America
Doane, Marion S. See:
WOODWARD, GRACE STEELE
Dobbin Thorpe. See:
DISCH, THOMAS M.
DOBELL, ISABEL MARIAN BARCLAY (1909-) [Canadian museum curator and author]
Isabel Barclay
DOBELL, SYDNEY THOMPSON (1824-74) [English poet]
Sydney Yendys
DOBER, CONRAD K. (1891-1938) [American pianist and composer]
Con Conrad
DOBNECK. See:
COCHLAEUS (DOBNECK), JOHANN
DOBRACZYNSKI, JAN (1910-) [Polish soldier and author]
Hozjusz
Eugeniusz Kurowski
DOBSON, E. PHILIP (1910-) [British editor and author]
Philip Spring
DOBSON, HENRY AUSTIN (1840-1921) [English poet, critic and biographer]
Austin Dobson
DOBSON, WILLIAM (1610-46) [English portrait and historical painter]
The English Tintoretto
The English Van Dyck
Doc. See:
BLANCHARD, FELIX ANTHONY
CHEATHAM, ADOLPHUS
CRAMER, ROGER M.
CRANDALL, MILTON
DOCK
Dock
EVANS, PAUL WESLEY
FARRELL, EDWARD STEPHEN
HOLLIDAY, JOHN H.
NEWELL, ROBERT
SEVERINSEN, CARL H.
SOUCHON, EDMOND II., M.D.
WEST, HAROLD
Doc, Papa. See:
DUVALIER, DR. FRANÇOIS
Doc Townsend of Florida. See:
HENDRICKS, JOSEPH EDWARD
Dock. See:
BARKER, ARTHUR

DOCK, CHRISTOPHER
(1698-1771) [German-American Mennonite schoolmaster]
The Pious Schoolmaster of Skippack
Docker's K.C., The. See:
BEVIN, ERNEST
Dockstader, Lew. See:
CLAPP, GEORGE ALFRED
Docteur. See:
Doctor
VÉRON, LOUIS DÉSIRÉ
Doctor [Dr.]. See:
CRIPPEN, DR. HAWLEY HARVEY
Docteur
FRANCIA, JOSÉ GASPAR RODRÍGUEZ
GRAHAM, JAMES
JOHNSON, DR. SAMUEL
NEWELL, ROBERT
ROSENBACH, ABRAHAM SIMON WOLF
SPALDING, GILBERT R.
SPOCK, BENJAMIN McLANE
TOWNSEND, FRANCIS EVERETT
Doctor, Angelic. See:
AQUINAS, ST. THOMAS
Doctor Angelicus. See:
ACQUINAS, ST. THOMAS
WICKLIFFE, JOHN
Dr. Billy Graham. See:
GRAHAM, WILLIAM FRANKLIN
Dr. Bruce Spencer. See:
ABEL, ALAN IRWIN
Dr. Caustic. See:
FESSENDEN, THOMAS GREEN
Doctor Charlie. See:
MAYO, CHARLES HORACE
Doctor Christianissimus. See:
GERSON, JEAN CHARLIER DE
Dr. Dolittle. See:
LOFTING, HUGH
Doctor Dulcifuus. See:
ANDREAS, ANTONY
Dr. Edzard Friese. See:
BUDDE, GERHARD AUGUST
Dr. Elisha Kent Kane. See:
FOX, MARGARET
Dr. F. Pezet. See:
ZAUNER, FRANZ PAUL
Dr. Frank Fredericks. See:
FRANCK, FREDERICK SIGFRED
Doctor Fundatissimus. See:
ROMANUS, AGEDIUS, OF COLONNA
Doctor Fundatus. See:
VARRO, WILLIAM
Doctor Illuminatus. See:
LULLY, RAYMOND
TAULER, JOHANN
Doctor Invincibilis. See:
OCKHAM (OCCAM), WILLIAM OF
Doctor Irrefragabilis. See:
ALEXANDER OF HALES
Dr. Jim. See:
JAMESON, SIR LEANDER STARR, 1ST BART.
Dr. Johannes Vogel. See:
HOFPREDIGER, JOHANNES MARTIN VOGEL
Dr. John Paxton. See:
LAWTON, SHERMAN PAXTON
Dr. Joyce Brothers. See:
BROTHERS, JOYCE DIANE BAUER
Doctor, Jungle. See:
WHITE, PAUL HAMILTON HUME
Dr. Mike. See:
MIKESELL, WILLIAM HENRY
Doctor Mirabilis (The Wonderful Doctor). See:
BACON, ROGER
Dr. Mises. See:
FECHNER, GUSTAV THEODOR
Doctor My-book. See:
ABERNETHY, JOHN
Dr. Noel Dunbar. See:
INGRAHAM, COLONEL PRENTISS

Doctor of the Incarnation, The.
See: CYRIL OF ALEXANDRIA, ST.

Dr. Owlglass. See:
BLAICH, HANS ERICH

Doctor Pifföel. See:
DUDEVANT, AMANDINE AURORE LUCIE DUPIN, "BARONNE"

Dr. Pommer. See:
BURGENHAGEN, JOHANN

Doctor Profundus (The Profound Doctor). See:
BRADWARDINE, THOMAS
MIDDLETON, RICHARD

Dr. Service. See:
ISENDAHL, WALTHER

Dr. Seuss. See:
GEISEL, THEODOR SEUSS

Doctor Slop. See:
STODDART, SIR JOHN

Doctor Subtilis (The Cunning Teacher). See:
DUNS SCOTUS, JOHN

Doctor, The. See:
SIDMOUTH, LORD VISCOUNT

Doctor, The Admirable. See:
BACON, ROGER

Doctor, The Authentic. See:
GREGORY OF RIMINI

Doctor, The Divine. See:
DE RUYSBROECK, JEAN

Doctor, The Ecstatic. See:
DE RUYSBROECK, JEAN

Doctor, The Eloquent. See:
AUREOLUS, PETER

Doctor, The Fighting. See:
REYNOLDS, JOHN CROMWELL

Doctor, The Gospel. See:
WICKLIFFE, JOHN

Doctor, The Illustrious. See:
HENRY OF GHENT

Doctor, The Invincible. See:
OCKHAM (OCCAM), WILLIAM OF

Doctor, The Irrefragable. See:
ALEXANDER OF HALES

Doctor, The Little. See:
HOUGHTON, DOUGLASS

Doctor, The Mellifluous. See:
BERNARD OF CLAIRVAUX

Doctor, The Most Resolute.
See: ST. POURÇAINE, GUILLAUME DURAND DE

Doctor, The Plain and Perspicuous. See:
BURLEIGH (BURLEY), WALTER

Doctor, The Plant. See:
CARVER, DR. GEORGE WASHINGTON

Doctor, The Profound (Doctor Profundus). See:
BRADWARDINE, THOMAS
MIDDLETON, RICHARD

Doctor, The Resolute. See:
BACONTHORPE (BACON) (BACHO), JOHN

Doctor, The Scholastic. See:
ANSELM OF LAON

Doctor, The Seraphic. See:
FIDANZA, GIOVANNI DI

Doctor, The Singular. See:
OCKHAM (OCCAM), WILLIAM OF

Doctor, The Solemn. See:
GOETHALS, HENRY

Doctor, The Solid. See:
BRADWARDINE, THOMAS

Doctor, The Touch. See:
GREATRAKES (GREATOREX), VALENTINE

Doctor, The Universal. See:
ALAIN DE LILLE (ALANUS DE INSULIS)

Doctor, The Wise. See:
WESSEL, JOHANN

Doctor, The Wonderful (Doctor Mirabilis). See:
BACON, ROGER

Doctor Universalis. See:
ALBERTUS MAGNUS, SAINT COUNT OF BOLLSTÄDT
AQUINAS, ST. THOMAS

Doctor Venerabilis (Venerable Doctor). See:
CHAMPEAUX, GUILLAUME DE

Doctor, Venerable (Doctor Venerabilis). See:
CHAMPEAUX, GUILLAUME DE

Doctor Will. See:
MAYO, WILLIAM JAMES
Dr. Willard Mackenzie. See:
STRATEMEYER, EDWARD L.
Doctors of France, The Eagle of the. See:
AILLY, PIERRE D'
Doctors, The Pillar of the. See:
CHAMPEAUX, GUILLAUME DE
Dod Grile. See:
BIERCE, AMBROSE GWINNETT
DODD, JAMES WILLIAM (1734-96) [English actor]
The Soul of Empty Eminence
DODDS, WARREN (1898-) [American jazz musician (drums)]
Baby Dodds
DODGE, MARY ABIGAIL (1833-96) [American editor, essayist and poet]
Gail Hamilton
DODGE, MARY ELIZABETH MAPES (1831-1905) [American author and editor]
Mary Mapes Dodge
J.S.
Joel Stacy
Dodge, Steve. See:
BECKER, STEPHEN DAVID
DODGSON, CHARLES LUTWIDGE (1832-98) [English mathematician and author]
Lewis Carroll
Dodo. See:
MARMAROSA, MICHAEL
Doe, John. See:
SCOTT, CLEMENT WILLIAM
Doeg. See:
SETTLE, ELKANAH
DOERFFLER, ALFRED (1884-) [American Lutheran clergyman and author]
Harris Dunn
Fred Ford
Carl H. Thomas
Doesticks, Q.K. Philander, P.B. See:
THOMSON, MORTIMER NEAL
Dog of Gangland, The Mad. See:
COLL, VINCENT
Dog, The Old. See:
BARTLETT, FREDERIC ORIN
Dogberry. See:
MULFORD, PRENTICE
Dogood, Mrs. Silence. See:
FRANKLIN, BENJAMIN
Dogood, Silence. See:
FRANKLIN, BENJAMIN
DOLE, JAMES DRUMMOND (1877-) [American pineapple grower and packer in Hawaii]
The Hawaiian Pineapple King
Jim Dole
DOLET, ÉTIENNE (1509-46) [French religious reformer]
The Martyr of the Renaissance
Dolin, Anton. See:
HEALEY-KAY, PATRICK
Dolittle, Dr. See:
LOFTING, HUGH
Doll, Baby. See:
SORRELL, VICTOR GARLAND
Doll Lady, The Texas. See:
WEAVER, GUSTINE NANCY COURSON
Doll, Tiddy. See:
GREENVILLE, RICHARD TEMPLE
Dollar. See:
BRAND, ADOLF JOHANNES
Dollar Beauty, The Ten Thousand. See:
KELLY, MICHAEL J.
Dollar Tabor, Silver. See:
TABOR, HORACE AUSTIN WARNER
DOLLEN, CHARLES JOSEPH (1926-) [American Roman Catholic priest, librarian and author]
Joseph Benedict
DOLLING, FATHER RICHARD RADCLYFFE (1851-1902)

[English humanist]
The Poor Man's Priest
Dolly. See:
MADISON, DOROTHY PAYNE TODD
MILLENDER, DHARATHULA HOOD
MORSE, THEODORA
Dolly Dawn, See:
STABILE, THERESA
Dolly, Quaker. See:
MADISON, DOROTHY PAYNE TODD
Dolly, Queen. See:
MADISON, DOROTHY PAYNE TODD
Dolo. See:
COKER, CHARLES MITCHELL
Dolores del Rio. See:
MARTÍNEZ, LOLITA DOLORES DE
Dolores Marbourg. See:
BACON, MARY SCHELL
Dolores Warwick. See:
FRESE, DOLORES WARWICK
Dom Denys Rutledge. See:
RUTLEDGE, EDWARD WILLIAM
Dom Manoel. See:
MANUEL II
Dome, Old Double. See:
BRISBANE, ARTHUR
Domecq, Honorio Bustos, B. Suarez Lynch, joint pseuds. of JORGE LUIS BORGES (1899-) and ADOLFO BIOY CASARES (-), [Argentinian authors and poets]
Domenichino, Il. See:
ZAMPIERI, DOMENICO
Domenico. See:
THEOTOKOPOULOS, KYRIAKOS
Domestic Novel, The Founder of the English. See:
RICHARDSON, SAMUEL
Domestic Poet, The. See:
COWPER, WILLIAM
DOMÍNGUEZ, MANUEL (1816-86)
[Spanish bullfighter]
Desperdicios
Dominguín. See:
DEL CAMPO, DOMINGO
GONZÁLEZ, LUIS MIGUEL
DOMINIC, ST. (c.1170-1221)
[Spanish friar]
Master of the Sacred Palace
Dominic, Sister Mary. See:
GALLAGHER, SISTER MARY DOMINIC
DOMINIQUE, ANATIE (1896-)
[American jazz musician (trumpet)]
Natty Dominique
Dominique, Captain. See:
YOU, DOMINIQUE
Don. See:
CARTER, DONALD JAMES
DONN
Donn
DRYSDALE, DONALD SCOTT
GARDNER, DONALD YETTER
HERBERT, DONALD JEFFRY
HUTSON, DONALD
McNEILL, DONALD THOMAS
MARQUIS, DONALD ROBERT PERRY
MURRAY, DONALD PATRICK
NEWCOMBE, DONALD
SCHOLLANDER, DONALD ARTHUR
SMITH, DONALD AUMONT
STANFORD, DONALD EWING
STEPHEN, SIR LESLIE
SUITER, ARLENDO D.
VOORHEES, DONALD
WALKER, DONALD JOHN
WHITEHEAD, DONALD FORD
Don A. Stuart. See:
CAMPBELL, JOHN WOOD
Don Ameche. See:
AMICI, DOMINIC
Don Barry. See:
D'ACOSTA, DONALD BARRY

Don Blunt. See:
BOOTH, EDWIN
Don Camilo. See:
CELA, CAMILO JOSÉ
Don Carlos. See:
BORBÓN, CARLOS LUIS FERNANDO DE, CONDE DE MONTEMOLÍN
BORBÓN, CARLOS MARÍA DE, INFANTE DE ESPAÑA
BORBÓN, CARLOS MARÍA DE LOS DOLORES DE, DUQUE DE MADRID
BORBON, CARLOS MARIA ISIDRO DE, CONDE DE MOLINA
CHARLES IV
Don Davis. See:
DRESSER, DAVIS
Don Demaine. See:
DRINKALL, GORDON DON
Don Donson. See:
SCARPA, SALVATORE
Don Elliott. See:
HELFMAN, DON ELLIOTT
Don, Hetman of the Cossacks of the. See:
PLATOV, MATVEI IVANOVICH, COUNT
Don John. See:
JOHN OF AUSTRIA
Don José. See:
MANAOIS, JOSEPH
Don Juan. See:
JOHN OF AUSTRIA
Don Luis Mazzantini. See:
MAZZANTINI, LUIS
Don Nicholas. See:
DE COLLIBUS, NICHOLAS
Don Quixote of the Jerseys. See:
LIVINGSTON, WILLIAM
Don Randi. See:
SCHWARTZ, DON
Don Raye. See:
WILHOITE, DONALD MACRAE, JR.
Don Ricardo. See:
RIDGELY, RICHARD
Don Rodney. See:
RAGONESE, DON
Don Stauffer. See:
BERKEBILE, FRED DONOVAN
Don Swan. See:
SCHWANDT, WILBUR
Don Tomasito. See:
ROBERTSON, THOMAS ANTHONY
DONAHUE, ALBERT FRANCIS (1904-) [American jazz musician (violin, leader)]
Al Donahue
Donald. See:
BLOOM, MURRAY
Donald Campbell. See:
GILFORD, CHARLES BERNARD
Donald Douglas. See:
KINLEYSIDE, DOUGLAS
Donald Duck. See:
BAILEY, DONALD ORLANDO
Donald Gordon. See:
PAYNE, DONALD GORDON
Donald Grey. See:
THOMAS, EUGENE
Donald Keith. See:
MONROE, KEITH
Donald Thistle. See:
BROWN, H. CLARK
Donald, Vivian. See:
MACKINNON, CHARLES ROY
Donald Winslow. See:
ZOLL, DONALD ATWELL
Donalds, Gordon. See:
SHIRREFFS, GORDON DONALD
Donatello. See:
BARDI, DONATO DI NICCOLÒ DI BETTO
Donato, Joao. See:
OLIVEIRA, JOAO DONATO DE
DONATUS (died c. 355) [Bishop of Carthage]
The Great
Done. See:
BROWN, WILLIAM JOHN
DUNN
Dunn
DUNNE

Dunne
Donelson, Hero of Fort. See:
GRANT, HIRAM ULYSSES
DONN [Donn]. See also:
Don
Donn Broward. See:
HALLERAN, EUGENE EDWARD
DONN-BYRNE, BRIAN OSWALD (1889-1928) [American novelist and short story writer]
Donn Byrne
Donn, Rob. See:
MACKAY, ROBERT
Donna Drake. See:
NOVELLA, RITA
Donna Reed. See:
MULLENGER, DONNA
DONNE, JOHN (1573-1631) [English poet and divine]
The Elder
DONNE, JOHN (1604-62) [English writer]
The Younger
DONNELLY, IGNATIUS (1831-1901) [American reformer and author]
The Sage of Nininger
DONO, PAOLO DE (1397-1475) [Florentine painter]
Paolo Uccello
DONOGHUE, STEVEN (1884-1945) [English jockey]
Steve Donoghue
Donohue, Troy. See:
JOHNSON, MERLE
Donovan, Dick. See:
MUDDOCK, JOYCE EMERSON PRESTON
Donovan, John. See:
DILLINGER, JOHN HERBERT
Donovan, William. See:
BERKEBILE, FRED DONOVAN
DONSON, CYRIL (1919-) [English educator, journalist and author]
Via Hartford
Russ Kidd
Donson, Don. See:
SCARPA, SALVATORE
DONUS (died 678) [Supreme Pontiff of Roman Catholic Church]
Pope Donus
Doodler, The Dipsy. See:
CLINTON, LARRY
Doog, K. Caj. See:
GOOD, IRVING JOHN
DOOLEY, ANITA DONNA (1899-1961) [Italian-American stage and motion picture actress]
Nita Naldi
Dooley, Mr. See:
DUNNE, FINLEY PETER
Doone Fargo. See:
NORWOOD, VICTOR GEORGE CHARLES
Doone, Jice. See:
MARSHALL, JAMES VANCE
Dor, Ana. See:
CEDER, GEORGIANA DORCAS
Dora Bryan. See:
BROADBENT, DORA
Dora d'Istria. See:
GHIKA, HELENA
Dora, Sister. See:
PATTISON, DOROTHY WYNDLOW
Dora Thorne. See:
BRAME, CHARLOTTE MARY
Dora Wordsworth. See:
QUILLINAN, DOROTHY WORDSWORTH
Dorant, Gene. See:
LENT, DORA GENEVA
DORAT. See:
DINEMANDY (DORAT), JEAN
Dore. See:
SCHARY, ISIDORE
DORE, CLAIRE MORIN (1934-) [Canadian teacher and author]
Claire France
Claire Morin
DORE, JOHN FRANCIS (1881-1938) [American politician; Mayor of Seattle, Washington]

The Labor Mayor
Doreen Ireland. See:
LORD, DOREEN MILDRED DOUGLAS
Doreen Wallace. See:
RASH, DORA EILEEN AGNEW WALLACE
DORGAN, THOMAS ALOYSIUS (1877-1929) [American cartoonist and sports writer]
Tad Dorgan
d'Orgemont. See:
BARRES, ADRIEN DES
DORHAM, McKINLEY HOWARD (1924-) [American jazz musician (trumpet, composer)]
Kenny Dorham
DORIA, ANDREA (c.1468-1560) [Genoese admiral and statesman]
The Father of Peace
Liberator and Father of his Country
The Liberator of Genoa
Doric Collyer. See:
HUNT, DOROTHY ALICE
Dorimond. See:
DROUIN, NICHOLAS
Doris Day. See:
VON KAPPELHOFF, DORIS
Doris Leslie. See:
FERGUSSON HANNAY, LADY
Doris Rybot. See:
PONSONBY, DORIS ALMON
DORLING. See also:
DARLING
Darling
DORLING, HENRY TAPRELL (1883-) [English author]
Taffrail
DORMAN, MICHAEL (1932-) [American journalist and author]
Jack Bishop
Dormie, M.A. See:
SHARROCK, MARIAN EDNA DORMITZER
Dormont de Belloy. See:
BUYRETTE, PIERRE LAURENT
Dorn, Philip. See:
VAN DUNGEN, FRITZ
Dornford Yates. See:
MERCER, CECIL WILLIAM
Dorothea Bennett. See:
YOUNG, DOROTHEA BENNETT
Dorothea Julia Ramsbottom. See: THACKERAY, WILLIAM MAKEPEACE
Dorothea Tinne. See:
STROVER, DOROTHEA
Dorothy Borne. See:
RICE, DOROTHY MARY
Dorothy Canfield. See:
FISHER, DOROTHY CANFIELD
Dorothy Cowlin. See:
WHALLEY, DOROTHY
Dorothy Dix. See:
GILMER, ELIZABETH MERIWETHER
Dorothy Gilman. See:
BUTTERS, DOROTHY GILMAN
Dorothy Gish. See:
GUICHE, DOROTHY DE
Dorothy Laird. See:
CARR, DOROTHY STEVENSON LAIRD
Dorothy Lamour. See:
KAUMEYER, DOROTHY
Dorothy Mackie Low. See:
LOW, LOIS DOROTHEA
Dorothy Malone. See:
MALONEY, DOROTHY
Dorothy Margaret Stuart. See:
BROWNE, DOROTHY MARGARET STUART
Dorothy Nyren. See:
CURLEY, DOROTHY NYREN
Dorothy Prescott. See:
POOR, AGNES BLAKE
Dorothy Q. See:
HOLMES, OLIVER WENDELL
Dorothy Terriss. See:
MORSE, THEODORA
Dorothy Thompson. See:
LEWIS, MRS. SINCLAIR

Dorothy Vicary. See:
RICE, DOROTHY MARY
Dorothy Wayne. See:
SAINSBURY, NOEL EVERINGHAM
DORR, JULIA CAROLINE RIPLEY (1825-1913) [American poet and novelist]
Caroline Thomas
Dors, Diana. See:
FLUCK, DIANA
Dorsage, Jean. See:
SIMENON, GEORGES
Dorsan, Luc. See:
SIMENON, GEORGES
D'ORSAY, ALFRED GUILLAUME GABRIEL, COUNT (1801-52) [French nobleman]
The Last of the Dandies
Dorsetshire Burns, The. See:
BARNES, WILLIAM
DORSEY, GERRY (1936-) [English singer of popular songs]
Engelbert Humperdinck
DORSEY, JAMES (1904-54) [American jazz musician (clarinet, saxophones, leader)]
Jimmy Dorsey
The World's Greatest Alto Saxophone Player
DORSEY, SARAH ANNE ELLIS (1829-79) [American author]
Filia
DORSEY, THOMAS (1905-56) [American jazz musician (trombone, trumpet, leader)]
T. D.
Tommy
The Sentimental Gentleman
The Sentimental Gentleman of Swing
DORST, JEAN PIERRE (1924-) [French ornithologist and author]
Pierre d'Urstelle
Dorvigny. See:
ARCHAMBAULT, LOUIS-FRANÇOIS
Dossage, Jean. See:
SIMENON, GEORGES
Douanier, Le. See:
ROUSSEAU, HENRI JULIEN FÉLIX
Double Dome, Old. See:
BRISBANE, ARTHUR
Double Quick. See:
HOLLINGSWORTH, JAMES H.
DOUBLEDAY, ABNER (1819-93) [American general officer and pioneer in the game of baseball]
The Father of Baseball
Old Forty-eight Hours
DOUBLEDAY, NELTZE DE GRAFF (1865-1918) [American author of books on birds and gardening]
Neltze Blanchan
DOUDY, REGINALD (1902-) [British stage and motion picture actor]
John Garrick
Doug. See:
GOODWIN, CHARLES D.
Doug Demarest. See:
BARKER, WILL
Doug, Dugout. See:
MacARTHUR, DOUGLAS
Doug Fairbanks. See:
ULLMAN, JULIUS
Dough Moose, The. See:
PERKINS, GEORGE WALBRIDGE
Doughboy's General, The. See:
BRADLEY, OMAR NELSON
Doughboys, The Mother of All the. See:
SCHUMANN-HEINK, MME. ERNESTINE
DOUGHERTY, DANIEL (1826-92) [American orator]
The Silver-tongued Orator
DOUGHERTY, WALTER HAMPDEN (1879-1955) [American actor]
Walter Hampden
DOUGHTON, ROBERT L. (1863-) [American politician, active in agricultural

legislation]
Farmer Bob
Muley Doughton
DOUGHTY, JAMES P. (1849-1922) [American cotton broker and cotton exchange official]
The Dean of Cotton Row
Uncle Jimmie
Doughty of the South, The. See: RICHARDS, THOMAS ADDISON
Douglas Ainslie. See: DUFF, DOUGLAS AINSLIE GRANT
Douglas, Albert. See: ARMSTRONG, DOUGLAS ALBERT
DOUGLAS, ARCHIBALD (1328?-1400) [Scottish nobleman; 3rd Earl of Douglas and Lord of Galloway]
The Black Douglas
The Grim
DOUGLAS, ARCHIBALD (1372-1424) [Scottish nobleman; 4th Earl of Douglas and 1st Duke of Touraine]
The Black Douglas
The Tyneman (Loser)
DOUGLAS, ARCHIBALD (1450?-1514) [Scottish nobleman; 5th Earl of Angus]
Bell-the-Cat
The Great Earl
The Red Douglas
DOUGLAS, ARCHIBALD (1489?-1557) [Scottish nobleman; 6th Earl of Angus]
The Red Douglas
DOUGLAS, ARCHIBALD (1555-88) [Scottish nobleman; 8th Earl of Angus]
The Good Earl
The Red Douglas
Douglas Coe. See: Allen, Adam
EPSTEIN, BERYL WILLIAMS
Douglas Collier. See: FELLOWES-GORDON, IAN DOUGLAS
Douglas, Donald. See: KINLEYSIDE, DOUGLAS
Douglas, Ellen. See: WILLIAMSON, ELLEN DOUGLAS
Douglas Fairbanks. See: ULLMAN, JULIUS
Douglas Farr. See: GILFORD, CHARLES BERNARD
DOUGLAS, GEORGE (1380?-1403) [Scottish nobleman; 1st Earl of Angus]
The Red Douglas
DOUGLAS, GEORGE (1412?-62) [Scottish nobleman; 4th Earl of Angus]
The Red Douglas
Douglas, George. See: BROWN, GEORGE DOUGLAS
Douglas Grant. See: OSTRANDER, ISABEL
Douglas Hardy. See: ANDREWS, CHARLES ROBERT DOUGLAS HARDY
Douglas Hogarth. See: PHILLIPS-BIRT, DOUGLAS
Douglas, Hudson. See: AITKEN, ROBERT
DOUGLAS, JAMES (1358?-88) [Scottish nobleman; 2nd Earl of Douglas]
The Black Douglas
The Dead Man Who Won a Fight
DOUGLAS, JAMES (1371-1443) [Scottish nobleman; 7th Earl of Douglas and Earl of Avondale]
The Black Douglas
The Fat
The Gross
DOUGLAS, JAMES (1426-88) [Scottish nobleman; 9th and last Earl of Douglas]
The Black Douglas
DOUGLAS, JOHN (1881-) [British educator and author]

Ian Douglas
DOUGLAS, JOHN SHOLTO (1844-1900) [British nobleman, athlete and patron of boxing]
The Marquis of Queensberry
Douglas, Kirk. See:
DEMSKY, ISSUR DANIELOVITCH
Douglas, Marian. See:
ROBINSON, ANNIE DOUGLAS GREEN
Douglas Marshall. See:
McCLINTOCK, MARSHALL
Douglas, Melvyn. See:
HESSELBERG, MELVYN
Douglas, Mike. See:
DOWD, MICHAEL DELANEY, JR.
Douglas, Olive. See:
BUCHAN, ANNA
Douglas Ring. See:
PRATHER, RICHARD SCOTT
Douglas, Robert. See:
ANDREWS, CHARLES ROBERT DOUGLAS HARDY
FINLAYSON, ROBERT DOUGLAS
Douglas Rutherford. See:
McCONNELL, JAMES DOUGLAS RUTHERFORD
Douglas, Shane. See:
WILKES-HUNTER, RICHARD
DOUGLAS, SIR JAMES (1286-c. 1330) [Lord of Douglas]
The Black Douglas
The Good
DOUGLAS, SIR JAMES (1803-77) [Canadian trader and public official]
The Father of British Columbia
DOUGLAS, SIR WILLIAM (1300?-53) [Scottish Nobleman]
The Flower of Chivalry
The Knight of Liddesdale
DOUGLAS, SIR WILLIAM OF (died 1298) [Scottish nobleman; 1st Lord of Douglas]
The Hardy
Douglas Sirk. See:
SIERCK, DETLEF
DOUGLAS, STEPHEN ARNOLD (1813-61) [American politician]
The Little Giant
Douglas, The Black. See:
DOUGLAS, ARCHIBALD
DOUGLAS, JAMES
DOUGLAS, SIR JAMES
DOUGLAS, WILLIAM
Douglas, The Red. See:
DOUGLAS, ARCHIBALD
DOUGLAS, GEORGE
Douglas Valentine. See:
WILLIAMS, GEORGE VALENTINE
DOUGLAS, WILLIAM (1327?-84) [Scottish nobleman; 1st Earl of Douglas]
The Black Douglas
DOUGLAS, WILLIAM (1724-1810) [British nobleman and sportsman]
The Duke of Queensberry
Old Q
Douglass. See:
MONTGOMERY, ROBERT DOUGLASS
Douglass, Frederick. See:
BAILEY, FREDERICK AUGUST WASHINGTON
DOUGLASS, WILLIAM (c. 1691-1752) [American physician, almanac maker and economist]
William Nadir
DOURAS, MARION (1900-61) [American motion picture actress]
Marion Davies
Douro, Old. See:
WELLINGTON, ARTHUR WELLESLEY, 1ST DUKE OF
Douro, The Marquis of. See:
BRONTË, CHARLOTTE
D'OUTREMEUSE, JEAN; See:
Mandeville, Jehan de (Sir John)

DOUVAIN, SANDRA (1942-) [American model and motion picture actress]
Sandra Dee
Dove, Billie. See:
BOHNY, LILIAN
DOVE, DAVID JAMES (c. 1696-1769) [Anglo-American educator and pamphleteer]
Philopatrius
Dover, Darry. See:
KHAURY, HERBERT BUCKINGHAM
Dow, Jr. See:
PAIGE, ELBRIDGE GERRY
DOW, LORENZO (1777-1834) [American preacher and eccentric]
Crazy Dow
DOW, NEAL (1804-97) [American prohibitionist]
The Father of the Maine Law
The Father of Prohibition
Dow, Peggy. See:
VARNADOW, PEGGY
Dowager, The. See:
MADISON, DOROTHY PAYNE TODD
Dowager, The Queen. See:
MADISON, DOROTHY PAYNE TODD
DOWD, MICHAEL DELANEY, JR. (1925?-) [American television personality]
Mike Douglas
Dowd, T.B. See:
PORTER, WILLIAM SYDNEY
DOWDEN, ANNE OPHELIA TODD (1907-) [American artist and author]
Anne Ophelia Todd
Dowdy, Mrs. Regera. See:
GOREY, EDWARD ST. JOHN
DOWELL, HORACE KIRBY (1904-) [American jazz musician (saxophone, composer, leader)]
Saxie Dowell
Dowers, Penn. See:
PENDOWER, JACQUES
DOWIE, JOHN ALEXANDER (1847-1907) [Scottish founder of Christian Catholic Church]
Elijah the Restorer
Dowling, Eddie. See:
GOUCHER, JOSEPH NELSON
DOWLING, VINCENT (-1852) [English sportsman]
Long Scribe
Downe, Patrick. See:
LASCELLES, WALTER
DOWNER, ELIPHALET (17??-1806) [American surgeon]
The Fighting Surgeon of the Revolution
DOWNEY, EDMUND (fl. late 19th-early 20th cent.) [Irish author]
F. N. Allen
DOWNEY, MORTON (1902-) [American singer]
The Irish Thrush
DOWNEY, RAYMOND JOSEPH (1914-) [American composer, singer and pianist]
Roy Wells
DOWNING, FRANCES MURDAUGH (1835-94) [American novelist and poet]
Frank Dashmore
Fanny Downing
Downing, J. See:
DAVIS, CHARLES AUGUSTUS
Downing, Major J. See:
DAVIS, CHARLES AUGUSTUS
Downing, Major Jack. See:
SMITH, SEBA
Downing of Downingville, Major Jack. See:
SMITH, SEBA
Downingville, Major Jack Downing of. See:
SMITH, SEBA
DOWNS, SARAH ELIZABETH (1843-) [American novelist]
Mrs. Georgie Sheldon
DOWSE, THOMAS (1772-1856) [American book collector]

The Literary Leather-
Dresser
DOWSETT, JOSEPH MOREWOOD (1864-) [English author]
Teswod
Traveller
Doyen of Mystery Writers in English and Probably in Any Language, The. See: STOUT, REX TODHUNTER
DOYLE, MARTHA CLAIRE MACGOWAN (1869-) [American author]
Martha James
DOYLE, SIR ARTHUR CONAN (1859-1930) [Scottish author and physician]
The Good Giant
DR. [Dr.]. Names so prefixed are indexed as though spelled "DOCTOR" or "Doctor"
DRACKETT, PAUL (1922-) [English author]
Paul King
Draco, F. See: DAVIS, JULIA
Drag, Slow. See: PAVAGEAU, ALCIDE
DRAGO, HENRY SINCLAIR (1888-) [American author]
Stewart Cross
Kirk Deming
Will Ermine
Bliss Lomax
J. Wesley Putnam
Grant Sinclair
Drake, Alfred. See: CAPURRO, ALFRED
Drake C. Denver. See: NYE, NELSON CORAL
Drake, Charles. See: RUPPERT, CHARLES
Drake, Donna. See: NOVELLA, RITA
Drake Elvin. See: BEHA, ERNEST
Drake, Fabia. See: McGLINCHY, F.D.
DRAKE, JOSEPH RODMAN. See: Croakers & Co.
Drake, Lisl. See: BEER, ELOISE C.S.
DRAKE, SIR FRANCIS (1545?-96) [English navigator, explorer and privateer]
Frankie Drake
Drake, Tom. See: ALDERDICE, ALFRED
Drama, The Father of American. See: DUNLAP, WILLIAM
Drama, The Father of Modern. See: IBSEN, HENRIK JOHAN
Drama, The Father of Portuguese. See: VICENTE, GIL
Drama, The Father of the French. See: JODELL, ÉTIENNE
Drama, The Father of the Spanish. See: CARPIO, LOPE FÉLIX DE VEGA
ENCINA (ENZINA), JUAN DEL
Drama, The Fielding of the. See: FARQUHAR, GEORGE
Drama, The Homer of the French. See: CORNEILLE, PIERRE
Drama, The Napoleon of the. See: BUNN, ALFRED
ELLISTON, ROBERT WILLIAM
Drama, The Virgil of the French. See: RACINE, JEAN BAPTISTE
Drama, The Wizard of American. See: BELASCO, DAVID
Dramatic Critics, The Dean of the. See: MANTLE, ROBERT BURNS
Dramatic Poets, The Homer of Our. See: SHAKESPEARE, WILLIAM
Dramatic Poets, The Horace of Our. See: SHAKESPEARE, WILLIAM
DRAPER, PAUL (1909-) [Anglo-American dancer]

Dancing Hamlet
Drapier, M.B. See:
SWIFT, JONATHAN
Drayne, George. See:
McCULLEY, JOHNSTON
Drayton, Alfred. See:
VARICK, ALFRED
Drayton, Lillian R. See:
CORYELL, JOHN RUSSELL
Drayton Mayrant. See:
SIMONS, KATHERINE DRAYTON MAYRANT
Dreadnaught, Old. See:
BOSCAWEN, EDWARD
Dreamer, The Immortal. See:
BUNYAN, JOHN
Dreary Wodge. See:
GOREY, EDWARD ST. JOHN
DREMANN, JANIS (c.1920-) [American radio and motion picture actress]
Janis Carter
Dresdel, Sonia. See:
OBEE, LOIS
DRESSEN, CHARLES WALTER (1898-1966) [American professional baseball manager]
Chuck Dressen
DRESSER, DAVIS (1904-) [American author of mystery stories]
Asa Baker
Matthew Blood
Kathryn Culver
Don Davis
Brett Halliday
Anthony Scott
Peter Shelley
Anderson Wayne
DRESSER, DAVIS. See also:
Debrett, Hal
Dresser, Louise. See:
KERLIN, LOUISE
Dresser, The Literary Leather. See: DOWSE, THOMAS
Dressler, Marie. See:
KOERBER, LEILA
DREW [Drew]. See also:
Dru
DREW, DANIEL (1797-1879) [American capitalist and stock market speculator]
Uncle Dan'l
Drew, Ellen. See:
RAY, TERRY
DREW, SAMUEL (1765-1833) [British smuggler, shoemaker and Wesleyan preacher]
The Cornish Metaphysician
Drexel, Jay B. See:
BIXBY, JEROME LEWIS
DREYFUS, JEAN-PAUL (1909-) [French motion picture director]
Jean-Paul le Chanois
Dring, Nathaniel. See:
McBROOM, R. CURTIS
DRINKALL, GORDON DON (1927-) [British journalist and author]
Don Demaine
DRINKER, ANNA (1827-) [American poet]
Edith May
Driving Force, The. See:
ROOSEVELT, THEODORE
Droch. See:
BRIDGES, ROBERT SEYMOUR
Droll, The. See,
BRUEGHEL (BREUGHEL), PIETER
DROOTIN, BENJAMIN (1920-) [Russian jazz musician (drums)]
Buzzy Drootin
Drop Shot. See:
CABLE, GEORGE WASHINGTON
DROUIN, NICHOLAS (c.1628-c.1664) [French provincial actor-manager]
Dorimond
DROUINEAU, FRANÇOIS (1917-) [French motion picture actor]
Frank Villard
DROUOT, ANTOINE, COMTE (1774-1847) [French general of artillery]
Le Sage de la Grande Armée
Drover. See:

WAYNE, ANTHONY
DROWER, ETHEL STEFANA MAY (1879-) [British author]
E. S. Stevens
Dru. See also:
DREW
Drew
Dru, Joanne. See:
LA COCK, JOANNE
Druce, Christopher. See:
PULLING, CHRISTOPHER ROBERT DRUCE
DRUCKER, PETER FERDINAND (1909-) [Austrian-American author, university professor and business consultant]
The Most Helpful Philosopher About the Business Scene We Have
Druid, The. See:
DIXON, HENRY HALL
DRUM, ROBERT F. (1918-) [American journalist, columnist and author]
Bob Drum
Drummer Boy of the Rappahannock, The. See:
HENDERSHOT, ROBERT HENRY
Drummer Man, That Ace. See:
KRUPA, EUGENE BERTRAM
DRUMMOND, EDITH MARIE DULCE CARMAN (1883-) [British author]
Dulce Carman
DRUMMOND, PATRICK HAMILTON (1857-) [Irish author]
Barton Shaw
Drummond, Walter. See:
SILVERBERG, ROBERT
Drums, King of the. See:
KRUPA, EUGENE BERTRAM
Drunkard, The. See:
MICHAEL III
WENCESLAUS IV
Dry Bishop from Virginia, The. See: CANNON, BISHOP JAMES, JR.
Dry Hole. See:
STEBBINS, GRANT CASE
Dry Plate Process in America, The Father of. See:
NEWTON, HENRY JOTHAM
Dry, The Kansas. See:
GUYER, ULYSSES SAMUEL
Dry Wind, The. See:
GUYER, ULYSSES SAMUEL
Dryasdust. See:
STRYPE, JOHN
DRYDEN, JOHN (1631-1700) [English playwright and poet]
The Father of English Criticism
The Greatest Writer of the Restoration Period
The Squab Poet
Dryden, John. See:
ROWLAND, DONALD SYDNEY
Dryden of Germany, The. See:
OPITZ, MARTIN
DRYSDALE, DONALD SCOTT (1936-) [American professional baseball player]
Don Drysdale
Duane. See:
JONES, DOROTHY HOLDER
DUANE, CHARLES P. (fl. mid-19th cent), [San Francisco politician; chief engineer of San Francisco fire department]
Dutch Charlie
Duane, Jim. See:
HURLEY, VIC
Duane Richards. See:
HURLEY, VIC
DuBARRY, MARIE JEANNE GOMARD DE VAUBERNIER, COMTESSE (1741-93) [Favorite of King LOUIS XV of France]
Madame Du Barry
du Blane, Daphne. See:
GROOM, ARTHUR WILLIAM
DuBOSE. See also:

DE BOIS
DUBUS
DuBOSE, LOUISE JONES (1901-) [American educator, editor and author]
Nancy Telfair
DUBUS. See also:
DE BOIS
DuBOSE
DUBUS, PIERRE-LOUIS (1721-99) [French comic actor]
Préville
Duca Minimo (The Least of the Dukes). See:
RAMPAGNETTO, GAETANO
Ducas. See:
JOHN III
MICHAEL VII
DUCASSE, ISIDORE LUCIEN (1846-70) [French prose-poet]
Le Comte de Lautréamont
Duce, Il. See:
MUSSOLINI, BENITO
Duch. See also:
Dutch
Duch Bill. See:
HICKOCK, JAMES BUTLER
DUCHAMP, GASTON ÉMILE (1875-) [French artist, engraver and lithographer]
Jacques Villon
DUCHÉ, JACOB (1737/8-98) [American clergyman, patriot and author]
T. Caspipina
DUCHESNE, ANDRÉ (1584-1640) [French historian]
The Father of French History
Duchesne, Jacques. See:
SAINT-DENIS, MICHEL JACQUES
Duchesne, Le Père. See:
HÉBERT, JACQUES RENÉ
DUCHESNE, ROSE PHILIPPINE (1769-1852) [French founder of Catholic convents in America]
The Woman Who Always Prays
Duchess of Gordon, The Beautiful. See:
GORDON, JANE MAXWELL
Duchess, The. See:
HARDING, FLORENCE KLING DE WOLFE
HUNGERFORD, MRS. MARGARET WOLFE
DUCHIN, EDWIN FRANK (1909-51) [American jazz musician (piano, leader)]
Eddie Duchin
The Magic Fingers of Radio
Duck Bill. See:
HICKOCK, JAMES BUTLER
Duck, Donald. See:
BAILEY, DONALD ORLANDO
Duckboard. See:
BUTLER, SMEDLEY DARLINGTON
Ducky Wuckie. See:
MEDWICK, JOSEPH M.
Dud. See:
BASCOMB, WILBUR ODELL
Dud, Cousin. See:
LEBLANC, DUDLEY J.
Dude President, The. See:
ARTHUR, CHESTER ALAN
DUDEVANT, AMANDINE AURORE LUCIE DUPIN, "BARONNE" (1804-76) [French novelist]
George Sand
Jules Sand
Doctor Piffoël
Dudley, Ernest. See:
COLTMAN-ALLEN, ERNEST
Dudley, Frank. See:
GREENE, WARD
Dudley, Jay. See:
CHAPMAN, J. DUDLEY
Dudley Manners. See:
KRUPP, MAJOR D. DUDLEY
Dudley, Nancy. See:
COLE, LOIS DWIGHT

Dudley, Robert. See:
BALDWIN, JAMES
DUDLEY, WALTER BRONSON (1877-1944) [American drama critic, playwright and humorist]
Bide Dudley
DUDLY, CAROLINE LOUISE (1862-1937) [American actress]
The American Bernhardt
Mrs. Leslie Carter
Duel Fighter, The. See:
JACKSON, ANDREW
Duel Fighter, The Kentucky. See: CLAY, CASSIUS MARCELLUS, SR.
Duff. See:
HARSTAD, ADOLPH
DUFF, CHARLES ST. LAWRENCE (1894-) [Irish author]
Cathal O'Dubh
DUFF, DOUGLAS AINSLIE GRANT (1865-) [English poet, critic and diplomat]
Douglas Ainslie
Duffy. See: LEWIS, GEORGE EDWARD
Dufour, Pierre. See:
LACROIX, PAUL
DUGANNE, AUGUSTINE JOSEPH HICKEY (1823-84) [American author of dime novels]
Motley Manners
Arthur Townley
DUGGAN, DENISE VALERIE (1909-) [English author]
Denise Egerton
DUGHET, GASPAR (1613-75) [French painter]
Gaspar Poussin
Dugout Doug. See:
MacARTHUR, DOUGLAS
DUGUESCLIN. See:
GUESCLIN (DUGUESCLIN), BERTRAND DU
Duguid, Robert. See:
PRINGMILL, ROBERT DUGUID FORREST
DUHAMEL, GEORGES (1884-1966) [French physician and writer]
Denis Thévenin
Duke. See:
DERRINGER, PAUL
ELLINGTON, EDWARD KENNEDY
JORDAN, IRVING SIDNEY
MORRISON, MARION MICHAEL
PEARSON, COLUMBUS CALVIN
SNIDER, EDWIN DONALD
WICKLIFFE, CHARLES ANDERSON
DUKE, ANNA MARIE PATRICIA (1946-) [American television and motion picture actress]
Patty Duke
Duke, Billy. See:
TESONE, WILLIAM N.
Duke Cuyler. See:
MESERVE, COLONEL ARTHUR LIVERMORE
DUKE, DONALD NORMAN (1929-) [American writer on railroads]
Roger Valentine
Duke Duncan. See:
RATHBONE, ST. GEORGE HENRY
Duke Humphrey, Good. See:
HUMPHREY
Duke of Birmingham, The. See:
POWELL, JAMES ROBERT
Duke of Braintree. See:
ADAMS, JOHN
Duke of Cumberland, The Bloody. See: CUMBERLAND, WILLIAM AUGUSTUS, DUKE OF
DUKE OF GORDON. See:
GEORGE, DUKE OF GORDON
Duke of Lower Lorraine. See:
GODFREY OF BOUILLON
Duke of Monmouth. See:
SCOTT, JAMES
Duke of Otranto, The. See:
MANOLESCO, GEORGE
Duke of Queensberry, The. See:

DOUGLAS, WILLIAM
Duke of Reichstadt. See:
BONAPARTE, NAPOLEON FRANÇOIS CHARLES JOSEPH
Duke of Somerset, The Proud. See: SEYMOUR, CHARLES, 6th DUKE OF SOMERSET
Duke of Summersetts, The. See: HOLMES, JOHN
Duke of Tralee, The. See:
BRESNAHAN, ROGER PATRICK
Duke of Windsor. See:
EDWARD VIII
Duke of Xensi. See:
HOLM, H.H. FRITZ VILHELM
Duke, The. See:
RUSSELL, JOSEPH
STOCKTON, RICHARD
Duke, The Great. See:
WELLINGTON, ARTHUR WELLESLEY, 1ST DUKE OF
Duke, The Iron. See:
MULDOON, WILLIAM
WELLINGTON, ARTHUR WELLESLEY, 1ST DUKE OF
Duke, The Little. See:
SCOTT, JAMES
Duke, The Protestant. See:
SCOTT, JAMES
Duke, The Silly. See:
CHURCHILL, JOHN
Duke, Vernon. See:
DUKELSKY, VLADIMIR
DUKELSKY, VLADIMIR (1903-) [Russian-American composer and pianist]
Vernon Duke
Dukes, The Least of the (Duca Minimo). See:
RAMPAGNETTO, WILLIAM
DUKINFIELD, WILLIAM CLAUDE (1879-1946) [American comedian, juggler, actor and script writer]
George Bogle
Otis Criblecoblis
Bill Fields
W.C. Fields
Mahatma Kane Jeeves
DULANY, DANIEL (1722-97) [American lawyer, statesman and pamphleteer]
Antilon
Dulce Carman. See:
DRUMMOND, EDITH MARIE DULCE CARMAN
Dulcie Gray. See:
BAILEY, DULCIE
Dulcifuus, Doctor. See:
ANDREAS, ANTONY
Dullness, The King of. See:
CIBBER, COLLEY
Dülmen, The Nun of. See:
EMMERICH, ANNA KATHARINA
DUMAS, ALEXANDRE (1802-70) [French novelist and playwright]
Alexander the Great
Dumas père
The Fourth Musketeer
DUMAS, ALEXANDRE (1824-95) [French novelist and playwright]
Dumas fils
DUMAS, ALEXANDRE DAVY DE LA PAILLETERIE (1762-1806) [French general officer]
Horatius Cocles of the Tyrol
Dumas of the Indians, The. See: CLOUS, OLIVIER
Dumb Ox. See:
AQUINAS, ST. THOMAS
Dumb Poet, The Deaf and. See:
NACK, JAMES M.
Dumb Prophet, The. See:
CLEVELAND, STEPHEN GROVER
Dum-Dum. See:
KENDALL, JOHN KAYE
Dunbar, Dr. Noel. See:
INGRAHAM, COLONEL PRENTISS

Duncan Clay. See:
DIEHL, WILLIAM WELLS
Duncan, Duke. See:
RATHBONE, ST. GEORGE HENRY
Duncan, Gregory. See:
McCLINTOCK, MARSHALL
Duncan, Jane. See:
CAMERON, ELIZABETH JANE
Duncan, Julia K. See:
KARIG, WALTER
STRATEMEYER, EDWARD L.
Duncan, Lois. See:
CARDOZO, LOIS STEINMETZ
DUNCAN, RENAULT RENALDO (1904-) [American painter and motion picture actor]
Duncan Renaldo
DUNCAN, WILLIAM MURDOCH (1909-) [Scottish author]
John Cassells
Neill Graham
Martin Locke
Peter Malloch
Lovat Marshall
Dunces, The King of. See:
CIBBER, COLLEY
DUNDAS, HENRY (1742-1811) [British political leader]
Starvation Dundas
The Uncrowned King of Scotland
Dundee, Bonny. See:
GRAHAM, JOHN
Dunelmus Bristoliensis. See:
CHATTERTON, THOMAS
DUNHAM, ELMER LEWIS (1914-) [American jazz musician (trombone, trumpet, leader)]
Sonny Dunham
DUNHAM, WILLIAM D. (1910-) [American composer and script writer]
By Dunham
DUNKERLEY, WILLIAM ARTHUR (1852-1941) [English novelist and religious poet]
John Oxenham
Dunlap, Colonel Walter P. See: COBB, SYLVANUS, JR.
Dunlap, Lon. See:
McCORMICK, WILFRED
DUNLAP, WILLIAM (1766-1839) [American playwright, theater manager, painter and historian]
A Citizen of New York
America's First Professional Playwright
An American
The Author of "The Archers"
The Author of "The Father"
The Father of American Drama
DUNLOP, AGNES MARY ROBERTSON (fl. mid-20th cent.) [British author]
Elizabeth Kyle
Jan Ralston
DUNN [Dunn]. See also:
Done
DUNNE
Dunne
Dunn, Blind Willie. See:
MASSARO, SALVATORE
Dunn Browne. See:
FISKE, SAMUEL WHEELOCK
DUNN, EMMETT CLARKE (1860-1938) [City manager of Alexandria, Virginia]
The Grand Old Man of Alexandria
Dunn, Harris. See:
DOERFFLER, ALFRED
Dunn, James. See:
WILKES-HUNTER, RICHARD
DUNN, MARIE BICKFORD (1898-1937) [Anglo-French motion picture actress]
Marie Prevost
DUNN, MARY ALICE (1897-) [Scottish author]
Mary Faid
Dunn, Michael. See:

MILLER, GARY NEIL
DUNNE [Dunne]. See also:
Done
DUNN
Dunn
Dunne, Desmond. See:
LEE-RICHARDSON, JAMES
DUNNE, FINLEY PETER (1867-1936) [American satirist]
Mr. Dooley
DUNNE, IRENE (1904-) [American motion picture actress]
The First Lady of Hollywood
DUNNER, JOSEPH (1908-) [German educator and author]
Germanicus
Alexander Roth
DUNNING, ANNIE KETCHUM (1831-) [American author]
Nellie Grahame
Dunning, Charlotte. See:
WOOD, CHARLOTTE DUNNING
DUNNINGER. See also:
DENNINGER
DUNNINGER, JOSEPH (1896-) [American mind reader and magician]
The Child Wonder Magician
The Man With the Miracle Mind
The Master Mind of Mental Mystery
DUNOIS, JEAN (1402-68) [natural son of LOUIS, Duke of Orleans; military associate of JOAN OF ARC]
The Bastard of Orleans
Count of Dunois and Longueville
DUNS SCOTUS, JOHN (1265?-1308?) [Scottish scholastic theologian and philosopher]
Doctor Subtilis (The Cunning Teacher)
DUNSANY, EDWARD JOHN MORETON DRAX PLUNKETT, 18TH BARON (1878-1957) [Irish poet, dramatist and novelist]
Lord Dunsany
Dunstan, Andrew. See:
CHANDLER, A. BERTRAM
DUNTON, EDITH KELLOGG (1875-) [American author]
Margaret Warde
DU PARC, RENÉ BERTHELOT (c. 1630-64) [French comic actor]
Gros-René
Du Perry, Jean. See:
SIMENON, GEORGES
DUPIN, ANDRÉ MARIE JEAN JACQUES (1783-1865) [French advocate]
The Elder
Duplessis, Yves. See:
JAURAND, YVONNE
DU PONT, ALFRED IRÉNÉE (1864-1935) [American industrialist]
Savior of the DuPonts
Dupont, Paul. See:
FREWIN, LESLIE RONALD
Dupres, Henri. See:
FAWCETT, FRANK DUBREZ
DUPUY, ELIZA ANN (1814-81) [American novelist and short story writer]
Annie Young
Durable Ned. See:
KALBFUS, EDWARD CLIFFORD
Duran, Carolus. See:
DURAND, CHARLES AUGUSTE ÉMILE
DURAND, CHARLES AUGUSTE ÉMILE (1837-1917) [French Painter]
Carolus Duran
Auguste Emile Carolus-Duran
DURAND, MME. ALICE FLEURY (1842-1902)

[French novelist]
Henry Gréville
DURANT, WILLIAM JAMES (1885-) [American author and historian]
Will Durant
DURANTE, JAMES FRANCIS (1893-) [American comedian, pianist and actor]
Jimmy Durante
Ragtime Jimmy
Schnozzola
Durazzo, Charles of. See: CHARLES III
DURBIN, EDNA MAE (1921-) [Canadian singer and motion picture actress]
Deanna Durbin
DÜRER, ALBRECHT (1471-1528) [German painter and engraver]
The Prince of Artists
D'URFEY, THOMAS (1653-1723) [English dramatist and humorous poet]
Tom D'Urfey
DURGIN, FRANCIS TIMOTHY (1922-) [American motion picture actor]
Rory Calhoun
DURGNAT, RAYMOND ERIC (1932-) [British author]
O.O. Green
DURHAM, EDWARD FANT (1908-) [American professional baseball player]
Bull Durham
DURIVAGE, FRANCIS ALEXANDER. See: Old 'un
DURKIN, TRENT (1915-35) [American juvenile motion picture actor]
Junior Durkin
DUROCHER, LEO ERNEST (1906-) [American baseball player and manager]
The Lip
Lippy Durocher
DURRELL, JACQUELINE SONIA RASEN (1929-) [British zoologist and author]
Jacquie Durrell
Durrell, Jane. See: FULKS, SARAH JANE
DURRELL, LAWRENCE GEORGE (1912-) [English author]
Charles Norden
Gaffer Peeslake
DURST, PAUL (1921-) [American journalist and author]
Peter Bannon
John Chelton
Jeff Cochran
John Shane
d'Urstelle, Pierre. See: DORST, JEAN PIERRE
Duse of the Dance, The. See: KOREFF, NORA
Duse, The Singing. See: ROQUER, EMMA DE
Du Shon, Jean. See: ATWELL, JEAN
Dusko Goykovich. See: GAJKOVIC, DUSAN
Duster. See: MAILS, WALTER
Duster, A Gentlemen With a. See: BEGBIE, HAROLD
Dusty. See:
COOKE, ALLEN LINDSEY
RHODES, JAMES LAMAR
RHODES, JOHN GORDON
Dutch. See:
CLARK, EARL
Duch
Dutch Bill. See: HICKOCK, JAMES BUTLER
Dutch Billy. See: WILLIAM III
Dutch Charlie. See: DUANE, CHARLES P.
Dutch Cleanser, Old. See: BLANKENBURG, RUDOLPH
Dutch Millionaire, The. See: PHILIPSE, FREDERICK

Dutch Poetry, The Father of.
See: VAN MAERLANT, JAKOB DE COSTER
Dutch Poets, The Father of.
See: VAN MAERLANT, JAKOB DE COSTER
Dutch Reformed Church in America, The Father of The. See:
LIVINGSTON, JOHN HENRY
Dutch Schultz. See:
FLEGENHEIMER, ARTHUR
Dutchman, The. See:
FLEGENHEIMER, ARTHUR
Dutchman, The Flying. See:
WAGNER, JOHN PETER
Dutchy. See:
PROVINE, JOHN WILLIAM
Duumvirs, The (The Duumvirate) joint name applied to THOMAS WOODROW WILSON (1856-1924), [28th President of the United States], and EDWARD MANDELL HOUSE (1858-1938) [American army officer and Wilson's confidential adviser]
Duumvirs, The (The Duumvirate). See also:
HOUSE, EDWARD MANDELL
WILSON, THOMAS WOODROW
DUVAL, MARTIN PAUL ALEXANDRE (1855-1906) [French novelist and short story writer]
Jean Lorrain
DUVALIER, DR. FRANÇOIS (1907-71) [President of Haiti]
Papa Doc
Dvorak, Ann. See:
McKIM, ANN
Dwarf Statesman, The. See:
STEPHENS, ALEXANDER HAMILTON
Dwight, Allan. See:
COLE, LOIS DWIGHT
Dwight Bennett. See:
NEWTON, DWIGHT BENNETT
Dwight David Eisenhower.
See: EISENHOWER, DAVID DWIGHT
Dwight McGlinn. See:
BRANNON, WILLIAM T.
DWIGHT, THEODORE. See:
Hartford Wits, The
DWIGHT, TIMOTHY. See:
Hartford Wits, The
DWYER, WILLIAM VINCENT (1883-1946) [American bootlegger, rum runner and racketeer]
Big Bill Dwyer
The King of the Bootleggers
DYER, CHARLES (1928-) [British playwright, novelist, actor and director]
C. Raymond Dyer
Raymond Dyer
R. Kraselchik
Charles Stretton
Renshaw Stretton
DYER, MARY (16??-1660) [Anglo-American Quaker martyr]
The Quaker Martyr
Dykeman, Wilma. See:
STOKELY, WILMA DYKEMAN
Dylan, Bob. See:
ZIMMERMAN, ROBERT
Dynamo of Power, The. See:
ROOSEVELT, THEODORE
Dynamo of the Italian Motion Picture Industry, The.
See: LAURENTIS, DINO DE
Dynely. See:
James, Dynely
DYSCOLUS, APOLLONIUS (fl. 2d cent. A.D.) [Alexandrian grammarian]
The Prince of Grammarians
Dyskolos (Ill Tempered). See:
APPOLONIUS

E

E.A. See:
ALEXANDER, ELEANOR JANE

E. A. B. See:
BAUGHAN, EDWARD ALGERNON
E. Arnot Robertson. See:
TURNER, EILEEN ARBUTHNOT ROBERTSON
E. B. See:
BEERS, ETHELINDA ELIOT
WHITE, ELWYN BROOKS
E. B. B. See:
BROWNING, ELIZABETH BARRETT
E. B. C. Jones. See:
LUCAS, EMILY BEATRIX COURSOLLES
E. B. Merritt. See:
WADDINGTON, MIRIAM
E. Barrington. See:
BECK, MRS. LILY MORESBY ADAMS
E. C. M. See:
McBRIDE, PETER
E. C. R. See:
HADFIELD, ELLIS CHARLES RAYMOND
E. Channing Matthews. See:
CHANNING-RENTON, LIEUT. ERNEST MATTHEWS
E. Chatterton Hodge. See:
HASTINGS, PHYLLIS DORA HODGE
E. D. M. See:
MANSFIELD, EDWARD DEERING
E. D. Tinne. See:
STROVER, DOROTHEA
E. de P. Flint. See:
FIELDEN, THOMAS PERCEVAL
e. e. See:
CUMMINGS, EDWARD ESTLIN
E. Foxton. See:
PALFREY, SARAH HAMMOND
E. G. Walraven. See:
JONES, EMMA GARRISON
E. H. Arr. See:
ROLLINS, MRS. ELLEN CHAPMAN HOBBS
E. H. Clements. See:
HUNTER, EILEEN HELEN
E. J. Richmond, Mrs. See:
RICHMOND, EUPHEMIA JOHNSON
E. K. See:
KORSOMO, EMIL
E. K. Seth-Smith. See:
MURRELL, ELSIE KATHLEEN
E. L. St. Vrain, Major. See:
MANNING, WILLIAM HENRY
E. L. Vincent. See:
MORRIS, CHARLES SMITH
E. L. Withers. See:
POTTER, GEORGE WILLIAM, JR.
E. M. See:
FORSTER, EDWARD MORGAN
HINDS, EVELYN MARGERY
E. M. Delafield. See:
DASHWOOD, MRS. EDMÉE ELIZABETH MONICA
E. M. England. See:
ANDERS, EDITH MARY ENGLAND
E. Morchard Bishop. See:
STONOR, OLIVER
E. P. See:
ROE, EDWARD PAYSON
E. P. H. See:
HOLLISTER, EDWARD PAYSON
E. R. Kern. See:
KERNER, FRED
E. R. Rangely. See:
KANTO, PETER
E. S. St. Mox- A U.S. Detective. See:
ELLIS, EDWARD SYLVESTER
E. S. Stevens. See:
DROWER, ETHEL STEFANA MAY
E. Souza. See:
SCOTT, EVELYN

E.T. See:
BELL, ERIC TEMPLE
E.V. Cunningham. See:
FAST, HOWARD MELVIN
E. Von Linden. See:
MAY, KARL FRIEDRICH
E.W. See:
HOWE, EDGAR WATSON
E. Ward Strayer. See:
STRATEMEYER, EDWARD L.
E.X. Ferrars. See:
BROWN, MORNA DORIS
EADGAR. See:
EDGAR (EADGAR)
EADMUND. See:
EDMUND (EADMUND)
EDMUND (EADMUND) II
EDMUND (EADMUND), ST.
EADWARD. See:
EDWARD (EADWARD)
Eadweard Muybridge. See:
MUGGERIDGE, EDWARD JAMES
EADWIG. See:
EDWY (EADWIG)
Eagle, Aged. See:
ELIOT, THOMAS STEARNS
Eagle, Gray. See:
NYE, JAMES WARREN
SPEAKER, TRISTRAM E.
Eagle of Brittany, The. See:
GUESCLIN (DUGUESCLIN), BERTRAND DU
Eagle of Edgefield, The Bald. See: GARY, MARTIN WITHERSPOON
Eagle of Illinois, Black. See:
LOGAN, JOHN ALEXANDER
Eagle of Meaux, The. See:
BOSSUET, JACQUES BÉNIGNE
Eagle of the Doctors of France, The. See:
AILLY, PIERRE D'
Eagle of the East, The. See:
WEBSTER, DANIEL
Eagle of Westchester, The Bald. See:
HUSTED, JAMES WILLIAM
Eagle Orator of South Carolina, The. See:
CALHOUN, JOHN CALDWELL
Eagle Orator of Tennessee, The. See:
HENRY, GUSTAVUS ADOLPHUS
Eagle Orator, The. See:
HENRY, GUSTAVUS ADOLPHUS
STOKES, WILLIAM BRICKLY
Eagle, Quentin the. See:
ROOSEVELT, QUENTIN
Eagle, Solomon. See:
SQUIRE, JOHN COLLINGS
Eagle, The Bald. See:
GARY, MARTIN WITHERSPOON
Eagle, The Great. See:
MAIMONIDES
Eagle, The Lone. See:
LINDBERGH, CHARLES AUGUSTUS
Eagle, The Theban. See:
PINDAR
Eaglet, The (l'Aiglon). See:
BONAPARTE, NAPOLEON FRANÇOIS CHARLES JOSEPH
Ealhwine. See:
ALCUIN
Eamon MacAedhagan. See:
EGAN, EDWARD WELSTEAD
Eando. See:
BINDER, OTTO OSCAR
Earhart, Amelia. See:
PUTNAM, AMELIA EARHART
Earl Holliman. See:
NUMKENA, ANTHONY
Earl, John Prescott. See:
GILCHRIST, BETH BRADFORD
Earl, Mary. See:
KING, ROBERT
Earl of Richmond, Henry. See: HENRY VII
Earl of Surrey. See:
HOWARD, HENRY
Earl, The Architect. See:

HERBERT, HENRY, 9TH
EARL OF PEMBROKE
Earl, The Good. See:
DOUGLAS, ARCHIBALD
Earl, The Great. See:
BOYLE, RICHARD, 1ST
EARL OF CORK
DOUGLAS, ARCHIBALD
Earl, The Wizard. See:
PERCY, SIR HENRY
Earle, W.J. See:
SENARENS, LUIS PHILIP
Earley, Martha. See:
WESTWATER, SISTER
AGNES MARTHA
EARLY, JUBAL ANDERSON
(1816-94) [American
Civil War general
officer]
The Bad Old Man
Crackers
Old Jube
Old Jubilee
Early Temperance Reformation,
The Luther of the. See:
HEWIT, NATHANIEL
EARNSHAW, GEORGE LIVING-
STON (1900-)
[American professional
baseball player]
Big Moose
Moose
Ears, Airplane. See:
ANDERSON, JOHN Z.
Earth-son, The Old Titanic.
See: WEBSTER, DANIEL
Earthquake. See:
ALLEN, WILLIAM
East, Michael. See:
WEST, MORRIS LANGLO
East Side Kids, The. See:
Dead End Kids, The.
East, The Eagle of the. See:
WEBSTER, DANIEL
EASTMAN, CHARLES
ALEXANDER (1858-1939)
[American Sioux Indian
physician and author]
Ohiyesa
EASTMAN, CHARLES GAMAGE
(1816-61) [American poet]
Burns of the Green Mountain
Burns of New England

EASTON, DALE (1918-)
[American motion picture
actor]
Greg McClure
EASTWOOD, HELEN (1892-)
[English author]
Olive Baxter
Fay Ramsay
Easy Boss Platt. See:
PLATT, THOMAS
COLLIER
Eat, Sleep'n. See:
BEST, WILLIE
Eater, The English Opium. See:
DE QUINCEY, THOMAS
Eaton, George L. See:
VERRAL, CHARLES
SPAIN
EATON, MARGARET O'NEILL
(1796-1879) [wife of
JOHN HENRY EATON,
secretary of War in
President ANDREW
JACKSON'S cabinet]
Bellona
The Gorgeous Hussy
Peggy O'Neill
Pothouse Peggy
Eaton, Peggy. See:
O'NEALE, MARGARET L.
EBASSUN, ANTONIO (fl. 18th
cent.) [Spanish bullfighter]
Martincho
EBERLE, IRMENGARDE
(1898-) [American author]
Allyn Allen
Phyllis Ann Carter
Ebony. See:
BLACKWOOD, WILLIAM
EBSEN, CHRISTIAN RUDOLF
(c. 1906-) [American
dancer and television and
motion picture actor]
Buddy Ebsen
ECCARD. See:
ECKHART (ECCARD)
(ECKARDT), JOHANNES
ECCLES, GEORGE CLINTON,
JR. (1916-) [American
theatrical producer]
The Dean of American Tent-
theater Showmen
St. John Terrell

Ecclesiastical History, The
Father of. See:
BEDE (BEDA) (BAEDA), ST.
EUSEBIUS OF CAESAREA
Echo, Proteus, Esq. See:
FRANKLIN, BENJAMIN
Eci. See:
McCONNELL, JOHN PRESTON
Ecijano. See:
JIMÉNEZ, JUAN
Eck, Johann. See:
MAYER, JOHANN ECK
ECKARDT. See:
ECKHART (ECCARD) (ECKARDT), JOHANNES
ECKE, BETTY TSENG YU-HO (1923-) [Chinese painter, educator and author]
Tseng Yu-ho
ECKER, JUDITH K. (1933-) [American composer and teacher]
Judith Koch
ECKHART (ECCARD) (ECKARDT) JOHANNES (c. 1260-1327) [German mystic and theologian]
Meister Eckhart
Eckmar, F.R. See:
DE HARTOG, JAN
ECKSTINE, WILLIAM CLARENCE (1914-) [American jazz musician (singer, valve trombone)]
Billy Eckstine
Mr. B.
Eclov, Shirley. See:
PFOUTZ, SHIRLEY ECLOV
Economy, Mr. See:
BYRD, HARRY FLOOD
Ecstatic Doctor, The. See:
DE RUYSBROECK, JEAN
Ed. See:
BEGLEY, EDWARD
FITZGERALD, EDWARD
GARDNER, EDWARD FRANCIS
HOWE, EDGAR WATSON
ILIFF, JOHN EDGAR
KIRKEBY, WALLACE T.
McKEEVER, EDWARD CLARK
SARDELLA, EDWARD A.
SULLIVAN, EDWARD VINCENT
WALSH, EDWARD AUGUSTIN
Ed, Cotton. See:
SMITH, ELLISON DuRANT
Ed McBain. See:
HUNTER, EVAN
Ed Wynn. See:
LEOPOLD, ISIAH EDWIN
Edana Romney. See:
RUBENSTEIN, EDANA
Edar. See:
ANTHONY, EDWARD
Eddie. See:
ARNOLD, RICHARD EDWARD
BUZZELL, EDWARD
CANO, EDWARD, JR.
COLLINS, EDWARD TROWBRIDGE
CONDON, ALBERT EDWARD
DE LANGE, EDGAR
DUCHIN, EDWIN FRANK
EDDY
Eddy
EDWARDS, EDWIN BRANFORD
FISHER, EDWIN JACK
GUEST, EDGAR ALBERT
HIGGINS, HAYDN
POE, EDGAR ALLAN
RICKENBACKER, EDWARD VERNON
SNYDER, EDWARD
SAWYER, EDWIN MILBY
SOUTH, EDWARD OTHA
STANKY, EDWARD RAYMOND
Eddie Albert. See:
HEIMBERGER, EDDIE ALBERT
Eddie Cantor. See:
ISKOWITZ, EDWARD ISRAEL
Eddie Dean. See:
GLOSSUP, EDGAR D.
Eddie Dowling. See:

GOUCHER, JOSEPH
NELSON
Eddie Fisher. See:
FISHER, EDWIN JACK
Eddie Fisher, Private. See:
FISHER, EDWIN JACK
Eddie Foy. See:
FITZGERALD, EDWIN
Eddie Lang. See:
MASSARO, SALVATORE
Eddie Leonard. See:
TONEY, LEMUEL
GORDON
Eddie Maxwell. See:
CHERKOSE, EDWARD
Eddie "Piano" Miller. See:
LISBONA, EDWARD
Eddie Shu. See:
SHULMAN, EDWARD
Eddy, Baseball. See:
KELLY, EDWARD
AUSTIN
EDDY, THOMAS (1758-1827)
[American philanthropist
and reformer]
The American Howard
Edgar. See:
WALLACE, RICHARD
HORATIO EDGAR
Edgar A. Perry. See:
POE, EDGAR ALLAN
Edgar Box. See:
VIDAL, GORE
EDGAR (EADGAR) (944-75)
[Saxon King of England]
The Peaceful
Edgar Poe. See:
LEVINE, PHILIP
Edgar Vance. See:
AMBROSE, ERIC
Edgefield, John. See:
ILIFF, JOHN EDGAR
Edgefield, The Bald Eagle of.
See: GARY, MARTIN
WITHERSPOON
Edgeworth Bess. See:
LYON, BESS
EDGEWORTH, HENRY ESSEX
(1745-1807) [Irish
churchman]
Abbé Edgeworth
De Firmont
Edie Adams. See:
KOVACS, EDITH ENKE
EDISON [Edison]. See also:
Edson
EDISON, HARRY (1915-)
[American jazz
musician (trumpet)]
Sweets
Edison of Crime Detection,
The. See:
HEINRICH, EDWARD
OSCAR
EDISON, THOMAS ALVA
(1847-1931) [American
Inventor]
The Father of the Phono-
graph
The Wizard of Menlo Park
The Wizard of the Wires
Edith de Born. See:
BISCH, EDITH
Edith Heal Barrien. See:
HEAL, EDITH
Edith Lindeman. See:
CALISCH, EDITH
Edith May. See:
DRINKER, ANNA
Edith Nesbit. See:
BLAND, MRS. HUBERT
Edith Piaf. See:
GASSION, EDITH
GIOVANNA
Edith Settle. See:
ANDREWS, WILLIAM
LINTON
Edith Van Dyne. See:
BAUM, LYMAN FRANK
Editors, The Dean of American
Magazine. See:
ALDEN, HENRY MILLS
EDMISTON, HELEN JEAN
MARY (1913-) [English
author]
Helen Robertson
Edmonds, Charles. See:
CARRINGTON, CHARLES
EDMUND
EDMONDS, HELEN WOODS
(1904-) [British author]
Anna Kavan
EDMUND (1245-96) [Earl of
Lancaster]
Crouchback
Edmund Breon. See:

MacLAVERTY, EDMUND
Edmund Carey. See:
KEAN, EDMUND
Edmund Crispin. See:
MONTGOMERY, ROBERT BRUCE
EDMUND (EADMUND) I (922?-46) [Saxon King of England]
The Deed-doer
The Magnificent
EDMUND (EADMUND) II (980?-1016) [Saxon King of England]
Ironside
EDMUND (EADMUND), ST. (841?-70) [King of the East Anglians]
The Martyr
Edmund Freebetter. See:
DABOLL, NATHAN
Edmund Kirke. See:
GILMORE, JAMES ROBERTS
Edmund Marshall. See:
HOPKINS, KENNETH
Edmund O. Scholefield. See:
BUTTERWORTH, WILLIAM EDMUND III
EDMUNDS, GEORGE FRANKLIN (1829-1919) [American politician; Senator from Vermont]
St. Jerome
Edna Lyall. See:
BAYLY, ADA ELLEN
Edna May Oliver. See:
COX-OLIVER, EDNA MAY
Edna Murray. See:
ROWLAND, DONALD SYDNEY
Edna Temple Crane. See:
EICHER, ETHEL ELIZABETH
Edna Winfield. See:
STRATEMEYER, EDWARD L.
Edogawa Rampo. See:
HIRAI, TARO
Edouard. See also:
Eduard
Eduardi
EDWARD
Edward
Edouard Benet. See:
EDWARDS, WILLIAM BENNETT
Edouard Grau. See:
WORTH, ADAM
Edouin. See also:
EDWIN
Edwin
Edouin, Willie. See:
BRYER, WILLIAM FREDERICK
Edschmid, Kasimir. See:
SCHMIDT, EDUARD
Edson. See also:
EDISON
Edison
Edson, N.I. See:
DENISON, MARY ANDREWS
Eduard. See also:
Edouard
Eduardi
EDWARD
Edward
Eduard Blutig. See:
GOREY, EDWARD ST. JOHN
Eduardi. See also:
Edouard
Eduard
EDWARD
Edward
Eduardi, Guillermo. See:
EDWARDS, WILLIAM BENNETT
Education, The Father of the System of Common-school. See:
TREADWELL, JOHN
EDWARD [Edward]. See also:
Edouard
Eduard
Eduardi
EDWARD I (1239-1307) [King of England]
The English Justinian
The Hammer of the Scots
Longshanks
The Scourge of Scotland
EDWARD II (1284-1327) [King of England]
Edward of Carnarvon
EDWARD III (1312-77) [King of

England]
Edward of Windsor
EDWARD IV (1441-83) [King of England]
The Robber
EDWARD VI (1537-53) [King of England]
The Pious
EDWARD VII (1841-1910) [King of England and Ireland]
The Peacemaker
EDWARD VIII (1894-) [King of England]
Duke of Windsor
Edward Arnold. See:
SCHNEIDER, GUENTHER
Edward Candy. See:
NEVILLE, BARBARA ALISON BOODSON
Edward Carrick. See:
CRAIG, EDWARD ANTHONY
EDWARD (EADWARD) (870?-924) [Saxon King of England]
The Elder
EDWARD (EADWARD) (c.963-78) [Saxon King of England]
The Martyr
The Philosopher
The Royal Martyr
EDWARD (EADWARD) (1002?-66) [Saxon King of England]
The Confessor
Edward G. Robinson. See:
GOLDENBERG, EMANUEL
Edward Grendon. See:
LeSHAN, LAWRENCE LEE
Edward Hope. See:
COFFEY, EDWARD HOPE
Edward, James. See:
STUART, JAMES FRANCIS EDWARD
Edward Lexy. See:
LITTLE, EDWARD GERALD
Edward Lytton. See:
MORRIS, CHARLES SMITH
WHEELER, EDWARD LYTTON
Edward Minturn. See:
JUDSON, EDWARD ZANE CARROLL
URNER, NATHAN DANE
EDWARD, PRINCE OF WALES (1330-76) [Son of EDWARD IV, King of England]
The Black Prince
Edward Search. See:
TUCKER, ABRAHAM
Edward Sterling. See:
LAMBERT, EDWARD
EDWARD, VISCOUNT GREY OF FALLODON (1862-) [British nobleman, military officer and author]
Grey of Fallodon
Edward William Sidney. See:
TUCKER, NATHANIEL BEVERLEY
Edward Young. See:
REINFELD, FRED
Edwards, Al. See:
NOURSE, ALAN EDWARD
EDWARDS, CLIFF (1895-) [American singer, entertainer and actor]
Ukulele Ike
EDWARDS, EDWIN BRANFORD (1891-1963) [American jazz musician (trombone)]
Daddy Edwards
Eddie Edwards
Edwards, Eleanor Lee. See:
VICTOR, MRS. METTA VICTORIA FULLER MORSE
Edwards, F.E. See:
NOLAN, WILLIAM FRANCIS
EDWARDS, GEORGE (1693-1773) [English ornithologist]
The Father of Ornithologists
EDWARDS, GEORGE GRAVELY (1896-) [American author]
George Graveley

EDWARDS, HERBERT CHARLES (1912-) [British teacher and author]
Bertram Edwards
EDWARDS, JANE CAMPBELL (1932-) [American author]
Jane Campbell
Edwards, John Milton. See: COOK, WILLIAM WALLACE
EDWARDS, JONATHAN (1703-58) [American Congregational clergyman and theologian]
The Artist of Damnation
The Elder
EDWARDS, JONATHAN (1745-1801) [American Congregational theologian]
The Younger
Edwards, Jules. See: JUDSON, EDWARD ZANE CARROLL
Edwards, Julia. See: CORYELL, JOHN RUSSELL
Edwards, Julie. See: STRATEMEYER, EDWARD L.
Edwards, Max. See: BENJAMIN, CLAUDE MAX EDWARD POHLMAN
Edwards, Michael. See: SLOWITZKY, MICHAEL
Edwards, Norman, joint pseud. of THEODORE EDWIN WHITE (1938-) and T. CARR (-) [American authors]
Edwards, Norman. See also: WHITE, THEODORE EDWIN
Edwards, Stephen. See: PALESTRANT, SIMON S.
Edwards, Vincent. See: ZOINO, VINCENT EDWARD
Edwards, Ward. See: RATHBONE, ST. GEORGE HENRY
Edwards, Warren. See: MANNING, WILLIAM HENRY
EDWARDS, WILLIAM BENNETT (1927-) [American ordnance expert and author]
Edouard Benet
Harvey Brandt
James L. Cranbrook
Guillermo Eduardi
Charles S. Johnson
Capt. Wilbur Jones
William C. L. Thompson
Edwige Feuillere. See: CUNATI, EDWIGE
EDWIN [Edwin]. See also: Edouin
Edwin Baldwin. See: GODWIN, WILLIAM
Edwin C. Burritt. See: BRILL, ETHEL CLAIRE
Edwin Caskoden. See: MAJOR, CHARLES
Edwin Emerson. See: ELLIS, EDWARD SYLVESTER
Edwin James. See: GUNN, JAMES E.
EDWIN, JOHN (1749-90) [English actor]
The Elder
Edwin South. See: CAMPBELL, BARTLEY T.
Edwin Winslow Martin. See: McCABE, JAMES DABNEY
Edwina Booth. See: WOODRUFF, EDWINA
EDWY (EADWIG) (c. 938-58) [King of Wessex]
The Fair
Edzard Friese, Dr. See: BUDDE, GERHARD AUGUST
Effie Johnson. See: RICHMOND, EUPHEMIA JOHNSON
Eflor, Colonel Oram. See: ROLFE, MARO O.
Eflor, Oram. See: ROLFE, MARO O.
EFROS, ISRAEL ISAAC (1891-) [Polish-American educator and author]

Efrot
Efrot. See:
EFROS, ISRAEL ISAAC
Egalité. See:
LOUIS-PHILIPPE
Egalité, Philippe. See:
JOSEPH, LOUIS-PHILIPPE
EGAN, EDWARD WELSTEAD (1922-) [American editor and author]
Eamon MacAedhagan
Egan, Lesley. See:
LININGTON, ELIZABETH
Egan O'Neill. See:
LININGTON, ELIZABETH
EGAN, PATRICK (1841-1919) [Irish-American politician]
Blaine's Irishman
The Escaped Jailbird
EGAN, PIERCE (1772-1849) [British sporting and humorous writer]
The Elder
EGAN, PIERCE (1814-80) [British artist and author]
The Younger
Egbert Augustus Cowslip, Esq. See: BARKER, BENJAMIN
Egbert S. Thomas. See:
ELLIS, EDWARD SYLVESTER
EGEDE, HANS (1686-1758) [Norwegian missionary]
The Apostle of Greenland
Egeria of Guizot, The. See:
LIEVEN, DOROTHEA, PRINCESS DE
Egerton, Denise. See:
DUGGAN, DENISE VALERIE
EGERTON, FRANCIS (1736-1803) [Duke of Bridgewater; projector of inland canals]
The Father of British Inland Navigation
Egerton, George. See:
BRIGHT, MRS. MARY CHAVELITA DUNNE
EGGLESTON, EDWARD (1837-1902) [American author]
Penholder
Eglinton, John. See:
MAGEE, WILLIAM KIRKPATRICK
EGNATZIK, JOSEPH (1920-) [American musician and composer]
Sandy Nelson
Egypt, St. Antony of. See:
ANTONY (ANTHONY), ST.
Egypt, The Big Man from Little. See:
KELLER, KENT ELLSWORTH
Egypt, The Peter the Great of. See: MEHEMET (MOHAMMED) ALI
Egyptian Miracle Man, The. See: BEY, RAHMAN
EHLERS, FRIEDRICH ROBERT (1858-) [German philosopher, psychologist and author]
Friedrich Robert
Ehrich von Stroheim. See:
VON NORDENWALL, HANS EHRICH MARIA STROHEIM
EHRLICH, BETTINA BAUER (1903-) [Austrian artist, illustrator and author]
Bettina
EHRLICH, JOHN GUNTHER (1930-) [American lawyer, newspaperman and author]
Jack Ehrlich
EICHBERGER, WILLY (1905-) [Austrian motion picture actor]
Carl Esmond
EICHER, ETHEL ELIZABETH (fl. 1934-65) [American psychologist and writer]
Edna Temple Crane
Emily Paul
William Paul
Eight to Seven, Old. See:
HAYES, RUTHERFORD BIRCHARD

1817, Somebody, M.D.C. See:
NEAL, JOHN
1812, The Land Hero of. See:
JACKSON, ANDREW
Eighteenth Amendment, The Father of the. See:
SHEPPARD, MORRIS
Eighteenth Century, The Most Thoroughgoing British Skeptic of the. See:
HUME, DAVID
Eighteenth Century, The Plato of the. See:
AROUET, FRANÇOIS MARIE
EIGNER, LAURENCE J. (1927-) [American author]
Larry Eigner
Eileen Elias. See:
DAVIES, EILEEN WINIFRED
Eileen McKeay. See:
McKEAG, ERNEST LIONEL
Eileen Page. See:
HEAL, EDITH
Eileen Thompson. See:
PANOWSKI, EILEEN THOMPSON
EINSELEN, ANNE F. (fl. 1939-49) [American novelist]
Anne Paterson
EINSTEIN, HARRY (1904-58) [American radio comedian]
Harry Parke
Parkyakarkus
Nick Parkyakarkus
Eirlys Trefor. See:
WILLIAMS, EIRLYS OLWEN
EISENHOWER, DAVID DWIGHT (1890-1969) [American general officer; thirty-fourth President of the United States]
Dwight David Eisenhower
General Ike
Ike
EISENSTAT, JANE SPERRY (1920-) [American artist and author]
J.E. Sperry
El de las Mercedes (He of the Largesse). See:
HENRY II
El Greco (The Greek). See:
THEOTOKOPOULOS, KYRIAKOS
El-Shabazz, Malik. See:
LITTLE, MALCOLM
Elagabalus (Heliogabalus). See: BASSIANUS, VARIUS AVITUS
Elaine May. See:
BERLIN, ELAINE
Elbertus, Fra. See:
HUBBARD, ELBERT
Elbur Ford. See:
HIBBERT, ELEANOR BURFORD
Elchi, The Great. See:
CANNING, SIR STRATFORD
Eichik Hiat. See:
KATZ, MENKE
Elder, Cosimo the. See:
MEDICI, COSIMO DE'
Elder, J.H. Rosny the. See:
BÖEX, JOSEPH HENRI HONORÉ
Elder, Jan the. See:
BRUEGHEL (BREUGHEL), JAN
Elder, Pieter the. See:
BRUEGHEL (BREUGHEL), PIETER
BURMAN (BURMANN), PIETER
ELDER, SUSAN BLANCHARD (1835-1923) [American poet, historian and miscellaneous writer]
Hermine
Elder, The. See:
APOLLINARIS
ARNOBIUS
BRUEGHEL (BREUGHEL), PIETER
BURMAN (BURMANN), PIETER
CALAMY, EDMUND
CATO, MARCUS PORCIUS
CEPHISODOTUS
CHANNING, WILLIAM ELLERY

COLMAN, GEORGE
CYRUS
DONNE, JOHN
DUPIN, ANDRÉ MARIE
JEAN JACQUES
EDWARD (EADWARD)
EDWARDS, JONATHAN
EDWIN, JOHN
EGAN, PIERCE
FLETCHER, GILES
GAMALIEL
HALS, FRANZ
HOLBEIN, HANS
KILLIGREW, THOMAS
MEER, JAN VAN DER
PALMA, JACOPO
PITT, WILLIAM
SCIPIO AFRICANUS,
PUBLIUS CORNELIUS
SECUNDUS, GAIUS
PLINIUS
SENECA, MARCUS LUCIUS
ANNAEUS
Smectymnuus
STONE, NICHOLAS
STRAUSS, JOHANN
STROZZI, FILIPPO
STURE, STEN
TAYLOR, ISAAC
TENIERS, DAVID
THEODOSIUS
VAN DE VELDE,
WILLEM
VISCHER, HERMANN
VISCHER, PETER
WARTON, THOMAS

Elder, The (El Viejo). See:
HERRERA, FRANCISCO

Elder, The (Hazaken). See:
HILLEL

Elder, The (Il Vecchio). See:
PALMA, JACOPO

Elder, The Blue Light. See:
JACKSON, THOMAS
JONATHAN

Elder, The Phenomenal Presiding. See:
WILSON, JOHN ALFRED
BAYNUM

Elder, William the. See:
VELDE, WILLEM VAN
DE

Elderly Spinster, An. See:
WILSON, MARGARET

Eldred Grayson. See:
HARE, ROBERT

ELDRIDGE, DAVID ROY (1911-) [American jazz musician (trumpet)]
Little Jazz
Roy Eldridge

Eldridge, Florence. See:
McKECHNIE, FLORENCE

Eleanor. See:
BELL, JESSIE MARY
ELEANOR
Elinor
ROOSEVELT, ANNA
ELEANOR

Eleanor Babbis. See:
FRIISBAASTAD, BABBIS
ELINOR

Eleanor Burford. See:
HIBBERT, ELEANOR
BURFORD

Eleanor Dorothy Glaser. See:
ZONIK, ELEANOR
DOROTHY

Eleanor Fox. See:
ST. JOHN, WYLLY FOLK

Eleanor Kirk. See:
AMES, ELEANOR
MARIA EASTERBROOK

Eleanor Lee Edwards. See:
VICTOR, MRS. METTA
VICTORIA FULLER
MORSE

ELEANOR OF BRITTANY (died 1241) [niece of JOHN LACKLAND, King of England]
The Damsel of Brittany

Eleanor Putnam. See:
BATES, ARLO
BATES, HARRIET
LEONORA VOSE

Eleanor Stewart. See:
PORTER, MRS. ELEANOR
HODGMAN

Eleanor Stuart. See:
CHILDS, ELEANOR STUART

Elector, The Great. See:
FREDERICK-WILLIAM

Electric Guitar, The King of the. See:

McBURNEY, ALBERT
Electric Light in Europe, The Father of. See:
LIEB, JOHN WILLIAM
Electrical Wizard, The. See:
STEINMETZ, CHARLES PROTEUS
Elegant Arthur. See:
ARTHUR, CHESTER ALAN
Elegant Fuentes, The. See:
FUENTES, ANTONIO
Elegant Oakey. See:
HALL, ABRAHAM OAKEY
Elephant. See:
PEARSON, ELIPHALET
Elephant Boy, The. See:
DASTAGIR, SABU
ELEUTHERUS (died 189) [Supreme Pontiff of Roman Catholic Church]
Pope Eleutherus
St. Eleutherus
Eli Perkins. See:
LANDON, MELVILLE DE LANCEY
Elia. See:
LAMB, CHARLES
Elia, Bridget. See:
LAMB, MARY ANN
Elia Kazan. See:
KAZANJOGLOUS, ELIA
ELIAS. See:
WILNA, ELIJAH (ELIAS)
Elias Boudinot. See:
GALAGINA
Elias, Eileen. See:
DAVIES, EILEEN WINIFRED
Elias (Elijah) Ben Solomon. See: WILNA, ELIJAH (ELIAS)
Eliberitanus. See:
ALWAZZAN (ALWEZAZ), ALHASSAN IBN MOHAMMED
Elijah (Elias) Ben Solomon. See:
WILNA, ELIJAH (ELIAS)
Elijah of the French Reformation, The. See:
FAREL, GUILLAUME
Elijah of Wilna, Gaon. See:
WILNA, ELIJAH (ELIAS)
Elijah the Restorer. See:
DOWIE, JOHN ALEXANDER
Elinor. See:
ELEANOR
Eleanor
GLYN, MRS. CLAYTON
Elinor Lyon. See:
WRIGHT, ELINOR BRUCE
Elinor Mordaunt. See:
MORDAUNT, MRS. EVELYN MAY CLOWES
Elinor Rice. See:
HAYS, ELINOR RICE
Eliot. See:
ELLET
Elliot
ELLIOTT
Elliott
Reed, Eliot
WARBURTON, ELLIOT GEORGE
Eliot, Alice. See:
JEWETT, SARAH ORNE
Eliot, Anne. See:
COLE, LOIS DWIGHT
Eliot Brewster. See:
GIFFORD, JAMES NOBLE
ELIOT, CHARLES WILLIAM (1834-1926) [American educator; president of Yale University]
America's First Citizen
The Greatest Citizen in the United States
Eliot, George. See:
CROSS, MARY ANN (MARIAN) EVANS
ELIOT, JOHN (1604-90) [Anglo-American evangelist among the American Indians]
The Apostle of the Indians
ELIOT, THOMAS STEARNS (1888-1965) [American poet, playwright, critic and essayist]
Charles Augustus Conybeare
Aged Eagle
T. S. Eliot
Reverend Charles James Grimble

Gus Krutzch
Deliberate Pedant
Old Possum
Muriel A. Schwartz
J. A. D. Spence
Helen B. Trundlett
Elisa Bialk. See:
KRAUTTER, ELISA BIALK
ELISABETH (1843-1916)
[Queen Consort of CHARLES I, King of Rumania; Rumanian writer]
Carmen Sylva
ELISABETH. See also:
ELIZABETH
Elizabeth
Elisha Kent Kane, Dr. See:
FOX, MARGARET
Elissa Landi. See:
ZANARDI-LANDI, ELIZABETH MARIE
Elizabeth. See:
BEAUCHAMP, MARY ANNETTE, COUNTESS RUSSELL (MRS.) HENNING ARNIM)
Elisabeth
ELIZABETH I (1533-1603)
[Queen of England and Ireland]
Good Queen Bess
The Untamed Heifer
The Virgin Queen
The World's Wonder
"Elizabeth and her German Garden," By the Author of. See:
BEAUCHAMP, MARY ANNETTE, COUNTESS RUSSELL (MRS. HENNING ARNIM)
Elizabeth Arden. See:
GRAHAM, FLORENCE NIGHTINGALE
Elizabeth Beaman John. See:
JOHN, ELIZABETH BEAMAN
Elizabeth Beatty. See:
HOLLOWAY, TERESA BRAGUNIER
Elizabeth Bott. See:
SPILLUS, ELIZABETH JANE
Elizabeth Burgoyne. See:
PICKLES, MABEL ELIZABETH
Elizabeth Cambridge. See:
HODGES, BARBARA K.
Elizabeth Cameron. See:
ROBINSON, ELIZABETH CAMERON
Elizabeth Clemons. See:
ROBINSON, ELIZABETH CAMERON
Elizabeth Feagles. See:
DAY, BETH FEAGLES
Elizabeth Ferrars. See:
BROWN, MORNA DORIS
Elizabeth Franklin. See:
CAMPBELL, HANNAH
Elizabeth Furness. See:
UPSON, DOROTHY BARBARA
Elizabeth Gregory. See:
GILFORD, CHARLES BERNARD
Elizabeth Grey. See:
HOGG, BETH TOOTILL
Elizabeth Grey Stewart. See:
REED, ELIZABETH STEWART
Elizabeth Harle. See:
ROBERTS, IRENE
Elizabeth Hastings. See:
SHERWOOD, MARGARET POLLOCK
Elizabeth Headley. See:
CAVANNA, ELIZABETH ALLEN
Elizabeth Houghton. See:
GILZEAN, ELIZABETH HOUGHTON BLANCHET
Elizabeth Howard. See:
MIZNER, ELIZABETH HOWARD
Elizabeth Janet Gray. See:
VINING, ELIZABETH GRAY
Elizabeth Kyle. See:
DUNLOP, AGNES MARY ROBERTSON
Elizabeth N. Graham, Mrs. See: GRAHAM, FLORENCE NIGHTINGALE
Elizabeth Oaksmith. See:
SMITH, ELIZABETH OAKES

Elizabeth Renier. See:
BAKER, BETTY DOREEN FLOOK
Elizabeth Risdon. See:
EVANS, ELIZABETH
Elizabeth Seifert. See:
GASPAROTTI, ELIZABETH SEIFERT
Elizabeth Sherman. See:
FRISKEY, MARGARET RICHARDS
Elizabeth Waud. See:
TATTERSALL, MURIEL JOYCE
Elizabeth Wesley. See:
McELFRESH, ELIZABETH ADELINE
Elizabeth West. See:
WILSON, MARGARET
Elizabeth Wetherell. See:
WARNER, SUSAN BOGERT
Elizabethans, The Last of the. See: FORD, JOHN
Elke Sommer. See:
SCHLETZ, ELKE
Ella
Birtha, joint pseuds. of PHILIP MORIN FRENEAU (1752-1832) and his wife ELEANOR FORMAN FRENEAU (-) [American poets]
Ella. See also:
FRENEAU, PHILIP MORIN
Ella Farman. See:
PRATT, ELIZA ANNA FARMAN
Ella Vater, By Miss. See:
SMITH, HARRY ALLEN
Ella Zoyara. See:
KINGSLEY, OMAR
Ellalice Tate. See:
HIBBERT, ELEANOR BURFORD
Ellen. See:
TERRY, DAME ELLEN ALICE
Ellen Alleyn. See:
ROSSETTI, CHRISTINA GEORGINA
Ellen Bogen, Miss. See:
ELLENBOGEN, HENRY
Ellen Burroughs. See:
JEWETT, SOPHIE
Ellen Douglas. See:
WILLIAMSON, ELLEN DOUGLAS
Ellen Drew. See:
RAY, TERRY
Ellen, Vera. See:
ROHE, VERA-ELLEN WESTMEYR
ELLENBOGEN, HENRY (1900-) [Austrian-American lawyer and politician]
Miss Ellen Bogen
Ellery. See:
Queen, Ellery
ELLET. See also:
ELIOT
Eliot
Elliot
ELLIOTT
Elliott
ELLET, CHARLES (1810-62) [American engineer]
The Brunel of America
ELLICOT, JOSEPH (1760-1859) [American land agent; surveyor of Buffalo, N.Y.]
The Father of Buffalo
Ellie Rae Fleuridas. See:
SHERMAN, ELEANOR RAE
ELLINGFORD, ROBERT FREDERICK (fl. early 20th cent.) [British organist and author]
Herbert Winter
ELLINGTON, EDWARD KENNEDY (1899-) [American jazz musician (piano, composer, leader)]
Duke Ellington
Ellington Gray. See:
JACOB, NAOMI ELLINGTON
Elliot. See:
ELIOT
Eliot
ELLET
ELLIOTT
Elliott

STEVENS, HAROLD
ELLIOTT [Elliott]. See also:
ELLET
ELIOT
Eliot
Elliot
Elliott, Don. See:
HELFMAN, DON ELLIOTT
ELLIOTT, EBENEZER (1781-1849) [British poet]
The Corn-law Rhymer
ELLIOTT, GORDON (1906-65) [American motion picture actor]
Wild Bill Elliott
ELLIOTT, JAMES THOMAS (1901-) [American professional baseball player]
Jumbo
ELLIOTT, JOHN R. (1914-) [American composer and author]
Jack Moon
Elliott Lawrence. See:
BROZA, ELLIOTT LAWRENCE
Elliott, Maxine. See:
DERMOT, JESSIE
ELLIOTT, ROBERT B. See:
Bob and Ray
Elliott Whitney. See:
SAYLER, HARRY LINCOLN
Ellis Bell. See:
BRONTË, EMILY JANE
ELLIS, EDWARD SYLVESTER (1840-1916) [American educator, poet and author of dime novels]
Captain Bruin Adams
Captain J. F. C. Adams
James Fenimore Cooper Adams
Boynton Belknap, M. D.
J. G. Bethune
Captain Latham C. Carleton
Edwin Emerson
Frank Faulkner
Col. H. R. Gordon
Oscar A. Gwynne
Oswald A. Gwynne
Captain R. M. Hawthorne
Lieut. Ned Hunter
Lieut. R. H. Jayne
Charles E. LaSalle
Seward D. Lisle
Captain H. R. Millbank
Billex Muller
Geoffrey Randolph
Lieut. J. H. Randolph
Rollo Robins
Seelin Robins
Emerson Rodman
E. S. St. Mox--A U. S. Detective
Egbert S. Thomas
Captain Wheeler
ELLIS, HENRY HAVELOCK (1859-1939) [English anthropologist and man of letters]
Havelock Ellis
Ellis, Hilda Roderick. See:
DAVIDSON, HILDA RODERICK ELLIS
ELLIS, MAGDALEN (1926-) [English-Russian motion picture actress]
Joan Lorring
ELLIS, MOLLY (1908-) [British motion picture actress]
Diana Napier
Ellis Peters. See:
PARGETER, EDITH MARY
Ellison, James. See:
SMITH, JAMES ELLISON
ELLISON, JAMES E. (1927-) [American Catholic priest educator and author]
Brother Flavius
ELLISTON, ROBERT WILLIAM (1774-1831) [English actor and manager; lessee of Drury Lane Theater, London]
The Napoleon of the Drama
ELLISTON, VALERIE MAE WATKINSON (1929-) [Australian author]
Valerie Watkinson
ELLSWORTH, GEORGE A. (fl. 1861-65) [American Civil War telegraph operator]
Lightning
ELLSWORTH, OLIVER (1745-1807)

[American politician;
Senator from Connecticut]
The Cerberus of the Treasury
ELLSWORTH, SALLIE BINGHAM (1937-) [American author]
Sallie Bingham
ELMAN, RICHARD MARTIN (1934-) [American author]
Eric Pearl
Elman, Ziggy. See:
FINKELMAN, HARRY
Elmer. See:
THOMAS, JOHN WILLIAM ELMER
Elmer A. Dawson. See:
STRATEMEYER, EDWARD L.
Elmer Eliot Saks. See:
FAWCETT, FRANK DUBREZ
Elmer Rice. See:
REIZENSTEIN, ELMER LEOPOLD
Elmer the Great. See:
BECK, WALTER WILLIAM
Elmo Lincoln. See:
LINKENHELT, OTTO ELMO
Elocution. See:
WALKER, JOHN
Eloquence, The Founder of Christian. See:
BOURDALONE, LOUIS
Eloquent, Blind Man. See:
WEST, WILLIAM HENRY
Eloquent Doctor, The. See:
AUREOLUS, PETER
Eloquent of the Senate, The Old Man. See:
HOAR, GEORGE FRISBIE
Eloquent Old Man. See:
ADAMS, JOHN QUINCY
COLERIDGE, SAMUEL TAYLOR
CUSTIS, GEORGE WASHINGTON PARKE
ISOCRATES
Eloquent, The Deafman. See:
POTTS, JAMES HENRY
ELPHICK, JEANETTE (1935-) [Australian motion picture actress]
Victoria Shaw
Elsa Falk. See:
ESCHERICH, ELSA FALK
Elsa Lanchester. See:
LAUGHTON, ELIZABETH SULLIVAN
Elsa Ruth Nast. See:
WATSON, JANE WERNER
Elsie Janis. See:
BIERBOWER, ELSIE
Elsom, Isobel. See:
REED, ISOBEL
Elspeth. See:
BRAGDON, ELSPETH MacDUFFIE
ELTING, MARY (1906-) [American journalist and author]
Davis Cole
Campbell Tatham
Eltinge, Julian. See:
DALTON, WILLIAM
Elton, John. See:
MARSH, JOHN
Éluard, Paul. See:
GRINDAL, EUGÉNE
Elvey, Maurice. See:
FOLKARD, WILLIAM
Elvin, Drake. See:
BEHA, ERNEST
Ely, Frederick. See:
KESSLER, JASCHA FREDERICK
Ely, Richard of. See:
FITZNEALE, RICHARD
ELY, WILLIAM HARVEY JOHNSON (1891-) [American judge, New Jersey State Senator and State WPA administrator]
Mickey Mouse
Elzey Hay. See:
ANDREWS, ELIZA FRANCES
Emancipation President, The. See: LINCOLN, ABRAHAM
Emancipation, The Advance Agent of. See:
MOTT, LUCRETIA
Emancipator, The Great. See:
LINCOLN, ABRAHAM

EMANUEL [Emanuel]. See also:
EMMANUEL
IMMANUEL
EMANUEL (MANUEL) I (1469-1521) [King of Portugal]
The Fortunate
The Great
The Happy
Emanuel Morgan. See:
Knish, Anne
Embey, Philip. See:
PHILIPP, ELLIOT ELIAS
Embodiment of Schweppervescence, The. See:
WHITEHEAD, WALTER EDWARD
Embodiment of Sea Power, The. See: NELSON, HORATIO, VISCOUNT NELSON
EMBREE, CHARLES, JR. (1919-) [American composer, writer and artist]
Riff Charles
Emerce. See:
CROWELL, MRS. MARY REED
Emeritus, America's Sweetheart. See:
SMITH, GLADYS MARY
Emerson, Alice B. See:
STRATEMEYER, EDWARD L.
Emerson, Edwin. See:
ELLIS, EDWARD SYLVESTER
EMERSON, HENRY OLIVER (1893-) [English educator and author]
Oliver Gordon
Emerson, Jane. See:
BIXBY, JEROME LEWIS
EMERSON, RALPH WALDO (1803-82) [American poet and essayist]
The American Montaigne
The Columbus of Modern Thought
The Sage of Concord
Emerson Rodman. See:
ELLIS, EDWARD SYLVESTER
Emery Bemsley Pottle. See:
POTTLE, GILBERT EMERY BEMSLEY
Emery Bonett. See:
COULSON, FELICITY CARTER
Emery, Gilbert. See:
POTTLE, GILBERT EMERY BEMSLEY
Emery Pottle. See:
POTTLE, GILBERT EMERY BEMSLEY
Emil Ludwig. See:
COHN, EMIL
Emil Nolde. See:
HANSEN, EMIL
Emil Richards. See:
RADDOCCHIA, EMILIO JOSEPH
Emil Sinclair. See:
HESSE, HERMANN
Emily. See:
David, Emily
Emily Brown. See:
STERNE, EMMA GELDERS
Emily Chubbuck. See:
JUDSON, EMILY CHUBBUCK
Emily Hare. See:
WINTHROP, LAURA
Emily Marshall. See:
HALL, BENNIE CAROLINE HUMBLE
Emily Mary Bell. See:
CASON, MABEL EARP
Emily Paul. See:
EICHER, ETHEL ELIZABETH
Emin Pasha. See:
SCHNITZLER, EDUARD
Eminence, Gray (Éminence Grise). See:
TREMBLAY, FRANÇOIS LE CLERC DU
Éminence Grise (Gray Eminence) See: TREMBLAY, FRANÇOIS LE CLERC DU
Eminence, Red (Éminence Rouge). See:
RICHELIEU, DUC DE, ARMAND JEAN DU PLESSIS

Éminence, Rouge (Red Eminence). See: RICHELIEU, DUC DE, ARMAND JEAN DU PLESSIS
Eminence, The Brown. See: BORMANN, MARTIN
Eminence, The Soul of Empty. See: DODD, JAMES WILLIAM
Eminent Prestidigitateur, The. See: CARTER, CHARLES J.
Emma Calvé. See: ROQUER, EMMA DE
Emma Carra. See: UNKNOWN
Emma, Dame. See: ALBANI, MARIE LOUISE CÉCILE LAJEUNESSE
Emma The Bell Gal, Sweet. See: BARRETT, EMMA
EMMANUEL. See:
EMANUEL
Emanuel
IMMANUEL
VICTOR EMMANUEL II
EMMERICH, ANNA KATHARINA (1774-1824) [German nun]
The Nun of Dülmen
Empecinado. See: DÍAZ, DON JUAN MARTÍN
Emperador, El (The Emperor). See: ALFONSO VII
Emperor. See also:
MACKENZIE, KENNETH
NORTON, JOSHUA A.
Emperor Nick of the Bribery Bank. See: BIDDLE, NICHOLAS
Emperor of Believers, The. See: OMAR I
Emperor of Jordan, The. See: GLUBB, SIR JOHN BAGOT
Emperor of the Mountains, The. See: PETER
Emperor of the West, The. See:
MACKENZIE, KENNETH
MURRAY, JOHN
Emperor, Parson's. See: CHARLES IV
Emperor, The (El Emperador). See: ALFONSO VII
Emperor, The Blind. See: LOUIS III
Emperor, The First. See: SHIH HUAN TI
Emperor, The Iron. See: NICHOLAS I
Emperor, The Marionette. See: MAXIMILIAN, FERDINAND JOSEPH
EMPEY, ARTHUR GUY (1883-) [American author and soldier]
Guy Empey
Empire Builder, The. See: HILL, JAMES JEROME
Empire, Restorer of the (Restitutor Orbis). See: AURELIANUS, LUCIUS DOMITIUS
Emplazado, El (The Summoned). See: FERDINAND IV
Emporia, The Sage of. See: WHITE, WILLIAM ALLEN
Empress Eugénie. See: GUZMAN, EUGÉNIE MARÍA DE MONTIJO, COMTESSE DE TEBA DE
Empress Maud, The. See: MATILDA
Empress of the Blues, The. See: SMITH, BESSIE
Empress, The Divine. See: WU, LADY
Empress Theodora, The. See: THEODORA
Empty Eminence, The Soul of. See: DODD, JAMES WILLIAM
Empty Jacket (Toom Tabard). See: JOHN DE BALIOL
Emslie, M. L. See: SIMPSON, MYRTLE LILLIAS
Enchanter, The. See: VAN BUREN, MARTIN
Enchanting Rebel, The. See: See: FUERTES, DOLORES ADIOS
ENCINA (ENZINA), JUAN DEL (1469?-1529?) [Spanish dramatist and poet]
The Father of the Spanish Drama

The Patriarch of the Spanish Theater
ENDICOTT, CHARLES MOSES (1793-1863) [American sea captain and author]
Junius Americanus
ENDICOTT, JOHN (1589-1665) [Anglo-American Governor of the Massachusetts Bay Colony]
The Father of New England
Enemy No. 1, Public. See:
DILLINGER, JOHN HERBERT
GILLIS, LESTER M.
Enfant du Miracle, l'. See:
CHAMBORD, HENRI CHARLES DIEUPONNÉ, COMTE DE
Enforcer, The. See:
NITTI, FRANK
ENG BUNKER. See:
Siamese Twins, The
Engelbert Humperdinck. See:
DORSEY, GERRY
Engineering, The Father of American. See:
WRIGHT, BENJAMIN
England, A Lady of (A. L. O. E.) See: TUCKER, CHARLOTTE MARIA
England, Cardinal of. See:
POLE, REGINALD
England, E. M. See:
ANDERS, EDITH MARY ENGLAND
England, John of (Joannes Anglicus). See:
JOAN
England, Lord Protector of. See: CROMWELL, OLIVER
CROMWELL, RICHARD
England, The Achilles of. See:
JOHN
England, The Aesop of. See:
GAY, JOHN
England, The Butcher of. See:
TIPTOFT, JOHN
England, The Father of the Enlightenment in. See:
LOCKE, JOHN
England, The First Victim in. See: SAWTREY, WILLIAM
England, The Hammer and Scourge of. See:
WALLACE, SIR WILLIAM
England, The Lady of. See:
MATILDA
England, The Patriarch of. See
COTTON, JOHN
England, The Raphael of. See:
REYNOLDS, SIR JOSHUA
England, The Solomon of. See:
JAMES I
England, The Terence of. See:
CUMBERLAND, RICHARD
England's First Home-grown Ballerina. See:
HOOKHAM, MARGARET
England's Viceroy, The King of. See: LOUIS XVIII
ENGLE, PETER KING (1916-) [American motion picture actor]
Peter Whitney
English Achilles, The. See:
TALBOT, JOHN
WELLINGTON, ARTHUR WELLESLEY, 1ST DUKE OF
English Actor, The Greatest. See:
GARRICK, DAVID
English Alexander, The. See:
HENRY V
English Aristophanes, The. See:
FOOTE, SAMUEL
English Atticus, The. See:
ADDISON JOSEPH
English Biographer, The First Professional. See:
WALTON, IZAAK
English Botany, The Father of. See: RAY, JOHN
English Cathedral Music, The Father of. See:
TALLIS, THOMAS
English Colonization in America, The Father of. See:
GORGES, FERDINANDO
English Criticism, The Father of. See:
DRYDEN, JOHN
English Criticism, The Sainte-Beuve of. See:
ARNOLD, MATTHEW
English Domestic Novel, The Founder of the. See:

RICHARDSON, SAMUEL
English Ennius, The. See:
LAYAMON (LAWEMAN)
English Geology, The Father of. See: SMITH, WILLIAM
English Hippocrates, The. See:
SYDENHAM, THOMAS
English Hobbema, The. See:
CROME, JOHN
English Horace, The. See:
JONSON, BENJAMIN
POPE, ALEXANDER
ENGLISH, JAMES EDWARD (1812-90) [American politician; Governor of Connecticut]
The Father of the Free School System
English Jim. See:
STUART, JAMES
English Joan of Arc, The. See: AMBREE, MARY
English Justinian, The. See:
EDWARD I
English Juvenal, The. See:
OLDHAM, JOHN
English Mercenne, The. See:
COLLINS, JOHN
English Milo, The. See:
TOPHAM, THOMAS
English Molière, The. See:
O'KEEFFE, JOHN
English Nation, Acting Governor of the. See:
CAXTON, WILLIAM
English Natural History, The Father of. See:
RAY (WARY), JOHN
English Navy, The Father of the. See:
HENRY VIII
English Novel, The Father of the. See:
FIELDING, HENRY
English Novelists, The Dean of Contemporary. See:
FORSTER, EDWARD MORGAN
English Opium-Eater, The See: DE QUINCEY, THOMAS
English Palestrina, The. See:
GIBBONS, ORLANDO
English Palladianism, The High Priest of. See:
BOYLE, RICHARD
English Palladio, The. See:
JONES, INIGO
English Petrarch, The. See:
SIDNEY (SYDNEY), SIR PHILIP
English Plato, The. See:
NORRIS, REV. JOHN
English Poetry, The Father of. See: CHAUCER, GEOFFREY
English Poussin, The. See:
COOPER, RICHARD
English Printing, The Father of. See: CAXTON, WILLIAM
English Prose, The Father of. See: ASCHAM, ROGER
English Prose, The First Master of. See:
NORTH, SIR THOMAS
English Prose Writers, The Spenser of. See:
TAYLOR, JEREMY
English Public School System, The Father of the. See:
WYKEHAM (WICKHAM), WILLIAM OF
English Rabelais, The. See:
AMORY, THOMAS
STERNE, LAURENCE
SWIFT, JONATHAN
English Revival, The Hymnist of the. See:
WESLEY, CHARLES
English Roscius, The. See:
BETTERTON, THOMAS
GARRICK, DAVID
English Salvator Rosa, The. See:
MORTIMER, JOHN HAMILTON
English Sappho, An. See:
PHILIPS, KATHERINE
English Sappho, The. See:
LANDON, LETITIA ELIZABETH
English Satirist, The First. See:
HALL, JOSEPH
English Seneca, The. See:
HALL, JOSEPH
English Socrates, The. See:
JOHNSON, DR. SAMUEL

English Solomon, The. See:
JAMES I
English Stage, The Last Minstrel of the. See:
SHIRLEY, JAMES
English Stage, The Queen of the. See: BROWN, ELIZABETH ANN
English Surgery, The Father of. See: WISEMAN, RICHARD
English Teniers, The. See:
MORLAND, GEORGE
English Terence, The. See:
CUMBERLAND, RICHARD
English, The Apostle of the. See:
AUGUSTINE (AUSTIN), ST.
English Theater, The Present Champion of the. See:
OLIVIER, SIR LAURENCE
ENGLISH, THOMAS DUNN (1819-1902) [American author]
Brigadier
English Tintoretto, The. See:
DOBSON, WILLIAM
English Unitarianism, The Father of. See:
BIDDLE, JOHN
English Van Dyck, The. See:
DOBSON, WILLIAM
Englishman, The Handsome. See:
CHURCHILL, JOHN
ENGSTROM, NORMA DOLORES (JEAN) (1920-) [American popular singer]
Peggy Lee
Enid Bergdahl. See:
GILLETTE, LELAND J.
Enid LaMonte Meadowcroft. See:
WRIGHT, ENID MEADOW-CROFT LaMONTE
Enlightened, The. See:
GAUTAMA SIDDHARTHA
Enlightenment in England, The Father of the. See:
LOCKE, JOHN
ENNIS, EDGAR CLYDE, JR. (1907-63) [American jazz musician (drums, singer, leader)]
Skinnay Ennis
Ennis Graham. See:
MOLESWORTH, MARY LOUISA
ENNIUS, QUINTUS (239 B.C. - 169 B.C.) [Roman Poet]
The Father of Roman Literature
The Father of Roman Poetry
Ennius, The English. See:
LAYAMON (LAWEMAN)
Ennius, The French. See:
CLOPINEL, JEAN
Ennius, The Spanish. See:
MENA, JUAN DE
Enoch Fitzwhistler, C.C.B. See: COBB, SYLVANUS, JR.
ENOS, WILLIAM BERKELEY (1895-) [American dance director]
Busby Berkeley
Enotrio Romano. See:
CARDUCCI, GIOSUE
Enrique, Erratic. See:
LUKENS, HENRY CLAY
ENS, JEWEL (1889-) [American professional baseball coach]
Mutt
Ensign Clark Fitch, U.S.N. See:
SINCLAIR, UPTON BEALL
Entertainer of the Ozarks, The Poet. See:
LUCEY, THOMAS ELMORE
Entomology, The Father of American. See:
SAY, THOMAS
Entomology, The Father of American Descriptive. See:
SAY, THOMAS
ENTON, DR. HARRY (1854-1927) [American physician and author of dime novels]
Mickey Free
Wenona Gilman
Harry Harrison
Ironclad
Val Versatile
Entrepreneur, Le Général (The Contractor General). See:
BONAPARTE, NAPOLEON
ENZINA. See:
ENCINA (ENZINA), JUAN DEL
ÉON DE BEAUMONT, CHARLES GENEVIÉVE TIMOTHÉE D'

(1728-1810) [French political agent and master fencer]
The Chevalier d'Éon

Epafrodito. See:
WAGNER, CHARLES PETER

Epernay, Mark. See:
GALBRAITH, JOHN KENNETH

Ephelia. See:
UNKNOWN

Ephesian. See:
ROBERTS, CARL ERIC BECHOFER

Ephesian Poet, The. See:
HIPPONAX

EPHRAEM. See:
EPHRAIM (EPHRAEM)

EPHRAIM (EPHRAEM) (c. 300-79) [Mesopotamian hermit, poet and apologist]
The Syrian

Epic Poetry, The Father of. See: HOMER

Epigrammaker, Little Owen the. See: OWEN, JOHN

Epiphanes. See:
ANTIOCHUS IV

Epiphanes (The Illustrious). See:
PTOLEMY V

EPIPHANIUS, ST. (c. 315-403) [Christian church father and writer]
The Scholastic

Épistolier de France, Le Grand. See: BALZAC, JEAN LOUIS GUEZ DE

EPP, MARGARET A. (fl. 1955-64) [Canadian author]
Agnes Goossen

Eppie. See:
FRIEDMAN, ESTHER PAULINE

EPSTEIN, BERYL WILLIAMS (1910-) [American editor and author]
Adam Allen
Douglas Coe
Beryl Williams

EPSTEIN, BERYL WILLIAMS. See also:
Allen, Adam

EPSTEIN, SAMUEL (1909-) [American author]
Bruce Campbell
Martin Colt
Charles Strong

EPSTEIN, SAMUEL. See also:
Allen, Adam

Equity in Tennessee, The Father of. See:
GREEN, NATHAN

Equity, The Father of. See:
FINCH, HENEAGE

Era-of-good-feeling President, The. See:
MONROE, JAMES

Erasmus, M. Nott. See:
STUBER, STANLEY IRVING

ERASTUS, THOMAS (1524-83) [Swiss theologian]
Lieber (Liebler)

Ercildoune, Thomas Rhymour of. See:
LEARMOUNT, THOMAS, OF ERCILDOUNE

Erckmann-Chatrian, joint pseud. of ÉMILE ERCKMANN (1822-99) and ALEXANDRE CHATRIAN (1826-90) [French novelists]

ERCOLANI, JAMES (1936-) [American motion picture actor]
James Darren

Ercole. See:
REEVES, STEPHEN

Eremita, Johannes. See:
CASSIANUS, JOHANNES

ERETRIA. See:
MENEDEMUS OF ERETRIA

Eretrian Bull, The. See:
MENEDEMUS OF ERETRIA

ERIC (fl. 1000) [Scandinavian navigator; reputed discoverer of America]
The Red

ERIC [Eric]. See also:
Erich
Erick

Eric Jameson. See:
TRIMMER, ERIC J.

Eric, Kenneth. See:

HENLEY, ARTHUR
Eric Pearl. See:
ELMAN, RICHARD MARTIN
Eric Thorstein. See:
GROSSMAN, JOSEPHINE JUDITH
Erica Fay. See:
STOPES, MRS. MARIE CHARLOTTE CARMICHAEL
Erich. See also:
ERIC
Eric
Erick
Erich Her. See:
PAETL, ERICH
Ehrich Maria Remarque. See:
REMARK, ERICH PAUL
Erick. See:
BEST, MRS. ALLENA CHAMPLIN
ERIC
Eric
Erich
Erick Berry. See:
BEST, MRS. ALLENA CHAMPLIN
ERICKSON [Erickson]. See also:
ERICSON
Ericson
Eriksson
Erickson, Leif. See:
ANDERSON, WILLIAM
ERICKSON, SABRA ROLLINS (1912-) [American editor and author]
Sabra Holbrook
ERICSON [Ericson]. See also:
ERICKSON
Erickson
Eriksson
Ericson, John. See:
MEIBES, JOSEPH
ERICSON, LEIF (died c. 1021) [Norse mariner and adventurer]
Leif the Lucky
ERICSON, ROLF (1927-) [Swedish-American jazz musician (trumpet)]
Roffe
Ericson, Walter. See:
FAST, HOWARD MELVIN
Erie, Prince of. See:
FISK, JAMES, JR.
Erie, The Hero of Lake. See:
PERRY, OLIVER HAZARD
ERIGENA, JOHANNES SCOTUS (815?-877?) [Medieval philosopher and theologian]
Johannes Ierugena (Irish-born)
Johannes Scotus
Eriksson. See:
ERICKSON
Erickson
ERICSON
Ericson
MAGNUS II
Eriksson, Gustavus. See:
GUSTAVUS I
Erlingsson. See:
MAGNUS V
Ermine, Will. See:
DRAGO, HENRY SINCLAIR
Ern, Cousin. See:
FORD, ERNEST JENNINGS
Ernan Mackey. See:
McINERNY, RALPH
Ernest. See:
BORGNINE, ERMES EFFRON
ERNST
Ernst
Ernest Bramah. See:
SMITH, ERNEST BRAMAH
Ernest Corley. See:
BULMER, HENRY KENNETH
Ernest Dudley. See:
COLTMAN-ALLEN, ERNEST
Ernest Hamilton. See:
GROSSMAN, JOSEPHINE JUDITH
Ernest Helfenstein. See:
SMITH, ELIZABETH OAKES
Ernest Lemoine. See:
ROY, EWELL PAUL
Ernest Small. See:
LENT, BLAIR
Ernest Thompson Seton. See:
THOMPSON, ERNEST SETON
Ernest Trevor. See:
POWELL, THOMAS
Ernest Vivian Coltman. See:
COLTMAN-ALLEN, ERNEST

Ernest, William. See:
BERKEBILE, FRED DONOVAN
Ernie. See:
BANKS, ERNEST
FORD, ERNEST B.
FREEMAN, ERNEST
NEVERS, ERNEST A.
PYLE, ERNEST TAYLOR
Ernie Allen. See:
BUNDGAARD, ERNEST
Ernie Burnett. See:
BERNADETTI, ERNEST MARCO
Ernie Ford, Tennessee. See:
FORD, ERNEST JENNINGS
Ernie Hare. See:
Happiness Boys, The
ERNST [Ernst]. See also:
Ernest
Ernst, Clara. See:
BARNES, CLARA ERNST
Ernst Theodor Amadeus Hoffmann. See:
HOFFMANN, ERNST THEODOR WILHELM
ERNST, ULRICH (1920-) [German-American artist]
Jimmy Ernst
Erratic Enrique. See:
LUKENS, HENRY CLAY
Erromango, The Martyr of. See:
WILLIAMS, JOHN
Errym, Malcolm J. See:
RYMER, JAMES MALCOLM
Erskine of the American Bar, The. See:
HOFFMAN, OGDEN
Erskine, Rosalind. See:
LONGRIGG, ROGER ERSKINE
Ertz, Susan. See:
McCRINDLE, MRS. RONALD
ERWIN [Erwin]. See also:
IRWIN
Irwin
ERWIN, GEORGE (1913-) [American jazz musician (trumpet, leader)]
Pee Wee Erwin
Erwin, Howard W. See:
INGRAHAM, COLONEL PRENTISS
Escape Artists, The King of. See: GARDNER, ROY
Escaped Jailbird, The. See:
EGAN, PATRICK
Escapologists, The King of. See:
WEISS, EHRICH (ERIK WEISZ)
ESCHERICH, ELSA FALK (1888-) [American artist and author]
Elsa Falk
ESCOFFIER, AUGUSTE (c.1847-1935) [French chef; creator of gourmet dishes]
The King of Chefs
ESCUDERO, IGNACIO RAFAEL GARCÍA Y (1919-) [Spanish bullfighter]
Albaicín
Esegar. See:
CURZON-SUGGERS, WILLIAM
Esek, Uncle. See:
SHAW, HENRY WHEELER
Esmeralda de Mar. See:
MELLEN, IDA MAY
Esmond, Carl. See:
EICHBERGER, WILLY
Esor B. MacIre. See:
AMBROSE, ERIC
Espartero. See:
GARCÍA, MANUEL
ESPEY, JAMES POLLARD (1785-1860) [American meteorologist]
The Storm King
ESPINOSA, FERMÍN (1911-) [Mexican bullfighter]
Armillita Chico
Espirit, Monsieur Sans. See:
FIELDING, HENRY
Esrom, D. A. See:
MORSE, THEODORA
Essex, Pepys in. See:
TOMPKINS, HERBERT WINCKWORTH
Essex, The Wood-thrush of. See: WHITTIER, JOHN GREENLEAF
ESTEBANEZ CALDERÓN, SERAFÍN (1799-1867)

[Spanish writer and politician]
El Solitario
Estelle. See:
LEWIS, SARAH ANN ROBINSON
ESTELLE, SISTER MARY (1907-) [American Roman Catholic nun and author]
Estelle Casalandra
Estelle Winwood. See:
GOODWIN, ESTELLE
ESTERHAZY, MARIE CHARLES FERDINAND WALSIN (1847-1923) [French army officer, forger and writer]
Comte de Voilemont
Esteven, John. See:
SHELLABARGER, SAMUEL
ESTEVES, JOSEPH (1921-) [American jazz musician (leader, arranger, piano)]
Joe Loco
Esther Cooper. See:
KELLNER, ESTHER
Esther Hope, Lady. See:
ST. JOHN, PERCY BOLLINGBROKE
Esther Phillips. See:
JONES, ESTHER MAY
Estoril, Jean. See:
ALLAN, MABEL ESTHER
Estrithson. See:
SWEYN II
Estudiante, El. See:
GÓMEZ, LUIS
Eterna Sonrisa, Niño de la. See:
TORRES, EMILIO
Eternal Flapper, The. See:
HOPPER, EDNA WALLACE
Ethel Barrymore. See:
COLT, ETHEL BLYTHE
Ethel Hamill. See:
WEBB, JEAN FRANCIS
Ethel Lynn. See:
BEERS, ETHELINDA ELIOT
Ethel Lynn Beers. See:
BEERS, ETHELINDA ELIOT
Ethel Merman. See:
ZIMMERMAN, ETHEL AGNES
Ethel Vance. See:
STONE, MRS. GRACE ZARING
ETHELBERT (AETHELBERT) (AEDILBERCT) (552?-616) [King of Kent]
Bretwalda (Ruler of the British)
ETHELE. See:
ATTILA (ETZEL) (ETHELE)
ETHELRED (AETHELRED) II (986?-1016) [King of England]
The Unready
ETHELWOLD OF WINCHESTER (died 984) [Christian churchman]
The Father of Monks
ETHERINGTON, MARY SUSAN (1864-1942) [English actress]
Marie Tempest
Ethiopia, The Apostle of. See:
FRUMENTIUS, ST.
Ethnology, The Father of American. See:
GALLATIN, ABRAHAM ALPHONSE ALBERT
Etienne. See:
KING-HALL, WILLIAM STEPHEN RICHARD
Ettrick Shepherd, The. See:
HOGG, JAMES
ETZEL. See:
ATTILA (ETZEL) (ETHELE)
ETZEL, FRANZ. See:
Three Wise Men
Eubie. See:
BLAKE, JAMES HUBERT
Eubulus. See:
BUTLER, SAMUEL
Euergetes (Benefactor). See:
ANTIOCHUS VII
DEMETRIUS III
PTOLEMY III
Euergetes II (Benefactor). See:
PTOLEMY VII (or VIII or IX)
Eugen Alban Corvin. See:

GATTERMANN, EUGEN LUDWIG
Eugène. See:
SUE, MARIE JOSEPH EUGÈNE
EUGENE (died 657) [Supreme Pontiff of Roman Catholic Church]
Pope Eugene I
St. Eugene
EUGENE (died 827) [Supreme Pontiff of Roman Catholic Church]
Pope Eugene II
Eugene III, Pope. See:
PAGANELLI, BERNARDO
Eugene IV, Pope. See:
CONDULMER, GABRIELE
Eugene Glen. See:
FAWCETT, FRANK DUBREZ
Eugene Martin. See:
STRATEMEYER, EDWARD L.
Eugenia Hale. See:
WOOLSEY, MARYHALE
Eugenia Miller. See:
MANDELKORN, EUGENIA MILLER
Eugénie, Empress. see:
GUZMÁN, EUGÉNIE MARÍA DE MONTIJO, COMTESSE DE TEBA DE
Eugeniusz Kurowski. See:
DOBRACZYNSKI, JAN
Eukairos. See:
DEMETRIUS III
Eulalie Steinmetz. See:
ROSS, EULALIE STEINMETZ
EULENSPIEGEL (ULENSPIEGEL), TILL (died 1350) [German peasant and clown]
Howleglass (Owlglass)
EUNSON, JOAN (c. 1932-) [American motion picture actress]
Joan Evans
Eunuch, The. See:
EUTROPIUS
Eupator. See:
MITHRIDATES VI
Europe, Le Cocher de l' (The Coachman of Europe). See:
CHOISEUL-AMBOISE, ÉTIENNE FRANÇOIS, DUC DE
Europe, The Coachman of (Le Cocher de l'Europe). See:
CHOISEUL-AMBOISE, ETIENNE FRANÇOIS, DUC DE
Europe, The Father of Electric Light in. See:
LIEB, JOHN WILLIAM
Europe, The First Gentlemen in. See: GEORGE IV
Europe, The Mystery Man of. See: ZACHARIAS, BASILEIOS
Europe, The Nestor of. See:
LEOPOLD I
Europe, The Nightmare of. See: BONAPARTE, NAPOLEON
European Confucius, The. See:
QUESNAY, FRANÇOIS
Europe's Liberator. See:
WELLINGTON, ARTHUR WELLESLEY, 1ST DUKE OF
EUSEBIUS (died 309/10) [Supreme Pontiff of Roman Catholic Church]
Pope Eusebius
St. Eusebius
EUSEBIUS OF CAESAREA (c. 264-c. 349) [Christian theologian and historian]
The Father of Church History
The Father of Ecclesiastical History
Pamphili
The Venerable Bede
EUTROPIUS (fl. c. 395-99) [Byzantine statesman]
The Eunuch
EUTYCHIAN (died 283) [Supreme Pontiff of Roman Catholic Church]
Pope Eutychian
St. Eutychian
Eva Bartok. See:
SJÖKE, EVA
Evald Maend. See:
MAND, EWALD
Evalina Mack. See:

McNAMARA, LENA
BROOKE
Evan Hall. See:
HALLERAN, EUGENE
EDWARD
Evan John. See:
SIMPSON, EVAN JOHN
Evangeline. See:
FRANCE-HAYHURST,
EVANGELINE
CHAWORTH-MUSTERS
EVANGELIST. See:
JOHN THE EVANGELIST,
ST.
Evangelist for Peace, The
Itinerant. See:
PAGE, KIRBY
Evangelist, The. See:
PHILIP
Evangelist, The Merchant. See:
CRITTENTON CHARLES
NELSON
Evangelist, The Mountain. See:
JONES, SAMUEL PORTER
Evangelist, The World's Most
Pulchritudinous. See:
McPHERSON, AIMEE
SEMPLE
Evans, Augusta Jane. See:
WILSON, AUGUSTA
JANE EVANS
EVANS, CHARLES E. (1857-
1945) [American blackface
minstrel and entertainer]
Honey Boy Evans
EVANS, CONSTANCE MAY
(1890-) [Canadian author]
Jane Gray
Mairi O'Nair
Evans, Dale. See:
SMITH, FRANCES OCTAVIA
EVANS, DAVIS (1878-1945)
[Welsh writer of short
stories]
Caradoc
EVANS, ELIZABETH
(1887-1958) [British
stage and motion picture
actress]
Elizabeth Risdon
EVANS, ERNEST (1941-)
[American composer,
author and singer]
Chubby Checker
Evans, Evin. See:
FAUST, FREDERICK
SCHILLER
EVANS, GEORGE BIRD. See:
Bird, Brandon
Evans, Gil. See:
GREEN, IAN ERNEST
GILMORE
Evans, Harris. See:
Bird, Brandon
EVANS, HILARY (1929-)
[American author]
H. E. Agard
EVANS, JEAN BELL SHAW
(1910-) [Scottish author]
Jane Shaw
Evans, Joan. See:
EUNSON, JOAN
EVANS-JONES, ALBERT (1895-)
[British Presbyterian
clergyman and author]
Cynam
EVANS, JULIA RENDEL (1913-)
[British author]
Polly Hobson
EVANS, KAY HARRIS. See:
Bird, Brandon
EVANS, MARGUERITE
FLORENCE HELENE
(1894-1964)
[English writer]
Countess Barcynska
Oliver Sandys
EVANS, MARY LORRAINE
STALLINGS (1939-)
[American jazz musician
(singer)]
Mary Stallings
Evans, Morgan. See:
DAVIES, LESLIE PURNELL
EVANS, OLIVER (1755-1819)
[American inventor]
The Watt of America
EVANS, PAUL WESLEY
(1907-) [American jazz
musician (cornet)]
Doc Evans
EVANS, REDD (1912-)
[American musician,
composer and recording
executive]
Louis Evans

Evans, Richard. See:
KUNITZ, RICHARD E.
EVANS, ROBLEY DUNGLISON (1847-1912) [American naval officer]
Fighting Bob Evans
Old Gimpy
EVARISTUS (died c. 105) [Supreme Pontiff of Roman Catholic Church]
Pope Evaristus
St. Evaristus
Eve Arden. See:
QUEDENS, EUNICE
Eve Larson. See:
ST. JOHN, WYLLY FOLK
Eve MacAdam. See:
LESLIE, CECILIE
Eve, Mr. New Year's. See:
LOMBARDO, GUY ALBERT
Eve Stewart. See:
NAPIER, PRISCILLA
Evelyn, Anthony. See:
WARD-THOMAS, EVELYN BRIDGET PATRICIA STEPHENS
Evelyn Goodenough. See:
PITCHER, EVELYN GOODENOUGH
EVELYN, JOHN MICHAEL (1916-) [British attorney, civil servant and author]
Michael Underwood
Evelyn McKenna. See:
JOSCELYN, ARCHIE L.
Evelyn Morchard Bishop. See: STONOR, OLIVER
Evelyn St. Leger. See:
RANDOLPH, EVELYN ST. LEGER
Even Firmer (Noch Vaster). See: STEENDAM, JACOB
Ever-Memorable, The. See:
HALES, JOHN
EVERETT, EDWARD (1794-1865) [American orator and statesman]
An American
Everett, Gail. See:
HALE, ARLENE
Everett, Wade. See:
COOK, WILLIAM EVERETT
Evergreen, Anthony. See:
IRVING WASHINGTON
Everitt Proctor. See:
MONTGOMERY, RUTHERFORD GEORGE
Everpoint. See:
FIELD, JOSEPH M.
EVERS, JOHN JOSEPH (1883-1947) [American professional baseball player]
Crab
The Trojan
EVERSLEY, DAVID EDWARD CHARLES (1921-) [German-British author]
William Small
EVERSON, WILLIAM OLIVER (1912-) [American poet]
Brother Antonius
Every. See:
AVERY, CAPTAIN JOHN
Everybody's Children, The Second Mother of. See:
ABBOTT, GRACE
Evil Genius, Adolf Hitler's. See:
BORMANN, MARTIN
Evil Genius of Maryland, The. See: CLAIBORNE, WILLIAM
Evil Genius of the German Horror Camps, The. See:
HIMMLER, HEINRICH
Evin Evans. See:
FAUST, FREDERICK SCHILLER
Evoe. See:
KNOX, EDMUND GEORGE VALPY
Evolution Poet, The. See:
CARRUTH, WILLIAM HERBERT
Ewan Mitchell. See:
JANNER, GREVILLE EWAN
EWART, ERNEST ANDREW (1878-) [English soldier and author]
Boyd Cable
EWBANK, WILBUR CHARLES (1907-) [American

professional football coach]
Weeb
Ewell, Tom. See:
TOMKINS, S. YEWELL
EWING, WILLIAM (1859-1906) [American professional baseball player]
Buck Ewing
Ex Flammis. See:
GLETCHEN, MAJOR GENERAL LORD EDWARD
Ex-R.S.M. See:
LINDSAY, HAROLD ARTHUR BILL
Exall, Barry. See:
NUGENT, JOHN PEER
Excursion, The Poet of the. See: WORDSWORTH, WILLIAM
Executioner, The Chief. See:
ROPER, DANIEL CALHOUN
Expatriate, America's Foremost. See:
STEARNS, HAROLD EDMUND
Experience, The Voice of. See: TAYLOR, MARION SAYLE
Experimental Physics, The Father of American. See: ROOD, OGDEN NICHOLAS
Experimental Physiology, The Father of. See:
GALEN
Explorer of the United States, The Picturesque. See:
LANMAN, CHARLES
Expounder of the Constitution, The. See:
WEBSTER, DANIEL
Express Rider, Wild Bill the Pony. See:
CODY, WILLIAM FREDERICK
Exterminator, The. See:
MONTBARS
Extra Billy. See:
SMITH, WILLIAM
Extraordinary Chancellor of the Rising State of New Jersey. See:
LIVINGSTON, WILLIAM
Eye, Big. See:
NELSON, LOUIS DELISLE
Eye, Old Gimlet. See:
BUTLER, SMEDLEY DARLINGTON
Eye, The. See:
PINKERTON, ALLAN
Eye, The Great. See:
SCHUYLER, PHILIP JOHN
Eye Witness. See:
BENNETT, JAMES O'DONNELL
FOE, DANIEL
EYERLY, JEANNETTE HYDE. See: Griffith, Jeannette
Eyes, All. See:
WEBSTER, DANIEL
Eyes, Banjo. See:
ISKOWITZ, EDWARD ISRAEL
Eyes, Bright (Inshtatheanba). See: LA FLESCHE, SUZETTE
Eyes, Four. See:
ROOSEVELT, THEODORE
Eyre, Annette. See:
WORBOYS, ANNETTE ISOBEL
EYSTER, PENELOPE ANNA MARGARETTA BLESSING (c. 1831-1922) [American lecturer and author]
Nellie Blessing Eyster
EYSTER, WILLIAM REYNOLDS (1841-1918) [American author of dime novels]
R. Hunt Wilby
EZDRAS. See:
EZRA (EZDRAS)
Ezekiel Jones. See:
WELD, HORATIO HASTINGS
Ezekiel, Old Captain. See:
GREELEY, EZEKIEL
Ezio.
See:
PINZA, FORTUNATO
EZRA, ABRAHAM BEN MEIR IBN (1092-1167) [Jewish-

Arabic scholar]
The Admirable
EZRA (EZDRAS) (5th cent. B.C.) [Hebrew priest and reformer]
The Scribe

F

F. Anstey. See:
GUTHRIE, THOMAS ANSTEY
F. Baldenne. See:
BALDENSPERGER, FERNAND
F. Brown. See:
MACKINNON, CHARLES ROY
F.D. See:
ROOSEVELT, FRANKLIN DELANO
F.D.R. See:
ROOSEVELT, FRANKLIN DELANO
F. de Lagenevais. See:
BLAZE, ANGE HENRI
F. Draco. See:
DAVIS, JULIA
F.E. Edwards. See:
NOLAN, WILLIAM FRANCIS
F.G.R. See:
ROE, FREDERIC GORDON
F.G. Trafford. See:
RIDDELL, CHARLOTTE ELIZA LAWSON
F.H. Partington. See:
YOXALL, HARRY WALDO
F.J. McCormick. See:
JUDGE, PETER
F.N. Allen. See:
DOWNEY, EDMUND
F.N. Vinard. See:
VINCENT, NATHANIEL HAWTHORNE
F.O.O. See:
STREET, CECIL JOHN CHARLES
F.O.O. Serrifile. See:
HOLMES, WILLIAM KERSLEY
F.P.A. See:
ADAMS, FRANKLIN PIERCE
F. Pezet, Dr. See:
ZAUNER, FRANZ PAUL
F.R. Eckmar. See:
DE HARTOG, JAN
F.S. Winton. See:
HARBAUGH, THOMAS CHALMERS
F. Van Wyck Mason. See:
MASON, FRANCIS VAN WYCK
F.W. Murnau. See:
PLUMPE, FRIEDRICH W.
Fa Presto (Hurry Up). See:
GIORDANO, LUCA
FABARES, NANETTE (1922-) [American singer, comedienne and actress]
Nanette Fabray
Faber. See:
GOLDSCHMIDT, DR. HERMANN
FABER, CECILIA BÖHL DE (1796-1877) [Spanish novelist]
Fernán Caballero
Faber, Hermann. See:
GOLDSCHMIDT, DR. HERMANN
FABER, JOHANN (1478-1541) [German controversialist; opponent of the Reformation]
The Hammer of the Heretics
Fabia Drake. See:
McGLINCHY, F.D.
Fabian. See:
FORTE, FABIAN
FABIAN (died 250) [Supreme Pontiff of Roman Catholic Church]
Pope Fabian
St. Fabian
Fabian, Warner. See:
ADAMS, SAMUEL HOPKINS
Fabius. See:
DICKINSON, JOHN
Fabius, The American. See:
WASHINGTON, GEORGE
Fabius, The French. See:
ANNE, DUC DE

MONTMORENCY
Fable, The Hero of the. See:
HENRI II
Fabray, Nanette. See:
FABARES, NANETTE
FABRE, JEAN HENRI (1823-1915) [French entomologist and writer]
The Insects' Homer
FABRICIUS, SARA (1880-) [Norwegian author]
Cora Sandel
Fabrick, Jonathan. See:
HOLBROOK, SILAS PINCKNEY
Fabrilo. See:
APARICI, JULIO
FACCHINETTI, GIOVANNI ANTONIO (1519-91) [Supreme Pontiff of Roman Catholic Church]
Pope Innocent IX
Face, Little Miss Poker. See:
WILLS, HELEN NEWINGTON
Face, Poker. See:
GARNER, JOHN NANCE
Face, The Great Stone. See:
WEBSTER, DANIEL
Faces, The Man of a Thousand. See:
CHANEY, LON
Faces, The Man of Many. See:
WEISENFREUND, MUNI
FACK, CAROLINE (1846-) [German author]
Lina Fack
FACTOR, JOHN (1890/92-) [Anglo-American (?) confidence man; victim of kidnap plot]
Jake the Barber
Norman D. Spencer
Factory King, The. See:
OASTLER, RICHARD
Fadette. See:
REEVES, MARIAN CALHOUN LEGARÉ
Fae Hewston Stevens. See:
STEVENS, FRANCES ISTED
FAGAN, INA (1898-) [American stage and motion picture actress]
Ina Claire
Faid, Mary. See:
DUNN, MARY ALICE
Fainéant, Le (The Sluggard). See: LOUIS V
Fair, A.A. See:
GARDNER, ERLE STANLEY
Fair Branch, The. See:
HYDE, DOUGLAS
Fair Geraldine, The. See:
FITZGERALD, LADY ELIZABETH
Fair God, The (Quetzalcóatl). See: CORTÉS, HERNÁN
Fair Maid of Anjou, The. See:
PLANTAGENET, LADY EDITH
Fair Maid of Galloway, The. See: MARGARET
Fair Maid of Kent, The. See:
JOAN
Fair Maid of Norway, The. See:
MARGARET
Fair Maid of Perth, The. See:
GLOVER, CATHERINE
Fair Perdida. See:
ROBINSON, MRS. MARY DARBY
Fair Quakeress, The. See:
LIGHTFOOT, HANNAH
Fair Rosamond. See:
CLIFFORD, ROSAMOND
Fair, The. See:
CHARLES IV
EDWY (EADWIG)
FREDERICK III
PHILIP IV
Fairbairn, Helen. See:
SOUTHARD, HELEN FAIRBAIRN
FAIRBANKS, CHARLES BULLARD (1827-59) [American travel writer]
Aguecheek
FAIRBANKS, CHARLES WARREN (1854-1918) [American statesman; Vice President of the United States]
Icebanks
Fairbanks, Doug. See:
ULLMAN, JULIUS
Fairbanks, Douglas. See:
ULLMAN, JULIUS

Fairbanks, Phyllis. See:
LANDESBERG, PHYLLIS G.
Fairbrother, Nan. See:
McKENZIE, NAN
Fairbrother, Sydney. See:
TAPPING, SYDNEY
Fairchild, Clarence. See:
CHAMPLIN, EDWIN ROSS
Fairfax, Beatrice. See:
GASCH, MARIE MANNING
FAIRFAX-BLAKEBOROUGH, JOHN (1883-) [British turf official and author]
Hambletonian
Fairfax, L. See:
CONNELLY, LELIA LOGAN
FAIRFIELD, CECILY ISABEL (1892-) [Irish novelist, critic and journalist]
Lynx
Rebecca West
Fairhaired (Haarfagr). See:
HAROLD I
Fairless, Michael. See:
BARBER, MARGARET FAIRLESS
FAIRS, SIR JOHN (1844-1921) [English actor-manager]
Sir John Hare
Fairstar, Mrs. See:
HORNE, RICHARD HENGIST (HENRY)
Faith, Adam. See:
NELHAMS, TERENCE
Faith Baldwin. See:
CUTHRELL, MRS. FAITH BALDWIN
Faith Perkins. See:
BRAMER, JENNIE PERKINS
Faith, Shelby's Man of. See:
ANTHONY, JOHN ALSTON
Faith, The Defender of the. See: ROBERTS, BRIGHAM HENRY
Faithful Andy. See:
SOMMERVILLE, ANDREW
Faithful, Commander of the. See: OMAR I
Faithful King, Most. See:
JOHN V
FALAY, ALMES MUVAFFAX (1930-) [Turkish jazz musician (trumpet, piano)]
Maffy
FALCA, PIETRO (1702-85) [Venetian painter]
Longhi
Falcon, Richard. See:
SHAPIRO, SAMUEL
Falconbridge. See:
KELLY, JONATHAN FALCONBRIDGE
Falconer, James. See:
KIRKUP, JAMES
Falconer, Lance. See:
HAWKER, MARY ELIZABETH
FALK, BIBB AUGUST (1899-) [American professional baseball player]
Jockey
Falk, Elsa. See:
ESCHERICH, ELSA FALK
Falkenburg, Jinx. See:
McCRARY, EUGENIA LINCOLN FALKENBURG
Falkland, Samuel. See:
HEIJERMANS (HEYERMANS), HERMAN
FALLA Y MATHEU, MANUEL MARÍA DE (1876-1946) [Spanish composer]
Manuel de Falla
Fallada, Hans. See:
DITZEN, RUDOLPH
Fallersleben, Hoffmann von. See: HOFFMAN, AUGUST HEINRICH
Fallodon, Grey of. See:
EDWARD, VISCOUNT GREY OF FALLODON
Fallon, Martin. See:
PATTERSON, HENRY
FALLON, WILLIAM J. (1886-1927) [American trial lawyer]
The Great Mouthpiece
Fallow Land (Novalis). See:
HARDENBERG, FRIEDRICH LEOPOLD, BARON VON

False Prophet, The. See:
MOHAMMED AHMED
Falstaff, Jake. See:
FETZER, HERMAN
Fame, Georgie. See:
POWELL, CLIVE
Famous Folk Singer of his Race, The Most. See:
WHITE, JOSHUA DANIEL
Famous People, New York City's Official Greeter of. See: WHALEN, GROVER ALOYSIUS
Fan Fan. See:
BLACKBURN, VICTORIA GRACE
Fancy Frank. See:
POWELL, DAVID FRANK
Fandom, The Idol of Baseball. See: COBB, TYRUS RAYMOND
Fane, Florence. See:
VICTOR, MRS. FRANCES FULLER BARRITT
Fane, Violet. See:
CURRIE, LADY MARY MONTGOMERY LAMB
FANNIN, JAMES W. (c.1800-36) [American soldier; hero at Battle of Concepción]
The Hero of Concepción
Fanny. See:
ANDREWS, ELIZA FRANCES
BURNEY, FRANCES
DOWNING, FRANCES MURDAUGH
KEMBLE, FRANCES ANNE
WRIGHT, FRANCES
Fanny, Aunt. See:
BARROW, FRANCES ELIZABETH MEASE
GAGE, FRANCES DANA BARKER
Fanny Brice. See:
BORACH, FANNY
Fanny Crosby. See:
VAN ALSTYNE, MRS. FRANCES JANE CROSBY
Fanny Fern. See:
PARTON, SARA PAYSON WILLIS
Fanny Forester. See:
JUDSON, EMILY CHUBBUCK
Fanny, Lord. See:
LORD HERVEY
Fanny Stirling. See:
KEHL, MARY ANNE
Faraday Keene. See:
JARRETT, CORA HARDY
FARBER, NATHANIEL C. (1918-) [American composer, pianist and arranger]
Nat Farber
Farel, Conrad. See:
BARDENS, DENNIS CONRAD
FAREL, GUILLAUME (1489-1565) [French reformer]
The Elijah of the French Reformation
The Scourge of the Priests
Fargo, Doone. See:
NORWOOD, VICTOR GEORGE CHARLES
Fargo, Joe. See:
RIKHOFF, JAMES C.
FARGUS, FREDERICK JOHN (1847-85) [English author of melodramatic novels]
Hugh Conway
FARIGOULE, LOUIS-HENRI JEAN (1885-) [French poet and novelist]
Jules Romains
Farinelli. See:
BROSCHI, CARLO
FARINOLA, VITO (c.1925-) [American entertainer and singer]
Vic Damone
FARJEON, ELEANOR (1881-) [British author]
Tomfool
FARLEY, JAMES ALOYSIUS (1888-) [American politician; Postmaster General of the United States]
Big Jim
Four-job Farley
Smiling Jim
A Political Thor

That Candid Spoilsman
FARLOW, TALMADGE HOLT (1921-) [American jazz musician (guitar)]
Tal Farlow
Farm Woman's Congresswoman, The. See:
KNUTSON, CORNELIA GJESDAL
Farmacevten. See:
HOLM, SVEN AAGE
Farman, Ella. See:
PRATT, ELIZA ANNA FARMAN
Farmer. See:
GEORGE III
SMITH, GEORGE HENRY
FARMER, BERNARD JONES (1902-) [British engineer and author]
Owen Fox
Farmer Bob. See:
DOUGHTON, ROBERT L.
SCOTT, ROBERT WALTER
Farmer Bob Scott. See:
SCOTT, ROBERT WALTER
Farmer Governor, The. See:
BOUCK, WILLIAM C.
Farmer King (Rei Lavrador). See: DINIZ (DENIS)
Farmer King, The. See:
GEORGE III
Farmer, Peter. See:
LLOYD, JOHN IVESTER
Farmer-President, The. See:
HARRISON, WILLIAM HENRY
WASHINGTON, GEORGE
Farmer, The Butterfly. See:
NEWMAN, LEONARD HUGH
Farmer, The Federal. See:
LEE, RICHARD HENRY
Farmer, The Golden. See:
DAVIS, WILLIAM
Farmer, The Pennsylvania. See:
DICKINSON, JOHN
Farmers' Dick. See:
OGLESBY, RICHARD JAMES
Farmer's Friend. See:
CAPPER, ARTHUR
Farnash, Hugh. See:
LUFF, STANLEY GEORGE ANTHONY
FARNESE, ALESSANDRO (1468-1549) [Supreme Pontiff of Roman Catholic Church]
Pope Paul III
Farnham, Burt. See:
CLIFFORD, HAROLD B.
FARNOL, JOHN JEFFRY (1878-1952) [British novelist]
Jeffery Farnol
FARNSWORTH, PHILO TAYLOR (1906-71) [American electrical engineer and inventor]
The Father of Television
FAROUK I (1920-) [ex-King of Egypt]
Prince Charming
FARQUHAR, GEORGE (1678-1707) [Irish playwright]
The Fielding of the Drama
The Smollett of the Stage
Farquharson, Martha. See:
FINLEY, MARTHA FARQUHARSON
FARR, DIANA PULLEIN-THOMPSON (fl. 1946-62) [British author]
Diana Pullein-Thompson
Farr, Douglas. See:
GILFORD, CHARLES BERNARD
Farra, Madame E. See:
FAWCETT, FRANK DUBREZ
FARRAGUT, DAVID GLASGOW (1801-70) [American naval officer]
The Hero of Mobile Bay
Farragut Fraddle. See:
MEARNS, DAVID CHAMBERS
Farrell, David. See:
SMITH, FREDERICK ESCREET
Farrell, Desmond. See:
ORGAN, JOHN
FARRELL, EDWARD STEPHEN (1902-) [American professional baseball player and dentist]

Doc Farrell
FARRELL, GILBERT HASTINGS (1845-1901) [English music-hall singer of patriotic songs]
Gilbert Hastings
MacDermott the Great
FARRELL, JAMES THOMAS (1904-) [American author]
Jonathan Titulescu Fogarty, Esq.
Farrell, Suzanne. See:
FICKER, ROBERTA SUE
Farrère, Claude. See:
BARGONE, FRÉDÉRIC CHARLES PIERRE EDOUARD
FARROW, MARIA DE LOURDES VILLIERS (1946-) [American actress]
Mia Farrow
FARWELL, CHARLES BENJAMIN (1823-1903) [American politician; senator from Illinois]
Poker Charley
Fashion Plate, The. See:
LEWIS, JAMES HAMILTON
Fashion, The First Gentleman of. See:
LELONG, LUCIEN
Fashion World's Most Irrepressible Master of Ceremonies. See:
CASSINI, OLEG LOIEWSKI
Fashion's Picasso. See:
BALENCIAGA, CRISTOBAL
FAST, HOWARD MELVIN (1914-) [American author]
E.V. Cunningham
Walter Ericson
Fasting Woman of Tutbury, The. See:
MOORE, ANNE PEGG
Fat. See also:
Fats
Fatty
Fat Adonis of Forty (or Fifty), The. See:
GEORGE IV
Fat, Alfonso The (Alfonso o Gordo). See:
ALFONSO II
Fat Contributor, The. See:
GRISWOLD, A. MINER
THACKERAY, WILLIAM MAKEPEACE
Fat Paunch (Physcon). See:
PTOLEMY VII (or VIII or IX)
Fat, The. See:
CHARLES II
DOUGLAS, JAMES
HENRY I
LOUIS VI
Fatha. See:
Father
HINES, EARL KENNETH
Fathead. See:
NEWMAN, DAVID
Father. See:
ABRAHAM
CATS, JACOB
COLE, AMBROSE N.
Fatha
FLANAGAN, EDWARD JOSEPH
MATHEW, THEOBALD
RYAN, ABRAM JOSEPH
SMITH, BERNARD
TABB, JOHN BANISTER
Father Abraham. See:
FRANKLIN, BENJAMIN
LINCOLN, ABRAHAM
Father and Glory of Boston, The. See: COTTON, JOHN
Father and Nursing Mother of the Gridiron Club, The. See: CARSON, JOHN MILLER
Father Bonaventura. See:
STUART, CHARLES EDWARD LOUIS PHILIP CASIMIR
Father Caedmon. See:
WAHL, CAEDMON THOMAS
Father Damien. See:
VEUSTER, JOSEPH DAMIEN DE
Father Divine. See:
BAKER, GEORGE
Father Fritz. See:

FREDERICK II
Father Goose. See:
SENNETT, MACK
Father Joseph (Père Joseph).
See: TREMBLAY,
FRANÇOIS LE CLERC
DU
Father Kit. See:
CARSON, CHRISTOPHER
Father, Loving His (New
Philopator). See:
PTOLEMY VII
Father, Loving His (Philopator).
See: PTOLEMY IV
Father M. Louis. See:
MERTON, THOMAS
JAMES
Father Noah. See:
WELLES, GIDEON
Father of Algebra, The. See:
DIOPHANTUS
Father of all the Yankees, The.
See: FRANKLIN,
BENJAMIN
Father of America, The. See:
ADAMS, SAMUEL
WASHINGTON, GEORGE
Father of American Anthropology, The. See:
MORGAN, LEWIS
HENRY
Father of American Apiculture,
The. See:
LANGSTROTH, LORENZO
LORRAINE
Father of American Ballad
Poetry, The. See:
HEWITT, JOHN HENRY
(HILL)
Father of American Baptists,
The. See:
CLARKE, JOHN
Father of American Botany, The.
See: BARTRAM, JOHN
Father of American Boxing, The.
See: MULDOON,
WILLIAM
Father of American Bridge
Building, The. See:
WHIPPLE, SQUIRE
Father of American Church
Music, The. See:
MASON, LOWELL
Father of American Commerce
with India, The. See:
DERBY, ELIAS HASKET
Father of American Conchology,
The. See:
SAY, THOMAS
Father of American Descriptive
Entomology, The. See:
SAY, THOMAS
Father of American Drama, The.
See: DUNLAP, WILLIAM
Father of American Engineering,
The. See:
WRIGHT, BENJAMIN
Father of American Entomology,
The. See:
SAY, THOMAS
Father of American Ethnology,
The. See:
GALLATIN, ABRAHAM
ALPHONSE ALBERT
Father of American Experimental
Physics, The. See:
ROOD, OGDEN NICHOLAS
Father of American Football,
The. See:
CAMP, WALTER
Father of American Geography,
The. See:
MORSE JEDIDIAH
Father of American Geology,
The. See:
MACLURE, WILLIAM
Father of American Geophysics,
The. See:
GOLYER, EVERETTE
LEE DE
Father of American Grape
Culture, The. See:
LONGWORTH, NICHOLAS
Father of American History,
The. See:
BRADFORD, WILLIAM
Father of American Independence,
The. See:
ADAMS, JOHN
Father of American Literature,
The. See:
IRVING, WASHINGTON
Father of American Manufacture,
The. See:
SLATER, SAMUEL
Father of American Map Making,

The. See:
GANNETT, HENRY
Father of American Mineralogy, The. See:
CLEAVELAND, PARKER
Father of American Minstrelsy, The. See: RICE, THOMAS DARTMOUTH
Father of American Newspapers, The. See:
HARRIS, BENJAMIN
Father of American Orchestral Music. See:
GRAUPNER, JOHANN CHRISTIAN GOTTLIEB
Father of American Poets, The. See: BRYANT, WILLIAM CULLEN
Father of American Prose, The. See: IRVING, WASHINGTON
Father of American Psychiatry, The. See: RUSH, BENJAMIN
Father of American Surgery, The. See:
PHYSICK, PHILIP SYNG
Father of American Universalism, The. See:
BALLOU, HOSEA
MURRAY, JOHN
Father of American Watchmaking, The. See:
DENNISON, AARON LUFKIN
Father of American Zoölogy, The. See:
SAY, THOMAS
Father of Anarchy, The. See:
WARREN, JOSIAH
Father of Anglican Church Music, The. See:
PURCELL, HENRY
Father of Angling, The. See:
WALTON, IZAAK
Father of Antiseptic Surgery, The. See:
LISTER, JOSEPH
Father of Arizona, The. See:
POSTON, CHARLES DEBRILL
Father of Automation, The. See: WIENER, NORBERT
Father of Baseball in the West, The. See:
WALDO, HIRAM H.
Father of Baseball, The. See:
CHADWICK, HENRY
DOUBLEDAY, ABNER
Father of Basketball, The. See:
NAISMITH, DR. JAMES A.
Father of Belgian Literature, The. See:
DE COSTER, CHARLES THEODORE HENRI
Father of Biblical Learning in America, The. See:
STUART, MOSES
Father of Bibliography, The. See:
TRITHEIM, JOHANNES
Father of British Columbia, The. See: DOUGLAS, SIR JAMES
Father of British Inland Navigation, The. See:
EGERTON, FRANCIS
Father of British Plastics, The. See: SWINBURNE, SIR JAMES, 9TH BARONET
Father of Buffalo, The. See:
ELLICOT, JOSEPH
Father of Burlesque Poetry, The. See: HIPPONAX
Father of Chautauqua County, The. See:
FOOTE, ELIAL TODD
Father of Chemistry, The. See:
VILLENEUVA, ARNAUD DE
Father of Christian Monachism, The. See:
ANTONY (ANTHONY), ST.
Father of Church History, The. See: EUSEBIUS OF CAESAREA
Father of Civil Service Reform, The. See:
JENCKES, THOMAS ALLEN
PENDLETON, GEORGE HUNT
Father of Comedy, The. See:
ARISTOPHANES
Father of Concrete Roads in New York, The. See:
GREENE, FREDERICK STUART
Father of Connecticut Jurisprudence, The. See:
LUDLOW, ROGER
Father of Cubism, The. See:

See: AESCHYLUS
THESPIS
Father of Greenbacks, The.
See: CHASE, SALMON PORTLAND
SPAULDING, ELBRIDGE GERRY
Father of Gymnastics (Turnvater).
See: JOHN, FRIEDRICH LUDWIG
Father of Harlequins, The. See:
RICH, JOHN
Father of His Country, Liberator and. See:
DORIA, ANDREA
Father of His Country, The. See:
WASHINGTON, GEORGE
Father of His Country, The (Pater Patriae). See:
ADRIAN (HADRIAN)
CICERO, MARCUS TULLIUS
MEDICI, COSIMO DE'
Father of Historical Societies in America, The. See:
PINTARD, JOHN
Father of History, The. See:
HERODOTUS
Father of Homeopathy in America, The. See:
HERING, CONSTANTINE
Father of Horticulture and Ornamental Gardening, The.
See: HENDERSON, PETER
Father of Humanism, The. See:
PETRARCH (FRANCESCO PETRARCA)
Father of Iambic Verse, The.
See: ARCHILOCHUS
Father of Indiana History, The. See:
DILLON, JOHN BROWN
Father of International Law, The. See:
GROTIUS, HUGO
Father of Iron Shipbuilding in America, The. See:
ROACH, JOHN
Father of Italian Poetry, The.
See: FREDERICK II
Father of Italian Prose, The.
See: BOCCACCIO, GIOVANNI
Father of Jests, The. See:
MILLER, JOSEPH
Father of Journalism in Mississippi, The. See:
MARSCHALK, ANDREW
Father of Journalism, The. See:
ARETINO, PIETRO
Father of Kant, The Spiritual.
See: HUME, DAVID
Father of Landscape Gardening, The. See:
LENÔTRE, ANDRÉ
Father of Letters, The. See:
FRANCIS I
Father of Lies, The. See:
HERODOTUS
Father of Logarithms, The. See:
NAPIER, JOHN
Father of Louisiana Jurisprudence, The. See:
MARTIN, FRANÇOIS XAVIER
Father of Massachusetts, The.
See: WINTHROP, JOHN
Father of Medicine, The. See:
HIPPOCRATES
Father of Middle Tennessee, The.
See: ROBERTSON, JAMES
Father of Minneapolis, The.
See: STEVENS, JOHN H.
Father of Minnesota, The.
See: SIBLEY, HENRY HASTINGS
Father of Modern Aerial Photography, The. See:
GODDARD, GEORGE WILLIAM
Father of Modern Agriculture, The. See:
YOUNG, ARTHUR
Father of Modern Amphibious Warfare, The. See:
SMITH, HOLLAND McTYEIRE
Father of Modern Ballet, The.
See: FOKINE, MICHEL
Father of Modern Baseball, The.
See: CARTWRIGHT, ALEXANDER JOY
Father of Modern Chemistry, The.
See: BOYLE, SIR ROBERT
Father of Modern Drama, The.
See: IBSEN, HENRIK JOHAN

Father of Modern French Songs, The. See: PANARD, CHARLES-FRANÇOIS
Father of Modern Geography, The. See: KREMER, GERHARD
Father of Modern Magic, The. See: ROBERT-HOUDIN, JEAN EUGÈNE
Father of Modern Missions, The. See: CAREY, WILLIAM
Father of Modern Norwegian Poetry, The. See: DASS, PETER
Father of Modern Painting, The. See: CIMABUE, GIOVANNI
Father of Modern Philosophy, The. See: DESCARTES, RENÉ
Father of Modern Prose Fiction, The. See: FOE, DANIEL
Father of Modern Theory, The. See: FERMAT, PIERRE DE
Father of Modernism, The. See: CÉZANNE, PAUL
SULLIVAN, LOUIS HENRI
Father of Monachism, The. See: ANTONY (ANTHONY), ST.
Father of Monks, The. See: ANTONY (ANTHONY), ST.
ETHELWOLD OF WINCHESTER
Father of More Brains Than Any Other Man in America. The. See: BEECHER, LYMAN
Father of Musick, The. See: PALESTRINA, GIOVANNI PIERLUIGI
Father of Music, The. See: BYRD (BIRDE), WILLIAM
Father of New England Commerce, The. See: ALLERTON, ISAAC
Father of New England, The. See: ENDICOTT, JOHN
Father of New France, The. See: CHAMPLAIN, SAMUEL DE
Father of Niagara Power, The. See: RANKINE, WILLIAM BIRCH
Father of Ohio Labor, The. See: CROSSER, ROBERT
Father of Ohio University, The. See: CUTLER, MANASSEH
Father of Orchestral Music, The. See: HAYDN, FRANZ JOSEPH
Father of Organized Alumni Work at Fisk University, The. See: PROCTOR, HENRY HUGH
Father of Ornithologists, The. See: EDWARDS, GEORGE
Father of Orthodoxy, The. See: ATHANASIUS, ST.
Father of Our Modern Fortifications, The. See: CRAIGHILL, WILLIAM PRICE
Father of Our Modern Navy, The. See: CHANDLER, WILLIAM EATON
Father of Parody, The. See: HIPPONAX
Father of Peace, The. See: DORIA, ANDREA
Father of Pennsylvania, The. See: PENN, WILLIAM
Father of Philosophy, The. See: BACON, ROGER
VON HALLER, ALBRECHT
Father of Photography, The. See: TALBOT, WILLIAM HENRY FOX
Father of Physiology, The. See: VON HALLER, ALBRECHT
Father of Pietism, The. See: SPENER, PHILIPP JAKOB
Father of Pitt Stadium, The. See: HAMILTON, ALFRED REED
Father of Pittsburgh, The. See: WASHINGTON, GEORGE
Father of Poetry, The. See: HOMER

Father of Portuguese Drama, The. See: VICENTE, GIL
Father of Presbyterianism in the State of New York, The. See: McNISH, GEORGE
Father of Presbyterianism in Virginia, The. See: MORRIS, SAMUEL
Father of Printing, The. See: GENSFLEISCH, JOHAN
Father of Prison Reform in the United States, The. See: OSBORNE, GEORGE O.
Father of Prohibition, The. See: DOW, NEAL
Father of Public Utility Regulation, The. See: NORRIS, GEORGE WILLIAM
Father of Radio Broadcasting, The. See: DAVIS, HARRY PHILLIPS
Father of Radio, The. See: FOREST, LEE DE
Father of Railroads, The. See: COOPER, PETER
Father of Realism, The. See: HOWELLS, WILLIAM DEAN
Father of Reclamation, The. See: WISNER, EDWARD
Father of Reform, The. See: CARTWRIGHT, JOHN
Father of Rhode Island, The. See: CLARKE, JOHN
Father of Ridicule, The. See: RABELAIS, FRANÇOIS
Father of Roman Literature, The. See: ENNIUS, QUINTUS
Father of Roman Philosophy, The. See: CICERO, MARCUS TULLIUS
Father of Roman Poetry, The. See: ENNIUS, QUINTUS
Father of Roman Satire, The. See: LUCILIUS, CAIUS
Father of Rural Credit in North Carolina, The. See: HILL, JOHN SPRUNT
Father of Rural Free Delivery, The. See: BUTLER, MARION
Father of Russian History, The. See: NESTOR
Father of Satire, The. See: ARCHILOCHUS
Father of Science Fiction, The. See: VERNE, JULES
Father of Scottish Poetry and History, The. See: BARBOUR, JOHN
Father of Scottish Presbytery, The. See: MELVILLE, ANDREW
Father of Secession, The. See: RHETT, ROBERT BARNWELL
Father of Ship-building, The. See: DICKIE, GEORGE WILLIAM
Father of Shorthand, The. See: BRIGHT, TIMOTHY
Father of Social Settlements. See: TOYNBEE, ARNOLD
Father of Song, The. See: HOMER
Father of State Universities, The. See: CUTLER, MANASSEH
Father of States' Rights, The. See: CALHOUN, JOHN CALDWELL
Father of Steamboat Navigation The. See: FULTON, ROBERT
Father of Swiss History, The. See: TSCHUDI, AEGIDIUS (GILG)
Father of Symphony, The. See: HAYDN, FRANZ JOSEPH
Father of Tacoma, The. See: WRIGHT, CHARLES BARSTOW
Father of Television, The. See: FARNSWORTH, PHILO TAYLOR
Father of Texas, The. See: AUSTIN, STEPHEN FULLER HOUSTON, SAMUEL
Father of the American Anthracite Iron Industry, The. See: THOMAS, DAVID

Father of the American Cotton Industry, The. See: COXE, TENCH
Father of the American Medical Association, The. See: DAVIS, NATHAN SMITH
Father of the American Navy, The. See: ADAMS, JOHN
BARRY, COMMODORE JOHN
HUMPHREYS, JOSHUA
Father of the American Revolution, The. See: ADAMS, SAMUEL
Father of the Automatic Rifle, The. See: BROWNING, JOHN MOSES
Father of the Bar of the State Of New York, The. See: VAN VECHEN, ABRAHAM
Father of the Barge Canal, The. See: CLINTON, GEORGE
Father of the Bathos and Indeed the Homer of It, The. See: BLACKMORE, SIR RICHARD
Father of the Blues, The. See: HANDY, WILLIAM CHRISTOPHER
Father of the Bonus, The. See: PATMAN, WRIGHT
VAN ZANT, JAMES E.
Father of the Breaker, The. See: MARKLE, GEORGE BUSHER
Father of the Brooklyn Institute of Arts and Sciences, The. See: HEALY, AARON AUGUSTUS
Father of the Chinese Republic, The. See: SUN YAT-SEN
Father of the City Manager Plan of Municipal Government, The. See: CHILDS, RICHARD SPENCER
Father of the Code, The. See: FIELD, DAVID DUDLEY
Father of the "Colyumnist," The. See: BAILEY, JAMES MONTGOMERY
Father of the Constitution, The. See: MADISON, JAMES
Father of the Continental Congress, The. See: FRANKLIN, BENJAMIN
Father of the Cotton Gin, The. See: WHITNEY, ELI
Father of the Country, The. See: CICERO, MARCUS TULLIUS
Father of the Criminal Bar, The. See: HOWE, WILLIAM FREDERICK
Father of the Czech Nationalist School of Composition. The. See: SMETANA, BEDŘICH
Father of the Declaration of Independence, The. See: JEFFERSON, THOMAS
Father of the Dry Plate Process in America, The. See: NEWTON, HENRY JOTHAM
Father of the Dutch Reformed Church in America, The. See: LIVINGSTON, JOHN HENRY
Father of the Eighteenth Amendment, The. See: SHEPPARD, MORRIS
Father of the English Navy, The. See: HENRY VIII
Father of the English Novel, The. See: FIELDING, HENRY
Father of the English Public School System, The. See: WYKEHAM (WICKHAM), WILLIAM OF
Father of the Enlightenment in England, The. See: LOCKE, JOHN
Father of the Federal Reserve System, The. See: GLASS, GEORGE CARTER
Father of the Florida Orange Industry, The. See: HARRIS, JAMES ARMSTRONG
Father of the Forward Pass,

Father of the University of
Virginia, The. See:
JEFFERSON, THOMAS
Father of the Vaudeville, The
Joyous. See:
BASSELIN, OLIVER
Father of the White Line, The.
See: HINES, EDWARD
NORRIS
Father of Thought, The. See:
CATINAT, NICOLAS
Father of Toxicology, The. See:
ORFILA, MATHIEU
JOSEPH BONAVENTURE
Father of Turenne, The. See:
BOUILLON, HENRI DE
LA TOUR D'AUVERGNE,
DUKE DE
Father of Universal Bibliography,
The. See:
GESSNER, KONRAD VON
Father of Universalism in America, The. See:
MURRAY, JOHN
Father of Variety, The. See:
PARNELL, THOMAS
FREDERICK
Father of Virginia, The. See:
SMITH, JOHN
Father of Western Mysticism,
The. See:
BERNARD OF CLAIRVAUX
Father of Whist, The. See:
HOYLE, EDMOND
Father Prout. See:
MAHONY, FRANCIS
SYLVESTER
Father Rondo. See:
DAVAUX, J.B.
Father Smith. See:
GALITZIN, DIMITRI
AUGUSTINE
Father", The Author of "The.
See: DUNLAP, WILLIAM
Father, The Bread (Der
Brodvater). See:
SOWER, CHRISTOPHER
Father Tom. See:
BEECHER, THOMAS
KINNICUT
Fathers, The Last of the. See:
BERNARD OF CLAIRVAUX
Fats. See:
Fat
Fatty
HEARD, EUGENE M.
HENRY, WILBUR F.
NAVARRO,
THEODORE
WALLER, THOMAS
WRIGHT
FATTORINO, BARTOLOMMEO
DI PAGOLO DEL
(1475-1517) [Italian
painter and
churchman]
Fra Bartolommeo
Baccio della Porta
Fatty. See:
ARBUCKLE, ROSCOE
Fat
Fats
Faubourg Saint-Germain, La
Sibylle du. See:
LENORMAND, MARIE
ANNE ADÉLAÏDE
FAUCONBERG, THOMAS (died
1471) [English rebel
soldier]
Thomas the Bastard
FAULEY, WILBUR FINLEY
(1872-) [American
journalist and playwright]
Wilbur Fawley
FAULKNER, ANNE IRVIN
(1906-) [American author]
Nancy Faulkner
FAULKNER,
CLIFFORD VERNON
(1913-) [Canadian editor
and author]
Pete Williams
Faulkner Conway. See:
PRICE, FRANK J.
Faulkner, Frank. See:
ELLIS, EDWARD SYLVESTER
FAULKNER, GEORGE (1699?-
1755) [Irish bookseller]
The Irish Atticus
FAULKNER, GEORGENE (1873-
) [American author of
stories for children]
The Story Lady
FAULKNER, WILLIAM (1897-1962)
[American novelist and

short story writer]
The American Balzac
FAULKS, MRS. FREDERIC J. (1874-) [American poet]
Theodosia Garrison
Faultless Painter, The. See: VANNUCCHI, ANDREA DOMENICO D'AGNOLO DI FRANCESCO DI LUCA
FAUST, FREDERICK SCHILLER (1892-1944) [American author]
George Owen Baxter
Max Brand
George Challis
Peter Dawson
Martin Dexter
Evin Evans
John Frederick
Heinie
The King of the Pulps
M. B.
David Manning
Peter Henry Moreland
Hugh Owen
Nicholas Silver
FAUST, GEORG (1480?-1540?) [German fortune teller and magician]
Johann (Johannes) Faust
Fausta Cialente. See: TERNI, FAUSTA CIALENTE
FAVIOT, ALIX (1621-70) [French actress]
Mademoiselle Desoeillets
Favorite Niece, Uncle Sam's. See: KAUMEYER, DOROTHY
Favorite Son of Texas, The. See: GARNER, JOHN NANCE
Favorite Television Comedian, America's. See: JACOBS, AMOS
Fawcett, Barbara. See: UPSON, DOROTHY BARBARA
FAWCETT, FRANK DUBREZ (1891-) [British author]
Henri Dupres
Madame E. Farra
Eugene Glen
Griff
Coolidge McCann
Elmer Eliot Saks
Ben Sarto
Simpson Stokes
FAWCETT, WILLIAM HAMILTON (1885-1940) [American humorist and publisher]
Captain Billy
Fawley, Wilbur. See: FAULEY, WILBUR FINLEY
Fay Chandos. See: TEMPEST, JAN
Fay, Erica. See: STOPES, MRS. MARIE CHARLOTTE CARMICHAEL
FAY, FRANCIS ANTHONY (1897- [American actor]
America's Foremost Master of Ceremonies
Frank Fay
Fay Holden. See: HAMMERTON, FAY
Fay Inchfawn. See: WARD, ELIZABETH REBECCA
FAY, LARRY (1889-1933) [American gangster]
The Beau Brummel of Broadway
Fay Ramsay. See: EASTWOOD, HELEN
Faye, Alice. See: LEPPERT, ALICE
Faye Huntington. See: FOSTER, THEODOSIA MARIA TOLL
FAYE, JULIAN LA (c. 1907-) [American singer and motion picture actor]
John Carroll
Fazola, Irving. See: PRESTOPNIK, IRVING
FAZZANO, JOSEPH E. (1929-) [American attorney and author]
John Fitzgerald
FEAGLES, ANITA MACRAE (1926-) [American author]

Travis MacRae
Feagles, Elizabeth See:
DAY, BETH FEAGLES
Fear and Without Reproach, The Knight Without. See:
BAYARD, PIERRE DU TERRAIL, CHEVALIER DE
FEARING, LILIAN BLANCHE (1863-1901) [American poet]
Blanche Fearing
Lillien Blanche Fearing
Raymond Russell
Fearless Frances. See:
PERKINS, FRANCES
Fearless, The. See:
JOHN
RICHARD I
Feathers, Old Fuss and. See:
SCOTT, WINFIELD
FEBIGER, CHRISTIAN (1746-96) [Danish-American Revolutionary general officer]
Old Denmark
FECHNER, GUSTAV THEODOR (1801-87) [German physicist and psychologist]
Dr. Mises
FEDDEN, KATHERINE WALDO DOUGLAS (died 1939) [American author]
Mrs. Romilly Fedden
FEDER, R.H. (1909-) [American motion picture producer]
Robert Arthur
Federal Bull-dog, The. See:
MARTIN, LUTHER
Federal Farmer, The. See:
LEE, RICHARD HENRY
Federal Reserve System, The Father of the. See:
GLASS, GEORGE CARTER
Fedor Sologub. See:
TETERNIKOV, FEDOR KUZMICH
Feds, The King of the. See:
HAMILTON, ALEXANDER
Feelin', A. Fellow. See:
FULLER, HENRY STARKEY
FEENEY, KATHARINE SCULLY (1928-) [American motion picture actress]
Sally Forrest
Feike Feikema. See:
MANFRED FREDERICK FEIKEMA
Feikema, Feike. See:
MANFRED, FREDERICK FEIKEMA
FEININGER, LYONEL (1871-) [American artist and cartoonist]
Your Uncle Feininger
FELDMAN, GERALD (1922-) [American jazz musician (leader, arranger)]
Jerry Fielding
FELDSTEIN, SAUL (1940-) [American musician, composer and teacher]
Sandy Feldstein
Felicia Quist. See:
HOBSON, LAURA ZAMETKIN
Felicien Marceau. See:
CARETTE, LOUIS-ALBERT
Felicité le Fevre. See:
SMITH-MASTERS, MARGARET
Felinus, Aretius. See:
KUHHORN, MARTIN
Felix. See:
SULLA, LUCIUS CORNELIUS
FELIX (died 274) [Supreme Pontiff of Roman Catholic Church]
Pope Felix I
St. Felix
FELIX (died 492) [Supreme Pontiff of Roman Catholic Church]
Pope Felix II
Pope Felix III
St. Felix
FELIX (died 530) [Supreme Pontiff of Roman Catholic Church]
Pope Felix III
Pope Felix IV
St. Felix
FÉLIX, ADÉLAÏDE (1828-72)

[French actress]
Lia
Felix Ago. See:
HALDEMAN, SAMUEL STEHMAN
Felix Aylmer. See:
JONES, FELIX EDWARD AYLMER
Felix C. Forest. See:
LINEBARGER, PAUL MYRON ANTHONY
Felix Carmen. See:
SHERMAN, FRANK DEMPSTER
FÉLIX, ÉLISA (1820-58) [French actress]
Rachel
Felix Guzmán. See:
SCHOPENHAUER, FELIX BEGLIO
Felix Hope. See:
WILLIAMSON, CLAUDE CHARLES H.
Felix Krull. See:
WHITE, JAMES DILLON
FÉLIX, MELANIE EMILIE (1836-1909) [French actress]
Dinah
Felix, Pastor. See:
LOCKHART, ARTHUR JOHN
FÉLIX, RACHEL (1829-54) [French actress]
Rebecca
Felix Salten. See:
SALZMANN, FELIX
FÉLIX, SOPHIE (1819-77) [French actress]
Sarah
Felix Summerley. See:
COLE, SIR HENRY
FELKIN, ALFRED LAURENCE (1856-) [British school inspector and author]
A. St. Laurence
FELLER, ROBERT WILLIAM ANDREW (1918-) [American professional baseball player]
Bob Feller
Rapid Robert
Feller, The Big. See:
SULLIVAN, TIMOTHY DANIEL
Feller, The Little. See:
SULLIVAN, TIMOTHY P.
Fellow Feelin'. A. See:
FULLER, HENRY STARKEY
Fellowes, Anne. See:
MANTLE, WINIFRED LANGFORD
FELLOWES-GORDON, IAN DOUGLAS (1921-) [British author]
Douglas Collier
Ian Gordon
FELSEN, HENRY GREGOR (1916-) [American author]
Angus Vicker
FELTON, CORNELIUS CONWAY (1807-62) [American professor at Harvard University]
The American Professor
FELTON, RONALD OLIVER (1909-) [British educator and author]
Ronald Welch
Female Howard, The. See:
FRY, MRS. ELIZABETH
Female Jesse James, The. See:
STARR, BELLE
Female Petrarch, The. See:
LEWIS, ESTELLE ANNA BLANCHE ROBINSON
Fence-rail. See:
JOHNSON, EDWARD
FENELLOSA, MARY McNEIL (fl. late 19th/early 20th cent.) [American novelist and poet]
Sidney McCall
Fénelon of Germany, The. See:
LAVATER, JOHANN CASPAR
Fénelon of the Reformation, The. See:
ARNDT, JOHN
Fêng, Chu. See:
BLOFELD, JOHN EATON CALTHORPE
FÊNG YU-HSIANG (1882-1948) [Chinese soldier and Christian convert]

The Christian General of China
Fenimore Cooper, The French. See: GLOUX, OLIVIER
Fennell, Connie. See: VAYSSE, CHARLES
Fenton, Freda. See: ROWLAND, DONALD SYDNEY
Fenwick, Kay. See: BEAN, KEITH FENWICK
Fenwick, Peter. See: HOLMES, PETER FENWICK
Fenworth Moore. See: STRATEMEYER, EDWARD L.
Feodorovich, Pëtr. See: PETER III
Fer, Bras de. See: BALDWIN
NOUE, FRANÇOIS DE
FERDINAND (1195-1231) [Portuguese Franciscan monk and preacher]
Anthony of Padua
FERDINAND I (1000?-65) [King of Castile and León]
En Magno (The Great)
FERDINAND I (1345-83) [King of Portugal]
The Handsome
FERDINAND I (1379?-1416) [King of Aragon and Sicily]
The Just
FERDINAND II (1452-1516) [King of Castile]
The Catholic
FERDINAND II (1810-59) [Ruler of the two Sicilies]
Bomba
King Bomba
FERDINAND III (1199-1252) [King of Castile and León]
El Santo (The Saint)
FERDINAND IV (1286?-1312) [King of Castile and León]
El Emplazado (The Summoned)
FERDINAND V (1452-1516) [King and Regent of Castile]
The Catholic
The Wily
FERDINAND VI (1713-59) [King of Spain]
El Sabio (The Learned)
Ferenc Molnár. See: NEUMANN, FERENC
Fergus. See: HUME, FERGUSON, WRIGHT
Fergus O'Dhu. See: TROTTER, CANON JOHN CRAWFORD
FERGUSON, CHARLES W. (1901-) [American Methodist minister and author]
Hilton Gregory
FERGUSON, MIRIAM A. (1875-) [American governor of Texas]
Ma Ferguson
FERGUSON, RICHARD (died 1800) [English highwayman]
Galloping Dick
FERGUSON, ROBERT (c.1637-1714) [British churchman; conspirer against the Stuart kings]
The Plotter
FERGUSON, WILLIAM BLAIR (1881-) [Irish-American novelist]
William Morton
FERGUSSON HANNAY, LADY (fl.1927-58) [British author]
Doris Leslie
Ferling, Lawrence. See: FERLINGHETTI, LAWRENCE MONSANTO
FERLINGHETTI, LAWRENCE MONSANTO (1919?-) [American poet and author]
Lawrence Ferling
FERMAT, PIERRE DE (1601-65) [French mathematician]
The Father of Modern Theory
FERMI, ENRICO (1901-54) [Italian physicist]
The Architect of the Atomic Bomb
Fern, Fanny. See: PARTON, SARA PAYSON WILLIS

Fernán Caballero. See:
FABER, CECILIA BÖHL DE
Fernand Gravet. See:
MARTENS, FERNAND
Fernandel. See:
CONTANDIN, FERNAND JOSEPH DÉSIRÉ
FERNÁNDEZ, EUGENIO (1923-) [Spanish bullfighter]
Angelete
FERNANDEZ, JOACHIM OCTAVE (1896-) [American politician; congressman from Louisiana]
Coroner
Ferney, The Patriarch of. See:
AROUET, FRANÇOIS MARIE
Ferney, The Philosopher of See: AROUET, FRANÇOIS MARIE
Ferrara, The Homer of. See:
ARIOSTO, LUDOVICO
Ferrars, E.X. See:
BROWN, MORNA DORIS
Ferrars, Elizabeth. See:
BROWN, MORNA DORIS
FERREIRA, ANTONIO (1528-69) [Portuguese poet]
The Portuguese Horace
Ferrer, José. See:
CINTRON, JOSÉ VINCENTE FERRER OTERO Y
FERRETTI, GIOVANNI MARIA MASTAI (1792-1878) [Supreme Pontiff of Roman Catholic Church]
Pope Pius IX
The Prisoner of the Vatican
Ferris, James Cody. See:
KARIG, WALTER
STRATEMEYER, EDWARD L.
Ferry Boy, The See:
CHASE, SALMON PORTLAND
FESSENDEN, THOMAS GREEN (1771-1837) [American journalist, poet and satirist]
The American Butler
Christopher Caustic
Dr. Caustic
Peter Pepper Box
Simon Spunkey
Fetchit, Stepin. See:
PERRY, LINCOLN
FETTER, ELIZABETH HEAD (1904-) [American author]
Hannah Lees
FETZER, HERMAN (1899-1935) [American columnist, novelist and poet]
Jake Falstaff
Feuillère, Edwige. See:
CUNATI, EDWIGE
Feuilletons, The King of. See:
JANIN, JULES GABRIEL
Fevre, Felicité le. See:
SMITH-MASTERS, MARGARET
Feyder, Jacques. See:
FREDERIX, JACQUES
Fibber McGee. See:
JORDAN, JAMES EDWARD
FICKE, ARTHUR DAVISON. See:
Knish, Anne
FICKER, ROBERTA SUE (1945-) [American ballerina]
Suzanne Farrell
FICKINGER, JAMES ALBERT (1853-1903) [American engineer]
Colonel
FICKLING, SKIP FORREST (1925-) [American author]
G. G. Fickling
Fiction, The Father of Modern Prose. See:
FOE, DANIEL
Fiction, The Father of Science. See: VERNE, JULES
FIDANZA, GIOVANNI DI (1221-74) [Italian scholar, mystic and churchman]
Giovanni Bonaventura
St. Bonaventura
The Seraphic Doctor
Fiddling Bob. See:
TAYLOR, ROBERT LOVE
Fidelio. See:
HUNT, EDGAR HUBERT
Fidget. See:
MONTAGU, ELIZABETH
Fidgety. See:
COLLINS, PHIL EUGENE
Fidler, Kathleen. See:
GOLDIE, KATHLEEN ANNIE
FIELD [Field]. See also:

FIELDS
Fields
Field, Andrew John. See:
WIEZELL, RICHARD
JOHN
Field, Charles. See:
ROWLAND, DONALD
SYDNEY
Field, Cheviot of the. See:
PARKER, ERIC
FIELD, DAVID DUDLEY (1805-94) [American lawyer]
The Father of the Code
FIELD, EUGENE (1850-95)
[American journalist and poet]
The Poet of Childhood
Field, Frank Chester. See:
ROBERTSON, FRANK
CHESTER
Field, Johanna. See:
MILNER, MARION
BLACKETT
FIELD, JOSEPH M. (1810-56)
[Irish-American actor, journalist and author]
Everpoint
FIELD, MARGARET CYNTHIA
(1917-) [British motion picture actress]
Virginia Field
Field, Michael, joint pseud. of
KATHARINE HARRIS BRADLEY (1848-1914) and her niece EDITH EMMA COOPER (1862-1913) [English authors of poetic dramas and lyrics]
FIELD, NATHAN (1587-1633)
[English actor and playwright]
Nathaniel Field
FIELDEN, THOMAS PERCEVAL
(1882-) [British musician and author]
P. de Fletin
E. de P. Flint
Fielding, Burke. See
DARGAN, OLIVE TILFORD
Fielding, Gabriel. See:
BARNSLEY, ALAN
GABRIEL
FIELDING, HENRY (1707-54)
[English jurist, playwright and novelist]
The Father of the English novel
The Hogarth of Novelists
Mr. Conny Keyber
Monsieur Sans Esprit
The Prose Homer of Human Nature
Scriblerus Secundus
Captain Hercules Vinegar
Fielding, Jerry. See:
FELDMAN, GERALD
Fielding, Michael. See:
SCIAPIRO, MICHEL
Fielding of the Drama, The.
See: FARQUHAR,
GEORGE
FIELDING, ROBERT (died 1712) [English rake of the restoration period]
Beau Fielding
Handsome Fielding
FIELDING, SARAH (1710-68)
[English writer]
A Lady
FIELDS [Fields]. See also:
FIELD
Field
FIELDS, ARTHUR B. (1889-1965) [Viennese-American Composer]
Buddy Fields
Fields, Bill. See:
DUKINFIELD, WILLIAM
CLAUDE
FIELDS, CARL DONNELL
(1915-) [American jazz musician (drums)]
Kansas
Fields, Gracie. See:
STANSFIELD, GRACE
Fields, Lew. See:
SCHANFIELD, LEWIS
MAURICE
Fields, Little Corporal of
Unsought. See:
McCLELLAN, GEORGE
BRINTON
Fields, Stanley. See:
AGNEW, WALTER L.
Fields, The Fighting Parson of
Bennington. See:

ALLEN, REVEREND THOMAS
Fields, W.C. See:
DUKINFIELD, WILLIAM CLAUDE
Fiend, The Corsican. See:
BONAPARTE, NAPOLEON
Fierabrace. See:
GUILLAUME D'ORANGE
Fierce, The. See:
ALEXANDER I
ALFONSO IV
FIESCHI, OTTOBONO (died 1276) [Supreme Pontiff of Roman Catholic Church]
Pope Adrian V
FIESCHI, SINIBALDI (c.1180-1254) [Supreme Pontiff of Roman Catholic Church]
Pope Innocent IV
Fiesole, Giovanni da. See:
PIETRO, GUIDO DI
Fifty), The Fat Adonis of Forty (or. See:
GEORGE IV
Figaro. See:
CLAPP, HENRY, JR.
FIGG, JAMES (1695-1734) [English professional boxer and athlete; first world's professional bareknuckles champion]
Jim Figg
Figgers, Old. See:
GROSVENOR, CHARLES HENRY
FIGGIS, DARRELL (1882-1925) [Irish poet and novelist]
Michael Ireland
Fight, The Dead Man Who Won a. See: DOUGLAS, JAMES
Fighter Pilot, A. See:
JOHNSON, HUGH ANTHONY STEPHEN
Fighter, The. See:
ALFONSO I
Fighter, The Duel. See:
JACKSON, ANDREW
Fighter, The Indian. See:
TALCOTT, JOHN
Fighter, The Kentucky Duel. See: CLAY, CASSIUS MARCELLUS, SR.
Fighter, The little Indian. See:
STANDISH, MILES (MYLES)
Fighting Bishop, The. See:
POLK, LEONIDAS
Fighting Bob. See:
EVANS, ROBLEY DUNGLISON
Fighting Chaplain, The. See:
CALDWELL, JAMES
Fighting Colonel, The. See:
GALBRAITH, FREDERICK WILLIAM
Fighting Commissary, The. See:
GINTER, LEWIS
Fighting Dick. See:
ANDERSON, RICHARD HERON
DALE, RICHARD
RICHARDSON, ISRAEL BUSH
Fighting Doctor, The. See:
REYNOLDS, JOHN CROMWELL
Fighting Jack. See:
HAYES, EDWARD MORTIMER
Fighting Jim. See:
LANE, JAMES HENRY
Fighting Joe. See:
HOOKER, JOSEPH
WHEELER, JOSEPH
Fighting Marine, The. See:
TUNNEY, JAMES JOSEPH
Fighting Nat. See:
FITZRANDOLPH, NATHANIEL
Fighting Parson of Bennington Fields, The. See:
ALLEN, REVEREND THOMAS
Fighting Parson, The. See:
ALLEN, REVEREND THOMAS
BALCH, BENJAMIN
BROWNLOW, WILLIAM GANNAWAY
DEWEY, JEDEDIAH
JONES, JOHN WILLIAM
KELLEY, DAVID CAMPBELL
SWALLOW, SILAS COMFORT
Fighting Prelate, The. See:
SPENSER, HENRY

Fighting Quaker, The. See:
GREENE, NATHANAEL
WANTON, JOHN
Fighting Surgeon of the Revolution, The. See:
DOWNER, ELIPHALET
Fighting Tom. See:
HOYNE, THOMAS
Fights, The Hero of a Hundred. See:
NELSON, HORATIO, VISCOUNT NELSON
WELLINGTON, ARTHUR WELLESLEY, 1ST DUKE OF
FIGLIA, GIORGIO (1924-) [Italian jazz musician (piano, composer)]
George Wallington
Filia. See:
DORSEY, SARAH ANNE ELLIS
Filibuster. See:
WALKER, WILLIAM
FILIPEPE, ALESSANDRO DI MARIANO DEI (1444?-1510) [Italian painter]
Sandro Botticelli
FILLEUL, ADÉLAÏDE MARIE ÉMILE (1761-1836) [French novelist]
Madame de Souza
FILLMORE, MILLARD (1800-74) [Thirteenth President of the United States]
An Accidental President
The American Louis Philippe
His Accidency
The Wool-carder President
Film. See: LAUDET, FERNAND CHARLES
Films, The Outdoor Girl of the. See:
VALLI, VIRGINIA
Filomena. See:
MILLER, FLORENCE FENWICK
fils. See:
DUMAS, ALEXANDRE
Finality John. See:
RUSSELL, LORD JOHN
Financier of the American Revolution, The. See:
MORRIS, ROBERT
Financier, The Great. See:
SHERMAN, JOHN
Financier, The Patriot. See:
MORRIS, ROBERT
FINCH, HENEAGE (1621-82) [Earl of Nottingham; English lawyer and statesman]
The Father of Equity
Finch, Matthew. See:
FINK, MERTON
Finder Generall, The Witch. See:
HOPKINS, MATTHEW
FINDLAY, MURIEL A. (1909-) [British motion picture actress]
Muriel Angelus
FINE, LARRY. See:
Stooges, The Three
FINEGAN, WILLIAM I. (1917-) [American jazz musician (arranger, leader, composer)]
Bill Finegan
FINEMAN, IRVING (1893-) [American screen writer and author]
Jonathan Joseph
Finger Brown, Three. See:
BROWN, MORDECAI PETER CENTENNIAL
LUCHESE, GAETANO
Fingered Jack, Three. See: GARCIA, MANUEL
Fingers Carr, Joe. See:
BUSCH, LOUIS F.
Fingers, Lightning. See:
LIGHT, BEN
Fingers of Radio, The Magic. See: DUCHIN, EDWIN FRANK
Fingers, Three. See:
FITZPATRICK, THOMAS
Fink, Brat. See:
DAVIS, GWEN
FINK, MERTON (1921-) [British dental surgeon and author]
Matthew Finch
FINK, MIKE (1770?-1823?) [American river boatman and Indian scout]

The King of the Keelboatmen
The Last of the Boatmen
The Snapping Turtle of the Ohio
FINKELMAN, HARRY (1914-68) [American jazz musician (trumpet, composer, leader)]
Ziggy Elman
FINKELSTEIN, LEONID VLADIMIROVITCH (1924-) [Russian journalist, editor and author]
Leonid Vladimirov
FINKELSTEIN, MEYER (1876-1951) [Russian revolutionist and Soviet diplomat]
Maksim Maksimovich Litvinov
Meyer Wallach
FINKLEA, TULA ELLICE (1923-) [American dancer and actress]
Cyd Charisse
Finlay. See also:
FINLEY
Finley
FINLAYSON, ROBERT DOUGLAS (1909-) [British stage and motion picture actor]
Robert Douglas
FINLEY [Finley]. See also:
Finlay
Finley, Glenna. See:
WITTE, GLENNA FINLEY
FINLEY, MARTHA FARQUHARSON (1828-1909) [American novelist and juvenile writer]
Martha Farquharson
FINN, DANIEL E. (1849-1910) [New York politician and police magistrate]
Battery Dan
FINN, NEAL FRANCIS (1903-) [American professional baseball player]
Mickey Finn
FINN, REGINALD PATRICK ARTHUR WELLDON (1900-) [British publishing executive, editor and author]
R. Welldon Finn
Rex Welldon Finn
Finn, The Flying. See:
NURMI, PAAVO
Finney, Mark. See:
MUIR, KENNETH ARTHUR
Finlay, Finona. See:
STUART, VIVIAN FINLAY
Finona Finlay. See:
STUART, VIVIAN FINLAY
Fiona Macleod. See:
SHARP, WILLIAM
FIRBANK, ARHUR ANNESLEY RONALD (1886-1926) [English novelist, dramatist and essayist]
Ronald Firbank
Firdausi (Firdusi) (Firdousi). See: MANSUR, ABDUL QASIM (HASAN)
Fire-alarm. See:
FORAKER, JOSEPH B.
Fire Angel, The. See:
HUDLUN, ANNA ELIZABETH
Fire Chief, The. See:
CARLEY, PATRICK J.
LEOPOLD, ISIAH EDWIN
Fire-eater, The Georgia. See:
TOOMBS, ROBERT
Firebrand. See:
PALMERSTON, HENRY JOHN TEMPLE, 3RD VISCOUNT
Firebrand of Florence, The. See:
CELLINI, BENVENUTO
Firebrand of France, The. See:
JOHN OF LANCASTER
Firebrand of the Universe, The. See: TUMUR LENK
Firebrand, The. See:
ALLEN, TERRY DE LA MESA
MARCANTONIO, VITO
Firmer, Even (Noch Vaster). See: STEENDAM, JACOB
Firmont, De. See:
EDGEWORTH, HENRY ESSEX
Firpo. See:
MARBERRY, FRED
FIRPO, LUIS ANGEL (1895-1960) [Argentine professional boxer]
The Wild Bull of the Pampas
First American Negro Novelist, The. See:
CHESNUTT,

First of the French Historians. See: VILLEHARDOUIN, GEOFFROI DE
First Professional English Biographer, The. See: WALTON, IZAAK
First Professional Playwright, America's. See: DUNLAP, WILLIAM
First Russian Philosopher, The. See: SOLOVIEV, VLADIMIR
First Scotch Reformer, The. See: HAMILTON, PATRICK
First Victim in England, The. See: SAWTREY, WILLIAM
First Whig, The. See: SACHEVERELL, WILLIAM
FISCHART, JOHANN BAPTIST (1546-89/90) [German satirist and reformer]
Mentzer
The Rabelais of Germany
FISCHER. See also: FISHER
Fisher
FISCHER, ROBERT JAMES (1943-) [American Grand Master of chess]
Bobby Fischer
The Boy Robot
The Corduroy Killer
The Sweatshirt Kid
Fisguill, Richard. See: WILSON, RICHARD HENRY
Fish. See: PALMER, DANIEL DAVID
FISH, HAMILTON, JR. (1888-) [American politician; Congressman from New York]
One-Man Patriot
The Great All-American
Fish Hooks. See: STOUT, ALLYN McCLELLAND
Fish, Julian. See: CAMPBELL, BLANCHE
FISH, ROBERT L. (1912-) [American plastics engineer and author]
Robert L. Pike
FISHER [Fisher]. See also: FISCHER
Fisher, Cyrus. See: TEILHET, DARWIN
FISHER, DOROTHY CANFIELD (1879-1958) [American novelist]
Dorothy Canfield
FISHER, EDWIN JACK (1928-) [American popular singer]
Eddie Fisher
Private Eddie Fisher
FISHER, HARRY CONWAY (1884-) [American cartoonist; creator of "Mutt and Jeff"]
Bud Fisher
FISHER, HENDRICK (1697-1779) [American Revolutionary War political leader]
The Samuel Adams of New Jersey
FISHER, JOHN (1909-) [English author]
Roger Piper
Fisher, Laine. See: HOWARD, JAMES ARCH
FISHER, LOIS JEANNETTE (1909-) [American artist, television performer and author]
Jeannette Jarrett
FISHER, REUBEN (1923-) [American composer]
Rube Fisher
Fisher, The Hero of Fort. See: LAMB, WILLIAM
Fisher, Wade. See: NORWOOD, VICTOR GEORGE CHARLES
FISHER, WELTHY BLAKESLEY HONSINGER (1879-) [American educator and organization official]
The First Lady of Literacy
FISK, JAMES, JR. (1834-72) [American financier and robber baron]
Colonel Fisk
Jubilee Jim
Prince of Erie
Fisk University, The Father of

Organized Alumni Work at. See: PROCTOR, HENRY HUGH
Fiske, John. See: GREEN, EDMUND FISK
Fiske, Jonathan, P.B. See: SHELLEY, PERCY BYSSHE
Fiske, Minnie Maddern. See: DAVEY, MARIE AUGUSTA
FISKE, SAMUEL WHEELOCK (1828-64) [American humorist]
Dunn Browne
FISKO, EUNICE CLELAND (1927-) [American writer and artist]
C.F. Griffin
Fitch, Clark. See: SINCLAIR, UPTON BEALL
Fitch, Ensign Clark, U.S.N. See: SINCLAIR, UPTON BEALL
FITCH, WILLIAM CLYDE (1865-1909) [American playwright]
Clyde Fitch
FITCHCOCK, REX (1892-1950) [Irish actor and motion picture director]
Rex Ingram
Fite, Mack. See: SCHNECK, STEPHEN
Fitz-Boodle, George. See: THACKERAY, WILLIAM MAKEPEACE
Fitz, Honey. See: FITZGERALD, JOHN F.
Fitz-John. See: WINTHROP, JOHN
FITZ-RANDOLPH, NATHANIEL (fl. 1776-80) [American Revolutionary War soldier]
Fighting Nat
Fitzgerald, Barry. See: SHIELDS, WILLIAM JOSEPH
FITZGERALD, EDWARD (1809-83) [English poet and translator]
Polonius
FITZGERALD, EDWARD (1898?-) [American radio commentator]
Ed Fitzgerald
FITZGERALD, EDWIN (1856-1928) [American actor and vaudevillian]
Eddie Foy
FITZGERALD, ELLA (1918-) [American Negro singer and composer]
The First Lady of Song
Fitzgerald, Jack. See: SHEA, JOHN GERALD
Fitzgerald, John. See: FAZZANO, JOSEPH E.
FITZGERALD, JOHN F. (1863-1950) [American politician; Mayor of Boston and grandfather of President JOHN FITZGERALD KENNEDY]
Honey Fitz
FITZGERALD, LADY ELIZABETH (c.1528-89) [supposed mistress of HENRY HOWARD, Earl of Surrey]
The Fair Geraldine
FITZGERALD, LAWRENCE PENNYBAKER (1906-) [American Baptist clergyman and author]
Jack Lawrence
FITZGERALD, PATRICK (1882-1965) [Irish motion picture actor]
Creighton Hale
FITZGERALD, ROY (1925-) [American motion picture actor]
Rock Hudson
Fitzgerald, Walter. See: BOND, WALTER
FITZGERALD, WILLIAM THOMAS (c.1759-1829) [English poet]
The Small-beer Poet
FITZHARDINGE, JOAN MARGARET (1912-) [Australian author]
Joan Phipson
Fitzherbert, Mrs. See: SMYTHE, MARIA ANNE
FITZHERBERT, RICHARD, 2ND

EARL OF PEMBROKE (c. 1130-76)
Strongbow
FITZHUGH, PERCY KEESE (1876-) [American author]
Hugh Lloyd
FITZNEALE, RICHARD (died 1198) [English cleric, author and statesman]
Richard of Ely
Fitznoodle. See:
VALLENTINE, BENJAMIN BENNATON
FITZPATRICK, MARGARET (c. 1913-) [American motion picture actress]
Gail Patrick
FITZPATRICK, THOMAS (c. 1799-1854) [Irish-American trapper, guide and Indian agent]
Broken Hand
Three Fingers
Fitzroy, James. See:
SCOTT, JAMES
FITZSIMMONS, ROBERT PROMETHEUS (1862-1917) [English professional boxer; world's heavyweight champion]
Champion of Champions
Bob Fitzsimmons
Ruby Robert
Fitzthunder, Robespierre Marat. See: SHAW, GEORGE BERNARD
Fitzvictor, John, P.B. See:
SHELLEY, PERCY BYSSHE
Fitzwhistler, Enoch, C.C.B. See: COBB, SYLVANUS, JR.
Five by Five, Mr. See:
RUSHING, JAMES ANDREW
500, Mr. See:
GRANATELLI, ANDREW
Five Members, The, joint nickname of JOHN HAMPDEN (c. 1595-1643), DENZIL HOLLES HOLLES (1599-1680), WILLIAM LENTHALL (1591-1662), JOHN PYM (1584-1643) and WILLIAM STRODE (1598-1645), [English statesmen and members of Parliament in opposition to CHARLES I of England]
Five Members, The. See also:
PYM, JOHN
Five P's. See:
OXBERRY, WILLIAM
Flaccus. See:
LEVY, NEWMAN
WARD, THOMAS
FLACCUS, QUINTUS HORATIUS (65 B.C.-8 B.C.) [Latin poet and satirist]
Horace
Flambeau, Viktor. See:
BRIGHAM, GERTRUDE RICHARDSON
Flammis, Ex. See:
GLETCHEN, MAJOR GENERAL LORD EDWARD
Flanagan, Bud. See:
FLANAGAN, EDWARD
WINTHROP, ROBERT
FLANAGAN, EDWARD (1908-) [American vaudevillian and motion picture actor]
Bud Flanagan
Dennis O'Keefe
FLANAGAN, EDWARD JOSEPH (1886-1948) [American Roman Catholic clergyman; founder of Boy's Town, home for homeless boys]
Father Flanagan
FLANAGAN, FLORENCE (1876-1940) [Australian music hall singer]
The Australian Marie Lloyd
Florrie Forde
FLANDERS, HENRY (1824-1911) [American lawyer and author]
Oliver Thurston
Flann O'Brien. See:
O'NUALLAIN, BRIAN
Flapper, The Eternal. See:
HOPPER, EDNA WALLACE
Flapper, The Grandma. See:
HOPPER, EDNA WALLACE
Flash, The Fordham. See:
FRISCH, FRANK FRANCIS

Flatboat Man, The. See:
LINCOLN, ABRAHAM
Flatworkers, The Prince of.
See: BURKE,
WILLIAM
FLAUBERT, GUSTAVE
(1821-80) [French
novelist]
The Master of Naturalism
Flavio. See:
SCALA, FLAMINIO
Flavius, Brother. See:
ELLISON, JAMES E.
Flavius Josephus. See:
BEN MATTATHIAS,
JOSEPH
Flavius, Snaeus. See:
KANTOROWICZ,
HERMANN
Flea. See:
CLIFTON, HERMAN E.
LEE, FITZHUGH
Flea of the Conventions, The.
See: FOLSOM, ABIGAIL
FLEAGLE, JACOB ROGER
(1906-) [American jazz
musician (arranger,
guitar)]
Brick Fleagle
FLÉCHIER, ESPRIT (1632-1710)
[French bishop and
pulpit orator]
The French Isocrates
FLECKER, HERMAN JAMES
ELROY (1884-1915)
[English dramatist,
translator and poet]
James Elroy Flecker
Flecnoc. See:
ADCOCK, ARTHUR ST.
JOHN
FLEGENHEIMER, ARTHUR
(1902-35) [American
gangster]
The Dutchman
Charles Harmon
Dutch Schultz
FLEISCHER, ANTHONY
CHARLES (1928-)
[South African author]
Hans Hofmeyer
FLEISCHMAN, ALBERT SIDNEY
(1920-) [American
author]
Sid Fleischman
FLEISCHMANN, WALTER (1919-)
[American stage and
motion picture actor]
Anthony Dexter
FLEITMAN, ALEX O. (1924-)
[American composer,
conductor and singer]
Al Foster
Flémalle, Master of. See:
CAMPIN, ROBERT
Fleming, George. See:
FLETCHER, JULIA
CONSTANCE
Fleming, Geraldine. See:
CORYELL, JOHN RUSSELL
FLEMING, IAN LANCASTER
(1908-64) [English corres-
pondent and author]
Atticus
Ian Fleming
FLEMING, MARGARET (1803-11)
[Scottish infant prodigy
and poet]
Pet Marjorie
FLEMING, MAY AGNES
(1840-80) [Canadian author]
Cousin May Carleton
Fleming, Oliver. See:
MACDONALD, PHILIP
Fleming, Rhonda. See:
LOUIS, MARILYN
FLEMING, THOMAS JAMES
(1927-) [American author
and editor]
Christopher Cain
T.J. James
J.F. Thomas
Flemish Blacksmith, The. See:
MATSYS, QUENTIN
Flemish Poets, The Father of.
See: VAN MAERLANT,
JAKOB DE COSTER
Flemish Raphael, The. See:
DE VRIENDT, FRANS
FLORIS
Fleschelles. See:
GAULTIER-GARGUILLE,
HUGHES GUÉRU
Fletcher, See:
HENDERSON, JAMES
FLETCHER

Fletcher, Adam. See:
FLEXNER, STUART BERG
FLETCHER, ADELE WHITLEY (1898-) [American editor and author]
Roberta Ormiston
FLETCHER, CHARLIE MAY HOGUE (1897-) [American author of books for children]
Charlie May Simon
FLETCHER, GILES (1549-1611) [English poet]
The Elder
FLETCHER, GILES (1588?-1623) [English poet]
The Younger
FLETCHER, HARRY LUFT VERNE (1902-) [British educator and author]
John Garden
John Hereford
FLETCHER, HELEN JILL (1911-) [American teacher and author]
Carol Lee
Charles Morey
FLETCHER, JOHN WILLIAM (1729-85) [Swiss Methodist churchman]
Wesley's Most Valuable Friend
FLETCHER, JOSEPH SMITH (1863-1935) [English author]
J.S. Fletcher
A Son of the Soil
FLETCHER, JULIA CONSTANCE (1858-1938) [American novelist]
George Fleming
Fletcher, Lucille. See:
WALLOP, LUCILLE FLETCHER
Fletin, P. de. See:
FIELDEN, THOMAS PERCEVAL
Fleuridas, Ellie Rae. See:
SHERMAN, ELEANOR RAE
FLEURY-HUSSON, JULES (1821-89) [French author]
Champfleury
FLEXNER, STUART BERG (1928-) [American editor, publisher and author]
Adam Fletcher
Steve Mees
Collier Santee
Flint. See also:
Flynt
Flint, E. de P. See:
FIELDEN, THOMAS PERCEVAL
Flint, Jack. See:
SIMPSON, EDWARD
Flintlock, Old. See:
HANSON, ROGER WEIGHTMAN
Flip. See:
PHILLIPS, JOSEPH EDWARD
WILSON, CLEROW
Flivver King, The. See:
FORD, HENRY
Flo. See:
ZIEGFELD, FLORENZ, JR.
Florella Rose. See:
CARLSON, VADA F.
FLOREN, LEE (1910-) [American teacher and author]
Brett Austin
Claudia Hall
Wade Hamilton
Marguerite Nelson
Lew Smith
Lee Thomas
Len Turner
Will Watson
Dave Wilson
Florence. See:
OSGOOD, FRANCES SARGENT LOCKE
Florence Austral. See:
WILSON, FLORENCE
Florence Bates. See:
RABE, FLORENCE
Florence Becker. See:
LENNON, FLORENCE BECKER TANNENBAUM
Florence Desmond. See:
DAWSON, FLORENCE
Florence Eldridge. See:
McKECHNIE, FLORENCE
Florence Fane. See:
VICTOR, MRS. FRANCES

FULLER BARRITT
Florence Marley. See:
SMEKALOVA, HANA
Florence Mary Pomeroy. See:
POWLEY, FLORENCE MARY POMEROY
Florence Nightingale of the Southern Army, The. See:
TRADER, ELLA KING NEWSOM
Florence Percy. See:
AKERS, ELIZABETH CHASE
Florence, The Firebrand of. See: CELLINI, BENEVENUTO
Florence, William James. See:
CONLIN, BERNARD
FLORENTIUS, GEORGIUS (538-94) [Catholic Bishop and historian]
St. Gregory of Tours
Flores. See:
MARTI, ISIDRO
FLORES, JOSÉ (1898-) [Spanish bullfighter]
Camará
Florice Norton, Mrs. See:
BRAME, CHARLOTTE MARY
Florida, Doc Townsend of. See: HENDRICKS, JOSEPH EDWARD
Florida Orange Industry, The Father of the. See:
HARRIS, JAMES ARMSTRONG
Florida, The King of. See:
PLANT, HENRY BRADLEY
Florine Ashby. See:
SHEAROUSE, FLORINE W.
Florio. See:
BROOKS, JAMES GORDON
FLORIO, JOHN (GIOVANNI) (1533?-1625) [British translator and lexicographer]
Resolute John Florio
Florrie Forde. See:
FLANAGAN, FLORENCE
FLORY, MEREDITH IRWIN (1926-) [American jazz musician (saxophone, arranger, leader)]
Med
Floss. See:
TERRY, FLORENCE
Flower. See:
BRUEGHEL (BREUGHEL), JAN
Flower, Captain John, M.P. See:
BRONTË, BRANWELL
Flower of Chivalry, The. See:
DOUGLAS, SIR WILLIAM
SIDNEY (SYDNEY), SIR PHILIP
Flower of Jesus, Little. See:
TERESA OF LISIEUX, ST.
Flower of Kings, The. See:
KING ARTHUR
Flower of Poets, The. See:
CHAUCER, GEOFFREY
Flower of Quakerism, The. See:
MOTT, LUCRETIA
Flower of Strathearn, The. See:
NAIRNE, CAROLINA OLIPHANT
Flower Painters, The King of the. See:
DE LONGPRÉ, PAUL
Flower, The Little. See:
LA GUARDIA, FIORELLO HENRY
FLOWERS, D'ARCY RAYMOND (1902-) [American professional baseball player]
Jake Flowers
Floyd Akens. See:
BAUM, LYMAN FRANK
FLOYD, CHARLES ARTHUR (1904-34) [American outlaw; member of the JOHN DILLINGER gang]
Pretty Boy Floyd
FLUCK, DIANA (1931-) [British motion picture actress]
Diana Dors
Fluctibus, Robertus, de. See:
FLUDD (FLUD), ROBERT
FLUDD (FLUD), ROBERT (1574-1637) [British physician and author of books on medicine]
Robertus de Fluctibus
Joachim Frizius
Rudolf Otreb
The Searcher

Flue, Nikolaus of. See:
LÖWENBRUGGER, NIKOLAS
Flycatcher, The Grey-crested. See: BURROUGHS, JOHN
Flying Dutchman, The. See:
WAGNER, JOHN PETER
Flying Finn, The. See:
NURMI, PAAVO
Flying Highwayman, The. See:
HARROW, WILLIAM
Flying Mantuan, The. See:
NUVOLARI, TAZIO
Flying Officer X. See:
BATES, HERBERT ERNEST
FLYNN, JANET (1909-) [Irish-German-American motion picture actress]
Gina Malo
Flynt. See also:
Flint
Flynt, Josiah. See:
WILLARD, JOSIAH FLINT
Foda, Aun. See:
FOXE, ARTHUR NORMAN
FOE, DANIEL (1659/61-1731) [English author, merchant, editor and pamphleteer]
Daniel De Foe
Daniel Defoe
Eye Witness
The Father of Modern Prose Fiction
Andrew Moreton, Merchant
The Sunny Gentleman
T. Taylor
Fog. See also:
FOGG
Fog Horn. See also:
Foghorn
Fog Horn, The. See:
ALLEN, WILLIAM
Fog, The Velvet. See:
TORME, MELVIN HOWARD
Fogarty, Jonathan Titulescu, Esq. See:
FARRELL, JAMES THOMAS
FOGG. See also:
Fog
FOGG, HENRY GEORGE WITHAM (1911-) [English author]
George Fyfield
Foghorn. See:
Fog Horn
FUNSTON, EDWARD HOGUE
WENZLAFF, GEORGE
FOIX, GASTON DE (1489-1512) [Duc de Nemours; French general officer]
The Thunderbolt of Italy
FOKINE, MICHEL (1880-1942) [Russian-American choreographer]
The Father of Modern Ballet
FOLENGO, TEOFILO (1491-1554) [Italian poet]
Merlinus Coccaius
FOLEY, CEDRIC JOHN (1917-) [British soldier and author]
John Sawyer
Ian Sinclair
Foley, Helen. See:
FOWLER, HELEN ROSA HUXLEY
FOLEY, PEARL (fl. 1921-37) [Canadian author]
Paul de Mar
Folio, Tom. See:
RAWLINSON, THOMAS
Folk Music, The Thomas Jefferson of. See:
SEEGER, PETER
Folk Singer of his Race, The Most Famous. See:
WHITE, JOSHUA DANIEL
Folk Singers, The Queen of the. See: BAEZ, JOAN
FOLKARD, WILLIAM (1887-) [British motion picture director]
Maurice Elvey
FOLSOM, ABIGAIL (c. 1792-1867) [Anglo-American reformer and anti-slavery advocate]
The Flea of the Conventions
FOLSOM, FRANKLIN BREWSTER (1907-) [American author]
Benjamin Brewster
Samuel Cutler
Michael Gorham

Lyman Hopkins
Troy Nesbit
FONTAINE [Fontaine]. See also:
Fonteyn
FONTAINE, FELIX GREGORY DE (1834-96) [American journalist and historian]
Personne
FONTAINE, JEAN DE LA (1621-95) [French fabulist]
The Aesop of France
Fontaine, Joan. See:
HAVILLAND, JOAN DE
FONTE, JEANNE DE LA (1898-1933) [French star of American silent films]
Renée Adorée
Fonteyn. See also:
FONTAINE
Fontaine
Fonteyn de Arias, Dame Margot. See: HOOKHAM, MARGARET
Fonteyn, Margot. See:
HOOKHAM, MARGARET
Foods Boys, The Best. See:
Happiness Boys, The
Fool Alive, The Luckiest. See:
KELLY, ALVIN
Fool in Christendom, The Most Learned. See:
JAMES I
Fool in Christendom, The Wisest. See: JAMES I
Fool, The Dancing. See:
McADOO, WILLIAM GIBBS
Fool, The Perfect. See:
LEOPOLD, ISAIAH EDWIN
Fool Tom. See:
JACKSON, THOMAS JONATHAN
Foolish, The. See:
CHARLES VI
FOOT. See also:
FOOTE
FOOT, HUGH MACKINTOSH (1907-) [British civil servant and author]
Lord Caradon
Football Coach in America, The Top. See:
PARKER, RAYMOND KLEIN
Football, The Caesar of. See:
LITTLE, LOUIS LAWRENCE
Football, The Dean of American. See: CAMP, WALTER
Football, The Father of American. See:
CAMP, WALTER
Football, The Grand Old Man of. See: STAGG, AMOS ALONZO
Football's Greatest Coach. See:
NEYLAND, GENERAL ROBERT REESE, JR.
Football's "Old Man River." See:
STAGG, AMOS ALONZO
FOOTE. See also:
FOOT
FOOTE, ELIAL TODD (1796-1877) [American physician, judge and historian]
The Father of Chautauqua County
FOOTE, HENRY STUART (1804-80) [American politician; Senator from Mississippi]
Hangman Foote
FOOTE, MICHAEL. See:
Cato
FOOTE, SAMUEL (1720-77) [English actor and playwright]
The English Aristophanes
The Modern Aristophanes
Foots. See:
THOMAS, WALTER PURL
FORAKER, JOSEPH B. (1846-1917) [American politician; Governor of Ohio]
Bloody Shirt Foraker
Fire-alarm Foraker
Forbes. See:
Rydell, Forbes
Forbes, Aleck. See:
RATHBONE, ST. GEORGE HENRY
FORBES, DELORIS STANTON (1923-) [American journalist and author]
De Forbes
Stanton Forbes
FORBES, DELORIS STANTON. See also:
Rydell, Forbes

Forbes, Graham B. See:
STRATEMEYER, EDWARD L.
Forbes, Kathryn. See:
McLEAN, KATHRYN ANDERSON
FORBES-ROBERTSON, MERIEL (1913-) [British stage and motion picture actress]
Meriel Forbes
Force, The Driving. See:
ROOSEVELT, THEODORE
Forces, The Father of the Mechanized. See:
CHAFFEE, ADNA ROMANZA
Ford, Albert Lee. See:
STRATEMEYER, EDWARD L.
FORD, COREY (1902-) [American humorist and parodist]
John Riddell
FORD, EDWARD CHARLES (1928-) [American professional baseball player]
Whitey Ford
Ford, Elbur. See:
HIBBERT, ELEANOR BURFORD
FORD, ERNEST B. (1916-) [American composer, publisher and journalist]
Ernie Ford
FORD, ERNEST JENNINGS (1919-) [American entertainer and singer]
Cousin Ern
Tennessee Ernie Ford
Ford, Fred. See:
DOERFFLER, ALFRED
FORD, GWYLLYN SAMUEL NEWTON (1916-) [Canadian-American actor]
Glenn Ford
FORD, HENRY (1863-1947) [American automobile manufacturer]
The Automobile Wizard
The Flivver King
The Genius of Motordom
Ford, Hildegarde. See:
MORRISON, VELMA FORD
FORD, JOHN (c. 1586-c. 1640) [English dramatist]
The Last of the Elizabethans
Ford, John. See:
O'FIENNE, SEAN
FORD, JOHN BAPTISTE (1811-1903) [American pioneer manufacturer of plate glass]
The Father of the Plate Glass Industry
Ford, Leslie. See:
BROWN, ZENITH JONES
Ford Logan. See:
NEWTON, DWIGHT BENNETT
Ford Madox Ford. See:
HUEFFER, FORD MADOX
Ford, Marcia. See:
RADFORD, RUBY LORRAINE
Ford, Mary. See:
SUMMERS, COLLEEN
Ford, Norrey. See:
DILCOCK, NOREEN
Ford of Aviation, The Henry. See: PIPER, WILLIAM THOMAS, SR.
Ford, Powell I. See:
DEMPSEY, JAMES E.
FORD, ROBERT (185?-84) [American outlaw; murderer of JESSE WOODSON JAMES]
Bob Ford
The Dirty Little Coward
Ford Sterling. See:
STITCH, GEORGE FORD
FORD, THELMA BOOTH (1907-) [American stage, motion picture and television actress]
Shirley Booth
Ford, Wallace. See:
GRUNDY, SAM
FORDE, FEODORA (1909-) [British stage and screen actress]
Jane Baxter
Forde, Florrie. See:
FLANAGAN, FLORENCE
Fordham Flash, The. See:

FRISCH, FRANK
FRANCIS
Foreign Mission Work in Christian America, The Father of. See:
MILLS, SAMUEL JOHN
Foremost Expatriate, America's. See: STEARNS, HAROLD EDMUND
Foremost Greek Scholar of Our Time, The. See:
MURRAY, GEORGE GILBERT AIMÉ
Foremost Master of Ceremonies, America's. See:
FAY, FRANCIS ANTHONY
Foremost Speculative Philosopher, America's. See: WEISS, PAUL
FOREST [Forest]. See also:
FORREST
Forrest
Fourest
Forest-born Demosthenes, The. See: HENRY, PATRICK
Forest, Felix C. See:
LINEBARGER, PAUL MYRON ANTHONY
FOREST, LEE DE (1873-1961) [American inventor and research engineer]
The Father of Radio
Forest, Mark. See:
DEGNI, LOU
Forest, The Robin Hood of the. See:
ALLEN, ETHAN
Forester. See:
PAINE, THOMAS
FORESTER, CECIL SCOTT (1899-) [British author]
C.S. Forester
Forester, Fanny. See:
JUDSON, EMILY CHUBBUCK
Forester, Francis. See:
WISE, DANIEL
Forester, Frank. See:
HERBERT, HENRY WILLIAM
Forestier, Auber. See:
WOODWARD, A. AUBERTINE
Forgotten Man, The. See:
BRADDOCK, JAMES J.
Forio, Robert. See:
WEISS, IRVING J.
Fork, America's Tuning. See:
SEEGER, PETER
Forkbeard. See:
SWEYN I
Form, Tom. See:
O'KEEFE, LESTER
FORMAN, DAVID (1745-97) [American Revolutionary soldier and anti-Loyalist]
Black David
Devil David
Formosan, The. See:
UNKNOWN
FORMOSUS (died 896) [Supreme Pontiff of Roman Catholic Church]
Pope Formosus
FORNIER, JACQUES (1285-1342) [Supreme Pontiff of Roman Catholic Church]
Pope Benedict XII
Forrest. See:
FOREST
Forest
Fourest
WILSON, ROBERT FORREST
Forrest, Colonel Cris. See:
STODDARD, WILLIAM OSBORN
FORREST, GEORGE (1915-) [American composer, conductor and pianist]
Chet Forrest
Forrest, Mary. See:
FREEMAN, JULIA DEANE
FORREST, NATHAN BEDFORD (1821-77) [American Civil War general officer]
The Swamp Fox of Mississippi
The Wizard of the Saddle
Forrest, Sally. See:
FEENEY, KATHARINE SCULLY
Forrest, Steve. See: ANDREWS, WILLIAM FORREST
Forrest, Sybil. See:
MARKUN, PATRICIA MALONEY

FORREST, THOMAS (fl. 1767)
[American writer of
comic opera]
Andrew Barton
FORRESTER. See also:
FORSTER
FOSTER
Foster
FORRESTER, ALFRED HENRY.
See: Crowquill, Alfred
FORRESTER, CHARLES
ROBERT (1803-50)
[English author and
illustrator]
Hal Willis
FORRESTER, CHARLES
ROBERT. See also:
Crowquill, Alfred
FORSTER. See also:
FORRESTER
FOSTER
Foster
FORSTER, EDWARD MORGAN
(1879-1970) [English
author]
The Dean of Contemporary
English Novelists
E.M. Forster
Forsythe, John. See:
FREUND, JOHN
Forsythe, Robert. See:
CRICHTON, KYLE
SAMUEL
Fort Donelson, Hero of. See:
GRANT, HIRAM ULYSSES
FORT, ELEANOR H. (1914-)
[American composer,
singer and actress]
Hank Fort
Fort Fisher, The Hero of. See:
LAMB, WILLIAM
Fort McHenry, The Hero of.
See: ARMISTEAD,
GEORGE
Fort Meigs, The Hero of. See:
CHRISTY, WILLIAM
Fort Mifflin, The Hero of.
See: THAYER, JOHN
Fort, Paul. See:
STOCKTON, FRANCIS
RICHARD
Fort Sumter, The Hero of. See:
BEAUREGARD, PIERRE
GUSTAVE TOUTANT

FORTE. See also:
Forty
FORTE, FABIAN (c.1938-)
[American teenage singer
and guitarist; motion picture
actor]
Fabian
FORTESCUE, MABEL (1894-1930)
[American silent motion
picture comedienne]
Mabel Normand
Forth. See also:
Fourth
Forth, George. See:
FREDERIC, HAROLD
Fortifications, The Father of
Our Modern. See:
CRAIGHILL, WILLIAM
PRICE
Fortuna. See:
MAZQUIARÁN, DIEGO
Fortunate, The. See:
EMANUEL (MANUEL) I
JOHN IV
Forty. See also:
FORTE
Forty-eight Hours, Old. See:
DOUBLEDAY, ABNER
Forty (or Fifty), The Fat
Adonis of. See:
GEORGE IV
Forward, Luke. See:
PATRICK, JOHNSTONE
GILLESPIE
Forward Pass, The Father of the.
See: HEISMAN, JOHN
WILLIAM
Forwards, Marshal. See:
BLÜCHER, GEBHARD
LEBERECHT VON, PRINCE
OF WAHLSTADT
FOSDICK, CHARLES AUSTIN (1842-
1915) [American writer of
juvenile fiction]
Harry Castlemon
Fossil. See:
SMITH, WILLIAM
FOSTER [Foster]. See also:
FORRESTER
FORSTER
Foster, Al. See:
FLEITMAN, ALEX O.
Foster, Dianne. See:
LURASKA, DIANNE

FOSTER, GEORGE MURPHY (1892-) [American jazz musician (bass)]
Pops Foster
Foster Johns. See: SELDES, GILBERT VIVIAN
FOSTER, MRS. LAURENCE (1907-) [English novelist]
Rumer Godden
Foster, Norman. See: HOEFFER, NORMAN
Foster, Richard. See: CROSSEN, KENDELL FOSTER
Foster, Susanna. See: LARSEN, SUZAN
FOSTER, THEODOSIA MARIA TOLL (1838-) [American author]
Faye Huntington
Fougasse. See: BIRD, CYRIL KENNETH
Foul Weather Jack. See: BYRON, JOHN
FOULKE, WILLIAM DUDLEY (1848-1935) [American lawyer and writer]
Robert Barclay Dillingham
FOULQUES. See: FULC (FULK) (FOULQUES) III
FOULQUES, GUY LE GROS (died 1268) [Supreme pontiff of Roman Catholic Church]
Pope Clement IV
Founder of Christian Eloquence, The. See: BOURDALONE, LOUIS
Founder of Christian Monasticism, The. See: ANTONY (ANTHONY), ST.
Founder of Danish Literature, The. See: HOLBERG, LUDVIG
Founder of Peace, The. See: BENEDICT OF NURSIA, ST.
Founder of Rome, The Third. See: CAIUS MARIUS
Founder of Rum Row, The. See: McCOY, CAPTAIN WILLIAM
Founder of Scene Painting, The. See: AGATHARCOS
Founder of the American Navy, The. See: PAUL, JOHN
Founder of the Critical Philosophy, The. See: KANT, IMMANUEL
Founder of the English Domestic Novel, The. See: RICHARDSON, SAMUEL
Founder of the Hudson River School of American Artists. See: COLE, THOMAS
Founder of the Science of Anthropology, The. See: BLUMENBACH, JOHANN FRIEDRICH
Founder of Vermont, The. See: ALLEN, IRA
Founder of Victoria, The. See: BATMAN, JOHN
Founder of Western Monasticism. See: BENEDICT OF NURSIA, ST.
Fountain of Life, The. See: ALEXANDER OF HALES
Fountain, The. See: ASHURST, HENRY FOUNTAIN
Four. See: Big Four, The; Immortal Four of Italy, The
Four-eyed George. See: MEADE, GEORGE GORDON
Four Eyes. See: ROOSEVELT, THEODORE
Four-job. See: FARLEY, JAMES ALOYSIUS
Four Marx Brothers, The.
The Four Nightingales, stage names of ADOLPH (ARTHUR) (Harpo) MARX (1893-1964); HERBERT (Zeppo) MARX (1901-); JULIUS HENRY (Groucho) MARX (1895-) and LEONARD (Chico) MARX (1891-1961) [American comedians and actors]
Four Marx Brothers, The. See also: MARX, MILTON

Four Nations, The Beloved
Man of the. See:
HAWKINS, BENJAMIN
Four Nightingales, The. See:
Four Marx Brothers, The
Four Straight Jake. See:
RUPPERT, JACOB, SR.
Fourest. See also:
FOREST
Forest
FORREST
Forrest
Fourest, Michel. See:
WYNNE-TYSON,
TIMOTHY JON LYADEN
FOURNIER, HENRI ALAIN
(1886-1914) [French
novelist]
Alain Fournier
Fourquet. See:
LAISNÉ, JEANNE
Fourth. See also:
Forth
Fourth Brother, The. See:
AUNG, MAUNG HTIN
Fourth, Clifton. See:
MORSE, H. CLIFTON
Fourth, Fum the. See:
GEORGE IV
Fourth Musketeer, The. See:
DUMAS, ALEXANDRE
ULLMAN, JULIUS
FOWLER, CHARLES HENRY
(1837-1908) [Canadian
Methodist missionary in
South America]
The Apostle of South America
The Great Commoner
FOWLER, CLARA ANN (1927-)
[American television
singer]
Patti Page
Fowler, Gene. See:
DEVLAN, EUGENE
FOWLER, HELEN ROSA
HUXLEY (1917-)
[British teacher and
author]
Helen Foley
Fowler, Henry the. See:
HENRY I
FOWLER, KENNETH ABRAMS
(1900-) [American
columnist, editor and
author]
Clark Brooker
FOWLER, WILLIAM RANDOLPH
(1922-) [American
composer, actor and
publicist]
Will Fowler
Fox. See:
FOXE
FOXX
WILLIAMS, GEORGE DALE
FOX, CATHERINE (KATE). See:
Fox Sisters, The
FOX, CHARLES (1921-)
[English author]
Richard Jeremy
FOX, CHARLES JAMES
(1749-1806) [English
statesman and orator]
Carlo Khan
The Man of the People
The Young Cub
FOX, CHARLES JAMES. See
also: Wondrous Three, The
Fox, David. See:
OSTRANDER, ISABEL
Fox, Eleanor. See:
ST. JOHN, WYLLY FOLK
FOX, ERVIN (1909-) [American
professional baseball
player]
Pete Fox
FOX, GARDNER FRANCIS
(1911-) [American
lawyer and author]
Jefferson Cooper
Jeffrey Gardner
James Kendricks
Kevin Matthews
Fox Jackson, Red. See:
JACKSON, WILLIAM
HICKS
FOX, JACOB NELSON
(1927-) [American pro-
fessional baseball player]
Nellie Fox
FOX, MARGARET (1833-93)
[American spiritualist and
medium]
Dr. Elisha Kent Kane
FOX, MARGARET. See also:
Fox Sisters, The

Fox, Marion. See:
WARD, MARION INEZ DOUGLAS
Fox of Kinderhook, The Red. See: VAN BUREN, MARTIN
Fox of Mississippi, The Swamp. See: FORREST, NATHAN BEDFORD
Fox of South Carolina, The Swamp. See:
MARION, FRANCIS
Fox of the Northland, The Silver. See: BIERMAN, BERNARD WILLIAM
Fox of the Tennessee Valley, The Swamp. See:
RODDEY, PHILIP DALE
Fox, Owen. See:
FARMER, BERNARD JONES
Fox, Red. See:
JACKSON, WILLIAM HICKS
Fox Sisters, The, joint nickname of CATHERINE (KATE) FOX (18??-) and her sister, MARGARET FOX (1833-93) [American spiritualists and mediums]
Fox Sisters, The. See also:
FOX, MARGARET
Fox, The. See:
VAN BUREN, MARTIN
Fox, The Desert. See:
ROMMEL, ERWIN JOHANNES EUGEN
Fox, The Gray. See:
CROOK, GEORGE
Fox, The Kinderhook. See:
VAN BUREN, MARTIN
Fox, The Old. See:
GRIFFITH, CLARK
WASHINGTON, GEORGE
Fox, The Old Swamp. See:
MARION, FRANCIS
Fox, The Red. See:
HAZELTON, JAMES
JEFFERSON, THOMAS
Fox, The Swamp. See:
MARION, FRANCIS
Fox, V. Helen. See:
COUCH, HELEN FOX
FOXE. See also:
FOX
Fox
FOXX
FOXE, ARTHUR NORMAN (1902-) [American psychiatrist and author]
Aun Foda
Foxholes, The Sweetheart of the. See:
KAUMEYER, DOROTHY
Foxton, E. See:
PALFREY, SARAH HAMMOND
FOXX. See also:
FOX
Fox
FOXE
FOXX, JAMES EMORY (1907-) [American professional baseball player]
Jimmy Foxx
Foy, Eddie. See:
FITZGERALD, EDWIN
FOYT, ANTHONY JOSEPH, JR. (1935-) [American automobile racing driver]
A. J. Foyt
The Houston Hurricane
Tony Foyt
Fqt. See:
FUNQUIST, HERMAN PETER ANTON
Fra Angelico. See:
PIETRO, GUIDO DI
Fra Bartolommeo. See:
FATTORINO, BARTOLOMMEO DI PAGOLO DEL
Fra Diavolo (Brother Devil). See: PEZZA, MICHELE
Fra Elbertus. See:
HUBBARD, ELBERT
Fra Galgario. See:
GHISLANDI, FRA VITTORE
Fra Guittone. See:
GUIDO D'AREZZO (GUIDO ARETINO)
Fra Paolo (Brother Paul). See:
SARPI, PIETRO (PAOLO)
Fra Paolotto. See:
GHISLANDI, FRA VITTORE
Fraddle, Farragut. See:
MEARNS, DAVID CHAMBERS

FRAENKEL, HEINRICH (1897-)
[German journalist and author]
Assiac
Caissa
Cinna
Fragson, Harry. See:
POTTS, HARRY
FRAHM, HERBERT ERNST KARL (1913-) [German journalist and political leader]
Willy Brandt
FRAHSE, MARY JANE (c.1919-) [American singer and motion picture actress]
Jane Frazee
Frame, Janet. See:
CLUTHA, JANET PATERSON FRAME
FRAMPTON, TREGONWELL (1641-1727) [English race-horse trainer]
The Father of the Turf
Fran. See:
LANDESMAN, FRANCES
TARKENTON, FRANCIS ASBURY
WINE-GAR, FRANK
FRANC-NOHAIN, CLAUDE (1903-) [French stage and motion picture actor]
Claude Dauphin
FRANCE. See:
Frans
Franz
ISABELLA OF FRANCE
MARGUERITE OF FRANCE
France, Anatole. See:
THIBAULT, JACQUES ANATOLE FRANÇOIS
France, Claire. See:
DORE, CLAIRE MORIN
FRANCE, CLAUDE DE (1499-1524) [daughter of LOUIS XIII, king of France]
La Bonne Reine
FRANCE-HAYHURST, EVANGELINE CHAWORTH-MUSTERS (1904-) [British author]
Evangeline France
France, Le Grande Épistolier de. See:
BALZAC, JEAN LOUIS GUEZ DE
France, Louis Charles de. See: LOUIS XVII
France, Margaret of. See:
MARGARET OF VALOIS
France, The Aesop of. See:
FONTAINE, JEAN DE LA
France, The Burns of. See:
BOÉ, JACQUES
France, The Caracci of. See:
JOUVENET, JEAN
France, The Chaucer of. See:
MAROT, CLÉMENT
France, The Cicero of. See:
MASSILLON, JEAN BAPTISTE
France, The Dick Turpin of. See: BOURGUIGNON, LOUIS-DOMINIQUE
France, The Eagle of the Doctors of. See:
AILLY, PIERRE D'
France, The Father of New. See: CHAMPLAIN, SAMUEL DE
France, The Firebrand of. See:
JOHN OF LANCASTER
France, The First Grenadier of. See:
LA TOUR D'AUVERGNE, THÉOPHILE MALO CORRET DE
France, The Horace of. See:
BÉRANGER, PIERRE-JEAN DE
France, The Plutarch of. See:
LE VAYER, FRANÇOIS DE LA MOTHE
France, The Prodigy of. See:
BUDÉ (BUDAEUS), GUILLAUME
France, The Pym of. See:
MOLÉ, MATHIEU
France, The She-Wolf of. See:
ISABELLA OF FRANCE
France, The Solomon of. See:
CHARLES V
LOUIS IX
France, The Terror of. See:

JOHN
France, The Theophrastus of. See: BRUYÈRE, JEAN DE LA
France, Victor. See: JORDAN, PHILIP FURNEAUX
Frances. See:
DEE, JEAN
FRANCIS
Francis
FRANÇOIS
François
Françoise
Frances Cowen. See: MUNTHE, FRANCES
Frances E. Huntly. See: MAYNE, ETHEL COLBURN
Frances, Fearless. See: PERKINS, FRANCES
France's Greatest Conductor. See: MÜNCH, CHARLES
Frances Helen Davenport. See: AIKEN, ALBERT W.
Frances Jessup. See: VAN BRIGGLE, MARGARET FRANCES JESSUP
Frances K. Judd. See: STRATEMEYER, EDWARD L.
Frances Lang. See: MANTLE, WINIFRED LANGFORD
Frances Little. See: MACAULAY, FANNIE CALDWELL
Frances McNab. See: FRASER, AGNES MAUDE
Frances Minto-Cowen. See: MUNTHE, FRANCES
Frances, Miss. See: HORWICH, FRANCES RAPPAPORT
Frances V. Scott. See: WING, FRANCES SCOTT
Frances Wayne. See:
BERTOCCI, CHIARINA FRANCESCA
WEDGE, FLORENCE
Frances Winwar. See: GREBANIER, FRANCESCA VINCIGUERRA
Frances Xavier Cabrini. See: CABRINI, MARY FRANCES
Francesca, Piero Della. See: FRANCHESI, PIERO DEI
Francesco Cavalli. See: CALETTI-BRUNI, FRANCESCO
FRANCESCO, GIORDANI. See: Three Wise Men
Franceska Gaal. See: ZILVERITCH, FANNY
Francey. See also: Francy
Francey Delaney. See: O'HARA, JOHN HENRY
FRANCHESI, PIERO DEI (c. 1420-92) [Italian painter of the Umbrian school]
Piero della Francesca
FRANCIA, JOSÉ GASPAR RODRÍGUEZ (1761?-1840) [Paraguayan dictator and lawyer]
Dr. Francia
Francine Davenport. See: TATE, VELMA
Franciosa, Anthony. See: PAPALEO, ANTHONY
Francis. See:
Frances
FRANÇOIS
François
Françoise
GUTHRIE, THOMAS ANSTEY
Richards, Francis
STOPPELMAN, FRANS
Sylvin, Francis
FRANCIS I (1494-1547) [King of France]
The Father of Letters
Francis, Arlene. See: KAZANJIAN, ARLINE FRANCIS
Francis Askham. See: GREENWOOD, JULIA EILEEN COURTNEY
Francis B. Williams. See: BROWIN, FRANCES WILLIAMS

FRANCIS, BASIL HOSKINS (1906-) [British banker, journalist and author]
Austen Rhode
Francis Beeding. See:
Beeding, Francis
PALMER, JOHN LESLIE
Francis Carco. See:
CARCOPINI-TUSOLI, FRANCIS
Francis Carlin. See:
MACDONNELL, JAMES FRANCIS CARLIN
Francis, Connie. See:
FRANCONERO, CONCETTA
FRANCIS, DAVID ALBERT (1918-) [American jazz musician (drums)]
Panama
Francis, Dee. See:
HAAS, DOROTHY
Francis Edward Clark. See:
SYMNES, FRANCIS EDWARD
Francis Forester. See:
WISE, DANIEL
Francis Gaite. See:
Coles, Manning
Francis Grierson. See:
SHEPARD, BENJAMIN HENRY JESSE FRANCIS
Francis Herbert. See:
BRYANT, WILLIAM CULLEN
Francis Hicks. See:
STEELE, SIR RICHARD
Francis Hunt. See:
STRATEMEYER, EDWARD L.
Francis Iles. See:
COX, ANTHONY BERKELEY
Francis, Kay. See:
GIBBS, KATHARINE
Francis, Mary E. See:
BLUNDELL, MRS. FRANCIS SWEETMAN
Francis Miltoun. See:
MANSFIELD, MILBURG FRANCISCO
Francis Newton. See:
HOBSBAWN, ERIC JOHN ERNEST
Francis of Assisi, St. See:
BERNARDONE, GIOVANNI FRANCESCO
Francis of Presbyterianism, The St. See:
MAKEMIE, FRANCIS
Francis, Philip. See:
LOCKYER, ROGER
FRANCIS, SIR PHILIP (1740-1818) [reputed British author of "Letters to Junius"; political pamphleteer]
Junius
Francis Snow Compton. See:
ADAMS, HENRY BROOKS
Francis Stuart Campbell. See:
KEUHNELT-LEDDIHN, ERIK RITTER VON
Francis Vielé-Griffin. See:
VIELÉ, EGBERT LUDOVICUS
Francis Vivian. See:
ASHLEY, ARTHUR ERNEST
Francisco Segura. See:
CANO, FRANCISCO SEGURA
Francisco Villa. See:
ARANGO, DOROTEO
Francisque. See:
MILLET, JEAN FRANÇOIS
FRANCK. See also:
Frank
FRANCK, FREDERICK SIGFRED (1909-) [Dutch author]
Dr. Frank Fredericks
Franco, Harry. See:
BRIGGS, CHARLES FREDERICK
Franco Zeffirelli. See:
CORSI, FRANCO ZEFFIRELLI
François. See:
BLANCHARD, JEAN PIERRE
Frances
FRANCIS
Francis
FRANÇOIS DE LORRAINE (1519-63) [second Duke of Guise]
Le Balafré (The Scarred)
François Perier. See:
PILU, FRANÇOIS
FRANÇOIS, PIERRE (fl. 1665) [French pirate]

Pierre Le Grand
François Villon. See:
MONTCORBIER, FRANÇOIS DE
Françoise. See:
Frances
FRANCIS
Francis
FRANÇOIS
François
SEIGNOBOSC, FRANÇOISE
Françoise Arnoul. See:
GAUTSCH, FRANÇOISE
Françoise Sagan. See:
QUOIREZ, FRANÇOISE
FRANCONERO, CONCETTA (1938-) [American popular singer and actress]
Connie Francis
Franconi, King. See:
MURAT, JOACHIM
Franconi of America, The. See:
CHIARINI, SIGNOR C.
Francy. See:
BOLAND, FRANÇOIS
Francey
Frank. See:
BEARD, THOMAS FRANCIS
CLUNE, FRANCIS PATRICK
COREY, FRANCIS ADELBERT
FAY, FRANCIS ANTHONY
FRANCK
HOGAN, FRANCIS T.
KNOX, WILLIAM FRANKLIN
LESLIE, MIRIAM FLORENCE FOLLINE
McAlister, Frank A.
NORRIS, BENJAMIN FRANKLIN
O'GRADY, FRANCIS DOMINIC
PRICE, FRANCIS WILSON
SEDGMAN, FRANCIS ARTHUR
SINATRA, FRANCIS ALBERT
SMEDLEY, FRANCIS EDWARD
WHITCHER, FRANCES MIRIAM BERRY
Frank A. Warner. See:
STRATEMEYER, EDWARD L.
Frank Allan. See:
LUNGSTRUM, FRANK ALLAN
Frank Anmar. See:
NOLAN, WILLIAM FRANCIS
Frank Boyd. See:
KANE, FRANK
Frank Brennand. See:
LAMBERT, ERIC
Frank Bruno. See:
ST. BRUNO, ALBERT FRANCIS
Frank Cauldwell. See:
KING, FRANCIS HENRY
Frank Chester Field. See:
ROBERTSON, FRANK CHESTER
Frank Cooper. See:
SIMMS, WILLIAM GILMORE
Frank Danby. See:
FRANKAU, JULIA
Frank Dashmore. See:
DOWNING, FRANCES MURDAUGH
Frank Dudley. See:
GREENE, WARD
Frank, Fancy. See:
POWELL, DAVID FRANK
Frank Faulkner. See:
ELLIS, EDWARD SYLVESTER
Frank Forester. See:
HERBERT, HENRY WILLIAM
Frank Fredericks, Dr. See:
FRANCK, FREDERICK SIGFRED
Frank Freelance. See:
BELLAW, AMERICUS WELLINGTON
Frank, Handsome. See:
PIERCE, FRANKLIN
Frank, Jacob. See:
LIEBOWICZ, JANKIEW
Frank Latimore. See:

KLINE, FRANK
Frank Leslie. See:
CARTER, HENRY
Frank Lester. See:
USHER, FRANK
Frank Linstow White. See:
WEITENKAMPF, FRANK
Frank Luther. See:
CROW, FRANCIS LUTHER
Frank Lynn. See:
LEISY, JAMES FRANKLIN
Frank McLowery. See:
KEEVIL, HENRY JOHN
Frank Madison. See:
HUTCHINS, FRANCIS GILMAN
Frank Merriwell. See:
WHITSON, JOHN HARVEY
Frank Miller. See:
LOOMIS, NOEL MILLER
Frank Morgan. See:
WUPPERMAN, FRANCIS
Frank O'Brian. See:
GARFIELD, BRIAN WYNNE
Frank O'Connor. See:
O'DONOVAN, MICHAEL
Frank, Old. See:
CHEATHAM, BENJAMIN FRANKLIN
Frank P. Armstrong, Captain. See: AIKEN, ALBERT W.
Frank Parker. See:
PAIKOWSKI, FRANCISZEK ANDZEJ
Frank Powell. See:
INGRAHAM, COLONEL PRENTISS
Frank Randle. See:
McEVOY, ARTHUR
Frank Richard Stockton. See:
STOCKTON, FRANCIS RICHARD
Frank Richards. See:
HAMILTON, CHARLES
Frank Rodgers. See:
INFIELD, GLENN BERTON
FRANK, RUTH VERD (1899-) [American composer, organist and pianist]
Ruth Uhl
Frank Shaul. See:
ROWLAND, DONALD SYDNEY
Frank Sullivan. See:
DILLINGER, JOHN HERBERT
Frank the Just. See:
MURPHY, FRANK
Frank V. Webster. See:
STRATEMEYER, EDWARD L.
Frank Villard. See:
DROUINEAU, FRANÇOIS
Frank W. Mason. See:
MASON, FRANCIS VAN WYCK
FRANK, WALDO DAVID (1889-1967) [American author]
Searchlight
Frank Watson. See:
AMES, FRANCIS H.
Frank Webber. See:
BUSHNELL, WILLIAM H.
Frank Wynne. See:
GARFIELD, BRIAN WYNNE
FRANKAU, JULIA (1864-1916) [English writer]
Frank Danby
FRANKAU, MARY EVELYN ATKINSON (1899-) [British playwright and author of books for children]
M. E. Atkinson
FRANKEN, ROSE D. (MRS.) WILLIAM BROWN MELONEY) (1898-) [American novelist and playwright]
Margaret Grant
FRANKEN, ROSE D. (MRS. WILLIAM BROWN MELONEY) See also:
Maloney, Franken
Frankfort Sommerville. See:
STORY, SOMMERVILLE
Frankie. See:
DRAKE, SIR FRANCIS
Frankie Avalon. See:
AVALLONE, FRANCIS
Frankie Carle. See:
CARLONE, FRANCIS N.
Frankie Darro. See:
JOHNSON, FRANK
Frankie Laine. See:
LOVECCHIO, FRANK PAUL

Frankie Masters. See:
MASTERMAN, FRANK EVANS
Frankie Yale. See:
UALE, FRANCESCO
FRANKLIN, BENJAMIN (1706-90) [American statesman, inventor, philanthropist and publisher]
Anthony Afterwit
The American Socrates
The Busybody
Father Abraham
The Father of All the Yankees
The Father of the Continental Congress
The Father of the Mail Order Catalog
The Father of the Stove
The Grand Old Man
The Liberator of the New World
The Many-sided Franklin
Mrs. Silence Dogood
Philomath
Poor Richard
Proteus Echo, Esq.
Richard Saunders
The Sage of America
Silence Dogood
The Tamer of Lightning
FRANKLIN, BENJAMIN (1862-) [American lawyer; advocate of New York's Tri-borough Bridge]
The Father of the Triborough Bridge
Franklin Calkins. See:
STRATEMEYER, EDWARD L.
Franklin, Charles. See:
USHER, FRANK
Franklin, Elizabeth. See:
CAMPBELL, HANNAH
Franklin Hadley. See:
WINTERBOTHAM, RUSSELL ROBERT
Franklin, Jay. See:
CARTER, JOHN FRANKLIN
FRANKLIN, MADELEINE (1918-) [Writer of juvenile literature]
Madeleine L'Engle
Franklin, May. See:
DEMING, RICHARD
Franklin of the West, The. See:
BRADFORD, JOHN
Franklin of Theology, The. See:
FULLER, ANDREW
Franklin, Sidney. See:
FRUMPKIN, SIDNEY
Franklin W. Dixon. See:
STRATEMEYER, EDWARD L.
Frans. See:
FRANCE
France
Franz
VAN ANROOY, FRANCINE
FRANSON, FREDRIK (1852-1908) [Swedish-American missionary]
The Man Sent from God
Franz. See also:
FRANCE
France
Frans
Franz Adamus. See:
BRONNER, FERDINAND
Franz Brand. See:
BONUS, ARTHUR
Franz, Robert. See:
KNAUTH, ROBERT
Franz Waxman. See:
WACHSMAN, FRANZ
FRANZERO, CARLO MARIA (1892-) [Italian author]
Charles Marie Franzero
FRASCH, HERMAN (1851-1914) [American industrialist; active in the sulphur industry]
The Sulphur King
Frascuelo. See:
SÁNCHEZ, SALVADOR
FRASER, AGNES MAUDE (1859-) [British author]
Frances McNab
Fraser, Alex. See:
BRINTON, HENRY
FRASER, HAROLD (1886-1962) [Australian-American silent motion picture comedian]
Snub Pollard

Fraser, Jane. See:
PILCHER, ROSAMUNDE
Fraser, Ronald. See:
TILTMAN, RONALD FRANK
Fraud President, The. See:
HAYES, RUTHERFORD BIRCHARD
Fraudulency, His. See:
HAYES, RUTHERFORD BIRCHARD
Fray Antonio Agapida. See:
IRVING, WASHINGTON
Frazer, Jane. See:
FRAHSE, MARY JANE
Fraser, Andrew. See:
MARLOWE, STEPHEN
FRAZER-HURST, REV. DOUGLAS (1883-) [Irish clergyman and author]
Hibbert Verne
FRAZIER, JAMEL (1922-) [American Negro child actor]
Buckwheat
Frazier, S.M. See:
MORRIS, CHARLES SMITH
Frece, Lady de. See:
POWLES, MATILDA ALICE
FRÉCHETTE, LOUIS HONORÉ (1839-1908) [Canadian attorney and author]
The Canadian Laureate
Freck. See:
OWEN, MARVIN JAMES
Freckles. See:
BARRY, WESLEY
Fred. See:
BASON, FREDERICK THOMAS
BORNET, FRANÇOIS
COGSWELL, FREDERICK WILLIAM
COE, FREDERICK
HALL, FREDERICK LEE
PERRY, FREDERICK JOHN
VINSON, FREDERICK MOORE
WALLER, FREDERIC
WILT, FREDERICK LOREN
Fred Allen. See:
SULLIVAN, JOHN FLORENCE
Fred Astaire. See:
AUSTERLITZ, FRED
Fred Ford. See:
DOERFFLER, ALFRED
Fred Niblo. See:
NOBILE, FEDERICO
Fred Russell. See:
PARNELL, THOMAS FREDERICK
Fred Silver. See:
SILVERBERG, FREDERICK
Fred, Uncle. See:
THOMPSON, FREDERICK B.
Freda. See:
COLLINS, FREDERICA JOAN HALE
Freda Fenton. See:
ROWLAND, DONALD SYDNEY
Freddie. See:
SLACK, FREDERICK CHARLES
FREDERIC [Frederic]. See also: FREDERICK
Frederick
Fredericks
FREDERIX
Fredric
Fredricks
FRIEDRICH
Friedrich
Frederic Dannay. See:
Queen, Ellery
Frederic Freyer. See:
BALLINGER, WILLIAM SANBORN
FREDERIC, HAROLD (1856-98)[American novelist]
George Forth
Frederic Martin. See:
CHRISTOPHER, MATTHEW F.
Frederic Ormund. See:
DEY, FREDERICK VAN RENSSELAER
Frederic Phelps. See:
McCULLEY, JOHNSTON
Frederick. See:
FREDERIC

Frederic
Fredericks
FREDERIX
Fredric
Fredricks
FRIEDRICH
Friedrich
LEMAITRE, ANTOINE-LOUIS PROSPER

FREDERICK I (1123?-90) [King of Germany and Italy; Holy Roman Emperor and Duke of Swabia (as FREDERICK II)]
Frederick Barbarossa
Redbeard

FREDERICK I (1369-1428) [Margrave of Meissen and Duke of Saxony]
The Warlike

FREDERICK I (1425-76) [Elector of Palatinate]
The Victorious

FREDERICK II (1194-1250) [Emperor of Germany and King of Sicily (as FREDERICK I]
The Father of Italian Poetry
The Wonder of the World

FREDERICK II (1411-64) [Elector and Duke of Saxony]
The Meek

FREDERICK II (died 1471) [Elector of Brandenburg]
Iron Tooth

FREDERICK II (1712-86) [King of Prussia]
Alaric-Cotin
Father Fritz
Frederick the Great
The Great
The Philosopher of Sans Souci

FREDERICK III (c.1286-1330) [King of Germany]
The Fair
Frederick of Austria
Frederick the Fair
Frederick the Handsome

FREDERICK III (1341-77) [King of Sicily]
The Simple

FREDERICK III (1415-93) [Emperor of the Holy Roman Empire]
The Pacific

FREDERICK III (1515-76) [Elector of Palatinate]
The Pious

FREDERICK IV (1574-1610) [Elector of Palatinate]
The Upright

FREDERICK V (1569-1632) [Elector of the Palatinate and King of Bohemia]
Goodman Palsgrave
The Snow King
The Winter King

FREDERICK AUGUSTUS I (1750-1827) [King of Saxony]
The Just

Frederick Benton Williams. See: HAMBLEN, HERBERT ELLIOTT

FREDERICK-CHARLES, PRINCE (1828-85) [Prussian field marshal]
The Red Prince

Frederick Christian. See: GEHMAN, RICHARD BOYD

Frederick, Dick. See: DEMPEWOLFF, RICHARD FREDERIC

Frederick Douglass. See: BAILEY, FREDERICK AUGUST WASHINGTON

Frederick Ely. See: KESSLER, JASCHA FREDERICK

Frederick Garrison. See: SINCLAIR, UPTON BEALL

Frederick Garrison, Lieut. See: SINCLAIR, UPTON BEALL

Frederick, George Augustus. See: GEORGE IV

Frederick Gordon. See: STRATEMEYER, EDWARD L.

Frederick J. Terrence. See: HAYES, JOHN F.

Frederick, John. See: FAUST, FREDERICK SCHILLER

Frederick Kerr. See:
KEEN, FREDERICK
KERNER, FRED
Frederick Lonsdale. See:
LEONARD, FREDERICK
FREDERICK LOUIS (1707-51)
[Prince of Wales; eldest son of GEORGE II of England]
Prince Titi
Frederick M. Dey. See:
DEY, FREDERICK VAN RENSSELAER
FREDERICK OF LORRAINE (died 1058) [Supreme Pontiff of Roman Catholic Church]
Pope Stephen X
Frederick, Oswald. See:
SNELLING, OSWALD FREDERICK
FREDERICK, WILHELMINA CAROLINA (1683-1737) [Queen of Great Britain and Ireland, wife of GEORGE III]
Caroline of Anspach
FREDERICK WILLIAM (1620-88) [Elector of Brandenburg]
The Great Elector
FREDERICK WILLIAM (1831-88) [Emperor of Germany]
Frederick the Noble
Our Fritz (Unser Fritz]
Frederick Wolf. See:
DEMPEWOLFF, RICHARD FREDERIC
Fredericks. See also:
FREDERIC
Frederic
FREDERICK
Frederick
FREDERIX
Fredric
Fredricks
FRIEDRICH
Friedrich
Fredericks, Arnold. See:
KUMMER, FREDERICK ARNOLD
Fredericks, Dr. Frank. See:
FRANCK, FREDERICK SIGFRED
Fredericksburg, The Hero of. See: KIRKLAND, RICHARD R.
FREDERIC. See also:
FERDERIC
Frederic
FREDERICK
Frederick
Fredericks
Fredric
Fredricks
FRIEDRICH
Friedrich
FREDERIX, JACQUES (1888-1948) [French actor and motion picture director]
Jacques Feyder
Fredric. See also:
FREDRIC
Frederic
FREDERICK
Frederick
Fredericks
FREDERIX
Fredricks
FRIEDRICH
Friedrich
Fredric March. See:
BICKEL, FREDERICK McINTYRE
Fredricks. See also:
FREDERIC
Frederic
FREDERICK
Frederick
Fredericks
FREDERIX
Fredric
FRIEDRICH
Friedrich
Fredricks, Frohm. See:
KERNERR, FRED
Free. See:
HOFFMAN, ABBIE
Free-born John. See:
LILBURNE, JOHN
Free Coinage for Silver, The Apostle of. See:
ST. JOHN, WILLIAM POPE
Free Delivery, The Father of Rural. See:
BUTLER, MARION

Free Dirt, The Orator of. See:
JULIAN, GEORGE WASHINGTON
Free, Mickey. See:
ENTON, DR. HARRY
Free School System in New Jersey, The Father of. See: CUTLER, AUGUSTUS WILLIAM
Free School System, The Father of the. See:
ENGLISH, JAMES EDWARD
Free Silver, The Father of. See:
BLAND, RICHARD PARKS
Free, The (Azad). See:
ABUL KALAM AZAD, MAULANA
Free Trade, The Apostle of. See: BRIGHT, JOHN
COBDEN, RICHARD
Freebetter, Edmund. See:
DABOLL, NATHAN
Freed, Arthur. See:
GROSSMAN, ARTHUR
Freelance, Frank. See:
BELLAW, AMERICUS WELLINGTON
FREEMAN, ANNE FRANCIS (1936-) [American author]
Anne Frances Huether
FREEMAN, AUSTIN (18??-62) [American pioneer in Kansas]
Old Kill Devil
FREEMAN, ERNEST (1922-) [American composer, conductor and arranger]
Ernie Freeman
FREEMAN, GRAYDON LA VERNE (1904-) [American educator, publishing official and author]
Larry Freeman
James H. Thompson
Serry Wood
Freeman, J.L. See:
ST. JOHN, PERCY BOLLINGBROKE
FREEMAN, JAMES DILLET (1912-) [American writer, teacher and lecturer on religion]
D.J. Mann
FREEMAN, JULIA DEANE (fl. mid 19th cent.) [American author]
Mary Forrest
FREEMAN, LAWRENCE (1906-) [American jazz musician (tenor saxophone)]
Bud Freeman
Freeman, Mrs. See:
JENNINGS, SARAH
FREEMAN, RICHARD AUSTIN (1862-1943) [English author of detective stories]
R. Austin Freeman
FREEMAN, RICHARD AUSTIN. See also:
Ashdown, Clifford
FREETH, JOHN (1730-1808) [British wit, poet, composer, publican and singer]
The Birmingham Poet
FREIHOFER, LOIS DIANE (1933-) [American author]
Lois Barth
FRELINGHUYSEN, THEODORE (1787-1861) [American politician; senator from New Jersey]
The Christian Statesman
FREMAULT, ANITA LOUISE (1915-) [American motion picture actress]
Anita Louise
Fremlin, Celia. See:
GOLLER, CELIA FREMLIN
FRÉMONT, JOHN CHARLES (1813-90) [American general officer and explorer]
The Gray Mustang
The Pathfinder
FRENCH, ALICE (1850-1934) [American novelist]
Octave Thanet
French Anacreon, The. See:
THIARD, PONTUS DE

French Aristophanes, The. See:
POQUELIN, JEAN BAPTISTE
French Burns, The. See:
BÉRANGER, PIERRE-JEAN DE
French Byron, The. See:
MUSSET, LOUIS CHARLES ALFRED DE
French Calliope, The. See:
DESHOULIÈRES, ANTOINETTE DU LIGIER DE LA GARDE
French Defoe, The. See:
RESTIF, NICHOLAS EDME
French Devil, The. See:
BART, JEAN
French Dickens, The. See:
DAUDET, ALPHONSE
French Drama, The Father of the. See:
JODELLE, ÉTIENNE
French Drama, The Homer of the. See:
CORNEILLE, PIERRE
French Drama, The Virgil of the. See:
RACINE, JEAN BAPTISTE
French Ennius, The. See:
CLOPINEL, JEAN
French Fabius, The. See:
ANNE, DUC DE MONTMORENCY
French Fenimore Cooper, The. See: GLOUX, OLIVIER
French Gamecock, The. See:
MOTIER, MARIE JEAN PAUL ROCH YVES GILBERT
French Historians, The First of the. See:
VILLEHARDOUIN, GEOFFROI DE
French History, The Father of. See: DUCHESNE, ANDRÉ
French, Horace, The. See:
BÉRANGER, PIERRE-JEAN DE
French Isocrates, The. See:
FLÉCHIER, ESPRIT
French John. See:
SIOUSSAT, JEAN PIERRE
French Landscape Gardening, The Creator of. See:
LENÔTRE, ANDRÉ
FRENCH, LUCY VIRGINIA SMITH (1825-81) [American editor, novelist, poet and essayist]
L'Inconnue
French Michelangelo, The. See:
COUSIN, JEAN
PUGET, PIERRE
French Ovid, The. See:
BELLAY, JOACHIM DU
French, Paul. See:
ASIMOV, ISAAC
French Petrarch, The. See:
AUBANEL, THÉODORE
French Phidias, The. See:
GOUJON, JEAN
PIGALLE, JEAN BAPTISTE
French Pindar, The. See:
DINEMANDY (DORAT), JEAN
French Poet, The. See:
RONSARD, PIERRE DE
French Prose, The Solon of. See: BALZAC, JEAN LOUIS GUEZ DE
French Quintilian, The. See:
HARPE, JEAN FRANÇOIS DE LA
French Raphael, The. See:
LE SUEUR, EUSTACHE
French Reformation, The Elijah of the. See:
FAREL, GUILLAUME
French Roscius, The. See:
BARON (BOYRON), MICHEL
TALMA, FRANÇOIS JOSEPH
French Sappho, The. See:
SCUDÉRI, MADELEINE DE
French Satire, The Father of. See: REGNIER, MATHURIN
French Shakespeare, The. See:
CORNEILLE, PIERRE
French Songs, The Father of Modern. See:
PANARD, CHARLES-FRANÇOIS

French Surgery, The Father of. See:
PARÉ, AMBROISE
French, The Apostle of the. See: DENIS (DENYS), ST.
French Tibullus, The. See:
DEFORGE, ÉVARISTE DÉSIRÉ
French Titian, The. See:
BLANCHARD, JACQUES
French Tragedy, The Father of. See:
CORNEILLE, PIERRE
GARNIER, ROBERT
French Van Dyck, The. See:
RIGAUD, HYACINTHE
FRENEAU, ELEANOR FORMAN. See:
Ella
FRENEAU, PHILIP MORIN (1752-1832) [American satirical poet and journalist]
P. F.
The Poet of the American Revolution
That Rascal, Freneau
Robert Slender, Stocking Weaver
FRENEAU, PHILIP MORIN. See also:
Ella
FREYBE, HEIDI HUBERTA (1914-) [German-American journalist and author]
Martha Albrand
Katrin Holland
Christine Lambert
FRERE, JOHN HOOKHAM (1769-1846) [English diplomat and author]
William and Robert Whistlecraft
FRESE, DOLORES WARWICK (1936-) [American social worker and author]
Dolores Warwick
Fresnay, Pierre. See:
LAUDENBACH, PIERRE-JULES
FREUD, SIGMUND (1856-1939) [Austrian founder of psychoanalysis]
The Copernicus of the Mind
FREUND, JOHN (1918-) [American stage and motion picture actor]
John Forsythe
FREWIN, LESLIE RONALD (1917-) [British motion picture executive and writer]
Paul Dupont
Freyer, Frederic. See:
BALLINGER, WILLIAM SANBORN
Friar. See:
BUNGAY, THOMAS
Frick, C.H. See:
IRWIN, CONSTANCE FRICK
Frick, Constance. See:
IRWIN, CONSTANCE FRICK
FRÍDA, EMIL (1853-1912) [Czech poet, dramatist, translator and critic]
Jaroslav Vrchlicky
FRIEDLAND, HARRY (1911-) [American jazz musician (violin, leader)]
Blue Barron
FRIEDLAND, VALENTIN (1490-1556) [German educator]
Trotzendorf
FRIEDLANDER, LEWIS (1901-62) [American motion picture director]
Lew Landers
FRIEDMAN, ESTHER PAULINE (1918-) [American newspaper columnist]
Ann Landers
Eppie
FRIEDMAN, EVE ROSEMARY TIBBER (1929-) [British author]
Robert Tibber
FRIEDMAN, THEODORE LEOPOLD (1891-1971) [American jazz musician (clarinet, alto saxophone, singer, composer, leader)]
The High-hatted Tragedian of Jazz
Ted Lewis

FRIEDRICH [Friedrich].
See also:
FREDERIC
Frederic
FREDERICK
Frederick
Fredericks
FREDERIX
Fredric
Fredricks
Friedrich Halm. See:
MÜNCH-BELLINGHAUSEN, ELIGIUS FRANZ JOSEPH, REICH-FREIHERR VON
FRIEDRICH, KARL EITEL (1839-1914) [King of Rumania]
Carol I
Friedrich Murnau. See:
PLUMPE, FRIEDRICH W.
Friedrich Robert. See:
EHLERS, FRIEDRICH ROBERT
Friedsam. See:
BEISSEL, JOHANN CONRAD
Friend, Farmer's. See:
CAPPER, ARTHUR
Friend of Helpless Children, The. See: HOOVER, HERBERT CLARK
Friend of Man, The. See:
RIQUETI, VICTOR
Friend of the Indian. See:
STUART, ROBERT
Friend of the People (l'Ami du Peuple). See:
MARAT, JEAN PAUL
Friend of the People, The. See: JEFFERSON, THOMAS
FRIEND, OSCAR JEROME (1897-) [American novelist]
Owen Fox Jerome
Friend, The Indian's. See:
WILLIAMS, ROGER
Friend, The Letter Carrier's. See: COX, SAMUEL SULLIVAN
Friend, The People's. See:
GORDON, WILLIAM
Friend, The Poor Man's. See:
COUZENS, JAMES
Friend, The Prisoner's. See:
BEAL, ABRAHAM
Friend, The Sailor's. See:
PLIMSOLL, SAMUEL
WESTON, AGNES
Friend, The Sinner's. See:
MATTHEW, FATHER THEOBALD
Friend, The Soldier's. See:
CURTIN, ANDREW GREGG
WARD, MARCUS LAWRENCE
Friend, Wesley's Most Valuable. See: FLETCHER, JOHN WILLIAM
Friendli, The Bernese. See:
MIND, GOTTFRIED
FRIENDLICH, RICHARD J. (1909-) [American author]
Dick Friendlich
FRIERSON, REVOYDA (1934-) [American jazz musician (singer)]
Ketty Lester
Friese, Dr. Edzard. See:
BUDDE, GERHARD AUGUST
Friesians, The Apostle of the. See: WILLIBRORD
FRIIS-BAASTAD, BABBIS ELINOR (1921-) [Norwegian author]
Babbis Friis Baastad
Eleanor Babbis
Babbis Friis
FRIML, CHARLES RUDOLF (1881-) [American composer]
Rudolf Friml
FRINGS, CATHERINE (fl. mid 20th cent.) [American scenarist]
Ketti Frings
FRISCH, FRANK FRANCIS (1898-) [American professional baseball player]
The Fordham Flash
FRISKEY, MARGARET RICHARDS (1901-) [American editor and author]
Elizabeth Sherman
FRITH, MARY (1584?-1659) [notorious English roisterer and pickpocket]

Moll Cutpurse
Fritz. See:
CRISLER, HERBERT ORIN
KNOTHE, WILFRED EDGAR
PALUDAN-MÜLLER, FREDERIK
WHITEHALL, HAROLD
Fritz Benthien. See:
BONUS, ARTHUR
Fritz, Father. See:
FREDERICK II
Fritz, Our (Unser Fritz). See:
FREDERICK WILLIAM
Fritz, Unser (Our Fritz). See:
FREDERICK WILLIAM
Frizius, Joachim. See:
FLUDD (FLUD), ROBERT
Frohm. See also:
From
Frome
Frohm Fredericks. See:
KERNER, FRED
FROISSART, JEAN (1337-c. 1410) [French chronicler]
The Walter Scott of the Middle Ages
Froissart, Jean. See:
DAUDET, ALPHONSE
From. See also:
Frohm
Frome
From Overseas (D'Outremer). See: LOUIS IV
From the Desk of Beri Headin. See: STORY, ISAAC
Frome. See also:
Frohm
From
Frome, David. See:
BROWN, ZENITH JONES
Fronde, The Soul of the. See:
LONGUEVILLE, ANNE, DUCHESSE DE
FROST, HAROLD G. (1893-1959) [American composer and musician]
Jack Frost
FROST, HELEN (1898-) [American ranch operator and author]
Dave Nichols
FROST, ROBERT LEE (1874-1963) [American lyric poet]
The Voice of New England
FROST, SARAH FRANCES (1866-1950) [Anglo-American actress]
Julia Marlowe
FROUDE, JAMES ANTHONY (1818-94) [English historian and novelist]
Zeta
Froy, Herald
Lee Gibb, joint pseuds. of GUY DEGHY (1912-) and KEITH WATERHOUSE (1929-) [British writers]
FRUMENTIUS, ST. (c. 300-c. 380) [Phoenician churchman; Bishop of Axum]
The Apostle of Ethiopia
FRUMPKIN, SIDNEY (1903-) [American bullfighter]
Sidney Franklin
Fry, Christopher. See:
HARRIS, CHRISTOPHER
FRY, MRS. ELIZABETH (1780-1845) [English prison reformer and humanitarian]
The Female Howard
FRYE, MARIE (1923-65) [American motion picture actress]
The Body
Marie McDonald
FUCHS, MURRAY LOUIS (1926-) [American dancer and choreographer]
Murray Louis
Fud. See:
LIVINGSTON, JOSEPH A.
FUENTES, ANTONIO (1869-1938) [Spanish bullfighter]
The Elegant Fuentes
FUENTES, MANUEL (1837-69) [Spanish bullfighter]
Bocanegra
FUERTES, DOLORES ADIOS (1835-68) [American actress]
The Enchanting Rebel
Adah Bertha Menken

Adah Isaacs Menken
FUGGER, JAKOB II (1459-1525) [German financier and merchant]
Fugger the Rich
Jakob the Rich
Führer, Der. See:
HITLER, ADOLF
FULC (FULK) (FOULQUES) III (972-1040) [Count of Anjou]
The Black
FULKS, SARAH JANE (1914-) [American motion picture actress]
Jane Durrell
Jane Wyman
FULLER, ANDREW (1754-1815) [English Baptist preacher and theologian]
The Franklin of Theology
FULLER, HENRY BLAKE (1857-1929) [American novelist, poet and essayist]
Stanton Page
FULLER, HENRY STARKEY (1852-) [American author]
A. Fellow Feelin'
Fuller, Iola. See:
McCOY, IOLA FULLER
FULLER, ROBERT MASON (1845-1919) [American physician, pharmacist and inventor]
The Father of the Tablet Triturate
Fuller, Roger. See:
TRACY, DONALD FISKE
FULLER, SAMUEL RICHARD, JR. (1879-) [American manufacturer and author]
Norman Brainerd
FULLER, SARAH MARGARET, MARCHIONESS OSSOLI (1810-50) [American feminist]
Margaret Fuller
FULLERTON, JEAN MUIR (1911-) [American motion picture actress]
Jean Muir
FULMER, HAMPTON PITTS (1875-1944) [American politician; Senator from South Carolina]
Horsepower
Fulton. See:
OURSLER, CHARLES FULTON
FULTON, ROBERT (1765-1815) [American inventor of first practical steamboat]
The Father of Steamboat Navigation
The Father of the Steamboat
Quicksilver Bob
Fum the Fourth. See:
GEORGE IV
FUMOLEAU, BLANCHE (1897-1964) [French motion picture actress]
Gaby Morlay
Functionary, Old Public. See:
BUCHANAN, JAMES
Fundatissimus, Doctor. See:
ROMANUS, AGAEDIUS, OF COLONNA
Fundatus, Doctor. See:
VARRO, WILLIAM
FUNG JING TOY (1865-97) [Chinese tong leader in San Francisco]
Little Pete
FUNICELLO, ANNETTE (1942-) [American motion picture actress]
Annette
Funniest Clown in the World, The. See: CLARK, ROBERT EDWIN
Funniest Woman, The World's. See: DAVIS, JOAN
FUNKQUIST, HERMAN PETER ANTON (1870-) [German author]
Fqt
FUNSTON, EDWARD HOGUE (1836-1911) [American politician; Congressman from Kansas]
Foghorn Funston
Furioso, Il. See:
ROBUSTI, JACOPO
Furious One (Xocoyotzin). See:

MONTEZUMA II
FURMAN, RICHARD (1755-1825) [American preacher]
The Boy Preacher
Furness, Elizabeth. See: UPSON, DOROTHY BARBARA
FURNESS, ELIZABETH MARY (1916-) [American actress and government official]
Betty Furness
Furnley, Maurice. See: WILMOT, FRANK LESLIE THOMSON
FURPHY, JOSEPH (1843-1912) [Australian novelist]
Tom Collins
FURUSETH, ANDREW (1854-1938) [Norwegian-American seaman and leader of the Seaman's Labor Union]
The Abraham Lincoln of the Sea
The Dean of the American Labor Movement
The Old Viking
Fury of the Gironde, The. See: TERWAGNE, ANNE JOSEPH
Fuseli, Henry. See: FÜSSLI, JOHANN HEINRICH
Fuss and Feathers, Old. See: SCOTT, WINFIELD
FUSS, MARTIN (c.1916-) [American motion picture producer]
Ross Hunter
FÜSSLI, JOHANN HEINRICH (1741-1825) [Swiss-born British painter and art critic]
Henry Fuseli
Fuzzy. See: KNIGHT, J. FORREST; ST. JOHN, AL
Fyfield, George. See: FOGG, HENRY GEORGE WITHAM

G

G.A. Birmingham. See: HANNAY, JAMES OWEN
G.A.L. Burgeon. See: BARFIELD, OWEN
G.B. See: BOAS, GUY HERMAN SIDNEY
G.B. Kirtland. See: HINE, SESYLE JOSLIN
G.B. Larking. See: SHAW, GEORGE BERNARD
G.B. Lovehill. See: BEAUMONT, CHARLES
G.B.S. See: SHAW, GEORGE BERNARD
G.B. Stern. See: HOLDSWORTH, GLADYS BRONWYN
G.E. Mitton. See: SCOTT, GERALDINE EDITH
G.E. Seebord. See: SODERBERG, PERCY MEASDAY
G.G. See: FICKLING, SKIP FORREST
G. Gearing-Thomas. See: NORWOOD, VICTOR GEORGE CHARLES
G. Hobab Kish. See: KENNEDY, GERALD HAMILTON
G.I.'s Own Songwriter, The. See: LOESSER, FRANK HENRY
G.J. See: JACKSON, REV. GEORGE
G.K.C. See: CHESTERTON, GILBERT KEITH
G.K. Thomas. See: DAVIES, LESLIE PURNELL
G. Noel Hatton. See: CAIRD, ALICE MONA
G.P.C. See: PANCONCELLI-CALZIA, GIULIO
G---, Percival. See: IRVING, PETER
G.R. Aldo. See: GRAZIATI, ALDO
G.R. Miller. See: JUDD, FREDERICK CHARLES
G.S. Page. See: GALBRAITH, GEORGIE STARBUCK
G. Vialio. See: SIMENON, GEORGES

G. Violis. See:
SIMENON, GEORGES
G.W. Alcalaw, Major. See:
HARBAUGH, THOMAS CHALMERS
G.W. Pabst. See:
WILHELM, GEORG
G. Waldo Browne. See:
BROWNE, GEORGE WALDO
Gaal, Franceska. See:
ZILVERITCH, FANNY
Gabby. See:
Gaby
HARTNETT, CHARLES LEO
HAYES, GEORGE FRANCIS
STREET, CHARLES EVARD
Gabin, Jean. See:
MONCOURGE, ALEXIS
GABLE, WILLIAM CLARK (1901-60) [American motion picture actor]
Clark Gable
GABOR, SARI (1921-) [Hungarian motion picture actress]
Zsa Zsa Gabor
Gabriel. See:
SPENCER, GABRIEL
Gabriel Fielding. See:
BARNSLEY, ALAN GABRIEL
Gabriel, The Twentieth Century. See:
HAWKINS, ERSKINE
Gabriela Mistral. See:
ALCAYAGA, LUCILLA GODOY DE
Gabriele d'Annunzio. See:
RAMPAGNETTO, GAETANO
Gabriele Rossetti. See:
CITERIORE, VASTO ABRUZZO
Gabrielle, La Belle. See:
D'ESTRÉES, GABRIELLE
Gabrielli. See:
MEEKE, MRS. MARY
Gaby. See:
Gabby
DESLYS, GABRIELLE
Gaby Morlay. See:
FUMOLEAU, BLANCHE
Gaddis, Peggy. See:
DERN, PEGGY GADDIS
Gael. See also:
Gail
Gale
Gael, The Achilles of the. See:
SETANTA
Gaffer Peeslake. See:
DURRELL, LAWRENCE GEORGE
Gag. See:
ATHERTON, CHARLES GORDON
GAGE, FRANCES DANA BARKER (1808-44) [American reformer and author]
Aunt Fanny
Gage, Wilson. See:
STEELE, MARY QUINTARD GOVAN
Gahagan, Major Goliah. See:
THACKERAY, WILLIAM MAKEPEACE
Gail. See also:
Gael
Gale
Gail Everett. See:
HALE, ARLENE
Gail Hamilton. See:
DODGE, MARY ABIGAIL
Gail Jordan. See:
DERN, PEGGY GADDIS
Gail Patrick. See:
FITZPATRICK, MARGARET
GAILLARD, BULEE (1916-) [American jazz musician (guitar, piano, vibraphone, singer)]
Slim Gaillard
GAINER, LAURA (1907-) [American motion picture actress]
Janet Gaynor
Gaines, Albert Cecil. See:
GRISSOM, ARTHUR COLFAX
Gaite, Francis. See:
Coles, Manning
GAIUS JULIUS CAESAR GERMANICUS (12-41 A.D.)

[Roman emperor]
Caligula
GAJKOVIC, DUSAN (1931-)
[Yogoslavian jazz musician (trumpet, composer)]
Dusko Goykovich
Gal, Sweet Emma the Bell. See: BARRETT, EMMA
GALAGINA (c.1803-1839) [Cherokee Indian editor and author]
Elias Boudinot
GALBRAITH, FREDERICK WILLIAM (1874-1921) [American World War I officer]
The Fighting Colonel
GALBRAITH, GEORGIE STARBUCK (1909-) [American versifier and author]
G. S. Page
Ann Patrice
Penny Pennington
Stuart Pennington
GALBRAITH, JOHN KENNETH (1908-) [Canadian economist, educator and author]
Mark Epernay
Herschel McLandress
Galdo Monk. See: RISELEY, JERRY BURR JR.
Gale. See also:
Gael
Gail
Gale Gallager. See: OURSLER, WILLIAM CHARLES
Gale, John. See: GAZE, RICHARD
Gale Page. See: RUTTER, SALLY
Gale Storm. See: COTTLE, JOSEPHINE
Gale Winterton. See: ADAMS WILLIAM TAYLOR
GALEN (131-201?) [Greek physician and philosopher]
The Father of Experimental Physiology
Galen, Philipp. See: LANGE, ERNST PHILIPP KARL
Galena, Butcher from. See: GRANT, HIRAM ULYSSES
Galena Tanner, The. See: GRANT, HIRAM ULYSSES
Galgario, Fra. See: GHISLANDI, FRA VITTORE
Galilean, The. See: JUDAS OF GALILEE
GALILEE. See: JUDAS OF GALILEE
GALILEI, GALILEO (1564-1642) [Italian scientist and astronomer]
Galileo
GALITZIN, DIMITRI AUGUSTINE (1770-1841) [Russian-American Catholic priest]
Father Smith
GALITZIN, PRINCE VASILI (1633-1713) [Russian commander and politician]
The Great
Gallager, Gale. See: OURSLER, WILLIAM CHARLES
GALLAGHER, RICHARD (c.1902-55) [American vaudevillian and motion picture actor]
Skeets Gallagher
GALLAGHER, SISTER MARY DOMINIC (1917-) [Canadian Roman Catholic nun and author]
Sister Mary Dominic
Gallant. See: PELHAM, JOHN
GALLATIN, ABRAHAM ALPHONSE ALBERT (1761-1849) [Swiss-American statesman, diplomat and ethnologist]
The Father of American Ethnology
Albert Gallatin
The Watchdog of the Treasury
GALLEGO, JOSÉ (1883-1910) [Spanish bullfighter]
Pepete III
Gallerite, The. See: BASON, FREDERICK THOMAS
GALLERY, DANIEL V. (1901-) [American Admiral; Little League

baseball commissioner in Latin America and author]
Dan Gallery
GALLICHAN, WALTER M. (1861-) [British author and journalist]
Anna Blount
January Mortimer
Gallinger, Osma Couch. See: TOD, OSMA GALLINGER
GALLITZIN, DEMETRIUS AUGUSTINE (1770-1840) [Dutch-American priest and missionary in America]
The Apostle of the Alleghenies
Augustine Smith
Gallo, El. See: GÓMEZ, RAFAEL
Galloping Dick. See: FERGUSON, RICHARD
Galloping Ghost, The. See: GRANGE, HAROLD EDWARD
GALLOWAY [Galloway]. See also: CALLOWAY
GALLOWAY, CHARLES BETTS (1849-1909) [American Methodist bishop]
Golden Mouthed
Prince Charley
Galloway, Lord of. See: DOUGLAS, ARCHIBALD, 3D LORD OF
Galloway, The Fair Maid of. See: MARGARET
GALSWORTHY, JOHN (1867-1933) [English novelist and playwright]
John Sinjohn
GALT, JOHN (1779-1839) [Scottish author]
T. Clark
Malachi Mailings
S. Prior
GALT, THOMAS FRANKLIN, JR. (1908-) [American author]
Tom Galt
GALVIN. See also: Calvin
GALVIN, GEORGE (1860-1904) [English comedian]
Dan Leno
Galway, Norman. See: GENTRY, BYRON B.
GAMALIEL (died 50 A.D. ?) [Rabbi of the Pharisees; President of the Sanhedrin]
The Elder
GAMALIEL OF JABNETH (died 115? A.D.) [Jewish scholar]
The Younger
Gambier, Kenyon. See: LATHROP, LORIN ANDREWS
GAMBLE, JUDY (1916-) [British motion picture actress]
Judy Campbell
Gambler, The Greatest. See: CANFIELD, RICHARD A.
Game Hunter, The Big. See: TINKHAM, GEORGE HOLDEN
Game of Whist, The Father of the. See: HOYLE, EDMOND
Game, One of the Gamest Players in the. See: MERKLE, FREDERICK C.
Gamecock of the Wilderness, The. See: MARBLE, DANFORTH
Gamecock, The. See: SUMTER, THOMAS
Gamecock, The Carolinian. See: SUMTER, THOMAS
Gamecock, The French. See: MOTIER, MARIE JEAN PAUL ROCH YVES GILBERT
Gamecock, The South Carolina. See: SUMTER, THOMAS
Gamest Players in the Game, One of the. See: MERKLE, FREDERICK C.
Ganassa, Zan. See: NASELI, ALBERTO
Gandalae, Lennard. See: BERNE, ERIC LENNARD
GANDHI, MOHANDAS KARAMCHAND (1869-1948) [Indian Nationalist leader]

Mahatma Gandhi
GANGANELLI, GIOVANNI (1705-74) [Supreme Pontiff of Roman Catholic Church]
Pope Clement XIV
Gangland, The Mad Dog of. See: COLL, VINCENT
GANNETT, HENRY (1846-1914) [American geographer and author]
The Father of American Map Making
GANNON, JAMES KIMBALL (1900-) [American lawyer and composer]
Kim Gannon
Ganny Cross, By. See: CROSS, OLIVER HARLAN
GANS, JOE (1874-1910) [American Negro professional boxer; world's lightweight champion]
The Old Master
Gant, Jonathan. See: ADAMS, CLIFTON
Gaon Elijah of Wilna. See: WILNA, ELIJAH (ELIAS)
Gap. See: MANGIONE, GASPARE CHARLES
GARBER, JAN (189?-) [American jazz musician (violin, leader)]
The Idol of the Airlanes
Garbo, Greta. See: GUSTAFFSON, GRETA LOVISA
GARCÍA. See: ESCUDERO, IGNACIO RAFAEL GARCÍA Y
GARCÍA, ARTURO (1908-) [Mexican motion picture actor]
Arturo de Cordova
GARCÍA, AUGUSTÍN (1886-1920) [Spanish bullfighter]
Malla
GARCÍA, FRANCISCO (1749?-1801) [Spanish bullfighter]
Perucho
GARCÍA, JOSÉ (1871-1947) [Spanish bullfighter]
Algabeño
GARCÍA, MANUEL (182?-53) [Mexican outlaw in California; lieutenant of JOAQUIN CARILLO (Joaquín Murieta)]
Three Fingered Jack
GARCÍA, MANUEL (1866-94) [Spanish bullfighter]
Espartero
GARCÍA, MANUEL (1896-1924) [Spanish bullfighter]
Maera
GARCÍA, MANUEL VARÉ (1894-1922) [Spanish bullfighter]
Varelito
GARCÍA, MARIÁ JURADO (1927-) [Mexican motion picture actress]
Katy Jurado
GARCÍA, RUSSELL (1938-) [American composer, conductor, arranger and trumpeter]
Russ García
GARCILASO DE LA VEGA (1539-c.1616) [Spanish-American historian]
El Inca
Garden," By the Author of "Elizabeth and her German. See: BEAUCHAMP, MARY ANNETTE, COUNTESS RUSSELL (MRS. HENNING ARNIM)
Garden, John. See: FLETCHER, HARRY LUFT VERNE
Garden Swan, The Theban. See: PINDAR
Gardener, The Market. See: BLACKMORE, RICHARD DODDRIDGE
Gardening, The Creator of French Landscape. See: LENÔTRE, ANDRÉ
Gardening, The Father of Horticulture and Ornamental. See: HENDERSON, PETER
Gardening, The Father of Landscape. See: LENOTRE, ANDRÉ
Gardens Joe, Pleasant. See:

McDOWELL, JOSEPH
GARDINER. See also:
GARDNER
Gardner
GARNER
Garner
GARNIER
GARDINER, ALFRED GEORGE (1865-) [British journalist and author]
Alpha of the Plough
GARDNER [Gardner]. See also:
GARDINER
GARNER
Garner
GARNIER
Gardner, Dave. See:
WEINGARTEN, DAVID
GARDNER, DONALD YETTER (1912-) [American composer and teacher]
Don Gardner
GARDNER, EDWARD FRANCIS (1905-) [American radio author and actor]
Archie the Manager
Ed Gardner
GARDNER, ERLE STANLEY (1889-1970) [American lawyer and writer of detective stories]
A. A. Fair
Charles M. Green
Carleton Kendrake
Charles J. Kenny
Gardner, Jeffrey. See:
FOX, GARDNER FRANCIS
Gardner, Lawrence. See:
BRANNON, WILLIAM T.
GARDNER, LEWIS J. (1836-1909) [American author]
Andrew Dearborn
Lewis J. Swift
Gardner Low. See:
RODDA, CHARLES
GARDNER, MAURICE (1909-) [American composer, conductor and arranger]
Robert Norman
Martin Pollock
Gerald Tolmage
GARDNER, NANCY BRUFF (1915-) [American poet and novelist]
Nancy Bruff
GARDNER, RICHARD (1931-) [American illustrator and author]
John Carver
Richard Cummings
Dic Gardner
Richard Orth
GARDNER, RICHARD. See also:
Anderson, Clifford
GARDNER, ROY (fl. 1921) [American train robber]
The King of Escape Artists
GARFIELD, BRIAN WYNNE (1939-) [American author]
Bennett Garland
Frank O'Brian
Brian Wynne
Frank Wynne
GARFIELD, JAMES ABRAM (1831-81) [twentieth President of the United States]
The Canal Boy
The Martyr President
The Preacher President
The Teacher President
GARFINKLE, JULIUS (1913-52) [American motion picture actor]
John Garfield
Garibaldi of the Italian Motion Picture Industry, The. See:
LAURENTIS, DINO DE
Garland, Bennett. See:
GARFIELD, BRIAN WYNNE
Garland, Beverly. See:
CAMPBELL, BEVERLY
GARLAND, DAVID JOHN (1864-) [Irish Church of England priest and author]
Joseph Mede
Garland, George. See:
ROARK, GARLAND
GARLAND, HANNIBAL HAMLIN (1860-1940) [American author]
Hamlin Garland
Garland, Judy. See:
GUMM, FRANCES
Garland, Luke. See:
WHITSON, JOHN HARVEY
GARLAND, WILLIAM M. (1923-) [American jazz musician (piano)]
Red Garland

GARMS, DEBS G. (1908-)
[American professional baseball player]
Tex Garms
GARNER [Garner]. See also:
GARDINER
GARDNER
Gardner
GARNIER
Garner, James. See:
BAUMGARNER, JAMES
GARNER, JOHN NANCE (1869-1967) [American statesman; Vice President of the United States]
Cactus Jack
The Favorite Son of Texas
Mohair Jack
The Owl
Poker Face
The Sage of Uvalde
Uvalde Jack
Garnet, Clew. See:
JUDSON, EDWARD ZANE CARROLL
GARNETT, DAVID (1892-)
[British bookman, publisher and author]
Leda Burke
GARNIER. See also:
GARDINER
GARDNER
Gardner
GARNER
Garner
GARNIER, BAPTISTE (fl. late 19th, early 20th cent.)
[Sioux Indian army scout and interpreter]
Little Bat
GARNIER, ROBERT (1534-90)
[French dramatic author]
The Father of French Tragedy
Garofalo. See:
TISI, BENVENUTO
GARRETSON, JAMES EDMUND (1828-95) [American educator, oral surgeon, dentist and author]
John Darby
GARRETT, RANDALL. See:
Phillips, Mark
GARRETT, THOMAS SAMUEL (1913-) [British missionary and author]
Tom Garrett
Garrett, Truman. See:
JUDD, MARGARET HADDICAN
GARRICK, DAVID (1717-79)
[English actor]
The English Roscius
The Greatest English Actor
The Silver-tongued
The Whitfield of the Stage
Garrick, John. See:
DOUDY, REGINALD
Garrison, Frederick. See:
SINCLAIR, UPTON BEALL
Garrison, Joan. See:
NEUBAUER, WILLIAM ARTHUR
Garrison, Lieut. Frederick. See:
SINCLAIR, UPTON BEALL
Garrison, Theodosia. See:
FAULKS, MRS. FREDERIC J.
GARRISON, WEBB BLACK (1919-) [American Methodist clergyman and author]
Gary Webster
Garrity. See:
GERRITY, DAVID JAMES
GARROWAY, DAVID CUNNINGHAM (1913-) [American radio and television personality]
Dave Garroway
GARROWAY, HENRY STEPHENSON (1871-1956)
[British stage and motion picture actor]
Henry Stephenson
Garry. See also:
Gary
Garry Marsh. See:
GERAGHTY, LESLIE MARCH
Garry Moore. See:
MORFIT, THOMAS GARRISON
GARSON, GREER (1912?-)
[Irish actress]
The First Lady of Hollywood
GARST, DORIS SHANNON (1894-) [American author]
Shannon Garst

Garstang, Basil. See:
BRERETON, JOHN LE GAY
GARSTANG, JAMES GORDON (1927-) [British physical educationalist and author]
Jack Garstang
Garth. See:
TOWNSEND, GEORGE ALFRED
Garth Hale. See:
CUNNINGHAM, ALBERT BENJAMIN
Garve, Andrew. See:
WINTERTON, PAUL
Gary. See:
COOPER, FRANK J.
Garry
Gary Cooper, The Buck Private's. See:
MacARTHUR, DOUGLAS
GARY, ELBERT HENRY (1846-1927) [American lawyer and corporation official]
Judge Gary
Gary, John. See:
STRADER, JOHN GARY
GARY, MARTIN WITHERSPOON (1831-81) [American general officer]
The Bald Eagle
The Bald Eagle of Edgefield
Gary Romero. See:
CATSOS, NICHOLAS A.
Gary Webster. See:
GARRISON, WEBB BLACK
Gas, The Napoleon of. See:
ADDICKS, JOHN EDWARD O'SULLIVAN
GASCH, MARIE MANNING (1878?-) [American columnist, reporter and author]
Beatrice Fairfax
Gaseous Cassius. See:
CLAY, CASSIUS MARCELLUS, JR.
GASKELL, ELIZABETH CLEGHORN STEVENSON (1810-65) [English author]
Mrs. Gaskell
GASKOIN, CHARLES JACINTH BELLAIRS (fl. early 20th cent.) [British educator and author]
Arthur Merridew
Gaspar Poussin. See:
DUGHET, GASPAR
GASPAROTTI, ELIZABETH SEIFERT (1897-) [American author]
Elizabeth Seifert
GASSION, EDITH GIOVANNA (1915-63) [French singer and entertainer]
Edith Piaf
GASTON (1331-93) [Comte de Foix; French nobleman]
Phoebus
Gaston, Marie. See:
DAUDET, ALPHONSE
Gaston Vialis. See:
SIMENON, GEORGES
Gaston Viallis. See:
SIMENON, GEORGES
Gate. See:
Golden Gate Trinity, The
Gate of Righteousness (Bab-ed-din). See:
MOHAMMED, MIRZA ALI
Gate, The Poet of the Golden. See: KIRCHOFF, THEODORE
GATES, HORATIO (1728-1806) [American Revolutionary War general officer]
Granny Gates
The Hero of Saratoga
GATES, JOHN WARNE (1855-1911) [American industrialist; barbed wire entrepreneur]
Bet-a-million Gates
Moonshine Gates
The Wire King of America
GATLEY, DOROTHY (1902-) [American motion picture actress]
Ann Harding
Gatling Gun. See:
PARKER, JOHN HENRY
Gato. See:
BARBIERI, LEANDRO
GATTERMANN, EUGEN LUDWIG (1886-) [German

author]
Eugen Alban Corvin
A.M. Renner
GAUGUIN, EUGÈNE HENRI PAUL (1848-1903) [French painter and sculptor]
Paul Gauguin
GAULDEN, RAY (1914-) [American author]
Wesley Ray
Gaulonite, The. See: JUDAS OF GALILEE
Gauls, The Apostle of the. See: IRENAEUS, ST.
Gault, Mark. See: COURNOS, JOHN
Gaultier, Bon. See: MARTIN, SIR THEODORE
GAULTIER-GARGUILLE, HUGUES GUÉRU (c. 1573-1633) [French actor and comedian]
Fleschelles
GAUNT, BERNICE (1909-) [American singer, pianist and motion picture actress]
Shirley Ross
Gaunt, Michael. See: ROBERTSHAW, JAMES DENIS
GAUTAMA, SIDDHARTHA (568 B.C. ?-483 B.C. ?) [founder of Buddhism]
Buddha
The Enlightened
Sakya Muni
GAUTHIER-VILLARS, HENRI (1859-1931) [French novelist]
Willy
GAUTHIER-VILLARS, HENRI. See also: Willy
GAUTSCH, FRANÇOISE (1931-) [French motion picture actress]
Françoise Arnoul
Gavarni. See: CHEVALIER, SULPICE GUILLAUME
Gavarni, Paul. See: CHEVALIER, SULPICE GUILLAUME
Gavin Black. See: WYND, OSWALD MORRIS
Gavin Brock. See: LINDSAY, JOHN MAURICE
Gavin Holt. See: RODDA, CHARLES
GAVIN, JAMES MAURICE (1907-) [American general officer, author and business executive]
Jumping Jim
Gavin, John. See: GOLENOR, JOHN ANTHONY
Gavin Ogilvy. See: BARRIE, SIR JAMES MATTHEW
Gavira. See: CANO, ENRIQUE
Gawkey, Lord. See: GRENVILLE, RICHARD TEMPLE
Gawsworth, John. See: ARMSTRONG, TERENCE IAN FYTTON
Gay Head. See: HAUSER, MARGARET LOUISE
GAY, JOHN (1685-1732) [English poet and dramatist]
The Aesop of England
The Orpheus of Highwaymen
Gay, Joseph. See: BREVAL, JOHN DURANT
Gaylord, Glance. See: BRADLEY, WARREN IVES
Gaynor, Janet. See: GAINER, LAURA
Gaynor, Mitzi. See: VON GERBER, FRANCESCA MITZI MARLENE DE CHARNEY
GAZE, RICHARD (1917-) [English author]
John Gale
Gazul, Clara. See: MÉRIMÉE, PROSPER
GAZZARA, BIAGO ANTHONY (1930-) [American actor]
Ben Gazzara
Bennie Gazzara
Gearing-Thomas, G. See: NORWOOD, VICTOR GEORGE CHARLES

GEBHARD, COUNT OF HIRSCHBERG (died 1057) [Supreme Pontiff of Roman Catholic Church]
Pope Victor II
Geddes, Barbara Bel. See: LEWIS, BARBARA GEDDES
GEDDES, JENNY (fl. 1637) [Scottish vegetable seller and religious fanatic]
Jenny Hamilton
The Immortal Janet Geddes
Jenny Mein
Geerlink, Will. See: HOFDROP, WILLIAM PIM
GEERTS, GEERT. See: GERHARDS, GERHARD (GEERT GEERTS)
Geffery. See also:
Geoffrey
Jeffery
JEFFREY
Jeffrey
JEFFREYS
Joffrey
Geffery Broadbottom. See: STANHOPE, PHILIP DORMER
GEHMAN, BETSY HOLLAND (1932-) [American journalist and author]
Anne Klainikite
GEHMAN, RICHARD BOYD (1921-) [American author]
Frederick Christian
Martin Scott
GEHRIG, HENRY LOUIS (1903-41) [American professional baseball player]
The Iron Horse
The Iron Man of Baseball
Larruping Lou
Lou Gehrig
Geilles. See:
GILES
Giles
Herring, Geilles
GEIS, BERNARD. See: Stevens, Peter
GEIS, DARLENE STERN (fl. 1947-64) [American author]
Ralph Kelly
Jane London
GEIS, DARLENE STERN. See also: Stevens, Peter
GEISE, DR. OTTO (1857-) [German author]
Otto Von Homberg
GEISEL, THEODOR SEUSS (1904-) [American illustrator and author]
Theo LeSieg
Dr. Seuss
GEISHUSLER, OSWALD (1488-1552) [Swiss reformer]
Oswald Myconius
GELASIUS (died 496) [Supreme Pontiff of Roman Catholic Church]
Pope Gelasius I
St. Gelasius
Gelasius II, Pope. See: CONIUOLO, GIOVANNI
GELÉE, CLAUDE (1600-82) [French landscape painter]
Claude Lorraine
GELIEN, ART (1931-) [American motion picture actor]
Tab Hunter
GELLERS, IRVING (1907-) [American composer, pianist and arranger]
Irv Carroll
GELLIS, ROBERTA L. JACOBS (1927-) [American chemist, bacteriologist and author]
Leah Jacobs
Gellone, St. Guillaume de. See: GUILLAUME D'ORANGE
Gem of Normandy, The. See: AELFGIFA, EMMA
GENDRE, LOUIS (1919-) [French motion picture actor]
Louis Jourdan
Gene. See:
ADKINSON, HARVEY E.
AMMONS, EUGENE
BUCK, EDWARD EUGENE
CASEY, WESLEY EUGENE
GLEASON, EUGENE FRANKLIN
HOOKS, GAYLOR EUGENE
KELLY, EUGENE JOSEPH
KLEBE, CHARLES EUGENE
KRUPA, EUGENE BERTRAM
LITTLER, EUGENE
LOCKHART, EUGENE
MORRA, EGIDIO

NOVELLO, EUGENE
SEDRIC, EUGENE PAUL
SHUFORD, CECIL EUGENE
STONE, EUGENIA
TUNNEY, JAMES JOSEPH
Gene Allen. See:
SUFANA, EUGENE
Gene Barry. See:
KLASS, EUGENE
Gene Dorant. See:
LENT, DORA GENEVA
Gene Fowler. See:
DEVLAN, EUGENE
Gene Gerrard. See:
O'SULLIVAN, EUGENE
Gene Inyart. See:
NAMOVICZ, GENE INYART
Gene Nelson. See:
BERG, GENE
Gene Raymond. See:
GUION, RAYMOND
Gene Willadsen. See:
LYNN, JANE THURSTON
General. See:
BOOTH, WILLIAM
COXEY, JACOB SECHLER
WELCH, RUFUS
General of the Armada, Captain. See:
COLUMBUS, CHRISTOPHER
General Baïonette. See:
CHASSÉ, DAVID HENDRIK, BARON
General of China, The Christian . See:
FENG YU-HSIANG
Général Entrepreneur, Le (The Contractor General). See: BONAPARTE, NAPOLEON
General Ike. See:
EISENHOWER, DAVID DWIGHT
General Lew Wallace. See:
WALLACE, LEWIS
General of the Mackerel Brigade, The. See:
McCLELLAN, GEORGE BRINTON
General Manager of the War, The. See:
SMITH, WALTER BEDELL
General Perron. See:
AULLIER, PIERRE
General for Runaway Slaves, Attorney. See:
CHASE, SALMON PORTLAND
General, The. See:
SINATRA, FRANCIS ALBERT
General, The Boy. See:
CUSTER, GEORGE ARMSTRONG
General, The Contractor (Le Général Entrepreneur). See: BONAPARTE, NAPOLEON
General, The Corsican. See:
BONAPARTE, NAPOLEON
General, The Doughboy's. See:
BRADLEY, OMAR NELSON
General, The Muscovy. See:
DALYELL (DALZELL), THOMAS
General, The Translator. See:
HOLLAND, PHILEMON
General Tom Thumb. See:
STRATTON, CHARLES SHERWOOD
Generall, The Witch Finder. See: HOPKINS, MATTHEW
Generation, The Voice of the Hangover. See:
O'HARA, JOHN HENRY
Generous, The. See:
KHUSRAU (CHOSROES) I
Genessee, The White Woman of the. See:
JEMISON, MARY
Geneva Bull, The. See:
MARSHALL, STEPHEN
Geneva, Citizen of. See:
ROUSSEAU, JEAN-JACQUES
Genevieve Ulmar. See:
COBB, WELDON J.
GENGA, ANNIBALE SERMATTEI DELLA (1760-1829) [Supreme Pontiff of Roman Catholic Church]
Pope Leo XII
Genghis Khan (Precious Warrior). See: TEMUJIN
Genghis Khan (Very Mighty Ruler). See:

TEMUJIN
Genial Reuben. See:
KOLB, REUBEN FRANCIS
Genial Showman, The. See:
BROWNE, CHARLES FARRAR
Genius, Adolf Hitler's Evil. See: BORMANN, MARTIN
Genius C.B. See:
BRONTË, CHARLOTTE
Genius of Maryland, The Evil. See: CLAIBORNE, WILLIAM
Genius of Motordom, The. See:
FORD, HENRY
Genius of Romance, The. See:
HAWTHORNE, NATHANIEL
Genius of the German Horror Camps, The Evil. See:
HIMMLER, HEINRICH
Genius on a Low Budget. See:
KRAMER, STANLEY E.
Genius, The Universal. See:
PETTY, WILLIAM
Genoa, The Liberator of. See:
DORIA, ANDREA
GENSFLEISCH, JOHAN (c. 1396-c. 1468) [German inventor of printing from movable type]
The Father of Printing
Johan Gutenberg
Gent., Thomas Morton of Clifford's Inn, See:
MORTON, THOMAS
Gentil Belleau, Le. See:
BELLEAU, REMI
Gentileschi, Artemisia. See:
LOMI, ARTEMISIA
Gentileschi, Orazio. See:
LOMI, ORAZIO
Gentiles, The Apostle of the. See: SAUL
Gentle Craft, The Laureate of the. See:
SACHS, HANS
Gentle Lochiel. See:
CAMERON, DONALD, OF LOCHIEL
Gentle Shepherd of Ohio, The. See: GROSVENOR, CHARLES HENRY
Gentle Shepherd, The. See:
GRENVILLE, GEORGE
Gentleman. See:
JACKSON, JOHN
PALMER, JOHN
SMITH, WILLIAM
Gentleman, America's First. See: ARTHUR, CHESTER ALAN
Gentleman, Arthur the. See:
ARTHUR, CHESTER ALAN
Gentleman from Hale, The. See:
TUNSTALL, ALFRED MOORE
Gentleman George. See:
BARRETT, GEORGE HOOKER (HORTON)
PENDLETON, GEORGE HUNT
Gentleman in Europe, The First. See:
GEORGE IV
Gentleman Jim. See:
CORBETT, JAMES JOHN
"Gentleman Joe," By the Author of. See:
BADGER, JOSEPH E., JR.
Gentleman of Connecticut, A. See:
HOPKINS, DR. LEMUEL
Gentleman of Fashion, The First. See: LELONG, LUCIEN
Gentleman of Maryland, A. See:
BRACKENRIDGE, HUGH HENRY
Gentleman of Oxford, A. See:
SHELLEY, PERCY BYSSHE
Gentleman of Swing, The Sentimental. See:
DORSEY, THOMAS
Gentleman of the Army, A. See:
STEELE, SIR RICHARD
Gentleman of the Land, First. See: ARTHUR, CHESTER ALAN
Gentleman of Virginia, By a. See:
DAWSON, WILLIAM
Gentleman Smuggler, The. See:
LAFITTE, JEAN
Gentleman, The Northumbrian. See: TEGNER, HENRY STUART

Gentleman, The Sentimental. See:
DORSEY, THOMAS
Gentleman, The Sunday. See:
FOE, DANIEL
Gentleman with a Duster, A.
See: BEGBIE, HAROLD
Gentlemanly Johnny. See:
BURGOYNE, JOHN
GENTRY, BYRON B. (1913-)
[American professional football player, attorney and author]
Norman Galway
Geoffrey. See:
Coffin, Geoffrey
Geffery
JEFFERY
Jeffery
JEFFREY
Jeffrey
JEFFREYS
Joffrey
Geoffrey, Charles. See:
MULLER, CHARLES GEORGE
Geoffrey Coffin. See:
MASON, FRANCIS VAN WYCK
Geoffrey Corson. See:
IRVING, WASHINGTON
SHOLL, ANNA McCLURE
Geoffrey Crayon. See:
IRVING, WASHINGTON
Geoffrey Crayon, Gent. See:
IRVING, WASHINGTON
Geoffrey Johns. See:
WARNER, GEORGE GEOFFREY JOHN
Geoffrey Randolph. See:
ELLIS, EDWARD SYLVESTER
Geoffrey Swayne. See:
CAMPION, SIDNEY RONALD
Geoffrey, Theodate. See:
WAYMAN, DOROTHY
Geography, The Father of American. See:
MORSE, JEDIDIAH
Geography, The Father of Modern. See:
KREMER, GERHARD
Geologist of Michigan, The Boy. See:
HOUGHTON, DOUGLASS
Geology, The Father of American. See:
MACLURE, WILLIAM
Geology, The Father of English.
See: SMITH, WILLIAM
Geometer, The Great. See:
APOLLONIUS OF PERGA
Geong, Hin me. See:
ARMITAGE, JOHN
Geophysics, The Father of American. See:
GOLYER, EVERETTE LEE DE
Georg Bauer. See:
AGRICOLA, GEORGIUS
George. See:
BARRINGTON, WALDRON
HOPLEY-WOOLRICH, CORNELL GEORGE
NASH, FRANK
RAPP, JOHANN GEORG
GEORGE I (1660-1727) [King of England]
The Turnip-hoer
GEORGE III (1738-1820) [King of England]
Farmer George
The Farmer King
GEORGE IV (1762-1830) [King of Great Britain and Ireland and King of Hanover]
The Beau of Princes
The Fat Adonis of Forty (or Fifty)
The First Gentleman in Europe
Fum the Fourth
George Augustus Frederick
The Prince of Princes
GEORGE V (1865-1936) [King of Great Britain and Northern Ireland and Emperor of India]
George Frederick Ernest Albert
The Sailor Prince
George A. Birmingham. See:
HANNAY, JAMES OWEN
George Adams. See:
LENGYEL, GEZA
George Anderson. See:
GROOM, ARTHUR

George Anderson. See:
GROOM, ARTHUR WILLIAM
WEISSMAN, JACK
George Archer. See:
HARDWICK, ARCHER
George Archibald, Mrs. See:
PALMER, ANNA CAMPBELL
George Arliss. See:
ANDREWS, GEORGE AUGUSTUS
George Bagby. See:
STEIN, AARON MARC
George Balanchine. See:
BALANCHIVADZE, GEORGEI MELITONOVITCH
George Beaton. See:
BRENAN, GERALD
George Bellairs. See:
BLUNDELL, HAROLD
George, Black (Karadjordje). See: CZERNY, GEORGE
George B. Lee. See:
HARBAUGH, THOMAS CHALMERS
George Bogle. See:
DUKINFIELD, WILLIAM CLAUDE
George Braith. See:
BRAITHWAITE, GEORGE
George Brent. See:
NOLAN, GEORGE
George, Brother. See:
LIBERACE, GEORGE J.
George Burns. See:
BIRNBAUM, NATHAN
George Challis. See:
FAUST, FREDERICK SCHILLER
GEORGE, CHARLIE (1912-) [American professional baseball player]
The Greek
GEORGE, DAVID LLOYD. See:
Big Three, The
George Douglas. See:
BROWN, GEORGE DOUGLAS
George Drayne. See:
McCULLEY, JOHNSTON
GEORGE, DUKE OF GORDON (1770-1836) [British nobleman]
The Cock of the North
George Egerton. See:
BRIGHT, MRS. MARY CHAVELITA DUNNE
George Eliot. See:
CROSS, MARY ANN (MARIAN) EVANS
George E. Sheldon. See:
STAHL, LEROY
George E. Stone. See:
STEIN, GEORGE
George, Farmer. See:
GEORGE III
George F. Harrington. See:
BAKER, WILLIAM MUMFORD
George Fitz-Boodle. See:
THACKERAY, WILLIAM MAKEPEACE
George Fleming. See:
FLETCHER, JULIA CONSTANCE
George Forth. See:
FREDERIC, HAROLD
George F. Preston. See:
WARREN, JOHN BYRNE LEICESTER
George, Four-eyed. See:
MEADE, GEORGE GORDON
George Fyfield. See:
FOGG, HENRY GEORGE WITHAM
George Garland. See:
ROARK, GARLAND
George, Gentleman; See:
BARRETT, GEORGE HOOKER (HORTON)
PENDLETON, GEORGE HUNT
George, Gladys. See:
CLARE, GLADYS
George Gordon. See:
BALDWIN, CHARLES CRITTENTON
George Graveley. See:
EDWARDS, GEORGE GRAVELEY
George Handy. See:
HENDLEMAN, GEORGE JOSEPH
George, Harry St. See:
RATHBONE, ST.

GEORGE HENRY
George Hembert Westley. See:
HIPPISLEY, GEORGE
GEORGE, HENRY (1839-97)
[American economist and author]
The Single Taxer
George, Honest. See:
MONK, GEORGE
George K. Arthur See:
BREST, GEORGE K. ARTHUR
George Kay. See:
LAMBERT, ERIC
George Kenny. See:
WHITCOMB, KENNETH G.
George Knowall. See:
O'NUALLAIN, BRIAN
George Leather. See:
SWALLOW, NORMAN
George L. Eaton. See:
VERRAL, CHARLES SPAIN
George, Live Oak. See:
LAW, GEORGE
George London. See:
BURNSON, GEORGE
George, Lonesome. See:
GOBEL, GEORGE LESLIE
George Ludlow. See:
KAY, ERNEST
George, Mademoiselle. See:
WEIMAR, MARGUERITE JOSÉPHINE
George, Marion E. See:
BENJAMIN, CLAUDE MAX EDWARD POHLMAN
George Measday. See:
SODERBERG, PERCY MEASDAY
George Metcalf. See:
JOHNSON, GEORGE METCALF
George Metesky. See:
HOFFMAN, ABBIE
George, Miss. See:
SIDUS, GEORGINA
George Montgomery. See:
LENZ, GEORGE MONTGOMERY
George Moran. See:
Two Black Crows
George Nelson. See:
GILLIS, LESTER M.
George O'Hanlon. See:
RICE, GEORGE
George, Old. See:
MONK, GEORGE
George Oliver. See:
ONIONS, GEORGE OLIVER
George Orwell. See:
BLAIR, ERIC
George Otis. See:
MELLEN, IDA MAY
George Owen Baxter. See:
FAUST, FREDERICK SCHILLER
George Pagnanelli. See:
DEROUNIAN, ARTHUR
George Powers. See:
INFIELD, GLENN BERTON
George Preedy. See:
LONG, MRS. GABRIELLE MARGARET VERE CAMPBELL
George Psalmanazar. See:
UNKNOWN
George Richmond. See:
BRISTER, RICHARD
GEORGE, ROBERT ESMONDE GORDON (1890-)
[New Zealand educator and author]
Robert Sencourt
George Robey. See:
WADE, GEORGE EDWARD
George Rosey. See:
ROSENBERG, GEORGE
George Rostrevor. See:
HAMILTON, GEORGE ROSTREVOR
George, Round House. See:
LEHMAN, GEORGE
GEORGE, ST. (died c. 303)
[Christian martyr and patron saint of England]
The Christian Hero
The Red Cross Knight
George Sand. See:
DUDEVANT, AMANDINE AURORE LUCIE DUPIN, "BARONNE"
George Santayana. See:
BORRAS, JORGE

AUGUSTÍN NICOLAS RUIZ DE SANTAYANA Y
George Seferis. See:
SEFERIADES, GIORGOS STYLIANOU
George Selden. See:
THOMPSON, GEORGE SELDEN
George Selmark. See:
SELDONSTRUSS, LESLIE
George Sidney. See:
GREENFIELD, SAMMY
George S. Kaine. See:
MORRIS, CHARLES SMITH
George Southcote. See:
ASHTON, SIR GEORGE GREY
George Stevens (Kingfish). See:
GOSDEN, FREEMAN F.
George Stolterfoth. See:
BONUS, ARTHUR
George, Tardy. See:
McCLELLAN, GEORGE BRINTON
George the Baker. See:
LEHMAN, GEORGE
George, The Chevalier de St. See: STUART, JAMES FRANCIS EDWARD
George, Uncle. See:
PERKINS, GEORGE DOUGLAS
THOMAS, GEORGE HENRY
George Wallington. See:
FIGLIA, GIORGIO
GEORGE, WALTER LIONEL (1882-1926) [English novelist and short story writer]
W. L. George
George Warwick. See:
DEEPING, GEORGE WARWICK
George Washington. See:
BLOOM, SOL
THOMAS, GEORGE HENRY
WASHINGTON, GEORGE
George Whitley. See:
CHANDLER, A. BERTRAM
George, Wilma. See:
CROWTHER, WILMA BERYL
George Wilson. See:
BLAND, GEORGE
George Windle Sandys. See:
CRAWFURD, OSWALD
George Winslow. See:
WENZLAFF, GEORGE
George Woden. See:
SLANEY, GEORGE WILSON
Georges Caraman. See:
SIMENON, GEORGES
Georges D'Isly. See:
SIMENON, GEORGES
Georges Guetary. See:
WORLOOU, LAMBROS
Georges Martin Georges. See:
SIMENON, GEORGES
Georges Sim. See:
SIMENON, GEORGES
Georgia Bar, The Scholar of the. See: HILL, WALTER BARNARD
Georgia Craig. See:
DERN, PEGGY GADDIS
Georgia, Distinguished Citizen of. See:
BERRY, MARTHA McCHESNEY
Georgia Fire-eater, The. See:
TOOMBS, ROBERT
Georgian Laureate, The. See:
ABERCROMBIE, LASCELLES
Georgia Peach, The. See:
COBB, TYRUS RAYMOND
Georgie. See:
JESSEL, GEORGE ALBERT
Georgie Auld. See:
ALTWERGER, JOHN
Georgie Fame. See:
POWELL, CLIVE
Georgie Sheldon, Mrs. See:
DOWNS, SARAH ELIZABETH
Georgina Masson. See:
JOHNSON, MARION GEORGINA WIKELEY
GERAGHTY, LESLIE MARCH

(1902-) [British motion picture actor]
Garry Marsh
Gerald. See:
HEARD, HENRY FITZ GERALD
Gerald, Jim. See:
GUENOD, JACQUES
Gerald McDow. See:
SCORTIA, THOMAS NICHOLAS
Gerald Tolmage. See:
GARDNER, MAURICE
Gerald Tyrwhitt. See:
BERNERS, GERALD HUGH TYRWHITT-WILSON, 14TH BARON
Gerald, Ziggy. See:
ZEIGERMAN, GERALD
Geralda, Lady. See:
BRONTË, ANNE
Geraldine Brooks. See:
STROOCK, GERALDINE
Geraldine Fleming. See:
CORYELL, JOHN RUSSELL
Geraldine, The Fair. See:
FITZGERALD, LADY ELIZABETH
GERARD (c. 1040-c. 1120) [Founder of the Order of St. John of Jerusalem]
The Blessed
Gerard de Nerval. See:
LABRUNIE, GERALD
GERARD, JEAN IGNACE ISIDORE (1803-47) [French caricaturist and book illustrator]
Grandville
Gerard Montgomery. See:
MOULTRIE, JOHN
Gérard Souzay. See:
TISSERAND, GÉRARD MARCEL
Gerardus Magnus. See:
GROOTE (GROOT) (GROETE), GERHARD
Geray, Steve. See:
GYERGYAY, STEFAN
GERHADR OF BURGUNDY (died 1061) [Supreme Pontiff of Roman Catholic Church]
Pope Nicholas II
GERHARDS, GERHARD (GEERT) GEERTS (1466?-1536) [Dutch scholar and humanist]
Desiderius Erasmus
Intellectual Father of the Reformation
The Prince of the Humanists
Gerhardus Mercator. See:
KREMER, GERHARD
GERICH, VALENTINE (1898-) [American composer and accordionist]
Val Valentine
Germain D'Antibes. See:
SIMENON, GEORGES
German-American Journalists, The Nestor of the. See:
PREETORIUS, EMIL
German Criticism, The Father of. See: LESSING, GOTTHOLD EPHRAIM
German Garden," By the Author of "Elizabeth and Her. See:
BEAUCHAMP, MARY ANNETTE, COUNTESS RUSSELL (MRS. HENNING ARNIM
German Horror Camps, The Evil Genius of the. See:
HIMMLER, HEINRICH
German Humanism, The Father of. See:
HUYSMAN, ROELOF
German Literature, The Father of. See:
LESSING, GOTTHOLD EPHRAIM
German Milton, The. See:
KLOPSTOCK, FRIEDRICH GOTTLIEB
German Plato, The. See:
JACOBI, FRIEDRICH HEINRICH
German Poetry, The Father of. See: OPITZ, MARTIN
German Rationalism, The Father of. See:
SEMLER, JOHANN SALOMO
German, The. See.
LOUIS II

German Trismegistus, The.
See: RUDOLF (RUDOLPH II)
German Zola, The. See: KRETZER, MARY
Germanicus. See: DUNNER, JOSEPH
Germans, The Apostle to the. See: GULDIN, JOHN C.
Germany, The Achilles of. See: ALBERT III
Germany, The Aesop of. See: LESSING, GOTTHOLD EPHRAIM
Germany, The Apostle of. See: WINIFRED (WYNFRITH)
Germany, The Cicero of. See: JOHANN
Germany, The Dryden of. See: OPITZ, MARTIN
Germany, The Fénelon of. See: LAVATER, JOHANN CASPAR
Germany, The Hector of. See: JOACHIM II
Germany, The Milton of. See: KLOPSTOCK, FRIEDRICH GOTTLIEB
Germany, The Nero of. See: WENCESLAUS IV
Germany, The Rabelais of. See: FISCHART, JOHANN BAPTIST
Germany, The Red Knight of. See: VON RICHTHOFEN, BARON MANFRED
Germany, The Sardanapalus of. See: WENCESLAUS IV
Germany, The Shakespeare of. See: VON KOTZEBUE, AUGUST FREDERICK FERDINAND
Germany, The Teacher of. See: SCHWARZERT, PHILIPP
Germany, The Ulysses of. See: ALBERT III
Germany, The Voltaire of. See: BAUER, BRUNO
WIELAND, CHRISTOPHER MARTIN
Germany's Greatest Modern Playwright. See: HAUPTMANN, GERHART
GERMAR, WILLIAM HERBERT (1911-)[American journalist, educator and author]
Herb Germar
Gerone Pilio. See: WHITFIELD, JOHN HUMPHREYS
Geronimo. See: GOYATHLAY
JOHN OF AUSTRIA
Gerrard, Gene. See: O'SULLIVAN, EUGENE
GERRITY, DAVID JAMES (1923-) [American author]
Garrity
Calli Goran
Mitch Hardin
Gerry. See: Jerrie
Jerry
MULLIGAN, GERALD JOSEPH
GERRY, PETER GOELET (1879-) [American politician; senator and congressman from Rhode Island]
The Millionaire
Gerry Travis. See: TRIMBLE, LOUIS P.
GERSON, JEAN CHARLIER DE (1363-1429) [French theologian and mystic]
Doctor Christianissimus
GERSTINE, JOHN (1915-) [American investment consultant and author]
Jack Gerstine
Gertie Gitana. See: ROSS, GERTRUDE MARY
Gertrude. See: LAWRENCE-KLASEN, ALEXANDRE DAGMAR
Gertrued Kingston. See: KONSTAM, GERTRUDE
GERTRUDE OF HELFTA, ST. (1256-1311) [German churchwoman and mystic]

The Great
Gertrude von Schwarzenfeld. See: COCHRANE DE ALENCAR, GERTRUDE E. L.
Gert W. Morrison. See: STRATEMEYER, EDWARD L.
GESSNER, KONRAD VON (1516-65) [Swiss naturalist and bibliographer]
The Father of Universal Bibliography
The Modern Pliny
Gesù, Giuseppe del (Giuseppe of Jesus). See: GUARNIERI, GIUSEPPE ANTONIO
Gettysburg, The Hero of the Battle of. See: BURNS, JOHN
GHAZNI. See: MAHMUD OF GHAZNI
GHENT. See: HENRY OF GHENT
Ghent, The Brewer of. See: VAN ARTEVELDE, JACOB
Ghetto Poet, The. See: WINCHEVSKY, MORRIS
Ghiberti, Lorenzo. See: BUONAC-CORSO, LORENZO DI CIONE DI SER
GHIKA, HELENA (1829-88) [Rumanian author and traveler]
Dora d'Istria
Ghine, Wunnakyawhtin U Ohn. See: MAURICE, DAVID JOHN KERR
Ghirlandajo. See: BIGORDI, RIDOLFO; BIGORDI, TOMMASO
GHISLANDI, FRA VITTORE (1655-1743) [Italian painter and Francescan monk]
Fra Galgario
Fra Paolotto
GHISLIERI, MICHELE (1504-72) [Supreme Pontiff of Roman Catholic Church]
Pope Pius V
St. Pius
Ghost, The. See: GREELEY, HORACE
Ghost, The Galloping. See: GRANGE, HAROLD EDWARD
Gia Scala. See: SCOGLIO, GIOVANNA
Giacomo Meyerbeer. See: BEER, JACOB LIEBMANN
Giant-killer, Jack the. See: DEMPSEY, WILLIAM HARRISON; JACKSON, ROBERT HOUGHWOUT; RANDOLPH, JOHN
Giant of Alexandria, The Little. See: NELSON, KNUTE
Giant of Literature, The. See: JOHNSON, DR. SAMUEL
Giant of Populism, The Intellectual. See: ALLEN, WILLIAM VINCENT
Giant of the Hills, The. See: CRAWFORD, ETHAN ALLEN
Giant, The Black. See: WEBSTER, DANIEL
Giant, The Good. See: DOYLE, SIR ARTHUR CONAN
Giant, The Little. See: DOUGLAS, STEPHEN ARNOLD; LEWIS, DAVID JOHN
Giant, The Massachusetts. See: WEBSTER, DANIEL
Giant, The White Mountain. See: CRAWFORD, ETHAN ALLEN
Gibb, Lee. See: Froy, Herald
Gibbon, Lewis Grassic. See: MITCHELL, JAMES LESLIE
GIBBONS, MRS. CEDRIC (1901-62) [American costume designer]
Irene
GIBBONS, ORLANDO (1583-1625) [English composer and organist]
The English Palestrina
GIBBS, COSMO HAMILTON (1877-1942) [British

novelist, dramatist and short story writer]
Cosmo Hamilton
Gibbs, Henry. See:
RUMBOLD-GIBBS, HENRY ST. JOHN CLAIR
GIBBS, JOHN (1810-89) [American actor]
John Gilbert
GIBBS, KATHARINE (1903-) [American stage and motion picture actress]
Kay Francis
GIBBS, RAPHAEL SANFORD (1912-) [American information officer and author]
Rafe Gibbs
GIBBS-SMITH, CHARLES HARVARD (1909-) [British aircraft authority and writer]
Charles Harvard
Gibbs, Terry. See:
GUBENKO, JULIUS
GIBSON, ALBERT ANDREW (1913-61) [American composer and arranger]
Andy Gibson
GIBSON, EDWARD RICHARD (1892-1962) [American rodeo champion and Western motion picture actor]
Hoot Gibson
Gibson, Harry Clark. See:
HUBLER, RICHARD GIBSON
Gibson, Josephine. See:
HINE, SESYLE JOSLIN
Gibson, Katharine. See:
WICKS, KATHARINE GIBSON
GIBSON, ROBERT (1935-) [American professional baseball player]
Bob Gibson
GIBSON, SAMUEL BRAXTON (1900-) [American professional baseball player]
Hoot Gibson
Gid. See:
WALDROP, GIDEON
GIFFORD, CHARLES L. (1871-1947) [American politician; congressman from Massachusetts]
Cranberry Gifford
GIFFORD, FRANKLIN KENT (1861-) [American Unitarian clergyman and author]
Richard Brinsley Newman
GIFFORD, JAMES NOBLE (c. 1897-1937) [American author]
Eliot Brewster
Warren Howard
Gift to the West, Harvard's. See:
CUTTING, BRONSON
Gig Young. See:
BARR, BYRON
Giggles. See:
VON ZELL, HARRY
Gigi. See:
PERREAU-SAUSSINE, GHISLAINE
Gil. See:
GILL
Gill
HODGES, GILBERT RAY
PATTEN, WILLIAM GILBERT
SLOTE, GILBERT
Gil Evans. See:
GREEN, IAN ERNEST GILMORE
Gil North. See:
HORNE, GEOFFREY
Gilbert. See:
O'SULLIVAN, RAYMOND
PATTEN, WILLIAM GILBERT
ROBINSON, WILLIAM STEVENS
GILBERT, CASS (1859-1934) [American architect]
The Father of the Skyscraper
Gilbert Emery. See:
POTTLE, GILBERT EMERY BEMSLEY
Gilbert Hastings. See:
FARRELL, GILBERT HASTINGS
Gilbert, John. See:
GIBBS, JOHN
PRINGLE, JOHN
GILBERT, MARIE DOLORES ELIZA ROSANNA (1818?-61) [Irish dancer and adventuress]
The Countess of Landsfield
The International Bad Girl of the Mid-Victorians

Lola Montez
The Woman in Black
Gilbert, Miriam. See:
PRESBERG, MIRIAM GOLDSTEIN
Gilbert, Nan. See:
GILBERTSON, MILDRED GEIGER
Gilbert, Paul. See:
MACMAHON, PAUL
GILBERT, RODRIGUE GABRIEL (1941-) [Canadian professional hockey player]
Rod Gilbert
Gilbert Roland. See:
ALONSO, LUIS ANTONIO DAMASO DE
GILBERT, RUTH GALLARD AINSWORTH (1908-) [British writer]
Ruth Ainsworth
GILBERT, SIR JOHN (1817-97) [English painter and illustrator]
The Scott of Painting
GILBERT, SIR WILLIAM SCHWENCK (1836-1911) [British parodist, playwright and librettist]
Bab
GILBERTSON, MILDRED GEIGER (1908-) [American radio and television director and author]
Nan Gilbert
GILCHRIST, ALAN W. (1912-) [British teacher and author]
Alan Cowan
GILCHRIST, BETH BRADFORD (1879-1957) [American author]
John Prescott Earl
Gilda Gray. See:
MICHAELSKA, MARIANNE
GILDAS (GILDUS) (c. 516-c. 570) [British historian]
The British Jeremiah
Gildas the Wise. See:
SAPIENS (BADONICUS), GILDAS
Gildersleeve, Professor. See:
URNER, NATHAN DANE
GILDUS. See:
GILDAS (GILDUS)
GILES [Giles]. See also:
Geilles
Giles, Blessed. See:
AEGIDIUS OF ASSISI
Giles, Gordon A. See:
BINDER, OTTO OSCAR
GILES, JOANNA ELDER. See:
Magill, Marcus
Giles, Johnny. See:
MELLENBRUCH, GILES EDWARD
Giles, Kris. See:
NIELSEN, HELEN BERNIECE
Giles Merton. See:
CURRAN, MONA ELISA
GILFORD, CHARLES BERNARD (1920-) [American educator and writer]
Donald Campbell
Douglas Farr
Elizabeth Gregory
GILG. See:
TSCHUDI, AEGIDIUS (GILG)
Gill. See:
Gil
Odell, Gill
GILL, RALPH (1919-) [American composer and singer]
Rusty Gill
GILL, TRAVISS. See:
Odell, Gill
Gillars, Mildred Elizabeth. See:
SISK, MILDRED ELIZABETH
GILLESE, JOHN PATRICK (1920-) [Irish author]
Dale O'Hara
John A. Starr
GILLESPIE, JOHN BIRKS (1917-) [American jazz musician (trumpet, arranger, singer and leader)]
Dizzy Gillespie
GILLETE, HARPER LEE (1884-1941) [American bullfighter]
Harper Lee
GILLETT, FREDERICK HUNTINGTON (1851-1935) [American politician; con-

gressman from Massachusetts]
The Father of the House
GILLETTE, LELAND J. (1912-)
[American composer, arranger, singer and producer]
Enid Bergdahl
Gillis, Ann. See:
O'CONNOR, ALMA
GILLIS, LESTER M. (1908-34)
[American gangster]
Baby Face Nelson
George Nelson
Public Enemy No. 1
GILLMORE. See also:
GILMER
GILMORE
Gilmore
GILLMORE, RUFUS HAMILTON (1879-1935) [American novelist]
Rufus Hamilton
GILMAN, CAROLINE HOWARD (1794-1888) [American poet, essayist and novelist]
Mrs. Clarissa Packard
Gilman, Dorothy. See:
BUTTERS, DOROTHY GILMAN
Gilman, Wenona. See:
ENTON, DR. HARRY
GILMER. See:
GILLMORE
GILMORE
Gilmore
GILMER, ELIZABETH MERIWETHER (1870-1951) [American author and journalist]
Dorothy Dix
GILMORE (Gilmore). See also:
GILLMORE
GILMER
GILMORE, JAMES ROBERTS (1822-1903) [American novelist and abolitionist]
Edmund Kirke
Gilmore, Marian. See:
DEY, FREDERICK VAN RENSSELAER
GILMORE, PATRICK SARSFIELD (1829-92) [American-Irish bandmaster and composer]
Louis Lambert
GILPIN, BERNARD (1517-83) [English clergyman and philanthropist]
The Apostle of the North
The Father of the Poor
Gilson, Jef. See:
QUIEVREUX, JEAN-FRANÇOIS
GILZEAN, ELIZABETH HOUGHTON BLANCHET (1913-) [Canadian nurse, interior decorator and author]
Elizabeth Houghton
Mary Hunton
Gimlet Eye, Old. See:
BUTLER, SMEDLEY DARLINGTON
Gimpy, Old. See:
EVANS, ROBLEY DUNGLISON
Gin, The Father of the Cotton. See: WHITNEY, ELI
Gina Bell. See:
BALZANO, JEANNE KOPPEL
Gina Bell-Zano. See:
BALZANO, JEANNE KOPPEL
Gina Malo. See:
FLYNN, JANET
Ginger Rogers. See:
McMATH, VIRGINIA KATHERINE
Ginger Snap Name, The Girl With the. See:
PITTS, ZASU
Gink. See:
HENDRICK, HARVEY
Ginny. See:
BROWN, VIRGINIA SHARPE
Jinny
Ginny Gorman. See:
KANTO, PETER
GINSBERG, SOL (1885-1963) [Russian-American composer, violinist and pianist]
Violinsky
GINTER, LEWIS (1824-97) [American Civil War general officer]
The Fighting Commissary

GINZBERG, ASCHER (1856-1927) [Russian author]
Achad Ha-am (One of the People)
GIORDANO, LUCA (1632-1705) [Neapolitan painter]
Fa Presto (Hurry Up)
Giorgione da Castelfranco. See: BARBARELLI, GIORGIO
Giorgione, Il. See: BARBARELLI, GIORGIO
Giotto. See: BONDONE, GIOTTO DI
Giovane, Il (The Younger). See: PALMA, JACOPO
Giovane, Palma (Young Palma). See: PALMA, JACOPO
GIOVANNI. See: FLORIO, JOHN (GIOVANNI)
Giovanni Bonaventura. See: FIDANZA, GIOVANNI DI
Giovanni da Fiesole. See: PIETRO, GUIDO DI
Giovanni Leone. See: ALWAZZAN (ALWEZAZ), ALHASSAN IBN MOHAMMED
GIOVANNONE, ANTHONY J. (1923-) [American composer and accordionist]
Chatta Johnson
GIPP, GEORGE (1896-1920) [American football player]
The Gipper
Gipsy. See: Gypsy
SMITH, RODNEY
Gipsy Boy, The. See: SMITH, RODNEY
Gipsy Glenn. See: BURTON, JENNIE DAVIS
GIRALDI, GIOVANNI BATTISTA (1504-73) [Italian novelist and tragic poet]
Cinthio (Cintio)
Girard. See: COLLINS, HERMAN LEROY
GIRARD, ANTOINE (died 1626) [French quack doctor and entertainer]
Tabarin
GIRARD, GABRIELLE (1926-) [French motion picture actress]
Daniele Delorme
GIRARD, PHILIPPE (fl. 1618) [French quack doctor]
Mondor
GIRAUDOUX, HIPPOLYTE JEAN (1882-1944) [French novelist and playwright]
Jean Giraudoux
Giri. See: VARAHAGIRI, VENKATA GIRI
Girl of the Films, The Outdoor. See: VALLI, VIRGINIA
Girl of the Mid-Victorians, The International Bad. See: GILBERT, MARIE DOLORES ELIZA ROSANNA
Girl, The Box Office. See: MICHAELSKA, MARIANNE
Girl, The It. See: BOW, CLARA
Girl, The Moon Over the Mountain See: SMITH, KATHRYN ELIZABETH
Girl, The O. Henry. See: AYRES, AGNES
Girl, The Oomph. See: SHERIDAN, CLARA LOU
Girl, The Original Bathing. See: STEADMAN, VERA
Girl, The Original Glamour. See: GOODMAN, THEODOSIA
Girl, The Original Radio. See: DE LEATH, VAUGHN
Girl, The Poor Little Rich. See: VANDERBILT, GLORIA
Girl, The Sarong. See: KAUMEYER, DOROTHY
Girl, The Screen's Bad. See: WEST, MAE
Girl, The Sweater. See: TURNER, JULIA JEAN MILDRED FRANCES
Girl, The Two-Gun. See: GUINAN, MARY LOUISE

CECELIA
Girl We Would Like to take a Slow Boat Back to the States With, The. See: VON KAPPELHOFF, DORIS
Girl With the Ginger Snap Name, The. See: PITTS, ZASU
Girls. See: Warner Girls, The
GIRON, FRANCISCO (1936-) [Venezuelan bullfighter]
Curro Girón
Gironde, The Fury of the. See: TERWAGNE, ANNE JOSEPH
GIRTIN, THOMAS (1913-) [British author]
Tom Girtin
GIRTY, SIMON (1741-1818) [American frontiersman, scout and traitor]
The Great Renegade
The White Savage
Gish, Dorothy. See: GUICHE, DOROTHY DE
Gish, Lillian. See: GUICHE, LILLIAN DE
GIST. See: GUESS (GIST), GEORGE
Gitana, Gertie. See: ROSS, GERTRUDE MARY
Gitanillo de Triana. See: REYES, FRANCISCO VEGA DE LOS
Gitanillo de Triana II. See: REYES, RAFAEL VEGA DE LOS
GITTINGS, JO GRENVILLE MANTON (1919-) [British broadcasting official and author]
Jo Manton
GIULIANI, PETER REBULI (1210/15-77) [Supreme Pontiff of Roman Catholic Church]
Pope John XXI
Giulio Romano. See: CACCINI, GIULIO
Giuseppe Blanco. See: WHITE, JOSEPH BLANCO
Giuseppe del Gesù (Giuseppe of Jesus). See: GUARNIERI, GIUSEPPE ANTONIO
Giuseppe of Jesus (Giuseppe del Gesù). See: GUARNIERI, GIUSEPPE ANTONIO
Give 'em Hell Harry. See: TRUMAN, HARRY S
Glacier Priest, The. See: HUBBARD, FATHER BERNARD ROSECRANS
GLADDEN, EDGAR NORMAN (1897-) [British civil servant and author]
Norman Mansfield
GLADSTONE, ARTHUR (1861-) [English merchant and author]
Arthur Stone
Gladstone of America. See: BLAINE, JAMES GILLESPIE
GLADSTONE, WILLIAM EWART (1809-98) [British statesman and Prime Minister]
The Grand Old Man
The Great Commoner
Gladys Armour. See: OSBORNE, DOROTHY GLADYS YEO
Gladys Condor. See: DAVISON, GLADYS PATTON
Gladys George. See: CLARE, GLADYS
Gladys Henson. See: GUNN, GLADYS
Gladys Mendl. See: SCHUTZE, GLADYS HENRIETTA
Gladys Pickford. See: SMITH, GLADYS MARY
Glamour Boy, Hollywood's No. 1. See: MATURE, VICTOR JOHN
Glamour Girl, The Original. See: GOODMAN, THEODOSIA
Glance Gaylord. See: BRADLEY, WARREN IVES
Glannege, Roger-Maxe de la. See: LEGMAN, GERSHON
Glaser, Eleanor Dorothy. See:

ZONIK, ELEANOR DOROTHY

GLASER, MILTON (1929-) [American artist, illustrator and author]
Max Catz

GLASS, GEORGE CARTER (1858-1946) [American politician; senator from Virginia]
The Father of the Federal Reserve System
The Snapping Turtle
Sound Money Glass
Unreconstructed Rebel

Glass Industry, The Father of the Plate. See:
FORD, JOHN BAPTISTE

Glass, Justine. See:
CORRALL, ALICE ENID

GLASSCO, JOHN (1909-) [Canadian poet, satirist and translator]
Silas N. Gooch
Miles Underwood

GLASSCOCK, ANNE BONNER (1924-) [American author]
Michael Bonner

GLAZER, MELVIN (1931-) [American pharmacist and musician]
Mel Glazer

GLEADOW, RUPERT SEELEY (1909-) [British poet, translator and author]
Justin Case

GLEASON, EUGENE FRANKLIN (1914-) [American author]
Gene Gleason

GLEASON, HERBERT JOHN (1916-) [American comedian and television personality]
The Great One
Jackie Gleason
Mr. Saturday Night

GLEASON, PATRICK JEROME (18??-1901) [American politician; Mayor of Long Island City, N.Y.]
Battle-axe Gleason

GLEASON, WILLIAM (1866-1933) [American professional baseball coach and player]
Kid Gleason

Glen, Eugene. See:
FAWCETT, FRANK DUBREZ

Glen Gray. See:
KNOBLAUGH, GLEN GRAY

Glen Trevor. See:
HILTON, JAMES

Glenn. See:
FORD, GWYLLYN SAMUEL NEWTON
MILLER, ALTON GLENN

GLENN, EVANS TYREE (1912-) [American jazz musician (composer, leader, trombone, vibraphone)]
Tyree Glenn

Glenn, Gipsy. See:
BURTON, JENNIE DAVIS

Glenn Kelly. See:
McNEILLY, MILDRED MASTERSON

Glenn Rollins. See:
OLSON, ROBERT G.

Glenna Finley. See:
WITTE, GLENNA FINLEY

GLETCHEN, MAJOR GENERAL LORD EDWARD (1863-) [British general officer and author]
Ex Flammis

GLICK, VIRGINIA KIRKUS (1893-) [American book critic, author and educator]
Virginia Kirkus

GLIDDEN, PATRICK DILLEY (1908-) [American author of western stories]
Luke Short

Gloomy Dean, The. See:
INGE, WILLIAM RALPH
SWIFT, JONATHAN

Gloria Grahame. See:
HALLWARD, GLORIA

Gloria Jean. See:
SCHOONOVER, GLORIA JEAN

Gloria Swanson. See:
SWENSON, JOSEPHINE MAY
Glorious Preacher, The. See:
CHRYSOSTOM, ST. JOHN
Glorious, The. See:
ATHELSTAN
Glory of Boston, The Father and. See:
COTTON, JOHN
GLOSSUP, EDGAR D. (c. 1908-) [American actor in Western motion pictures]
Eddie Dean
GLOUX, OLIVIER (1818-83) [French-American frontiersman and author]
Gustave Aimard
The Dumas of the Indians
The French Fenimore Cooper
GLOVER, CATHERINE (fl. 19th cent.) [Beautiful young woman of Perth, Scotland]
The Fair Maid of Perth
Glovet, Jules de. See:
QUESNAY DE BEAUREPAIRE, JULES
Glovichisch, Jurni. See:
GLOVIO, GIULIO
GLOWACKI, ALEXANDER (1847-1912) [Polish novelist and short story writer]
Boleslaw Prus
GLUBB, SIR JOHN BAGOT (1897-) [British soldier]
The Emperor of Jordan
Glubb Pasha
GLUCK, BARBARA ELIZABETH (1814-94) [Austrian poet and short story writer]
Betty Paoli
GLÜCK, CHRISTOPHER WILLIBALD (1714-87) [German operatic composer]
The Hercules of Music
The Michelangelo of Music
Glyn Carr. See:
STYLES, FRANK SHOWELL
GLYN, MRS. CLAYTON (1864-1943) [British novelist]
Elinor Glyn
Glyndon, Howard. See:
SEARING, LAURA CATHERINE REDDEN
GOBEL. See also:
GOEBEL
GOBEL, GEORGE LESLIE (1920-) [American television comedian]
Lonesome George
God-bearer (Theophoros). See:
IGNATIUS OF ANTIOCH, ST.
God-given. See:
LOUIS XIV
God-like Daniel, The. See:
WEBSTER, DANIEL
God of All Philosophers, The. See: CICERO, MARCUS TULLIUS
God of Dancing, The. See:
VESTRIS GAETANO APOLLINO
God, Splendor of (Baha Ullah) See:
MIRZA HUSEYN ALI
God, The Fair (Quetzalcóatl). See: CORTÉS, HERNÁN
God, The Lion of. See:
ALI, CALIPH
God, The Man Sent from. See:
FRANSON, FREDRIK
God, The Scourge of. See:
ATTILA (ETZEL) (ETHELE)
God, The Supreme Power of. See:
SIMON MAGUS
God, The Sword of. See:
KHALID (KALED)
God (Theos). See:
ANTIOCHUS II
GODDARD, GEORGE WILLIAM (1889-) [Anglo-American general officer]
The Father of Modern Aerial Photography
GODDARD, JOSEPHINE LAWRENCE (1920-) [American motion picture actress]
Jody Lawrance
Godden, Rumer. See:
FOSTER, MRS. LAURENCE
Goddess of Health, The. See:

HAMILTON, EMMA LYON
GODE VON AESCH, ALEXANDER GOTTFRIED FRIEDRICH (1906-) [German educator, editor and author]
Alexander Gode
Goderich, Goosey. See: ROBINSON, FREDERICK JOHN
Godfre Ray King. See: BALLARD, GUY WARREN
GODFREY, ARTHUR MICHAEL (1903-) [American radio and television personality]
Arthur Godfrey
Red Godfrey, The Warbling Banjoist
The Red Head
GODFREY, HOLLEN (fl. 1865) [American plainsman and Indian fighter]
Old Wicked
GODFREY OF BOUILLON (c. 1061-1100 [French nobleman and soldier; leader of First Crusade]
Baron and Defender of the Holy Sepulcher
Defender of the Holy Sepulcher
Duke of Lower Lorraine
GODIVA (GODGIFU) (1040-80) [English noblewoman; wife of LEOFRIC, Earl of Mercia]
Lady Godiva
Godless Anne Royall. See: ROYALL, ANNE NEWPORT
Godley, John. See: KILBRACKEN, JOHN RAYMOND GODLEY
Godmother of Detective Stories, The. See: GREEN, ANNA KATHARINE
Godolphin, Mary. See: AIKIN, LUCY
GODOY, MANUEL DE (1767-1851) [Duke of Alcudia]
The Prince of the Peace
GODWIN. See also: GOODWIN
Goodwin
GODWIN, JOHN (1928-) [Australian author]
John Stark
GODWIN, WILLIAM (1756-1836) [English philosopher and author]
Edwin Baldwin
GOEBBELS, JOSEPH (1897-1945) [German Nazi politician]
Jupp
GOEBEL. See also: GOBEL
GOEBEL, WILLIAM (1856-1900) [American politician; leader of Kentucky Democratic party]
Dictator Goebel
GOERING, HERMAN WILHELM (1893-1946) [Nazi German politico-military leader]
Sawdust Caesar
GOETHALS, HENRY (1227-93) [French schoolman]
The Solemn Doctor
GOETHE. See: VON GOETHE, JOHANN WOLFGANG
GOFFAGE, JOHN (1909-) [Australian motion picture actor]
Chips Rafferty
Goffe. See: GOW, CAPTAIN JOHN
GOGGAN, JOHN PATRICK (1902-) [American playwright]
John Patrick
GOHMAN, FRED JOSEPH (1918-) [American author and illustrator]
Spider Webb
Gold Bug, The. See: BENTON, THOMAS HART
Gold, Hal. See: GOLDBERG, HARRY
Gold Humbug. See: BENTON, THOMAS HART
GOLD, JACOB (1921-) [American composer, publisher and record executive]
Jack Gold
Gold, Michael. See: GRANICH, IRVING
Gold, Stream of (Chrysorrhoas). See: JOHN OF DAMASCUS

(JOHANNES DAMASCENUS)
GOLDBERG. See also: GOLDENBERG
GOLDBERG, ELVIRA REOD (1928-) [American jazz musician (singer, alto saxophone, soprano saxophone)]
Vi Redd
GOLDBERG, HARRY (1912-) [American composer, drummer and teacher]
Hal Gold
GOLDBERG, ISRAEL (1887-) [Polish-American author]
Rufus Learsi
GOLDBERG, REUBEN LUCIUS (1883-1970) [American cartoonist, author and comic strip artist]
Rube Goldberg
GOLDBERG, RICHARD (1928-) [American jazz musician (drums)]
Richie Goldberg
GOLDBOGEN, AVROM HIRSCH (1909-58) [American promoter and producer]
Mike Todd
Golden Arm, The Man With the. See: KOUFAX, SANFORD
Golden Boy. See: HORNUNG, PAUL VERNON
Golden Calves of the People, The, joint nickname of DANIEL WEBSTER (1782-1852) and HUGH LAWSON WHITE (1773-1840) [American statesmen]
Golden Calves of the People, The. See also: WEBSTER, DANIEL
WHITE, HUGH LAWSON
Golden Farmer, The. See: DAVIS, WILLIAM
Golden Gate, The Poet of the. See: KIRCHOFF, THEODORE
Golden Gate Trinity, The
The Overland Three, joint nicknames of IDA DONNA COOLBRITH (1842-1928), FRANCIS BRETT HARTE (1836-1902) and CHARLES WARREN STODDARD (1843-1909) [American writers]
Golden Gate Trinity, The. See also: COOLBRITH, IDA DONNA
HARTE, FRANCIS BRETT
STODDARD, CHARLES WARREN
Golden-hearted, The Silver-tongued and. See: WILLARD, FRANCES ELIZABETH
Golden MacDonald. See: BROWN, MARGARET WISE
Golden Man of the Gridiron, The. See: WILKINSON, CHARLES BURNHAM
Golden Mouthed. See: CHRYSOSTOM, ST. JOHN
GALLOWAY, CHARLES BETTS
Golden Nose. See: BRAHE, TYCHO
Golden Rule. See: JONES, SAMUEL MILTON
Golden Spurs, The Knight of the. See: STUART, JAMES EWELL BROWN
Golden Tonsil, The. See: VON KAPPELHOFF, DORIS
Golden Voice of Radio, The. See: MUNN, FRANK
GOLDENBERG. See also: GOLDBERG
GOLDENBERG, EMANUEL (1893-) [Rumanian-born motion picture actor]
Edward G. Robinson
Steve Wilson
GOLDENTHAL, ALLAN BENARRIA (1920-) [American pharmacist, business executive and

author]
Allan Benarria
GOLDFISH, SAMUEL (1884-) [Polish-American motion picture producer]
Samuel Goldwyn
GOLDFRANK, HELEN COLODNY (1912-) [American author]
Helen Kay
GOLDIE, KATHLEEN ANNIE (fl. mid-20th cent.) [English author]
Kathleen Fidler
Goldin, Horace. See: GOLDSTEIN, HYMAN
GOLDING, MORTON JAY (1925-) [American editor and author]
Stephanie Lloyd
Jay Martin
M. M. Michaeles
Patricia Morton
GOLDMANN, MAX (1873-1943) [Austrian-American actor and theatrical producer]
Max Reinhardt
GOLDONI, CARLO (1707-93) [Italian playwright]
The Italian Molière
GOLDSCHMIDT, DR. HERMANN (1860-) [German author]
Hermann Faber
Faber Goldschmidt
Goldschmidt, Madame Otto. See: LIND, JOHANNA MARIA
Goldsmith of America, The Oliver. See: TAYLOR, BENJAMIN FRANKLIN
GOLDSMITH, OLIVER (1728-74) [English poet, novelist and playwright]
Goldy
The Inspired Idiot
Goldsmith, The American. See: IRVING, WASHINGTON
GOLDSTEIN, HYMAN (1867-1939) [Jewish illusionist and magician]
Horace Goldin
GOLDSTEIN, WILLIAM ISAAC (1932-) [American writer]
Rex Lode
GOLDSTEIN, WILLIAM ISAAC
See also: Bolo, Solomon
GOLDSTON, ROBERT CONROY (1927-) [American author]
James Stark
Goldwyn, Samuel. See: GOLDFISH, SAMUEL
Goldy. See: GOLDSMITH, OLIVER
GOLENOR, JOHN ANTHONY (1928-) [American actor]
John Gavin
Golf, The Nestor of. See: MORRIS, TOM
Goliah Gahagan, Major. See: THACKERAY, WILLIAM MAKEPEACE
Goliath of His Party, The. See: BAYARD, JAMES ASHETON
GOLLER, CELIA FREMLIN (1914-) [British author]
Celia Fremlin
GOLYER, EVERETTE LEE DE (1886-1956) [American geologist and geophysicist]
The Father of American Geophysics
Gom Gut. See: SIMENON, GEORGES
GÓMEZ, JOSÉ (1895-1920) [Spanish bullfighter]
Joselito
The Pontiff of Bullfighting
GÓMEZ, LUIS (1911-) [Spanish bullfighter]
El Estudiante
GÓMEZ, RAFAEL (1882-1960) [Spanish bullfighter]
El Gallo
GOMPERS, SAMUEL (1850-1924) [American labor leader]
The Grand Old Man of Labor
Gonatas. See: ANTIGONUS II
Goncourts, The, joint pseud. of EDMOND LOUIS ANTOINE HUOT DE GONCOURT (1822-96) and his brother JULES ALFRED HUOT DE GONCOURT (1830-70) [French novelists and historians]

Gone, Long. See:
MILES, LUKE
Gong, The Ohio. See:
ALLEN, WILLIAM
GONSALVES, JOHN P. (1925-) [American composer, singer and recording executive]
Joli
GONZAGA, LUIGI (1568-91) [Italian Jesuit priest]
St. Aloysius
GONZAGA, TOMÁS ANTÓNIO (1744-1809) [Brazilian and Portuguese poet]
Dirceu
GONZÁLES, BLI (died 1756) [Spanish criminal]
John Symmonds
Spanish Jack
GONZÁLES, FRANCISCO (1784-1843) [Spanish bullfighter]
Panchón
GONZÁLES, LUCIANO (1920-48) [Cuban jazz musician (bongo and conga drums)]
Chano Pozo
GONZÁLES, RICHARD (1928-) [American tennis player]
Pancho Gonzáles
GONZÁLEZ, HILARIO (1883-1908) [Spanish bullfighter]
Serranito
GONZÁLEZ, JOSÉ (1907-47) [Mexican bullfighter]
Carnicerito de México
GONZÁLEZ, LUIS MIGUEL (1926-) [Spanish bullfighter]
Dominguín
GONZÁLEZ, RAFAEL (1880-1955) [Spanish bullfighter]
Machaquito
GONZALO DE CÓRDOBA (GONSALVO DI CORDOVA) (1453-1515) [Spanish military commander]
El Gran Capitán (The Great Captain
Gooch, Silas N. See:
GLASSCO, JOHN
GOOCH, WAYNE R. (fl. 1906) [American bootlegger and moonshiner]
The King of Moonshiners
Good Bishop, The. See:
OTEY, JAMES HARVEY
Good Duke Humphrey. See:
HUMPHREY
Good Earl, The. See:
DOUGLAS, ARCHIBALD
Good Giant, The. See:
DOYLE, SIR ARTHUR CONAN
Good Governor of Virginia, The. See: BOTETOURT, LORD NORBORNE BERKELEY
Good Gray Poet, The. See:
WHITMAN, WALTER
Good, Grover the. See:
CLEVELAND, STEPHEN GROVER
GOOD, IRVING JOHN (1916-) [British computer engineer and author]
K. Caj Doog
Good King Wenceslaus. See:
WENCESLAUS
Good Lord Cobham, The. See:
OLDCASTLE, SIR JOHN
Good Lord Lyttelton, The. See:
LYTTELTON, GEORGE, 1ST LORD LYTTELTON
Good Physician, The. See:
HIGBEE, CHESTER GOSS
Good Queen Bess. See:
ELIZABETH I
Good Regent, The. See:
STUART, JAMES
Good Roads. See:
CARTWRIGHT, WILBURN
KING, CYRUS MURDOCK
Good Roads, The Father of. See: SPROUL, WILLIAM CAMERON
Good, The. See:
ALBERT
ALFONSO IX
DOUGLAS, SIR JAMES
GRAHAM, JAMES
HAAKON I
MAGNUS I
PHILIP
RENÉ I
RICHARD II

WILLIAM II
Good, The (Le Bon). See:
JOHN II
Good, Will B. See:
ARBUCKLE, ROSCOE
Good Will, The Ambassador of. See: ROGERS, WILLIAM PENN ADAIR
Good Works, The Father of. See: MOHAMMED II
Goodall, Daphne Machin. See:
MACHIN GOODALL, DAPHNE
Goodenough, Evelyn. See:
PITCHER, EVELYN GOODENOUGH
GOODMAN, BENJAMIN DAVID (1909-) [American jazz musician (clarinet, leader)]
B. G.
Benny Goodman
The King of Swing
GOODMAN, GEORGE J. W. (1930-) [American journalist and author]
Adam Smith
Goodman, Murray. See:
SCHACHT, ALEXANDER
Goodman of Ballengeigh, The. See: JAMES V
Goodman Palsgrave. See:
FREDERICK V
GOODMAN, THEODOSIA (1890-1955) [American motion picture actress]
Theda Bara
The Original Glamour Girl
The Queen of the Vampires
GOODRICH, FRANK BOOTT (1826-94) [American playwright and miscellaneous writer]
Dick Tinto
GOODRICH, SAMUEL GRISWOLD (1793-1860) [American author and publisher]
Peter Parley
GOODSPEED, MARJORIE (1921-) [American television and motion picture actress]
Marjorie Reynolds
GOODWIN [Goodwin]. See also:
GODWIN
GOODWIN, CHARLES D. (1929-) [American composer and author]
Doug Goodwin
GOODWIN, ESTELLE (1883-) [British stage and motion picture actress]
Estelle Winwood
GOODWIN, HANNAH ELIZABETH BRADBURY (1827-93) [American author]
H. B. G.
GOODWIN, HAROLD LELAND (1914-) [American author]
John Blaine
Hal Goodwin
Blake Savage
Goodwin, Mark. See:
MATTHEWS, STANLEY GOODWIN
GOODWIN, NATHANIEL CARL (1857-1919) [American actor and vaudeville entertainer]
Nat Goodwin
Goody. See:
GOWDY
KNIGHT, GOODWIN JESS
Goody Palsgrave. See:
STUART, ELIZABETH
Goose. See:
GOSLIN, LEON ALLEN
Goose, Father. See:
SENNETT, MACK
Goosey Goderich. See:
ROBINSON, FREDERICK JOHN
Goossen, Agnes. See:
EPP, MARGARET
Gopaleen, Myles na. See:
O'NUALLAIN, BRIAN
Goran, Calli. See:
GERRITY, DAVID JAMES
GORCEY, LEO. See:
Dead End Kids, The
Gordie. See:
HOWE, GORDON
Gordito. See:
CARMONA, ANTONIO
Gordo. See:

BALDWIN, GORDON C.
Gordo, Alfonso o (Alfonso the Fat). See: ALFONSO II
Gordo, Cerro. See: KELLY, JONATHAN FALCONBRIDGE
GORDON. See: GEORGE, DUKE OF GORDON
Gordon A. Giles. See: BINDER, OTTO OSCAR
Gordon, A.M.R. See: ROSE, A. McGREGOR
Gordon Ashe. See: CREASEY, JOHN
GORDON, CHARLES GEORGE (1833-85) [English general officer and administrator]
Chinese Gordon
Gordon Pasha
GORDON, CHARLES WILLIAM (1860-1937) [Canadian novelist]
Ralph Connor
Gordon, Colonel H.R. See: ELLIS, EDWARD SYLVESTER
Gordon Daviot. See: MACINTOSH, ELIZABETH
Gordon Davis. See: DIETRICH, ROBERT SALISBURY
Gordon, Donald. See: PAYNE, DONALD GORDON
Gordon Donalds. See: SHIRREFFS, GORDON DONALD
Gordon, Frederick. See: STRATEMEYER, EDWARD L.
Gordon, George. See: BALDWIN, CHARLES CRITTENTON
GORDON, GORDON. See: Gordons, The
Gordon Grimsley. See: GROOM, ARTHUR WILLIAM
Gordon, Ian. See: FELLOWES-GORDON, IAN DOUGLAS
GORDON, JANE MAXWELL (c.1749-1812) [Scottish noblewoman]
The Beautiful Duchess of Gordon
GORDON, JUDAH LOEB (1830-92) [Hebrew poet]
Y.L.G.
Yalag
Yehudah Lieb
Yehudah Lion
Gordon, Julien. See: CHANCE, JULIE GRINNELL
Gordon, Lew. See: BALDWIN, GORDON C.
Gordon MacLaren. See: PATTEN, WILLIAM GILBERT
GORDON, MILDRED. See: Gordons, The
Gordon, Neil. See: MACDONNELL, ARCHIBALD GORDON
Gordon, Oliver. See: EMERSON, HENRY OLIVER
Gordon, Peter. See: WILKES-HUNTER, RICHARD
Gordon, Rex. See: HOUGH, STANLEY BENNETT
Gordon, Ruth. See: JONES, RUTH
Gordon Scott. See: WERSCHKUL, GORDON M.
Gordon Semple. See: NEUBAUER, WILLIAM ARTHUR
Gordon Shayne. See: WINTER, BEVIS
Gordon Shepherd. See: BROOK-SHEPHERD, GORDON
Gordon Stewart. See: RATHBONE, ST. GEORGE HENRY
Gordon, Stewart. See: SHIRREFFS, GORDON DONALD
Gordon Stuart. See: SAYLER, HARRY LINCOLN

STEWART, ROBERT ARMISTEAD
Gordon Summers. See: HORNBY, JOHN
Gordon, Tom. See: THOMAS, GORDON
Gordon, Uncle. See: ROE, FREDERIC GORDON
GORDON, WILLIAM (1801-49) [English philanthropist]
The People's Friend
Gordons, The, joint pseud. of GORDON GORDON (1912-) and his wife, MILDRED GORDON (1912-) [American authors]
GORE, THOMAS PRYOR (1870-) [American politician; senator from Oklahoma]
The Blind Savant
GORENKO, ANNA ANDREYEVNA (1888-) [Russian poet]
Anna Akhmatova
GOREY, EDWARD ST. JOHN (1925-) [American designer, illustrator, author and editor]
Eduard Blutig
Mrs. Regera Dowdy
Redway Grode
O. Mude
Ogdred Weary
Dreary Wodge
Gorgeous Hussy, The. See: EATON, MARGARET O'NEILL
GORGES, FERDINANDO (c. 1565-1647) [British proponent of American colonization]
The Father of English Colonization in America
GORHAM, MAURICE ANTHONY CONEYS (1902-) [British editor and author]
Walter Rault
Gorham, Michael. See: FOLSOM, FRANKLIN BREWSTER
Gorion, M.Y. Ben. See: BERDICHEVSKY, MIKAH YOSEF
Gorju, Guillot. See: ST. JACQUES, BERTRAND HARDOUIN
Gorky, Maxim. See: PESHKOV, ALEKSEI MAKSIMOVICH
GORM (died c. 940) [first King of United Denmark]
The Old
Gorman, Ginny. See: KANTO, PETER
GORMAN, THOMAS FRANCIS XAVIER (1913-) [American organization official and writer]
Mike Gorman
Gorney, Charles. See: RUDOLPH, WILLIAM
Goryan, Sirak. See: SAROYAN, WILLIAM
GOSDEN, FREEMAN F. (1899-) [American radio actor]
Amos Jones
Kingfish (George Stevens)
Lightnin'
GOSDEN, FREEMAN F. See also:
Amos and Andy
GOSLIN, LEON ALLEN (1900-71) [American professional baseball player]
Goose Goslin
Gospel Doctor, The. See: WICKLIFFE, JOHN
Gospel Song, Queen of the. See: JACKSON, MAHALIA
GOSSART, JAN (c. 1470-1532) [Flemish painter]
Jan Mabuse
Gossips, The Prince of. See: PEPYS, SAMUEL
Gosslet, Paul. See: LEVER, CHARLES JAMES
GOSTING, RICHARD (1941-) [American composer and singer]
Dick St. John

GOT, BERTRAND DE
(1260-1314) [Supreme Pontiff of Roman Catholic Church]
Pope Clement V
Gothicus. See:
CLAUDIUS (MARCUS AURELIUS CLAUDIUS)
Goths, The Last of the. See:
RODERICK
GOTTFRIED. See:
VON BERLICHINGEN, GÖTZ (GOTTFRIED)
Gotthelf, Jeremias. See:
BITZIUS, ALBERT
GOTTLIEB, JOSEPH ABRAHAM
(1919-) [American comedian, actor and television personality]
Joey Bishop
GOTTLIEB, LOUIS E.
(1923-) [American jazz musician (composer, arranger, singer, bass)]
Lou Gottlieb
Gottschalk, Laura Riding.
See: JACKSON, LAURA RIDING
GOTTSHALL, FRANKLIN HENRY (1902-)
[American illustrator and author]
H. Borneman
Götz with the Iron Hand.
See: VON BERLICHINGEN, GÖTZ (GOTTFRIED)
GOUCHER, JOSEPH NELSON
(1894-) [American actor, playwright, director and producer]
Eddie Dowling
Gouge, Orson. See:
LARNER, JEREMY
Gough, Kathleen. See:
ABERLE, KATHLEEN GOUGH
GOUJON, JEAN (1515-68)
[French sculptor and architect]
The Correggio of Sculpture
The French Phidias
GOULD, JASON (1836-92)
[American financier and robber baron]
Jay Gould
The Railroad King
Gould, Michael. See:
AYRTON, MICHAEL
GOULD, MORTON (1913-)
[American composer and conductor]
The Most Talented Young Composer in America
GOULD, NATHANIEL (1857-1919) [English sporting novelist]
Nat Gould
GOULDING, RAYMOND W.
See: Bob and Ray
Gourmets, The Prince of. See:
BRILLAT-SAVARIN, ANTHELME
Gouty, Piero the. See:
MEDICI, PIERO DE'
GOVAN, CHRISTINE NOBLE
(1898-) [American author]
Mary Allerton
J.N. Darby
Government, The Father of the City Manager Plan of Municipal. See:
CHILDS, RICHARD SPENCER
Governor of the English Nation, Acting. See:
CAXTON, WILLIAM
Governor of Virginia, The Good. See:
BOTETOURT, LORD NORBORNE BERKELEY
Governor, Spurious. See:
LIVINGSTON, WILLIAM
Governor, The Bachelor. See:
HILL, DAVID BENNETT
Governor, The Boy. See:
MASON, STEVENS THOMSON
Governor, The Farmer. See:
BOUCK, WILLIAM C.
Governor, The Great War.
See: CURTIN, ANDREW GREGG
Governor, The One-legged. See:
STUYVESANT, PETER
Governor, The Revel. See:

TRUMBULL, JONATHAN
Governor, The Reform. See:
CLEVELAND, STEPHEN GROVER
Governor, The Veto. See:
CLEVELAND, STEPHEN GROVER
WINSTON, JOHN ANTHONY
Governor, The War. See:
MORTON, OLIVER HAZARD PERRY THROCK
GOW, CAPTAIN JOHN (died 1725) [Scottish pirate]
Goffe
Smith
GOWANS, ARTHUR BRADFORD (1903-54) [American jazz musician (trombone, clarinet, arranger)]
Brad Gowans
GOWANS, WILLIAM (1803-70) [Scottish-American bibliophile, publisher and bookseller]
The Antiquarian of Nassau Street
GOWDY. See also:
Goody
GOWDY, CURTIS (1919-) [American sportscaster]
Curt Gowdy
GOWER, JOHN (c. 1325-1408) [English poet]
Moral Gower
GOYATHLAY (1829-1909) [American Apache Indian chief]
Geronimo
Goykovich, Dusko. See:
GOJKOVIC, DUSAN
Gozzoli, Benozzo. See:
SANDRO, BENOZZO DI LESE DI
GRABER, ALEXANDER (1914-) [English author]
Alexander Cordell
GRABOWSKI, ZBIGNIEW ANTHONY (1903-) [Polish journalist and author]
Axel Heyst
Gracchus. See:
BABEUF, FRANÇOIS NOEL
Gracchus, The Modern. See:
RIQUETTI, HONORÉ GABRIEL
Grace Brooks Hill. See:
STRATEMEYER, EDWARD L.
Grace Darling of America, The. See: WILSON, IDA LEWIS
Grace Greenwood. See:
LIPPINCOTT, SARA JANE CLARKE
Grace, Joseph. See:
HORNBY, JOHN
Grace of Baal, The. See:
HANNIBAL
Grace Richmond. See:
MARSH, JOHN
Graces, The Painter of the. See: APPIANO, ANDREA
Gracie Fields. See:
STANSFIELD, GRACE
Gracious Majesty, Consort of Her Most. See:
ALBERT
Gradelino. See:
CONSTANTINI, CONSTANTINO
Graduate of Oxford, A. See:
RUSKIN, JOHN
Grady. See:
CASH, GRACE
Graham Adamson. See:
GROOM, ARTHUR WILLIAM
Graham Allen. See:
ARNOLD, GEORGE
Graham Ashley. See:
ORGAN, JOHN
Graham B. Forbes. See:
STRATEMEYER, EDWARD L.
Graham, Ennis. See:
MOLESWORTH, MARY LOUISA
GRAHAM, FLORENCE NIGHTINGALE (1884-1966) [Canadian beautician, horsewoman and business executive]
Elizabeth Arden

Mrs. Elizabeth N. Graham

Graham, Hugh. See: BARROWS, MARJORIE

GRAHAM, JAMES (c. 1631-69) [Scottish nobleman; 2nd Marquis of Montrose]
The Good

GRAHAM, JAMES (1745-94) [Scottish quack doctor]
Dr. Graham
The Servant of the Lord
O. W. L. (Oh Wonderful Love)

GRAHAM, JOHN (c. 1649-89) [1st Viscount Dundee; Scottish soldier and nobleman]
Bloody Claverse
Bonny Dundee
Graham of Claverhouse

Graham, John. See: PHILLIPS, DAVID GRAHAM

Graham, Lieut. Preston. See: INGRAHAM, COLONEL PRENTISS

GRAHAM, MAUDE FITZ-GERALD SUSAN (1912-) [New Zealand journalist and author]
Susan

Graham, Neill. See: DUNCAN, WILLIAM MURDOCH

Graham, Ramona. See: COOK, RAMONA GRAHAM

Graham, Sheilah. See: SHEIL, LILY

GRAHAM, SYLVESTER (1794-1851) [American minister and advocate of nutrition reform]
The Poet of Bran Meal and Pumpkins

Graham, Tom. See: LEWIS, HARRY SINCLAIR

Graham, Virginia. See: KOMISS, VIRGINIA

GRAHAM, WILLIAM FRANKLIN (1918-) [American Baptist clergyman, evangelist and author]
Billy Graham
Dr. Billy Graham

Graham, Winifred. See: CORY, WINIFRED MURIEL

Grahame, Gloria. See: HALLWARD, GLORIA

Grahame, Nellie. See: DUNNING, ANNIE KETCHUM

Gramercy Park, The Sage of. See: JONES, SAMUEL TILDEN

Gramiades. See: HORTON-SMITH, LIONEL GRAHAM HORTON

Grammar, Above (Supra Grammaticam). See: SIGISMUND

Grammar, The Scourge of. See: JACOB, GILES

Grammarians, The Coryphaeus of. See: ARISTARCHUS

Grammarians, The Prince of. See: DYSCOLUS, APOLLONIUS

Grammaticam, Supra (Above Grammar). See: SIGISMUND

Grammaticus. See:
AELFRIC
BLAIKLOCK, EDWARD MUSGRAVE

Gran Capitán, El (The Great Captain). See: GONZALO DE CÓRDOBA (GONSALVO DI CORDOVA)

GRANATELLI, ANDREW (1923-) [American automobile racing promoter and manufacturing executive]
Andy Granatelli
Mr. 500
Mr. S. T. P.

Granby Dixon. See: KINGSLEY, HENRY

Grand Corneille, Le. See: CORNEILLE, PIERRE

Grand Corrupter, The. See:
WALPOLE, SIR ROBERT
Grand, Le. See:
HENDERSON, LE GRAND
Grand Monarch, The. See:
LOUIS XIV
Grand Monarque, Le. See:
LOUIS XIV
Grand Old Lady, Chicago's. See:
HUDLUN, ANNA ELIZABETH
Grand Old Lady of Opera, The. See: SCHUMANN-HEINK, MME. ERNESTINE
Grand Old Lady of the Movies, The. See:
KOERBER, LEILA
Grand Old Man from Maryland, The. See:
WHYTE, WILLIAM PINKNEY
Grand Old Man, Hollywood's. See: BLYTHE, LIONEL
Grand Old Man of Alexandria, The. See:
DUNN, EMMETT CLARKE
Grand Old Man of Football, The. See:
STAGG, AMOS ALONZO
Grand Old Man of Labor, The. See: GOMPERS, SAMUEL
Grand Old Man of Missouri, The. See:
KIRK, JOHN ROBERT
Grand Old Man of the Screen, The. See:
ROBERTS, THEODORE
Grand Old Man, The. See:
FRANKLIN, BENJAMIN
GLADSTONE, WILLIAM EWART
PITT, WILLIAM
SAVAGE, GEORGE MARTIN
Grand Old Man, The Union's. See: SAVAGE, GEORGE MARTIN
Grand, Pierre le. See:
FRANÇOIS, PIERRE
Grand, Sarah. See:
McFALL, FRANCES ELIZABETH CLARK
Grand Wrestler, The. See:
LINCOLN, ABRAHAM
Grande Armée, Le Sade de la. See: DROUOT, ANTOINE, COMTE
Grande Épistolier de France, Le. See:
BALZAC, JEAN LOUIS GUEZ DE
Grande Mademoiselle, La. See:
MONTPENSIER, ANNE MARIE LOUISE D'ORLÉANS, DUCHESSE DE
Grande Vitesse. See:
WALKERLEY, RODNEY LEWIS
Grandest Roman of Them All, The. See:
McMILLIN, BENTON
Grandfather. See also:
Gran'ther
Grandfather, Baby McKee's. See: HARRISON, BENJAMIN
Grandfather Greenway. See:
CANNON, CHARLES JAMES
Grandfather of the Missionaries, The. See:
ROBERTS, ROBERT RICHFORD
Grandfather of Yale Rowing, The. See: SHEFFIELD, GEORGE ST. JOHN
Grandfather, The Son of His. See: HARRISON, BENJAMIN
Grandfather's Hat. See:
HARRISON, BENJAMIN
Grandison Cromwell. See:
MOTIER, MARIE JEAN PAUL ROCH YVES GILBERT
Grandma. See:
MOSES, ANNA MARY ROBERTSON
Grandma Flapper, The. See:
HOPPER, EDNA WALLACE
Grandmother of Boston, The. See: PEABODY, ELIZABETH PALMER

Grandmother of the Russian Revolution, The Little. See: BRESHKOVSKY, CATHERINE
Grandpa's Grandson. See: HARRISON, BENJAMIN
Grandson, Grandpa's. See: HARRISON, BENJAMIN
GRANDSTAFF, KATHERINE (1933-) [American actress; wife of HARRY LILLIS (Bing) CROSBY]
Kathryn Grant
Grandville. See: GÉRARD, JEAN IGNACE ISIDORE
GRANGE, CYRIL (1900-) [British agriculturist and author]
Onlooker
Quill
GRANGE, HAROLD EDWARD (1903-) [American football player and sports commentator]
The Galloping Ghost
Red Grange
The Wheaton Iceman
Granger, Stewart. See: STEWART, JAMES
GRANICH, IRVING (1896-) [American author and journalist]
Michael Gold
Granite, Tony. See: POLITELLA, DARIO
Granny. See:
GATES, HORATIO
HAYES, RUTHERFORD BIRCHARD
RICE, GRANTLAND
Granny, Old. See: HARRISON, WILLIAM HENRY
Grant. See: ALLEN, CHARLES GRANT BLAIRFINDIE
Grant, Allen. See: WILSON, JAMES GRANT
GRANT, ANNE MACVICAR (1755-1838) [Scottish author]
Mrs. Grant of Laggan
Grant, Cary. See: LEACH, ALEXANDER ARCHIBALD
Grant, Charles. See: LENGEL, WILLIAM CHARLES
Grant, Douglas. See: OSTRANDER, ISABEL
GRANT, HILDA KAY (1910-) [Canadian author]
Jan Hilliard
GRANT, HIRAM ULYSSES (1822-85) [American general officer; eighteenth President of the United States]
The American Caesar
Butcher Grant
Butcher from Galena
The Galena Tanner
Great Hammerer
Great Peacemaker
Hero of Appomattox
Hero of Fort Donelson
Hug Grant
Ulysses Simpson Grant
Lyss
Old Three Stars
Sam
Silent Man
The Tanner President
Texas
Uncle Sam
Unconditional Surrender
Uniformed Soldier
Union Safeguard
United States
United States Grant
Unprecedented Strategist
Unquestionably Skilled
Useless Grant
Grant, Joan. See: KELSEY, JOAN MARSHALL
Grant, Kathryn. See: GRANDSTAFF, KATHERINE
Grant, Kirby. See: HORN, KIRBY GRANT
Grant, Major A. F. See: HARBAUGH, THOMAS CHALMERS
Grant, Margaret. See:

CORYELL, JOHN
RUSSELL
FRANKEN,
ROSE D. (MRS.)
WILLIAM BROWN
MELONEY)
GRANT, SEAFIELD (1909-)
[South-African born
stage and motion picture
actor]
Louis Hayward
Grant Sinclair. See:
DRAGO, HENRY
SINCLAIR
GRANT-WATSON, ELLIOT
LOVEGOOD (1885-)
[English author]
John Lovegood
GRANTHAM, GEORGE
FARLEY (1900-)
[American professional
baseball player]
Boots Grantham
Gran'ther. See:
Grandfather
HOAR, GEORGE
FRISBIE
GRANTIANUS, JOHANNES
(died 1048) [Supreme
Pontiff of Roman
Catholic Church]
Pope Gregory VI
Grantland, Keith. See:
BEAUMONT, CHARLES
Grape Culture, The Father
of American. See:
LONGWORTH, NICHOLAS
Grapho. See:
OAKLEY, ERIC GILBERT
GRATTAN, HENRY (1746-1820)
[Irish orator and
statesman]
The Patriot of Humanity
Grau, Edouard. See:
WORTH, ADAM
GRAUER, BENJAMIN
FRANKLIN (1908-)
[American radio and
television announcer]
Ben Grauer
GRAUPNER, JOHANN
CHRISTIAN GOTTLIEB
(1767-1836) [German-
American musician and
composer]
The Father of American
Orchestral Music
GRAVELET, JEAN FRANÇOIS
(1824-97), [French
tightrope walker]
Charles Blondin
The Little Wonder
Graveley, George. See:
EDWARDS, GEORGE
GRAVELEY
GRAVES, CLOTILDE INEZ
AUGUSTA MARY (1863-
1932) [English author]
Richard Dehan
Graves, Harley. See:
WILKINSON, MRS.
MARGUERITE OGDEN
GRAVES, JOHN PARLIN
(1911-) [American
author]
John Parlin
Graves, Peter. See:
ARNESS, PETER
Gravet, Fernand. See:
MARTENS, FERNAND
GRAY [Gray]. See also:
Grey
Gray, Barry. See:
COFFIN, ROBERT BARRY
Gray, Barton. See:
SASS, GEORGE HERBERT
Gray, Coleen. See:
JENSEN, DORIS
GRAY, DONALD M. (1928-)
[British stage, motion
picture and television
actor]
Charles Gray
Gray, Dulcie. See:
BAILEY, DULCIE
Gray Eagle. See:
NYE, JAMES WARREN
SPEAKER, TRISTRAM E.
Gray, Elizabeth Janet. See:
VINING, ELIZABETH
GRAY
Gray, Ellington. See:
JACOB, NAOMI
ELLINGTON
Gray Eminence (Éminence Grise).
See: TREMBLAY,

FRANÇOIS LE CLERC DU
GRAY, FINLY HUTCHINSON (1864-) [American politician; Democratic representative from Indiana]
The Hoosier Shakespeare
Gray Fox, The. See: CROOK, GEORGE
GRAY, GEORGE HUGH (1922-) [Irish journalist, television script writer and author]
Tony Gray
Gray, Gilda. See: MICHAELSKA, MARIANNE
Gray, Glen. See: KNOBLAUGH, GLEN GRAY
Gray, Jane. See: EVANS, CONSTANCE MAY
Gray Mustang, The. See: FRÉMONT, JOHN CHARLES
Gray, Nadia. See: KUJNIR-HERESCU, NADIA
Gray Poet, The Good. See: WHITMAN, WALTER
Gray, Sally. See: STEVENS, CONSTANCE
GRAY, SIMON (1936-) [English author and playwright]
James Holliday
Hamish Reade
GRAY, THOMAS (1716-71) [British poet]
The British Pindar
Gray, Walter T. See: VICTOR, MRS. METTA VICTORIA FULLER MORSE
GRAY, WILLIAM BITTLE (1891-) [British marine biologist]
Captain Bill Gray
Grayfell. See: HAROLD II
Grayson, David. See: BAKER, RAY STANNARD
Grayson, Eldred. See: HARE, ROBERT
Grayson, Kathryn. See: HEDRICK, ZELMA
Grayson, Paul. See: DEMPSEY, JAMES E.
GRAZIATI, ALDO (1902-53) [Italian cinematographer]
G.R. Aldo
Great Agnostic, The. See: INGERSOLL, ROBERT GREEN
Great, Albert the. See: ALBERTUS MAGNUS, SAINT, COUNT OF BOLLSTÄDT
Great, Alexander the. See: ALEXANDER III
DUMAS, ALEXANDRE
WILLIAMS, ALEX
Great All American, The. See: FISH, HAMILTON, JR.
Great American Commoner, The. See: STEVENS, THADDEUS
Great American Democrat, The First. See: WISE, JOHN
Great American Showman, The. See: BARNUM, PHINEAS TAYLOR
Great American Traveler, The. See: PRATT, DANIEL
Great Arnauld, The. See: ARNAULD, ANTOINE
Great Bastard, The. See: BOURGOGNE, ANTOINE DE
Great Captain, The (El Gran Capitán). See: GONZALO DE CÓRDOBA (GONSALVO DI CORDOVA)
Great, Catherine the. See: ANHALT-ZERBST, SOPHIA AUGUSTA FREDERICA OF
Great Cham of Literature, The. See: JOHNSON, DR. SAMUEL
Great, Charles the. See: CHARLEMAGNE
Great Commoner, The. See: BRYAN, WILLIAM JENNINGS
CLAY, HENRY

FOWLER, CHARLES HENRY
GLADSTONE, WILLIAM EWART
HOGG, JAMES STEPHEN
PITT, WILLIAM
STEVENS, THADDEUS
Great Compromiser, The. See: CLAY, HENRY
Great, Constantine the. See: CONSTANTINIUS, FLAVIUS VALERIUS AURELIUS
Great, Cosimo the. See: MEDICI, COSIMO DE'
Great Democratic Warwick, The. See: SWEENEY, PETER BARR
Great Detective, A. See: SCHINDLER, RAYMOND C.
Great Duke, The. See: WELLINGTON, ARTHUR WELLESLEY, 1ST DUKE OF
Great Eagle, The. See: MAIMONIDES
Great Earl, The. See: BOYLE, RICHARD, 1ST EARL OF CORK
DOUGLAS, ARCHIBALD
Great Elchi, The. See: CANNING, SIR STRATFORD
Great Elector, The. See: FREDERICK-WILLIAM
Great, Elmer the. See: BECK, WALTER WILLIAM
Great Emancipator, The. See: LINCOLN, ABRAHAM
Great Eye, The. See: SCHUYLER, PHILIP JOHN
Great Father of Detroit, The. See: CASS, LEWIS
Great Financier, The. See: SHERMAN, JOHN
Great Geometer, The. See: APOLLONIUS OF PERGA
Great Hammerer. See: GRANT, HIRAM ULYSSES
Great Head (Canmore). See: MALCOLM III
Great Heart, The Man of. See: HOOVER, HERBERT CLARK
Great, Houdini the. See: WEISS, EHRICH (ERIK WEISZ)
Great Interpreter, The. See: WEBSTER, DANIEL
Great John L., The. See: SULLIVAN, JOHN LAWRENCE
Great Khan, The. See: KUBLAI KHAN (KHUBILAI KHAN) (KUBLA KHAN)
Great Leader (Quaid-i-azam). See: JINNAH, MOHAMMED ALI
Great Left-Handed Press Agent, The. See: MAILS, WALTER
Great Liberal, The. See: WHEELER, BURTON KENDALL
Great, MacDermott the. See: FARRELL, GILBERT HASTINGS
Great Magician of the North, The. See: SCOTT, SIR WALTER
Great Magician, The. See: SCOTT, SIR WALTER
Great Mails, The. See: MAILS, WALTER
Great Marcher, The. See: SHERMAN, WILLIAM TECUMSEH
Great Marquis, The. See: POMBAL, MARQUÉS DE, SEBASTIÃO JOSÉ DE CARVALHO E MELLO
Great Master of Love, The. See: DANIEL, ARNAUD (ARNAUT)
Great Merlini, The. See: RAWSON, CLAYTON
Great Minstrel, The. See: SCOTT, SIR WALTER
Great Moralist, The. See: JOHNSON, DR. SAMUEL
Great Mouthpiece, The. See: FALLON, WILLIAM J.
Great Nullifier, The. See: CALHOUN, JOHN CALDWELL
Great Objector, The. See: HOLMAN, WILLIAM STEELE

Great Ocean, The Prose Homer of the. See:
RUSSELL, WILLIAM CLARK
Great of Egypt, The Peter the. See:
MEHEMET (MOHAMMED) ALI
Great One, The. See:
BEBAN, GARY JOSEPH
GLEASON, HERBERT JOHN
Great Pacificator, The. See:
CLAY, HENRY
COCHRANE, CLARK BETTON
Great Pan, The. See:
AROUET, FRANÇOIS MARIE
Great Peacemaker. See:
GRANT, HIRAM ULYSSES
Great Profile, The. See:
BLYTHE, JOHN
Great Purist, The. See:
NORRIS, GEORGE WILLIAM
Great Renegade, The. See:
GIRTY, SIMON
Great Repealer, The. See:
BARTON, BRUCE
Great, St. Albert the. See:
ALBERTUS MAGNUS, SAINT, COUNT OF BOLLSTÄDT
Great Scouts, The Last of the. See: CODY, WILLIAM FREDERICK
Great Seer, The. See:
JOHNSON, DR. SAMUEL
Great Sow, The. See:
ISABELLA OF BAVARIA
Great Stone Face, The. See:
WEBSTER, DANIEL
Great, The. See:
AGISILAUS
ALBERTUS MAGNUS, SAINT, COUNT OF BOLLSTÄDT
ALBUQUERQUE, AFFONSO D'
ALEXANDER III
ALFONSO III
ALFRED (AELFRED)
AMADEUS V
ANTIOCHUS III
ANTONY (ANTHONY), ST.
ARNAULD, ANTOINE
ASOKA (ADAOKA)
BASIL, ST.
BERNARD, ROGER
BONAPARTE, NAPOLEON
BRUNO (BRUN), ST.
CANUTE (CNUT) (KNUT) II
CARTER, CHARLES J.
CASIMIR III
CHARLES II
CHARLES EMMANUEL I
CHULALONGKORN
CONDÉ, LOUIS II, PRINCE DE CONDÉ
CYRUS
DARIUS I
DIONYSIUS OF ALEXANDRIA ST.
DONATUS
DUMAS, ALEXANDRE
EMANUEL (MANUEL) I
FREDERICK II
GALITZIN, PRINCE VASILI
GERTRUDE OF HELFTA, ST.
GREGORY
GUSTAVUS II
HANNO
HENRY IV
HEROD
HERRMANN, ALEXANDER
HUGUES (HUGH)
IVAN III VASILIEVICH
JOHN I
JUSTINIAN I (FLAVIUS ANICUS JUSTINIANUS)
KHUSRAU (CHOSROES) I
LENORMAND, MARIE ANNE ADÉLAÏDE
LEO
LEO I
LLYWELYN
LOUIS I
LOUIS XIV
MAHMUD OF GHAZNI
MAILS, WALTER
MATTHIAS I
MAXIMILIAN I

MITHRIDATES VI
MOHAMMED II
NICHOLAS
OTTO I
PEDRO III
PETER I
POMPEY, GNAEUS
POMPEIUS MAGNUS
PROCOPIUS, ANDREW
RATOFF, GERGORY
SANCHO III
SAPOR II
SHAW, RALPH ROBERT
SIGISMUND I
THEODORIC
THEODOSIUS I
TIGRANES I
VISCONTI, MATTEO
VLADIMIR I
WALDEMAR I
WILD, JONATHAN

Great, The (Akbar). See: JELAL-ED-DIN-MOHAMMED

Great, The (El Magno). See: FERDINAND I

Great, The (Nui). See: KAMEHAMEHA I

Great Thundering Rooster, The. See: JOHNSON, HUGH SAMUEL

Great Triumvirate of Italian Literature, The, joint appellation of DURANTE ALIGHIERI (Dante Alighieri) (1265-1321), GIOVANNI BOCCACCIO (1313-75) and PETRARCH (FRANCESCO PETRARCA) (1304-74) [Italian poets]

Great Triumvirate of Italian Literature, The. See also:
ALIGHIERI, DURANTE
BOCCACCIO, GIOVANNI
Immortal Four of Italy, The
PETRARCH (FRANCESCO PETRARCA)

Great Triumvirate, The
The Immortal Trio, collective nicknames of JOHN CALDWELL CALHOUN (1782-1850), HENRY CLAY (1777-1852), and DANIEL WEBSTER (1782-1852), [American statesmen]

Great Triumvirate, The. See also:
CALHOUN, JOHN CALDWELL
CLAY, HENRY
WEBSTER, DANIEL

Great Unknown, The. See: SCOTT, SIR WALTER

Great, Vance the. See: STEVENS, ALFRED PECK

Great War Governor, The. See: CURTIN, ANDREW GREGG

Great White Chief. See: ROOSEVELT, THEODORE

Great White Devil, The. See: VAN CORTLANDT, PHILIP

Great Witch of Balwery, The. See: AIKEN, MARGARET

Great Wizard of the North, The. See: ANDERSON, JOHN HENRY

Great Wolf, The. See: TRYON, WILLIAM

Great Wrestler, The. See: LINCOLN, ABRAHAM

Greater, New York, The Father of. See: GREEN, ANDREW HASWELL

Greater Philadelphia, The Father of. See: BULLITT, JOHN CHRISTIAN

Greater Than the Throne Itself, One Behind the Throne. See: STUART, JOHN

Greatest Alto Saxophone Player, The World's. See: DORSEY, JAMES

Greatest American Jurist, The. See: MARSHALL, JOHN

Greatest Botanist in the World, The. See: BARTRAM, JOHN

Greatest Citizen in the United States, The. See: ELIOT, CHARLES WILLIAM

Greatest Coach, Football's.

See: NEYLAND, GENERAL ROBERT REESE, JR.
Greatest Conductor, France's. See: MÜNCH, CHARLES
Greatest English Actor, The. See: GARRICK, DAVID
Greatest Gambler, The. See: CANFIELD, RICHARD A.
Greatest Inventors, One of America's. See: BOYDEN, SETH
Greatest Lover, The Screen's. See: D'ANTONGUOLLA, RODOLPHO ALFONZO RAFAELO PIERRE FILIBERT GUGLIELMO DI VALENTIN
Greatest Modern Playwright, Germany's. See: HAUPTMANN, GERHART
Greatest Pilot in the World, Bar None, The. See: BALCHEN, BERNT
Greatest Poet Who Wrote in Sanscrit, The. See: BHARTRIHARI (BHARTRHARI)
Greatest Pope, Rome's. See: GREGORY
Greatest Showman Since Barnum, The. See: NORTH, JOHN RINGLING
Greatest Theoretical Physicist of the Nineteenth Century, The. See: MAXWELL, JAMES CLERK
Greatest Traveler, Detroit's. See: STEARNS, FREDERICK KIMBALL
Greatest Writer of the Restoration Period, The. See: DRYDEN, JOHN
GREATRAKES (GREATOREX), VALENTINE (1629-83) [Irish physician]
The Touch Doctor
Greaves, Richard. See: McCUTCHEON, GEORGE BARR
GREB, HENRY EDWARD (1894-1926) [American professional boxer; world's middleweight champion]
Harry Greb
GREBANIER, FRANCESCA VINCIGUERRA (1900-) [Italian-American critic and novelist]
Frances Winwar
Grecian. See: DAVIES, CHARLES STEWART
Grecian Literature, The Voltaire of. See: LUCIAN OF SAMOSATA
GRECO, ARMANDO (1926-) [American jazz musician (piano, arranger, singer)]
Buddy Greco
GRECO, COSTANZO (1918-) [Spanish dancer and choreographer]
José Greco
Greco, El (The Greek). See: THEOTOKOPOULOS, KYRIAKOS
Greece. See: Seven Sages of Greece, The
Greece, The Leonidas of Modern. See: BOZZARIS (BOTZARIS), MARKOS
Greece, The Muse of. See: XENOPHON
Greece, The Seven Wise Men of. See: Seven Sages of Greece, The.
Greece, The Wisest Man of. See: SOCRATES
Greedy Woman, A. See: PENNELL, ELIZABETH
Greek Commentator, The. See: GUZMAN, FERNANDO NUÑEZ DE
Greek Music, The Father of. See: TERPANDER
Greek Prose, The Father of. See: HERODOTUS
Greek Revolution, The Lafayette of the. See: HOWE, SAMUEL GRIDLEY
Greek Scholar of Our Time, The Foremost. See:

MURRAY, GEORGE
GILBERT AIMÉ
Greek, The. See:
GEORGE, CHARLIE
Greek, The (El Greco). See:
THEOTOKOPOULOS,
KYRIAKOS
Greek Tragedy, The Father
of. See:
AESCHYLUS
THESPIS
Greeks, The Last of the. See:
PHILOPOEMEN
GREELEY, EZEKIEL (1725-93)
[American lawyer,
farmer, sea-faring man
and community leader]
Old Captain Ezekiel
GREELEY, HORACE (1811-72)
[American newspaper
editor, publisher and
moral leader]
The Ghost
Old White Hat
The Prince of Journalists
The Sage of Chappaqua
GREEN [Green]. See also:
GREENE
Greene
GREIN
GREEN, ANDREW HASWELL
(fl. last quarter of
19th cent.) [American
civic leader in New York]
The Father of Greater New
York
GREEN, ANNA KATHARINE
(1846-1935) [American
writer of detective
fiction]
The Godmother of Detective
Stories
The Mother of Detective
Stories
Green, Bryan. See:
DAVIS, HORACE BANCROFT
Green, Charles M. See:
GARDNER, ERLE
STANLEY
Green Count, The. See:
AMADEUS VI
Green, D. See:
CASEWIT, CURTIS
GREEN, DAVID (1886-)
[Jewish leader; Premier
of Israel]
David Ben-Gurion
GREEN, EDMUND FISK
(1842-1901) [American
philosopher and historian]
John Fiske
Green-eyed Man of Destiny,
The. See:
WALKER, WILLIAM
GREEN, HENRIETTA
HOWLAND (1834-1916)
[American financier]
Hetty Green
The Witch of Wall Street
Green, Henry. See:
YORKE, HENRY VINCENT
GREEN, HENRY HAWES
CRAVEN (1837-1910)
[English scene painter]
Hawes Craven
GREEN, IAN ERNEST
GILMORE (1912-)
[Canadian jazz musician
(piano, composer)]
Gil Evans
Green Isle, The Orpheus of the.
See: O'CAROLAN,
TURLOCH
GREEN, JOHN (1908-)
[American composer,
conductor, arranger and
pianist]
Johnny Green
GREEN, JULIEN HARTRIDGE
(1900-) [French-
American educator and
author]
Theophile Delaporte
Julien Green
David Irland
Green, L. Dunton. See:
GREIN, JACOB THOMAS
Green Man, The. See:
DE SALVO, ALBERT H.
Green Mountain, Burns of the.
See: EASTMAN,
CHARLES GAMAGE
GREEN, NATHAN (1792-1866)
[American jurist]
The Father of Equity in
Tennessee

The Hardwicke of Tennessee
Green, O.O. See:
DURGNAT, RAYMOND ERIC
Green, Olive. See:
REED, MYRTLE
GREEN, PETER (fl. early 20th cent.) [British clergyman and author]
Artifex
GREEN, PETER MORRIS (1924-) [British educator, editor and author]
Denis Delaney
GREEN, SHEILA ELLEN (1934-) [American author]
Sheila Greenwald
Green, The. See:
AMADEUS VI
GREEN, URBAN CLIFFORD (1926-) [American jazz musician (trombone)]
Urbie Green
GREEN, VERNICE, JR. (1935-) [American jazz musician (saxophone, flute, clarinet)]
Bunky Green
GREEN-WANSTALL, KENNETH (1918-) [British journalist and author]
Ken Wanstall
Greenbacks, The Father of. See:
CHASE, SALMON PORTLAND
SPAULDING, ELBRIDGE GERRY
GREENBERG, HENRY BENJAMIN (1911-) [American professional baseball player]
Hank Greenberg
GREENE [Greene]. See also:
GREEN
Green
GREIN
Greene, Adam. See:
SCOTT, PETER DALE
GREENE, FREDERICK STUART (1870-1939) [American civil engineer and politician]
The Father of Concrete Roads in New York
GREENE, GLADYS (1908-) [American stage and motion picture actress]
Jean Arthur
GREENE, NATHANAEL (1742-86) [American Revolutionary War general officer]
The Fighting Quaker
Greene, Robert. See:
DEINDORFER, ROBERT GREENE
GREENE, SARAH PRATT McLEAN (1856-1935) [American author]
Sally Pratt McLean
GREENE, WARD (1892-) [American novelist]
Frank Dudley
GREENFIELD, ELIZABETH TAYLOR (1808-76) [American Negro singer]
The Black Swan
GREENFIELD, JEROME (1923-) [Hebrew educator and author]
Jerry Greenfield
GREENFIELD, SAMMY (1878-1945) [American vaudeville comedian and motion picture actor]
George Sidney
Greenfingers, Mr. See:
WALLS, IAN GASCOIGNE
GREENHOOD, CLARENCE DAVID (1895-) [American author]
Mark Sawyer
Greenhorn. See:
THOMPSON, GEORGE
GREENHOW, ROSE O'NEAL (fl. 1861-65) [American Civil War Confederate spy]
The Queen of the Rosewater Administration
Greenland, The Apostle of. See:
EGEDE, HANS
Greenock, Lord. See:
CATHCART, CHARLES MURRAY, 2D EARL

GREENSPUN, HERMAN MILTON (1909-) [American attorney and author]
Hank Greenspun
Greenwald, Sheila. See: GREEN, SHEILA ELLEN
Greenway, Grandfather. See: CANNON, CHARLES JAMES
Greenwood, Grace. See: LIPPINCOTT, SARA JANE CLARKE
GREENWOOD, JULIA EILEEN COURTNEY (1910-) [British journalist and broadcaster]
Francis Askham
GREER, WILLIAM ALEXANDER (1903-) [American jazz musician (drums, leader)]
Sonny Greer
Greet, Sir Ben. See: BARLING, PHILIP
Greeter of Famous People, New York City's Official. See: WHALEN, GROVER ALOYSIUS
Greg McClure. See: EASTON, DALE
Gregg Palmer. See: LEE, PALMER
Gregoire Aslan. See: ASLANIAN, KRIDOR
Gregor. See: MENDEL, JOHANN
Gregor Lang. See: BIRREN, FABER
GREGORY [Gregory]. See also: Grigory
GREGORY (c. 540-604) [Supreme Pontiff of Roman Catholic Church]
The Great
Pope Gregory I
Rome's Greatest Pope
St. Gregory
GREGORY (died 731) [Supreme Pontiff of Roman Catholic Church]
Pope Gregory II
St. Gregory
GREGORY (died 741) [Supreme Pontiff of Roman Catholic Church]
Pope Gregory III
St. Gregory
GREGORY (died 844) [Supreme Pontiff of Roman Catholic Church]
Pope Gregory IV
GREGORY (died 999) [Supreme Pontiff of Roman Catholic Church]
Pope Gregory V
Gregory VI, Pope. See: GRATIANUS, JOHANNES
Gregory VII, Pope. See: HILDEBRAND
Gregory VIII, Pope. See: MORRA, ALBERTO DI
Gregory IX, Pope. See: UGOLINI, COUNT OF SEGNI
Gregory X, Pope. See: VISCONTI, TEOBALDO
Gregory XI, Pope. See: BEAUFORT, PIERRE ROGER DE
Gregory XII, Pope. See: CARRARIO, ANGELO
Gregory XIII, Pope. See: BUONCOMPAGNI, UGO
Gregory XIV, Pope. See: SFONDRATI, NICCOLÒ
Gregory XV, Pope. See: LUDOVISI, ALESSANDRO
Gregory XVI, Pope. See: CAPPELLARI BARTOLOMMEO ALBERTO
Gregory Duncan. See: McCLINTOCK, MARSHALL
GREGORY, EDMUND (1925-) [American jazz musician (alto and baritone saxophones, flute, composer)]
Sahib Shihab
Gregory, Elizabeth. See: GILFORD, CHARLES BERNARD
Gregory, Hilton. See: FERGUSON, CHARLES W.
Gregory, Lady Augusta. See: PERSSE, ISABELLA AUGUSTA

GREGORY, MRS. HORACE
MARYA (1902-) [Russian poet]
Maria Zaturenska
GREGORY OF ARMENIA, ST. (c. 257-c. 332) [first patriarch and patron saint of the Armenian Church]
The Apostle of Armenia
The Illuminator
GREGORY OF NAZIANZUS, ST. (325?-90) [Christian Church father and Bishop of Constantinople]
The Theologian
Theologus
GREGORY OF RIMINI (died 1358) [Italian schoolman]
The Authentic Doctor
Gregory of Tours, St. See:
FLORENTIUS, GEORGIUS
Gregory, Paul. See:
LENHART, JASON GREGORY
Gregory, St. See:
GREGORY
HILDEBRAND
Gregory, Sean. See:
HOSSENT, HARRY
GREGORY THAUMATURGUS (c. 210-c. 270) [Greek church father]
Wonderworker
Gregory the Great. See:
GREGORY
RATOFF, GREGORY
GREGSON, MICHAEL (1928-) [British motion picture actor]
Michael Craig
Gregson, Paul. See:
OAKLEY, ERIC GILBERT
GREIG, MAYSIE COUCHER (1901-) [Australian author]
Jennifer Ames
GREIN. See also:
GREEN
Green
GREENE
Greene
GREIN, JACOB THOMAS (1862-1935) [Dutch-English playwright, dramatic critic and theatre manager]
J. T. G.
Jack Grein
James Grein
L. Dunton Green
GRELLET, ETIENNE DE (1773-1855) [French Quaker, traveler and evangelist]
Stephen
Grenadier of France, The First. See:
LA TOUR D'AUVERGNE, THÉOPHILE MALO CORRET DE
Grendon, Edward. See:
LeSHAN, LAWRENCE LEE
Grendon, Stephen. See:
DERLETH, AUGUST WILLIAM
Grenelle, Lisa. See:
MUNROE, ELIZABETH LEE
Grenfell, Joyce. See:
PHIPPS, JOYCE
GRENFELL, SIR WILFRED THOMASON (1865-1940) [English physician, missionary and author]
Grenfell of Labrador
GRENVILLE, GEORGE (1712-70) [British statesman and Prime Minister]
The Gentle Shepherd
GRENVILLE, RICHARD TEMPLE (1711-79) [Earl Temple; English politician]
Lord Gawkey
Tiddy-Doll
GRESHAM, CLAUDE HAMILTON, JR. (1922-) [American conversationist and author]
Grits Gresham
Greta Garbo. See:
GUSTAFFSON, GRETA LOVISA
Greta Gynt. See:
WOXHOLT, GRETA
Gréville, Henry. See:

DURAND, MME. ALICE
FLEURY
Grey. See:
GRAY
Gray
ROWLAND-BROWN,
LILIAN
Grey, Beryl. See:
SVENSON, MRS. SVEN
GUSTAV
Grey, Brenda. See:
MACKINLAY, LEILA
ANTOINETTE
STERLING
Grey-crested Flycatcher, The.
See: BURROUGHS,
JOHN
Grey, Donald. See:
THOMAS EUGENE
Grey, Elizabeth. See:
HOGG, BETH TOOTILL
Grey-eyed Man of Destiny,
The. See:
WALKER, WILLIAM
Grey, Nan. See:
MILLER, ESCHAL
Grey of Fallodon. See:
EDWARD, VISCOUNT
GREY OF FALLODON
Greystone, The Sage of. See:
TILDEN, SAMUEL
JONES
GRIBBIN, KATHERINA HOUSTON
(1902-) [British
vaudevillian, stage and
motion picture actress]
Renée Houston
Gridiron Club, The Father
and Nursing Mother of
the. See:
CARSON, JOHN MILLER
Gridiron, The Golden Man of
the. See:
WILKINSON, CHARLES
BURNHAM
Gridiron, The Old Man of the.
See: KENNEALLY,
GEORGE V
GRIER, JAMES W. (1902-59)
[American jazz musician
(saxophone, leader,
composer, arranger)]
The Host to the Coast
Jimmie Grier
Grierson, Francis. See:
SHEPARD, BENJAMIN
HENRY JESSE FRANCIS
GRIEVE, CHRISTOPHER
MURRAY (1892-)
[Scottish author, poet,
journalist and essayist]
Isobel Guthrie
A.K. Laidlaw
Hugh MacDiarmid
James MacLaren
Pteleon
Grievous, Peter, Esq. See:
HOPKINSON, FRANCIS
Griff. See:
FAWCETT, FRANK
DUBREZ
McKEAG, ERNEST LIONEL
WILLIAMS, GRIFFITH E.,
III
Griffin, C. F. See:
FISKO, EUNICE CLELAND
GRIFFIN, DEBRALEE (1933-)
[American stage and
motion picture actress]
Debra Paget
GRIFFIN, MERVYN EDWARD, JR.
(1925-) [American tele-
vision personality and pro-
ducer]
Merv Griffin
GRIFFIN, JOSEPH K. (born 1852)
[American Indian scout,
lecturer and author]
Tahan
GRIFFITH, ANDREW SAMUEL
(1926-) [American actor]
Andy Griffith
GRIFFITH, CLARK (1869-1955)
[American professional
baseball player]
The Old Fox
Griffith, Jeannette, joint. pseud.
of JEANNETTE HYDE
EYERLY (1908-) and
VALERIA WINKLER
GRIFFITH (-) [American
authors]
Grigory. See also:
GREGORY
Gregory
Grigory Vinokur. See:

WEINRAUCH, HERSCHEL
Grile, Dod. See:
BIERCE, AMBROSE GWINNETT
Grillandajo. See:
BIGORDI, RIDOLFO
BIGORDI, TOMMASO
GRILLO, FRANK (1912-) [Cuban jazz musician (leader)]
Machito
Grim Chieftain, The. See:
LANE, JAMES HENRY
Grim Old Lion of Athens, The. See: GROSVENOR, CHARLES HENRY
Grim, The. See:
DOUGLAS, ARCHIBALD
GRIMALDI, JOSEPH (1779-1837) [English clown and pantominist]
Joey
Grimble, Reverend Charles James. See:
ELIOT, THOMAS STEARNS
GRIMES, BURLEIGH A. (1893-) [American professional baseball player]
Senator
GRIMES, LLOYD (1915-) [American jazz musician (guitar)]
Tiny Grimes
Grimm. See:
Brothers Grimm, The
GRIMM, JACOB LUDWIG KARL. See: Brothers Grimm, The
GRIMM, WILHELM KARL. See: Brothers Grimm, The
Grimm of Iceland, The. See:
ARNASON, JÓN
GRIMOND, JOSEPH (1913-) [British political leader]
Jo Grimond
GRIMORD, GUILLAUME DE (1309-70) [Supreme Pontiff of Roman Catholic Church]
Pope Urban V
Grimshaw, Mark. See:
McKEAG, ERNEST LIONEL
Grimsley, Gordon. See:
GROOM, ARTHUR WILLIAM
GRIMSON, MARGARET BRUNTON (1849-1935 [English actress]
Madge Kendal
GRIMSTON, WILLIAM HUNTER (1843-1917) [English actor-manager]
William Hunter Kendal
GRINDAL, EUGENE (1895-1952) [French poet]
Paul Eluard
GRINGHUIS, RICHARD H. (1913-) [American author]
Dirk Gringhuis
Gringo, Harry. See:
WISE, HENRY AUGUSTUS
Grinnell, David. See:
WOLLHEIM, DONALD ALLEN
GRIS, JOSÉ VITTORIANO GONZÁLEZ (1887-1927) [Spanish-French cubist painter]
Juan Gris
Grise, Éminence (Gray Eminence). See:
TREMBLAY, FRANÇOIS LE CLERC DU
Grise, Redingote. See:
BONAPARTE, NAPOLEON
GRISSOM, ARTHUR COLFAX (1869-1901) [American journalist and author of dime novels]
Albert Cecil Gaines
GRISWOLD, A. MINER (1834-91) [American journalist and humorist]
The Fat Contributor
Sandy Griswold
GRISWOLD, FRANCES IRENE BURGE (1826-1900) [American author]
Mrs. S.B. Phelps
GRISWOLD, RUFUS WILMOT (1815-57) [American editor and anthologist]
Ludwig

Grits. See:
GRESHAM, CLAUDE HAMILTON, JR.
Groaner, The. See:
CROSBY, HARRY LILLIS
GROAT, RICHARD MORROW (1930-) [American professional baseball player]
Dick Groat
Grock. See:
WETTACH, ADRIAN (ARNOLD)
Grode, Redway. See:
GOREY, EDWARD ST. JOHN
GROETE. See:
GROOTE (GROOT) (GROETE), GERHARD
Grog, Old. See:
VERNON, EDWARD
GROOM, ARTHUR WILLIAM (1898-1964) [British author]
Graham Adamson
George Anderson
Daphne du Blane
Gordon Grimsley
Bill Pembury
John Stanstead
Maurice Templar
Martin Toonder
GROOTE (GROOT) (GROETE), GERHARD (1340-84) [Dutch preacher]
Gerardus Magnus
Groove. See:
HOLMES, RICHARD ARNOLD
Gros-Guillaume. See:
GUÉRIN, ROBERT
Gros-René. See:
DU PARC, RENÉ BERTHELOT
Grosofsky, Leslie. See:
GROSS, LESLIE
GROSS, LESLIE (1927-) [American author]
Leslie Grosofsky
Gross, The. See:
DOUGLAS, JAMES
GROSSBERG, YITZROCH LOIZA (1923-) [American painter]
Larry Rivers
GROSSEL, IRA (1918-61) [American radio, stage and motion picture actor]
Jeff Chandler
GROSSMAN, ARTHUR (1894-) [American lyricist of popular songs]
Arthur Freed
GROSSMAN, JOSEPHINE JUDITH (1923-) [American author]
Ernest Hamilton
Judith Merrill
Rose Sharon
Eric Thorstein
GROSSMAN, JOSEPHINE JUDITH. See also:
Judd, Cyril
GROSVENOR, CHARLES HENRY (1833-1917) [American politician; congressman from Ohio]
The Gentle Shepherd of Ohio
The Grim Old Lion of Athens
Old Figgers
GROTIUS, HUGO (1583-1645) [Dutch theologian and historian]
The Father of International Law
GROTO, LUIGI (1541-85) [Italian dramatist and poet]
The Blind Man of Adria
The Blind Poet
Groton, The Heroine of. See:
BAILEY, ANNA WARNER
Groucho Marx. See:
Four Marx Brothers, The
GROUÈS, HENRI ANTOINE (1912-) [French priest]
Abbé Pierre
GROVE, ROBERT MOSES (1900-) [American professional baseball player]
Lefty Grove
Grove, Will O. See:
BRISTER, RICHARD
Grover. See:
CLEVELAND, STEPHEN GROVER

GROVER, MARTIN (1811-75)
[American attorney]
The Ragged Lawyer
Grover, Old. See:
CLEVELAND, STEPHEN GROVER
Grover, Our. See:
CLEVELAND, STEPHEN GROVER
Grover the Good. See:
CLEVELAND, STEPHEN GROVER
GROW, GALUSHA AARON (1823-1907) [American politician; congressman from Pennsylvania]
The Father of the Homestead Law
GRUBER, FRANK (1904-69) [American journalist and author]
Stephen Acre
Charles K. Boston
John K. Vedder
Gruelle, Johnny. See:
BARTON, JOHN
Grumbler, Anthony. See:
HOFFMAN, DAVID
Grün, Anastasius. See:
AUERSPERG, ANTON ALEXANDER, GRAF VON
GRUNDY, SAM (1897-1966) [British motion picture actor]
Wallace Ford
GRUNDY, WILFRED WALKER (1884-) [British educator and author]
Aber
Guano Statesman. See:
BLAINE, JAMES GILLESPIE
Guard of New York, The Father of the National. See:
PHISTERER, FREDERICK
Guard, The Boy. See:
WHITMAN, JOHN LORIN
Guard, Theodore de la. See:
WARD, NATHANIEL
Guardian of Civil Service, The. See:
RAMSPECK, ROBERT
GUARDIOLA, SANTOS (1810-62) [Central American general officer; President of Honduras]
The Tiger of Central America
Guarnerius, Tobias, Jr. See:
DIMITRY, CHARLES PATTON
GUARNIERI, GIUSEPPE ANTONIO (1683-1745) [Italian violin maker]
Giuseppe del Gesù (Giuseppe of Jesus)
GUARNIERI, PIETRO (1695-1765) [Italian violin maker]
Peter of Venice
GUARNIERI, PIETRO GIOVANNI (1655-1728) [Italian violin maker]
Peter of Mantua
GUBENKO, JULIUS (1924-) [American jazz musician (vibraphone, leader)]
Terry Gibbs
GUCKENHEIMER, DR. FRITZ (1906-) [American composer, clarinetist and business executive]
Richard Gump
GUDJONSSEN, HALLDÓR (1902-) [Icelandic author]
Halldór Kiljan Laxness
Guelphs, Head of the. See:
HENRY
GUENOD, JACQUES (1889-) [French stage and motion picture actor]
Jim Gerald
Guercino (Squint-Eyed). See:
BARBIERI, GIOVANNI FRANCESCO
GUÉRIN, ROBERT (fl. 1600-34) [French farce-player and actor]
Gros-Guillaume
GUERRA, RAFAEL (1862-1941) [Spanish bullfighter]
Guerrita
Llaverito
GUERRINI, OLINDO (1845-1916) [Italian poet]
Lorenzo Stecchetti
Guerrita. See:
GUERRA, RAFAEL
GUESCLIN (DUGUESCLIN),

BERTRAND DU (1320-80) [French commander]
The Eagle of Brittany

GUESS (GIST), GEORGE (c. 1770-1843) [American newspaper man; creator of the Cherokee alphabet]
Sequoyah

GUEST, EDGAR ALBERT (1881-1959) [American newspaper columnist and poet]
Eddie Guest

Guetary, Georges. See: WORLOOU, LAMBROS

GUEVARA, DR. SERNA ERNESTO (1928-) [Cuban political leader]
Che

GUFFEY, JOSEPH F. (1875-) [American politician; senator from Pennsylvania]
The King-maker

Guglielmi, Rudolph. See: D'ANTONGUOLLA, RODOLPHO ALFONZO RAFAELO PIERRE FILIBERT GUGLIELMO DI VALENTIN

GUICHE, DOROTHY DE (1898-1968) [American motion picture actress]
Dorothy Gish

GUICHE, LILLIAN DE (1896-) [American motion picture actress]
Carrots
The First Lady of the Screen
Lillian Gish

Guideo, Manoello. See: IMMANUEL BEN SOLOMON

GUIDI, TOMMASO (1401-28?) [Italian painter]
Masaccio

GUIDO D'AREZZO (GUIDO ARETINO) (c. 995-c. 1050) [Benedictine monk and reformer of music]
Fra Guittone

Guillaume Apollinaire. See: KOSTROWITSKY, APOLLINARIS

GUILLAUME D'ORANGE (c. 750-812) [leader of Charlemagne's armies]
Fierabrace
Marquis au Court Nez (Marquis Short-nose)
St. Guillaume de Gellone

Guillaume, Gros. See: GUÉRIN, ROBERT

Guillaume, Robert. See: SNEDDON, ROBERT WILLIAM

Guillén, Curro. See: RODRÍGUEZ, FRANCISCO HERRERA

GUILLERM NELLY (1933-) [French ballerina]
Violette Verdy

Guillermo Eduardi. See: EDWARDS, WILLIAM BENNETT

Guillot-Gorju. See: ST. JACQUES, BERTRAND HARDOUIN

Guillotina, The. See: HOPKINS, DR. LEMUEL

Guillotine, The Anacreon of The. See: VIEUZAC, BERTRAND BARÈRE DE

GUINAN, MARY LOUISE CECELIA (1884-1933) [American night club entertainer and motion picture actress]
The Nightclub Queen
Texas Guinan
The Two-gun Girl

GUION, RAYMOND (1908-) [American stage and motion picture actor]
Gene Raymond
Mr. Malone

GUISE, MARY (1515-60) [French noblewoman; mother of MARY, QUEEN OF SCOTS
Mary of Lorraine

Guiseppe Mario. See: CANDIA, DON GIOVANNI DE

Guitar, The King of the Electric. See: McBURNEY, ALBERT

Guittone, Fra. See: GUIDO D'AREZZO (GUIDO ARETINO)

GUIU, JOSÉ MELIS (1920-)

[Cuban composer, pianist and conductor]
José Melis
Guizot, The Egeria of. See:
LIEVEN, DOROTHEA, PRINCESS DE
GULDIN, JOHN C. (1799-1863) [American clergyman; editor of German religious literature]
The Apostle to the Germans
Gulf, The Pirate of the. See:
LAFITTE, JEAN
Gulf, The Terror of the. See:
LAFITTE, JEAN
Gulliver, Lemuel. See:
SWIFT, JONATHAN
Gulliver, The Whig. See:
WEBSTER, DANIEL
GUMM, FRANCES (1922-69) [American singer and motion picture actress]
Judy Garland
Gummo. See:
MARX, MILTON
Gump, Richard. See:
GUCKENHEIMER, DR. FRITZ
Gumshoe. See:
HUNTER, WHITESIDE GODFREY
Gunboat. See:
HUDSON, WALTER
GUNN, GLADYS (1897-) [Irish stage and motion picture actress]
Gladys Henson
GUNN, JAMES E. (1923-) [American educator, editor and author]
Edwin James
GUNN, WILLIAM HARRISON (1934-) [American actor, playwright and novelist]
Bill Gunn
Gunther, William. See:
SPRECHER, WILLIAM GUNTHER
GUPTA, RAM CHANDRA (1927-) [Indian educator and author]
Rama
GURDIN, NATASHA (1938-) [American actress]
Natalie Wood
Gurie, Sigrid. See:
HAUKELID, SIGRID GURIE
GURNEY, JOHN CHANDLER (1896-) [American politician; senator from South Dakota]
Chan Gurney
Gus. See:
ADDICKS, JOHN EDWARD O'SULLIVAN
MANCUSO, RONALD BERNARD
TRAVO, GUS
Guz Krutzch. See:
ELIOT, THOMAS STEARNS
Gus McNaughton. See:
HOWARD, AUGUSTUS
Gus, Uncle. See:
REY, HANS AUGUSTO
Gushington, Impulsia. See:
SHERIDAN, LADY HELEN SELINA
Gustaf. See:
GUSTAVUS V
GUSTAFFSON, GRETA LOVISA (1905-) [Swedish motion picture actress]
Greta Garbo
GUSTAFSON, AXEL (c.1847-) [Swedish author]
Carl Bremer
Gustav Troll. See:
BRESTOWSKI, CARL AUGUST
Gustave Aimard. See:
GLOUX, OLIVIER
GUSTAVUS I (1496-1560) [King of Sweden]
Gustavus Eriksson
Gustavus Vasa
GUSTAVUS II (1594-1632) [King of Sweden]
The Great
Gustavus Adolphus
The Lion of the North
The Snow King
The Star of the North
The Swedish Maccabaeus
GUSTAVUS IV (1778-1837) [King of Sweden]

Gustavus Adolphus
GUSTAVUS V (1858-1950)
[King of Sweden]
Gustaf
Gut, Gom. See:
SIMENON, GEORGES
Gutenberg, Johan. See:
GENSFLEISCH, JOHAN
GUTHRIE, ALFRED BERTRAM, JR. (1901-) [American journalist, teacher and novelist]
A. B. Guthrie, Jr.
Guthrie, Isobel. See:
GRIEVE, CHRISTOPHER MURRAY
Guthrie, Ramsay. See:
BOWRAN, JOHN GEORGE
GUTHRIE, THOMAS ANSTEY (1856-1934) [English humorist and story writer]
F. Anstey
Francis
GUTHRIE, WOODROW WILSON (1912-) [American folk singer, composer and writer]
Woody Guthrie
Guts, Old Blood and. See:
PATTON, GEORGE SMITH JR.
Guy. See:
DE MAUPASSANT, HENRI RENÉ ALBERT GUY
EMPEY, ARTHUR GUY
Guy Bruce. See:
PUNNETT, IVOR McCAULEY
Guy Carlton Lee. See:
AYER, JOHN
Guy de Montfort. See:
JOHNSON, DONALD McINTOSH
Guy Madison. See:
MOSELEY, ROBERT
GUY OF BURGUNDY (died 1124) [Supreme Pontiff of Roman Catholic Church]
Pope Callistus II
Guy Pearce. See:
PILLEY, CHARLES
Guy, The Big. See:
DIMAGGIO, JOSEPH PAUL, JR.
WILLIAMS, THEODORE SAMUEL
GUYER, ULYSSES SAMUEL (1863-) [American politician; congressman from Kansas]
The Dry Wind
The Kansas Dry
Guyon, Madame. See:
MOTTE-GUYON, JEANNE MARIE BOUVIER DE LA
GUYONVARCH, IRENE CECILIA (1915-) [English author]
Irene Pearl
GUZMAN, ALPHONSO PEREZ DE (1258-1320) [Spanish general officer]
The Spanish Brutus
GUZMAN, EUGÉNIE MARIA DE MONTIJO, COMTESSE DE TEBA DE (1853-71) [Empress of the French]
Empress Eugénie
Guzmán, Felix. See:
SCHOPENHAUER, FELIX BEGLIO
GUZMAN, FERNANDO NUÑEZ DE 1473-1553) [Spanish savant]
The Greek Commentator
Gwalia, Alfred. See:
THOMAS, ALFRED
GWALTNEY, PEMBROKE DECATUR (1836-1914) [American agriculturist; pioneer in the peanut industry]
The Peanut King
Gwen. See:
VERDON, GWYNETH EVELYN
Gwynne, Anne. See:
TRICE, MARGUERITE GWYNNE
Gwynne, Oscar A. See:
ELLIS, EDWARD SYLVESTER
GYERGYAY, STEFAN (1904-) [Hungarian stage and motion picture actor]
Steve Geray
Gymnastics, Father of

(Turnvater). See:
JAHN, FRIEDRICH LUDWIG
Gynt, Greta. See:
WOXHOLT, GRETA
Gyp. See:
MARTEL, COMTESSE DE MIRABEAU DE
Gypsies, The Queen of the. See:
ADAMS, ROSE
Gypsy. See also:
Gipsy
GWYN (GWYNNE), ELEANOR (1650-87) [English actress; mistress of CHARLES II]
Nell Gwyn (Gwynne)
Pretty, Witty Nellie
Gypsy Rose Lee. See:
HOVICK, ROSE LOUISE

H

H. See:
BEDFORD-JONES, HENRY JAMES O'BRIEN
H.A. Page. See:
JAPP, ALEXANDER HAY
H. Allen Smith. See:
SMITH, HARRY ALLEN
H.B.G. See:
GOODWIN, HANNAH ELIZABETH BRADBURY
H. Baldwin Taylor. See:
WAUGH, HILLARY BALDWIN
H. Borneman. See:
GOTTSHALL, FRANKLIN HENRY
H. Braxton Hull. See:
JACOBS, HELEN HULL
H.C.H.C. See:
CANDY, HUGH CHARLES HERBERT
H.C. Thomas. See:
KEATING, LAWRENCE A.
H.D. See:
ALDINGTON, HILDA DOOLITTLE
H.E. See:
BATES, HERBERT ERNEST
WATTERS, HENRY EUGENE
H.E. Agard. See:
EVANS, HILARY
H.F. See:
HEARD, HENRY FITZ GERALD
H.G. See:
WELLS, HERBERT GEORGE
H.H. See:
JACKSON, HELEN MARIA FISKE HUNT
H.H.H. See:
HUMPHREY, HUBERT HORATIO
H.H. Holmes. See:
WHITE, WILLIAM ANTHONY PARKER
H.J.M. See:
MASSINGHAM, HAROLD JOHN
H.J. Schlosberg. See:
MAY, HENRY JOHN
H.L. See:
DAVIS, HAROLD LENOIR
MENCKEN, HENRY LOUIS
H.L. Howard. See:
WELLS, CHARLES JEREMIAH
H. Lowe Lawson. See:
LAWSON, HORACE LOWE
H.M. See:
TOMLINSON, HENRY MAJOR
H.O. Ward, Mrs. See:
MOORE, CLARA SOPHIA JESSUP
H.P. Siwéermill. See:
SHARP, WILLIAM
H.R. Gordon, Colonel. See:
ELLIS, EDWARD SYLVESTER
H.R. Millbank, Captain. See:
ELLIS, EDWARD SYLVESTER
H. Rebak. See:
BAKER, HENRY
H. Rider Haggard. See:
HAGGARD, HENRY RIDER
H.S.T. See:
TRUMAN, HARRY S
H.T.P. See:
PARKER, HENRY TAYLOR

H. Trusta. See:
PHELPS, ELIZABETH STUART
H.W. Chevalier. See:
SEARS, EDWARD I.
Ha-ari. See:
LURIA, ISAAC BEN SOLOMON
HAAKON I (c. 914-961) [King of Norway]
The Good
HAAKON II (1147-62) [King of Norway]
Herdebred (Broad Shouldered)
HAAKON IV HAAKONSSON (1204-63) [King of Norway]
The Old
HAAKON V (1217-c. 1263) [King of Norway]
The Old
HAAKON V MAGNUSSON (1270-1319) [King of Norway]
Haalegg (Longlegs)
HAARER, ALEC ERNEST (1894-) [British civil servant and author]
Shanwa
Haarfagr (Fairhaired). See:
HAROLD I
Haarlem, Jan Vermeer van. See:
MEER, JAN VAN DER
HAAS, DOROTHY F. (fl. 1957-63) [American author]
Dee Francis
HAAS, GEORGE W. (1903-) [American professional baseball player]
Mule
Hababli (The Babylonian). See:
HILLEL
Habbema, Joos. See:
HEIJERMANS (HEYERMANS), HERMAN
Habe, Hans. See:
BEKESSY, JEAN
Habeas Corpus. See:
HOWE, WILLIAM FREDERICK
HABLA, MANUEL DE LA (1868-1936) [Spanish bullfighter]
Zurito
Hachette, Jeanne. See:
LAISNÉ, JEANNE
Hack. See:
WILSON, LEWIS ROBERT
HACKENSCHMIDT, GEORGE (-1968) [Estonian heavyweight wrestler]
The Russian Lion
HACKER, LEONARD (1924-) [American comedian and actor]
Buddy Hackett
Hackett, Buddy. See:
HACKER, LEONARD
Haddock, Albert. See:
HERBERT, SIR ALAN PATRICK
Haddon, Christopher. See:
PALMER, JOHN LESLIE
Haderman, Janet H. See:
WALWORTH, JEANETTE RITCHIE HADERMAN
Hadewjich. See:
UNKNOWN
HADFIELD, ELLIS CHARLES RAYMOND (1909-) [British editor and author]
Charles Alexander
E.C.R. Hadfield
Hadley, Franklin. See:
WINTERBOTHAM, RUSSELL ROBERT
HADLEY, IRVING D. (1904-) [American professional baseball player]
Bump
HADRIAN (ADRIAN) (76-138 A.D.) [Roman emperor]
Pater Patriae (The Father of His Country)
Háfiz (One Who Remembers). See:
SHAMS UN-DIN MOHAMMED
HAFTEL, MARTHA (1930?-) [Austrian singer and actress]
Martha Schlamme
Hagen, Jean. See:
VERHAGEN, JEAN
HAGGARD, HENRY RIDER (1856-1925) [English author]
H. Rider Haggard

Haggard, Paul. See:
LONGSTREET, STEPHEN
Haggard, William. See:
CLAYTON, RICHARD HENRY MICHAEL
HAGNER, PETER (1772-1850) [Auditor of United States Treasury]
The Watch-dog of the Treasury
HAGUE, FRANK (1876-1956) [American political boss; Mayor of Jersey City, N.J.]
Boss Hague
The Dictator of Jersey City
HAHNEMANN, CHRISTIAN SAMUEL FREDERICK (1755-1843) [German physician; founder of homeopathy]
The Prodigy of Learning
HAILE SELASSIE, RAS TAFFARI (TAFARI) (1891-) [Emperor of Ethiopia and Eritrea]
The Lion of Judah
HAIME, AGNES IRVINE CONSTANCE ADAMS (1884-) [British teacher, reformer and author]
Persis
HAJMASSY, ILONA (1912-) [Hungarian motion picture actress]
Ilona Massey
Hakim, Sadik. See:
THORNTON, ARGONNE DENSE
Hal. See:
ALOMA, HAROLD DAVID
BORLAND, HAROLD GLEN
BOYLE, HAROLD VINCENT
Debrett, Hal
DICKINSON, HAROLD H., JR.
GOODWIN, HAROLD LELAND
HOLBROOK, HAROLD ROWE, JR.
HOPPER, HAROLD S.
MOONEY, HAROLD
ROSSON, HAROLD
SCHAEFER, HAROLD HERMAN
SHARP, HAROLD SPENCER
Hal, Big. See:
SHARP, HAROLD SPENCER
Hal, Bluff King. See
HENRY VIII
Hal Clement. See:
STUBBS, HARRY CLEMENT
Hal Dane. See:
MACFALL, CHAMBERS HALDANE COOKE
Hal Gold. See:
GOLDBERG, HARRY
Hal Harkaway. See:
STRATEMEYER, EDWARD L.
Hal Tate. See:
TEITELMAN, ALEX
Hal Willis. See:
FORRESTER, CHARLES ROBERT
HALDANE, JAMES ALEXANDER. See:
Scottish Boanerges, The
BALDANE, ROBERT. See:
Scottish Boanerges, The
HALDEMAN, SAMUEL STEHMAN (1812-80) [American educator, author, naturalist and philologist]
Felix Ago
HALLWARD, GLORIA (1924-) [American motion picture actress]
Gloria Grahame
HALE [Hale]. See also:
HALLE
Halle
Hale, Alan. See:
McKAHAN, RUFUS ALAN
HALE, ARLENE (1924-) [American author]
Louise Christopher
Gail Everett
Mary Anne Tate
HALE, ARNEL ODELL (1909-) [American

professional baseball
player]
Chief
Hale, Binnie. See:
MUNRO, BERNICE
HALE
Hale, Creighton. See:
FITZGERALD, PATRICK
Hale, Eugenia. See:
WOOLSEY, MARYHALE
Hale, Garth. See:
CUNNINGHAM, ALBERT
BENJAMIN
Hale, Helen. See:
MULCAHY, LUCILLE
BURNETT
Hale, Jonathan. See:
HATLEY, JONATHAN
HALE, MARIE LOUISE
GIBSON (1886-)
[American novelist]
Marice Rutledge
Maryse Rutledge
Hale, Mary. See:
WOOLSEY, MARYHALE
Hale, Michael. See:
BULLOCK, MICHAEL
Hale of the South, The Nathan.
See: DAVIS, SAM
HALE, SARAH JOSEPHA
(1788-1879) [American poet,
author and editor]
S. J. H.
The Mother of Thanksgiving
Hale, Sonnie. See:
MONRO, ROBERT HALE
Hale, The Gentleman from.
See: TUNSTALL,
ALFRED MOORE
HALES. See:
ALEXANDER OF HALES
HALS
HALES, JOHN (1584-1656)
[English scholar and
divine]
The Ever-memorable
The Walking Library
HALL, ABRAHAM OAKEY
(1826-98) [Mayor of New
York City; member of
Tweed Ring]
The Admirable Crichton of
our City Politicians
Elegant Oakey
Mayor Von O'Hall
Hall, Adam. See:
TREVOR, ELLESTON
HALL, ALFRED (1895-1946)
[American jazz musician
(drums)]
Tubby Hall
HALL, BAYNARD RUSH
(1821-71) [American
Presbyterian clergyman
and novelist]
Robert Carlton
HALL, BENNIE CAROLINE
HUMBLE (fl. 1950-60)
[American author]
Hall Bennett
Emily Marshall
Hall Caine. See:
CAINE, THOMAS HENRY
HALL
Hall Caine, Sir. See:
CAINE, THOMAS
HENRY HALL
Hall, Claudia. See:
FLOREN, LEE
HALL, ELIZABETH WATSON
(1912-) [American
author]
Betty Watson
Hall, Evan. See:
HALLERAN, EUGENE
EDWARD
HALL, FREDERICK LEE
(1916-) [American
lawyer and politician;
Governor of Kansas)]
Fred Hall
HALL, HENRY (1920-)
[American motion picture
actor]
Huntz Hall
HALL, HENRY. See also:
Dead End Kids, The
Hall, Holworthy. See:
PORTER, HAROLD
EVERETT
HALL, HOWARD (18??-1921)
[American novelist, poet
and playwright]
Charles Sumner
Hall Hunter. See:
MARSHALL, EDISON
Hall, J. De P. See:
McKELWAY, ST. CLAIR

Hall, Jarvis. See:
BAGG, HELEN F.
Hall, Jon. See:
LOCHER, CHARLES
HALL, JOSEF WASHINGTON (1894-) [American radio commentator, writer and lecturer]
Upton Close
HALL, JOSEPH (1574-1656) [English bishop and author]
The Christian Seneca
The English Seneca
The First English Satirist
HALL, MAJOR SAMUEL STONE (1838-86) [American soldier, adventurer and author]
Buckskin Sam
HALL, MARGUERITE RADCLYFFE (1886-1943) [English novelist and poet]
Radclyffe Hall
HALL, MARIE BOAS (1919-) [American author]
Marie Boas
Hall, Marjory. See:
YEAKLEY, MARJORY HALL
Hall, Midshipman Tom W. See:
INGRAHAM, COLONEL PRENTISS
HALL, MINOR (1897-) [American jazz musician (drums)]
Ram Hall
HALL, MUSA L. (1877-) [American educator]
The Madonna of Hall-Moody
HALL, OAKLEY MAXWELL (1920-) [American author]
O. M. Hall
Jason Manor
Hall, Owen. See:
DAVIS, JAMES
Hall Philips, Log. See:
PHILIPS, MARDIN WILSON
Hall, The Sachem of Tammany. See:
KELLY, JOHN
TWEED, WILLIAM MARCY
Hall, The Sage of Log. See:
PHILIPS, MARDIN WILSON
HALL, WENDELL WOODS (1896-) [American composer, singer, entertainer and ukulele player]
The Red-headed Music-maker
Hallam Whitney. See:
WHITTINGTON, HARRY
Halldór Kiljan Laxness. See: GUDJONSSEN, HALLDÓR
HALLE [Halle]. See also:
HALE
Hale
HALLE, ADAM DE LA (c. 1240-c. 1286) [French minstrel]
Le Bossu d'Arras
Halle Bach, The. See:
BACH, WILHELM FRIEDMANN
HALLECK, FITZ-GREEN. See:
Croakers & Co.
HALLECK, HENRY WAGER (1815-72) [American Civil War general officer]
Old Brains
HALLERAN, EUGENE EDWARD (1905-) [American author]
Donn Broward
Evan Hall
HALLEY, EDMUND (1656-1742) [English astronomer]
The Southern Tycho
Halliburton, Hugh. See:
ROBERTSON, JAMES LOGIE
HALLIBURTON, THOMAS CHANDLER (1796-1865) [Canadian humorist and satirist]
Sam Slick
Halliday. See also:
Holiday
HOLLIDAY
Holliday
Halliday, Ben. See:
MANNING, WILLIAM HENRY
Halliday, Brett. See:

DRESSER, DAVIS
Halliday, Michael. See:
CREASEY, JOHN
Halliday Witherspoon. See:
NUTTER, WILLIAM H.
HALLOWAY, MARIAN M. RUNNELS (1934-) [American jazz singer]
Marian Montgomery
Halls, The Father of the See: MORTON, CHARLES
Halm, Friedrich. See:
MUNCH-BELLINGHAUSEN, ELIGIUS FRANZ JOSEPH, REICHFREIHERR VON
HALOP, BILLY. See:
Dead End Kids, The.
HALPINE, CHARLES GRAHAM (1829-68) [American journalist, poet and miscellaneous writer]
Miles O'Reilly
HALS. See also:
HALES
HALS, FRANZ (c.1580-1666) [Dutch portrait and genre painter]
The Elder
HALS, FRANZ (fl.1637-69) [Dutch portrait and genre painter]
The Younger
HALSEY, FRANK DAVIS. See: McAlister, Frank A.
HALSEY, HARLAN P. (fl. mid-19th cent.) [American author of dime novels]
Judson R. Taylor
HALSEY, WILLIAM FREDERICK (1882-1959) [American Admiral of the Fleet]
Bull Halsey
HALVERSTADT, CONSTANCE (1910-) [American stage and motion picture actress]
Constance Cummings
Halyard, Harry. See:
UNKNOWN
Ham. See:
YOUNG, WILLIAM HAMILTON
Ham (Cham). See:
NOE, AMÉDÉE DE
Ham, The Prisoner of. See:
BONAPARTE, CHARLES LOUIS NAPOLEON
HAMANN, JOHANN GEORG (1730-88) [German philosophical writer]
The Magician of the North
The Magnus of the North
HAMBLEN, HERBERT ELLIOTT (1849-) [American author]
Frederick Benton Williams
Hambletonian. See:
FAIRFAX-BLAKEBOROUGH, JOHN
Hamburg Bach, The. See:
BACH, KARL PHILIPP EMANUEL
HAMILCAR BARCA (c.270-228 B.C.)[Carthaginian general officer; father of HANNIBAL]
Lightning
Hamill, Ethel. See:
WEBB, JEAN FRANCIS
HAMILTON, ALEXANDER (1757-1804) [American statesman; Secretary of the Treasury]
Alexander the Coppersmith
Caesar
The Father of the Tariff
The King of the Feds
The Little Lion
HAMILTON, ALEXANDER. See: also: Publius
HAMILTON, ALFRED REED (1872-1927) [Planner of stadium at the University of Pittsburgh]
The Father of Pitt Stadium
Hamilton, Alice. See:
CROMIE, ALICE HAMILTON
HAMILTON, ANDREW (c.1676-1741) [Scottish-American patriot]
The Day-star of the Revolution

Hamilton, Betsy. See:
MOORE, IDORA McCLELLAN

HAMILTON, CHARLES (1875-) [English author of books for boys]
Frank Richards

Hamilton, Clive. See:
LEWIS, CLIVE STAPLES

Hamilton, Cosmo. See:
GIBBS, COSMO HAMILTON

HAMILTON, DR. ALEXANDER (1712-56) [Scottish-American diarist, essayist and physician]
Loquacious Scribble, Esq.

HAMILTON, EMMA LYON (1761?-1815) [Mistress of HORATIO NELSON, VISCOUNT NELSON]
The Goddess of Health
Lady Hamilton

Hamilton, Ernest. See:
GROSSMAN, JOSEPHINE JUDITH

HAMILTON, FORESTSTORN (1921-) [American jazz musician (drums, composer)]
Chico Hamilton

Hamilton, Gail. See:
DODGE, MARY ABIGAIL

HAMILTON, GEORGE (1901-57) [American jazz musician (composer, leader)]
Spike Hamilton

HAMILTON, GEORGE ROS-TREVOR (1888-) [British poet and writer]
George Rostrevor

Hamilton Holmes, Captain. See:
HARBAUGH, THOMAS CHALMERS

Hamilton, Jack. See:
BRANNON, WILLIAM T.

Hamilton, Jenny. See:
GEDDES, JENNY

HAMILTON, JOHN DANIEL MILLER (1892-) [American politician; campaign manager for ALFRED M. LANDON in 1936]
Torchy

Hamilton, Kay. See:
DE LEEUW, CATEAU WILHELMINA

HAMILTON, MARY AGNES (1883-) [Scottish novelist and political writer]
Iconoclast

Hamilton, Michael. See:
CHETHAM-STRODE, WARREN

HAMILTON, PATRICK (1498?-1529) [Scottish churchman, martyr and reformer]
The First Scotch Reformer
The Protomartyr of the Scottish Reformation

HAMILTON, RICHARD F. (1847-1916) [American circus press agent]
Tody Hamilton

Hamilton, Robert W. See:
STRATEMEYER, EDWARD L.

Hamilton, Rufus. See:
GILLMORE, RUFUS HAMILTON

Hamilton, W. J. See:
CLARK, CHARLES DUNNING

Hamilton, Wade. See:
FLOREN, LEE

HAMILTON, WILLIAM GERARD (1729-96) [English politician]
Single Speech Hamilton

Hamish Reade. See:
GRAY, SIMON

Hamlet, Dancing. See:
DRAPER, PAUL

Hamlin. See:
GARLAND, HANNIBAL HAMLIN

HAMMARSKJÖLD, DAG HJALMAR CARL AGNE (1905-61) [Secretary-General of the United Nations]

The Curator of the Secrets of 82 Nations
Hammer and Scourge of England, The. See: WALLACE, SIR WILLIAM
Hammer, Charles The. See: CHARLES MARTEL
Hammer of the Heretics, The. See: AILLY, PIERRE D'
AUGUSTINIUS, AURELIUS
FABER, JOHANN
Hammer of the Monks, The. See: CROMWELL, THOMAS
Hammer of the Scots, The. See: EDWARD I
Hammer of Thor, The. See: TOWNSEND, FRANCIS EVERETT
Hammer, Old Stone. See: METCALFE, THOMAS
Hammer, The. See: CHARLES MARTEL
MACCABAEUS, JUDAS
Hammerer, Great. See: GRANT, HIRAM ULYSSES
Hämmerlein, Thomas. See: KEMPEN, THOMAS HAMERKEN VAN
HAMMERTON, FAY (1895-) [British stage and motion picture actress]
Fay Holden
HAMMETT, SAMUEL ADAMS (1816-65) [American novelist and merchant]
Philip Paxton
Sam Slick, Jr.
HAMMETT, SAMUEL DASHIELL (1894-1961) [American author of detective stories]
Peter Collinson
Dash Hammett
Dashiell Hammett
HAMMOND, ANTHONY (1668-1738) [English miscellaneous writer]
The Silver-tongued
HAMMOND, HENRIETTA HARDY (1854-83) [American novelist]
Lou Capsadell
Henri Daugé
HAMMOND INNES, RALPH (1913-) [British journalist and author]
Hammond Innes
Ralph Hammond
HAMMOND JAMES HENRY (1807-64) [American politician; senator from South Carolina]
Mudsill Hammond
Hammond, Kay. See: STANDING, DOROTHY
Hamp, Pierre. See: BOURILLON, PIERRE
Hamp, The. See: HAMPTON, LIONEL
Hampden. See: HAMPTON
Hampton
HART, ADOLPHUS MORDECAI
Hampden County Bar, The Father of the. See: BATES,WILLIAM GELSTON
Hampden County Bar, The Historian of the. See: BATES, WILLIAM GELSTON
Hampden County Bar, The Nestor of the. See: BATES, WILLIAM GELSTON
HAMPDEN, JOHN. See: Five Members, The
Hampden, Walter. See: DOUGHERTY, WALTER HAMPDEN
HAMPOLE, RICHARD ROLLE DE (c. 1290-1349) [English hermit and poet]
The Hermit of Hampole
Hampshire, The Monarch of. See: WILLIAMS, ISRAEL
HAMPTON [Hampton]. See also: Hampden
HAMPTON, KATHLEEN (1923-) [American author]
Lee Street
HAMPTON, LIONEL (1915-) [American jazz musician (vibraphone, drums, piano, leader)]
The Hamp
HAMPTON, LOCKSLEY WELLINGTON (1932-) [American jazz musician (trombone,

tuba, composer)]
Slide Hampton
Hampton, Mark. See:
NORWOOD, VICTOR GEORGE CHARLES
Hampton Stone. See:
STEIN, AARON MARC
Hampton, The Poet of Low. See: MILLER, WILLIAM
Hamsun, Knut. See:
PEDERSEN, KNUT
HANCOCK, CLARENCE EUGENE (fl. 1927-47) [American lawyer and politician; representative from New York]
Banty
HANCOCK, CORNELIA (fl. 1863-65) [American volunteer nurse in Civil War]
The Battlefield Angel
HANCOCK, JOHN (1737-93) [American patriot, shipowner, smuggler and signer of the Declaration of Independence]
King Hancock
King of the Smugglers
HANCOCK, WINFIELD SCOTT (1824-86) [American Civil War general officer]
The Superb
Hand and Pen of the Congress, The. See:
THOMPSON, CHARLIE
Hand, Broken. See:
FITZPATRICK, THOMAS
Hand, Götz with the Iron. See:
VON BERLICHINGEN, GÖTZ (GOTTFRIED)
Hand, Impartial. See:
JOHNSON, DR. SAMUEL
STEELE, SIR RICHARD
Handcuff King, The. See:
WEISS, EHRICH (ERIK WEISZ)
Handcuffs, The King of. See:
WEISS, EHRICH (ERIK WEISZ)
Handcuffs, Undisputed King of. See: WEISS, EHRICH (ERIK WEISZ)
HÄNDEL, GEORG FRIEDRICH (1685-1759) [German composer]
The Thunderbolt
Handkerchief. See:
MOODY, JOSEPH
Hands, By Several. See:
BEHN, MRS. APHRA
Handsome. See:
FIELDING, ROBERT
Handsome Conway. See:
RUGG, WILLIAM AUGUSTUS
Handsome Englishman, The. See: CHURCHILL, JOHN
Handsome Frank. See:
PIERCE, FRANKLIN
Handsome Jack. See:
TUCKER, JOHN RANDOLPH
Handsome Swordsman (Beau Sabreur). See:
MURAT, JOACHIM
Handsome, The. See:
FERDINAND I
FREDERICK III
PHILIP I
Handy Andy. See:
SOMMERVILLE, ANDREW
Handy, George. See:
HENDLEMAN, GEORGE JOSEPH
HANDY, WILLIAM CHRISTOPHER (1873-1958) [American jazz cornetist, composer and orchestra leader]
The Father of the Blues
Hanging. See:
HAWKINS, HENRY, 1ST BARON BRAMPTON
Hanging Judge, The. See:
JEFFREYS, GEORGE, 1ST BARON JEFFREYS OF WEM
NORBURY, THE EARL OF
Hangman. See:
FOOTE, HENRY STUART
Hangman, The. See:
HEYDRICH, REINHARD
Hangman, The Buffalo. See:
CLEVELAND, STEPHEN GROVER

Hangover Generation, The Voice of the. See: O'HARA, JOHN HENRY
Hank. See:
BAUER, HENRY ALBERT
CRAWFORD, BENNY ROSS, JR.
D'AMICO, HENRY JOHN
FORT, ELEANOR H.
GREENBERG, HENRY BENJAMIN
GREENSPUN, HERMAN MILTON
HOBSON, HARRY
JONES, HENRY Z., JR.
KETCHAM, HENRY KING
MONK, HENRY
SANICOLA, HENRY W.
Hank Janson. See:
HOBSON, HARRY
NORWOOD, VICTOR GEORGE CHARLES
Hank Madison. See: ROWLAND, DONALD SYDNEY
HANKE, ROBERT LOWERY (1916-) [American motion picture actor]
Robert Lowery
Hankins, Clabe. See: McDONALD, ERWIN LAWRENCE
HANKINSON, CHARLES JAMES (1866-) [British author]
Clive Holland
HANLEY, CLIFFORD (1922-) [Scottish journalist and author]
Henry Calvin
HANLON, EDWARD HUGH (1857-1937) [American professional baseball player]
Ned Hanlon
HANNA, MARCUS ALONZO (1837-1904) [American politician and businessman]
Mark Hanna
HANNAGAN, STEPHEN JEROME (1899-) [American publicity agent]
Steve Hannagan
Hannah Lees. See: FETTER, ELIZABETH HEAD
Hannah More of America, The See: MERCER, MARGARET
Hannah Warner. See: JEWETT, JOHN HOWARD
HANNAY, JAMES OWEN (1865-1950) [Irish clergyman and novelist]
G. A. Birmingham
George A. Birmingham
J. O. Hannay
J. Owen Hannay
James O. Hannay
HANNIBAL (247-c. 183 B.C.) [Carthaginian general officer]
The Carthaginian Lion
The Grace of Baal
HANNO (fl. 3rd cent. B.C.) [Pro-Roman politician of Carthage]
The Great
Hans. See:
ARP, JEAN
VIRCHOW, HANS JAKOB PAUL
WAGNER, JOHN PETER
Hans Breitmann. See: LELAND, CHARLES GODFREY
Hans Fallada. See: DITZEN, RUDOLPH
Hans Habe. See: BEKESSY, JEAN
Hans Hofmeyer. See: FLEISCHER, ANTHONY CHARLES
Hans Pfaal. See: POE, EDGAR ALLAN
Hans Stockfisch. See: SPENCER, JOHN
Hans Wagner-Schonkirch. See: WAGNER, HANS
Hans Warner. See: BLAZE, ANGE HENRI
HANSEN, EMIL (1867-1956) [German artist]
Emil Nolde
HANSEN, ROY FORD (1910-)

[American professional baseball player]
Snipe
Hansi. See:
WALTZ, J. JACQUES
HANSON, ROGER WEIGHTMAN (1827-63) [American Confederate Army officer]
Old Flintlock
HANSON, WINIFRED (1901-) [American vaudeville comedienne and motion picture actress]
Winnie Lightner
Hap. See:
ARNOLD, HENRY HARLEY
Happiness Boys, The
The Best Food Boys
The Interwoven Pair
The Taystee Loafers, joint stage names of ERNEST HARE (Ernie Hare) (1884-1939) and WILLIAM JONES (Billy Jones) (1889-1940) [American singers and Entertainers]
Happy. See:
CALDWELL, ALBERT
CHANDLER, ALBERT BENJAMIN
TURNER, JOHN C.
Happy Jack. See:
SNELLEN, JOHN H.
Happy, The. See:
EMANUEL (MANUEL) I
Happy Unhappy Answers, The Man of. See:
TARLTON, RICHARD
Happy Valley, The Sage of. See: TAYLOR, ALFRED ALEXANDER
Happy Warrior, The. See:
ROOSEVELT, THEODORE
SHEETS, FREDERICK HILL
SMITH, ALFRED EMANUEL
Haraldsson. See:
MAGNUS II
OLAF II
OLAF III
HARBAGE, ALFRED BENNETT (1901-) [American educator and author]
Thomas Kyd
HARBAUGH, THOMAS CHALMERS (1849-1924) [American poet and author of juvenile literature and dime novels]
Major G.W. Alcalaw
Colonel T.B. Bostwick
Major Walter Brisbane
Nick Carter
Bertha M. Clay
Major A.F. Grant
Isaac Hawkes
Captain Hamilton Holmes
Captain Howard Holmes
Charles Howard
Captain J.L. Kennedy
Jackson Knox
George B. Lee
Howard Lincoln
Major S.S. Scott
Captain Dick Steadman
Major Walt Wilmot
Captain Walt Winton
F.S. Winton
Harry Winton
HARBERGER, JOHN PICO (1906-) [Italian-American millinery designer and couturier]
John Pico John
Mr. John
Harbinson, Robert. See:
BRYANS, ROBERT HARBINSON
HARBURG, E.Y. (1898-) [American librettist and author]
Yip
HARCOURT, MELVILLE (1909-) [British Anglican clergyman and author]
Criticus
Hard-headed Pete. See:
STUYVESANT, PETER
Hard Rock. See:
O'CONNELL, DANIEL J.
Hard Ruler. See:
HAROLD III
Hardeen. See:

WEISS, THEO
Harden. See:
WEISS, THEO
HARDENBERG, FRIEDRICH LEOPOLD, BARON VON (1772-1801) [German poet and writer of philosophical romances]
Novalis (Fallow Land)
The Prophet of Romanticism
HARDER, MELVIN LEROY (1909-) [American professional baseball player]
Chief
HARDIE, JAMES KEIR (1856-1915) [Scottish labor leader and member of parliament]
Keir Hardie
HARDIE, LAURA CONSTANCE (1878? 1880?-1955) [British stage and motion picture actress]
Constance Collier
HARDIN, BENJAMIN (1784-1852) [American politician; congressman from Kentucky]
The Terror of the House
Hardin, Clement. See:
NEWTON, DWIGHT BENNETT
HARDIN, LOUIS THOMAS (1916-) [American jazz musician (miscellaneous instruments)]
Moondog Hardin
Hardin, Mitch. See:
GERRITY, DAVID JAMES
Hardin, Peter. See:
VACZEK, LOUIS
Hardin, Tom. See:
BAUER, ERWIN A.
Hardin, Wes. See:
KEEVIL, HENRY JOHN
Harding, Ann. See:
GATLEY, DOROTHY
Harding, Austin. See:
LENDON, ALFRED AUSTIN
Harding, Bertita. See:
RADETZKY VON RADETZ, COUNTESS BERTHA LEONARTZ DE HARDING
HARDING, DAVID LLEWELLYN (1867-1952) [British stage and motion picture actor]
Lyn Harding
HARDING, FLORENCE KLING DE WOLFE (1860-1924) [wife of President WARREN G. HARDING]
The Duchess
HARDING, LAVERE (1917-) [American jazz musician (composer, arranger)]
Buster Harding
HARDMAN, RICHARDS LYNDEN (1924-) [American motion picture producer and author]
Bronson Howitzer
Hardrata (Stern in Council). See: HAROLD III
HARDT, RICHARD (1907-) [American composer and pianist]
Paul Kapp
Hardwick, Adam. See:
CONNOR, JOHN ANTHONY
HARDWICK, ARCHER (1918-) [American composer, pianist and teacher]
George Archer
HARDWICK, RICHARD HOLMES, JR. (1923-) [American businessman, interpreter and author]
Rick Holmes
Hardwicke of Tennessee, The. See: GREEN, NATHAN
HARDWICKE, OTTO (1904-) [American jazz musician (saxophone)]
Toby Hardwicke
Hardy, Alice Dale. See:
STRATEMEYER, EDWARD L.
Hardy, Douglas. See:
ANDREWS, CHARLES ROBERT DOUGLAS HARDY
Hardy, The. See:
DOUGLAS, SIR WILLIAM OF

Hare, Emily. See:
WINTHROP, LAURA
HARE, ERNEST (Ernie Hare). See: Happiness Boys, The
Hare, Martin. See:
ZAJDLER, ZOË GIRLING
HARE, ROBERT (1781-1858) [American chemist and novelist]
Eldred Grayson
Hare, Sir John. See:
FAIRS, SIR JOHN
HARE, WILLIAM HOBART (1838-1909) [American Episcopal Bishop; missionary to Sioux Indians]
The Apostle to the Sioux Indians
Swift Bird
Harefoot. See:
HAROLD I
HARGRAVE, WILLIAM McKINLEY (1900-) [American professional baseball player]
Pinkey
HARGREAVES-MAWDSLEY, WILLIAM NORMAN (1921-) [British educator and author]
Norman Mawdsley
HARGREAVES, REGINALD CHARLES (1888-) [British soldier and author]
Aiguillette
Hari, Mata. See:
ZELLE, MAGARETE GERTRUDE
HÄRING, GEORG WILHELM HEINRICH (1798-1871) [German historical novelist]
Willibald Alexis
HARIRI, ABU MOHAMMED AL KASIM IBN ALI (1054-1122)] [Arabic writer]
The Silk-merchant
Harjo, Chinnubbie. See:
POSEY, ALEXANDER LAWRENCE
Hark, Mildred. See:
McQUEEN, MILDRED HARK
Harkaway, Hal. See:
STRATEMEYER, EDWARD L.
HARLAND, HENRY (1861-1905) [American editor and novelist]
Sidney Luska
Harland, Marion. See:
TERHUNE, MARY VIRGINIA HAWKES
Harle, Elizabeth. See:
ROBERTS, IRENE
Harlequin. See:
REED, ALEXANDER WYCLIF
Harlequins, The Father of. See: RICH, JOHN
Harley Graves. See:
WILKINSON, MRS. MARGUERITE OGDEN
Harley, John. See:
MARSH, JOHN
HARLEY, JOHN HUNTER (1866-) [British journalist and author]
J. H. H.
Harley Thorne. See:
BRAYMAN, JAMES O.
Harlow, Jean. See:
CARPENTER, HARLEAN
HARMAN. See also:
HARMON
Harmon
HERMAN
HERMANN
Hermann
Hermanns
Hermine
HERRMANN
HARMAN, RICHARD ALEXANDER (1917-) [British educator, musician and author]
Alec Harman
HARMENSEN (HERMANSZ), JACOB (1560-1609) [Dutch reformed theologian; founder of Arminianism]
Jacobus Arminius
HARMER, ALFRED CROUT (1825-1900) [American politician; Congressman from Pennsylvania]

The Father of the House
HARMON [Harmon]. See also:
HARMAN
HERMAN
HERMANN
Hermann
Hermanns
Hermine
HERRMANN
Harmon, Charles. See:
FLAGENHEIMER, ARTHUR
HARMON, JAMES JUDSON (1933-) [American performer and writer]
Jim Harmon
HARNETT. See also:
HARTNETT
HARNETT, CORNELIUS (c. 1723-81) [American statesman]
The Samuel Adams of North Carolina
HAROLD (died c. 985) [King of Denmark]
Blue-tooth
HAROLD [Harold]. See also:
Herald
HAROLD I (c. 850-c. 933) [King of Norway]
Haarfagr (Fairhaired)
HAROLD I (died 1040) [King of England]
Harold Harefoot
HAROLD II (930?-70?) [King of Norway]
Grayfell
HAROLD II (c. 1022-66) [King of the English]
The Last of the Saxons
HAROLD III (1015-66) [King of Norway]
Hard Ruler
Hardrata (Stern in Council)
Harold Arlen. See:
ARLUCK, HYMEN
Harold Heartman. See:
MEBANE, JOHN HARRISON
Harold, Honest. See:
ICKES, HAROLD LeCLAIRE
Harold Kyrle. See:
BELLEW, HAROLD KYRLE
Harold Payne. See:
KELLY, GEORGE C.
Harold Robbins. See:
RUBIN, HAROLD
Harold West. See:
WILSON, ROGER C.
Harolde, Ralf. See:
WIGGER, RALF HAROLDE
Haroun-al-Roosevelt. See:
ROOSEVELT, THEODORE
Harp of the North, David's.
See: WALLIN, JOHAN OLOF
HARPE, JEAN FRANÇOIS DE LA (1739-1803) [French poet and critic]
The French Quintilian
HARPER, JAMES CUNNINGHAM (1893-) [American band director and business executive]
Captain Harper
Harper Lee. See:
GILLETE, HARPER LEE
Harpo Marx. See:
Four Marx Brothers, The
HARRELL, IRENE BURK (1927-) [American librarian and author]
Amos Amor
Mildred Waylan
HARRELSON. See also:
HARRISON
Harrison
HARRELSON, KENNETH SMITH (1941-) [American professional baseball player]
Ken Harrelson
Harriet Hilliard. See:
NELSON, PEGGY LOU SNYDER
Harriet Kathryn Myers. See:
WHITTINGTON, HARRY
Harriet Stuart. See:
LENNOX, CHARLOTTE RAMSAY
Harrigan and Hart. See:
ABARBANELL, JACOB RALPH
HARRIGAN, EDWARD (1845-1911) [American playwright, actor and producer]
Ned Harrigan
HARRIMAN, EDWARD H. (1848-1909) [American railroad magnate and financier]
The Colossus of the Roads
HARRINGTON, FRANCIS C. (1887-1940) [American army

officer and politician]
Pinky
Harrington, George F. See:
BAKER, WILLIAM MUMFORD
Harrington Hastings. See:
MARSH, JOHN
Harrington Hext. See:
PHILLPOTTS, EDEN
Harrington, K. See:
BEAN, KEITH FENWICK
HARRINGTON, MARK RAYMOND (1882-) [American archaeologist and writer]
Ramón de las Cuevas
Jiskogo
Tonashi
Harrington Strong. See:
McCULLEY, JOHNSTON
HARRIS, BENJAMIN (fl. 1673-1716) [Anglo-American pioneer bookseller, author and publisher]
The Father of American Newspapers
HARRIS, BENJAMIN (1919-) [American jazz musician (trumpet)]
Little Benny
HARRIS, CHRISTOPHER (1907-) [English dramatist]
Christopher Fry
HARRIS, DAVID STANLEY (1903-) [American professional baseball player]
Sheriff
Harris Dunn. See:
DOERFFLER, ALFRED
Harris Evans. See:
Bird, Brandon
HARRIS, FRANK BRAYTON (1932-) [American publisher and author]
Kirkpatrick West
HARRIS, GEORGE WASHINGTON (1814-69) [American humorist]
Sut Lovingood
Sugartail
HARRIS, JAMES (1709-80) [English scholar]
Hermes Harris
HARRIS, JAMES ARMSTRONG (1847-1921) [American pioneer in establishing Florida orange industry]
The Father of the Florida Orange Industry
The Orange King
HARRIS, JOEL CHANDLER (1848-1908) [American humorist, story teller and editor]
Obediah Skinflint
Uncle Remus
Harris, Kathleen. See:
HUMPHRIES, ADELAIDE M.
Harris, Larry M. See:
JANIFER, LAURENCE MARK
Harris, MacDonald. See:
HEINEY, DONALD WILLIAM
Harris, Marilyn. See:
SPRINGER, MARILYN HARRIS
HARRIS, MARION ROSE YOUNG (1925-) [British journalist and author]
Rose Young
Harris, Roger. See:
WILSON, ROGER HARRIS LEBUS
HARRIS, SIR ARTHUR TRAVERS (1892-) [British airman in World Wars I and II]
Bomber Harris
HARRIS, SIR CHARLES ALEXANDER (1855-) [British statesman, barrister and author]
Nemesis
HARRIS, STANLEY RAYMOND (1896-) [American baseball manager]
The Boy Wonder
Bucky Harris
HARRISON [Harrison]. See also:
HARRELSON
Harrison Adams. See:
RATHBONE, ST. GEORGE HENRY
STRATEMEYER, EDWARD L.

HARRISON, BENJAMIN (1833-1901) [Twenty-third President of the United States]
Baby McKee's Grandfather
The Centennial President
Chinese Harrison
Grandfather's Hat
Grandpa's Grandson
Kid-gloves Harrison
Little Ben
The Son of His Grandfather

Harrison Denmark. See: ZELAZNY, ROGER

HARRISON, GEORGE. See: Beatles, The

Harrison, Harry. See: ENTON, DR. HARRY

HARRISON, HENRY SNYDOR (1880-1930) [American novelist]
Henry Second

Harrison Hunt. See: BALLARD, WILLIS TODHUNTER

HARRISON, JAMES (1937-) [American author]
Jim Harrison

HARRISON, MARIA LILLI PEISER (1914-) [Viennese actress]
Lilli Palmer

HARRISON, MARY ST. LEGER KINGSLEY (1852-1931) [English novelist]
Lucas Malet

Harrison, Rex. See: CAREY, REGINALD

Harrison, Whit. See: WHITTINGTON, HARRY

HARRISON, WILLIAM HENRY (1773-1841) [Ninth President of the United States]
The Farmer-President
The Hero of Tippecanoe
The Log Cabin Candidate
Log Cabin Harrison
Old Granny
Old Tip
Old Tippecanoe
Tippecanoe
The Washington of the West

HARRON, ROBERT (1894-1920) [American motion picture actor]
Bobby Harron

HARROW, WILLIAM (died 1763) [English highwayman]
The Flying Highwayman

Harry. See:
ARMSTRONG, HENRY W.
BELAFONTE, HAROLD GEORGE, JR.
CAREY, HENRY DE WITT
GREB, HENRY EDWARD
HEINE, HEINRICH
KEMP, HIBBARD
MENCKEN, HENRY LOUIS
PATTERSON, HENRY

Harry Archer. See: AURACHER, HARRY

Harry Austin. See: McINERNY, RALPH

HARRY, BLIND (fl. 1470-92) [Scottish minstrel, blind from birth]
Blind Harry
Henry the Minstrel

Harry Bluff. See: MAURY, MATTHEW FONTAINE

Harry C. Laurie. See: CAHN, ZVI

Harry Carmichael. See: OGNALL, LEOPOLD HORACE

Harry Castlemon. See: FOSDICK, CHARLES AUSTIN

Harry Cavendish. See: ST. JOHN, PERCY BOLLINGBROKE

Harry Clark Gibson. See: HUBLER, RICHARD GIBSON

Harry Dangerfield. See: PATTEN, WILLIAM GILBERT

Harry Dennies Perry. See: INGRAHAM, COLONEL PRENTISS

Harry Dubois Milman. See: CORYELL, JOHN RUSSELL

Harry Fragson. See: POTTS, HARRY

Harry Franco. See:
BRIGGS, CHARLES FREDERICK
Harry, Give 'em Hell. See:
TRUMAN, HARRY S
Harry Gringo. See:
WISE, HENRY AUGUSTUS
Harry Halyard. See:
UNKNOWN
Harry Harrison. See:
ENTON, DR. HARRY
Harry Hazard. See:
BADGER, JOSEPH E., JR.
Harry Hazel. See:
JONES, JUSTIN
Harry Hazelton. See:
BADGER, JOSEPH E., JR.
Harry, High Tax. See:
TRUMAN, HARRY S.
Harry Houdini. See:
WEISS, EHRICH (ERIK WEISZ)
Harry, King. See:
HENRY VIII
Harry, Light Horse. See
LEE, HENRY
WATTERSON, HENRY
Harry Mason Rowe. See:
STRATEMEYER, EDWARD L.
Harry, Mile-a-Minute. See:
SELFRIDGE, HARRY GORDON
Harry Morgan. See:
BRATSBURG, HARRY
Harry Neal. See:
BIXBY, JEROME LEWIS
Harry of the West. See:
CLAY, HENRY
Harry Parke. See:
EINSTEIN, HARRY
Harry Percy of the House, The. See: WISE, HENRY ALEXANDER
Harry St. George. See:
RATHBONE, ST. GEORGE HENRY
Harry Twitcher. See:
BROUGHAM, HENRY PETER
Harry Walker. See:
WAUGH, HILLARY BALDWIN
Harry White. See:
WHITTINGTON, HARRY
Harry Winton. See:
HARBAUGH, THOMAS CHALMERS
HARSTAD, ADOLPH (1916-) [American drum major and band director]
Duff Harstad
Hart. See:
CRANE, HAROLD HARTE
HART, ADOLPHUS MORDECAI (1813-79) [Canadian-American author]
Hampden
Hart, Harrigan and. See:
ABARBANELL, JACOB RALPH
HART, MOSS (1904-61) [American playwright, director and author]
Robert Arnold Conrad
HART, ROBERT ALTON (1906-) [American motion picture director]
Robert Alton
Hart Thorne. See:
CARHART, ARTHUR HAWTHORNE
Hart, Tony. See:
CANNON, ANTHONY
HART, WILLIAM S. (1872-1946) [American motion picture actor and author]
Bill Hart
HART, WILLIAM STERLING (1917-) [American motion picture actor]
Robert Sterling
HARTE, FRANCIS BRETT (1836-1902) [American humorist, author, story-teller and poet]
Bret Harte
HARTE, FRANCIS BRETT. See: also: Golden Gate Trinity, The
Harte, Marjorie. See:
McEVOY, MARJORIE HARTE
HARTER, DOW WATTERS (1885-) [American politician; congressman from Ohio]

The Rubber King
Hartford, Via. See:
DONSON, CYRIL
Hartford Wits, The, joint nickname of RICHARD ALSOP (1761-1815), JOEL BARLOW (1754-1812), THEODORE DWIGHT (1764-1846), TIMOTHY DWIGHT (1752-1817), DR. LEMUEL HOPKINS (1750-1801), DAVID HUMPHREYS (1752-1818) and JOHN TRUMBULL (1750-1831) [American professional men and literary aspirants]
Hartford Wits, The. See also:
HOPKINS, DR. LEMUEL
TRUMBULL, JOHN
Hartley Howard. See:
OGNALL, LEOPOLD HORACE
Hartley, Little. See:
COLERIDGE, DAVID HARTLEY
HARTLEY, VIVIAN MARY (1913-67) [British actress
Vivien Leigh
Hartman, Patience. See:
ZAWADSKY, PATIENCE
HARTMAN, RACHEL FRIEDA (1920-) [American editor and author]
Janice Ward
Hartmann, Roger. See:
MEHTA, RUSTAM JEHANGIR
HARTMANN, SADAKICHI (1869-1944) [Japanese author]
Sidney Allan
HARTNETT. See also:
HARNETT
HARTNETT, CHARLES LEO (1900-) [American professional baseball player]
Gabby Hartnett
HARTREE, CHARLES (1914-) [British stage and motion picture comedian]
Charles Hawtrey

HARTSHORNE, HENRY (1823-97) [American novelist, poet and physician]
Corinne L'Estrange
Hartwell, Nancy. See:
CALLAHAN, CLAIRE WALLIS
HARTWIG, EVA BRIGITTA (1917-) [German ballet dancer and motion picture actress]
Vera Zorina
HARUN-AL-RASHID (763 or 766-809) [Fifth of the Abassid caliphs of Islam]
Aaron the Upright
Harvard, Charles. See:
GIBBS-SMITH, CHARLES HARVARD
Harvard, Haughton of. See:
HAUGHTON, PERCY DUNCAN
Harvard Playwright, The First. See: CROWNE, JOHN
Harvard's Gift to the West. See: CUTTING, BRONSON
Harvester, Simon. See:
RUMBOLD-GIBBS, HENRY ST. JOHN CLAIR
HARVET, INEZ (c.1920-) [American singer and motion picture actress]
Irene Manning
HARVEY [Harvey]. See also:
HERVEY
Hervey
Harvey Brandt. See:
EDWARDS, WILLIAM BENNETT
Harvey D. Richards. See:
SAINSBURY, NOEL EVERINGHAM
HARVEY, GABRIEL (c.1545-1630) [English writer, poet and pamphleteer]
Hobynoll
Martin Marprelate
Harvey Hicks. See:
STRATEMEYER, EDWARD L.
Harvey Lant. See:

ROWLAND, DONALD
SYDNEY
Harvey, Laurence. See:
SKIKNE, LARUSHKA
MISCHA
HARVEY, PAUL (1918-)
[American news analyst
and columnist]
America's Most Honored
Broadcaster
HARVEY, WILLIAM HOPE
(1851-1936) [American
formulator of plans for
coinage of silver]
Coin Harvey
Harwin, Brian. See:
HENDERSON, LeGRAND
Harwood, Gina. See:
BATTISCOMBE, ESTHER
GEORGINA HARWOOD
HARWOOD, ISABELLA
(1840?-88) [British
dramatist and novelist]
Ross Neil
Hasaan. See:
ALI, HASAAN IBN
HASAN. See:
MANSUR, ABDUL
QASIM (HASAN)
HASAN-IBN-AL-SABBAH
(fl. 1090) [Grand Master
of the Assassins ("Hashish
Eaters")]
The Old Man of the Mountain
Sheik-al-Jebal
Hashknife. See:
SIMPSON, JOHN
NICHOLAS
HASKIN, DOROTHY CLARK
(1905-) [American
author]
Howard Clark
HASLAM, ROBERT (fl. 1860-61)
[American Pony Express
rider]
Pony Bob
Hasler, Martin. See:
SHURLY, ERNEST
WILLIAM
HASSE, JOHANN ADOLF
(1699-1783) [German
composer]
Il Sassone
HASSELGARD, AKE (1922-48)
[American jazz musician
(clarinet)]
Stan Hasselgard
Hasso, Signe. See:
LARSSON, SIGNE
Hastings, Alan. See:
WILLIAMSON, GEOFFREY
Hastings, Elizabeth. See:
SHERWOOD, MARGARET
POLLOCK
Hastings, Gilbert. See:
FARRELL, GILBERT
HASTINGS
Hastings, Harrington. See:
MARSH, JOHN
HASTINGS, PHYLLIS DORA
HODGE (fl. 1952-62)
[British author]
John Bedford
E. Chatterton Hodge
Rosina Land
Julia Mayfield
HASTINGS, WILLIAM WIRT
(1866-1938) [American
politician; congressman
from Oklahoma]
Cherokee Bill
Hat, Grandfather's. See:
HARRISON, BENJAMIN
Hat, Old White. See:
GREELEY, HORACE
Hat, The Last Cocked. See:
MONROE, JAMES
Hat, The Man in the Straw.
See: CHEVALIER,
MAURICE AUGUSTE
HATAR, GYOZO VICTOR
JOHN (1914-) [Hungarian
author]
Medveczky
HATCH, CARL ATWOOD
(1889-1963) [American
politician; senator from
New Mexico]
Cowboy Carl
Hatchet, The Lady With the.
See: NATION, CARRY
AMELIA MOORE
HATFIELD, BAZIL MUSE
(1870-) [American
proponent of Texas canals]
Admiral of the Trinity

First Lord of the Marshes
Johnny Simmonseed
Master of the Swamps
HATFIELD, CHARLES FOLSOM (1862-) [American advertising executive]
The Dean of Community Advertising
HATFIELD, CLARENCE E. (fl. 1902-37) [American novelist]
Takkie Caution
HATFIELD, JOHN. See: ROBINSON, MARY
Hathaway, Jan. See: NEUBAUER, WILLIAM ARTHUR
HATLEY, JONATHAN (1892-1966) [American motion picture actor]
Jonathan Hale
Hatmaker, The (El Sombrerero). See: RUIZ, ANTONIO
Hats, The Last of the Cocked. See: MEASE, JOHN
Hattie, Aunt. See: BAKER, HARRIETTE NEWALL WOODS
Hattie, Knitting. See: CARAWAY, HATTIE WYATT
HATTO II (died c. 970) [Archbishop of Mainz]
Bishop Hatto
HATTON, CHRISTOPHER (1540-91) [Chancellor of England]
The Dancing Chancellor
Hatton, G. Noel. See: CAIRD, ALICE MONA
HATZIDAKIS, NICHOLAS (1872-) [German educator and author]
Zeffros Vradinos
HAUCK, LOUISE PLATT (1883-1943) [American novelist]
Lane Archer
Peter Ash
Louise Landon
Jean Randall
HAUGHTON, PERCY DUNCAN (1876-1924) [American football coach]
Haughton of Harvard
P.D.
Hauk, Maung. See: HOBBS, CECIL CARLTON
HAUKELID, SIGRID GURIE (1915-) [American-Norwegian motion picture actress]
Sigrid Gurie
HAUPTMANN, GERHART (1862-1946) [German playwright]
Germany's Greatest Modern Playwright
HAUSER, KASPAR (c. 1812-33) [German foundling]
The Wild Boy
HAUSER, MARGARET LOUISE (1909-) [American journalist, editor and author]
Gay Head
Havelock. See: ELLIS, HENRY HAVELOCK
Havelock of America, The. See: HOWARD, OLIVER OTIS
HAVEN, EMILY BRADLEY NEAL (1827-63) [American editor and writer]
Cousin Alice
Clara Cushman
Alice B. Haven
Alice G. Lee
Haver, June. See: STOVENOUR, JUNE
HAVILLAND, JOAN DE (1917-) [Anglo-American stage and motion picture actress]
Joan Fontaine
Having an Immortal Soul (Anushirvan). See: KHOSRAU I
Havoc, June. See: HOVICK, JUNE
Haw. See: TABOR, HORACE AUSTIN WARNER
Haw Haw, Lord. See: JOYCE, WILLIAM
Hawaiian Pineapple King, The.

See: DOLE, JAMES D.
Hawes Craven. See:
GREEN, HENRY HAWES CRAVEN
Hawk. See:
HAWKINS, COLEMAN
Hawk, The. See:
CHARLES, EZZARD
HAWKINS, COLEMAN
HAWKER, MARY ELIZABETH (1848-1908) [Scottish short story writer]
Lance Falconer
Hawkes, Isaac. See:
HARBAUGH, THOMAS CHALMERS
Hawkeye Man, The Burlington. See: BURDETTE, ROBERT JONES
HAWKINS, BENJAMIN (1754-1816) [American Indian agent; senator from North Carolina]
The Beloved Man of the Four Nations
HAWKINS, COLEMAN (1904-69) [American jazz musician (saxophone)]
Bean
Hawk
The Hawk
HAWKINS, ERSKINE (1914-) (American jazz musician (trumpet, leader, composer)]
The Twentieth Century Gabriel
HAWKINS, HENRY, 1ST BARON BRAMPTON (1817-1907) [British judge]
Hanging Hawkins
HAWKINS, SIR ANTHONY HOPE (1863-1933) [English novelist and playwright]
Anthony Hope
Hawkshaw the Detective. See:
IRON, NATHANIEL COLCHESTER
HAWLEY, JOSEPH (1723-88) [American political leader; advisor to JOHN ADAMS and others]
The Nestor of the Patriots
Hawley, Mabel C. See:
STRATEMEYER, EDWARD L.
Hawley Williams. See:
HEYLIGER, WILLIAM
Hawser Martingale. See:
SLEEPER, JOHN SHERBURNE
Hawthorne, Alice. See:
WINNER, SEPTIMUS
Hawthorne, Captain R.M. See:
ELLIS, EDWARD SYLVESTER
HAWTHORNE, NATHANIEL (1804-64) [American novelist and short story writer]
The Genius of Romance
Oberon
Ashley A. Royce
HAWTON, HECTOR (1901-) [British journalist, editor and author]
Virginia Curzon
Hawtrey, Charles. See:
HARTREE, CHARLES
Hay, Elzey. See:
ANDREWS, ELIZA FRANCES
Hay, Ian. See:
BEITH, JOHN HAY
HAY, JOHN MILTON (1838-1905) [American poet]
Little Breeches
HAYAKAWA, KINTARO (1890-) [Japanese character actor]
Sessue Hayakawa
HAYDEN, ERIC WILLIAM (1919-) [British Baptist pastor and author]
Cire
Hayden, Melissa. See:
HERMAN, MELISSA
HAYDN, FRANZ JOSEPH (1732-1809) [Austrian composer]
The Father of Orchestral Music
The Father of Symphony
Joseph Haydn
Papa Haydn

Haydn's Wife. See:
BOCCHERINI, LUIGI
HAYDON, ARTHUR LINCOLN (1872-) [British author and journalist]
Arthur Lincoln
HAYES [Hayes]. See also:
HAYS
HAYES, CLARENCE (1908-) [American jazz musician (singer, guitar, composer)]
Clancy Hayes
HAYES, EDWARD BRIAN (1935-) [English jazz musician (saxophones, flute, vibraharp)]
Tubby Hayes
HAYES, EDWARD MORTIMER (1842-1912) [American general officer]
Fighting Jack
HAYES, GEORGE FRANCIS (1886-1969) [American motion picture actor]
Gabby Hayes
Hayes, Helen. See:
BROWN, HELEN HAYES
Hayes, Henry. See:
KIRK, ELLEN WARNER OLNEY
HAYES, JOHN F. (1904-) [Canadian business executive and author]
Frederick J. Terrence
HAYES, JOSEPH (1918-) [American playwright and novelist]
Joseph H. Arnold
HAYES, LUCY WARE WEBB (1831-89) [wife of President RUTHERFORD BIRCHARD HAYES]
Lemonade Lucy
HAYES, MARY JANE (1930-) [American motion picture actress]
Allison Hayes
Hayes, Peter Lind. See:
LIND, JOSEPH CONRAD
HAYES, ROBERT LEE (1942-) [American Negro professional football player]
Bob Hayes
HAYES, RUTHERFORD BIRCHARD (1822-93) (Nineteenth President of the United States]
The Dark Horse President
The Fraud President
Granny Hayes
The Hero of '77
His Fraudulency
Old Eight to Seven
The President de Facto
Hayman. See:
PEEL, HAZEL MARY
HAYNE, PAUL HAMILTON (1830-86) [American poet and editor]
The Last Literary Cavalier
The Laureate of the South
The Poet Laureate of the South
The Poet of Charleston
HAYNES, ALFRED HENRY (1910-) [British Civil servant and author]
Keith Christie
Haynes, Anna. See:
MADLEE, DOROTHY HAYNES
Haynes, Linda. See:
SWINFORD, BETTY JUNE WELLS
Haynes, Pat. See:
McKEAG, ERNEST LIONEL
HAYS. See also:
HAYES
Hayes
HAYS, ELINOR RICE (fl. 1952) [American author]
Elinor Rice
Haythorne, Joan. See:
HAYTHORNTHWAITE, JOAN
HAYTHORNTHWAITE, JOAN (1915-) [British stage and motion picture actress]
Joan Haythorne
HAYTON, LEONARD GEORGE (1908-) [American pianist, composer, conductor and arranger]
Lennie Hayton
Hayward, Louis. See:
GRANT, SEAFIELD

Hayward, Richard. See:
KENDRICK, BAYNARD HARDWICK
Hayward, Susan. See:
MARRINER, EDYTHE
Haywarde, Richard. See:
COZZENS, FREDERICK SWARTWOUT
HAYWOOD, WILLIAM DUDLEY (1869-1928) [American labor leader]
Big Bill Haywood
Hayworth, Rita. See:
CANSINO, MARGARITA CARMEN
Hazaken (The Elder). See:
HILLEL
Hazard, Harry. See:
BADGER, JOSEPH E., JR.
Hazard, Jack. See:
BOOTH, EDWIN
HAZARD, JONATHAN J. (c. 1744-c. 1824) [American politician]
Beau Jonathan
Hazard, Laurence, joint pseud. of PATRICIA MIRIAM BARR (1934-) and her husband, JOHN MARSHALL BARR (-) [British authors]
HAZARD, THOMAS ROBINSON (1797-1886) [American author]
Shepherd Tom
Hazel Allen. See:
HERSHBERGER, HAZEL KUHNS
HAZEL, ARTHUR (1903-) [American jazz musician (drums, cornet, mellophone, leader)]
Monk Hazel
Hazel Baxter. See:
ROWLAND, DONALD SYDNEY
Hazel, Harry. See:
JONES, JUSTIN
Hazel Shepard. See:
SMITH, HELEN AINSLIE
Hazel, Witch. See:
SMITH, FRANCIS SHUBAEL
Hazell, Hy. See:
O'HIGGINS, HYACINTH HAZEL
Hazeltine, Horace. See:
WAYNE, CHARLES STOKES
Hazelton, Alexander. See:
ARMSTRONG, WILLIAM ALEXANDER
Hazelton, Captain. See:
WHITSON, JOHN HARVEY
Hazelton, Colonel. See:
WHITSON, JOHN HARVEY
Hazelton, Harry. See:
BADGER, JOSEPH E., JR.
HAZELTON, JAMES (fl. 1861-65) [American Civil War soldier]
The Red Fox
He of the Largesse (El de las Mercedes). See:
HENRY II
Head, Ann. See:
MORSE, ANNE CHRISTENSEN
Head, Gay. See:
HAUSER, MARGARET LOUISE
Head, Great (Canmore). See:
MALCOLM III
Head, Matthew. See:
CANADAY, JOHN EDWIN
Head of the Guelphs. See:
HENRY
Head, The Red. See:
BOW, CLARA
GODFREY, ARTHUR MICHAEL
Redhead
Head, Woolly. See:
JULIAN, GEORGE WASHINGTON
Headin, From the Desk of Beri. See: STORY, ISAAC
Headley, Elizabeth. See:
CAVANNA, ELIZABETH ALLEN
HEADLEY, JOEL TYLER (1813-97) [American author]
The Autocrat of the Quacks
Headliner, Vaudeville's Youngest. See: WEST, MAE
Headsman. See:

CLARKSON, JAMES SULLIVAN
Headstrong Peter. See: STUYVESANT, PETER
HEAGERTY, TRAVERS (1874-) [British stage and motion picture actor]
Henry Travers
HEAL, EDITH (1903-) [American author]
Edith Heal Barrien
Eileen Page
Margaret Powers
HEALEY. See also: HEALY
HEALEY-KAY, PATRICK (1904-) [American dancer and choreographer]
Anton Dolin
Health, The Goddess of. See: HAMILTON, EMMA LYON
HEALY. See also: HEALEY
HEALY, AARON AUGUSTUS (1850-1921) [American art collector and philanthropist]
The Father of the Brooklyn Institute of Arts and Sciences
HEARD, EUGENE M. (1923-) [American jazz musician (drums)]
Fats Heard
HEARD, HENRY FITZ GERALD (1889-) [English editor, author and researcher]
Gerald Heard
H.F. Heard
HEARD, JAMES CHARLES (1917-) [American jazz musician (drums)]
J.C. Heard
HEARD, JOSEPH NORMAN (1922-) [American librarian and author]
Joe Norman
HEARN, PATRICIO LAFCADIO TESSIMA CARLOS (1850-1904) [Irish-Greek writer]
Lafcadio Hearn
Yakumo Koizumi
Hearne, Huxley. See: BROOKER, BERTRAM
HEARST, WILLIAM RANDOLPH (1863-1952) [American capitalist, newspaper and magazine publisher]
The Lord of San Simeon
Heart, The Man of Great. See: HOOVER, HERBERT CLARK
Heartman, Harold. See: MEBANE, JOHN HARRISON
Hearts, The Queen of. See: STUART, ELIZABETH
HEATH, ALBERT (1935-) [American jazz musician (drums)]
Tootie Heath
HEATH, EDWARD (1900-) [English jazz musician (leader, composer, trombone)]
Ted Heath
HEATH, JAMES EDWARD (1926-) [American jazz musician (saxophone)]
Little Bird
Heath, Veronica. See: BLACKETT, VERONICA HEATH STUART
Heath, W. Shaw. See: WILLIAMSON, WILLIAM HENRY
Heathcott, Mary. See: KEEGAN, MARY HEATHCOTT
Heaven-sent Angel of Mercy and of Prison Reform, The. See: DIX, DOROTHEA LYNDE
Heaven-sent Minister, The. See: PITT, WILLIAM
Heaven-taught Plowman, A. See: BURNS, ROBERT
Heavenlier Birth, The Twin of. See: BEAUMONT, FRANCIS
Heavenly Archer (Ilhuicamia). See: MONTEZUMA I
Heber. See: NEWTON, RICHARD HEBER
HEBER, REGINALD (1783-1826) [English prelate and

hymn writer]
The Christian Atticus
HÉBERT. See also:
HERBERT
Hébert
HÉBERT, JACQUES RENÉ (1755-94) [French revolutionist and editor]
Le Père Duchesne
HECK, BARBARA RUCKLE (1744-1804) [Irish-Canadian Methodist organizer in North America]
The Mother of Methodism in the United States
Hector of Germany, The. See:
JOACHIM II
Hedbrooke, Andrew. See:
SILL, EDWARD ROWLAND
Hedda. See:
HOPPER, ELDA FURRY
Hedda Sterne. See:
LINDENBERG, HEDDA
HEDDEN, WORTH TUTTLE (1896-) [American educator and author]
Winifred Woodley
HEDRICK, ZELMA (1922-) [American singer and motion picture actress]
Kathryn Grayson
Hedy Lamarr. See:
LIESLER, HEDWIG
Heels, Silver. See:
MARSHALL, JOHN
HEENAN, JOHN CAMEL (1835-73) [American pugilist]
The Benicia Boy
HEFFELFINGER, WILLIAM W. (1867-1954) [American football player]
Pudge Heffelfinger
HEFLIN, EMMET EVAN, JR. (1910-71) [American motion picture actor]
Van Heflin
Hegesippus. See:
SCHONFIELD, HUGH JOSEPH
Heifer, The Untamed. See:
ELIZABETH I
HEIJERMANS (HEYERMANS), HERMAN (1864-1924) [Dutch-Jewish playwright, novelist and short story writer]
Ivan Jelakomitch
Koos Habbema
Samuel Falkland
HEIMBERGER, EDDIE ALBERT (1908-) [American actor and film producer]
Eddie Albert
Heine. See:
MEINE, HENRY WILLIAM
SHARP, HAROLD SPENCER
HEINE, HEINRICH (1797-1856) [German poet and journalist]
Harry
HEINEY, DONALD WILLIAM (1921-) [American author]
MacDonald Harris
Heinie. See:
BEAU, HENRY J.
FAUST, FREDERICK SCHILLER
MANUSH, HENRY A.
SCHUBLE, HENRY GEORGE, JR.
HEINLEIN, ROBERT ANSON (1907-) [American author]
Anson MacDonald
Lyle Monroe
John Riverside
Caleb Saunders
Heinrich. See:
MEINE, HENRY WILLIAM
HEINRICH, EDWARD OSCAR (fl. 1916-23) [American detective]
The Edison of Crime Detection
Heir of the Republic, The. See: BONAPARTE, NAPOLEON
HEISMAN, JOHN WILLIAM (1869-1936) [American football coach]
The Father of the Forward Pass

Old John W.
Helen. See:
VALENTINE, SISTER MARY HESTER
Helen B. Trundlett. See:
ELIOT, THOMAS STEARNS
Helen Beecher Long. See:
STRATEMEYER, EDWARD L.
Helen Berkley. See:
MOWATT, ANNA CORA OGDEN RITCHIE
Helen Berry. See:
ROWLAND, DONALD SYDNEY
Helen Dickson. See:
REYNOLDS, HELEN MARY GREENWOOD
Helen Fairbairn. See:
SOUTHARD, HELEN FAIRBAIRN
Helen Foley. See:
FOWLER, HELEN ROSA HUXLEY
Helen Hale. See:
MULCAHY, LUCILLE BURNETT
Helen Hayes. See:
BROWN, HELEN HAYES
Helen Hill. See:
MILLER, HELEN HILL
Helen Hinckley. See:
JONES, HELEN HINCKLEY
Helen Hunt Jackson. See:
JACKSON, HELEN MARIA FISKE HUNT
Helen Kay. See:
GOLDFRANK, HELEN COLODNY
Helen Langley. See:
ROWLAND, DONALD SYDNEY
Helen Louise Thorndyke. See:
STRATEMEYER EDWARD L.
Helen Lourie. See:
STORR, CATHERINE COLE
Helen Luqueer. See:
BUSHNELL, MRS. WILLIAM H.
Helen Robertson. See:
EDMISTON, HELEN JEAN MARY
Helen Twelvetrees. See:
JURGENS, HELEN
Helen Vinson. See:
RULFS, HELEN
Helen Westcott. See:
HICKMAN, MYRTHAS HELEN
HELENA (c.250-c.330) [mother of CONSTANTINE THE GREAT]
Augusta
Helena Carter. See:
RICKERTS, HELEN
Helfenstein, Ernest. See:
SMITH, ELIZABETH OAKES
HELFMAN, DON ELIOTT (1926-) [American jazz musician (vibraphone, mellophone, trumpet, bongo drums, singer)]
Don Elliott
Heliogabalus (Elagabalus). See:
BASSIANUS, VARIUS AVITUS
Hell. See:
BRUEGHEL (BREUGHEL), PIETER
Hell and Maria. See:
DAWES, CHARLES GATES
Hell Harry, Give 'em. See:
TRUMAN, HARRY S
Hell Hound. See:
ROGERS, HENRY HUTTLESTON
Hellmuth the Taciturn. See:
VON MOLTKE, HELLMUTH KARL BERNHARD
Hell's Devil Butler. See:
BUTLER, SMEDLEY DARLINGTON
Helm, Brigitte. See:
SCHITTENHELM, GISELE EVE
Helma. See:
DE BOIS, WILHELMINA J.E.
Helmi, Jack. See:
SANDS, LEO GEORGE
Heloise. See:
CRUSE, HELOISE
Helpful Philosopher About the Business Scene We Have,

The Most. See:
DRUCKER, PETER FERDINAND
Helpless Children, The Friend of. See:
HOOVER, HERBERT CLARK
HEMANS, FELICIA DOROTHEA (1793-1835) [English poet]
Mrs. Hemans
Hemans of America, The Mrs. See:
SIGOURNEY, LYDIA HUNTLEY
Hemans, The American. See:
SIGOURNEY, LYDIA HUNTLEY
Hemingway, Taylor. See:
RYWELL, MARTIN
HEMPHILL, JOSEPH (1770-1842) [American legislator and jurist]
Single Speech Hemphill
HEMSKERK. See:
VON HEEMSKERK (HEMSKERK), MARTIN
Henderley, Brooks. See:
STRATEMEYER, EDWARD L.
HENDERSHOT, ROBERT HENRY (1850-c. 1925) [American Civil War drummer boy in Union army]
The Drummer Boy of the Rappahannock
Henderson, J. Stanley. See:
WILLETT, EDWARD
HENDERSON, JAMES FLETCHER (1898-1952) [American jazz musician (piano, leader, arranger)]
Fletcher Henderson
Smack
HENDERSON, LeGRAND (1901-) [American author and illustrator]
LeGrand
Brian Harwin
HENDERSON, LISLE (1904-) [American motion picture actor]
Lyle Talbot
HENDERSON, LYLE CEDRIC (1918-) [American jazz musician (piano, leader, composer)]
Skitch Henderson
Henderson, Marc Antony. See:
STRONG, REV. GEORGE A.
Henderson, Mary. See:
MAVOR, DR. OSBORNE HENRY
HENDERSON, PETER (1823-90) [American horticulturist]
The Father of Horticulture and Ornamental Gardening
HENDLEMAN, GEORGE JOSEPH (1920-) [American jazz musician (piano, composer)]
George Handy
HENDRICK, HARVEY (1897-) [American professional baseball player]
Gink
HENDRICKS, FREDERICK WILMOTH (1901-) [West Indian calypso singer]
Wilmouth Houdini
HENDRICKS, JOHN CARL (1921-) [American jazz song-writer and singer]
Jon Hendricks
HENDRICKS, JOSEPH EDWARD (1903-) [American politician; congressman from Florida]
Doc Townsend of Florida
HENDRICKS, NAMÉE (1890-) [American lecturer and author]
Sah-nee-weh
Hendrix, Sonny. See:
BARKAN, STANLEY HOWARD
HENEGAR, RUSSELL DALE (1897-) [American military band conductor]
Russ Henegar
HENHAM, ERNEST GEORGE (1870-) [British author]
John Trevena
HENLEY, ARTHUR (1921-) [American lecturer and

author]
Kenneth Eric
Webb Jones
HENLEY, JOHN (1692-1756) [English preacher and eccentric]
Orator Henley
HENREY. See also:
HENRI
Henri
Henriques
HENRY
Henry
HENREY, MADELEINE (1906-) [French-English author]
Mrs. Robert Henrey
Henri. See:
BLAZE, ANGE HENRI
HENREY
Henriques
HENRY
Henry
TAINE, HIPPOLYTE ADOLPHE
HENRI I (1550-88) [Duke of Guise]
Le Balafré (The Scarred)
HENRI II (1614-64) [Duke of Guise]
The Hero of the Fable
Henri D'Arles. See
BEAUDE, HENRI
Henri Daugé. See:
HAMMOND, HENRIETTA HARDY
Henri Dupres. See:
FAWCETT, FRANK DUBREZ
Henri Le Caron, Major. See: BEACH, THOMAS
Henri le Reunét. See:
POE, EDGAR ALLAN
Henri-Louis Lekain. See:
CAÏN, HENRI-LOUIS
Henri Wiener. See:
LONGSTREET, STEPHEN
Henrich von der Cläna. See:
WEISS, ALBERT MARIA
Henreid, Paul. See:
VON HERNREID, PAUL
Henrietta Baker. See:
DAVIS, JEANNETTE
Henrietta Leslie. See:
SCHUTZE, GLADYS HENRIETTA
Henriques. See also:
HENREY
HENRI
Henri
HENRY
Henry
Henriques, Affonso. See:
ALFONSO I
HENRY (1129-95) [Duke of Saxony and Bavaria]
Head of the Guelphs
The Lion
HENRY (1394-1460) [Prince of Portugal]
Henry the Navigator
Prince Henry the Navigator
Henry. See:
Adams, Henry
HENREY
HENRI
Henri
Henriques
WILSON, JEREMIAH JONES COLBATH
HENRY I (876?-936) [Duke of Saxony and King of Germany]
Henry the Fowler
HENRY I (1068-1135) [King of England]
Henry Beauclerc (Henry the Scholar)
HENRY I (1210?-74) [King of Navarre]
The Fat
HENRY II (c. 972-1024) [King of Germany and Holy Roman Emperor]
The Lame
The Saint
St. Henry
HENRY II (1133-89) [King of England]
Curtmantle
HENRY II (1333-79) [King of Castile and León]
El de las Mercedes (He of the Largesse)
HENRY III (1017-56) [Holy Roman Emperor]
The Black
HENRY III (1379-1406) [King of Castile]
The Sickly

HENRY III (1551-89) [King of France]
The Man Milliner
HENRY IV (1367-1413) [King of England]
Bolingbroke
Henry of Lancaster
HENRY IV (1553-1610) [King of Navarre (as HENRY III) and of France (as HENRY IV)]
Le Béarnais
Henry of Navarre
Henry the Great
The King of Brave Men
Mon Soldat (My Soldier)
HENRY V (1387-1422) [King of England]
The English Alexander
Henry V. See:
CHAMBORD, HENRI CHARLES DIEUPONNÉ, COMTE DE
HENRY VI (1421-71) [King of England]
The Martyr King
HENRY VII (1275-1313) [King of Germany and Holy Roman Emperor]
Henry of Luxemburg
HENRY VII (1457-1509) [King of England]
Henry Tudor
Henry, Earl of Richmond
HENRY VIII (1491-1547) [King of England]
Bluff King Hal
The Father of the English Navy
King Harry
Henry Tudor
Henry Allen, Esq., The Late. See: HOPE, JAMES BARRON
Henry Armstrong. See:
JACKSON, HENRY
Henry B. Beston. See:
SHEAHAN, HENRY BESTON
Henry B. Stoddard, Major. See: INGRAHAM, COLONEL PRENTISS
Henry Beston. See:
SHEAHAN, HENRY BESTON
Henry C. Browning. See:
MOWATT, ANNA CORA OGDEN RITCHIE
Henry Calvin. See:
HANLEY, CLIFFORD
Henry Churton. See:
TOURGEE, ALBION WINEGAR
Henry Compton. See:
MACKENZIE, CHARLES
Henry, Daniel, Jun. See:
HOLMES, HENRY DANIEL
Henry Dee. See:
TORBETT, HARVEY DOUGLAS LOUIS
Henry Ford of Aviation, The. See: PIPER, WILLIAM THOMAS, SR.
Henry Fuseli. See:
FÜSSLI, JOHANN HEINRICH
Henry G. Aikman. See:
ARMSTRONG, HAROLD HUNTER
Henry Gibbs. See:
RUMBOLD-GIBBS, HENRY ST. JOHN CLAIR
Henry Girl, The O. See:
AYRES, AGNES
Henry Green. See:
YORKE, HENRY VINCENT
Henry Gréville. See:
DURAND, MME. ALICE FLEURY
HENRY, GUSTAVUS ADOLPHIS (1804-80) [American orator]
The Eagle Orator
The Eagle Orator of Tennessee
Henry Handel Richardson. See:
RICHARDSON, HENRIETTA
Henry Hayes. See:
KIRK, ELLEN WARNER OLNEY
Henry Holbeach. See:
RANDS, WILLIAM BRIGHTY
Henry Homespun. See:
SOUTHWICK, SOLOMON
Henry Howard of Kenninghall. See: HOWARD, HENRY
Henry, Hurry Up. See:

KAISER, HENRY J.
Henry Irving, Sir. See:
BRODRIBB, JOHN HENRY
Henry Jenner, Mrs. See:
JENNER, KATHERINE LEE
Henry Koster. See:
KOSTERLITZ, HERMANN
Henry L. Boone. See:
ST. JOHN, PERCY BOLLINGBROKE
Henry Lansing. See:
ROWLAND, DONALD SYDNEY
Henry, Marse. See:
WATTERSON, HENRY
Henry Martyn. See:
PERRY, MARTIN HENRY
Henry Moorshead. See:
PINE, LESLIE GILBERT
Henry Morgan. See:
VON OST, HENRY LERNER, JR.
Henry Morton Stanley, Sir
See: ROWLANDS, JOHN
Henry, O. See:
PORTER, WILLIAM SYDNEY
HENRY OF GHENT (c.1217-93)
[scholastic philosopher]
The Illustrious Doctor
Henry of Lancaster. See:
HENRY IV
Henry of Navarre. See:
BLAINE, JAMES GILLESPIE
HENRY IV
WATTERSON, HENRY
Henry, Old Sir. See:
VANE, SIR HENRY
Henry, Olivier. See:
PORTER, WILLIAM SYDNEY
Henry Oscar. See:
WALE, HENRY
Henry, Our Patrick. See:
KOLB, REUBEN FRANCIS
HENRY, PATRICK (1736-99)
[American lawyer, orator and revolutionist]
The Forst-born Demosthenes
The Man of the People
The Prophet of the Revolution
The Voice of the Revolution
Henry Pu-Yi. See:
HSUAN-T'UNG
Henry Rabasseire. See:
PACHTER, HENRY MAXIMILIAN
Henry Russell. See:
OLSON, HENRY RUSSELL
Henry Second. See:
HARRISON, HENRY SNYDOR
Henry Seton Merriman. See:
Merriman, Henry Seton
SCOTT, HUGH STOWELL
Henry Soudley. See:
WOOD, JAMES PLAYSTED
Henry Stephenson. See:
GARROWAY, HENRY STEPHENSON
Henry Stratton. See:
NELSON, MICHAEL HARRINGTON
Henry Sutton. See:
SLAVITT, DAVID R.
Henry T. Adams. See:
RANSOM, JAY ELLIS
Henry the Minstrel. See:
BLIND HARRY
Henry Thomas. See:
SCHNITTKIND, HENRY THOMAS
Henry Travers. See:
HEAGERTY, TRAVERS
Henry, Uncle. See:
SMITH, GEORGE HENRY
Henry van Porter. See:
CORRELL, CHARLES J.
Henry Wade. See:
AUBREY-FLETCHER, HENRY LANCELOT
HENRY, WILBUR F. (1897-1952)
[American football player]
Fats Henry
Henry Wilson. See:
COLBATH, JEREMIAH JONES
Henry Wishart. See:
SHEPHERD, ROBERT HENRY WISHART
Henry Wood, Mrs. See:
WOOD, ELLEN PRICE

Henry, Young Sir. See:
VANE, SIR HENRY
Henson, Gladys. See:
GUNN, GLADYS
Hepburn, Audrey. See:
VAN HEEMSTRA, EDDA HEPBURN
Her, Erich. See:
PAETL, ERICH
HERACLITUS (c. 540-475 B.C.) [Greek Philosopher]
The Dark Philosopher
The Weeping Philosopher
Herald. See:
Froy, Herald
Herb. See:
GERMAR, WILLIAM HERBERT
MAGIDSON, HERBERT
Herbert. See:
BEST, OSWALD HERBERT
HÉBERT
Herbert, Arthur. See:
SHAPPIRO, HERBERT ARTHUR
Herbert Arthur. See:
SHAPPIRO, HERBERT ARTHUR
Herbert Bellwood. See: PATTEN, WILLIAM GILBERT
Herbert Carter. See:
RATHBONE, ST. GEORGE HENRY
HERBERT, DONALD JEFFRY (1917-) [American television personality]
Don Herbert
Mr. Wizard
Herbert, Francis. See: BRYANT, WILLIAM CULLEN
HERBERT, HENRY, 9th EARL OF PEMBROKE (1693-1751) [English builder of first Westminster bridge]
The Architect Earl
HERBERT, HENRY WILLIAM (1807-58) [English author]
Frank Forester
Herbert, Holmes. See:
SANGER, EDWARD
Herbert Lom. See:
SCHLUDERPACHERU, HERBERT CHARLES ANGELO KUCHACEVICH ZE
Herbert, Mort. See:
PELOVITZ, MORTON HERBERT
HERBERT, SIR ALAN PATRICK (1890-) [English writer]
Albert Haddock
Herbert Wade. See:
WALES, HUGH GREGORY
HERBERT, WILLIAM (1580-1630) [Third Earl of Pembroke]
Mr. W.H.
Herbert Winter. See:
ELLINGFORD, ROBERT FREDERICK
Herbie Mann. See:
SOLOMON, HERBERT JAY
Herbst, Josephine. See:
HERMANN, MRS. JOHN
Hercules Mary. See:
PROMITIS, MARY
Hercules of Music, The. See:
GLUCK, CHRISTOPHER WILLIBALD
Hercules Romanus. See:
COMMODUS, LUCIUS AELIUS AURELIUS
Hercules Vinegar, Captain. See:
FIELDING, HENRY
Herdebred (Broad Shouldered) See: HAAKON II
Hereford, John. See:
FLETCHER, HARRY LUFT VERNE
Heretics, The Hammer of the. See: AILLY, PIERRE D'
AUGUSTINIUS, AURELIUS
FABER, JOHANN
HEREWARD (fl. c. 1070) [English outlaw and patriot]
The Wake
HERING. See also:
HERRING
Herring
HERING, CONSTANTINE (1800-80) [German-American homeopath]
The Father of Homeopathy in America
HERMAN. See also:
HARMAN

HARMON
Harmon
HERMANN
Hermann
Hermanns
Hermine
HERRMANN
HERMAN, FLOYD CAVES (1903-) [American professional baseball player]
Babe Herman
Herman Knott. See: SMITH, WALTER CHALMERS
HERMAN, MELISSA (1928-) [Canadian ballerina
Melissa Hayden
HERMAN, NICHOLAS (c.1605-91) [Carmelite mystic]
Brother Lawrence
HERMAN, WOODROW CHARLES (1913-) [American jazz musician (clarinet, alto saxophone, singer, leader)]
Woody Herman
HERMANN [Hermann]. See: HERMAN etc.
HERMANN (1013-54) [German historian]
The Lame
Hermann Burte. See: STRUBE, HERMANN
Hermann Faber. See: GOLDSCHMIDT, DR. HERMANN
Hermann Lauscher. See: HESSE, HERMANN
HERMANN, MRS. JOHN (1897-) [American novelist]
Josephine Herbst
Hermanns. See also:
HARMAN
HARMON
Harmon
HERMAN
HERMANN
Hermann
Hermine
HERRMANN
Hermanns, Peter. See: BRANNON, WILLIAM T.
Hermes. See: HARRIS, JAMES
Hermine. See:
ELDER, SUSAN BLANCHARD
HARMAN
HARMON
Harmon
HERMAN
HERMANN
Hermann
Hermanns
HERRMANN
Hermit Author of Palo Alto, The. See: HOOVER, HERBERT CLARK
Hermit of Hampole, The. See: HAMPOLE, RICHARD ROLLE DE
Hermit of Newfane, The. See: BROWN, DAVID
Hermit of Slabsides, The. See: BURROUGHS, JOHN
Hermit of the Abolitionist Movement, Peter-the-. See: LUNDY, BENJAMIN
Hermit of Walden, The. See: THOREAU, HENRY DAVID
Hermit, Peter the. See: PETER
Hermitage, The Sage of the. See: JACKSON, ANDREW
HERN, GEORGE ANTHONY (1916-) [English editor and author]
Andrew Hope
HERN, GEORGE ANTHONY See also: Potiphar
Hernia Whittlebot. See: COWARD, NOEL PEIRCE
Hero Husband, The. See: WANDERER, CARL
Hero of a Hundred Fights, The. See: NELSON, HORATIO VISCOUNT NELSON
WELLINGTON, ARTHUR WELLESLEY, 1st DUKE OF
Hero of Appomattox. See: GRANT, HIRAM ULYSSES
Hero of Charleston, The. See: LEE, CHARLES
Hero of Chippewa, The. See: SCOTT, WINFIELD
Hero of Concepción, The. See: FANNIN, James W.
Hero of 1812, The Land. See: JACKSON, ANDREW

Hero of Fort Donelson. See:
GRANT, HIRAM ULYSSES
Hero of Fort Fisher, The. See: LAMB, WILLIAM
Hero of Fort McHenry, The. See: ARMISTEAD, GEORGE
Hero of Fort Meigs, The. See: CHRISTY, WILLIAM
Hero of Fort Mifflin, The. See: THAYER, SIMEON
Hero of Fort Sumter, The. See: BEAUREGARD, PIERRE GUSTAVE TOUTANT
Hero of Fredericksburg, The. See: KIRKLAND, RICHARD E.
Hero of King's Mountain, The. See: CLEVELAND, BENJAMIN
Hero of Lake Erie, The. See: PERRY, OLIVER HAZARD
Hero of Little Round Top, The. See: CHAMBERLAIN, JOSHUA LAWRENCE
Hero of Manila, The. See: DEWEY, GEORGE
Hero of Mobile Bay, The. See: FARRAGUT, DAVID GLASGOW
Hero of New England, The. See: STANDISH, MILES (MYLES)
Hero of New Orleans, The. See: JACKSON, ANDREW
Hero of Reunion, The. See: SMITH, HENRY BOYNTON
Hero of San Juan Hill, The. See: ROOSEVELT, THEODORE
Hero of Saratoga, The. See: GATES, HORATIO
Hero of '77, The. See: HAYES, RUTHERFORD BIRCHARD
Hero of Stony Point, The. See: WAYNE, ANTHONY
Hero of the Battle of Gettysburg, The. See: BURNS, JOHN
Hero of the Confederacy, The Boy. See: DAVIS, SAM
Hero of the Crater, The. See: MAHONE, WILLIAM
Hero of the Fable, The. See: HENRY II
Hero of the Hornet's Nest, The. See: PRENTISS, BENJAMIN MAYBERRY
Hero of the Nile, The. See NELSON, HORATIO, VISCOUNT NELSON
Hero of Tippecanoe, The. See: HARRISON,WILLIAM HENRY
Hero of Vincennes, The. See: CLARK, GEORGE ROGERS
Hero Strong. See: TRASK, CLARA AUGUSTA JONES
Hero, The Christian. See: GEORGE, ST.
Hero, The Kansas. See: MONTGOMERY, JAMES
Hero, The Little. See: WHEELER, JOSEPH
Hero, The Martyr. See: BROWN, JOHN
Hero, The Traitorous. See: ARNOLD, BENEDICT
Hero, The Waterloo. See: HILL, VISCOUNT ROWLAND
HEROD (37?-4 B.C.) [Procurator of Judea]
The Great
HERODOTUS (c. 484-c. 424 B.C.) [Greek historian]
The Father of Greek Prose
The Father of History
The Father of Lies
Herodotus, The Northern. See: STURLESON, SNORRE
Heroine of Groton, The. See: BAILEY, ANNA WARNER
Herr N. Osey. See: WEISS, EHRICH (ERIK WEISZ)
HERRERA, FRANCISCO (1622-85) [Spanish painter]
El Mozo (The Younger)
HERRERA, FRANCISCO (1576-1656) [Spanish painter]
El Viejo (The Elder)
HERRERA, FRANCISCO ARJONA (1818-68) [Spanish bullfighter]

Cúchares
HERRICK, MARVIN THEODORE,
See: Smith, John
HERRING [Herring]. See also:
HERING
HERRING, ARTHUR L. (1907-)
[American professional baseball player]
Sandy Herring
Herring, Geilles
Martin Ross, joint pseuds. of EDITH ANNA OENINE SOMERVILLE (1861-1949) and her cousin VIOLET FLORENCE MARTIN (1862-1915) [Irish authors]
Herring, Geilles. See also:
MARTIN, VIOLET FLORENCE
HERRMANN. See also:
HARMAN
HARMON
Harmon
HERMAN
HERMANN
Hermann
Hermanns
Hermine
HERRMANN, ALEXANDER (1844-98) [Viennese illusionist and magician]
Herrmann the Great
Herrnstein, Barbara. See:
SMITH BARBARA HERRNSTEIN
HERSHBERGER, HAZEL KUHNS (1910-) [American author]
Hazel Allen
Herschel McLandress. See:
GALBRAITH, JOHN KENNETH
Hershey, Sheaf. See:
NEWELL, PETER
Hertha Pretorius. See:
KOUTS, HERTHA PRETORIUS
HERTZ, NELLIE SOLANGE STRONG (1920-)
[American author]
Solange Strong
Hervey. See:
ALLEN, WILLIAM HERVEY
HARVEY
Harvey
LORD HERVEY
Hervey, Irene. See:
HERWICK, IRENE
Hervey, Jane. See:
McGAW, NAOMI BLANCHE THOBURN
HERWICK, IRENE (c.1916-)
[American motion picture actress]
Irene Hervey
HERZOG, ÉMILE SALAMON WILHELM (1885-1967)
[French writer]
André Maurois
Hesba Stretton. See:
SMITH, SARAH
HESELTINE, PHILIP ARNOLD (1894-1930) [English musicologist and composer]
Peter Warlock
HESIOD (fl. 735 B.C.)
[Greek poet]
The Ascraean Sage
Hesiod. See:
COOKE, THOMAS
HESKETT, ANNE ELIZABETH CAMPBELL BARD (1908-) [American author]
Betty MacDonald
HESS, RUDOLPH (1894-)
[German politician and Nazi leader]
Mad Rudi
HESSE. See:
PHILIP OF HESSE
HESSE, HERMAN (1877-1962)
[Swiss poet and novelist]
Hermann Lauscher
Emil Sinclair
HESSELBERG, MELVYN (1901-)
[American stage and motion picture actor]
Melvyn Douglas
HESTON, WILLIAM M. (1878-1963) [American football player]
The Michigan Terror
HESYCHIUS (fl. early 6th cent.)
[Greek historical and biographical writer]

The Illustrious
Hetman of the Cossacks of the Don. See:
PLATOV, MATVEI IVANOVICH, COUNT
Hetty. See:
GREEN, HENRIETTA HOWLAND
HEWIT, AUGUSTINE FRANCIS (1820-97) [American Roman Catholic teacher and editor]
The Newman of America
HEWIT, NATHANIEL (1788-1867) [American clergyman and temperance advocate]
The Luther of the Early Temperance Reformation
HEWITT, JOHN HENRY (HILL) (1801-90) [American composer and ballad poet]
The Father of American Ballad Poetry
Hext, Harrington. See:
PHILLPOTTS, EDEN
Hextall, David. See:
PHILLIPS-BIRT, DOUGLAS
HEYDRICH, REINHARD (1904-42) [Nazi terrorist; deputy chief of the Gestapo]
The Hangman
HEYERMANS. See:
HEIJERMANS (HEYERMANS), HERMAN
HEYLIGER, WILLIAM (1884-) [American author]
Hawley Williams
Heyst, Axel. See:
GRABOWSKI, ZBIGNIEW ANTHONY
Heywood, Anne. See:
STROSS, MRS. RAYMOND
Hi De Ho Man, The. See:
CALLOWAY, CABELL, 3RD
Hi De Ho, The King of. See:
CALLOWAY, CABELL, 3RD
Hiat, Elchik. See:
KATZ, MENKE
HIBBERT, ELEANOR BURFORD (1906-) [British merchant and author]
Eleanor Burford
Elbur Ford
Victoria Holt
Kathleen Kellow
Jean Plaidy
Ellalice Tate
Hibbert Verne. See:
FRAZER-HURST, REV. DOUGLAS
Hibernia. See:
POTTEN, HENRY THOMAS
HICKMAN, MYRTHAS HELEN (1929-) [American motion picture actress]
Helen Westcott
HICKOCK, JAMES BUTLER (1837/9-70) [American frontiersman]
Duck Bill
Duch Bill
Dutch Bill
The Prince of Pistoleers
Shanghai Bill
Wild Bill Hickock
Hickory Hill, The Sage of. See:
WATSON, THOMAS EDWARD
Hickory, Old. See:
JACKSON, ANDREW
Hickory, Young. See:
HILL, DAVID BENNETT
POLK, JAMES KNOX
TYLER, JOHN
Hicks, Francis. See:
STEELE, SIR RICHARD
Hicks, Harvey. See:
STRATEMEYER, EDWARD L.
HICKS, TOMMY (1936-) [British singer and motion picture actor]
Tommy Steele
HICKS, WILLIAM (1830-83) [British officer]
Hicks Pasha
Hieronymus Aleander. See:
ALEANDRO, GIROLAMO
Hieronymus Bosch (Bos). See: VAN AEKEN, HIERONYMUS

Hieronymus Lorm. See:
LANDESMANN, HEINRICH
HIGBEE, CHESTER GOSS
(1835-1908) [American
physician and surgeon]
The Good Physician
HIGDON, HAL (1931-) [American editor and author]
Lafayette Smith
HIGGINBOTHAM, JACK
(1906-) [American
jazz musician (trombone)]
Jay C. Higginbotham
J.C. Higginbotham
HIGGINS, ANDREW JACKSON
(1886-) [American
shipbuilder]
America's No. 1 Boatbuilder
Money-maker and Hoopla-artist
The Shipyard Bunyan
HIGGINS, EUGENE (1874-)
[American painter of
rural life]
The Millet of America
HIGGINS, HAYDN (1932-)
[American jazz musician
(piano, organ, vibraphone)]
Eddie Higgins
HIGGINS, MATTHEW JAMES
(1810-68) [British
controversialist]
Jacob Omnium
HIGGINS, RICHARD C.
(1938-) [British essayist,
editor and author]
Dick Higgins
HIGGINS, ROSALYN COHEN
(1937-) [British educator,
lawyer and author]
Rosalyn Cohen
HIGGINSON, JOSEPH
VINCENT (1896-) [American composer, organist
and teacher]
Cyr de Brant
High-born Demosthenes, The.
See: WILLIAM I
High-hatted Tragedian of
Jazz, The. See:
FRIEDMAN, THEODORE
LEOPOLD
High Priest of English
Palladianism, The. See:
BOYLE, RICHARD
High Priest of the Constitution,
The. See:
BAYARD, JAMES
ASHETON
High Tax Harry. See:
TRUMAN, HARRY S
Highland Laddie, The. See:
STUART, CHARLES
EDWARD LOUIS PHILIP
CASIMIR
Highland Mary. See:
CAMPBELL, MARY
MORISON, MARY
Highlanders, The Apostle of the.
See: COLUMBA, ST.
Highlands, The Cowper of the.
See: BUCHANAN, DUGALD
Highlands, The Ulysses of the.
See: CAMERON, SIR
EVAN
Highness Prince Lahovary, His.
See: MANOLESCO,
GEORGE
Highness, Royal. See:
ALBERT
Highwayman, The Flying. See:
HARROW, WILLIAM
Highwaymen, The Orpheus of.
See: GAY, JOHN
Hilaire. See:
BELLOC, JOSEPH
HILARY PIERRE
Hilary. See:
TUNSTALL-BETHRENS,
MARTIN HILARY
HILARY (died 468) [Supreme
Pontiff of Roman
Catholic Church]
Pope Hilary
St. Hilary
Hilary Neal. See:
NORTON, OLIVE MARION
HILARY OF POITIERS
(c. 300-367) [Bishop of
Poitiers]
The Athanasius of the West
Hilary Rose. See:
MACKINNON, CHARLES
ROY
Hilda Boden. See:
BODENHEIM, HILDA MORRIS

Hilda Roderick Ellis. See:
DAVIDSON, HILDA RODERICK ELLIS
Hilda Simms. See:
MOSES, HILDA
Hilda Tablet. See:
SWANN, DONALD IBRAHIM
Hilda Trevelyan. See:
TUCKER, HILDA
Hilda Vaughan. See:
MORGAN, HILDA CAMPBELL
Hilde Spiel. See:
DE MENDELSSOHN, HILDE MARIA
HILDEBRAND (c. 1021-85) [Supreme Pontiff of Roman Catholic Church]
Pope Gregory VII
St. Gregory
Hildebrand. See:
BEETS, NICOLAAS
Hildegard Neff. See:
KNEF, HILDEGARDE
Hildegarde. See:
SELL, HILDEGARDE LORETTA
Hildegarde Ford. See:
MORRISON, VELMA FORD
Hildegarde, The Incomparable. See: SELL, HILDEGARDE LORETTA
Hill, Anne. See:
MUSKETT, NETTA
HILL, BERTHA (1905-50) [American jazz musician (singer)]
Chippie Hill
HILL, BRIAN. See:
Magill, Marcus
HILL, DANIEL HARVEY (1821-89) [American Confederate Army officer]
Bethel Hill
HILL, DAVID BENNETT (1843-1910) [American politician; Governor of New York]
The Bachelor Governor
Young Hickory
HILL, DAVID CHARLES (1936-) [American author]
Dave Hill
Hill, Dee. See:
ZUCKER, DOLORES MAE BOLTON
HILL, GEORGE CANNING (1825-98) [American attorney, biographer and author]
Lewis Myrtle
HILL, GEORGE HANDEL (1809-48) [American actor]
Yankee Hill
Hill, Grace Brooks. See:
STRATEMEYER, EDWARD L.
HILL, GRACE LIVINGSTON (1865-) [American novelist]
Marcia MacDonald
Hill, Helen. See:
MILLER, HELEN HILL
Hill, Hyacinthe. See:
ANDERSON, VIRGINIA R. CRONIN
HILL, JAMES JEROME (1838-1916) [American railway executive and financier]
The Empire Builder
Jim Hill
HILL, JOHN SPRUNT (1869-) [American proponent of low-interest credit for farmers]
The Father of Rural Credit in North Carolina
Hill, K. F. See:
BAER, MRS.
Hill, Kate F. See:
BAER, MRS.
HILL, KATHLEEN LOUISE (1917-) [Canadian author]
Kay Hill
Hill, King. See:
ROBERTSON, FRANK CHESTER
HILL, MARGARET OHLER (1915-) [American educator and author]
Rachel Bennett
Andrea Thomas

Hill, Mrs. K. F. See:
BAER, MRS.
Hill, Monica. See:
WATSON, JANE WERNER
Hill, Murray. See:
HOLLIDAY, ROBERT CORTES
Hill, Polly. See:
HUMPHREYS, MARY EGLANTYNE HILL
Hill, Professor Bunker C. See: ABEL, ALAN IRWIN
Hill, Ruth A. See:
VIGUERS, RUTH HILL
Hill, The Hero of San Juan. See: ROOSEVELT, THEODORE
Hill, The Sage of Hickory. See: WATSON, THOMAS EDWARD
Hill, The Sage of Potato. See:
HOWE, EDGAR WATSON
HILL, VISCOUNT ROWLAND (1772-1842) [English general officer]
The Waterloo Hero
HILL, WALTER BARNARD (1851-1905) [American lawyer, scholar and temperance advocate]
The Apostle of Prohibition
The Scholar of the Georgia Bar
HILL, WILLIAM JOSEPH (1889-1940) [American composer]
Billy Hill
HILL, WILLIAM KIRKPATRICK (1862-) [British author]
John Asterisk
Hillas. See also:
HILLIS
Hillas, Julian. See:
DASHWOOD, ROBERT JULIAN
Hillbilly Cat, The. See:
PRESLEY, ELVIS ARON
HILLEL (c. 60 B.C.-10 A.D.) [Doctor of Jewish law]
Hababli (The Babylonian)
Hazaken (The Elder)
HILLHOUSE, WILLIAM (1728-1816) [American politician in Connecticut]
Sachem
Hilliard, Harriet. See:
NELSON, PEGGY LOU SNYDER
Hilliard, Jan. See:
GRANT, HILDA KAY
HILLIS. See also:
Hillas
HILLIS, CHARLES RICHARD (1913-) [Canadian missionary]
Dick Hillis
Hillo, Pepe. See:
DELGADO, JOSÉ
Hills, The Giant of the. See:
CRAWFORD, ETHAN ALLEN
Hills, The Patriarch of the. See:
CRAWFORD, ABEL
Hills, The Sage of the Verduga. See: McGROARTY, JOHN STEVEN
Hills, The Seer of Wellesley. See: BABSON, ROGER WARD
HILTON, CONRAD NICHOLSON (1887-) [American hotel executive]
The Biggest Hotel Man in the World
The No. 1 Innkeeper
Hilton Gregory. See:
FERGUSON, CHARLES W.
HILTON, JAMES (1900-54) [English author]
Glen Trevor
HILTON, RICHARD (1894-) [British general officer and author]
Zakhmi Dil
HIMMLER, HEINRICH (1900-45) [German Nazi official and chief of the Gestapo]
The Evil Genius of the German Horror Camps
The Scourge of the Swastika
Himmler of Russia, The. See:
BERIA, LAVRENTI PAVLOVICH
Himself. See:
SHAW, RALPH ROBERT
Hin me Geong. See:

ARMITAGE, JOHN
Hinckley, Helen. See:
JONES, HELEN HINCKLEY
HINDMAN, THOMAS CARMICHAEL (1828-68) [American army officer]
The Lion of the South
HINDS, EVELYN MARGERY (fl. 1946-63) [British educator and author]
E. M. Hinds
HINE, SESYLE JOSLIN (1929-) [American journalist, editor and author]
Josephine Gibson
Sesyle Joslin
G. B. Kirtland
HINES, EARL KENNETH (1905-) [American jazz musician (piano, leader)]
Fatha Hines
HINES, EDWARD NORRIS (1870-) [American road commissioner in Michigan]
The Father of the White Line
HINES, MILTON (1926?-) [American comedian and television personality]
Soupbone
Soupy Sales
HINGLE, MARTIN PATTERSON (1924-) [American actor]
Pat Hingle
HINKSON, MRS. KATHARINE TYNAN (1861-1931) [Irish author]
Katharine Tynan
Hinton, Richard W. See:
ANGOFF, CHARLES
HIPPISLEY, GEORGE (1865-1936) [American columnist and author]
George Hembert Westley
HIPPLE, HUGH (1920-) [American radio announcer and motion picture actor]
Hugh Marlowe
Hippo, The Bishop of. See:
AUGUSTINIUS, AURELIUS
HIPPOCRATES (460?-377? B.C.) [Greek physician]
The Father of Medicine
Hippocrates, The English. See:
SYDENHAM, THOMAS
Hippocrates, The Roman. See:
CELSUS, AULUS CORNELIUS
HIPPONAX (fl. 6th cent. B.C.) [Greek iambic poet]
The Ephesian Poet
The Father of Burlesque Poetry
The Father of Parody
Hipsch Martin. See:
SCHONGAUER, MARTIN
HIRAI, TARO (1894-) [Japanese author]
Edogawa Rampo
Hirsch, William Randolph, joint pseud. of MARVIN KITMAN (-), RICHARD ROBERTS LINGEMAN (1931- and VICTOR S. NAVASKY (1932-) [American authors
Hirsch, William Randolph. See also: LINGEMAN, RICHARD ROBERTS
HIRSCHBERG. See:
GEBHARD, COUNT OF HIRSCHBERG
HIRST, HENRY BECK (1817-74) [American lawyer, poet and journalist]
Anna Maria Hirst
HIRT, ALOIS MAXWELL (1922-) [American jazz musician (trumpet, leader)]
Al Hirt
Trumpeting Behemoth
His Accidency. See:
ARTHUR, CHESTER ALAN
CLEVELAND, STEPHEN GROVER
FILLMORE, MILLARD
JOHNSON, ANDREW
TYLER, JOHN
His Country, The Saviour of. See:
OATES, TITUS
His Fraudulency. See:
HAYES, RUTHERFORD BIRCHARD
His Highness Prince Lahovary. See: MANOLESCO, GEORGE

His Rotundity. See:
ADAMS, JOHN
Hislop, Andrew See:
CLARKE, MARCUS
Historian of America, The First. See:
ANGHIERA, PIETRO MARTIRE
Historian of Printing, The. See: AMES, JOSEPH
Historian of the Café Society, The Social. See:
BEEBE, LUCIUS
Historian of the Hampden County Bar, The. See:
BATES, WILLIAM GELSTON
Historian, The Plastic. See:
DAVIDSON, JO
Historians, The First of the French. See:
VILLEHARDOUIN, GEOFFROI DE
Historical Novel, The Father of the. See:
SCOTT, SIR WALTER
Historical Societies in America, The Founder of. See: PINTARD, JOHN
History, The Father of. See:
HERODOTUS
History, The Father of American. See:
BRADFORD, WILLIAM
History, The Father of Church. See:
EUSEBIUS OF CAESAREA
History, The Father of Ecclesiastical. See:
BEDE (BEDA) (BAEDA), ST.
EUSEBIUS OF CAESAREA
History, The Father of English Natural. See:
RAY (WRAY), JOHN
History, The Father of French. See:
DUCHESNE, ANDRÉ
History, The Father of Indiana. See: DILLON, JOHN BROWN
History, The Father of Russian. See: NESTOR
History, The Father of Scottish Poetry and. See:
BARBOUR, JOHN
History, The Father of Swiss. See: TSCHUDI, AEGIDIUS (GILG)
History, The Sculptor of American. See:
KELLY, JAMES EDWARD
Hit Parade, The Army's One-man. See: LOESSER, FRANK HENRY
HITCHCOCK, ALFRED JOSEPH (1899-) [British motion picture and television producer]
The Cherubic Master of Suspense
The Portly Master of the Involuntary Scream
HITCHCOCK, THOMAS (1900-44) [American polo player and military aviator]
Tommy Hitchcock
HITCHIN, MARTIN MEWBURN (1917-) [British author]
Martin Mewburn
HITLER, ADOLF (1889-1945) [German dictator; Führer and Chancellor of the Third German Reich]
Der Führer
Adolf Schicklgrüber
Hitler's Evil Genius, Adolf. See: BORMANN, MARTIN
HOAD, LEWIS A. (1934-) [Australian tennis player]
Lew Hoad
Hoagy. See:
CARMICHAEL, HOAGLUND HOWARD
HOAR, GEORGE FRISBIE (1826-1904) [American politician; senator from Massachusetts]
Gran'ther Hoar
The Moon-faced Senator from Worcester
The Old Man Eloquent of the Senate
Pre-Adamite
HOAR-STEVENS, THOMAS TERRY (1911-) [British comedian and motion picture actor

Terry-Thomas
Hoarse One, Little (Ronquillo). See: PELAYO, LUIS
HOBART, ALICE NOURSE (1882-) [American author]
Alice Tisdale Hobart
Hobart, Black. See: SAUNDERS, ED
HOBART, GEORGE VERE (1867-1926) [American journalist, humorist and playwright]
Hugh McHugh
HOBART-HAMPDEN, AUGUST CHARLES (1822-86) [British admiral; naval adviser to Turkey]
Captain Roberts
Hobart Pasha
Hobart, Rose. See: KEEFER, ROSE
Hobbema, The English. See: CROME, JOHN
Hobbema, The Scotch. See: NASMYTH, PATRICK (PETER)
Hobbes Inverted. See: HUME, DAVID
Hobbes, John Oliver. See: CRAIGIE, PEARL MARY TERESA RICHARDS
HOBBES, THOMAS (1588-1679) [English philosopher]
The Philosopher of Malmesbury
HOBBS, CECIL CARLTON (1907-) [American Methodist clergyman and author]
Maung Hauk
HOBMAN, JOSEPH BURTON (1872-) [British political journalist]
The Man from the North
Hobo, The Millionaire. See: HOW, JAMES EADS
HOBSBAWN, ERIC JOHN ERNEST (1917-) [British educator and author]
Francis Newton
HOBSON, HARRY (1908-) [British musician and author]
Hank Hobson
Hank Janson
HOBSON, LAURA ZAMETKIN (1900-) [American journalist and author]
Felicia Quist
Hobson, Polly. See: EVANS, JULIA RENDEL
HOBSON, RICHMOND PEARSON (1870-1937) [American naval officer]
Kissing-bug Hobson
Parson Hobson
Hobynoll. See: HARVEY, GABRIEL
Hocus, Humphrey. See: CHURCHILL, JOHN
Hodge, E. Chatterton. See: HASTINGS, PHYLLIS DORA HODGE
HODGES, BARBARA K. (1893-) [English novelist]
Elizabeth Cambridge
HODGES, GILBERT RAY (1924-) [American professional baseball player]
Gil Hodges
HODGES, JOHN CORNELIUS (1906-) [American jazz musician (composer, alto saxophone)]
Johnny Hodges
Rabbit
Hodges, Turner. See: MOREHEAD, ALBERT HODGES
HODGKINSON, ISABEL (1918-) [British stage and motion picture actress]
Isabel Dean
HODGSON, AGNES (fl. late 18th-early 19th cents.) [British author and journalist]
Mrs. Willoughby Hodgson
Hodgson, Norma. See: RUSSELL, NORMA HULL LEWIS
HODGSON, WILLIAM ARCHER (1887-) [British dental surgeon and author]
Thearcher

HODSON, ARNOLD WEINHOLT (fl. early 20th cent) [British author]
Delphi
HOEFFER, NORMAN (1900-) [American motion picture actor]
Norman Foster
Hoey. See also:
Hooey
Hoey, Dennis. See:
HYAMS, SAMUEL DAVID
HOFDROP, WILLIAM PIM (1912-) [Dutch author]
Will Geerlink
HOFER, ANDREAS (1767-1810) [Tyrolese patriot]
The Wallace of Switzerland
Hoff. See:
HOFFMAN, PIERCY J.
HOFF, HARRY SUMMERFIELD (1910-) [British scientist and author]
William Cooper
HOFFENBERG, MASON. See:
Kenton, Maxwell
HOFFMAN. See also:
HOFFMAN
Hofman
HOFFMAN, ABBIE (1936-) [American civil rights worker and author]
Free
Spiro Igloo
George Metesky
HOFFMAN, CLARE E. (1875-) [American lawyer and politician; representative from Michigan]
CIO Hoffman
The Sit-down Striker
HOFFMAN, DAVID (1784-1854) [American lawyer, educator and historian]
Anthony Grumbler
HOFFMAN, MICHAEL (1787-1848) [American politician; congressman from New York]
Admiral Hoffman
HOFFMAN, OGDEN (1793-1856) [American criminal lawyer]
The Erskine of the American Bar
HOFFMAN, PIERCY J. (1896-) [American cartoonist]
Hoff
HOFFMANN. See also:
HOFFMAN
Hofman
HOFFMANN, AUGUST HEINRICH (1798-1874) [German poet and philologist]
Hoffmann von Fallersleben
HOFFMANN, ERNST THEODOR WILHELM (1776-1822) [German writer, music critic and caricaturist]
Amadeus
Ernst Theodor Amadeus Hoffmann
HOFFMANN, MARGARET JONES (1910-) [American organist and author]
Peggy Hoffmann
Hofman. See also:
HOFFMAN
HOFFMANN
Hofman, Anton. See:
HOLLO, ANSELM
Hofmeyer, Hans. See:
FLEISCHER, ANTHONY CHARLES
HOFMEYR, JAN HENDRIK (1845-1909) [South African statesman]
Onze Jan
HOFPREDIGER, JOHANNES MARTIN VOGEL (1873-) [German clergyman and author]
Dr. Johannes Vogel
HOGAN, FRANCIS T. (1916-) [American composer]
Frank Hogan
HOGAN, JAMES FRANCIS (1906-) [American professional baseball player]
Shanty Hogan
HOGAN, WILLIAM BENJAMIN (1912-) [American professional golfer]
Ben Hogan
Hogarth, Douglas. See:

PHILLIPS-BIRT, DOUGLAS
Hogarth, Jr. See:
KENT, ROCKWELL
Hogarth of Novelists, The. See:
FIELDING, HENRY
Hogarth, The American. See:
SHAHN, BENJAMIN
Hogarth, The Scottish. See:
ALLAN, DAVID
HOGARTH, WILLIAM (1697-1764) [English painter and engraver]
The Juvenal of Painters
HOGG, BETH TOOTILL (1917-) [British author]
Elizabeth Grey
HOGG, JAMES (1770-1835) [Scottish poet]
The Ettrick Shepherd
HOGG, JAMES STEPHEN (1851-1906) [American politician; Governor of Texas]
The Great Commoner
HOGSETT, ELON CHESTER (1903-) [American professional baseball player]
Chief Hogsett
Hohenthal, Karl. See:
MAY, KARL FRIEDRICH
Holbeach, Henry. See:
RANDS, WILLIAM BRIGHTY
HOLBECHE, PHILIPPA (1919-) [English author]
Philippa Shore
HOLBEIN, HANS (1465?-1524) [German portrait painter]
The Elder
HOLBEIN, HANS (1497?-1543) [German portrait painter]
The Younger
HOLBERG, LUDVIG (1684-1754) [Danish writer]
The Founder of Danish Literature
HOLBROOK, HAROLD ROWE, JR. (1925-) [American monologist and actor]
Hal Holbrook
Holbrook, Sabra. See:
ERICKSON, SABRA ROLLINS
HOLBROOK, SILAS PINCKNEY (1796-1835) [American lawyer, editor and author]
Jonathan Fabrick
HOLCOMBE, SOLOMON (1789-1871) [American capitalist]
King Solomon
HOLD, MARGARET VAN VECHTEN SAUNDERS (1899-) [American author]
Rackham Holt
Hold That Line. See:
BLANTON, THOMAS LINDSAY
Holden, Fay. See:
HAMMERTON, FAY
HOLDEN, MARTHA EVERTS (1844-96) [American author]
Amber
HOLDEN, RAYMOND PECKHAM (1894-) [American editor and author]
Richard Peckham
Holden, William. See:
BEEDLE, WILLIAM FRANKLIN
HOLDSWORTH, GLADYS BRONWYN (1890-) [British author]
G. B. Stern
Hole Stebbins, Dry. See:
STEBBINS, GRANT CASE
Holiday. See also:
Halliday
HOLLIDAY
Holliday
Holiday, Billie. See:
McKAY, ELEANOR GOUGH
Holiday, Joe. See:
BEFUMO, JOSEPH A.
HOLIFIELD, CHESTER EARL (1903-) [American businessman and politician; representative from California]
Chet Holifield
Holiness, Beauty of. See:
HURD, RICHARD
Holland, Clive. See:
HANKINSON, CHARLES JAMES

HOLLAND, EDWIN CLIFFORD
(c. 1794-1824) [American
verse writer]
Orlando
HOLLAND, HERBERT LEE
(1910-) [American
jazz musician (trumpet)]
Peanuts Holland
HOLLAND, JOSIAH GILBERT
(1819-81) [American
author, editor and
journalist]
The American Tupper
Timothy Titcomb
Holland, Katrin. See:
FREYBE, HEIDI
HUBERTA
Holland, Kel. See:
WHITTINGTON, HARRY
HOLLAND, PHILEMON
(1552-1637) [English
linguist and translator]
The Translator General
The Translator-General in
His Age
HOLLAND, RAY P. (1884-)
[American editor and
conservationist]
Bob White
HOLLAND, ROBERT EMORY
(1911-) [American
musician and educator]
Bob Holland
Holland, The Raphael of.
See: VON HEEMSKERK
(HEMSKERK), MARTIN
Holland, William of. See:
WILLIAM
HOLLENBECK, WEBB
PARMELEE (1893-1966)
[American singer, dancer,
stage and motion picture
actor]
Clifton Webb
HOLLES, DENZIL HOLLES. See:
Five Members, The
HOLLEY. See also:
HOLLY
HOLLEY, MAJOR QUINCY JR.
(1924-) [American jazz
musician (bass)]
Mule Holley
HOLLEY, MARIETTA (1836-1926)
[American humorist,
novelist, essayist and poet]
Josiah Allen's Wife
HOLLIDAY [Holliday]. See also:
Halliday
Holiday
Holliday, James. See:
GRAY, SIMON
HOLLIDAY, JOHN H. (184?-87)
[American frontier
gunfighter; contemporary
of WYATT EARP]
Doc Holliday
Holliday, Judy. See:
TUVIM, JUDITH
HOLLIDAY, ROBERT CORTES
(1880-1947) [American
author]
Murray Hill
Holliman, Earl. See:
NUMKENA, ANTHONY
HOLLINGSWORTH, JAMES H.
(1830-c. 1894) [American
Civil War officer]
Double Quick
Hollis, Jim. See:
SUMMERS, HOLLIS
SPURGEON, JR.
HOLLISTER, EDWARD PAYSON
(1839-77) [American lawyer,
writer and biographer]
E. P. H.
HOLLO, ANSELM (1934-)
[Finnish journalist, radio
producer, translator
and author]
Sergei Bielyi
Anton Hofman
HOLLOWAY, BRENDA WILMAR
(1908-) [British author]
Sarah Verney
HOLLOWAY, JAMES L.
(1927-) [American jazz
musician (tenor saxophone)]
Red Holloway
HOLLOWAY, TERESA BRAGUNIER
(1906-) [American teacher
and author]
Elizabeth Beatty
Margaret Vail McLeod
HOLLY. See also:
HOLLEY
HOLLY, JOAN CAROL (1932-)

[American author]
J. Hunter Holly
Hollywood Plutarch, The. See:
DIETERLE, WILHELM
Hollywood, Queen Marie of.
See: KOERBER, LEILA
Hollywood Ten, The total nick-name of
ALVAN BESSIE (-),
HERBERT J. BIBERMAN (1900-),
LESTER COLE (-),
EDWARD DMYTRYK (1908-)
RING LARDNER, JR. (-)
JOHN HOWARD LAWSON (1886-),
ALBERT MALTZ (1908-),
SAM ORNITZ (-),
ADRIAN SCOTT (1912-),
and DALTON TRUMBO (1905-) [Hollywood writers, producers and directors; in 1947 refused to tell the Un-American Activities Committee whether or not they were Communists]
Hollywood Ten, The. See also:
TRUMBO, DALTON
Hollywood, The First Lady of.
See: DUNNE, IRENE
GARSON, GREER
KING, MOIRA SHEARER
Hollywood's Busiest and Most Versatile Woman. See:
HOPPER, ELDA FURRY
Hollywood's Grand Old Man.
See: BLYTHE, LIONEL
Hollywood's No. 1 Glamour Boy.
See:
MATURE, VICTOR JOHN
HOLM, H.H. FRITZ VILHELM (1881-) [Danish nobleman, general officer, statesman and author]
Duke of Xensi
Holm, Saxe. See:
JACKSON, HELEN MARIA FISKE HUNT
HOLM, SVEN AAGE (1902-) [Danish broadcaster and author]
Farmacevten
Holman. See:
HULMAN
HUNT, WILLIAM HOLMAN
HOLMAN, JAMES (1787-1857) [British naval officer and author of travel books]
The Blind Traveler
HOLMAN, WILLIAM STEELE (1822-97) [American politician; representative from Indiana]
The Great Objector
The Watchdog of the Treasury
HOLMES [Holmes]. See also:
HOMES
HOLMES, ABIEL (1763-1837) [American Congregational clergyman]
Myron
Holmes, Captain Hamilton. See:
HARBAUGH, THOMAS CHALMERS
Holmes, Captain Howard. See:
HARBAUGH, THOMAS CHALMERS
HOLMES, DAVID CHARLES (1919-) [American engineer and author]
David Charlson
Holmes, H.H. See:
WHITE, WILLIAM ANTHONY PARKER
HOLMES, HENRY DANIEL (1851-1908) [American poet]
Daniel Henry, Jun.
Holmes Herbert. See:
SANGER, EDWARD
HOLMES, JOHN (1773-1843) [American politician; representative and senator from Massachusetts]
The Duke of Summersetts
HOLMES, JOSEPH EVERETT (1922-) [American editor and author]
Jay Holmes
HOLMES, ODETTA (1930-) [American Negro folk singer]

Odetta
HOLMES, OLIVER WENDELL (1809-94) [American physician, poet, essayist and novelist]
The Autocrat
Dorothy Q.
HOLMES, PETER FENWICK (1932-) [English author]
Peter Fenwick
HOLMES, RICHARD ARNOLD (1931-) [American jazz musician (organ)]
Groove Holmes
Holmes, Rick. See:
HARDWICK, RICHARD HOLMES, JR.
HOLMES, WILFRED JAY (1900-) [American retired naval officer, educator and writer]
Alec Hudson
HOLMES, WILLIAM KERSLEY (1882-) [British editor and author]
F.O.O. Serrifile
HOLMVIK, OYVIND (1914-) [Norwegian editor and author]
Oy-vik
Paprika
Sepia
Holt, Gavin. See:
RODDA, CHARLES
HOLT, ISAAC (1924-) [American jazz musician (baritone saxophone, composer)]
Red Holt
Holt, Margaret. See:
PARISH, MARGARET HOLT
Holt Marvell. See:
MASCHWITZ, ERIC
Holt, Rackham. See:
HOLD, MARGARET VAN VECHTEN SAUNDERS
Holt, Stephen. See:
THOMPSON, HARLAN H.
Holt, Tex. See:
JOSCELYN, ARCHIE L.
Holt, Victoria. See:
HIBBERT, ELEANOR BURFORD
Holton, Leonard. See:
WIBBERLEY, LEONARD PATRICK O'CONNOR
Holworthy Hall. See:
PORTER, HAROLD EVERETT
Holy Devil, The. See:
RASPUTIN, GREGORY
Holy Horatio. See:
ALGER, HORATIO, JR.
Holy Sepulcher, Baron and Defender of the. See:
GODFREY OF BOUILLON
Holy Sepulchre, Defender of the. See:
GODFREY OF BOUILLON
Holy, The. See:
JUDAH I
HOLYWOOD, JOHN (died 1244 or 1256) [English mathematician]
Johannes de Sacrobosco
HOLZAPFEL, RUDOLF PATRICK (1938-) [Irish essayist, poet and translator]
Rudi Holzapfel
Rooan Hurkey
R. Patrick Ward
Homberg, Otto Von. See:
GEISE, DR. OTTO
Home, Cecil. See:
WEBSTER, JULIA AUGUSTA
Home-Grown Ballerina, England's First. See:
HOOKHAM, MARGARET
Home Run. See:
BAKER, JOHN FRANKLIN
Homeopathy in America, The Father of. See:
HERING, CONSTANTINE
HOMER (lived c. 850 B.C. or later; according to some, lived as early as 1200 B.C.) [Greek epic poet]
The Blind Bard of the Chian Strand
The Blind Old Bard
The Blind Old Man of Scio's Rocky Isle
The Father of Epic Poetry
The Father of Song
The Maeonian Swan

The Man of Chios
The Prince of Poets
Scio's Blind Old Bard
The Swan of the Meander
HOMER (fl. 3rd cent. B.C.)
[Greek tragic poet]
The Younger
Homer, Louise. See: BEATTY, LOUISE DILWORTH
Homer of Ferrara, The. See: ARIOSTO, LUDOVICO
Homer of His Age, The. See: ANGILBERT, ST.
Homer of Human Nature, The Prose. See: FIELDING, HENRY
Homer of It, The Father of the Bathos and Indeed the. See: BLACKMORE, SIR RICHARD
Homer of Orators, The. See: CHRYSOSTOM, ST. JOHN
Homer of Our Dramatic Poets, The. See: SHAKESPEARE, WILLIAM
Homer of Persia, The. See: MANSUR, ABDUL QASIM (HASAN)
Homer of Philosophers, The. See: ARISTOCLES
Homer of Portugal, The. See: CAMOENS, LUIZ DE
Homer of the French Drama, The. See: CORNEILLE, PIERRE
Homer of the Great Ocean, The Prose. See: RUSSELL, WILLIAM CLARK
Homer of the Middle West, The. See: MASON, WALT
Homer of the Novel, The. See: SCOTT, SIR WALTER
Homer Stansbury Leeds. See: BERNARD, PIERRE A.
Homer, The Attic. See: SOPHOCLES
Homer, The British. See: MILTON, JOHN
Homer, The Insects'. See: FABRE, JEAN HENRI
Homer, The Scottish. See: WILKIE, WILLIAM
Homer, The Scourge of (Homeromastix). See: ZOILUS
HOMES. See also:
HOLMES
Holmes
HOMES, MARY SOPHIE SHAW ROGERS (c. 1830-)
[American poet and novelist]
Millie Mayfield
Homespun, Henry. See: SOUTHWICK, SOLOMON
Homestead Act, The Father of the. See: JOHNSON, ANDREW
Homestead Law, The Father of The. See: GROW, GALUSHA, AARON
Homme de Décembre, l' (The Man of December). See: BONAPARTE, CHARLES LOUIS NAPOLEON
Homme Rouge, Le Petit. See: VIZETELLY, ERNEST ALFRED
Homo Universale (The Universal Man). See: VINCI, LEONARDO DA
Hondo Wells. See: WHITTINGTON, HARRY
Honest Abe. See: LINCOLN, ABRAHAM
Honest Allan. See: CUNNINGHAM, ALLAN
Honest Allan Cunningham. See: CUNNINGHAM, ALLAN
Honest George. See: MONK, GEORGE
Honest Harold. See: ICKES, HAROLD LeCLAIRE
Honest Jack. See: LORD ALTHORP
Honest John. See:
BRICKER, JOHN WILLIAM
COVODE, JOHN
KELLY, JOHN

LORD ALTHORP
STEPHENSON, JOHN
Honest King, The. See:
VICTOR EMMANUEL II
Honest Lawyer, The. See:
OGDEN, ROBERT
Honey. See:
WALKER, WILLIAM
Honey Bear. See:
SEDRIC, EUGENE PAUL
Honey Boy. See:
EVANS, CHARLES E.
Honey Fitz. See:
FITZGERALD, JOHN F.
Honeyed Teacher, The. See:
BERNARD OF CLAIRVAUX
HONEYMAN, JOHN (fl. late 18th cent.) [American spy]
The Tory Traitor
Honor. See:
Honour
Honorable Order of Starvation, Knight of the Most. See:
LIVINGSTON, WILLIAM
Honorable Wilhelmina Amelia Skeggs, The. See:
THACKERAY, WILLIAM MAKEPEACE
Honored Broadcaster, America's Most. See:
HARVEY, PAUL
Honorio. See:
Domecq, Honorio Bustos
HONORIUS (died 638) [Supreme Pontiff of Roman Catholic Church]
Pope Honorius I
Honorius II, Pope. See:
SCANNABECCHI, LAMBERTO
Honorius III, Pope. See:
SAVELLI, CENCIO
Honorius IV, Pope. See:
SAVELLI, GIACOMO
Honour, A Person of. See:
SOUTHLAND, T.
SWIFT, JONATHAN
Honus. See:
WAGNER, JOHN PETER
HOOD, DOROTHY BROWNING (1914-) [adopted daughter of EDWARD BROWNING
Sunshine
HOOD, JOHN BELL (1831-79) [American Confederate general officer]
Butcher Hood
Hood of Missouri, The Robin. See: JAMES, JESSE WOODSON
Hood of the Forest, The Robin. See: ALLEN, ETHAN
Hood of the Sierras, Robin. See:
CARILLO, JOAQUIN
Hooey. See:
Hoey
LONG, HUEY PIERCE
HOOKER, JOSEPH (1814-79) [American Civil War general officer]
Fighting Joe Hooker
HOOKER, LOIS (1927-) [Canadian motion picture actress]
Lois Maxwell
HOOKER, THOMAS (1586-1641/47) [Anglo-American Congregational churchman]
The First Democrat
The Light of the Western Churches
HOOKER, WILLIAM BRIAN (1880-1946) [American author of opera librettos]
Brian Hooker
HOOKHAM, MARGARET (1919-) [English ballerina]
Dame Margot Fonteyn de Arias
England's First Home-grown Ballerina
Margot Fonteyn
Hooks, Fish. See:
STOUT, ALLYN McCLELLAND
HOOKS, GAYLOR EUGENE (1927-) [American author]
Gene Hooks
Hoop (Du Cerceau). See:
ANDROUET, JACQUES
Hooper, Byrd. See:
ST. CLAIR, BYRD HOOPER
HOOPER, JOHNSON J. (1815-63) [American journalist and

humorist]
Simon Suggs
HOOPER, NESBERT (1938-) [American jazz musician (drums)]
Sticks Hooper
Stix Hooper
HOOPER, ROBERT (1709-90) [American philanthropist]
King Hooper
Hoopington, Ambrose. See:
BINNEY, CECIL
Hoopla-artist, Money-maker and. See:
HIGGINS, ANDREW JACKSON
Hoosier Orator, The. See:
ORTON, HARLOW S.
Hoosier Poet, The. See,
RILEY, JAMES WHITCOMB
Hoosier Shakespeare, The. See:
GRAY, FINLY HUTCHINSON
Hoot. See:
GIBSON, EDWARD RICHARD
GIBSON, SAMUEL BRAXTON
Hootie. See:
McSHANN, JAY
Hooton, Charles. See:
ROWE, VIVIAN CLAUDE
HOOVER, HELEN DRUSILLA BLACKBURN (1910-) [American chemist, metallurgist and author]
Jennifer Price
HOOVER, HERBERT CLARK (1874-1964) [thirty-first President of the United States]
The Chief
The Friend of Helpless Children
The Hermit Author of Palo Alto
The Man of Great Heart
HOPE [Hope]. See also:
HOPP
HOPPE
Hope, Andrew. See:
HERN, GEORGE ANTHONY
Hope, Anthony. See:
HAWKINS, SIR ANTHONY HOPE
Hope Daring. See:
JOHNSON, ANNA
Hope, Edward. See:
COFFEY, EDWARD HOPE
Hope, Felix. See:
WILLIAMSON, CLAUDE CHARLES H.
HOPE, JAMES BARRON (1829-87) [American poet]
The Late Henry Allen, Esq.
Hope, Lady Esther. See:
ST. JOHN, PERCY BOLLINGBROKE
Hope, Laura Lee. See:
STRATEMEYER, EDWARD L.
Hope, Laurence. See:
NICOLSON, ADELA FLORENCE
HOPE, LESLIE TOWNES (1904-) [Anglo-American comedian, radio, motion picture and television actor]
Bob Hope
Ski-nose
Hope, The Bard of. See:
CAMPBELL, THOMAS
HOPF, ALICE LIGHTNER (1904-) [American author]
A.M. Lightner
HOPKINS, DR. LEMUEL (1750-1801) [American physician and poet]
A Bludgeon Satirist
A Gentleman of Connecticut
The Democratiad
The Guillotina
HOPKINS, DR. LEMUEL. See: also: Hartford Wits, The
Hopkins, Jeremiah. See:
NOTT, HENRY JUNIUS
HOPKINS, KENNETH (1914-) [American author]
Christopher Adams
Anton Burney
Warwick Mannon
Paul Marsh
Edmund Marshall
Arnold Meredith
Hopkins, Lyman. See:
FOLSOM, FRANKLIN BREWSTER
HOPKINS, MARK. See:

Big Four, The
HOPKINS, MATTHEW (died 1647)
[British author and
"witch finder"
The Witch Finder Generall
Hopkins, Puffer. See:
MATHEWS, CORNELIUS
HOPKINS, SAM (1912-)
[American jazz musician
(singer, guitar)]
Lightnin'
HOPKINSON, FRANCIS
(1737-91) [American
author; signer of Declaration of Independence]
Calumet
Cautious
Peter Grievous, Esq.
A Lover of Candour
One of the People
HOPLEY-WOOLRICH, CORNELL
GEORGE (1903-)
[American writer of
mystery stories]
George Hopley
William Irish
Cornell Woolrich
HOPP. See also:
HOPE
Hope
HOPPE
HOPP, SIGNE MARIE
(1905-) [Norwegian
author]
Zinken
HOPPE. See also:
HOPE
Hope
HOPP
HOPPE, WILLIAM
FREDERICK (1887-)
[American billiard
player]
The Boy Wonder
Willie Hoppe
HOPPER, EDNA WALLACE
(1864-1959) [American
actress and beauty
specialist]
The Eternal Flapper
The Grandma Flapper
HOPPER, EDWARD
(1882-1967) [American
painter]
The Painter of Loneliness
HOPPER, ELDA FURRY
(1890-1966) [American
newspaper and radio columnist and actress]
Hedda Hopper
Hollywood's Busiest and Most
Versatile Woman
HOPPER, HAROLD S. (1912-)
[American composer and
author]
Hal Hopper
HOPPER, WILLIAM DE WOLF
(1858-1935) [American
actor and musical comedy
star]
De Wolf Hopper
Horace. See:
FLACCUS, QUINTUS
HORATIUS
SMITH, HORATIO
VERNET, EMILE JEAN
HORACE
WALPOLE, HORATIO
Horace Goldin. See:
GOLDSTEIN, HYMAN
Horace Hazeltine. See:
WAYNE, CHARLES
STOKES
Horace Mann of the South,
The. See:
RUFFNER, WILLIAM
HENRY
Horace of France, The. See:
BÉRANGER, PIERRE-
JEAN DE
Horace of Our Dramatic Poets,
The. See:
SHAKESPEARE, WILLIAM
Horace, The English. See:
JONSON, BENJAMIN
POPE, ALEXANDER
Horace, The French. See:
BÉRANGER, PIERRE-
JEAN DE
Horace, The Portuguese. See:
FERREIRA, ANTONIO
Horaces. See:
Spanish Horaces, The
HORAN, JOHN MICHAEL
(1838-1938) [American
railroad employee for 83

years]
Soda Ash Johnny
Horatio, Holy. See:
ALGER, HORATIO, JR
Horatio Ribbonson. See:
SHAW, GEORGE BERNARD
Horatius Cocles of the Tyrol. See:
DUMAS, ALEXANDRE DAVY DE LA PAILLETERIE
Horizontal Bill. See:
MORRISON, WILLIAM RALLS
HORMISDAS (died 523) [Supreme Pontiff of Roman Catholic Church]
Pope Hormisdas
St. Hormisdas
HORN [Horn]. See also:
HORNE
HORN, KIRBY GRANT (1914-) [Scottish-American motion picture actor]
Kirby Grant
Horn, The Fog. See:
ALLEN, WILLIAM
Horn, Trader. See:
SMITH, ALFRED ALOYSIUS
Hornbook, Adam. See:
COOPER, THOMAS
HORNBY. See also:
HORNSBY
HORNBY, JOHN (1913-) [British author]
Joseph Grace
Gordon Summers
HORNBY, LESLIE (1949-) [British fashion model]
Twiggy
HORNE. See also:
HORN
Horn
HORNE, CYNTHIA MIRIAM (1939-) [British author]
Cynthia Pilkington
HORNE, GEOFFREY (1916-) [British civil servant and author]
Gil North
HORNE, HUGH ROBERT (1915-) [American Baptist minister, television broadcaster and author]
Jane Madison
HORNE, JOHN (1736-1812) [English politician and philologist]
The Philosopher of Wimbledon
Horne Tooke
HORNE, RICHARD HENGIST (HENRY) (1803-84) [English author]
Mrs. Fairstar
Hornet's Nest, The Hero of the See: PRENTISS, BENJAMIN MAYBERRY
HORNSBY. See also:
HORNBY
HORNSBY, ROGERS (1896-) [American professional baseball player]
Rajah
HORNUNG, PAUL VERNON (1935-) [American professional football player]
Golden Boy
Horowitz, The Black. See:
WALLER, THOMAS WRIGHT
HORROCKS, PETER (1926-) [British motion picture actor]
Peter Reynolds
Horror Camps, The Evil Genius of the German. See:
HIMMLER, HEINRICH
Horse Charlie, Wild. See:
ALEXANDER, CHARLES W.
Horse, Death on a Pale. See:
WIRZ, CAPTAIN HENRY
Horse Harry, Light. See:
LEE, HENRY
WATTERSON, HENRY
Horse, Lee's Old War. See:
LONGSTREET, JAMES
Horse of Reform, The Old War. See: BLANKENBURG, RUDOLPH
Horse of Sumner County, The War. See:
TROUSDALE, WILLIAM
Horse of Tennessee, The

Democratic War. See:
McMILLIN, BENTON
Horse of the Confederacy, The War. See:
LONGSTREET, JAMES
Horse of the Senate, The Wheel. See:
RUGGLES, BENJAMIN
Horse President, The Dark. See: HAYES RUTHERFORD BIRCHARD
Horse, The. See:
AMECHE, ALAN
TWIGGS, DAVID EMANUEL
Horse, The Democratic War. See: McMILLIN, BENTON
Horse, The First Dark. See:
POLK, JAMES KNOX
Horse, The Iron. See:
GEHRIG, HENRY LOUIS
Horse, The Old War. See:
COOK, PHILIP
DEVIN, THOMAS CASIMIR
Horseback, The Man on. See:
BOULANGER, GEORGES ERNEST JEAN MARIE
ROOSEVELT, THEODORE
Horsely, Ramsbottom. See:
BERNE, ERIC LENNARD
Horsepower. See:
FULMER, HAMPTON PITTS
Horticulture and Ornamental Gardening, the Father of. See:
HENDERSON, PETER
HORTON, JUANITA (1898-) [American motion picture actress]
Bessie Love
HORTON-SMITH, LIONEL GRAHAM HORTON (1871-) [British barrister and author]
Gramiades
HORWICH, FRANCES RAPPAPORT (1908-) [American educator and author]
Miss Frances
Hosea Biglow. See:
LOWELL, JAMES RUSSELL
HOSEMANN, ANDREAS (1498-1552) [German theologian and reformer]
Andreas Osiander
HOSKEN, ALICE CECIL SEYMOUR (1877-) [British novelist]
Coralie Stanton
HOSKEN, CLIFFORD (1882-) [British author and journalist]
Richard Keverne
HOSKEN, ERNEST CHARLES HEATH (1875-) [British author]
Pierre Costello
Hospitality. See:
King and Queen of Hospitality, The
Hospitals, Brigadier Commanding. See: BICKERDYKE, MARY ANN BALL
Hoss, Old. See:
STEPHENSON, JACKSON RIGGS
HOSSENT, HARRY (1916-) [British journalist, editor and author]
Sean Gregory
Kevin O'Malley
Host to the Coast, The. See:
GRIER, JAMES W.
Hostess, The Nation's. See:
MADISON, DOROTHY PAYNE TODD
HOSTETTER, IRIS A. (1913-) [American dancer and motion picture actress]
Iris Adrian
Hot Lips. See:
BURNETT, CAROL
PAGE, ORAN
Hot Oil. See:
MARLAND, ERNEST WHITWORTH
Hot Paprika from Hungary, The. See:
BANKY, VILMA
Hot Stove Jimmy. See:
QUINN, JAMES ALOYSIUS
Hot Toddy. See:
TODD, THELMA
Hotel, Katie from the Kostur.

See: CUMPANAS, ANA
Hotel Man in the World, The Biggest. See:
HILTON, CONRAD NICHOLSON
Hotspur. See:
PERCY, SIR HENRY
Hotspur of Debate, The. See:
LORD STANLEY
Hotspur, Young. See:
INGERSOLL, RALPH ISAACS
Hotte. See:
BUCHHOLZ, HORST WERNER
Houdini, Harry. See:
WEISS, EHRICH (ERIK WEISZ)
Houdini in the White House, The. See:
ROOSEVELT, FRANKLIN DELANO
Houdini the Great. See:
WEISS, EHRICH (ERIK WEISZ)
Houdini, The Legal Successor of. See:
WEISS, THEO
Houdini, Wilmouth. See:
HENDRICKS, FREDERICK WILMOTH
HOUGH, CLARA SHARPE (1893-) [American author]
C. Sharpe
HOUGH, RICHARD (1922-) [British editor and author]
Bruce Carter
HOUGH, STANLEY BENNETT (1917-) [British author]
Rex Gordon
Bennett Stanley
Houghton, Claude. See:
OLDFIELD, CLAUDE HOUGHTON
HOUGHTON, DOUGLASS (1809-45) [American physician, surgeon and geologist]
The Boy Geologist of Michigan
The Little Doctor
Houghton, Elizabeth. See:
GILZEAN, ELIZABETH HOUGHTON BLANCHET
HOUGHTON, RICHARD MONCKTON MILNES, 1ST BARON (1809-85) [English poet]
Single Speech Milnes
HOUGHTON, WILLIAM HENRY (1887-1946) [American Baptist evangelist and pastor]
Will H. Houghton
HOUK, RALPH GEORGE (1919-) [American professional baseball mqnager]
Major
Hound Rogers, Hell. See:
ROGERS, HENRY HUTTLESTON
Hours, Old Forty-eight. See:
DOUBLEDAY, ABNER
House. See also:
White House
House, Anne W. See:
McCAULEY, ELFRIEDA BABNICK
HOUSE, EDDIE JAMES, JR. (1902-) [American jazz musician (singer, guitar)]
Son House
HOUSE, EDWARD MANDELL (1858-1938) [American army officer and confidential adviser to President THOMAS WOODROW WILSON]
Colonel House
HOUSE, EDWARD MANDELL. See also:
Duumvirs, The (The Duumvirate)
House of Commons, The Father of the. See:
O'CONNOR, THOMAS POWER
VILLIERS, CHARLES PELHAM
House, The Choirmaster of the. See:
WOODRUM, CLIFTON ALEXANDER
House, The Dean of the. See:

SABATH, ADOLPH
JOACHIM
House, The Father of the. See:
BINGHAM, HENRY
HARRISON
DALZELL, JOHN
GILLETT, FREDERICK
HUNTINGTON
HARMER, ALFRED CROUT
KELLEY, WILLIAM
DARRAGH
MACON, NATHANIEL
O'NEILL, CHARLES
WILLIAMS, LEWIS
House, The Harry Percy of
the. See:
WISE, HENRY ALEXANDER
House, The Terror of the.
See: HARDIN, BENJAMIN
HOUSEPIAN, VANIG
(1918-) [American
jazz musician
(arranger, guitar)]
Turk Van Lake
HOUSMAN, ALFRED EDWARD
(1859-1936) [English
poet and critic]
A. E. Housman
Houston Hurricane, The. See:
FOYT, ANTHONY
JOSEPH, JR.
Houston, Renée. See:
GRIBBIN, KATHERINA
HOUSTON
HOUSTON, SAMUEL
(1793-1863) [American
frontier hero and
soldier; President of
Texas]
The Father of Texas
Sam Houston
Houston, The Builder of the
City of. See:
WILSON, WILLIAM
ABNER
HOVELL, LUCILLE A.
PETERSON (1916-) [American author]
Lucy A. Hovell
HOVICK, JUNE (1916-)
[American marathon
dancer, motion picture
actress and playwright]
Dainty Baby June the Pocket-sized Pavlova
June Havoc
Jean Reed
HOVICK, ROSE LOUISE
(1914-70) [American
burlesque stripper,
author and actress]
Gypsy Rose Lee
HOW. See also:
HOWE
Howe
HOW, JAMES EADS (1868-1930)
[American inheritor of
wealth; lived voluntarily
in poverty]
The Millionaire Hobo
The Millionaire Tramp
Howadji. See:
CURTIS, GEORGE
WILLIAM
Howard. See:
Cory, Howard L.
KEEL, HAROLD
HOWARD, AUGUSTUS (1884-)
[British singer and
motion picture actor]
Gus McNaughton
HOWARD, AVERY (1908-66)
[American jazz musician
(trumpet)]
Kid Howard
Howard, Barbara. See:
CORYELL, JOHN
RUSSELL
Howard, Charles. See:
HARBAUGH, THOMAS
CHALMERS
Howard Clark. See:
HASKIN, DOROTHY CLARK
PORTER, WILLIAM
SYDNEY
Howard, Constance. See:
WHITE, CONSTANCE M.
Howard, Coralie. See:
COGSWELL, CORALIE
NORRIS
HOWARD, CORRIE. See:
Cory, Howard L.
Howard, Curly. See:
Stooges, The Three
Howard, Elizabeth. See:
MIZNER, ELIZABETH
HOWARD

Howard Glyndon. See:
SEARING, LAURA CATHERINE REDDEN
Howard, H. L. See:
WELLS, CHARLES JEREMIAH
Howard, Hartley. See:
OGNALL, LEOPOLD HORACE
HOWARD, HENRY (c. 1517-47) [English poet]
Earl of Surrey
Henry Howard of Kenninghall
Howard Holmes, Captain. See:
HARBAUGH, THOMAS CHALMERS
Howard, Jack. See:
RATHBONE, ST. GEORGE HENRY
HOWARD, JAMES ARCH (1922-) [American psychologist and author]
Laine Fisher
HOWARD, JEROME. See:
Stooges, The Three
Howard, John. See:
COX, JOHN
Howard Lincoln. See:
HARBAUGH, THOMAS CHALMERS
HOWARD, LORD WILLIAM (1563-1640) [English border nobleman]
Belted Will
Howard, Mark. See:
RIGSBY, HOWARD
Howard, Mr. Thomas. See:
JAMES, JESSE WOODSON
HOWARD, MOE. See:
Stooges, The Three
HOWARD, MUNROE (1913-) [American advertising executive and author]
Philip St. Clair
HOWARD, OLIVER OTIS (1830-1909) [American soldier and religious humanitarian]
The Havelock of America
HOWARD, PETER DUNSMORE. See: Cato
Howard, Police Captain. See:
SENARENS, LUIS PHILIP
HOWARD, ROBERT WEST (1908-) [American newspaperman and author]
Michael Case
HOWARD, SHEMP. See:
Stooges, The Three
HOWARD, SIR JOHN (c. 1430-85) [1st Duke of Norfolk; British nobleman]
Jack of Norfolk
The Jockey of Norfolk
Howard, The American. See:
EDDY, THOMAS
Howard, The Female. See:
FRY, MRS. ELIZABETH
Howard, Vechel. See:
RIGSBY, HOWARD
Howard W. Erwin. See:
INGRAHAM, COLONEL PRENTISS
Howard, Warren. See:
GIFFORD, JAMES NOBLE
HOWARTH, ELLEN C. (1827-99) [American poet]
Clementine
HOWE [Howe]. See also:
HOW
HOWE, EDGAR WATSON (1853-1937) [American newspaper editor, publisher and philosopher]
E. W. Howe
Ed Howe
The Sage of Potato Hill
HOWE, ELIAS (1819-67) [American inventor]
The Father of the Sewing Machine
HOWE, GORDON (1928-) [Canadian professional hockey player]
Gordie Howe
Howe, James Wong. See:
WONG TUNG JIM
HOWE, JOHN (1630-1705) [English Puritan clergyman; chaplain to OLIVER CROMWELL]
The Platonic Puritan
The Puritan Plato

HOWE, JULIA WARD (1819-1910)
[American poet and social reformer]
A Lady
HOWE, MURIEL (fl. 1945-58)
[British author]
Barbara Redmayne
HOWE, RICHARD, 1ST EARL (1726-99) [British nobleman]
Black Dick]
HOWE, SAMUEL GRIDLEY (1801-76) [American humanitarian, active in aiding Greek revolutionists]
The Lafayette of the Greek Revolution
HOWE, WILLIAM FREDERICK (1828-1902) [American criminal lawyer]
The Father of the Criminal Bar
Habeas Corpus Howe
HOWE, WILLIAM WIRT (1833-1909) [American lawyer and author]
Mohammed Pasha
Howell, S. See:
STYLES, FRANK SHOWELL
HOWELLS, WILLIAM DEAN (1837-1920) [American author]
The Dean of American Letters
The Father of Realism
Howitzer, Bronson. See:
HARDMAN, RICHARDS LYNDEN
HOWLAND, FRANCES LOUISE MORSE (1855-)
[American author]
Kenyon West
Howleglass (Owlglass). See:
EULENSPIEGEL (ULENSPIEGEL), TILL
Howlin' Mad. See:
SMITH, HOLLAND McTYEIRE
HOYLE, EDMOND (1672-1769)
[English writer on card games]
The Father of the Game of Whist
The Father of Whist
HOYNE, THOMAS (1817-83)
[American lawyer, District Attorney and U. S. Marshal in Illinois]
Fighting Tom Hoyne
HOYSRADT, JOHN (1905-)
[American motion picture actor]
John Hoyt
Hoyt, John. See:
HOYSRADT, JOHN
Hoyt, W. M. See:
MANNING, WILLIAM HENRY
Hozjusz. See:
DOBRACZYNSKI, JAN
Hristo Andonov Poljanski. See:
ANDONOV-POLJANSKI, HRISTO
Hsia, Hsiao. See:
LIU, WU-CHI
Hsiao Hsia. See:
LIU, WU-CHI
HSÜAN T'UNG (1906-67)
[Tenth and last Chinese emperor of the Manchu dynasty]
Henry Pu-Yi
Kang Teh
Hub Pomeroy. See:
CLAASEN, HAROLD
HUBAY, JENÓ (1858-1937)
[Hungarian composer and violinist]
Hubay von Szlatna
HUBBARD, ELBERT (1856-1915)
[American inspirational essayist]
Fra Elbertus
HUBBARD, FATHER BERNARD ROSECRANS (1888-)
[American Catholic priest, explorer, scientist and author]
The Glacier Priest
HUBBARD, FRANK McKINNEY (1868-1930) [American humorist, journalist and cartoonist]

Kin Hubbard
Abe Martin
Hubbard, Margaret Ann. See:
PRILEY, MARGARET HUBBARD
HUBBARD, RICHARD BENNETT (1832-1901) [American lawyer, soldier and politician]
The Demosthenes of Texas
HUBEL, EDUARD (1879-) [Estonian author]
Mait Metsanurk
HUBER, FRANÇOIS (1750-1831) [Swiss naturalist]
The Blind Naturalist
HUBER, JOHANN RUDOLPHE (1658-1748 [Swiss painter]
The Tintoretto of Switzerland
Hubert Bagster. See:
TRUMPER, HUBERT BAGSTER
HUBERT, ST. (died 727) [Bishop of Liege]
The Apostle of Ardennes and of Brabant
HUBLER, RICHARD GIBSON (1912-) [American editor and author]
Harry Clark Gibson
Hubsch Martin. See:
SCHONGAUER, MARTIN
HUC, PHILIPPE (1889-1941) [French poet]
Tristan Derème
Huck. See:
BETTS, WALTER M.
HUCKO, MICHAEL ANDREW (1918-) [American jazz musician (clarinet, tenor saxophone)]
Peanuts Hucko
Huckster, The. See:
DARIUS I
HUDDLESTON, SISLEY (1883-) [British journalist and author]
Peter Vernon
HUDLUN, ANNA ELIZABETH (fl. 1871 and 1874) [American Negro social welfare worker]
Chicago's Grand Old Lady
The Fire Angel
Hudson. See:
MAXIM, ISAAC
Hudson, Alec. See:
HOLMES, WILFRED JAY
Hudson Douglas. See:
AITKIN, ROBERT
HUDSON, GEORGE (1800-71) [English speculator and railway promoter]
The Railway King
HUDSON, HOYT HOPEWELL. See: Smith, John
HUDSON, JEFFERY (1619-82) [British dwarf and jester]
Sir Jeffery Hudson
Hudson River School of American Artists, Founder of the. See:
COLE, THOMAS
Hudson, Rock. See:
FITZGERALD, ROY
Hudson, Stephen. See:
SCHIFF, SYDNEY
HUDSON, WALTER (1898-) [American newspaper baseball writer]
Gunboat
HUDSON, WILLIAM HENRY (1841-1922) [English author]
W. H. Hudson
HUEFFER, FORD MADOX (1873-1939) [English journalist and author]
Ford Madox Ford
HUESTON, BILLY (1896-1957) [American composer, publisher and producer]
Bruce Morgan
Huether, Anne Francis. See:
FREEMAN, ANNE FRANCIS
Hug. See:
GRANT, HIRAM ULYSSES
HUGGINS, MILLER JAMES
HUGENSZ, LUCAS (1494-1533) [Dutch engraver and painter]
Lucas Van Leyden
HUGGINS, MILLER JAMES (1879-1929) [American professional baseball player and manager]
Hug
HUGGINS, WILLIAM (1821-84) [English painter of animals]

The Liverpool Landseer
HUGH. See:
HUGHES (HUGH)
HUGUES (HUGH) II
Hugh Allen. See:
MORRIS, CHARLES SMITH
Hugh Cleland. See:
CLARKE, JOHN CAMPBELL
Hugh Conrad. See:
SCHOENFELD, WILLIAM C.
Hugh Conway. See:
FARGUS, FREDERICK JOHN
Hugh Farnash. See:
LUFF, STANLEY GEORGE ANTHONY
Hugh Graham. See:
BARROWS, MARJORIE
Hugh Halliburton. See:
ROBERTSON, JAMES LOGIE
Hugh Laing. See:
SKINNER, HUGH
Hugh Lloyd. See:
FITZHUGH, PERCY KEESE
Hugh MacDiarmid. See:
GRIEVE, CHRISTOPHER MURRAY
Hugh McHugh. See:
HOBART, GEORGE VERE
Hugh Marlowe. See:
HIPPLE, HUGH
PATTERSON, HENRY
Hugh Matheson. See:
MACKAY, LEWIS HUGH
Hugh Morton. See:
McLELLAN, CHARLES MORTON STEWART
Hugh O'Brian. See:
KRAMPKE, HUGH
Hugh Owen. See:
FAUST, FREDERICK SCHILLER
Hugh Sturton. See:
JOHNSON, HUGH ANTHONY STEPHEN
Hugh Venning. See:
VAN ZELLER, HUBERT
Hugh Walters. See:
HUGHES, WALTER LLEWELLYN
Hugh Warren. See:
MANNING, WILLIAM HENRY
HUGHES, CHARLES JAMES PENNETHORNE (1907-67) [British educator, broadcaster and author]
C. J. Pennethorne Hughes
James Pennethorne Hughes
HUGHES, JAMES LANGSTON (1902-67) [American Negro writer]
Langston Hughes
HUGHES, JOHN CEIRIOG (1832-87) [Welsh poet]
Ceiriog
Hughes, Matilda. See:
MACLEOD, CHARLOTTE MATILDA HUGHES
HUGHES PATRICK C. (1908-) [English jazz musician (arranger)]
Spike Hughes
HUGHES, ROBERT J. (1916-) [American musician]
James Denton
James Moffatt
HUGHES, THOMAS (1822-96) [English jurist, reformer and author]
Tom Brown
HUGHES, WALTER LLEWELLYN (1910-) [English author]
Hugh Walters
Hughie. See:
JENNINGS, HUGH AMBROSE
PRINCE, HUGH DENHAM
Hugo. See:
THEORELL, AXEL HUGO
Hugo Langway. See:
LANG, ANDREW
Hugo Paul. See:
LITTLE, PAUL H.
Hugo Wast. See:
MARTÍNEZ ZUVIRÍA GUSTAVO ADOLFO
HUGUES (HUGH) (died 956) [Count of Paris and Duke of France]
The Great

The White
HUGUES (HUGH) II (1102-42) [Duke of Burgundy]
Borel
HULL, CORDELL (1871-1955) [American lawyer and statesman; Secretary of State]
Cord
Hull, H. Braxton. See: JACOBS, HELEN HULL
Hull, Josephine. See: SHERWOOD, JOSEPHINE
Hull, Richard. See: SAMPSON, RICHARD HENRY
HULL, ROBERT MARVIN, JR. (1939-) [Canadian professional hockey player]
Bobby Hull
HULMAN. See also: HOLMAN
Holman
HULMAN, ANTON, JR. (1901-) [American business executive, race track official and philanthropist]
Tony Hulman
Human Nature, The Prose Homer of. See: FIELDING, HENRY
Human Race, The Orator of the. See: CLOOTZ, JEAN BAPTISTE DE VAL DE GRÂCE
Humanism, The Father of. See: PETRARCH (FRANCESCO PETRARCA)
Humanism, The Father of German. See: HUYSMAN, ROELOF
Humanists, The Prince of the. See: GERHARDS, GERHARD (GEERT GEERTS)
Humanity. See: MARTIN, RICHARD
Humanity, The Anatomist of. See: POQUELIN, JEAN BAPTISTE
Humanity, The Patriot of. See: GRATTAN, HENRY
Humanity, The Sweet-spirited Advocate of Justice, Love and. See: MOTT, LUCRETIA
Humanus. See: PAINE, THOMAS
Humbug, Gold. See: BENTON, THOMAS HART
Humbug, Old. See: BENTON, THOMAS HART
Humbugs, Prince of. See: BARNUM, PHINEAS TAYLOR
HUME, DAVID (1711-76) [Scottish philosopher, political economist and and historian
Hobbes Inverted
The Spiritual Father of Kant
The Most Thoroughgoing British Skeptic of the Eighteenth Century
HUME, FERGUSON WRIGHT (1859-1932) [English novelist and playwright]
Fergus Hume
HUME, JOSEPH (1777-1855) [English politician]
Adversity Hume
Humfrey. See also: HUMPHREY
Humphrey
Humphry
Humfrey, C. See: OSBORNE, CHARLES HUMFREY CAULFIELD
Humming Bird, The Arkansas. See: WARNECKE, LONNIE
Humor, Master of Undergraduate. See: SHULMAN, MAX
Humorist of the Pacific Slope, The Wild. See: CLEMENS, SAMUEL LANGHORNE
Humorists, The Prince of. See: CLEMENS, SAMUEL LANGHORNE
Hump. See: CAMPBELL, BRUCE DOUGLAS
Hump, The. See:

HUMPHREYS, MURRAY
HUMPERDINCK, ENGELBERT (1854-1921) [German composer]
The Modern Wagner
Humperdinck, Engelbert. See: DORSEY, GERRY
HUMPHREY [Humphrey]. See also: Humfrey
Humphry
HUMPHREY (1391-1447) [Duke of Gloucester; patron of learning and book collector]
Good Duke Humphrey
Humphrey Hocus. See: CHURCHILL, JOHN
HUMPHREY, HUBERT HORATIO (1911-) [Vice President of the United States]
H. H. H.
Humphrey, Old. See: MOGRIDGE, GEORGE
Humphrey Philroye. See: STEELE, SIR RICHARD
Humphrey St. Kayne. See: CRAWFURD, OSWALD
HUMPHREYS. See also: HUMPHRIES
Humphries
HUMPHREYS, BENJAMIN GRUBB (1808-82) [American soldier and politician; Governor of Mississippi]
Old Veto
HUMPHREYS, DAVID. See: Hartford Wits, The
HUMPHREYS, ELIZA MARGARET (-1938) [English novelist]
Rita
HUMPHREYS, JOSHUA (1751-1838) [American shipbuilder]
The Father of the American Navy
HUMPHREYS, MARY EGLANTYNE HILL (1914-) [British economist and author]
Polly Hill
HUMPHREYS, MURRAY (- 1965) [American gangster and kidnapper]
The Camel
The Hump
HUMPHRIES [Humphries]. See also: HUMPHREYS
HUMPHRIES, ADELAIDE M. (1898-) [American author]
Kathleen Harris
Wayne Way
Token West
Humphries, Jack. See: KELLY, JONATHAN FALCONBRIDGE
HUMPHRIES, SIDNEY VERNON (1907-) [English author]
Michael Vane
Humphry. See also: Humfrey
HUMPHREY
Humphrey
Humphry Ward, Mrs. See: ARNOLD, MARY AUGUSTA
Hun, Attila The. See: ATTILA (ETZEL) (ETHELE)
Hundred Fights, The Hero of a. See: NELSON, HORATIO VISCOUNT NELSON
WELLINGTON, ARTHUR WELLESLEY, 1ST DUKE OF
Hungarians, The Apostle of the. See: ANASTASIUS, ST.
Hungary, The Hot Paprika from. See: BANKY, VILMA
Hunger. See: OLAF I
HUNGERFORD, MRS. MARGARET WOLFE (1850-97) [Irish novelist]
The Duchess
Hungerford, Pixie. See: BRINSMEAD, HESBA FAY
Hunk, The. See: MATURE, VICTOR JOHN
Hunt Collins. See: HUNTER, EVAN
HUNT, DOROTHY ALICE (1896-) [English author]

Doric Collyer
HUNT, EDGAR HUBERT (1909-) [British musician and author]
Fidelio
Hunt, Francis. See: STRATEMEYER, EDWARD L.
Hunt, Harrison. See: BALLARD, WILLIS TODHUNTER
HUNT, HENRY (1773-1835) [English political demagogue]
Orator Hunt
HUNT, JAMES HENRY LEIGH (1784-1859) [English essayist and poet]
Leigh Hunt
Hunt, Kyle. See: CREASEY, JOHN
HUNT, MARCIA (1917-) [American motion picture actress]
Marsha Hunt
Hunt, Penelope. See: NAPIER, PRISCILLA
HUNT, WALTER (1907-) [American jazz musician (singer, trombone, leader)]
Pee Wee Hunt
HUNT, WILLIAM HOLMAN (1827-1910) [English painter]
Holman Hunt
Hunter, Anson. See: ORRMONT, ARTHUR
Hunter, Clingham, M.D. See: ADAMS, WILLIAM TAYLOR
Hunter D'Allard. See: BALLARD, WILLIS TODHUNTER
HUNTER, EILEEN HELEN (1905-) [English author]
E.H. Clements
HUNTER, EVAN (1926-) [American detective story writer]
Hunt Collins
Ed McBain
Richard Marsten
Hunter, Hall. See: MARSHALL, EDISON
Hunter, Jeffrey. See: McKINNIES, HENRY H.
Hunter, John. See: BALLARD, WILLIS TODHUNTER
Hunter, Kim. See: COLE, JANET
Hunter, Lieut. Ned. See: ELLIS, EDWARD SYLVESTER
HUNTER, MAUD LILY (1910-) [British teacher and author]
Christine Hunter
John Hunter
Charlotte Steer
Hunter, Mrs. See: BARKER, KATE CLARK
Hunter of the Plains, The Champion Buffalo. See: CODY, WILLIAM FREDERICK
Hunter, Paul. See: WEAVER, BERTRAND
Hunter-Preacher, The. See: LYNN, BENJAMIN
Hunter, Ross. See: FUSS, MARTIN
Hunter, Tab. See: GELIEN, ART
Hunter, The Big Game. See: TINKHAM, GEORGE HOLDEN
Hunter, The Lion. See: CUMMING, ROUALEYN GEORGE GORDON
TINKHAM, GEORGE HOLDEN
HUNTER, THOMAS LOMAX (1875-1948) [American poet]
The Cavalier
HUNTER, VICTORIA ALBERTA (1929-) [American educator and author]
Vickie MacLean Hunter
HUNTER, WHITESIDE GODFREY (1841-1917) [American politician; Congressman from Kentucky]

Gumshoe
HUNTER, WILLIAM RANDOLPH (1843-86) [American actor, journalist, poet and playwright]
Jay Bee
Joseph Bradford
HUNTINGDON, SELINA, COUNTESS OF (1707-91) [English Methodist leader]
The Countess of Huntingdon's Connection
HUNTINGTON, COLLIS POTTER. See: Big Four, The
Huntington, Faye. See: FOSTER, THEODOSIA MARIA TOLL
HUNTLEY, CHESTER ROBERT (1911-) [American radio and television journalist]
Chet Huntley
Huntley Paterson. See: LUDOVICI, ANTHONY MARIO
Huntly, Frances E. See: MAYNE, ETHEL COLBURN
Hunton, Mary. See: GILZEAN, ELIZABETH HOUGHTON BLANCHET
Huntz Hall. See: Dead End Kids, The
HALL, HENRY
HUNZICKER, BEATRICE PLUMB (1886-) [Anglo-American author]
Beatrice Plumb
HURD, EDITH THATCHER. See: Sage, Juniper
HURD, PERCY ANGIER (fl. early 20th cent.) [British journalist and member of Parliament]
Windermere
HURD, RICHARD (1720-1808) [English prelate and writer]
Beauty of Holiness
Hurkey, Rooan. See: HOLZAPFEL, RUDOLF PATRICK
HURLEY, DORAN (1900-) [American journalist, radio station manager and author]
McGregor
HURLEY, VIC (1898-) [American naval officer and author]
Jim Duane
Duane Richards
Hurricane, The. See: RIQUETI, HONORÉ GABRIEL
Hurricane, The Houston. See: FOYT, ANTHONY JOSEPH, JR.
Hurry Up. See: YOST, FIELDING HARRIS
Hurry Up (Fa Presto). See: GIORDANO, LUCA
Hurry Up Henry. See: KAISER, HENRY J.
Husband, The Hero. See: WANDERER, CARL
HUSING, EDWARD BRITT (1901-) [American radio announcer]
Ted Husing
Husk. See: CHANCE, FRANK LeROY
MATHEWSON, CHRISTOPHER
Hussaini Muhammad Askari. See: PEREIRA, HAROLD BERTRAM
Hussar of Literature, The Black. See: SCOTT, SIR WALTER
HUSSGEN, JOHANNES (1482-1531) [Swiss reformer]
Johannes Oecolampadius
Hussy, The Gorgeous. See: EATON, MARGARET O'NEILL
HUSTED, JAMES WILLIAM (1833-92) [American politician and National Guard general officer]
The Bald Eagle of Westchester
HUTCHINS, FRANCIS GILMAN (1939-) [American educator and author]
Frank Madison

Hutchins, William. See:
TYNDALE (TINDALE), WILLIAM
HUTCHINSON, ARTHUR STUART MENTETH (1879-) [English author]
A. S. M. Hutchinson
HUTSON, DONALD (1913-) [American football player]
Don Hutson
Hutton, Betty. See:
THORNBURG, BETTY JANE
Hutton, Marion. See:
THORNBURG, MARION
Hutton, Robert. See:
WINNE, ROBERT BRUCE
Huxley Hearne. See:
BROOKER, BERTRAM
HUXLEY, HERBERT HENRY (1916-) [British educator and author]
Stenus
HUXLEY, JULIAN SORELL (1887-) [English author and biologist]
Balbus
HUYSMAN, ROELOF (1443-85) [Dutch scholar]
Rodolphus Agricola
The Father of German Humanism
HUYSMANS, CHARLES MARIE GEORGES (1848-1907) [French novelist]
J. K. Huysmans
Joris-Karl Huysmans
Huyukiko Yosimura. See:
TEREDA, TORAHIKO
Hviezdoslav. See:
ORSZÁGH, PAVOL
Hwei, Chen. See:
STEVENSON, WILLIAM
Hy. See:
MAYER, HENRY
Hy Hazell. See:
O'HIGGINS, HYACINTH HAZEL
Hyacinthe. See:
LOYSON, CHARLES
Hyacinthe, Père. See:
LOYSON, CHARLES
Hyacinthe Hill. See:
ANDERSON, VIRGINIA R. CRONIN
HYAMS, SAMUEL DAVID (1893-1960) [British singer, stage and motion picture actor]
Dennis Hoey
HYDE, DOUGLAS (1860-1949) [Irish nationalist and writer]
The Fair Branch
Hyde Park, The Squire of. See:
ROOSEVELT, FRANKLIN DELANO
HYGINUS (died c. 140) [Supreme Pontiff of Roman Catholic Church]
Pope Hyginus
St. Hyginus
HYMAN, JOHN WIGGINTON (1899-) [American jazz musician (clarinet, violin, leader)]
Johnny Wiggs
Hymnist of the English Revival, The. See:
WESLEY, CHARLES
Hyndman. Jane Lee. See:
WYNDHAM, LEE
HYNES, CAPTAIN ALFRED D. (fl. 1871-72) [American author of dime novels]
Ralph Ringwood
HYNES, FRANCES HEENAN (1910-) [American figure in notorious lawsuit]
Peaches
Hystaspis. See:
DARIUS I

I

I. See:
ROBERTS, IRENE
I. Playfair. See:
WILDE, OSCAR FINGAL O'FLAHERTIE WILLS
I. S. See:
SCHNEIDER, ISIDOR
Iain. See also:
Ian

Iain Torr. See:
MACKINNON, CHARLES ROY
Iain Waltmore. See:
WALTMAN, WILLIAM JOHN
Iambic Verse, The Father of. See: ARCHILOCHUS
IAMS, SAMUEL H., JR. (1910-) [American author]
Jack Iams
Ian. See:
DOUGLAS, JOHN
FLEMING, IAN LANCASTER
Iain
Ian Bond. See:
WILLETT, BROTHER FRANCISCUS
Ian Cameron. See:
PAYNE, DONALD GORDON
Ian Gordon. See:
FELLOWES-GORDON IAN DOUGLAS
Ian Hay. See:
BEITH, JOHN HAY
Ian Jefferson. See:
DAVIES, LESLIE PURNELL
Ian Keith. See:
ROSS, KEITH
Ian Lewis. See:
BENSMAN, JOSEPH
Ian Maclaren. See:
WATSON, JOHN
Ian Sinclair. See:
FOLEY, CEDRIC JOHN
IBARRA, CASTOR JAUREGUIBEITIA (1876-) [Spanish bullfighter]
Cocherito de Bilbao
IBN GABIROL, SOLOMON BEN JUDAH (c.1021-c. 1058) [Hebrew poet and philosopher]
Avicebron
Ibn-Sina. See:
AVICENNA
IBSEN, HENRIK JOHAN (1828-1906) [Norwegian dramatist]
The Father of Modern Drama
Ice-bear. See:
KROEGER, HENRY
Ice King, The. See:
MORSE, CHARLES WYMAN
TUDOR, FREDERIC
Icebanks. See:
FAIRBANKS, CHARLES WARREN
Iceland, King of. See:
JÖRGENSSEN, JÖRGEN
Iceland, The Grimm of. See:
ARNASON, JÓN
Iceman, The Wheaton. See:
GRANGE, HAROLD EDWARD
Ichabod Crane, Jr. See:
SMITH, FRANCIS SHUBAEL
ICKES, HAROLD LeCLAIRE (1874-1952) [American statesman; Secretary of the Interior]
The Curmudgeon
Honest Harold
Iconoclast. See:
BRADLAUGH, CHARLES
HAMILTON, MARY AGNES
Iconoclast, Brann the. See:
BRANN, WILLIAM COWPER
Ida Raymond. See:
TARDY, MARY T.
Idaho Lion, The. See:
BORAH, WILLIAM EDGAR
IDE, FRANCES OTIS OGDEN (1853-1927) [American writer of children's books]
Ruth Ogden
Ideal Scientific Witness, The. See: SPILSBURY, SIR BERNARD HENRY
IDELL, ALBERT E. (1901-) [American novelist]
Phillips Rogers
Idiot, The. See:
BANGS, JOHN KENDRICK
Idiot, The Inspired. See:
GOLDSMITH, OLIVER
Idol of Baseball Fandom, The.

COBB, TYRUS RAYMOND
Idol of Ohio, The. See:
MCKINLEY, WILLIAM
Idol of the Airlanes, The. See:
GARBER, JAN
Idol of the American Boy, The. See:
RUTH, GEORGE HERMAN
Idol of the Rabble, The. See:
PENKETHMAN (PINKETHMAN), WILLIAM
Idol of the Temple, The. See:
MARIE CHARLOTTE
Ierugena, Johannes (Irish-born). See: ERIGENA, JOHANNES SCOTUS
Ifano. See:
JONES, IFANO
Igloo, Spiro. See:
HOFFMAN, ABBIE
IGNATIUS. See:
LOYOLA, IGNATIUS OF, ST. (IÑIGO DE OÑEZ Y LOYOLA)
Ignatius Loyola Robertson. See: KNAPP, SAMUEL LORENZO
IGNATIUS OF ANTIOCH, ST. (fl. 100 A.D.) [early Christian prelate and martyr]
Theophoros (God-bearer)
Ignotus. See:
ADAMS, HENRY JOSEPH
Ignotus, Pauper et. See:
THATCHER, JOHN WELLS
IGOE, OWEN JOSEPH (1923-) [American jazz musician (drums)]
Sonny Igoe
IJAMES, MARY TUNSTALL (1894-1963) [American composer, actress and singer]
Marion Sunshine
Ik Marvel. See:
MITCHELL, DONALD GRANT
Ike. See:
EISENHOWER, DAVID DWIGHT
Ike, Boardwalk. See:
BACHARACH, ISAAC
Ike, General. See:
EISENHOWER, DAVID DWIGHT
Ike Marvel. See:
MITCHELL, DONALD GRANT
Ike, Ukulele. See:
EDWARDS, CLIFF
Ikey Solomons, Esq., Junior. See: THACKERAY, WILLIAM MAKEPEACE
Il Divino. See:
VECELLI (VECELLIO), TIZIANO
Il Maestro. See:
NUVOLARI, TAZIO
Il Tintoretto. See:
ROBUSTI, JACOPO
Ilderim (Lightning). See:
BAJAZET I
Iles, Francis. See:
COX, ANTHONY BERKELEY
Ilhuicamia (Heavenly Archer). See: MONTEZUMA I
ILIFF, JOHN EDGAR (1852-1917) [American author and storekeeper]
John Edgefield
Ed Iliff
Ilin, M. See:
MARSHAK, I. A.
Ill Tempered (Dyskolos). See:
APPOLONIUS
Illington, Margaret. See:
LIGHT, MAUDE ELLEN
Illinois. See:
JACQUET, BATTISTE ILLINOIS
Illinois Baboon, The. See:
LINCOLN, ABRAHAM
Illinois, The Black Eagle of. See: LOGAN, JOHN ALEXANDER
Ilona Massey. See:
HAJMASSY, ILONA
Illuminator, The. See:
GREGORY OF ARMENIA, ST.
Illuminatus, Doctor. See:
LULLY, RAYMOND
TAULER, JOHANN

Illustrious Defender, The.
See: WEBSTER, DANIEL
Illustrious Doctor, The. See: HENRY OF GHENT
Illustrious Infidel, The. See: INGERSOLL, ROBERT GREEN
Illustrious, The. See: HESYCHIUS
Illustrious, The (Epiphanes). See: PTOLEMY V
Imagination, The Bard of the. See: AKENSIDE, MARK
IMMANUEL. See also:
EMANUEL
Emanuel
EMMANUEL
IMMANUEL BEN SOLOMON (c. 1265-c. 1330) [Hebrew poet and Bible commentator]
Manoello Guideo
Immaterial John Jameson See: JAMESON, JOHN
Immerito, M. See: SPENSER, EDMUND
Immortal. See:
KEATS, JOHN
WEBSTER, DANIEL
Immortal Bard, The. See: SHAKESPEARE, WILLIAM
Immortal Dreamer, The. See: BUNYAN, JOHN
Immortal Four of Italy, The, joint appellation of DURANTE ALIGHIERI (Dante Alighieri) (1265-1321), LUDOVICO ARIOSTO (1474-1533), PETRARCH (FRANCESCO PETRARCA) (1304-74) and TORQUATO TASSO (1544-95) [Italian poets]
Immortal Four of Italy, The. See also:
ALIGHIERI, DURANTE
ARIOSTO, LUDOVICO
Great Triumvirate of Italian Literature, The
PETRARCH (FRANCESCO PETRARCA)
Immortal Janet Geddes, The. See: GEDDES, JENNY
Immortal Soul, Having an (Anushirvan). See: KHOSRAU I
Immortal Tinker, The. See: BUNYAN, JOHN
Immortal Trio, The. See: Great Triumvirate, The
Impartial Hand. See:
JOHNSON, DR. SAMUEL
STEELE, SIR RICHARD
Impeachment. See: THOMAS, JOHN PARNELL
Imperial Peacock of Park Avenue, The. See: BONAPARTE, CHARLES JOSEPH
Impulsia Gushington. See: SHERIDAN, LADY HELEN SELINA
Ina Claire. See: FAGAN, INA
INABNETT, MARVIN (1938-) [American composer and singer]
Marvin Ingram
Inca, El. See: GARCILASO DE LA VEGA
Incarnation, The Doctor of the. See: CYRIL OF ALEXANDRIA, ST.
Incas, The Last of the. See: ATAHUALPA
Incendiary of the White House, Chief. See: ADAMS, SAMUEL
Inceptor, Venerabilis. See: OCKHAM (OCCAM), WILLIAM OF
INCHBALD, ELIZABETH SIMPSON (1753-1821) [English novelist, playwright and actress]
Mrs. Inchbald
Inchfawn, Fay. See: WARD, ELIZABETH REBECCA
Incogniteau, Jean-Louis. See: KEROUAC, JEAN-LOUIS LEBRID DE
Incomparable Hildegarde, The. See: SELL, HILDEGARDE LORETTA

Incomparable Max, The. See:
BEERBOHM, SIR HENRY MAXIMILLIAN
Inconnue, L'. See:
FRENCH, LUCY VIRGINIA SMITH
Incorruptible, The. See:
ROBESPIERRE, FRANÇOIS-JOSEPH MAXIMILIEN ISIDORE DE
Incorruptible, The Sea-Green. See: ROBESPIERRE, FRANÇOIS-JOSEPH MAXIMILIEN ISIDORE DE
IND, ALLISON (1903-) [American journalist and author]
Phil Stanley
Richard Wallace
Independence, Atlas of. See:
ADAMS, JOHN
Independence, Colossus of. See: ADAMS, JOHN
Independence, Colossus of American. See:
ADAMS, JOHN
Independence, Partisan of. See: ADAMS, JOHN
Independence, The Father of American. See:
ADAMS, JOHN
Independence, The Father of the Declaration of. See:
JEFFERSON, THOMAS
Independence, The Man of. See: TRUMAN, HARRY S
Independent. See:
MEAD, EDWIN DOAK
India, Clive of. See:
CLIVE, ROBERT, BARON CLIVE OF PLASSEY
India, The Bayard of. See:
OUTRAM, SIR JAMES
India, The Father of American Commerce with. See:
DERBY, ELIAS HASKET
India, The Nestor of the Methodist Conference in. See: BOWEN, GEORGE
India, Viceroy of. See:
CORNWALLIS, CHARLES CORNWALLIS, 1ST MARQUIS
Indian. See also:
Indienne
Indian Dan. See:
WEBSTER, DANIEL
Indian Fighter, The. See:
TALCOTT, JOHN
Indian Fighter, The Little. See:
STANDISH, MILES (MYLES)
Indian, Friend of the. See:
STUART, ROBERT
Indiana History, The Father of. See: DILLON, JOHN BROWN
Indianapolis Potato Mayor, The. See: SHANK, SAMUEL LEWIS
Indian's Friend, The. See:
WILLIAMS, ROGER
Indians, The Apostle of the. See: ELIOT, JOHN
LAS CASAS, BARTOLOME DE
Indians, The Apostle to the Sioux. See:
HARE, WILLIAM HOBART
Indians, The Dumas of the. See:
GLOUX, OLIVIER
Indians, The Patriarch of the. See: MAYHEW, THOMAS
Indians, The Protector of the. See: LAS CASAS, BARTOLOME DE
Indienne. See also:
Indian
Indienne, La Belle. See:
MAINTENON, MADAME DE
Indies, The Apostle of the. See:
XAVIER, ST. FRANCIS
Industrial Architect, The World's No. 1. See:
KAHN, ALBERT
Industry, The Czar of the Liquor. See:
MORGAN, WILLIAM FORBES
Industry, The Dynamo of the Italian Motion Picture. See:
LAURENTIS, DINO DE
Industry, The Father of the American Anthracite Iron.

See: THOMAS, DAVID
Industry, The Father of the American Cotton. See: COXE, TENCH
Industry, The Father of the Florida Orange. See: HARRIS, JAMES ARMSTRONG
Industry, The Father of the Plate Glass. See: FORD, JOHN BAPTISTE
Industry, The Father of the Silk. See: RYLE, JOHN
Industry, The Garibaldi of the Italian Motion Picture. See: LAURENTIS, DINO DE
Industry, The Kingfish of the Italian Motion Picture. See: LAURENTIS, DINO DE
Infant Prodigy, The. See: MANTLE, MICKEY CHARLES
Infant Roscius, The. See: BETTY, WILLIAM HENRY WEST
Infidel, The Illustrious. See: INGERSOLL, ROBERT GREEN
Infidelity, The Apostle of. See: AROUET, FRANÇOIS MARIE
INFIELD, GLENN BERTON (1920-) [American author]
George Powers
Frank Rodgers
Arthur Tolby
INGALLS, MARILLA BAKER (1828-1902) [American Baptist missionary to India and Burma]
The Lady of the Iron Watchdog
INGE, WILLIAM RALPH (1860-1954) [English divine]
The Gloomy Dean
INGELOW, JEAN (1820-97) [British poet, novelist and writer of children's stories]
Orris
Ingelow of America, The Jean. See: CAREY, ALICE
Inger Stevens. See: STENSLAND, INGER
INGERSOLL, RALPH ISAACS (1788-1872) [American politician; Congressman from Connecticut]
Young Hotspur
INGERSOLL, ROBERT GREEN (1833-99) [American lawyer, politician, lecturer, soldier and agnostic]
The Great Agnostic
The Illustrious Infidel
Ingo. See: JOHANSSON, INGEMAR
Ingoldsby North. See: URNER, NATHAN DANE
Ingoldsby, Thomas, Esq. See: BARHAM, RICHARD HARRIS
INGOLIA, CONCETTA (1938-) [American motion picture actress]
Connie Stevens
INGRAHAM, COLONEL PRENTISS (1843-1904) [American soldier, adventurer and author of dime novels, plays and poems]
Dangerfield Burr
Dr. Noel Dunbar
Howard W. Erwin
Lieut. Preston Graham
Midshipman Tom W. Hall
T.W. King
Colonel Leon Lafitte
W.B. Lawson
J.B. Omahundro
Harry Dennies Perry
Frank Powell
Major Henry B. Stoddard
Captain Alfred B. Taylor
Ingram, Marvin. See: INABNETT, MARVIN
Ingram, Rex. See: FITCHCOCK, REX
Iñigo López de Recalde. See: LOYOLA, IGNATIUS OF, ST. (ÍÑIGO DE OÑEZ Y LOYOLA)

Initiator, The Venerable. See:
OCKHAM (OCCAM), WILLIAM OF
Inland Navigation, The Father of British. See:
EGERTON, FRANCIS
Inman, R.R. See:
MORRIS, CHARLES SMITH
Inn, Gent., Thomas Morton of Clifford's. See:
MORTON, THOMAS
Innes, Hammond. See:
HAMMOND INNES, RALPH
Innes, Michael. See:
STEWART, JOHN INNES MACINTOSH
Innkeeper, The No. 1. See:
HILTON, CONRAD NICHOLSON
INNOCENT (died 417)
[Supreme Pontiff of Roman Catholic Church]
Pope Innocent I
St. Innocent
Innocent II, Pope. See:
PAPARESCHI, GREGORIO
Innocent III, Pope. See:
SEGNI, LOTHAIR OF
Innocent IV, Pope. See:
FIESCHI, SINIBALDI
Innocent V, Pope. See:
TARENTAISE, PETER OF
Innocent VI, Pope. See:
AUBERT, ÉTIENNE
Innocent VII, Pope. See:
MIGLIORATI, COSIMO DE
Innocent VIII, Pope. See:
CIBO, GIOVANNI BATTISTA
Innocent IX, Pope. See:
FACCHINETTI, GIOVANNI ANTONIO
Innocent X, Pope. See:
PAMPHILI, GIOVANNI BATTISTA
Innocent XI, Pope. See:
ODESCALCHI, BENEDICT
Innocent XII, Pope. See:
PIGNATELLI, ANTONIO
Innocent XIII, Pope. See:
CONTI, MICHELANGELO
Innocentius M. Bochenski. See:
BOCHENSKI, JOSEPH M.
Innsley, Owen. See:
JENNISON, LUCIA
INÖNÜ, ISMET (1884-)
[Turkish soldier and politician]
Ismet Pasha
Insects' Homer, The. See:
FABRE, JEAN HENRI
Inshtatheanba (Bright Eyes). See: LA FLESCHE, SUZETTE
Inside, Mr. See:
BLANCHARD, FELIX ANTHONY
Insight, James. See:
COLEMAN, ROBERT WILLIAM ALFRED
Inspired Idiot, The. See:
GOLDSMITH, OLIVER
Institute of Arts and Sciences, The Father of the Brooklyn. See: HEALY, AARON AUGUSTUS
Institution, An International. See:
ANKA, PAUL ALBERT
INSULIS. See:
ALAIN DE LILLE (ALANUS DE INSULIS)
Insult, Mr. See:
LEONARD, JACK E.
Insurance Business, The King of the Marine. See:
TOWNSEND, HAWORTH NOTTINGHAM
Intellectual Father of the Reformation. See:
GERHARDS, GERHARD (GEERT, GEERTS)
Intellectual Giant of Populism, The. See:
ALLEN, WILLIAM VINCENT
Intelligence Officer, The. See:
JAMES, LIONEL
Intelligent of American Sopranos, The Most. See:
SMITH, PHYLLIS
International Bad Girl of the Mid-Victorians, The. See:
GILBERT, MARIE DOLORES ELIZA ROSANNA

International Institution, An. See: ANKA, PAUL ALBERT
Interpreter of the Constitution, The Legal. See: MARSHALL, JOHN
Interpreter, The Great. See: WEBSTER, DANIEL
Interviewers, The Prince of. See: SENIOR, NASSAU WILLIAM
Interwoven Pair, The. See: Happiness Boys, The
Inventors, One of America's Greatest. See: BOYDEN, SETH
Inverted, Hobbes. See: HUME, DAVID
Inverurie, The Weaver-Poet of. See: THOM, WILLIAM
Investigator, Ohio's Ace. See: SLATER, ORA E.
Investigator, The. See: BELL, CHARLES JASPER
Investigators, King of the. See: KING, WILLIAM HENRY
Investor, Academic. See: REDDAWAY, WILLIAM BRIAN
Invincibilis, Doctor. See: OCKHAM (OCCAM), WILLIAM OF
Invincible Doctor, The. See: OCKHAM (OCCAM), WILLIAM OF
Invincible Stonewall, The. See: JACKSON, THOMAS JONATHAN
Invincible Warrior in Righteous Causes, The. See: MOTT, LUCRETIA
Involuntary Scream, The Portly Master of the. See: HITCHCOCK, ALFRED JOSEPH
Inyart, Gene. See: NAMOVICZ, GENE INYART
Iola Fuller. See: McCOY, IOLA FULLER
Iolo Morgannwg. See: WILLIAMS, EDWARD
Iona, Andy. See: LONG, ANDY IONA
Ione Leigh. See: MASSADA, IONE
Ione Saunders. See: COLE, MARGARET ALICE
IPPOLITOV-IVANOV, MIKHAIL MIKHAILOVICH (1859-1935) [Russian composer]
People's Artist of the Republic
Iqua. See: BORCHARD, RUTH BERENDSOHN
Ira. See: WALKER, IRMA RUTH RODEN
Ireland, Baron. See: SALSBURY, NATE
Ireland, Doreen. See: LORD, DOREEN MILDRED DOUGLAS
Ireland, Michael. See: FIGGIS, DARRELL
Ireland, The Apostle of. See: PATRICK, ST.
Ireland, The Pearl of. See: BRIDGET, ST.
Ireland, The Uncrowned King of. See: PARNELL, CHARLES STEWART
IRENAEUS, ST. (fl. 1st cent. A.D.) [Greek church father]
The Apostle of the Gauls
The Peacemaker
Irene. See: GIBBONS, MRS. CEDRIC
Irene Adler. See: STORR, CATHERINE COLE
Irene Day. See: ORME, EVE
Irene Hervey. See: HERWICK, IRENE
Irene Lynn. See: ROWLAND, DONALD SYDNEY
Irene Manning. See: HARVET, INEZ
Irene Pearl. See: GUYONVARCH, IRENE CECILIA
Irene Ray. See:

SUTTON, RACHEL
IRENE BEEBE
Irene Ryan. See:
RIORDAN, IRENE
Irina. See:
KIRK, IRENE
Iris Adrian. See:
HOSTETTER, IRIS A.
Iris Corbin. See:
CLINTON, IRIS A.
CORBIN
Iris Rowland. See:
ROBERTS, IRENE
Irish Atticus, The. See:
FAULKNER, GEORGE
Irish-born (Johannes Ierugena).
See: ERIGENA, JOHANNES
SCOTUS
Irish Novelist, M. O'Rolfe,
the. See:
ROLFE, MARO O.
Irish Roscius, The. See:
BARRY, SPRANGER
Irish Thrush, See:
DOWNEY, MORTON
Irish, William. See:
HOPLEY-WOOLRICH,
CORNELL GEORGE
Irishman, An. See:
MOORE, THOMAS
Irishman, Blaine's. See:
EGAN, PATRICK
Irland, David. See:
GREEN, JULIEN
HARTRIDGE
IRNERIUS (died before 1140)
[Italian jurist]
The Lucerna Juris
Iron Chancellor, The. See:
VON BISMARCK,
PRINCE OTTO
EDUARD LEOPOLD
Iron Czar, The. See:
NICHOLAS I
Iron Duke, The. See:
MULDOON, WILLIAM
WELLINGTON, ARTHUR
WELLESLEY, 1ST
DUKE OF
Iron Emperor, The. See:
NICHOLAS I
Iron Hand, Götz with the. See:
VON BERLICHINGEN,
GÖTZ (GOTTFRIED)
Iron Horse, The. See:
GEHRIG, HENRY LOUIS
Iron Industry, The Father of
the American Anthracite.
See: THOMAS, DAVID
Iron, John. See:
CARLILE, JOHN CHARLES
Iron Kelley, Pig. See:
KELLEY, WILLIAM
DARRAGH
Iron Man. See:
Ironman
McGINNITY, JOSEPH
JEROME
Iron Man of Baseball, The.
See:
GEHRIG, HENRY LOUIS
Iron Mask, The Man in the.
See: MOODY,
WILLIAM VAUGHAN
UNKNOWN
IRON, NATHANIEL COLCHESTER
(fl. 1861-66) [American
author of dime novels]
Hawkshaw the Detective
Old Cap Collier
Iron Pants, Old. See:
JOHNSON, HUGH SAMUEL
Iron, Ralph. See:
SCHREINER, OLIVE
EMILIE ALBERTINA
Iron Shipbuilding in America,
The Father of. See:
ROACH, JOHN
Iron, The Man of Blood and.
See: VON BISMARCK,
PRINCE OTTO EDUARD
LEOPOLD
Iron Tooth. See:
FREDERICK II
Iron Watchdog, The Lady of the.
See: INGALLS, MARILLA
BAKER
Ironclad. See:
ENTON, DR. HARRY
Ironhorse. See:
SCHULMERICH, EDWARD
WESLEY
Ironman. See:
Iron Man
STARR, RAYMOND
FRANCIS

Ironmaster Maximus. See:
See: WILKINSON, JOHN DONALD
Ironquill. See:
WARE, EUGENE FITCH
IRONS, LETTIE ARTLEY (-1875) [American novelist]
Paul J. Prescott
Ironside. See:
EDMUND (EADMUND) II
IRONSIDE, HENRY ALLAN (1876-1951) [Canadian-American clergyman]
The Boy Preacher of Los Angeles
Ironside, Nestor. See:
STEELE, SIR RICHARD
Ironsides. See:
CROMWELL, OLIVER
Irrefragabilis, Doctor. See:
ALEXANDER OF HALES
Irrefragable Doctor, The. See:
ALEXANDER OF HALES
Irrepressible Master of Ceremonies, The Fashion World's. See:
CASSINI, OLEG LOIEWSKI
Irv Carroll, See:
GELLERS, IRVING
IRVIN, CECIL P. (1906-) [American football player]
Tex Irvin
Irving. See:
CRUMP, JAMES IRVING
Irving Berlin. See:
BALINE, ISRAEL
Irving Brown. See:
ADAMS, WILLIAM TAYLOR
Irving, Christopher. See:
JOHNSTON, SIR REGINALD FLEMING
IRVING, CLIFFORD. See:
Anderson, Clifford
Irving Fazola. See:
PRESTOPNIK, IRVING
IRVING, JOHN TREAT (1812-1906) [American novelist and essayist]
John Quod
IRVING, PETER (1771-1838) [American author]
Percival G-
Irving, Reginald. See:
JOHNSTON, SIR REGINALD FLEMING
Irving, Robert. See:
ADLER, IRVING
Irving Rose. See:
BROWNE, ERNEST D.
Irving, Sir Henry. See:
BRODRIBB, JOHN HENRY
Irving Stone. See:
TANNENBAUM, IRVING
IRVING, WASHINGTON (1783-1859) [American author]
The American Goldsmith
Fray Antonio Agapida
Geoffrey Corson
Geoffrey Crayon
Geoffrey Crayon, Gent.
Anthony Evergreen
The Father of American Literature
The Father of American Prose
Diedrich Knickerbocker
Jonathan Oldstyle
Jonathan Oldstyle, Gent.
The Prince of American Letters
IRVING, WASHINGTON;
See also:
Langstaff, Launcelot
IRVING, WILLIAM See:
Langstaff, Launcelot
IRWIN [Irwin]. See also:
ERWIN
Erwin
IRWIN, CONSTANCE FRICK (1913-) [American librarian and author]
C.H. Frick
Constance Frick
Irwin Longman. See:
LOCKWOOD, INGERSOLL
IRWIN, WILLIAM C.K. (1907-) [American composer, conductor and arranger]
Will Irwin
Isa. See:
CRAIG, ISA
Isaac Bashevis. See:
SINGER, ISAAC
Isaac Bickerstaff. See:

STEELE, SIR RICHARD
SWIFT, JONATHAN
WEST, BENJAMIN
Isaac Hawkes. See:
HARBAUGH, THOMAS CHALMERS
Isaac Warshofsky. See:
SINGER, ISAAC
Isabel. See:
ISABELLA
Isabella
Isabelle
Isobel
MOWATT, ANNA CORA OGDEN RITCHIE
Isabel Barclay. See:
DOBELL, ISABEL MARIAN BARCLAY
Isabel Bolton. See:
MILLER, MARY BRITTON
Isabel Dean. See:
HODGKINSON, ISABEL
ISABELLA [Isabella]. See also:
Isabel
Isabelle
Isobel
ISABELLA I (1451-1504) [Queen of Castile]
The Catholic
Isabella Bird. See:
BISHOP, ISABELLA BIRD
Isabella Castelar. See:
WINTER, ELIZABETH CAMPBELL
ISABELLA OF BAVARIA (1360-1435) [queen consort of CHARLES VI of France]
The Great Sow
ISABELLA OF FRANCE (1292-1358) [Wife of EDWARD II of England and daughter of PHILIP THE FAIR, King of France]
The She-Wolf of France
ISABELLA OF VALOIS (1389-1409) [Queen of England]
The Little Queen
Isabelle. See also:
Isabel
ISABELLA
Isabella
Isobel
Isabelle London. See:
Child, Alan
Isak Dinesen. See:
BLIXEN-FINECKE, BARONESS KAREN
ISAURE, CLÉMENCE (c. 1450-c. 1500) [French poet]
The Sappho of Toulouse
Isaurian, The. See:
LEO III
ZENO
ISENDAHL, WALTHER (1877-) [German engineer and author]
Dr. Service
Isis. See:
TORBETT, HARVEY DOUGLAS LOUIS
ISKOWITZ, EDWARD ISRAEL (1892-1964) [American actor and comedian]
Banjo Eyes
Eddie Cantor
Iss Iskowitz
Island, The Sphinx of the Rock. See: MOORE, WILLIAM HENRY
Isle, The Blind Old Man of Scio's Rocky. See: HOMER
Isle, The Orpheus of the Green. See: O'CAROLAN, TURLOCH
Islebius, Magister. See: SNEIDER (SCHNITTER), JOHANNES
ISLEY, PHYLLIS (1919-) [American motion picture actress]
Jennifer Jones
ISMAY, HASTINGS LIONEL, 1ST BARON (1887-1965) [British general officer and Secretary General to NATO]
Pug
Ismet Pasha. See:
INÖNÜ, ISMET
Isobel. See also:
Isabel
ISABELLA

Isabella
Isabelle
Isobel Elson. See:
REED, ISOBEL
Isobel Guthrie. See:
GRIEVE, CHRISTOPHER MURRAY
Isobel Saxe. See:
RAYNER, CLAIRE
ISOCRATES (436-338 B.C.) [Athenian orator and teacher of rhetoric]
Old Man Eloquent
Isocrates, The French. See:
FLÉCHIER, ESPRIT
ISRAELS, CHARLES H. (1936-) [American jazz musician (bass)]
Chuck Israels
Israfel. See:
POE, EDGAR ALLAN
Iss. See:
ISKOWITZ, EDWARD ISRAEL
Issachar. See:
STANFORD, JOHN KEITH
Istria, Dora d'. See:
GHIKA, HELENA
Istvan Tatray. See:
RUPERT, RAPHAEL RUDOLPH
It Girl, The. See:
BOW, CLARA
Italian Literature. See:
Great Triumvirate of Italian Literature, The
Italian Molière, The. See:
GOLDONI, CARLO
Italian Motion Picture Industry, The Dynamo of the. See:
LAURENTIS, DINO DE
Italian Motion Picture Industry, The Garibaldi of the. See: LAURENTIS, DINO DE
Italian Motion Picture Industry, The Kingfish of the. See:
LAURENTIS, DINO DE
Italian Nightingale, The. See:
CATALANI, ANGELICA
Italian Pindar, The. See:
CHIABRERA, GABRIELLO
Italian Poetry, The Father of. See: FREDERICK II
Italian Prose, The Father of. See: BOCCACCIO, GIOVANNI
Italian Race, That Singular Splendor of the. See:
ALIGHIERI, DURANTE
ITALIANO, ANNEMARIE (ANNA MARIA) (1931-) [American actress]
Anne Bancroft
Italo Svevo. See:
SCHMITZ, ETTORE
Italy, The Mary Stuart of. See:
JANE I
Italy, The Racine of. See:
TRAPASSI, PIETRO ANTONIO DOMENICO BONAVENTURA
Italy, The Thunderbolt of. See:
FOIX, GASTON DE
Ithacus. See:
SHAW, JOHN
Itinerant Evangelist for Peace, The. See:
PAGE, KIRBY
Itself, One Behind the Throne Greater Than the Throne. See: STUART, JOHN
ITURBIDE, AGUSTÍN DE (1783-1824) [Mexican revolutionist, afterwards emperor]
The Napoleon of Mexico
Iva Kitchell. See:
BAUGH, EMMA
IVAN I DANILOVICH (died 1341) [Grand Prince or Duke of Moscow]
Ivan Kalita (The Moneybag]
IVAN II (1326-59) [Grand Prince or Duke of Moscow]
Ivan Krasny (The Red)
IVAN III VASILIEVICH (1440-1505) [Grand Duke of Moscow]
Ivan the Great
IVAN IV VASILIEVICH (1530-84) [Grand Duke of Moscow and Czar of Russia]

Ivan the Terrible
Jonah
IVAN, GUSTAVE E. See:
Tavo, Gus
Ivan Jelakomitch. See:
HEIJERMANS (HEYERMANS), HERMAN
Ivan Kalita (The Moneybag).
See: IVAN I DANILOVICH
IVAN, MARTHA MILLER PFAFF (1909-) [American author]
Martha Miller
IVAN, MARTHA MILLER PFAFF. See also:
Tavo, Gus
Ivan Rosedale. See:
DITMAS, FRANCIS IVAN LESLIE
Ivan T. Ross. See:
ROSSNER, ROBERT
IVANHOE, BURL ICLE (1909-) [American ballad singer, stage and motion picture actor]
Burl Ives
Ivar Jorgenson. See:
SILVERBERG, ROBERT
Ives, Burl. See:
IVANHOE, BURL ICLE
Ives, Lawrence. See:
WOODS, FREDERICK
Ivor. See:
ROBERTS, IRENE
Ivor Novello. See:
DAVIES, IVOR NOVELLO
Ivory Black. See:
JANVIER, THOMAS ALLIBONE
Ivy B. Summerforest. See:
KIRKUP, JAMES
Ivy, Poison. See:
ANDREWS, IVY PAUL

J

J.A.B. See:
BERINGER, JOSEPH AUGUST
J.A.D. Spence. See:
ELIOT, THOMAS STEARNS
J.A.K. See:
WILLIAMS, ANNA BOLLES
J. Arbuthnot Wilson. See:
ALLEN, CHARLES GRANT BLAIRFINDIE
J.B. See:
PRIESTLEY, JOHN BOYNTON
SELKIRK, JAMES BROWN
J.B. Omahundro. See:
INGRAHAM, COLONEL PRENTISS
J. Bejla. See:
RZEWUSKI, COUNT HENRYK
J.C. See:
HEARD, JAMES CHARLES
HIGGINBOTHAM, JACK
J.D. See:
SALINGER, JEROME DAVID
J.D. Ballard. See:
MORRIS, CHARLES SMITH
J.D. Conroy. See:
RYMER, JAMES MALCOLM
J.D. Stevens. See:
ROWLAND, DONALD SYDNEY
J. De P. Hall. See:
McKELWAY, ST. CLAIR
J. Downing. See:
DAVIS, CHARLES AUGUSTUS
J. Downing, Major. See:
DAVIS, CHARLES AUGUSTUS
J.E. Buckrose. See:
JAMESON, ANNIE EDITH
J.E.M. Arden. See:
CONQUEST, GEORGE ROBERT ACWORTH
J.E. Marsh. See:
MARSHALL, EVELYN
J.E. Sperry. See:
EISENSTAT, JANE SPERRY
J.E.T. See:
TUEL, JOHN E.
J. Eddie Weems, Jr. See:
WEEMS, JOHN EDWARD

J.F.C. Adams, Captain. See:
ELLIS, EDWARD SYLVESTER

J.F.K. See,
KENNEDY, JOHN FITZGERALD

J.F. Thomas. See:
FLEMING, THOMAS JAMES

J.G. BETHUNE See:
ELLIS, EDWARD SYLVESTER

J.H.H. See:
HARLEY, JOHN HUNTER

J.H. Randolph, Lieut. See:
ELLIS, EDWARD SYLVESTER

J.H. Rosny the Elder. See:
BOËX, JOSEPH HENRI HONORÉ

J.H. Rosny the Younger. See:
BOËX, SERAPHIN JUSTIN FRANÇOIS

J.H. Southard. See:
MORRIS, CHARLES SMITH

J. Hammond Trumbull. See:
TRUMBULL, JOHN

J. Harvey Bond. See:
WINTERBOTHAM, RUSSELL ROBERT

J. Hector St. John. See:
CRÈVECOEUR, MICHAEL-GUILLAUME JEAN DE

J. Hunter Holly. See:
HOLLY, JOAN CAROL

J.J. See:
JAY JAY
JOHNSON, JAMES LOUIS

J.J.C. See:
VON GRIMMELSHAUSEN, JOHANN HANS JAKOB CHRISTOFFEL

J.J. Connington. See:
STEWART, ALFRED WALTER

J.J. Coupling. See:
PIERCE, JOHN ROBINSON

J.J. Marric. See:
CREASEY, JOHN

J.K. See:
HUYSMANS, CHARLES MARIE GEORGES

J.K.B. See:
BANGS, JOHN KENDRICK

J.K. Marvel. See:
MITCHELL, DONALD GRANT

J.L. Freeman. See:
ST. JOHN, PERCY BOLLINGBROKE

J.L.H. Whitney. See:
TRIMBLE, JACQUELYN WHITNEY

J.L. Kennedy, Captain. See:
HARBAUGH, THOMAS CHALMERS

J. Lincoln Paine. See:
KRAMISH, ARNOLD

J. Marjoram. See:
MOTTRAM, RALPH HALE

J.N. Darby. See:
GOVAN, CHRISTINE NOBLE

J.N. Ding. See:
DARLING, JAY NORWOOD

J.O. Hannay. See:
HANNAY, JAMES OWEN

J. Odem. See:
RUBIN, JACOB A.

J. Owen Hannay. See:
HANNAY, JAMES OWEN

J.P. See:
LESLEY, PETER

J.P.M. See:
WHEELER, ANDREW CARPENTER

J.P. Mowbray. See:
WHEELER, ANDREW CARPENTER

J.R. See:
RUSKIN, JOHN

J. Riemens-Reurslag. See:
REURSLAG, GUURTJE JOHANNA HENDRIKA

J. Russell. See:
BIXBY, JEROME LEWIS

J.S. See:
DODGE, MARY ELIZABETH MAPES
FLETCHER, JOSEPH SMITH

J.S. of Dale. See:

STIMSON, FREDERIC
JESUP
J. Stanley Henderson. See:
WILLETT, EDWARD
J. T. See:
TROWBRIDGE, JOHN
TOWNSEND
J. T. Brougham. See:
ST. JOHN, PERCY
BOLLINGBROKE
J. T. G. See:
GREIN, JACOB THOMAS
J. T. McIntosh. See:
MACGREGOR, JAMES
MURDOCH
J. T. Warren. See:
MANNING, WILLIAM
HENRY
J. Tweedale. See:
BICKLE, JUDITH
BRUNDRETT
J. Wellington Wells. See:
DE CAMP, LYON
SPRAGUE
J. Wesley Putnam. See:
DRAGO, HENRY
SINCLAIR
Jaan Kenbrovin. See:
VINCENT, NATHANIEL
HAWTHORNE
Jabbo. See:
SMITH, CLADYS
Jabez. See:
NICOL, ERIC PATRICK
JABNETH. See:
GAMALIEL OF JABNETH
Jac. See also:
Jack
Jacque
Jacques
Jock
Jac, Papa. See:
ASSUNTO, JAC
Jack. See:
BENSON, JOHN J.
CADE, JOHN
CLEMO, REGINALD JOHN
CONROY, JOHN WESLEY
COPE, ROBERT KNOX
DEMPSEY, WILLIAM
HARRISON
EHRLICH, JACK GUNTHER
FROST, HAROLD G.
GARSTANG, JAMES
GORDON
GERSTINE, JOHN
GOLD, JACOB
GREIN, JACOB THOMAS
IAMS, SAMUEL H., JR.
Jac
Jacque
Jacques
JACKSON, EUGENE
BERNARD
Jock
JOHNSON, JOHN
ARTHUR
KENNEDY, JOHN
FITZGERALD
KEROUAC, JEAN-LOUIS
LEBRID DE
KETCH, JOHN
KRAMER, JOHN ALBERT
KROLL, JOHN JACOB
LAINE, GEORGE VITELLE
LASLEY, JOHN WAYNE
III
LEMMON, JOHN UHLER,
III
LONDON, JOHN GRIFFITH
McBRIDE, JOHN JOSEPH
O'CONNOR, JOHN WOOLF
OLSEN, JOHN EDWARD
RUSSELL, JOHN
SEWARD, JOHN NEIL
SHARKEY, JOHN MICHAEL
SHARPE, JOHN RUFUS III
SHEPPARD, JOHN
SIEGEL, JACOB
STEFFAN, ALICE KENNEDY
TEAGARDEN, WELDON
JOHN
VAN COEVERING, JAN
ADRIAN
WILLIAMSON, JOHN
STEWART
Jack Alden. See:
BARROWS, MARJORIE
Jack-all-alone. See:
COWPER, FRANK
Jack Amend-all. See:
CADE, JOHN
Jack Barrymore. See:
BLYTHE, JOHN
Jack Bassett. See:
ROWLAND, DONALD SYDNEY

Jack Benny. See:
KUBELSKY BENNY
Jack Benny, An Aggressive. See: KNIBERG, IRWIN ALAN
Jack Bishop. See:
DORMAN, MICHAEL
Jack, Black. See:
KEMBLE, JOHN PHILIP
LOGAN, JOHN ALEXANDER
PERSHING, JOHN JOSEPH
Jack Brag, Sir. See:
BURGOYNE, JOHN
Jack, Cactus. See:
GARNER, JOHN NANCE
Jack, Calico. See:
RACKHAM, JOHN
Jack, Captain. See:
CRAWFORD, JOHN WALLACE
Jack, Colonel. See:
KROHN, JOHN ALBERT
Jack Danvers. See:
CASELEYR, CAMILLE AUGUSTE MARIE
Jack Dempsey. See:
DEMPSEY, WILLIAM HARRISON
KELLY, JOHN
Jack Downing, Major. See:
SMITH, SEBA
Jack Downing of Downingville, Major. See:
SMITH, SEBA
Jack, Fighting. See:
HAYES, EDWARD MORTIMER
Jack Fitzgerald. See:
SHEA, JOHN GERALD
Jack, Flint. See:
SIMPSON, EDWARD
Jack, Foul Weather. See:
BYRON, JOHN
Jack Hamilton. See:
BRANNON, WILLIAM T.
Jack, Handsome. See:
TUCKER, JOHN RANDOLPH
Jack, Happy. See:
SNELLEN, JOHN H.
Jack Hazard. See:
BOOTH, EDWIN
Jack Helmi. See:
SANDS, LEO GEORGE
Jack, Honest. See:
LORD ALTHORP
Jack Howard. See:
RATHBONE ST. GEORGE HENRY
Jack Humphries. See:
KELLY, JONATHAN FALCONBRIDGE
Jack La Bolina. See:
VECCHI, AUGUSTUS VICTOR
Jack La Rue. See:
BIONDOLILLO, GASPARE
Jack Lawrence. See:
FITZGERALD, LAWRENCE PENNYBAKER
Jack Liston. See:
MALONEY, RALPH LISTON
Jack Little, Little. See:
LITTLE, JOHN
Jack McCready. See:
POWELL, TALMAGE
Jack, Mad. See:
BYRON, CAPTAIN JOHN
PERCIVAL, JOHN
Jack Maxwell. See:
McKEAG, ERNEST LIONEL
Jack, Mohair. See:
GARNER, JOHN NANCE
Jack Moon. See:
ELLIOTT, JOHN R.
Jack Oakie. See:
OFFIELD, LEWIS D.
Jack of Clubs, The. See:
SHERIDAN, PHILIP HENRY
Jack of Knaresborough, Blind. See: METCALF, JACK
Jack of Newbury. See:
WINCHCOMB, JOHN
Jack of Norfolk. See:
HOWARD, SIR JOHN
Jack of Spades, The. See:
LOGAN, JOHN ALEXANDER
Jack, Oklahoma. See:
NICHOLS, JOHN CONOVER
Jack, Old. See:
JACKSON, THOMAS JONATHAN
Jack Palance. See:

PALANUIK, WALTER
Jack Paulson. See:
JACKSON, CAARY PAUL
Jack Paxton. See:
LAWTON, SHERMAN PAXTON
Jack Phillips. See:
SANDBURG, CARL AUGUST
Jack Sharpe. See:
RATHBONE, ST. GEORGE HENRY
SHARPE, JOHN RUFUS III
Jack, Sixteen-String. See:
RANN, JOHN
Jack, Spanish. See:
GONZALES, BLI
Jack, Texas. See:
OMOHUNDRO, JOHN B.
Jack the Giant-killer. See:
DEMPSEY, WILLIAM HARRISON
JACKSON, ROBERT HOUGHWOUT
RANDOLPH, JOHN
Jack the Ripper. See:
UNKNOWN
Jack, Three Fingered. See:
GARCIA, MANUEL
Jack, Uvalde. See:
GARNER, JOHN NANCE
Jack Waller, Swearing. See:
WALLER, JOHN
Jack Warner. See:
WATERS, JACK
Jack Wilson. See:
WOVOKA
Jack Winters. See:
TALENT, LEO
Jack Woodford. See:
WOOLFOLK, JOSIAH PITTS
JACKET. See:
RED JACKET
Jacket, Empty (Toom Tabard). See: JOHN DE BALIOL
Jackie. See:
CAIN, JACQUELINE RUTH
DAVIS, JACKSON
GLEASON, HERBERT JOHN
Jacquie
Jaki
JENSEN, JACK EUGENE
KENNEDY, JACQUELINE BOUVIER (MRS. ARISTOTLE SOCRATES ONASSIS)
MARTIN, CECILIA
ROBINSON, JACK ROOSEVELT
Jackrabbit. See:
ABBITT, JIM
JACKSON, ANDREW (1767-1845) [American general officer; seventh President of the United States]
The Duel Fighter
The Hero of New Orleans
King Andrew the First
The Land Hero of 1812
Mischievous Andy
Old Hickory
The People's President
The Pointed Arrow
The Sage of the Hermitage
The Sharp Knife
JACKSON, ANDREW. See also:
King and Queen of Hospitality, The
JACKSON, ANTHONY (1876-1921) [American jazz musician (piano, singer, composer)]
Tony Jackson
JACKSON, CAARY PAUL (1902-) [American author]
Colin Lochlons
Jack Paulson
JACKSON, EUGENE BERNARD (1915-) [American librarian]
Jack Jackson
JACKSON, FREDERICK (1886-1953) [American playwright and novelist]
Victor Thorne
JACKSON, GREIG STEWART (1918-) [American jazz musician (bass, songwriter)]
Chubby Jackson
JACKSON, HELEN MARIA FISKE HUNT (1830-85) [American novelist, poet and essayist]
H. H.

Saxe Holm
Helen Hunt Jackson
JACKSON, HENRY (1912-) [American professional boxer; world's featherweight, welterweight and lightweight champion]
Henry Armstrong
Jackson, Joe. See:
JIRANEK, JOSEPH FRANCIS
JACKSON, JOHN (1769-1845) [British pugilist]
Gentleman Jackson
JACKSON, JOSEPH JEFFERSON (1888-1951) [American professional baseball player]
Shoeless Joe Jackson
Jackson Knox. See:
HARBAUGH, THOMAS CHALMERS
JACKSON, LAURA RIDING (1901-) [American poet and author]
Laura Riding Gottschalk
Barbara Rich
Laura Riding
Jackson, Lucille. See:
STRAUSS, MARY LUCILLE JACKSON
JACKSON, MAHALIA (1911-1972) [American Negro singer]
Queen of the Gospel Song
JACKSON, MILTON (1923-) [American jazz musician (vibraphone, piano, guitar, singer)]
Bags Jackson
Milt Jackson
Jackson Mitchel. See:
MATCHA, JACK
Jackson, Nora. See:
TENNANT, NORA JACKSON
JACKSON, QUENTIN LEONARD (1909-) [American jazz musician (trombone)]
Butter Jackson
JACKSON, RACHEL DONELSON (1767-1828) [Wife of President ANDREW JACKSON]
Aunt Rachel
The Bonny Brown Wife
JACKSON, RACHEL DONELSON. See also: King and Queen of Hospitality, The.
JACKSON, REV. GEORGE (1864-) [British clergyman, educator and author]
G. J.
JACKSON, ROBERT HOUGHWOUT (1892-) [American politician, Assistant Attorney General of the United States]
Jack the Giant-killer
Jackson, Sally. See:
KELLOGG, JEAN
Jackson, Sam. See:
TRUMBO, DALTON
JACKSON, SHELDON (1834-1909) [American missionary]
The Bishop of All Outdoors
JACKSON, THOMAS JONATHAN (1824-63) [American Confederate general officer]
The Blue Light Elder
Fool Tom Jackson
The Invincible Stonewall
Old Jack
Old Tom Jackson
Stonewall Jackson
The Sword of the Confederacy
JACKSON, WILLIAM HICKS (1835-1903) [American Confederate general officer and stock breeder]
Red Fox Jackson
JACOB [Jacob]. See also: Jakob
Jacob Frank. See:
LIEBOWICZ, JANKIEW
JACOB, GILES (1686-1744) [English lawyer and dramatic writer]
The Scourge of Grammar
JACOB, NAOMI ELLINGTON (1889-) [English novelist]
Ellington Gray
Jacob Omnium. See:
HIGGINS, MATTHEW JAMES
Jacob, P. L., Bibliophile. See:
LACROIX, PAUL

JACOB, PIERS ANTHONY
DILLINGHAM (1934-)
[British teacher and
author]
Piers Anthony
Jacob Tonson. See:
BENNETT, ENOCH
ARNOLD
JACOB, ZACHARIE (1600-67)
[French actor and
playwright]
Montfleury
JACOBI, FRIEDRICH HEINRICH
(1743-1819) [German
philosopher]
The German Plato
JACOBS, AMOS (1914-)
[American actor and
television personality]
America's Favorite Tele-
vision Comedian
Danny Thomas
JACOBS, HELEN HULL
(1908-) [American tennis
player and author]
H. Braxton Hull
Jacobs, Leah. See:
GELLIS, ROBERT L.
JACOBS
JACOBS, ROSETTA (1932-)
[American motion
picture actress]
Piper Laurie
Jacobs, T. C. H. See:
PENDOWER, JACQUES
Jacobs, Thomas Curtis Hicks.
See: PENDOWER,
JACQUES
JACOBS, WALTER DARNELL
(1922-) [American
research scientist and
author]
Peter Oboe
JACOBS, WILLIAM WYMARK
(1863-1943) [English short
story writer and play-
wright]
W. W. Jacobs
Jacobus Arminius. See:
HERMANSEN (HERMANSZ),
JACOB
JACOBY, LEE (1911-) [American
stage and motion picture
actor]
Lee J. Cobb
Jacopo Bassano. See:
PONTE, GIACOMO DA
Jacopo da Pontormo. See:
CARRUCCI, JACOPO
JACOT DE BOINOD, BERNARD
LOUIS (1898-) [British
attorney and author]
B. L. Jacot
Jacque. See also:
Jac
Jack
Jacques
Jock
Jacque Braza. See:
McKEAG, ERNEST LIONEL
Jacque, Christian. See:
MAUDET, CHRISTIAN
Jacqueline Blairman. See:
PINTO, JACQUELINE
HARRIS
Jacques. See also:
Jac
Jack
Jacque
Jock
Jacques Bonhomme. See:
CAILLET, GUILLAUME
Jacques Chardonne. See:
BOUTELLEAU, JACQUES
Jacques Croise. See:
SCHAKOVSKOY,
PRINCESS ZINAIDA
Jacques Dersonne. See:
SIMENON, GEORGES
Jacques Duchesne. See:
SAINT-DENIS, MICHEL
JACQUES
Jacques Feyder. See:
FREDERIX, JACQUES
Jacques Jasmin. See:
BOÉ, JACQUES
Jacques Reval. See:
LAVER, JAMES
Jacques Tati. See:
TATISCHEFF, JACQUES
Jacques Villon. See:
DUCHAMP, GASTON
ÉMILE
JACQUET, BATTISTE ILLINOIS
(1921-) [American jazz
musician (tenor saxophone,

leader)]
Illinois Jacquet
Jacquie. See:
DURRELL, JACQUELINE SONIA RASEN
Jackie
Jaki
JADEN, DONNA MAE (1922-) [American motion picture actress]
Janis Paige
JAEGHER, RAYMOND-JOSEPH DE (1905-) [Belgian Roman Catholic priest, missionary and author]
Lei Chen Yuan
Jafah Clarke, Captain. See:
NESMITH, ROBERT I.
JAFFE, GABRIEL VIVIAN (1923-) [British physician and author]
Vivian Poole
Jafsie. See:
CONDON, DR. JOHN FRANCIS
JAGELKA, CHARLES (1923-) [American jazz musician (guitar, banjo)]
Chuck Wayne
JAHANGIR (1569-1627) [Mogul emperor]
The Conqueror of the World
JAHN. See also:
JOHN
John
Jon
JAHN, FRIEDRICH LUDWIG (1778-1852) [Prussian patriot and teacher of gymnastics]
Turnvater (Father of Gymnastics)
Jail Breaker, Champion. See:
WEISS, EHRICH (ERIK WEISZ)
Jailbird, The Escaped. See:
EGAN, PATRICK
Jailer, The Beloved. See:
WHITMAN, JOHN LORIN
Jake. See:
FLOWERS, D'ARCY RAYMOND
KRAMER, JOHN ALBERT
RUPPERT, JACOB, SR.
Jake Falstaff. See:
FETZER, HERMAN
Jake, Four Straight. See:
RUPPERT, JACOB, SR.
Jake Kramer. See:
KRAMER, JOHN ALBERT
Jake Kramer, Big. See:
KRAMER, JOHN ALBERT
Jake the Barber. See:
FACTOR, JOHN
Jaki. See:
BYARD, JOHN A., JR.
Jackie
Jacquie
Jakob. See also:
JACOB
Jacob
Jakob Corvinus. See:
RAABE, WILHELM
Jakob the Rich. See:
FUGGER, JAKOB II
Jamal, Ahmad. See:
JONES, FRITZ
James. See:
GREIN, JACOB THOMAS
Jeames
NAPJUS, ALICE JAMES
JAMES I (1208-76) [King of Aragon]
El Conquistador (The Conqueror)
JAMES I (1566-1625) [King of England]
The British Solomon
The English Solomon
The Most Learned Fool in Christendom
The Scottish Solomon
The Second Solomon
The Solomon of England
The Wisest Fool in Christendom
JAMES II (c. 1260-1327) [King of Aragon]
The Just
James III. See:
STUART, JAMES FRANCIS EDWARD
JAMES V (1512-42) [King of Scotland]
The Goodman of Ballengeigh

The King of the Commons
James A. Bailey. See:
McGINNIS, JAMES ANTHONY
James A. Maitland. See:
SMITH, FRANCIS SHUBAEL
James Allen. See:
ADER, PAUL FASSETT
James, Andrew See:
KIRKUP, JAMES
James Barbary. See:
BEECHING, AMY BROWN
BEECHING, JACK
James, Beau. See:
WALKER, JAMES JOHN
James Bond, Mrs. See:
BOND, MARY FANNING WICKHAM
James, Brian. See:
THOMAS, GORDON
TIERNEY, JOHN LAWRENCE
James Bridie. See:
MAVOR, DR. OSBORNE HENRY
James Byrom. See:
BRAMWELL, JAMES GUY
James Cody Ferris. See:
KARIG, WALTER
STRATEMEYER, EDWARD L.
JAMES, CORNELIUS (1927-)
[American jazz singer]
Pinocchio
James Craig. See:
MEADOR, JAMES
James Crofts. See:
SCOTT, JAMES
James Cross. See:
PARRY, HUGH JONES
James Cruze. See:
BOSEN, JENS CRUZ
James Darren. See:
ERCOLANI, JAMES
JAMES, DAVID BURNETT STEPHEN (1919-)
[British author, critic and editor]
Stephen Vizard
James Dean. See:
BYRON, JAMES
James Dean, The Teutonic.
See: BUCHHOLZ, HORST WERNER
James Denton. See:
HUGHES, ROBERT J.
James Dewey. See:
McNEILLY, MILDRED MASTERSON
James DeWitt. See:
LEWIS, MILDRED D.
James Dunn. See:
WILKES-HUNTER, RICHARD
James, Dynely, joint pseud. of
WILLIAM JAMES CARTER MAYNE (1928-) and
R.D. CAESAR (-)
[British authors]
James Edward. See:
STUART, JAMES FRANCIS EDWARD
James, Edwin. See:
GUNN, JAMES E.
James Ellison. See:
SMITH, JAMES ELLISON
James Elroy Flecker. See:
FLECKER, HERMAN JAMES ELROY
James Falconer. See:
KIRKUP, JAMES
James Fenimore Cooper Adams.
See: ELLIS, EDWARD SYLVESTER
James Fitzroy. See:
SCOTT, JAMES
James Garner. See:
BAUMGARNER, JAMES
James H. Thompson. See:
FREEMAN, GRAYDON LA VERNE
James Hadley Chase. See:
RAYMOND, RENÉ
James Holliday. See:
GRAY, SIMON
James Insight. See:
COLEMAN, ROBERT WILLIAM ALFRED
James James. See:
ADAMS, ARTHUR HENRY
James Jershom Jezreel. See:
WHITE, JAMES
JAMES, JESSE WOODSON (1847-82) [American outlaw]
Mr. Thomas Howard
The Robin Hood of Missouri
James, Josephine, joint pseud. of EMMA GELDERS

STERNE (1894-) and
BARBARA LINDSAY (-)
[American authors]
James, Josephine. See also:
STERNE, EMMA
GELDERS
James, Judith. See:
JENNINGS, LESLIE
NELSON
James Keene. See:
COOK, WILLIAM
EVERETT
James Kendricks. See:
FOX, GARDNER
FRANCIS
James King of William. See:
KING OF WILLIAM,
JAMES
James Knight. See:
SCHNECK, STEPHEN
James L. Bliss. See:
PORTER, WILLIAM
SYDNEY
James L. Cranbrook. See:
EDWARDS, WILLIAM
BENNETT
James Lewis (Louis) Macie. See:
SMITHSON, JAMES
JAMES, LIONEL (1871-)
[British army officer
and author]
The Intelligence Officer
James McGregor Cartwright.
See: JENNINGS, LESLIE
NELSON
James MacLaren. See:
GRIEVE, CHRISTOPHER
MURRAY
James MacNell. See:
MACDONNELL, JAMES
EDMOND
James Marshall. See:
RISTER, CARL COKE
James, Martha. See:
DOYLE, MARTHA CLAIRE
MACGOWAN
James Moffatt. See:
HUGHES, ROBERT J.
James Munro. See:
CAVE, RODERICK
GEORGE JAMES MUNRO
MITCHELL, JAMES
James Norman. See:
SCHMIDT, JAMES NORMAN
James O. Hannay. See:
HANNAY, JAMES OWEN
James Otis. See:
KALER, JAMES OTIS
James Owen Hannay. See:
HANNAY, JAMES OWEN
James Parker. See:
NEWBY, ERIC
James, Paul. See:
WARBURG, JAMES PAUL
James Pennethorne Hughes. See:
HUGHES, CHARLES
JAMES PENNETHORNE
James Peterson. See:
ZEIGER, HENRY ANTHONY
James Peto. See:
WHITE, JAMES DILLON
James Preston. See:
UNETT, JOHN
James Prior. See:
KIRK, JAMES PRIOR
James R. Cooper. See:
STRATEMEYER,
EDWARD L.
James, Ronald. See:
PRESTON, JAMES
James, St. See:
STRANG, JAMES JESSE
James St. Briavels. See:
WOOD, JAMES PLAYSTED
James Seymour. See:
CUNNINGHAM, JAMES
James Stark. See:
GOLDSTON, ROBERT
CONROY
James Steward, Reverend. See:
TRUMBULL, HENRY
James T.C. Yu. See:
TSUNE-CHI YU
James, T.F. See:
FLEMING, THOMAS
JAMES
James, The Female Jesse. See:
STARR, BELLE
JAMES THE GREATER, ST.
(died c. 44 A.D.) [brother
of ST. JOHN THE
EVANGELIST; one of the
Twelve Apostles]
Bonerge (Son of Thunder)
JAMES THE LESS (died c. 62
A.D.) [Apostle]

The Brother of the Lord
The Little
James Updyke. See:
BURNETT, WILLIAM RILEY
James Van Heusen. See:
BABCOCK, EDWARD CHESTER
James Vance Marshall. See:
PAYNE, DONALD GORDON
James Wong Howe. See:
WONG TUNG JIM
JAMESON [Jameson]. See also:
Jamieson
Jamison
JEMISON
JAMESON, ANNIE EDITH (1794-1860) [Irish author]
J. E. Buckrose
Jameson, Eric. See:
TRIMMER, ERIC J.
JAMESON, JOHN (1802-55) [American lawyer and politician; congressman from Missouri]
Immaterial John Jameson
JAMESON, MARGARET STORM (1897-) [English novelist]
Storm Jameson
JAMESON, SIR LEANDER STARR, 1ST BART. (1853-1917) [South African statesman and physician]
Dr. Jim
Jamie. See:
Jymie
Jamieson. See:
BROWN, WILLIAM JAMES CLARK
JAMESON
Jameson
Jamison
JEMISON
Jamison. See also:
JAMESON
Jameson
Jamieson
JEMISON
Jamison, Jane. See:
TRACHSEL, MYRTLE JAMISON
Jams Lite. See:
SCHNECK, STEPHEN
Jan. See:
SARNOFF, JANYC
WROBLEWSKI, PTASZYN
YOUNG, JANET RANDALL
Jan Hathaway. See:
NEUBAUER, WILLIAM ARTHUR
Jan Hilliard. See:
GRANT, HILDA KAY
Jan Mabuse. See:
GOSSART, JAN
Jan, Onze. See:
HOFMEYR, JAN HENDRIK
Jan Peerce. See:
PERELMAN, JACOB PINCUS
Jan Ralston. See:
DUNLOP, AGNES MARY ROBERTSON
Jan Reling. See:
DAVIS, HORACE BANCROFT
Jan Sterling. See:
ADRIANCE, JAN STERLING
Jan Struther. See:
MAXTONE GRAHAM, MRS. JOYCE ANSTRUTHER
Jan the Elder. See:
BRUEGHEL (BREUGHEL), JAN
Jan the Younger. See:
BRUEGHEL (BREUGHEL), JAN
Jan Valtin. See:
KREBS, RICHARD JULIUS HERMAN
Jan Van Der Meer Van Delft. See: VERMEER, JAN
Jan Vermeer van Haarlem. See:
MEER, JAN VAN DER
JANE [Jane]. See also:
Jayne
JANE I (1325-82) [Queen of Naples]
The Mary Stuart of Italy
Jane Annixter. See:
STURTZEL, JANE LEVINGTON
Jane Baxter. See:
FORDE, FEODORA

Jane Bryan. See:
O'BRIEN, JANE
Jane Burr. See:
WINSLOW, ROSE GUGGENHEIM
Jane, Calamity. See:
BURKE (CANARY), MARTHA JANE
Jane Campbell. See:
EDWARDS, JANE CAMPBELL
Jane Chichester. See:
LONGRIGG, JANE CHICHESTER
Jane Collier. See:
SHUMSKY, ZENA FELDMAN
Jane, Crazy. See:
LA LOCA, JOANNA
Jane Darwell. See:
WOODWARD, PATTI
Jane Duncan. See:
CAMERON, ELIZABETH JANE
Jane Durrell. See:
FULKS, SARAH JANE
Jane Fraser. See:
PILCHER, ROSAMUNDE
Jane Frazee. See:
FRAHSE, MARY JANE
Jane Gray. See:
EVANS, CONSTANCE MAY
Jane Hervey. See:
McGAW, NAOMI BLANCHE THOBURN
Jane Jamison. See:
TRACHSEL, MYRTLE JAMISON
Jane Langford. See:
MANTLE, WINIFRED LANGFORD
Jane Lee Hyndman. See:
WYNDHAM, LEE
Jane Levington Comfort. See:
STURTZEL, JANE LEVINGTON
Jane London. See:
GEIS, DARLENE STERN
Jane McIlvaine. See:
McCLARY, JANE STEVENSON
Jane Madison. See:
HORNE, HUGH ROBERT
Jane Mast. See:
WEST, MAE
Jane Muir. See:
PETRONE, JANE MUIR
Jane Oliver. See:
REES, HELEN CHRISTINA EASSON EVANS
Jane Oxford. See:
WILLIAMS, ELMA MARY
Jane Patterson. See:
BRITTON, MATTIE LULA COOPER
Jane Powell. See:
BURCE, SUZANNE
Jane Scott. See:
McELFRESH, ELIZABETH ADELINE
Jane Shaw. See:
EVANS, JEAN BELL SHAW
Jane Thayer. See:
WOOLLEY, CATHERINE
Jane Vansittart. See:
MOORHOUSE, HILDA VANSITTART
Jane Wyman. See:
FULKS, SARAH JANE
Janet Beecher. See:
MEYSENBURG, JANET BEECHER
Janet D. Wheeler. See:
STRATEMEYER, EDWARD L.
Janet Frame. See:
CLUTHA, JANET PATERSON FRAME
Janet Gaynor. See:
GAINER, LAURA
Janet Geddes, The Immortal. See:
GEDDES, JENNY
Janet H. Haderman. See:
WALWORTH, JEANETTE RITCHIE HADERMAN
Janet Leigh. See:
MORRISON, JEANETTE
Janet Lewis. See:
WINTERS, JANET LEWIS
Janet Randall. See:
YOUNG, JANET RANDALL
JANIFER. See also:
Jennifer
JANIFER, LAURENCE MARK (fl. 1959-63) [American

author]
Andrew Blake
Larry M. Harris
JANIFER, LAURENCE MARK. See also:
Phillips, Mark
Janice. See also:
Janis
Janice Ward. See:
HARTMAN, RACHEL FRIEDA
JANIN, JULES GABRIEL (1804-74) [French journalist]
The King of "Feuilletons"
Janina, The Lion of. See:
ALI
Janis. See also:
Janice
Janis, Byron. See:
YANKS, BYRON
Janis Carter. See:
DREMANN, JANIS
Janis, Elsie. See:
BIERBOWER, ELSIE
Janis Paige. See:
JADEN, DONNA MAE
JANNER, GREVILLE EWAN (1928-) [British barrister and author]
Ewan Mitchell
Jans, Emerson See:
BIXBY, JEROME LEWIS
Janson. See also:
Janssen
JANSZOON
JENSEN
Jensen
Janson, Hank. See:
HOBSON, HARRY
NORWOOD, VICTOR GEORGE CHARLES
Janssen. See also:
Janson
JANSZOON
JENSEN
Jensen
Janssen, David. See:
MEYER, DAVID HAROLD
JANSZOON. See also:
Janson
Janssen
JENSEN
Jensen
JANSZOON, LAURENS (c.1370-1440) [Dutch claimant to the invention of printing]
Coster
January Mortimer. See:
GALLICHAN, WALTER M.
Janus Weathercock. See:
WAINEWRIGHT, THOMAS GRIFFITHS
JANVIER MARGARET THOMPSON (1844-1913) [American poet]
Margaret Vandegrift
JANVIER, THOMAS ALLIBONE (1849-1913) [American journalist and author]
Ivory Black
Japan, The Billy Sunday of. See:
KIMURA, HENRY SEIMATSU
JAPP, ALEXANDER HAY (1839?-1905) [Scottish author]
H.A. Page
JARDINE, JACK (1931-) [American author]
Larry Maddock
JARDINE, JACK. See also:
Cory, Howard L.
Jaroslav Vrchlicky. See:
FRÍDA, EMIL
JARRETT, CORA HARDY (1877-) [American novelist]
Faraday Keene
Jarrett, Jeannette. See:
FISHER, LOIS JEANNETTE
Jarvis Hall. See:
BAGG, HELEN F.
Jasmin, Jacques. See:
BOÉ, JACQUES
Jason Manor. See:
HALL, OAKLEY MAXWELL
Jason Ridgway. See:
MARLOWE, STEPHEN
Jason, William. See:
MACHLIN, MILTON ROBERT
JAURAND, YVONNE (1912-) [French educator and author]
Yves Duplessis

Javali. See:
BEADNELL, CHARLES MARSH
JAW-YUANRENN (1892-) [Chinese researcher and author]
Y.R. Chao
Jay. See:
GOULD, JASON
HOLMES, JOSEPH EVERETT
THOMPSON, JENNINGS L., JR.
Jay B. Drexel. See:
BIXBY, JEROME LEWIS
Jay Barbette. See:
SPICER, BART
Jay Bee. See:
HUNTER, WILLIAM RANDOLPH
Jay Bender. See:
DEINDORFER, ROBERT GREENE
Jay Bentham. See:
BENSMAN, JOSEPH
Jay C. See:
HIGGINBOTHAM, JACK
Jay Dender. See:
DEINDORFER, ROBERT GREENE
Jay Dudley. See:
CHAPMAN, J. DUDLEY
Jay Franklin. See:
CARTER, JOHN FRANKLIN
JAY, HARRIET (1853-) [British dramatist and author]
Charles Marlowe
Jay Jay. See:
J.J.
JOHNSON, JAMES LOUIS
JAY, JOHN. See:
Publius
Jay Martin. See:
GOLDING, MORTON JAY
Jay Martins. See:
TENER, MARTIN J.
Jay Raphael. See:
JOSEPHS, RAY
Jay, Simon. See:
ALEXANDER, COLIN JAMES
Jay Stewart. See:
PALMER, STUART
Jay, W. M. L. See:
WOODRUFF, JULIA LOUISA
Jayne. See also:
JANE
Jane
Jayne, Lieut. R.H. See:
ELLIS, EDWARD SYLVESTER
Jayne Mansfield. See:
PALMER, JAYNE
Jaynes, Claire, joint pseud. of JANE ROTHSCHILD MAYER (1903-) and CLARA SPIEGEL (1904-) [American authors]
Jazz, King of. See:
WHITEMAN, PAUL
Jazz, Little. See:
ELDRIDGE, DAVID ROY
Jazz, The Ananias of. See:
MESIROW, MILTON
Jazz, The High-hatted Tragedian of. See:
FRIEDMAN, THEODORE LEOPOLD
Jazz, The Queen of. See:
ABUZA, SOPHIE
SCRUGGS, MARY ELFRIEDA
Jeake, Samuel, Jr. See:
AIKEN, CONRAD POTTER
Jeames. See also:
JAMES
James
Jeames de la Pluche. See:
THACKERAY, WILLIAM MAKEPEACE
Jean. See:
GIRAUDOUX, HIPPOLYTE JEAN
JEANNE
Jeanne
SIBELIUS, JOHANN JULIUS CHRISTIAN
SMITH, FRANCES CHRISTINE
WEBSTER, ALICE JANE CHANDLER
Jean Arthur. See:

GREENE, GLADYS
Jean Dale. See:
DIESTELHORST, H. JEAN
Jean de Meung. See:
CLOPINEL, JEAN
Jean Dorsage. See:
SIMENON, GEORGES
Jean Dossage. See:
SIMENON, GEORGES
Jean Du Perry. See:
SIMENON, GEORGES
Jean Du Shon. See:
ATWELL, JEAN
Jean Estoril. See:
ALLAN, MABEL ESTHER
Jean Froissart. See:
DAUDET, ALPHONSE
Jean Gabin. See:
MONCOURGE, ALEXIS
Jean, Gloria. See:
SCHOONOVER, GLORIA JEAN
Jean Hagen. See:
VERHAGEN, JEAN
Jean Harlow. See:
CARPENTER, HARLEAN
Jean Ingelow of America, The. See: CAREY, ALICE
Jean Kent. See:
SUMMERFIELD, JOAN
Jean Kirby. See:
McDONNELL, VIRGINIA BLEECKER
ROBINSON, CHAILLE PAYNE
Jean Lorrain. See:
DUVAL, MARTIN PAUL ALEXANDER
Jean-Louis. See:
KEROUAC, JEAN-LOUIS LEBRID DE
Jean-Louis Incogniteau. See:
KEROUAC, JEAN-LOUIS LEBRID DE
Jean Marais. See:
VILLAIN-MARAIS, JEAN
Jean Marsh. See:
MARSHALL, EVELYN
Jean Moréas. See:
PAPADIAMANTOPOULOS, IOANNES
Jean Muir. See:
FULLERTON, JEAN MUIR
Jean Paul. See:
RICHTER, JOHANN PAUL FRIEDRICH
Jean-Paul Le Chanois. See:
DREYFUS, JEAN-PAUL
Jean-Pierre Aumont. See:
SALOMONS, JEAN-PIERRE
Jean Plaidy. See:
HIBBERT, ELEANOR BURFORD
Jean Randall. See:
HAUCK, LOUISE PLATT
Jean Reed. See:
HOVICK, JUNE
Jean Sandor. See:
SIMENON, GEORGES
Jean Scott. See:
MUIR, MARIE
Jean Sterling. See:
TAYLOR, MARY VIRGINIA
Jean Valjean, Philadelphia's. See: BURKE, WILLIAM
Jean Vigo. See:
ALMEREYDA, JEAN
Jean Wallace. See:
WALLASEK, JEAN
Jeanne Bowman. See:
BLOCKLINGER, PEGGY O'MORE
JEANNE D'ARC. See:
JOAN OF ARC, ST. (JEANNE D'ARC)
Jeanne Hachette. See:
LAISNÉ, JEANNE
JEANNERET-GRIS, CHARLES ÉDOUARD (1887-1965) [Swiss architect and artist]
Charles-Edward Jeanneret
Le Corbusier
Jeannette. See:
Griffith, Jeannette
Jeannette Jarrett. See:
FISHER, LOIS JEANNETTE
Jeannie Carson. See:
SHUFFLEBOTTOM, JEAN
Jeans, Ursula. See:
McMINN, URSULA
Jeans Williams, Blue. See:
WILLIAMS, JAMES DOUGLAS

Jeb. See:
STUART, JAMES EWELL BROWN
Jeb, Old. See:
STUART, JAMES EWELL BROWN
Jebal, Sheik-al. See:
HASAN-IBN-AL-SABBAH
Jedediah Cleisbotham. See:
SCOTT, SIR WALTER
JEDLITZKA, MARIE (1887-) [Austrian dramatic soprano]
Maria Jeritza
Jeeves, Mahatma Kane. See:
DUKINFIELD, WILLIAM CLAUDE
Jef Gilson. See:
QUIEVREUX, JEAN-FRANÇOIS
Jeff. See:
SUTTON, JEFFERSON H.
Jeff Chandler. See:
GROSSEL, IRA
Jeff Clinton. See:
BICKHAM, JACK MILES
Jeff Cochran. See:
DURST, PAUL
JEFFERSON, ARTHUR STANLEY (1890-1965)[British actor and motion picture comedian]
Stan Laurel
Stanley Laurel
Jefferson Cooper. See:
FOX, GARDNER FRANCIS
Jefferson, Ian. See:
DAVIES, LESLIE PURNELL
Jefferson Jim. See:
WILSON, JAMES FALCONER
JEFFERSON, JOSEPH (1829-1905) [American actor and playwright]
The Dean of the American Stage
Jefferson of Folk Music, The Thomas. See:
SEEGER, PETER
JEFFERSON, THOMAS (1743-1826) [Third President of the United States]
The Apostle of Liberty
The Father of the Declaration of Independence
The Father of the University of Virginia
The Friend of the People
Long Tom
The Man of the People
The Pen of the Revolution
The Philosopher of Democracy
The Red Fox
The Sage of Monticello
The Scribe of the Revolution
Jeffery. See:
FARNOL, JOHN JEFFREY
Geffery
Geoffrey
JEFFREY
Jeffrey
JEFFREYS
Joffrey
JEFFERY, GRANT (1924-) [Canadian financial writer]
Peter Paul Turner
Jeffery Hudson, Sir. See:
HUDSON, JEFFERY
Jeffery, Jeffery E. See:
MARSTON, JEFFERY EARDLEY
JEFFREY [Jeffrey]. See also:
Geffrey
Geoffrey
JEFFERY
Jeffery
JEFFREYS
Joffrey
Jeffrey Ashford. See:
UNKNOWN
Jeffrey Church. See:
KIRK, RICHARD EDMUND
Jeffrey Collins. See:
WILCOX, COLLIN
Jeffrey Gardner. See:
FOX, GARDNER FRANCIS
Jeffrey Hunter. See:
McKINNIES, HENRY H.
Jeffery Lynn. See:
LIND, RAGNAR
JEFFREY, ROSA GRIFFITH VERTNER JOHNSON (1828-94) [American poet and novelist]
Rosa
Jeffrey, Ruth. See:
BELL, LOUISE PRICE

JEFFREY-SMITH, MAY THORNTON (1882-) [English author]
Aunt Maysie
Maimee Thornton
JEFFREYS. See also:
Geffery
Geoffrey
JEFFERY
Jeffery
JEFFREY
Jeffrey
Joffrey
JEFFREYS, GEORGE, 1ST BARON JEFFREYS OF WEM (1648-89) [English jurist]
The Hanging Judge
Jehan. See: Mandeville, Jehan de (Sir John)
Jehu O'Cataract. See: NEAL, JOHN
Jelakomitch, Ivan. See: HEIJERMANS (HEYERMANS), HERMAN
JELAL-ED-DIN-MOHAMMED (1542-1605) [Mogul emperor of India]
Akbar (The Great)
Jelly. See: NASH, FRANK
Jelly Roll Morton. See: LA MENTHE, FERDINAND JOSEPH
JEMISON. See also:
JAMESON
Jameson
Jamieson
Jamison
JEMISON, MARY (1743-1833) [American woman; captive of Indians]
Deh-he-wŏ-mis
The White Woman of the Genessee
Jemmy. See:
Jimmie
Jimmy
Jemmy Twitcher. See: MONTAGU, JOHN
JENCKES. See also:
JENKS
JENCKES, THOMAS ALLEN (1818-75) [American politician; congressman from Rhode Island]
The Father of Civil Service Reform
JENCKES, VIRGINIA ELLIS (1882-) [American farmer and politician; congresswoman from Indiana]
The Cherry-trees Nemesis
Jenghiz Khan (Precious Warrior). See: TEMUJIN
Jenkins, Allen. See: McGONEGAL, AL
JENKINS, FREDDY (1906-) [American jazz musician (trumpet)]
Posey
JENKINS, JACKIE (1938-) [American child motion picture actor]
Butch Jenkins
JENKINS, JAMES (1764-1847) [American preacher]
Bawling Jenkins
Thundering Jimmy
JENKINS, MacGREGOR (1869-1940) [American publisher and author]
Rusticus
JENKINS, RICHARD (1925-) [Welsh stage and motion picture actor]
Richard Burton
JENKINS, WENDY (1912-) [British motion picture actress]
Wendy Barrie
JENKINS, WILLIAM FITZGERALD (1896-) [American author of mystery and adventure stories for boys]
Murray Leinster
JENKS. See also:
JENCKES
JENKS, GEORGE CHARLES (1850-1929) [Anglo-American writer of dime novels]
Nicholas Carter
Nick Carter

W. B. Lawson
JENNER, KATHERINE LEE (1853-) [British novelist]
Mrs. Henry Jenner
Katherine Lee
Jenneval. See:
DECHEZ, LOUIS A.
Jennifer. See also:
JANIFER
Jennifer Ames. See:
GREIG, MAYSIE COUCHER
Jennifer Jones. See:
ISLEY, PHYLLIS
Jennifer Price. See:
HOOVER, HELEN DRUSILLA BLACKBURN
JENNINGS, HUGH AMBROSE (1870-1928) [American professional baseball player]
Hughie Jennings
JENNINGS, JOHN E., JR. (1906-) [American author]
Bates Baldwin
Joel Williams
JENNINGS, LESLIE NELSON (1890-) [American editor, poet and author]
A. B. Brooke
Cyril Carfagne
James McGregor Cartwright
Baroness Julie Desplaines
Judith James
Paul Rayson
Jennings, S. M. See:
MEYER, JEROME SYDNEY
JENNINGS, SARAH (1660-1744) [Duchess of Marlborough]
Mrs. Freeman
Queen Sarah
Jennison, C. S. See:
STARBIRD, KAYE
JENNISON, LUCIA (1850-) [American author of love songs and sonnets]
Owen Innsley
Jenny. See:
LIND, JOHANNA MARIA
SHORT, DEWEY
Jenny Hamilton. See:
GEDDES, JENNY
Jenny June. See:
CROLY, JANE CUNNINGHAM
Jenny Mein. See:
GEDDES, JENNY
JENSEN [Jensen]. See also:
Janson
Janssen
JANSZOON
Jensen, Bank. See:
OTTESEN, THEA TAUBER
JENSEN, DORIS (1922-) [American motion picture actress]
Coleen Gray
JENSEN, FORREST (1909-) [American professional baseball player]
Woody Jensen
JENSEN, JACK EUGENE (1927-) [American professional baseball player]
Jackie Jensen
JENSEN, PAULINE MARIE LONG (1900-) [American author]
Ann Marie Long
Jephtha. See:
RIXEY, EPPA, JR.
JEPSON-TURNER, GLADYS (1924-) [British ice-skating star and motion picture actress]
Belita
Jeremiah Digges. See:
BERGER, JOSEF
Jeremiah Hopkins. See:
NOTT, HENRY JUNIUS
Jeremiah, The British. See:
GILDAS (GILDUS)
Jeremias Gotthelf. See:
BITZIUS, ALBERT
Jeremy. See:
BENNETT, JOHN JEROME NELSON
Martin, Jeremy
Jeremy Kemp. See:
WALKER, EDMUND
Jeremy Lord. See:
REDMAN, BEN RAY
Jeremy Pitt. See:
WYNNE-TYSON, TIMOTHY

JON LYADEN
Jeremy Premont, Brother. See:
WILLETT, BROTHER FRANCISCUS
Jeremy, Richard. See:
FOX, CHARLES
Jeremy York. See:
CREASEY, JOHN
Jerezano. See:
LARA, MANUEL
Jeritza, Maria. See:
JEDLITZKA, MARIE
Jerman, Sylvia Paul. See:
COOPER, SYLVIA
Jerome, Owen Fox. See:
FRIEND, OSCAR JEROME
Jerome Robbins. See:
RABINOWITZ, JEROME
Jerome, St. See:
EDMUNDS, GEORGE FRANKLIN
Jerret, Nick. See:
BERTOCCI, NICHOLAS
Jerrie. See:
COBB, GERALDYN M.
GERRY
Gerry
Jerry
Jerrold, Mary. See:
ALLEN, MARY
Jerry. See:
ABERSHAW, LOUIS JEREMIAH
BARBER, CARL JEROME
COLONNA, GERARD
GERRY
Gerry
GREENFIELD, JEROME
Jerrie
KERN, JEROME DAVID
LESHAY, JEROME
ORBACH, JEROME
WALD, JEROME IRVING
Jerry Fielding. See:
FELDMAN, GERALD
Jerry Lewis. See:
LEVITCH, JOSEPH
Jerry Marlowe. See:
MAUTNER, JEROME
Jerry, Sockless. See:
SIMPSON, JERRY
Jerry, Uncle. See:
RUSK, JEREMIAH McLAIN
Jerry West. See:
STRATEMEYER, EDWARD L.
SVENSON, ANDREW E.
Jersey City, The Dictator of. See: HAGUE, FRANK
Jersey Joe. See:
STRIPP, JOSEPH VALENTINE
Jersey Joe Walcott. See:
CREAM, ARNOLA RAYMOND
Jersey Lily, The. See:
BRETON, EMILY CHARLOTTE LE
Jersey Slick. See:
TICHENOR, ISAAC
Jerseys, Don Quixote of the. See:
LIVINGSTON, WILLIAM
Jeru. See:
MULLIGAN, GERALD JOSEPH
Jesse. See:
Jessey
Jessie
OWENS, JAMES CLEVELAND
Jesse James, The Female. See:
STARR, BELLE
Jesse, Michael. See:
BALDWIN, MICHAEL
Jesse Webster. See:
CASSILL, RONALD VERLIN
JESSEL, GEORGE ALBERT (1898-) [American actor and toastmaster]
The Boy Monologist
Georgie Jessel
Jessey. See also:
Jesse
Jessie
Jessey, Cornelia. See:
SUSSMAN, CORNELIA SILVER
Jessica Lyon. See:
DE LEEUW, CATEAU WILHELMINA
Jessie. See also:
Jesse
Jessey
Jessie Bonstelle See:
BONESTEELE, LAURA

JUSTINE
Jessie Ralph. See:
CHAMBERS, JESSIE RALPH
Jessup, Frances. See:
VAN BRIGGLE, MARGARET FRANCES JESSUP
Jester, The. See:
LINCOLN, ABRAHAM
Jests, The Father of. See:
MILLER, JOSEPH
Jesuit, The Seditious. See:
CAMPION, EDMUND
Jesus, Giuseppe of (Guiseppe del Gesù). See: GUARNIERI, GIUSEPPE ANTONIO
Jesus, Little Flower of. See:
TERESA OF LISIEUX, ST.
Jesus, Mother Raymond de. See:
DION, SISTER RAYMOND DE JESUS
Jesus, Theresa de. See:
TERESA OF AVILA
Jet. See:
TUEL, JOHN E.
Jet Luber. See:
MEULENBELT-LUBER HENRIETTA C. A.
Jeune, Le (The Young). See:
LOUIS VII
JEWETT, JOHN HOWARD (1843-1925) [American author]
Hannah Warner
JEWETT, SARAH ORNE (1849-1909) [American author]
Alice Eliot
JEWETT, SOPHIE (1861-1909) [American poet]
Ellen Burroughs
Jewish Negro, America's One-eyed. See:
DAVIS, SAMMY, JR.
Jewish Plato, The. See:
PHILO JUDAEUS
Jezreel, James Jershom. See:
WHITE, JAMES
Jice Doone. See:
MARSHALL, JAMES VANCE
Jiggs. See:
McMANUS, GEORGE
WHIGHAM, HAYDN
Jill Christian. See:
DILCOCK, NOREEN
Jill St. John. See:
OPPENHEIM, JILL
Jim. See:
ATKINS, JAMES G.
BACKUS, JAMES
BEATTY, JAMES TULLY
BERRY, JAMES
BISHOP, JAMES ALONZO
BOWIE, JAMES
BRIDGER, JAMES
BROSNAN, JAMES PATRICK
CLAY, JAMES
CRANE, JAMES GORDON
DILLES, JAMES
DOLE, JAMES DRUMMOND
FIGG, JAMES
HARMON, JAMES JUDSON
HARRISON, JAMES
HILL, JAMES JEROME
JORDAN, JAMES EDWARD
KIRKWOOD, JAMES
KONSTANTY, CASIMER JAMES
NABORS, JAMES THURSTON
RYUN, JAMES RONALD
TATUM, JAMES MOORE
THORPE, JAMES FRANCIS
TULLY, JAMES
WOODMAN, JAMES MONROE
Jim, Big. See:
COLOSIMO, JAMES
FARLEY, JAMES ALOYSIUS
Jim Bob Tinsley. See:
TINSLEY, JAMES ROBERT
Jim Bowie. See:
BOWIE, JAMES
NORWOOD, VICTOR GEORGE CHARLES
STRATEMEYER, EDWARD L.
Jim Circus. See:
ROSEVEAR, JOHN
Jim Cornwall. See:
RIKHOFF, JAMES C.
Jim Daly. See:

STRATEMEYER, EDWARD L.
Jim, Diamond. See:
BRADY, JAMES BUCHANAN
Jim, Dr. See:
JAMESON, SIR LEANDER STARR, 1ST BART.
Jim Duane. See:
HURLEY, VIC
Jim, English. See:
STUART, JAMES
Jim, Fighting. See:
LANE, JAMES HENRY
Jim, Gentleman. See:
CORBETT, JAMES JOHN
Jim Gerald. See:
GUENOD, JACQUES
Jim Hollis. See:
SUMMERS, HOLLIS SPURGEON, JR.
Jim, Jefferson. See:
WILSON, JAMES FALCONER
Jim-Jim Crowd, The, joint nickname of JAMES SMITH, JR. (1851-1927) and JAMES NUGENT (1864-1927) [American politicians and public officials]
Jim, Jubilee. See:
FISK, JAMES, JR.
Jim, Jumping. See:
GAVIN, JAMES MAURICE
Jim, Puddler, See:
DAVIS, JAMES JOHN
Jim Roberts. See:
BATES, BARBARA SNEDEKER
Jim, Silent. See:
MOORE, JAMES TATUM
Jim Smiley. See:
SPEARS, RAYMOND SMILEY
Jim, Smiling. See:
FARLEY, JAMES ALOYSIUS
Jim, Sunny. See:
WATSON, JAMES ELI
Jim, Tama. See:
WILSON, JAMES
Jim, Texas. See:
ROBERTSON, JAMES B.
Jim Tressidy. See:
NORWOOD, VICTOR GEORGE CHARLES
Jiménez, José. See:
DANA, WILLIAM
JIMÉNEZ, JUAN (1858-99) [Spanish bullfighter]
Ecijano
JIMÉNEZ, JUAN (1939-) [Spanish bullfighter]
Trianero
JIMÉNEZ, MANUEL (1814-52) [Spanish bullfighter]
El Cano
JIMÉNEZ, MANUEL (1932-60) [Spanish bullfighter]
Chicuelo II
JIMÉNEZ, RAFAEL (1941-) [Spanish bullfighter]
Chicuelo
Jimmie. See:
GRIER, JAMES W.
Jemmy
Jimmy
LUNCEFORD, JAMES MELVIN
NOONE, JAMES
Jimmie Lawrence. See:
DILLINGER, JOHN HERBERT
Jimmie, Uncle. See:
DOUGHTY, JAMES P.
Jimmy. See:
BROWN, JAMES NATHANIEL
BRUNO, JAMES
BYRNES, JAMES FRANCIS
CAGNEY, JAMES
DORSEY, JAMES
DURANTE, JAMES FRANCIS
ERNST, ULRICH
FOXX, JAMES EMORY
Jemmy
Jimmie
McHUGH, JAMES FRANCIS
MONACO, JAMES V.
ROWLES, JAMES GEORGE
RULE, JAMES A.
RUSHING, JAMES ANDREW
STEWART, JAMES MAITLAND
STOCKARD, JAMES WRIGHT, JR.

WALKER, JAMES JOHN
Jimmy, Beanpole. See:
JONES, JAMES C.
Jimmy, Hot Stove. See:
QUINN, JAMES ALOYSIUS
Jimmy Jones, Lean. See:
JONES, JAMES C.
Jimmy, Ragtime. See:
DURANTE, JAMES FRANCIS
Jimmy, Son. See:
ROOSEVELT, JAMES
Jimmy, Ten-cent. See:
BUCHANAN, JAMES
Jimmy, Thundering. See:
JENKINS, JAMES
Jimmy Valentine. See:
LYTELL, BERT
Jingle Money. See:
SMITH, JAMES MONROE
JINNAH, MOHAMMED ALI (1876-1948) [Pakistanian statesman]
Quaid-i-azam (Great Leader)
Jinny. See:
Ginny
McDONNELL, VIRGINIA BLEECKER
Jinx Falkenburg. See:
McCRARY, EUGENIA LINCOLN FALKENBURG
JIRANEK, JOSEPH FRANCIS (-1942) [American vaudeville comedian]
Joe Jackson
Jiskogo. See:
HARRINGTON, MARK RAYMOND
Jo. See:
GRIMMOND, JOSEPH
Joe
SWERLING, JOSEPH
Jo, Damita. See:
BLANC, DAMITA JO DE
Jo-Jo. See:
WHITE, JOYNER
Jo King. See:
BELLAW, AMERICUS WELLINGTON
Jo Mendel. See:
BOND, GLADYS PARKER
Jo Pierce. See:
MANNING, WILLIAM HENRY
MORRIS, CHARLES SMITH
Jo Sinclair. See:
SEID, RUTH
Jo Valentine. See:
ARMSTRONG, CHARLOTTE
JOACHIM II (1514-71) [Elector of Brandenburg]
The Hector of Germany
Joachim Camerarius. See:
LIEBHARD, JOACHIM
Joachim Frizius. See:
FLUDD (FLUD), ROBERT
JOAN (fl. 855) [mythical female pope, supposed to have occupied papal chair in guise of a man]
Joannes Anglicus (John of England)
Pope Joan
Pope John VIII
JOAN (1321-62) [Queen of Scotland]
Joan Makepeace
Joan of the Tower
JOAN (1328-85) [wife of EDWARD, The Black Prince]
The Fair Maid of Kent
Joan, Bobbing. See:
MAR, JOHN ERSKINE, 6TH OR 11TH EARL OF
Joan Crawford. See:
LE SUEUR, LUCILLE
Joan Evans. See:
EUNSON, JOAN
Joan Fontaine. See:
HAVILLAND, JOAN DE
Joan Gale Thomas. See:
ROBINSON, JOAN MARY GALE THOMAS
Joan Garrison. See:
NEUBAUER, WILLIAM ARTHUR
Joan Grant. See:
KELSEY, JOAN MARSHALL
Joan Haythorne. See:
HAYTHORNTHWAITE, JOAN
Joan Leslie. See:
BRODELL, JOAN
Joan Lorring. See:
ELLIS, MAGDALEN

Joan Medhurst. See:
LIVERTON, JOAN
Joan of Arc of the Modern Religious World, The. See:
UTLEY, ULDINE
JOAN OF ARC, ST. (JEANNE D'ARC) (1412-31) [French saint, national heroine and martyr]
The Maid
The Maid of Orleans (La Pucelle d'Orléans)
The Wondrous Maid
Joan of Arc, The English. See:
AMBREE, MARY
Joan Pepper. See:
WETHERELL-PEPPER, JOAN ALEXANDER
Joan Phipson. See:
FITZHARDINGE, JOAN MARGARET
Joan Rivers. See:
MOLINSKY, JOAN
Joan Sherman. See:
DERN, PEGGY GADDIS
Joanna Catlow. See:
LOWRY, JOAN CATLOW
Joanna Wade. See:
BERCKMAN, EVELYN DOMENICA
Joanne Dru. See:
LA COCK, JOANNE
Joannes Anglicus (John of England). See:
JOAN
João Donato. See:
OLIVEIRA, JOÃO DONATO DE
Joaquin. See:
MILLER, CINCINNATUS HEINE (HEINER)
Joaquin Murieta. See:
CARILLO, JOAQUIN
Jocelyn Arundel. See:
ALEXANDER, JOCELYN ANNE ARUNDEL
Jocelyn, Richard. See:
CLUTTERBUCK, RICHARD
Jock. See:
Jac
Jack
Jacque
Jacques
SUTHERLAND, DR. JOHN BAIN
WHITNEY, JOHN HAY
Jock Mahoney. See:
O'MAHONEY, JACQUES
Jockey. See:
FALK, BIBB AUGUST
Jockey of Norfolk, The. See:
HOWARD, SIR JOHN
Jodelet. See:
BEDEAU, JULIEN
JODELLE, ÉTIENNE (1532-73) [French poet and dramatist]
The Father of the French Drama
Jody Lawrance. See:
GODDARD, JOSEPHINE LAWRENCE
Joe. See:
BAKER, GEORGE
BUSHKIN, JOSEPH
BYRD, GENE
CRONIN, JOSEPH EDWARD
DIMAGGIO, JOSEPH PAUL, JR.
Jo
KELLY, JOSEPH WILLIAM
McCARTHY, JOSEPH VINCENT
MILLER, JOSEPH
NAMATH, JOSEPH WILLIAM
PAGE, JOSEPH FRANCIS
RINES, JOSEPH
SANDERS, JOSEPH L.
TINKER, JOSEPH BERT
VAN WORMER, JOSEPH EDWARD
VENUTI, GIUSEPPE
WEBER, JOSEPH M.
Joe, Alfalfa. See:
WING, JOSEPH ELWYN
Joe Bari. See:
BENEDETTO, ANTHONY DOMINICK
Joe, Big. See:
TURNER, JOSEPH
Joe Brandon. See:
DAVIS, ROBERT P.
Joe, Broadway. See:
NAMATH, JOSEPH WILLIAM
Joe", By the Author of "Gentleman. See:
BADGER, JOSEPH E., JR.
Joe Cain, See:

CAIANI, JOSEPH
Joe, California. See:
MILNER, MOSES EMBREE
Joe Fargo. See:
RIKHOFF, JAMES C.
Joe, Fighting. See:
HOOKER, JOSEPH
WHEELER, JOSEPH
Joe Fingers Carr. See:
BUSCH, LOUIS F.
Joe Holiday. See:
BEFUMO, JOSEPH A.
Joe Hooker, Fighting. See:
HOOKER, JOSEPH
Joe Jackson. See:
JIRANEK, JOSEPH FRANCIS
Joe, Jersey. See:
STRIPP, JOSEPH VALENTINE
Joe Jot, Jr. See:
BELLAW, AMERICUS WELLINGTON
Joe, Little. See:
WHEELER, JOSEPH
Joe Loco. See:
ESTEVES, JOSEPH
Joe Louis. See:
BARROW, JOSEPH LOUIS
Joe Manton. See:
GITTINGS, JO GRENVILLE MANTON
Joe, Marse. See:
McCARTHY, JOSEPH VINCENT
Joe May. See:
MANDEL, JOSEPH
Joe Norman. See:
HEARD, JOSEPH NORMAN
Joe Pass. See:
PASSALAQUA, JOSEPH ANTHONY
Joe Penner. See:
PINTER, JOSEPH
Joe, Philly. See:
JONES, JOSEPH RUDOLPH
Joe, Pleasant Gardens. See:
McDOWELL, JOSEPH
Joe, Pushful. See:
CHAMBERLAIN, JOSEPH
Joe, Quaker Meadows. See:
McDOWELL, JOSEPH
Joe, Shoeless. See:
JACKSON, JOSEPH JEFFERSON
Joe Sullivan. See:
O'SULLIVAN, DENIS PATRICK TERENCE JOSEPH
Joe, Uncle. See:
CANNON, JOSEPH GURNEY
STILWELL, JOSEPH WARREN
SWING, JOSEPH MAY
Joe, Vinegar. See:
STILWELL, JOSEPH WARREN
Joe Walcott, Jersey. See:
CREAM, ARNOLA RAYMOND
Joe Willie. See:
NAMATH, JOSEPH WILLIAM
Joe, Wooden. See:
NICHOLAS, JOE
Joel Reeve. See:
COX, WILLIAM R.
Joel Stacy. See:
DODGE, MARY ELIZABETH MAPES
Joel Williams. See:
JENNINGS, JOHN E., JR.
Joey. See:
GRIMALDI, JOSEPH
Joey Bishop. See:
GOTTLIEB, JOSEPH ABRAHAM
Joffrey. See also:
Geffery
Geoffrey
JEFFERY
Jeffery
JEFFREY
Jeffrey
JEFFREYS
Joffrey, Robert. See:
KHAN, ABDULLAH JAFFA ANVER BEY
Johan Gutenberg. See:
GENSFLEISCH, JOHAN
Johan, Karl (Charles John). See:
BERNADOTTE, JEAN BAPTISTE JULES
JOHANN (fl. late 15th cent.)
[Elector of Brandenburg]

The Cicero of Germany
JOHANN. See also:
JOHN (JOHANN)
Johann Eck. See:
MAYER, JOHANN ECK
Johann Friedrich Blunck. See:
BLUNCK, HANS FRIEDRICH
Johann (Johannes) Faust. See:
FAUST, GEORG
Johann Strauss, The American Successor to. See:
ROMBERG, SIGMUND
Johanna Field. See:
MILNER, MARION BLACKETT
Johanna Leigh. See:
SAYERS, DOROTHY LEIGH
Johanna Menzel. See:
MESKILL, JOHANNA MENZEL
JOHANNES. See:
JOHN (JOHANNES) OF SWABIA
Johannes Agricola. See:
SNEIDER (SNITTER), JOHANNES
JOHANNES DAMASCENUS. See:
JOHN OF DAMASCUS (JOHANNES DAMASCENUS)
Johannes de Sacrobosco. See:
HOLYWOOD, JOHN
Johannes Eremita. See:
CASSIANUS, JOHANNES
Johannes Ierugena (Irish-born). See: ERIGENA, JOHANNES SCOTUS
Johannes (Johan) Faust. See:
FAUST, GEORG
Johannes Leo. See:
ALWAZZAN (ALWEZAZ), ALHASSAN IBN MOHAMMED
Johannes Massiliensis. See:
CASSIANUS, JOHANNES
Johannes Oecolampadius. See:
HUSSGEN, JOHANNES
Johannes Scotus. See:
ERIGENA, JOHANNES SCOTUS
Johannes Sleidanus. See:
PHILIPPI, JOHANNES
Johannes Vogel, Dr. See:
HOFPREDIGER, JOHANNES MARTIN VOGEL
JOHANSSON. See also:
JOHNSON
Johnson
Johnston
Johnstone
JONSON
JOHANSSON, INGEMAR (1932-) [Swedish professional boxer; world's heavyweight champion]
Ingo
John. See:
BRAHM, HANS
BROMFIELD, FARRON
CARRADINE, RICHMOND REED
CHRYSOSTOM, ST. JOHN
HUNTER, MAUD LILY
JAHN
Jon
KEROUAC, JEAN-LOUIS LEBRID DE
O'HARA, JOHN HENRY
Smith, John
WILSON, CHRISTOPHER NORTH
JOHN (died 526) [Supreme Pontiff of Roman Catholic Church]
Pope John I
St. John
JOHN (died 574) [Supreme Pontiff of Roman Catholic Church]
Pope John III
JOHN (died 642) [Supreme Pontiff of Roman Catholic Church]
Pope John IV
JOHN (died 686) [Supreme Pontiff of Roman Catholic Church]
Pope John V
JOHN (died 705) [Supreme Pontiff of Roman Catholic Church]
Pope John VI
JOHN (died 707) [Supreme Pontiff of Roman Catholic Church]
Pope John VII
JOHN (died 882), [Supreme Pontiff of Roman Catholic Church]
Pope John VIII
JOHN (died 900) [Supreme Pontiff

of Roman Catholic Church]
Pope John IX
JOHN (died 928) [Supreme Pontiff of Roman Catholic Church]
Pope John X
JOHN (died 935) [Supreme Pontiff of Roman Catholic Church]
Pope John XI
JOHN (died 972) [Supreme Pontiff of Roman Catholic Church]
Pope John XIII
JOHN (died 996) [Supreme Pontiff of Roman Catholic Church]
Pope John XV
JOHN (died 1003) [Supreme Pontiff of Roman Catholic Church]
Pope John XVII
JOHN (died 1009) [Supreme Pontiff of Roman Catholic Church]
Pope John XVIII
JOHN (died 1032) [Supreme Pontiff of Roman Catholic Church]
Pope John XIX
JOHN (c.1370-1419) [Duke of Burgundy]
The Fearless
JOHN (c.1373-1453) [First Earl of Shrewsbury]
The Achilles of England
The Terror of France
JOHN I (925-76) [Emperor of the Byzantine (Eastern Roman) Empire]
Zimisces
JOHN I (1167-1216) [King of England]
John Lackland
Sansterre
JOHN I (1357-1433) [King of Portugal]
The Bastard
The Great
JOHN I (1459-1501) [King of Poland]
John Albert
JOHN I (1487-1540) [King of Hungary]
Zápolya (Szapolyai)
John I of Vancouver, The Archbishop. See: WOLSEY, WILLIAM FRANKLYN
JOHN II (1088-1143) [Emperor of the Byzantine (Eastern Roman) Empire]
Comnenus
Kalojoannes
JOHN II (1319-64) [King of France]
Le Bon (The Good)
JOHN II (1455-95) [King of of Portugal]
The Perfect
The Perfect Prince
JOHN II (1540-71) [King of Hungary]
Sigismund Zápolya (Szapolyai)
JOHN II (1609-72) [King of Poland]
Casimir
Casimir V
JOHN III (1193-1254) [Emperor of the Byzantine (Eastern Roman) Empire]
Ducas
Vatatzes
JOHN III (1624-96) [King of Poland]
Sobieski
JOHN IV (1250?-1300?) [Emperor of the Byzantine (Eastern Roman) Empire]
Lascaris
JOHN IV (1605-56) [King of Portugal]
The Fortunate
JOHN IV (1839-89) [Emperor of Ethiopia]
Dejaz Kassai
JOHN V (or VI) (1332-91) [Emperor of the Byzantine (Eastern Roman) Empire]
Palaeologus
JOHN V (died 1399) [Duke of Brittainy]
The Valiant
JOHN V (1689-1750) [King of Portugal]
Most Faithful King
JOHN VI (or V) (1292?-1383) [Emperor of the Byzantine (Eastern Roman) Empire]
Cantacuzene
JOHN VII (1360-1412) [Emperor of the Byzantine (Eastern

Roman) Empire]
Palaeologus
JOHN VIII (1391-1448) [Emperor of the Byzantine (Eastern Roman) Empire]
Palaeologus
JOHN II, Pope. See:
MERCURIUS
John VIII, Pope. See:
JOAN
JOHN
John XII, Pope. See:
OTTAVIANO
John XIV, Pope. See:
PETER OF PAVIA
John XXI, Pope. See:
GIULIANI, PETER REBULI
John XXII, Pope. See:
D'EUSE, JACQUES
John XXIII, Pope. See:
RONCALLI, ANGELO GIUSEPPE
John A. Starr. See:
GILLESE, JOHN PATRICK
John A. Summers. See:
LAWSON, HORACE LOWE
John Adams. See:
SMITH, ALEXANDER
John Andrews. See:
CAMPBELL, ANDREW
John Anthony. See:
BECKETT, RONALD BRYMER
SABINI, JOHN ANTHONY
John Archer. See:
BOWMAN, RALPH
John Ashlin. See:
CUTFORTH, JOHN ASHLIN
John Asterisk. See:
HILL, WILLIAM KIRKPATRICK
John August. See:
DE VOTO, BERNARD AUGUSTINE
John Austwick. See:
LEE, AUSTIN
John Ayscough. See:
BICKERSTAFFE-DREW, FRANCIS BROWNING DREW, COUNT
John Barrymore. See:
BLYTHE, JOHN
John Barrymore, Jr. See:
BLYTHE, JOHN, JR.
John Beal. See:
BLIEDUNG, ALEXANDER
John Bedford. See:
HASTINGS, PHYLLIS DORA HODGE
John Bell. See:
JOHNSON, VICTOR HUGO
John Bickerdyke. See:
COOK, CHARLES HENRY
John, Big. See:
PATTON, JOHN
John Blaine. See:
GOODWIN, HAROLD LELAND
John Bledlow. See:
VALE, HENRY EDMUND THEODORIC
John Bonett. See:
COULSON, JOHN HUBERT ARTHUR
John Boswell. See:
KING, JOHN BOSWELL
John Brandane. See:
MACINTYRE, DR. JOHN
John Brown John. See:
TALBOT, CHARLES REMINGTON
John Buchan. See:
TWEEDSMUIR, BARON JOHN BUCHAN
John Bud. See:
BRONTË, BRANWELL
John Burger. See:
MARQUARD, LEOPOLD
John Burgess Wilson. See:
BURGESS, ANTHONY
John Byron. See:
ARMSTRONG, JOHN BYRON
John Cameron. See:
MACDONELL, ARCHIBALD GORDON
John Carrick. See:
CROSBIE, HUGH PROVAN
John Carroll. See:
FAYE, JULIAN LA
John Carver. See:
GARDNER, RICHARD
John Casells. See:
DUNCAN, WILLIAM MURDOCH
John, Charles (Karl Johan). See:
BERNADOTTE, JEAN BAPTISTE JULES

John Charlton. See:
WOODHOUSE, MARTIN
John Chelton. See:
DURST, PAUL
John Chester. See:
MITCHELL, DR. SILAS WEIR
John Clarke. See:
LAUGHLIN, VIRGINIA CARLI
SONTUP, DANIEL
John Cleveland. See:
McELFRESH, ELIZABETH ADELINE
John Clifford. See:
BAYLISS, JOHN CLIFFORD
John Coleridge. See:
BINDER, OTTO OSCAR
John Coolwater. See:
CONNIFF, JAMES CLIFFORD GREGORY
John, Corporal. See:
CHURCHILL, JOHN
JOHN, COUNT OF TUSCULUM (died 1058) [Supreme Pontiff of Roman Catholic Church]
Pope Benedict X
John Courtney. See:
COURNOS, JOHN
JUDD, FREDERICK CHARLES
John Coventry. See:
PALMER, JOHN WILLIAMSON
John Crompton. See:
LAMBURN, JOHN BATTERSBY CROMPTON
John Curtis. See:
PREBBLE, JOHN EDWARD CURTIS
John D. See:
ROCKEFELLER, JOHN DAVISON
John Dall. See:
THOMPSON, JOHN JENNER
John Dangerfield. See:
CRAWFURD, OSWALD
John Darby. See:
GARRETSON, JAMES EDMUND
JOHN DE BALIOL (1249-1315) [King of Scotland]
Toom Tabard (Empty Jacket)
John Dexter. See:
KANTO, PETER
John Doe. See:
SCOTT, CLEMENT WILLIAM
John, Don. See:
JOHN OF AUSTRIA
Juan, Don
John Donovan. See:
DILLINGER, JOHN HERBERT
John Dryden. See:
ROWLAND, DONALD SYDNEY
John Edgefield. See:
ILIFF, JOHN EDGAR
John Eglinton. See:
MAGEE, WILLIAM KIRKPATRICK
John Eland Craig. See:
CHIPPERFIELD, JOSEPH EUGENE
JOHN, ELIZABETH BEAMAN (1907-) [American camp director, Red Cross official and author]
B. John
Betty John
Beth St. John
John Elton. See:
MARSH, JOHN
John Ericson. See:
MEIBES, JOSEPH
John Esteven. See:
SHELLABARGER, SAMUEL
John, Evan. See:
SIMPSON, EVAN JOHN
John, Finality. See:
RUSSELL, LORD JOHN
John Fiske. See:
GREEN, EDMUND FISK
John Fitzgerald. See:
FAZZANO, JOSEPH E.
John Fitzvictor, P.B. See:
SHELLEY, PERCY BYSSHE
John Florio, Resolute. See:
FLORIO, JOHN (GIOVANNI)
John Flower, M. P. Captain. See:
BRONTË, BRANWELL
John Ford. See:
O'FIENNE, SEAN
John Forsythe. See:
FREUND, JOHN

John Francis Tuohy. See:
TUOHY, FRANK
John Frederick. See:
FAUST, FREDERICK SCHILLER
JOHN FREDERICK I (1503-54) [Elector of Saxony]
The Magnanimous
John, Free-born. See:
LILBURNE, JOHN
John, French. See:
SIOUSSAT, JEAN PIERRE
John Gale. See:
GAZE, RICHARD
John Garden. See:
FLETCHER, HARRY LUFT VERNE
John Garfield. See:
GARFINKLE, JULIUS
John Garrick. See:
DOUDY, REGINALD
John Gary. See:
STRADER, JOHN GARY
John Gavin. See:
GOLENOR, JOHN ANTHONY
John Gawsworth. See:
ARMSTRONG, TERENCE IAN FYTTON
John Gilbert. See:
GIBBS, JOHN
PRINGLE, JOHN
John Godley. See:
KILBRACKEN, JOHN RAYMOND GODLEY
John Graham. See:
PHILLIPS, DAVID GRAHAM
John Harley. See:
MARSH, JOHN
John Hereford. See:
FLETCHER, HARRY LUFT VERNE
John, Honest. See:
BRICKER, JOHN WILLIAM
COVODE, JOHN
KELLY, JOHN
LORD ALTHORP
STEPHENSON, JOHN
John Howard. See:
COX, JOHN
John Hoyt. See:
HOYSRADT, JOHN
John Hunter. See:
BALLARD, WILLIS TODHUNTER
John Iron. See:
CARLILE, JOHN CHARLES
John Jameson, Immaterial. See:
JAMESON, JOHN
John Jervis Connington. See:
STEWART, ALFRED WALTER
JOHN (JOHANN) (1468-1532) [Elector of Saxony]
The Constant
JOHN (JOHANNES) OF SWABIA [1290-1313) [German prince; murderer of ALBERT I]
The Parricide
John, John Brown. See:
TALBOT, CHARLES REMINGTON
John Jorrocks. See:
SURTEES, ROBERT SMITH
John K. Vedder. See:
GRUBER, FRANK
John Keith Bassett. See:
KEATING, LAWRENCE A.
John Kelly, Honest. See:
KELLY, JOHN
John Kildare. See:
KING, JOHN BOSWELL
John King. See:
McKEAG, ERNEST LIONEL
John L. See:
SULLIVAN, JOHN LAWRENCE
John L., The Great. See:
SULLIVAN, JOHN LAW-RENCE
John Lacy. See:
DARLEY, GEORGE
John Latouche. See:
CRAWFURD, OSWALD
John le Carre. See:
CORNWELL, DAVID JOHN MOORE
John Lindsey. See:
MURIEL, JOHN
John Loder. See:
LOWE, JOHN
John, Long. See:

WENTWORTH, JOHN
John Longsword. See:
LONG, JOHN FREDERICK LAWRENCE
John Lovegood. See:
GRANT-WATSON, ELLIOT LOVEGOOD
John McArthur. See:
WISE, ARTHUR
John Macdonald. See:
MILLAR, KENNETH
John MacGrom. See:
McMASTER, GUY HUMPHRIES
John Main. See:
PARSONS, MRS. ELSIE WORTHINGTON CLEWS
John Mandeville, Sir. See:
Mandeville, Johan de (Sir John)
John Martin. See:
SHEPARD, MORGAN VAN ROERBACH
TATHAM, LAURA ESTHER
John Miles. See:
BICKHAM, JACK MILES
John Miller. See:
SAMACHSON, JOSEPH
John Milton Edwards. See:
COOK, WILLIAM WALLACE
John, Mr. See:
HARBERGER, JOHN PICO
John Moreton. See:
COHEN, MORTON NORTON
John N. H. Brennan. See:
WELCOME, JOHN
John Norcross. See:
CONROY, JOHN WESLEY
John o'Birds. See:
BURROUGHS, JOHN
John of Antioch. See:
CHRYSOSTOM, ST. JOHN
JOHN OF AUSTRIA (1547-78) [Spanish general officer]
Don John
Don Juan
Gerónimo
Juan de Austria
JOHN OF DAMASCUS (JOHANNES DAMASCENUS) (700?-54?) [Syrian theologian, writer and scholar]
Chrysorrhoas (Stream of Gold)
John of England (Joannes Anglicus). See:
JOAN
JOHN OF LANCASTER (1389-1435) [Duke of Bedford, Regent of England and France]
The Firebrand of France
Protector and Defender of the Kingdom
JOHN OF SALISBURY (c. 1115-80) [English ecclesiastic, scholar and author]
The Little (Parvus)
John of the Cross, St. See:
ÁLVAREZ, JUAN DE YAPES Y
John Oliver Hobbes. See:
CRAIGIE, PEARL MARY TERESA RICHARDS
John Oxenham. See:
DUNKERLEY, WILLIAM ARTHUR
John P. Squibob. See:
DERBY, GEORGE HORATIO
John Parlin. See:
GRAVES, JOHN PARLIN
John Parry. See:
WHELPTON, GEORGE ERIC
John Partridge. See:
PAGE, JOHN
John Patrick. See:
GOGGAN, JOHN PATRICK
John Paul. See:
WEBB, CHARLES HENRY
John Paul Jones. See:
PAUL, JOHN
John Paxton, Dr. See:
LAWTON, SHERMAN PAXTON
John Phillips. See:
MARQUAND, JOHN PHILLIPS
John Philo Robinson. See:
CRIPPEN, DR. HAWLEY HARVEY
John Phoenix. See:
DERBY, GEORGE HORATIO
MAYLEM, JOHN
John Pickard Owen. See:
BUTLER, SAMUEL

John Pico John. See:
HARBERGER, JOHN PICO
John, Pious. See:
WANAMAKER, JOHN
John Prentice Langley. See:
RATHBONE, ST. GEORGE HENRY
John Prescott Earl. See:
GILCHRIST, BETH BRADFORD
John Presland. See:
BENDIT, GLADYS WILLIAMS
John, Prince. See:
BEAUREGARD, PIERRE GUSTAVE TOUTANT
VAN BUREN, JOHN
John, Private. See:
ALLEN, JOHN MILLS
John Qualen. See:
OLESON, JOHN
John Quod. See:
IRVING, JOHN TREAT
John R. Cooper. See:
STRATEMEYER, EDWARD L.
John Rae. See:
POMPEO, JOHN ANTHONY
John Randolph of Roanoke. See:
RANDOLPH, JOHN
John Rhode. See:
STREET, CECIL JOHN CHARLES
John Riddell. See:
FORD, COREY
John Ridgeley. See:
REA, JOHN HUNTINGDON
John Riverside. See:
HEINLEIN, ROBERT ANSON
John Roche. See:
LE ROI, DAVID DE ROCHE
John, Rosamund. See:
JONES, NORA R.
John Ross. See:
COOWESCOOWE (KOOWESKOOWE)
John Ross Macdonald. See:
MILLAR, KENNETH
John Roy Carlson. See:
DEROUNIAN, ARTHUR
John S. Daniels. See:
OVERHOLSER, WAYNE D.
John St. John. See:
SALE, RICHARD
John Sawyer. See:
FOLEY, CEDRIC JOHN
John Saxon. See:
ORRICO, CARMEN
John Search. See:
WHATELY, RICHARD
John, Second. See:
ADAMS, JOHN QUINCY
John Sedges. See:
BUCK, PEARL SYDENSTRICKER
John Sellers, Brother. See:
SELLERS, JOHN B.
John Shane. See:
DURST, PAUL
John Shepherd. See:
BALLARD, WILLIS TODHUNTER
John Sinjohn. See:
GALSWORTHY, JOHN
John Smith. See:
VAN ORDEN, ROBERT
John Smith, Captain. See:
SMITH, JOHN
John Smith of Cambridge. See:
SMITH, JOHN
John Sproston. See:
SCOTT, PETER DALE
John Stanstead. See:
GROOM, ARTHUR WILLIAM
John Stark. See:
GODWIN, JOHN
John Strange Winter. See:
STANNARD, HENRIETTA ELIZA VAUGHAN
John Stratten. See:
ALLDRIDGE, JOHN STRATTEN
John Stuart. See:
CROALL, JOHN
John Symmonds. See:
GONZALES, BLI
John Syntax. See:
DENNETT, HERBERT VICTOR
John T. Raymond. See:
O'BRIEN, JOHN
John Taine. See:
BELL, ERIC TEMPLE
John Tanner. See:

MATCHA, JACK
John Taylor of Caroline. See:
TAYLOR, JOHN
JOHN THE EVANGELIST, ST. (died c. 101) [one of the Twelve Apostles]
Bonerge (Son of Thunder)
St. John the Divine
John Timon. See:
MITCHELL, DONALD GRANT
John Trevena. See:
HENHAM, ERNEST GEORGE
John Turncoat. See:
THAYER, JOHN
John, Tuscarora. See:
BARNWELL, JOHN
John, Uncle. See:
SEDGWICK, JOHN
John W. Allen, Jr. See:
LESLEY, PETER
John W., Old. See:
HEISMAN, JOHN WILLIAM
John Warwick. See:
BEATTIE, JOHN McINTOSH
John Wayne. See:
MORRISON, MARION MICHAEL
John Weir. See:
CROSS, COLIN JOHN
John Welcome. See:
BRENNAN, JOHN NEEDHAM HUGGARD
John William Calcraft. See:
COLE, JOHN WILLIAM
John Winch. See:
LONG, MRS. GABRIELLE MARGARET VERE CAMPBELL
John Winton. See:
PRATT, JOHN
John Worne. See:
WYLIE, JAMES
John Wycliffe. See:
BEDFORD-JONES, HENRY JAMES O'BRIEN
John Wylcotes. See:
RANSFORD, OLIVER
Johnnie. See:
DILLINGER, JOHN HERBERT
Johnny
RAY, JOHN ALVIN
Johnnie Luce. See:
LUCCIOLA, JOHN
Johnny. See:
CARSON, JOHN
CASH, JOHN R.
GREEN, JOHN
HODGES, JOHN CORNELIUS
Johnnie
LUJACK, JOHN
MANDEL, JOHN ALFRED
MARKS, JOHN D.
MARVIN, JOHN
MATHIS, JOHN ROYCE
MERCER, JOHN H.
NOBLE, JOHN AVERY
UNITAS, JOHN
WINTERS, JONATHAN HARSHMAN
Johnny Appleseed. See:
CHAPMAN, JOHN
Johnny Cale. See:
CALABRO, JOHN A.
Johnny Carlo. See:
SELVAGGIO, JOHN R.
Johnny Dark. See:
NORWOOD, VICTOR GEORGE CHARLES
Johnny, Gentlemanly. See:
BURGOYNE, JOHN
Johnny Giles. See:
MELLENBRUCH, GILES EDWARD
Johnny Gruelle. See:
BARTON, JOHN
Johnny Laredo. See:
CAESAR, EUGENE LEE
Johnny Mince. See:
MUENZENBERGER, JOHN HENRY
Johnny Richards. See:
CASCALES, JOHN
Johnny Ringo. See:
KEEVIL, HENRY JOHN
Johnny Simmonseed. See:
HATFIELD, BAZIL MUSE
Johnny, Soda Ash. See:
HORAN, JOHN MICHAEL
Johnny Wiggs. See:
HYMAN, JOHN WIGGINTON
Johns, Avery. See:
COUSINS, MARGARET
Johns, Foster. See:
SELDES, GILBERT VIVIAN

Johns, Geoffrey. See:
WARNER, GEORGE GEOFFREY JOHN
Johns, Kenneth, joint pseud. of HENRY KENNETH BULMER (1921-) and JOHN NEWMAN (-) [British authors]
Johns, Kenneth. See also:
BULMER, HENRY KENNETH
JOHNSON [Johnson]. See also:
JOHANSSON
Johnston
Johnstone
JONSON
Johnson, A. E., joint pseud. of ANNABELL JONES JOHNSON (1921-) and her husband, EDGAR RAYMOND JOHNSON (1912-) [American authors]
Johnson, A. E. See also:
JOHNSON, ANNABELL JONES
JOHNSON, ALBERT J. (1910-) [American jazz musician (tenor saxophone, composer)]
Budd Johnson
JOHNSON, ANDREW (1808-75) [Seventeenth President of the United States]
The Daddy of the Baby
The Father of the Homestead Act
His Accidency
King Andy
King Andy the First
Old Andy
Old Veto
Sir Veto
The Tennessee Tailor
The Veto President
JOHNSON, ANNA (1860-) [American author]
Hope Daring
JOHNSON, ANNABELL JONES (1921-) [American librarian, secretary and author]
A. Johnson
JOHNSON, ANNABELL JONES. See also:
Johnson, A. E.
Johnson, Benjamin F., of Boone. See: RILEY, JAMES WHITCOMB
JOHNSON, BYRON BANCROFT (1864-1931) [American baseball official]
Ban Johnson
JOHNSON, CAROL DIAHANN (1935-) [American Negro actress, singer and television personality]
Diahann Carroll
Johnson, Charles S. See:
EDWARDS, WILLIAM BENNETT
Johnson, Chatta. See:
GIOVANNONE, ANTHONY J.
JOHNSON, CHRISTOPHER (1931-) [British editor, correspondent and author]
Louis McIntosh
JOHNSON, CLAUDIA ALTA TAYLOR (1912-) [wife of President LYNDON BAINES JOHNSON]
Lady Bird
Johnson, Crockett. See:
LEISK, DAVID JOHNSON
JOHNSON, DAVID CLAYPOOLE (1797-1865) [American engraver and caricaturist]
The American Cruikshank
JOHNSON, DR. SAMUEL (1709-84) [English lexicographer, poet, playwright and wit]
Dr. Johnson
The English Socrates
The Giant of Literature
The Great Cham of Literature
The Great Moralist
The Great Seer
Impartial Hand
The Leviathan of Literature
The Literary Colossus
The Polyphemus of Literature
Ursa Major
JOHNSON, DR. SAMUEL. See: also: JOHNSON, SAMUEL
JOHNSON, DONALD McINTOSH (1903-) [British barrister,

medical officer, man of letters and author]
Guy de Montfort
JOHNSON, EDGAR RAYMOND. See: Johnson, A. E.
JOHNSON, EDWARD (1816-73) [American general officer]
Allegheny Johnson
Fence-rail Johnson
Johnson, Effie. See: RICHMOND, EUPHEMIA JOHNSON
JOHNSON, ESTHER (1681-1728) [Englishwoman, loved by JONATHAN SWIFT; possibly his wife]
Stella
JOHNSON, FRANK (1917-) [American motion picture actor]
Frankie Darro
JOHNSON, FREDERIC H. (1908-) [American jazz musician (trombone)]
Keg Johnson
JOHNSON, GEORGE METCALF (1885-) [American novelist]
George Metcalf
JOHNSON, HAROLD (fl. mid 20th. cent.) [American editor]
Speed Johnson
Speed McGee
JOHNSON, HEWLETT (1874-1966) [English ecclesiastic]
The Red Dean
JOHNSON, HOWARD BRENNAN (1932-) [American business executive and restaurateur]
Bud Johnson
JOHNSON, HUGH ANTHONY STEPHEN (1913-67) [Irish civil servant and author]
A Fighter Pilot
Hugh Sturton
JOHNSON, HUGH SAMUEL (1882-1943) [American general officer, lawyer, journalist and N. R. A. administrator]
The Babe Ruth of the New Deal
Crack-Down Johnson
The Crack-Down Czar of the N. R. A.
The Great Thundering Rooster
The King of the Never-Made-Good Crack Downs
The N. R. A. Czar
Old Iron Pants
JOHNSON, JAMES LOUIS (1924-) [American jazz musician (trombone)]
J. J.
Jay Jay
JOHNSON, JAMES WESLEY (1850-) [American Methodist clergyman and author]
Annan Dale
JOHNSON, JOHN ARTHUR (1878-1946) [American Negro professional boxer; world's heavyweight champion]
Jack Johnson
JOHNSON, JOHN MONROE (1878-) [American civil engineer and Assistant Secretary of Commerce]
Rowboat Johnson
JOHNSON, LARAINE (1920-) [American stage and motion picture actress]
Laraine Day
JOHNSON, LAWRENCE (1908-) [British stage and motion picture actor]
Laurence Naismith
JOHNSON, LYNDON BAINES (1908-) [Thirty-sixth President of the United States]
L. B. J.
JOHNSON, MARION GEORGINA WIKELEY (1912-) [British correspondent and author]
Georgina Masson
Johnson, Mary Louise. See: KING, MARY LOUISE
JOHNSON, MARY McDONOUGH (1783-1856) [Mother of President ANDREW JOHNSON]
Polly the Weaver
JOHNSON, MERLE (1937-) [American motion picture

actor]
Troy Donohue
JOHNSON, PAMELA HANSFORD. See: Lombard, Nap
Johnson, Randolph. See: RASLEY, JOHN M.
JOHNSON, ROBERT LEE (1908-) [American professional baseball player]
Cherokee
JOHNSON, RONALD. See: Chamberlain, Theodore
JOHNSON, SAMUEL (1649-1703) [English clergyman and pamphleteer]
The Whig
JOHNSON, SAMUEL. See also: JOHNSON, DR. SAMUEL
JOHNSON, VICTOR HUGO (1912-) [American author]
John Bell
JOHNSON, VIRGINIA WALES (1849-1916) [American juvenile and miscellaneous writer]
Cousin Virginia
Johnson, W. Bolingbroke. See: BISHOP, MORRIS
JOHNSON, WALTER PERRY (1887-1946) [American professional baseball player]
Barney
The Big Train
JOHNSON, WILLIAM EUGENE (1862-1945) [American prohibition enforcement agent]
Pussyfoot Johnson
JOHNSON, WILLIAM GEARY (1879-1949) [American jazz musician (cornet, trumpet)]
Bunk Johnson
JOHNSON, WILLIAM RANSOM (1782-1849) [American horse trainer and sportsman]
The Napoleon of the Turf
JOHNSON, WOODROW WILSON (1915-) [American jazz musician (leader, arranger, piano)]
Buddy Johnson
JOHNSTON [Johnston]. See also:
JOHANSSON
JOHNSON
Johnson
Johnstone
JONSON
JOHNSTON, HENRY ERSKINE (1777-1845) [Scottish actor]
The Scottish Roscius
JOHNSTON, SIR REGINALD FLEMING (1874-) [British educator and author]
Christopher Irving
Reginald Irving
Lin Shao-Yang
Sanction
Johnston Smith. See: CRANE, STEPHEN
JOHNSTON, WILLIAM M. (1895-1946) [American tennis player]
Little Bill Johnston
Johnstone. See also:
JOHANSSON
JOHNSON
Johnson
Johnston
JONSON
Johnstone, Ted. See: McDANIEL DAVID EDWARD
Joli. See: GONSALVES, JOHN P.
Jolie. See: YOELSON, ASA
Jolly Millionaire, The. See: O'BRIEN, WILLIAM SHONEY
Jolly, Pete. See: CERAGIOLI, PETER A.
Jolly Roger. See: BRADFIELD, ROGER
Jolson, Al. See: YOELSON, ASA
JOLYOT, PROSPER, SIEUR DE CRAIS-BILLON (1674-1762) [French poetic dramatist]
Crébillon
Jon. See: HENDRICKS, JOHN CARL JAHN

JOHN
John
THIELMANS, JEAN
Jon Hall. See:
LOCHER, CHARLES
Jon Roberts. See:
OLSON, ROBERT G.
Jón Trausti. See:
MAGNÚSSON, GUDMUNDUR
Jonah. See:
IVAN IV VASILIEVICH
JONES, ROBERT ELLIOTT
Jonas, Justus. See:
KOCH, JODOCUS
Jonas Ward. See:
ARD, WILLIAM THOMAS
Jonathan. See:
BURKE, JOHN FREDERICK
WHITE, JAMES
Jonathan, Beau. See:
HAZARD, JONATHAN J.
Jonathan Brooks. See:
MELLETT, JOHN CALVIN
Jonathan, Brother. See:
LAMBERT, JONATHAN
TRUMBULL, JONATHAN
Jonathan Fabrick. See:
HOLBROOK, SILAS PINCKNEY
Jonathan Fiske, P.B. See:
SHELLEY, PERCY BYSSHE
Jonathan Gant. See:
ADAMS, CLIFTON
Jonathan Hale. See:
HATLEY, JONATHAN
Jonathan Joseph. See:
FINEMAN, IRVING
Jonathan Oldcastle. See:
MEYNELL, WILFRID
Jonathan Oldstyle. See:
IRVING, WASHINGTON
Jonathan Oldstyle, Gent. See:
IRVING, WASHINGTON
Jonathan Rhodes. See:
OLSEN, JOHN EDWARD
Jonathan Slick. See:
STEPHENS, ANN SOPHIA WINTERBOTHAM
Jonathan Stagge. See:
Quentin, Patrick
Jonathan Titulescu Fogarty, Esq. See: FARRELL, JAMES THOMAS
Jones, Amos. See:
GOSDEN, FREEMAN F.
Jones, Billy. See:
Happiness Boys, The
JONES, BURGHER WILLIAM (1924-) [American jazz musician (bass tuba)]
Buddy Jones
Jones, Candy. See:
WILCOX, JESSICA
Jones, Capt. Wilbur. See:
EDWARDS, WILLIAM BENNETT
JONES, CHARLES (1889-1942) [American Western motion picture actor]
Buck Jones
JONES, CHARLES COLCOCK (1831-93) [American historian of Georgia]
The Macaulay of the South
JONES, CHARLES JESSE (1844-) [American buffalo hunter, later conservationist]
Buffalo Jones
JONES, DOROTHY HOLDER (1925-) [American author]
Duane Jones
Jones, E.B.C. See:
LUCAS, EMILY BEATRIX COURSOLLES
JONES, EMMA GARRISON (1833-98) [American author]
E.G. Walraven
JONES, ESTHER MAY (1935-) [American jazz musician (singer)]
Esther Phillips
Jones, Ezekiel. See:
WELD, HORATIO HASTINGS
JONES, FELIX EDWARD AYLMER (1889-) [British actor and author]
Felix Aylmer
JONES, FRITZ (1920-) [American jazz musician (piano)]
Ahmad Jamal
JONES, HELEN HINCKLEY (1903-) [American educator and author]
Helen Hinckley

JONES, HENRY (1831-99)
[English physician and author of books on card games]
Cavendish
JONES, HENRY Z., JR. (1940-) [American musician, actor and publisher]
Hank Jones
JONES, IFANO (fl. late 19th-early 20th cent.) [British librarian and author]
Ifano
JONES, INIGO (1573-1652)
[English architect and scenery designer]
The English Palladio
JONES, JAMES ATHEARN (1791-1854) [American editor and author]
Matthew Murgatroyd
JONES, JAMES C. (1809-59)
[American politician; Governor of Tennessee]
Beanpole Jimmy
Lean Jimmy Jones
Jones, Jennifer. See:
ISLEY, PHYLLIS
JONES, JOHN LUTHER (1863-1900) [American locomotive engineer; hero of the ballad "Casey Jones"]
Casey Jones
Jones, John Paul. See:
PAUL, JOHN
JONES, JOHN PERCIVAL (1829-1912) [Anglo-American politician; senator from Nevada]
The Nevada Commoner
JONES, JOHN WILLIAM (1836-1909) [American Baptist clergyman, soldier and author]
The Fighting Parson
JONES, JOSEPH RUDOLPH (1923-) [American jazz musician (drums)]
Philly Joe
JONES, JUSTIN (fl. 1844-67)
[American writer of melodramatic novels]
Harry Hazel
JONES, LILLIE MAE (1930-)
[American jazz musician (singer)]
Betty Carter
JONES, LINDLEY ARMSTRONG (1912-65) [American jazz musician (drums, leader)]
Spike Jones
Jones, Major. See:
THOMPSON, WILLIAM TAPPAN
JONES, MARVIN (1886-)
[American lawyer and politician; congressman from Texas]
Agricultural Jones
JONES, MARY HARRIS (1830-1930) [Irish-American reformer and labor leader]
Mother Jones
JONES, NORA R. (1913-)
[British motion picture and stage actress]
Rosamund John
Jones of the South, Paul. See:
SEMMES, RAPHAEL
JONES, ROBERT ELLIOTT (1909-) [American jazz musician (trumpet, leader)]
Jonah Jones
JONES, ROBERT TYRE, JR. (1902-71) [American golfing champion]
Bobby Jones
The King of the Links
JONES, RUFUS (1936-)
[American jazz musician (drums)]
Speedy Jones
JONES, RUTH (1896-)
[American actress and playwright]
Ruth Gordon
JONES, RUTH (1924-)
[American jazz musician (singer)]
Dinah Washington
JONES, SAMUEL (1734-1819)
[American attorney and law reformer]
The Father of the New York Bar

JONES, SAMUEL MILTON (1846-1904) [Anglo-American manufacturer]
Golden Rule Jones
JONES, SAMUEL PORTER (1847-1906) [American evangelist, lecturer and author]
The Mountain Evangelist
Sam Jones
JONES, SAMUEL POUND (1892-) [American professional baseball player]
Sad Sam
JONES, SISSIERRETTA JOYNER (1869-) [American Negro opera and concert singer]
Black Patti
Jones, Tom. See: WOODWARD, THOMAS JONES
JONES, VIRGIL CARRINGTON (1906-) [American editor and author]
Pat Jones
JONES, VIRGINIA (1928-) [American motion picture actress]
Virginia Mayo
Jones, Webb. See: HENLEY, ARTHUR
JONES, WILLIAM (1726-1800) [English clergyman and theological writer]
Trinity Jones
JONES, WILLIAM. See also: Happiness Boys, The
JONES, WILLIAM ANDREW (c.1905-) [American motion picture comedian]
Billy de Wolfe
JONES, WILMORE (1907-) [American jazz musician (drums)]
Slick Jones
JONSON. See also:
JOHANSSON
JOHNSON
Johnson
Johnston
Johnstone
JONSON, BENJAMIN (c.1573-1637) [English poet and playwright]
The English Horace
Ben Jonson
Rare Ben Jonson
Joos Habbema. See: HEIJERMANS (HEYERMANS), HERMAN
JOPLIN, SCOTT (1868-1917) [American jazz musician (piano, composer)]
The King of the Ragtime Composers
JORDAN [Jordan]. See also: Jourdan
JORDAN, BAXTER BYERLEY (1908-) [American professional baseball player]
Bucky Jordan
Jordan, Gail. See: DERN, PEGGY GADDIS
JORDAN, IRVING SIDNEY (1922-) [American jazz musician (piano, composer)]
Duke Jordan
JORDAN, JAMES EDWARD (1896-) [American radio performer]
Jim Jordan
Fibber McGee
JORDAN, JAMES TAFT (1915-) [American jazz musician (trumpet, singer, leader)]
Taft Jordan
JORDAN, LOUIS THOMAS (1908-) [American jazz musician (alto saxophone, singer, leader)]
Louie Jordan
JORDAN, MARIAN DRISCOLL (1896-1961) [American radio comedienne]
Molly McGee
JORDAN, PHILIP FURNEAUX (1902-) [British author and publisher]
Victor France
Jordan, The Emperor of. See: GLUBB, SIR JOHN BAGOT
JORGENSEN, MARY VENN (fl. 1929-45) [American author]

Mary Adrian
Jorgenson, Ivar. See:
SILVERBERG, ROBERT
JÖRGENSSEN, JÖRGEN (1779-c.1845) [Danish adventurer]
King of Iceland
Joris-Karl. See:
HUYSMANS, CHARLES MARIE GEORGES
Jorrocks, John. See:
SURTEES, ROBERT SMITH
JOSCELYN, ARCHIE L. (1899-) [American author]
A. A. Archer
Al Cody
Tex Holt
Evelyn McKenna
Lynn Westland
José. See:
GRECO, COSTANZO
José Canusi. See:
BARKER, S. OMAR
José, Don. See:
MANAOIS, JOSEPH
José Ferrer. See:
CINTRON, JOSÉ VINCENTE FERRER OTERO Y
José Jiménez. See:
DANA, WILLIAM
José Melis. See:
GUIU, JOSÉ MELIS
Josef. See also:
JOSEPH
Joseph
Josef Miche. See:
BOCHENSKI, JOSEPH M.
Joselillo. See:
LOPES, JOSÉ LAURENTINO
Joselillo de Colombia. See:
ZÚÑIGA, JOSÉ
Joselito. See:
GÓMEZ, JOSÉ
Joseph. See:
COOK, FLAVIUS JOSEPHUS
HAYDN, FRANZ JOSEPH
Josef
Rosny, Joseph Henri
Joseph Atterley. See:
TUCKER, GEORGE
Joseph Benedict. See:
DOLLEN, CHARLES JOSEPH
Joseph Bradford. See:
HUNTER, WILLIAM RANDOLPH
Joseph Brant. See:
THAYENDANEGEA
JOSEPH, CHARLES (1735-1814) [Prince de Ligne; German field marshal]
The Prince of Coxcombs
Joseph Conrad. See:
KORZENIOWSKI, TEODOR JOZEF KONRAD
Joseph, Father (Père Joseph). See: TREMBLAY, FRANÇOIS LE CLERC DU
Joseph Gay. See:
BREVAL, JOHN DURANT
Joseph Grace. See:
HORNBY, JOHN
Joseph H. Arnold. See:
HAYES, JOSEPH
JOSEPH, JAMES HERZ (1924-) [American author]
Lowell Adams
Joseph, Jonathan. See:
FINEMAN, IRVING
Joseph Kambu. See:
AMAMOO, JOSEPH GODSON
Joseph Kell. See:
BURGESS, ANTHONY
JOSEPH, LOUIS PHILIPPE (1747-93) [Duke of Orléans; French nobleman]
Philippe Egalité
Joseph Louis Russo. See:
RUSSO, GIUSEPPE LUIGI
Joseph Mede. See:
GARLAND, DAVID JOHN
Joseph Nelson. See:
MITCHELL, ISAAC
Joseph Novak. See:
KOSINSKI, JERZY NIKODEM
Joseph, Père (Father Joseph). See: TREMBLAY, FRANÇOIS LE CLERC DU
Joseph Sawyer. See:
SAUER, JOSEPH
Joseph Shearing. See:
LONG, MRS. GABRIELLE MARGARET VERE CAMPBELL
Joseph Stalin. See:

Big Three, The
DJUGASHVILI, YOSIF VISSARIONOVICH
Joseph Strange. See:
CRAWFURD, OSWALD
Joseph Von Sternberg. See:
STERN, JOE
Joseph Walker. See:
McSPADDEN, JOSEPH WALKER
Joseph Wayne. See:
OVERHOLSER, WAYNE D.
Josephine. See:
James, Josephine
Josephine Bell. See:
BALL, DORIS BELL COLLIER
Josephine Gibson. See:
HINE, SESYLE JOSLIN
Josephine Herbst. See:
HERMANN, MRS. JOHN
Josephine Hull. See:
SHERWOOD, JOSEPHINE
Josephine Plain. See:
MITCHELL, ISABEL MARY
Josephine Story. See:
LORING, EMILIE BAKER
Josephine Tey. See:
MACINTOSH, ELIZABETH
JOSEPHS, RAY (1912-)
[American correspondent and author]
Jay Raphael
Josephus, Flavius. See:
BEN MATTATHIAS, JOSEPH
Josh. See:
WHITE, JOSHUA DANIEL
Josh Billings. See:
SHAW, HENRY WHEELER
Josh, Silver-tongued. See:
LEE, JOSHUA BRYAN
Joshua Coffin. See:
LONGFELLOW, HENRY WADSWORTH
Joshua Stark. See:
OLSEN, THEODORE VICTOR
Josiah Allen's Wife. See:
HOLLEY, MARIETTA
Josiah Flynt. See:
WILLARD, JOSIAH FLINT
Josiah the First, King. See:
QUINCY, JOSIAH
Josie Alton. See:
DEUBLER, MARY
Josie Arlington. See:
DEUBLER, MARY
Joslin, Sesyle. See:
HINE, SESYLE JOSLIN
Jot, Joe, Jr. See:
BELLAW, AMERICUS WELLINGTON
Jourdan. See also:
JORDAN
Jordan
Jourdan, Louis. See:
GENDRE, LOUIS
Journalism in Mississippi, The Father of. See:
MARSCHALK, ANDREW
Journalism, The Father of. See:
ARETINO, PIETRO
Journalists, The Nestor of the German-American. See:
PREETORIUS, EMIL
Journalists, The Prince of. See:
GREELEY, HORACE
Journeyman. See:
NOCK, ALBERT JAY
JOUVENET, JEAN (1644-1717)
[French historical painter]
The Caracci of France
Joy, Leatrice. See:
ZEIDLER, LEATRICE JOY
Joyce. See:
CARY, ARTHUR JOYCE LUNEL
KILMER, ALFRED JOYCE
Joyce, Brenda. See:
LEABO, BETTY
Joyce Carey. See:
LAWRENCE, JOYCE
Joyce Collins. See:
SEARLE, JOYCE COLLINS
Joyce Grenfell. See:
PHIPPS, JOYCE
Joyce Mortimer Batten. See:
MANKOWSKA, JOYCE KELLS BATTEN
JOYCE, WILLIAM (1906-46)
[American Nazi radio propaganda broadcaster]

Lord Haw Haw
Joyous Father of the Vaudeville, The. See:
BASSELIN, OLIVER
Juan. See:
GRIS, JOSÉ VITTORIANO GONZÁLEZ
LEWIS, JOHN WOODRUFF
Juan Belmonte. See:
BELMONTE Y GARCÍA, JUAN
Juan Belmonte, Jr. See:
CAMPOY, JUAN BELMONTE Y
Juan de Austria. See:
JOHN OF AUSTRIA
JUAN DE AVILA (1500-69) [Spanish writer and preacher]
The Apostle of Andalusia
Juan, Don. See:
John, Don
JOHN OF AUSTRIA
Juanito. See:
CAMPOY, JUAN BELMONTE Y
Juba. See:
ALLEN, BENJAMIN
Jube, Old. See:
EARLY, JUBAL ANDERSON
Jubilee Jim. See:
FISK, JAMES, JR.
Jubilee, Old. See:
EARLY, JUBAL ANDERSON
Jud. See:
DeNAUT, GEORGE MATTHEWS
JUDD
Judd
JUDAEUS. See:
PHILO JUDAEUS
JUDAH I (fl. 190-220) [President of the Sanhedrin]
The Holy
The Prince
JUDAH, SAMUEL BENJAMIN HELBERT (c. 1799-1876) [American playwright and poet]
Terentius Phlogobombos
Judah, The Lion of. See:
HAILE SELASSIE, RAS TAFFARI (TAFARI)
Judah, A Thrice-accursed. See:
BERIA, LAVRENTI PAVLOVICH
JUDAS OF GALILEE (fl. 6 A.D.) [Jewish leader of revolt] against QUIRINUS]
The Galilean
The Gaulonite
JUDD [Judd]. See also:
Jud
Judd, Cyril, joint pseud. of JOSEPHINE JUDITH GROSSMAN (1923-) and C.M. KORNBLUTH (-) [American authors]
Judd, Cyril. See also:
GROSSMAN, JOSEPHINE JUDITH
Judd, Frances K. See:
STRATEMEYER, EDWARD L.
JUDD, FREDERICK CHARLES (1914-) [British electrical engineer and writer]
John Courtney
A. Lester-Rands
G.R. Miller
JUDD, MARGARET HADDICAN (1906-) [American librarian and author]
Truman Garrett
JUDD, MARY ANN (1922-) [American song composer and singer]
Marianne O'Brien
JUDD, NADINE (1927-) [English ballerina]
Nadia Nerina
Judge. See:
BEAN, ROY
GARY, ELBERT HENRY
LANDIS, KENESAW MOUNTAIN
LINDSEY, BENJAMIN BARR
RUTHERFORD, JOSEPH FRANKLIN
Judge, Big. See:
CONNOLLY, RICHARD
JUDGE, PETER (1891-1947) [Irish stage and motion

picture actor]
F. J. McCormick
Judge Powell Big. See:
POWELL, JOHN STEPHEN
Judge, The Hanging. See:
JEFFREYS, GEORGE, 1ST BARON JEFFREYS OF WEM
NORBURY, THE EARL OF
Judge, The Virginia. See:
KELLY, WALTER C.
Judith. See:
Berrisford, Judith M.
Judith Campbell. See:
PARES, MARION STAPYLTON
Judith James. See:
JENNINGS, LESLIE NELSON
Judith Koch. See:
ECKER, JUDITH K.
Judith Merrill. See:
GROSSMAN, JOSEPHINE JUDITH
JUDSON, EDWARD ZANE CARROLL (1821?-86) [American writer of dime novels]
Ned Buntline
Charles H. Cranston
Jules Edwards
Clew Garnet
Julia Manners
Edward Minturn
JUDSON, EMILY CHUBBUCK (1817-54) [American author]
Emily Chubbuck
Fanny Forester
Judson R. Taylor. See:
HALSEY, HARLAN P.
Judy. See:
TURNER, JULIA JEAN MILDRED FRANCES
Judy Campbell. See:
GAMBLE, JUDY
Judy Garland. See:
GUMM, FRANCES
Judy Holliday. See:
TUVIM, JUDITH
Judy Varga. See:
STANG, JUDIT
JUDY, WILL (1891-) [American lawyer, publisher and author]
Wymar Port
Jug. See:
AMMONS, EUGENE
Juhani, Aho. See:
BROFELDT, JUHANI
Juice, Orange. See:
SIMPSON, ORENTHAL JAMES
Jukes, The King of the. See:
COMO, PIERINO
Jules Berry. See:
PAUFICHET, JULES
Jules Claretie. See:
ARNAUD, ARSÈNE
Jules de Glouvet. See:
QUESNAY DE BEAUREPAIRE, JULES
Jules Edwards. See:
JUDSON, EDWARD ZANE CARROLL
Jules Loring. See:
MacKaye, Loring
Jules Romains. See:
FARIGOULE, LOUIS-HENRI JEAN
Jules Sand. See:
DUDEVANT, AMANDINE AURORE LUCIE DUPIN, "BARONNE"
SANDEAU, JULES
Julia Child. See:
McWILLIAMS, JULIA
Julia Edwards. See:
CORYELL, JOHN RUSSELL
Julia K. Duncan. See:
KARIG, WALTER
STRATEMEYER, EDWARD L.
Julia Mannering. See:
BINGHAM, MADELEINE
Julia Manners. See:
JUDSON, EDWARD ZANE CARROLL
Julia Marlowe. See:
FROST, SARAH FRANCES
Julia Mayfield. See:
HASTINGS, PHYLLIS DORA HODGE
Julia Renton. See:
COLE, MARGARET ALICE

Julia Virginia. See:
LAENGSDORFF, JULIA VIRGINIA
JULIAN [Julian]. See also:
Julien
Julian Callender. See:
LEE, AUSTIN
Julian David. See:
MacKaye, Loring
Julian Eltinge. See:
DALTON, WILLIAM
Julian Fish. See:
CAMPBELL, BLANCHE
JULIAN, GEORGE WASHINGTON (1817-99) [American abolitionist and co-founder of the Free Soil Party]
The Apostle of Disunion
The Orator of Free Dirt
Woolly-head
Julian Hillas. See:
DASHWOOD, ROBERT JULIAN
Julian Prescot. See:
BUDD, JOHN
Julian Roberts. See:
BARDENS, DENNIS CONRAD
Julian St. Dare. See:
PATTEN, WILLIAM GILBERT
JULIAN SEBASTIAN (1910-) [American jazz musician (guitar)]
Zeb Julian
JULIANUS, FLAVIUS CLAUDIUS (331-63) [Roman Emperor]
The Apostate
Julius
Julie Andrews. See:
WALTON, JULIA ELIZABETH WELLS
Julie Arnoldy. See:
BISCHOFF, JULIA BRISTOL
Julie Edwards. See:
STRATEMEYER, EDWARD L.
Julien. See:
GREEN, JULIEN HARTRIDGE
JULIAN
Julian
Julien Gordon. See:
CHANCE, JULIE GRINNELL
Julius. See:
JULIANUS, FLAVIUS CLAUDIUS
JULIUS (died 352) [Supreme Pontiff of Roman Catholic Church]
Pope Julius I
St. Julius
Julius II, Pope. See:
ROVERE, GIULIANO DELLA
Julius III, Pope. See:
MONTE, GIOVANNI MARIA CIOCCHI DEL
Julius Bristol. See:
ABEL, ALAN IRWIN
Julius, Charles. See:
BERTRAM, CHARLES
Julius, Moritz. See:
BONN, MORITZ JULIUS
Jumbo. See:
ELLIOTT, JAMES THOMAS
Jumbo, Uncle. See:
CLEVELAND, STEPHEN GROVER
Jumillano. See:
ORTUÑO, EMILIO
Jumping Jim. See:
GAVIN, JAMES MAURICE
June. See:
ALLYSON, JAN
June, Caroline Silver. See:
SMITH, LAURA ROUNTREE
June Christy. See:
LUSTER, SHIRLEY
June Haver. See:
STOVENOUR, JUNE
June Havoc. See:
HOVICK, JUNE
June, Jenny. See:
CROLY, JANE CUNNINGHAM
June Lang. See:
VLASEK, JUNE
June the Pocket-Sized Pavlova, Dainty Baby. See:
HOVICK, JUNE
June Wells. See:
SWINFORD, BETTY JUNE WELLS
JUNG, JOHANN HEINRICH (1740-1817) [German mystic and writer]
Jung Stilling

Jungle Doctor. See:
WHITE, PAUL HAMILTON HUME
Junior. See:
COOK, HERMAN
COUGHLAN, FRANK
DAVIS, GLENN
DURKIN, TRENT
MANCE, JULIAN C., JR.
RAGLIN, ALVIN
WELLS, AMOS, JR.
Junior, Democritus. See:
BURTON, ROBERT
Junior, Diogenes. See:
COWPER, FRANK
Junior, Dow. See:
PAIGE, ELBRIDGE GERRY
Junior, Ikey Solomons, Esq. See: THACKERAY, WILLIAM MAKEPEACE
Junior Sub. See:
BEITH, JOHN HAY
Juniper. See:
Jupiter
Sage, Juniper
Junius. See:
COLTON, CALVIN
FRANCIS, SIR PHILIP
Junius Americanus. See:
ENDICOTT, CHARLES MOSES
LEE, ARTHUR
Junius, Thomas. See:
Smectymnuus
YOUNG, THOMAS
JUNOT, ANDOCHE (1771-1813) [French general officer]
The Tempest
Jupiter. See:
CARLYLE, ALEXANDER
Juniper
Jupiter Scapin. See:
BONAPARTE, NAPOLEON
Jupp. See:
GOEBBELS, JOSEPH
Jurado, Katy. See:
GARCÍA, MARÍA JURADO
JURGENS, HELEN (1908-58) [American motion picture actress]
Helen Twelvetrees
JURGENS, RICHARD HENRY (1910-) [American jazz musician (trumpet, leader)]
Dick Jurgens
Juris, The Lucerna. See:
IRNERIUS
Jurisprudence, The Father of Connecticut. See:
LUDLOW, ROGER
Jurisprudence, The Father of Louisiana. See:
MARTIN, FRANÇOIS XAVIER
Jurist, The Greatest American. See: MARSHALL, JOHN
Jurni Glovichisch. See:
CLOVIO, GIULIO
Just, Frank the. See:
MURPHY, FRANK
Just, The. See:
ARISTIDES (ARISTEIDES)
CASIMIR II
FERDINAND I
FREDERICK AUGUSTUS I
JAMES II
KHUSRAU (CHOSROES) I
LOUIS XIII
Justice, Love and Humanity, The Sweet-spirited Advocate of. See: MOTT, LUCRETIA
Justice of Worcester County, The Marrying. See:
DAVIS, WALTER ALONZO
Justiciary, The. See:
PEDRO I
Justin Case. See:
GLEADOW, RUPERT SEELEY
JUSTIN, ST. (c. 100-c. 165) [Early father of the Christian church]
The Martyr
Justine Glass. See:
CORRALL, ALICE ENID
JUSTINIAN I (FLAVIUS ANICIUS JUSTINIANUS) (c. 483-c. 565) [Ruler of the Byzantine (Eastern Roman) empire]
The Great
Justinian, The English. See:
EDWARD I
Justus Jonas. See:
KOCH, JODOCUS
JUVENAL (fl. c. 60-140) [Roman rhetorician and

satirical poet]
The Aquinian Sage
Juvenal of Painters, The. See:
HOGARTH, WILLIAM
Juvenal of the Provençals, The.
See: CARDINAL, PIERRE
Juvenal, The English. See:
OLDHAM, JOHN
Juvenal, The Young.
See: LODGE, THOMAS
Juvenile Court, The Father of the.
See: LINDSEY,
BENJAMIN BARR
Juvenis. See:
CAWSTON, FREDERICK
GORDON
Jymie. See:
Jamie
MERRITT, JAMES